Graphic Communications

THE PRINTED IMAGE

by
Z. A. "Zeke" Prust

South Holland, Illinois
The Goodheart-Willcox Company, Inc.
Publishers

Library of Congress Catalog Card Number 93-26404
International Standard Book Number 0-87006-080-5

2 3 4 5 6 7 8 9 10   94   98 97 96 95

+--+
| **Library of Congress Cataloging in Publication Data** |
| |
| Prust, Z. A. |
| Graphic communications: the printed image / |
| by Zeke Prust. |
| |
| p. cm. |
| Includes index. |
| ISBN 0-87006-080-5 |
| 1. Printing, Practical--United States. I. Title. |
| Z244.P958 1994 |
| 686.2--dc20   93-26404 |
| CIP |
+--+

The cover photograph of monitor and screen image is courtesy of Radius, Inc.

The photograph is reproduced as a 150-line screen; the background image was enlarged from a portion of the photo to show the halftone at a resolution of 10 dots per inch.

INTRODUCTION

Graphic communications, sometimes called graphic arts or just printing, has seen drastic changes in the past few years. The influx of electronics and computers has affected almost all areas of production. Electronic scanners, electronic color correction systems, electronic publishing, electronically controlled cameras, electronic monitoring and control systems on presses, and other advancements have changed almost every aspect of printing technology to some extent.

GRAPHIC COMMUNICATIONS will help you learn about the rapidly changing field of printing quickly and easily. It "tells and shows" how various methods are used to take an original idea and convert it into a finished printed product.

This book is designed to explain the numerous technological advancements and to also describe conventional methods for producing printed products. This should give you the knowledge needed to understand all major aspects of graphic communications.

The text is divided into 33 chapters. Each chapter starts out with objectives so you will know what you are expected to learn. Know These Terms, at the end of chapters, will help you make sure you have learned the language of the industry. Technical terms are printed in italics and immediately defined. A good selection of Review Questions will test your comprehension of the chapter material.

Since "a picture paints a thousand words," this text uses hundreds of illustrations to clarify the complex processes of the industry. Color is used to enhance the educational value of many of these illustrations and to also stress safety rules given throughout the book.

GRAPHIC COMMUNICATIONS is a valuable source of information for anyone entering any area of the printing industry. This text will help you become well versed in all aspects of printing technology.

Z. A. Prust

CONTENTS

1 Overview of Graphic Communications 7

2 Graphic Communications Careers 27

3 Safety and Health 41

4 Measurement 53

5 Typefaces 69

6 Design 87

7 Copyfitting, Specifications 95

8 Relief Composition 107

9 Cold Composition 119

10 Layout 141

11 Proofreading 169

12 Electronic Production 177

13 Line Photography, Process Cameras 191

14 Halftone Reproduction 215

15 Color Theory and Reproduction, Scanners 235

16 Photomechanical and Electronic Modifications 257

17 Processing Photographic Material 269

18 Stripping and Imposition 281

19 Contacting and Color Proofing 299

20 Offset Lithographic Platemaking 311

21 Relief Plates 329

22 Lithographic Press Systems 339

23 Offset Press Operation and Troubleshooting 357

24 Letterpress Imposition and Lockup 383

25 Relief Printing Presses 391

26 Gravure Printing 405

27 Screen Printing and Other Processes 419

28 Substrates 447

29 Ink 463

30 Finishing and Binding 471

31 Trade Customs 499

32 Designing For Efficiency, Entrepreneurship 505

33 The Changing Technology 517

Index-Glossary Reference 524

IMPORTANT SAFETY NOTICE

The theory, procedures, and safety rules given in this book are typical to the industry. However, they are general and do NOT apply to all situations. For this reason, it is very important that you refer to the manufacturer's instructions when using any product or machine. These factory directions will give the details needed to work safely while producing quality printed products.

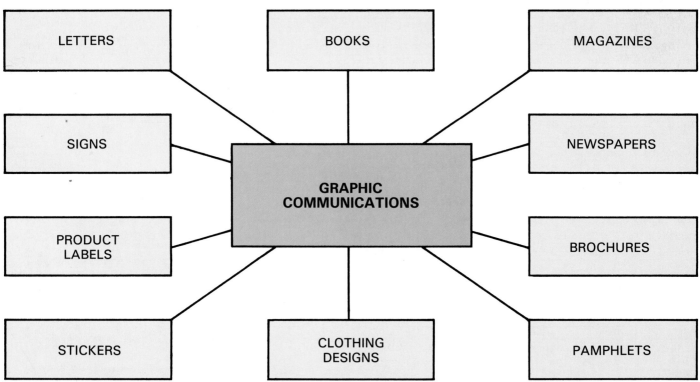

LETTERS

BOOKS

MAGAZINES

SIGNS

NEWSPAPERS

PRODUCT LABELS

BROCHURES

GRAPHIC COMMUNICATIONS

STICKERS

CLOTHING DESIGNS

PAMPHLETS

Graphic communications is a vast industry that produces a wide variety of products. This chapter will quickly review the major areas that you will learn about when studying this book.

Chapter 1

OVERVIEW OF GRAPHIC COMMUNICATIONS

After studying this chapter, you will be able to:
• Explain the important role of graphic communications in our technological society.
• Identify the major processes commonly associated with the graphic communications industry.
• Summarize the four printing classifications.
• Describe the operations normally found in the binding and finishing departments of printing plants.
• Summarize the flow of a product through a graphic communications facility.
• More fully comprehend the subjects covered in later chapters of this book.

The term *"graphic"* relates to things we can see or to the visual. The term *"communication"* refers to the exchange of information in any form. Therefore, *graphic communication* means the exchange of information in visual form: words, drawings, photographs, etc.

The purpose of this chapter is to briefly explain the role of graphic communications in a technological society and to identify the basic processes of the industry. As a result, this chapter will help prepare you to more fully comprehend later chapters that discuss the many aspects of graphic communications in more detail.

WHY IS COMMUNICATION IMPORTANT?

People are communicators! We exchange messages when we talk, send a letter, watch television, phone someone, read directions, or observe a stop light. This exchange of complex data sets humans apart from other living organisms. Without this communication, the human race would become chaotic and could quickly self-destruct.

The method or *medium* of communication will vary based on the specific needs of the individuals. For example, talking or verbal expression is satisfactory in certain situations, but it has limitations. People can often be misunderstood or thoughts can be forgotten with verbal communication. There is no record of the exchange of ideas or thoughts. Therefore, *graphic images* (visual images) have and will continue to be extremely important to our rapidly advancing society, Fig. 1-1.

PRODUCING VISUAL IMAGES

In the past, the term "printing" was used to imply all facets of the graphic communications industry. However, with present technology, printing is too limited to include the advanced technology found in a typical facility. Many allied systems, mostly electronic, have been added to the production of graphic images.

Printing is now understood to imply using ink to place an image on a *substrate* (paper, plastic, etc.). Today, printing is just one part or aspect of the rapidly growing graphic communications industry.

Graphic communications has become more acceptable and accurate to reflect today's modern, highly sophisticated industry. It implies exchanging data visually, in any form:

Fig. 1-1. Graphic communications involves the exchange of messages in visual form. Here employees in a graphic communications facility work as a ''team'' to exchange ideas verbally for printed product. (Screaming Color-Chapter One)

Fig. 1-2. Communication is critical to the human race. Without communication, society would become chaotic. Communication can take many forms. When talking on the phone, using verbal communication, you may also be using satellite communication to send your messages. (Policrom Screens)

printing, satellite communication of documents, computer generated images, monitor display of words, etc., Fig. 1-2.

As you will learn, technological changes in equipment have provided some sophisticated control devices to assist operators to produce quality printed products more efficiently.

PURPOSE OF GRAPHIC COMMUNICATIONS

Graphic communications is the "lifeblood" of our technological society. The industry is directing and influencing the population of the world wherever and whenever a product is printed.

A common description of printing is that it is "the art preservative of all arts." It is a primary means of storing information.

Textbooks, magazines, and journals all advance the knowledge of our society. The variety of printed products seems to be endless: books, newspapers, greeting cards, packages, stamps, fabrics, labels, order forms, advertisements, manuals, and maps are a few examples. Take away any one of these and think how it would affect society.

Truly, graphic communications is a major contributor to the advancement of civilization. It affects education to a very high degree—how individuals think; how individuals see things; and how they draw conclusions. Knowledge can become obsolete, but scholars often refer to the past to derive conclusions and direction for the future.

Printing also plays a very important role in the leisure time of our society. Printed materials take a wide variety of forms for recreational purposes.

People are often seeking knowledge which is very practical and is in immediate need. An example is someone referring to a service manual that explains how to repair a certain make of car. Textbooks are a form of storing knowledge for immediate use or for future reference. Take away the books in the libraries across the country and those seeking knowledge would be greatly deprived. Most of our heritage and knowledge would be lost.

Advertising is another form of information. The printed "ad" is a common means of conveying advertising messages to potential buyers. The ad in a newspaper is an example of informing people of a product generally available in a local area. A magazine advertisement is a method of telling people of a product on a regional or national basis. Advertisement takes on many forms.

The visual impression of an ad creates a great impact on the selection of a product. Focusing attention helps in directing a buyer's decision-making or purchasing process.

DESIGN, SPECIFICATIONS, QUOTES

Before any job can be printed, the product must be thought out from beginning to end. It must be properly designed. Specifications or measurements for all variables must be given and a quote of costs must be calculated.

Design

Design assures that the printed image conveys the intended message. Many forms of art medium are used by the graphic designer. Taking an idea and putting the idea in an appropriate visual presentation is a very important skill. The selection of the type style and pictorial material, which includes art forms and photographs, can make the final product either acceptable or unacceptable.

Specifications

Specifications are guidelines used to determine the format and cost of the final product. This would include such items as *paper weight* (thickness), color use, type of binding, and finishing methods. The development of specifications varies considerably from one facility to another.

Quotes

A *quote* or *quotation* lists the specific prices and quantities for production of printed goods and services. It is a cost agreement between two parties. The cost estimate is based on the job specifications. The cost values represent the final cost to manufacture the printed product, Fig. 1-3.

COPY AND ART PREPARATION

Most printed products have a combination of written material, called *copy* (words), and pictures, called *artwork* (line art and photographs). Both are equally important in graphic communications, Fig. 1-4.

Fig. 1-3. The quote is given to the customer after evaluation of the cost of materials, size of run, color use, etc. (Screaming Color-Chapter One)

Fig. 1-4. Editor must ready copy for typesetting and check art for layout. This is important aspect of production. Mistakes waste time and money.

Copy

The copy, also termed the *manuscript* or *text,* must be composed by a person having writing talent and a grasp of the subject. The amount of copy will vary with each type of job. For instance, a magazine article and an advertisement will vary tremendously in length, style, content, and purpose.

Many of today's writers use a computer to input their knowledge or message. Some still use a typewriter. The computer or word processor is becoming more popular because it allows for easy modification of copy. Spelling, sentence

Fig. 1-5. The computer is moving into almost every facet of graphic communications. Writers and editors commonly use computer or word processor because it allows for easy change in wording, spelling, sequence, etc. (Screaming Color-Chapter One)

structure, and punctuation can all be corrected on the display terminal or monitor. Then, a printer will output the copy onto paper. Refer to Fig. 1-5.

Line art

Line art is an image consisting of solid lines on a white or contrasting background. A number of techniques are used to produce line art. In most cases, technical ink pens are utilized to manually make solid black lines on a white background. However, computers tied to *plotters* (automated drafting machines) or *optical exposure units* (scanner-type device explained shortly) will also produce very high quality line art.

Note! Copy, since it is usually solid black type on white, is commonly referred to as *line copy*. Look at Fig. 1-6.

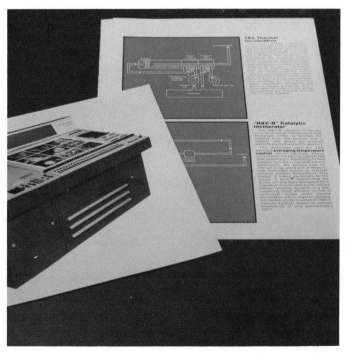

Fig. 1-6. Written material, line art, and photos are three types of matter in printed products. As you will learn, each must be handled differently when moving through production.

9

Continuous tone

Continuous tone copy has gradations of tones or shades from light to dark. A photograph is an example of a continuous tone. It has a range from the very lightest shade to the darkest shade. Continuous tone copy must be handled differently than line art when moving through some stages of production.

Halftones

A *halftone* is a continuous tone photograph that has been broken into TINY DOTS with a screening process. Halftones are needed to run an image on a press. The press plate or image carrier needs distinct solid and nonsolid areas (non-image areas) to place inked images on the substrate.

If you use a magnifying glass to look at any of the photos in this textbook, you will be able to see that the images are halftones and have a dot pattern. Fig. 1-7 shows a greatly magnified view of the dots in a halftone.

Separations

Separations are needed for each primary color of a four color illustration. Each separation is a positive or negative representing one primary color: cyan (blue), magenta (red), yellow, and black. Each separation is used to make the image carrier (plate) for that color. When run on the press, each color is printed in *register* (alignment) with the other to produce a full color illustration. See Fig. 1-8.

As you will learn later, highly sophisticated equipment is commonly used to make separations for full color reproduction.

Editing

Editing is the final preparation of the author's or writer's manuscript for publication. It involves checking the text,

Fig. 1-8. To print four-color, color separations have to be made of full color photo. Each separation represents one of the four primary colors. Then, four colors of ink can be deposited in register or on top of each other on the paper when running through press. (Westvaco Corp.)

Fig. 1-7. An original photo is a continuous tone that has different shades or gradations of color or darkness. A halftone is screened and is made up of tiny dots that look like a continuous tone. Screen or dot pattern is needed so different amounts of ink can be printed on substrate. Look at the photos in this book closely with a magnifying glass. Can you see the dots on the halftones?

line art, and photographs. There are two classifications of editing: content editing and copy editing.

Content editing, as the name implies, is more involved with the subject matter than with spelling and punctuation. The editor checks the material to make sure it is up-to-date, technically accurate, covers all important ideas, is organized into a logical sequence, and is interesting. Some of the manuscript may have to be rewritten during content editing. More thought is given to the ideas presented than to whether a "t" is crossed or an "i" is dotted.

Copy editing is usually done after content editing. After all of the thoughts are organized in sequence, copy editing is done to correct spelling and punctuation, to mark for style, and to assure proper grammar. Consistency within the designated format or style is critical during copy editing.

As with writing, editing is frequently done on a computer. The writer's manuscript may even come in as a floppy disk. When on a "floppy," the manuscript can be altered while still as digital data in the computer. The edited material can usually be transferred directly to the typesetting equipment, using floppy disks. Changes to meet specifications in type style, line length, and type size can then be made on the typesetting equipment.

Copyfitting

Copyfitting is the planned fitting together of three separate elements: the copy, the art, and the area. Copy that is too long or too short for the space in a given job will change the planned design of the job. Several copyfitting methods are used today. Professional writers very seldom have difficulty in submitting the right number of words for the layout. The computer is a valuable tool because it can evaluate the area, modify type or art size, or alter other factors to meet the job specifications.

IMAGE GENERATION

Image generation is the process of making high quality reproduction copy. These images can be produced manually by the graphic designer or by very sophisticated, computerized equipment. Refer to Figs. 1-9 and 1-10.

Cold composition

The term *"cold composition"* was derived as the opposite of hot composition. *Hot composition* is associated with molten metal, such as was used by older line casting machines of the past. Cold composition is a broad term that includes present typesetting methods other than hot type.

Examples of ways of producing words in cold type are: composing or image generation machines, strike-on devices, freehand lettering or writing, transfer letters, and lettering devices or guides.

Photocomposing

Photocomposing is the generation of an image using light and a light sensitive material. A very high percentage of all copy set today is by phototypesetting or image generation machines. These machines make it possible to create various

Fig. 1-9. Cold composition refers to modern methods of setting type. Hot type was older method when characters were formed from molten metal. This typesetter is working at modern photocomposing machine. Input is stored on computer disk. Disk can then be sent to laser machine that places high quality type image on light sensitive paper.

Fig. 1-10. This full-function workstation offers complex page layout, color correction, and retouching. (Scitex America Corporation)

Fig. 1-11. Modern facilities use computer-controlled equipment to set text, create art, or modify images quickly and accurately.

Hard and soft copy

Soft copy refers to data that is stored as computer information, usually on a *floppy disk* (magnetic storage disk). The data on the floppy disk can be stored or recalled for editing on the monitor when a change in copy is needed. Refer to Fig. 1-12.

Fig. 1-12. Personal computers can be interfaced or linked with typesetting equipment. The writer can set copy on the computer. Then, the floppy disk inputs data into typesetting equipment computer storage for programming in type style, type size, and line length. (R.R. Donnelley)

size images (letters, numbers, etc.) that are very sharp and accurately positioned. Look at Fig. 1-11.

The text material is assembled by automatic or computer-controlled typesetting equipment. A typical means of inputting the copy is by using a keyboard that looks like a typewriter or computer keypad. The computer circuitry deposits the image on light sensitive paper with a laser (concentrated light beam) or CRT (cathode ray tube or electron beam). This produces a *latent image* (image not visible or permanent) on the light sensitive material.

A *processor,* also called a *developing unit,* is then used to treat the light sensitive paper and make the latent image of the copy permanent and visible. Chemicals in the processor cause a chemical reaction on the light sensitive paper's surface. This develops the image, similar to that of developing a photograph.

Galleys (proofs)

A *galley* is the copy output from the image generation machine and the processor. It is the light sensitive paper after it has been developed. The copy is very clean and precise, making it suitable for reproduction.

The galley can be proofread and used as camera ready copy. The negative or positive is used to make the printing plate after being positioned or organized properly with the other elements of the printed product.

Camera-ready copy

Camera-ready copy refers to images that are good enough to be used in a printed product. For example, a dot matrix printer (printer that produces small dots to form each character) is NOT high quality. It is difficult to read and is not commonly used as camera-ready copy. However, the words or letters produced by phototypesetting equipment are suitable as camera-ready copy. Each letter or character is shaped perfectly and positioned in a straight line across the page or sheet.

The term *hard copy* indicates copy printed on a substrate. For example, the soft copy on a floppy disk can be made into hard copy with a low cost printer. Then, the text can be checked or proofed before placing the text image on more expensive photographic paper. The hard copy from the printer can be sent to other employees or a client for review. Look at Fig. 1-13.

Strike-on

Regular office typewriters or special typewriters designed for producing copy for reproduction are called *strike-on type composers*. Special computer-controlled typewriters are also available for producing camera-ready copy.

Freehand lettering or writing

Hand lettering or *writing* is sometimes used for reproduction, Fig. 1-14. The images must be very dense using black ink, red ink, or paint. Discussed in later chapters, special pens, ink, and other equipment are needed.

Transfer letters

Transfer letters are printed on large sheets. These can be removed and placed on another sheet of material to be reproduced. An adhesive type substance makes the letters bond to the new substrate.

Lettering devices

All layout people are not capable of drawing images freehand; therefore, special *lettering guides* are used to assist

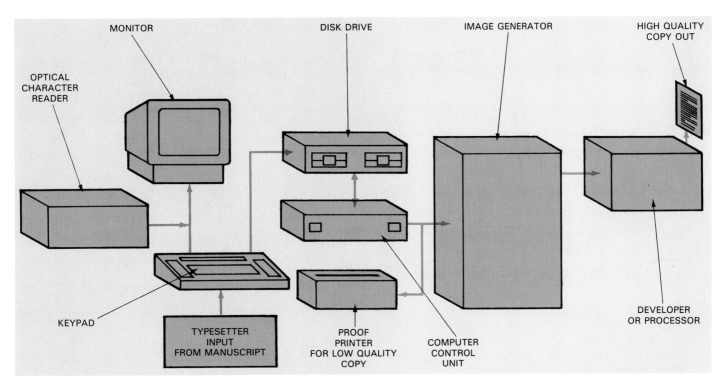

MONITOR   DISK DRIVE   IMAGE GENERATOR   HIGH QUALITY COPY OUT

OPTICAL CHARACTER READER

KEYPAD

TYPESETTER INPUT FROM MANUSCRIPT

PROOF PRINTER FOR LOW QUALITY COPY

COMPUTER CONTROL UNIT

DEVELOPER OR PROCESSOR

Fig. 1-13. Drawing shows fundamental parts of modern computerized, typesetting equipment. Optical character reader is advanced unit that can change hand-typed copy into computer digital code automatically. Monitor or screen is television type picture tube for observing what is in computer. Keypad is for inputing data manually into computer. Disk drive inputs or stores data. Computer control unit interfaces various units. Printer is for low quality proof copies of text. Image generator commonly uses a laser or cathode ray tube to place text on light sensitive paper. Developer or processor makes image on paper visible and permanent.

in creating the images in a professional manner. They serve as template devices for forming character shapes.

Fig. 1-15 shows a machine, called a *typositor,* which can generate extremely large characters for reproduction.

Fig. 1-14. Hand composition of type is needed with special applications. Here layout artist is pasting up extremely large type for poster. (Lehigh Press)

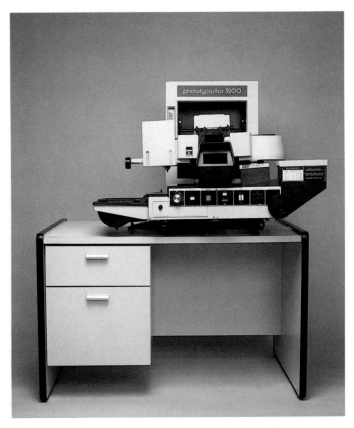

Fig. 1-15. Typositor can be used to make very large characters that cannot be generated on phototypesetting equipment. (Visual Graphics Corporation)

LAYOUT

It is essential that the printed material be attractive in design, hold attention, transmit the message, as well as stimulate the reader. Refer to Fig. 1-16.

Layouts are the arrangement of all component parts of a printed product. All of the parts (type, line art, photos) must be organized to form an attractive printed product. See Fig. 1-17. Three types of layouts are: thumbnail sketch, rough, and comprehensive.

Fig. 1-16. Layout brings all parts of graphic product together. Here artist is working with overlays to produce color line drawing. (Lehigh Press)

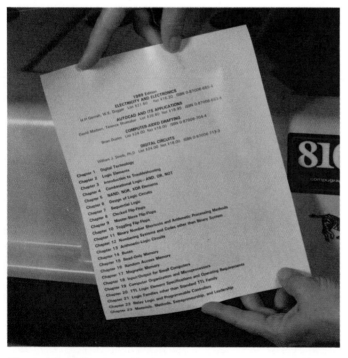

Fig. 1-17. Galley is normally text as it comes out of developer or processor after phototypesetting. It must be checked carefully.

The *thumbnail sketch* is the idea in basic form. Time and money can be saved by first submitting a series of hand-made thumbnail sketches to the client.

The *rough* is an actual size visual of the page that accurately shows the space for type and position of different illustrations.

The *comprehensive* is the most detailed sketch. It clearly shows style, size, and format to be used in the final printed piece.

Mechanical

The *mechanical* is the assembly of all the components or elements as camera-ready copy during layout. Another term commonly used in place of the mechanical is the *pasteup*. Look at Fig. 1-18.

Fig. 1-18. Making mechanical or pasteup requires layout person to position all elements on layout sheet properly.

The mechanical is usually layed out to exact size of the finished job. This allows body copy, page numbers, etc. to be set to the finished size. The galleys are cut and adhered in place on the layout sheets. These elements can be bonded into position with melted wax, rubber cement, tape, or pressure sensitive adhesive.

The space for photographs, and other special art must be accurately indicated on the mechanical. Photos are not pasted down during layout. A *blue pencil* is used to write all of the instructions and guide lines on the layout sheets because it will not reproduce and show on the final product.

Electronic pagination

Electronic pagination is a form of computerized layout, Fig. 1-19. Discussed later, a machine is used to convert the text, line art, and photos into electronic data. The electronic images can then be viewed on a monitor. The operator can size and organize all of the elements by computer. A total page can be composed and final copy assembled electronically. Then, the computer can be used to output the data as a single sheet of camera-ready copy, Fig. 1-20.

Fig. 1-19. Electronic pagination is form of computerized layout. Computer uses digital data to show images on monitor. Computer can be programmed to position type, size art, etc., so that page is made up electronically and then generated into hard copy of final product.

Fig. 1-20. Here operator is programming information for electronic cropping and sizing of four color photo.

PHOTOCONVERSION

Photoconversion generally implies using light to place the original image onto a light sensitive material. This new image is needed to make the printing plate or image carrier. The press or other device is then capable of using the image carrier to reproduce the original image in large quantities.

Process cameras

The originals can be photographically converted or altered using a *process camera*, Fig. 1-21. The process camera either has a horizontal or vertical facing lens. Some must be used in a darkroom (area void of light). Others are *daylight cameras* and can be used in normal room light.

In the various reproduction processes involving the process camera, a *film negative* (opposite original), a *film positive* (film like original), or a *print* (photo like original) can be produced. Presently, the process camera is commonly used to make enlargements, reductions, and same size reproductions. It is sometimes used to make screened photos. See Fig. 1-22.

Fig. 1-21. Process camera will make duplicates of originals of varying sizes. It can also make screened positives and negatives. This horizontal camera is computerized. (AGFA)

Fig. 1-22. This is a vertical camera. Note controls for automatic exposure, sizing, etc. It is designed to be used in normal room light. Film or photopaper is roll fed. This type camera is commonly used to make stats, enlarge or reduce copies, screen halftones, and make film positives or negatives. (Visual Graphics Corporation)

Discussed briefly, a *screened photo* has been changed from a continuous tone photograph to a halftone. The halftone has tiny dots that produce the image. The tiny dot patterns are needed for printing. A press needs these small dots so that dots of ink can be deposited on the paper to produce an image that looks like a photograph.

Photos can be screened electronically or by placing a *screen* (dot pattern image) over the film during reproduction.

Darkroom

A *darkroom* is an area that can be made devoid of light for working with photographic materials. Although daylight handling films are becoming very popular, many films must be developed in a special darkroom which keeps out white light. Special lights are used in the darkroom for safe film handling before and after exposure.

Fig. 1-23. This is a camera-developer system. It automatically reproduces image after being programmed properly. (Visual Graphics Corporation)

Fig. 1-23 shows a camera with an automatic or computer-controlled developing system. The processor develops the light sensitive material into a permanent, visible image.

Scanners

Scanners provide an electronic means of placing an image onto a light sensitive material or onto *magnetic disks* (computer data storage devices). They are commonly used to make screened halftones and more commonly, color separations. Scanners will also allow images to be modified electronically to improve color, alter contrast, change sizes, etc.

The scanner is slowly replacing the process cameras for many tasks. One is pictured in Fig. 1-24.

For example, a four-color transparency can be placed on the input drum of the scanner. The scanner spins the transparency. A sensor and electronic circuitry convert the image into an electronic, digital, or computer code. This allows the image to be stored or modified electronically, Fig. 1-25. The output drum of the scanner will produce a screened image or color separations of the original.

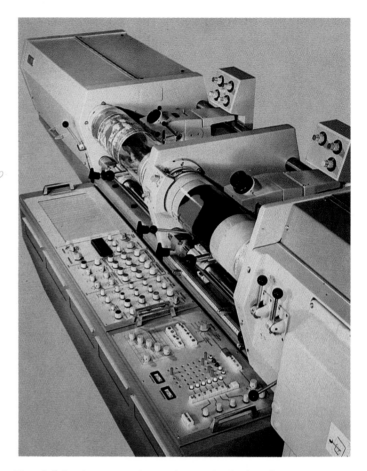

Fig. 1-24. A scanner is an electronic device that converts a visual image into a digital code. When in electronic or digital form, the image can be easily separated into primary colors, modified, enlarged, reduced, or screened. (Linotype-Hell)

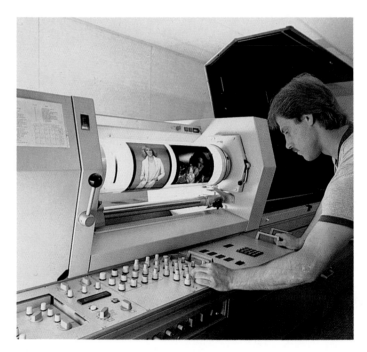

Fig. 1-25. Operator is scanning two four-color transparencies. Scanner drum spins transparencies and optical pickup converts images into electrical data representing images. (Screaming Color-Chapter One)

Fig. 1-26 shows computer-aided scanning. The operator is correcting the color of a photo on a monitor.

Fig. 1-27 shows the storage disks for scanned images. This saves considerable space over storing actual films.

A monitor, showing an actual scanned photograph, is given in Fig. 1-28. Note how the computer can be used to close in on minute details of the photo. The color of the woman's eyes can be changed electronically before going to film.

Fig. 1-29 illustrates how computer-aided scanning can be used to modify a transparency.

After the image has been corrected or modified as needed, the scanner will output the new image directly onto film. In most cases, the electronically or contact screened images on film are needed to produce the printing plates.

Fig. 1-26. Once scanner has converted images into digital code, computer can be used to modify images by changing electrical data. Here operator is using computer-aided scanning system to richen color of transparencies. (Chemco)

Fig. 1-27. Instead of huge stacks of film, magnetic disks store images more efficiently. A—This rack of disks contains a tremendous amount of data. (Lehigh Press) B—The CD is another storage medium.

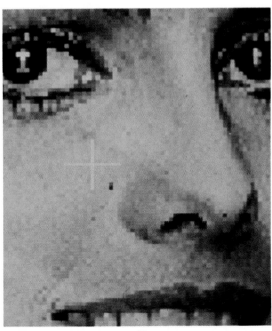

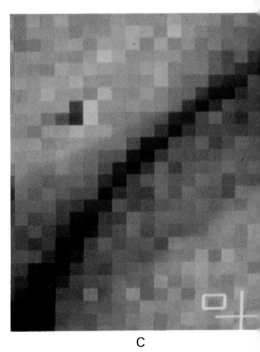

A   B   C

Fig. 1-28. Note how computerized-scanning or preview system lets you use monitor to zoom in on specific area of image. A—Full view of transparency, for general evaluation. B—Close-up of facial details. C—Extreme close-up for making eyes a richer color, called color correction.

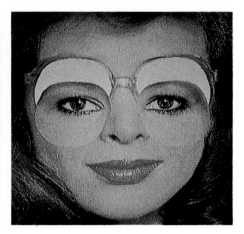

Fig. 1-29. Here a computer is being used to actually alter the content of the image. Note how eye position has been altered electronically. All three are from the same original.

Control instruments

Numerous types of control instruments are used in graphic communications to assure consistent quality. One example is the densitometer, Fig. 1-30.

The *densitometer* will measure the density, opacity, or light stopping ability of an image. This will allow the image to be reproduced properly. You will learn about many types of similar instruments in this book.

STRIPPING

Stripping is the process of film assembly before printing. It involves the assembling of line and halftone negatives or positives. All of the negatives or positives, when assembled, make up a single page or several pages, called a *flat*. See Fig. 1-31. The film is attached to a base or flat which supports the individual pieces of film.

As is occuring in other areas, changes are taking place in the stripping department. The application of the computer is very evident since all of the films can be assembled electronically. This eliminates the tedious work now being done by the stripper.

Fig. 1-32 shows an automatic stripping or computer stripping type system.

PLATEMAKING

Platemaking is the process of placing an image on an *image carrier* or *plate*. The method varies with each printing process. Carriers can be produced mechanically, electronically, or photographically. The plates are the means by which MANY COPIES can be made as duplicates of the original. All image carriers must have the quality to transfer identical images into a substrate.

Today, it is possible to place the stored images on the image carrier or plate without intermediate steps. For example, images can be placed directly on plates using a computer-controlled laser. Look at Fig. 1-33.

Fig. 1-30. Densitometer is common tool used in graphic communications. It will measure contrast or density of images for assuring quality reproduction.

Fig. 1-31. Stripping involves working with films that have been converted from layout sheets and continuous tone photos. All images must be located on flat properly before making press plate or image carrier.

Fig. 1-32. This is an automatic or computerized stripping system. "Mouse" or handset can be moved around to outline or denote images for sizing, masking, etc. It saves time over hand stripping in some applications. (Screaming Color-Chapter One)

Fig. 1-33. Control room of computerized graphic communications facility. Some facilities can go directly to plate electronically. Plate or image carrier is needed so that press can deposit ink on substrate.

PRESSWORK

Presswork, in all printing processes, is the transfer of an image from an image carrier to a substrate. The most commonly used *substrate* is paper. Printing presses are the "production machines" of the graphic communications industry. They will make duplicates in large quantities.

Sheet and web presses

Presses are of two types: sheet-fed and roll-fed. As the name implies, the *sheet-fed press* uses single or individual sheets of paper. A *roll-fed* or *web-fed press* uses a long, single sheet or ribbon of paper. See Fig. 1-34.

Fig. 1-35 shows a sheet-fed press. Fig. 1-36 shows a web-fed press. Web presses are used for longer *"runs"* (press operation for complete job) than sheet-fed presses.

Letterpress printing

Letterpress is a relief printing process that requires a raised image, Fig. 1-37A. Technological changes have brought about various kinds of letterpress duplicate image carriers. Some of today's newspapers are printed by the relief process.

The range of products printed by the letterpress process appears to be limitless. Examples are as follows: business cards, stationery, labels, business forms, tickets, cartons, magazines, reports, wrappings, newspapers, books, and many other products.

Flexography uses a flexible plastic or synthetic plate and has a relief or raised image to print on a substrate. Plastic bags, labels, and other packaging materials are commonly printed by this process.

Offset-lithography printing

Offset-lithography printing means that the image is on a flat surface and transferred to a substrate. The technical term used to identify this process is *planography*. The process is based on the concept that water and oil do NOT

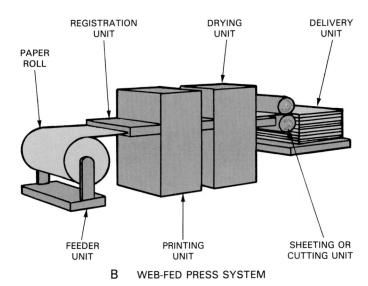

Fig. 1-34. Two basic types of presses. A—Sheet-fed press moves single sheets of paper through impression system. B—Web-press prints on long ribbon of paper. It is used for larger press runs.

Fig. 1-35. This is a sheet-fed offset-litho press. Paper sheets are picked up on right. They are then pulled to left for printing.

A

B

Fig. 1-36. This modern web press has computerized controls that increase production and quality. A—Press control center.
B—Web printing unit. (Hantscho)

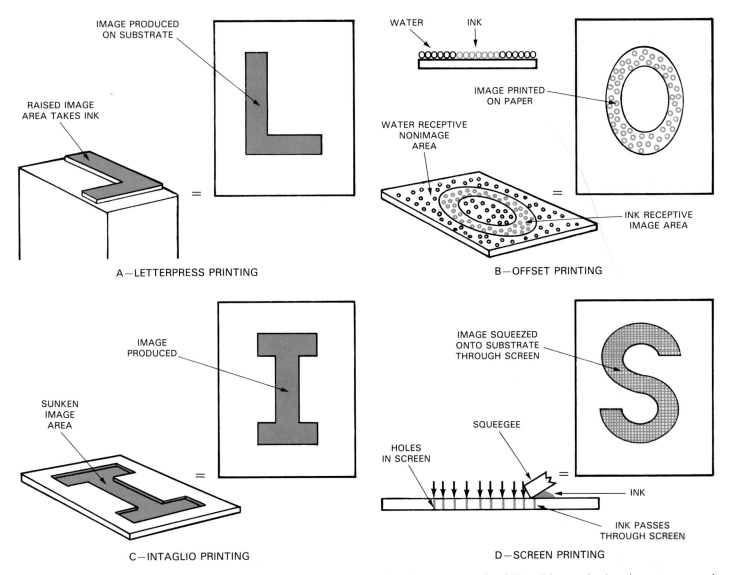

IMAGE PRODUCED ON SUBSTRATE

RAISED IMAGE AREA TAKES INK

A—LETTERPRESS PRINTING

WATER   INK

IMAGE PRINTED ON PAPER

WATER RECEPTIVE NONIMAGE AREA

INK RECEPTIVE IMAGE AREA

B—OFFSET PRINTING

IMAGE PRODUCED

SUNKEN IMAGE AREA

C—INTAGLIO PRINTING

IMAGE SQUEEZED ONTO SUBSTRATE THROUGH SCREEN

SQUEEGEE

HOLES IN SCREEN

INK

INK PASSES THROUGH SCREEN

D—SCREEN PRINTING

Fig. 1-37. Note four basic press systems. A—Letterpress has raised image area. B—Offset-lithography has image area and nonimage areas on same plane. Image area is receptive to ink. Nonimage area is only receptive to water. C—Gravure or intaglio has image area sunken to hold ink. D—Screen printing has small holes in image for ink to pass through and deposit on substrate.

readily mix, Fig. 1-37B. Both offset, sheet-fed, and web-fed presses may be commonly found in the same plant.

Waterless printing is a form of offset lithography that is growing in popularity for both quality and environmental reasons. It uses ink viscosity, rather than a dampening solution, to keep image and non-image areas separate.

Gravure printing

Gravure printing is a printing method most commonly known in the graphic communications industry as the *intaglio process*. The image area is sunken in the carrier, as shown in Fig. 1-37C.

Two characteristics are common to the gravure process. First, both line work and photographs are screened. Secondly, the image and nonimage areas of the carrier are inked and the ink must be scraped off the carrier surface by a doctor blade. This only leaves ink in the sunken image area.

The process is considered to be an excellent, high speed, long run means of producing a superior product. Some of

the typical materials printed by this method are: magazines, catalogs, newspaper supplements, package printing, metal surfaces, and vinyl surfaces.

The presses are often very large, Fig. 1-38, but smaller units are being manufactured. The trend is to also use gravure for some shorter run materials.

Screen printing

The *screen printing* process is the most used of the porous printing methods. Any stencil process is a form of porous printing. The image carrier is attached to the screen (porous image) and ink is forced through the open meshed areas. Refer to Fig. 1-37D.

A wide variety of applications exists. Many tiny electronic circuits are produced with a type of screen process. Another unusual application is printing the conductive materials on rear windows of automobiles to defrost the window.

The presses for the screen process can be hand operated or highly automated, Fig. 1-39.

Fig. 1-38. Press size varies tremendously. Here workers are preparing for long run. This is a gravure press.

Fig. 1-39. This is a screen press for special applications.

Impactless (pressureless) printing

Impactless or *pressureless printing* does not require direct contact between an image carrier and the substrate. Impactless printing, unlike the previously discussed processes, does not require that an ink be pressed against a substrate.

Ink jet printing is one of the examples of the impactless process. Ink droplets are formed and forced through very small nozzles onto the substrate. Most of the units use a computer to control the image generation. The computer controls where, and how much, ink is forced onto the substrate.

Laser printers are also being used to produce images which are high quality, Fig. 1-40. The *electrostatic method* uses the forces of an electric current and static electricity. It is commonly found in office copying machines. Some of today's machines are capable of producing copies in multiple colors.

BINDING AND FINISHING

Once an image has been printed on a substrate, some form of binding and/or finishing is usually required. One or the other or both are the final steps to complete the printing job.

Binding

Binding generally involves attaching several pages of a printed product together. Binding requires complex equipment, as shown in Fig. 1-41.

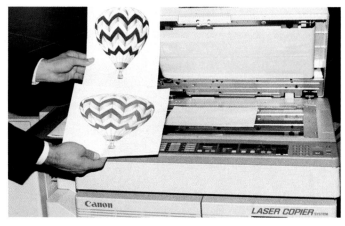

Fig. 1-40. A laser copier will produce quality images in full color. Copier technology has advanced tremendously in recent years.   (Canon)

Fig. 1-41. A bindery uses various methods to hold multiple sheets together to form one product; this book is an example.

Most printing requires one or more of the following steps: scoring, folding, gathering, stitching, and trimming.

Scoring is the creasing of a heavier sheet of paper or paperboard to assist in the folding of the material.

Folding is required, for example, when a large sheet contains more than one page of a product, Fig. 1-42.

Gathering is the assembling of single pages or *signatures* (group of pages).

Collating requires that the pages be placed in the right sequence, Fig. 1-43.

Stitching is one means by which the collated materials are held or bound together. Many magazines are stitched to hold all the pages so that the magazine does not fall apart.

Trimming is the cutting of the stock to produce even edges. Fig. 1-44 shows an example of a semi-automatic operation for cutting stock. *Robotics* (automated machines) are used extensively in modern facilities to complete this cumbersome operation.

Finishing

Finishing is a term which includes operations that enhance the final printed product. Some of the more common operations are: embossing, die cutting, stamping, laminating, and coating. Additional specialities include: punching, drilling, round cornering, padding, guilding, etc.

Embossing is the process of producing a raised design on paper or other material. This finishing process uses pressure, heat, and dwell-time (contact time) to mold fibers of the paper into a design.

Die cutting is a process of cutting paper, paperboard, or other materials with regular or irregular designs formed by the die cutting rules or blades.

Stamping generally refers to the application of a metal foil to almost any type of material, such as leather, paper,

Fig. 1-43. Gathering is done to collect sheets or signatures into one product. This shows newspaper pages after gathering. (USA Today)

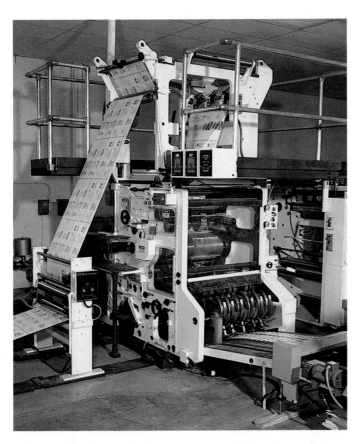

Fig. 1-42. Here you can see printed images leaving web press to start binding process. This machine folds, perforates, and chops web sheet into signatures. (Hantscho)

Fig. 1-44. Trimming is done to make all sheets even on edges. This is large computer-controlled cutter that automatically trims stock to size.

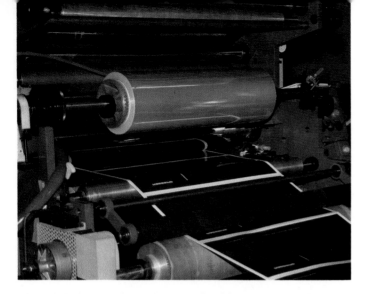

Fig. 1-45. Laminating is just one finishing operation that puts protective coating over image.

or cloth. A combination of embossing and foil stamping can also be done in one operation.

Lamination is the process of bonding plastic film, by heat and pressure, to a sheet of paper to protect the paper and improve its appearance. Rather than laminating stock, a *coating* can also be placed on the sheet to protect or to spot coat an area to draw attention. A common term that refers to coating is *varnishing*. Look at Fig. 1-45.

Many additional finishing operations are used in the industry and will be discussed in later chapters.

GRAPHIC COMMUNICATION SEGMENTS

The graphic communications industry can be divided into segments or classifications. A few of the segments are: commercial printing, periodical printing, newspaper printing, book publishing and printing, in-plant printing, and forms printing. See Fig. 1-46.

Commercial printing

The *commercial printer* is a printer for hire and has a very complex product variety. Typical products produced by this plant would revolve around job printing (flyers, brochures, letterheads, envelopes, etc.), advertising printing (events, products, etc.), and annual reports (financial statements of large companies). One printing process, offset lithography, appears to stand out in the commercial printing segment.

Periodical printing

Periodical printing consists of those establishments that print magazines. Publishers of periodicals are found in nearly every state of the United States. It appears that a shift to gravure is taking place in periodical production.

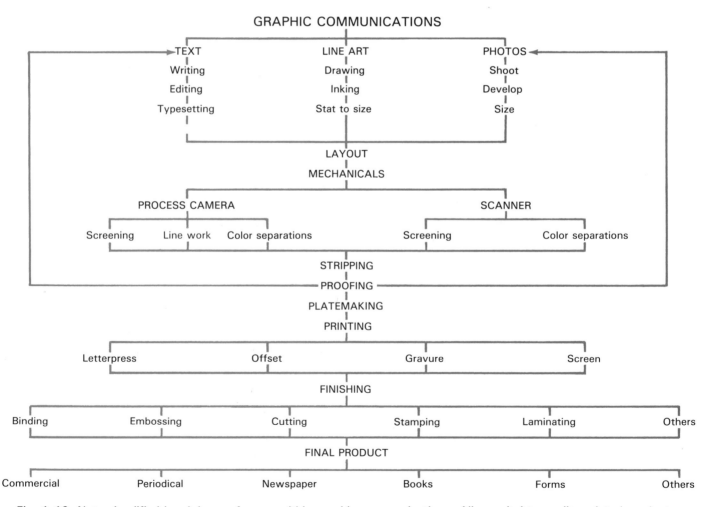

Fig. 1-46. Note simplified breakdown of areas within graphic communications. All are vital to quality printed products.

Newspaper printing

Newspaper printing provides news and advertising to various markets. The computer is very evident in today's facility. Satellite transmission makes it possible to have newspapers with national information on a daily basis.

Book publishing and printing

Book publishing and *printing* provides many types of books found in bookstores, drugstores, and general store displays. A large variety of subjects are found in textbooks. Most of the printing facilities use large web presses.

As you will learn, the book publishing industry is witnessing great changes in copy and pictorial handling hardware.

In-plant printing

The *in-plant printing* segment of the industry is commonly found as a printing facility that is located as a part of a non-printing industry. Most large companies have their own in-plant printing facility.

Forms printing

Forms printers design and print special forms used in business. The types of forms might include those for acquisition (obtaining), manipulation (changing), routing (moving), and recording (storing) of data or information. The "paperless" technologies (computers, microfilm, etc.) are altering the needs in some businesses.

KNOW THESE TERMS

Medium, Visual image, Substrate, Printing, Design, Specifications, Quotation, Manuscript, Line art, Continuous tone, Halftone, Content editing, Copy editing, Copyfitting, Image generation, Cold composition, Hot composition, Photocomposing, Floppy disk, Hard copy, Soft copy, Strike-on, Transfer lettering, Typositor, Galley, Proof, Layout, Thumbnail sketch, Rough, Comprehensive, Mechanical, Paste-up, Blue pencil, Electronic pagination, Full color, Process camera, Darkroom, Scanner, Computer-aided scanning, Densitometer, Stripping, Platemaking, Presswork, Sheet-fed press, Web-fed press, Letterpress, Flexography, Offset-lithography, Planography, Gravure, Intaglio, Screen printing, Inkjet printing, Impactless printing, Binding, Scoring, Gathering, Stitching, Trimming, Finishing, Embossing, Die cutting, Stamping, Laminating, Commercial printing, Periodical printing, Newspaper printing, Book printing, In-plant printing, Forms printing.

REVIEW QUESTIONS—CHAPTER 1

1. Which of the following is NOT considered a visual image?
   a. Written word. c. Photograph.
   b. Latent image. d. Line drawing.

2. A _____ is the material used for printing: paper, plastic, etc.
3. _____ assures that the printed image conveys the desired message.
4. What are specifications?
5. A quote gives the specific _____ and _____ for production of printed goods and services.
6. The manuscript can also be called the copy or text. True or False?
7. Line art includes drawings consisting of continuous tones. True or False?
8. Explain the term "halftone."
9. Explain the difference between content editing and copy editing.
10. This is the most common way of generating copy for printing.
    a. Strike-on.
    b. Hot type.
    c. Scanning.
    d. Photocomposing.
11. How does modern typesetting equipment store information?
12. How do you make a mechanical?
13. What is the difference between an original continuous tone photo and a screened halftone?
14. How can a photo be modified electronically?
15. In your own words, explain the following types of printing: Letterpress, Flexography, Planography, Gravure, Screen printing, Impactless printing.
16. _____ involves attaching several pages of a printed product together.
17. _____ is creasing a heavier sheet of paper to assist in folding.
18. _____ is the assembling of single pages or signatures.
19. _____ requires that the gathered pages be in the right sequence.
20. Explain four processes commonly associated with finishing.

SUGGESTED ACTIVITIES

1. Visit a commercial plant and identify the types of products produced by the facility.
2. Visit a quick-copy facility and identify its main objective in a technological society.
3. Select a printed product. Summarize the basic steps for producing the product.
4. Visit a commercial plant and identify the different graphic processes used in creating the product. Include: method of image generation, how halftones are produced, whether layout is done electronically, method of platemaking, and type of presswork used for production.

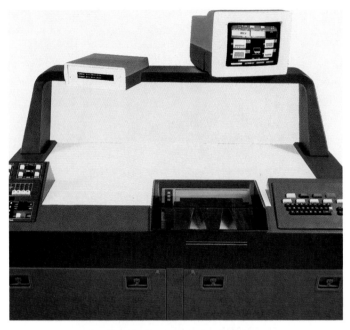

A—Electronic press control system.

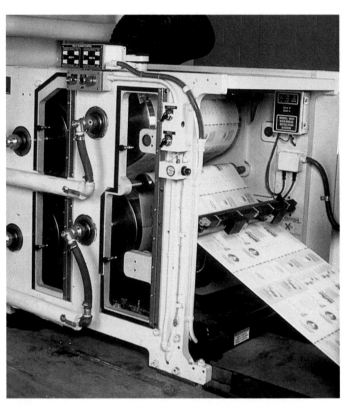

B—Web press.

C—Electronic image retouching station.

D—Electronic graphics tablet.

Graphic communications offers a wide variety of challenging jobs. These, and numerous other advanced machines, are used to produce quality printing products.   (Hantscho, Lehigh)

Chapter 2

GRAPHIC COMMUNICATIONS CAREERS

After studying this chapter, you will be able to:
- Identify the variety of jobs available within the graphic communications industry.
- Separate creative, skill, and management type positions.
- Explain the characteristics common to a selected position in graphic communications.
- Select a graphic communications career that matches your interests and abilities.

The graphic communications industry encompasses a multitude of challenging positions for creative, skilled, and management personnel. This chapter will summarize and help you more fully understand these positions.

CHOOSING A CAREER

Making a career choice is one of the most important decisions you will ever make. It can affect many aspects of your life. It will determine your income, your work surroundings, and the kinds of people you will be around all day. A career choice can also affect your family. It could determine where you live, how you dress for work, your geographic location, and many other considerations.

Job satisfaction

Above all, your career choice can affect your satisfaction with life in general. Satisfaction with your career is very important. You need to feel good about what you are doing all day and about the future it offers. You need to enjoy and be proud of your work.

Choosing the right graphic communications career requires you to look to the future. What kind of work do you expect to be doing five years from now? What do you want to be doing in ten years? Which occupation will offer advancement and give satisfaction? In what area is there going to be a demand?

First, you must know your interests and any special talents. Then you will need to identify the requirements of different printing jobs. This will let you select a career that fits your interests, abilities, and goals.

Categories of careers

The graphic communications industry needs people with many different talents, abilities, and interests. In general, the entire workforce can be organized into five different categories:
1. CREATIVE PEOPLE who are skilled at writing, art, and design.
2. SKILLED PEOPLE who can operate machines. Some of the machines are very complicated and require great skill.
3. MANAGERIAL types who like to work with people and supervise the work of others.
4. SCIENTIST with a deep interest in science and scientific research.
5. TECHNICAL PEOPLE who can complete tasks to improve the machines, materials, and printing products. They may experiment with and test machines, inks, and printing paper.

TECHNOLOGICAL GROWTH

Graphic arts industries, in recent years, have had a marked growth in use of technology. What was formerly an industry heavily oriented to printing crafts now has a huge commitment to state-of-the-art equipment. See Fig. 2-1.

The term commonly used to reflect the sophistication of the industry is *"high technology"* or "high tech." In the graphic communications industry, this means the use of computers, electronic devices, lasers, robotics, and similar technological advancements.

Computers and electronics

Computers are very much a part of the graphic communications industry. Computer applications in the future appear to be great. Fig. 2-2.

A very common example is the use of the computer to set type. Advancement has greatly increased the number of characters that can be set per second. The computer is also adaptable to many other uses: quality assurance, cost analysis, inventory, color separations, production scheduling, robot control, etc.

Fig. 2-1. Computers and electronics are moving into almost all career areas of graphic communications. (Scitex America Corporation)

Fig. 2-2. You might want to consider enrolling in some electronic or computer courses. This knowledge would be very helpful if you are seeking a career in graphic communications. In this illustration, employee is defining exposure parameters for computer-driven opti-copy system.   (Jonathan Rawle)

With the increased use of computers in graphic communications, a basic knowledge of electronics is imperative. Technical level training will be essential for many of the positions in modern industry. Look at Fig. 2-3.

Another electronics application is facsimile transmission of images over telephone lines or by satellite. Facsimile systems give the industry the capability of almost instant transportation of images as well as proofs across the coun-

try. The images are digitized (computer coded) and transmitted (sent electronically). The images can be stored or ready for display and use.

The adaptation is very functional for national and regional publications. The editor, production personnel, and others can call for copy and format as required for pagination. The format can be stored in the memory of the computer. The applications appear to be limitless.

You should consider enrolling in a few courses in basic electronics or computers. This could help you when trying to get a job in graphic communications.

Robotics

Robotics involves using machines to do repetitive tasks. It is being considered in various locations of the manufacturing facility. For example, a robot is ideal for the bindery area where highly repetitive tasks are found. The movement of stock from one location to another is also found in some plants. Positioning can be accurately accomplished by robotic applications. Robotic action is consistent, accurate, and it eliminates human error.

Common labor type activities may be eliminated by robots, but again, a higher technical skill will be required at other work locations.

A dramatic change in areas of the industry is expected in the future. Gaining information in this area certainly will benefit the future graphic communications employee.

Lasers

The *laser* (light amplification by stimulated emission of radiation) is just making itself known in the graphic

Fig. 2-3. This computer is capable of altering photograph electronically. A competent technician is needed to operate this type of sophisticated equipment.   (Scitex America Corporation)

communications industry. Its projected use is phenomenal. Research shows that it could affect most workers in the industry. Laser applications are being considered in nearly every area of production. You will learn about these laser applications later in the text.

Micro imaging

The limited storage space for printed materials has forced the development of *micro imaging* of materials on film. No longer are daily newspapers or technical drawings stored on shelves for future use. The drawings, maps, and graphs are placed in graphic recorders or on microfilm. A variety of film exposures assures high quality microform image recordings. A variety of employment opportunities are available. An interest in photographic techniques is essential.

SERVICE OPERATIONS

Printing is a cooperative enterprise. One component depends on another. Since most firms do not have an integrated facility, service companies are essential to contribute to the completion of a product.

Agency, studio

An *agency* or *studio* is an example of a service company. It will help a larger company with advertisements, packaging, and other printed or media-oriented materials. There are many graphic communications positions available in agencies, Fig. 2-4.

Quick printing/copy services

The role of quick printing or copy services is very evident. Speed is very important and varying degrees of quality may be acceptable to the client.

The persons employed in these facilities vary greatly from the standpoint of technical knowledge. The skill required by operators also varies. Many operators are "button pushers" while others have high technical skill and operate systems that are very sophisticated.

The other positions in this area require employees to be very versatile. The job specification might require that they manage, sell services, estimate job costs, or operate equipment. Knowing what is required by the owner or franchise is imperative.

Specialty printing service

Specialty printing shops do not have a wide market but provide a service for specialized products. They do engraving, labels, and other similar types of printing. For example, engraving would be needed for high quality business cards, stationery, invitations, and special treatment to posters or covers of reports.

Screen process service

The screen process area has many specialty type printing facilities. Some applications are for sign printing while others are for placing images on fabrics. Vinyl application is also found as a specialized form of screen printing.

Fig. 2-4. Service companies include advertising agencies, quick printing shops, specialty printing shops, composing service companies, etc. They are smaller companies that do work for larger companies or individuals.

A wide variety of skills are required in screen process printing. One example, the electronics industry is using very sophisticated screen printing systems to manufacture electronic circuits and components.

Composing service

Although many firms have *composing* or typesetting as an integral part of their operation, others rely on outside typographic service companies to supply their typesetting needs. Some typographic processes are very sophisticated. In the last few years, typography has experienced many changes brought about by technological advances in the industry. Research and development is evident and continued changes are expected in this exciting area.

Bindery and finishing service

Bindery and finishing operations are often beyond the capability of the facility. The basic requirements of binding and finishing are common to many facilities. However, processes that require a special application are subcontracted. The subcontracted company may have special equipment with rapid capability of folding, trimming, and packaging of the printed product.

Many of the positions in binding and finishing do not require extensive training. Therefore, this is one area of the industry ideal for the application of robotics. Once robots are in place in a bindery facility, a higher skill level will be needed by the employees. They must be able to maintain the robots and related equipment.

Manufacturers

The graphic communications industry depends on many types of machines to meet all the needs of a manufacturing facility. Someone must manufacture and service the cameras, platemakers, processors, presses, scanners, cutters, folders, inks, and paper. There are many job openings for people to sell and service products manufactured for the graphic communciations industry.

One example of an operation which fulfills a great need in the industry is the ink manufacturer. For instance, the chemist has the important job of compounding ink; the ink must be compatible with the press, substrate, and any other requirement of the process. Research and testing are imperative to guarantee the proper results.

CLASSIFICATION OF PERSONNEL

A closer look at the graphic communications industry shows that personnel fall under different classifications. It is important for you to understand these classifications. Four organization charts representing firms with size categories of 17, 50, 68, and 170 employees are shown in Figs. 2-5 through 2-8. The charts show how personnel in management

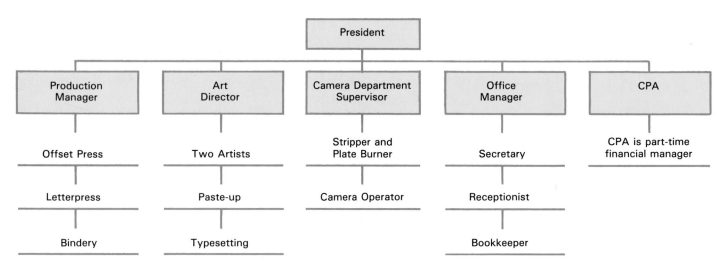

ORGANIZATION CHART
For Company with 17 Employees

Fig. 2-5. Study this organizational chart for a small company.

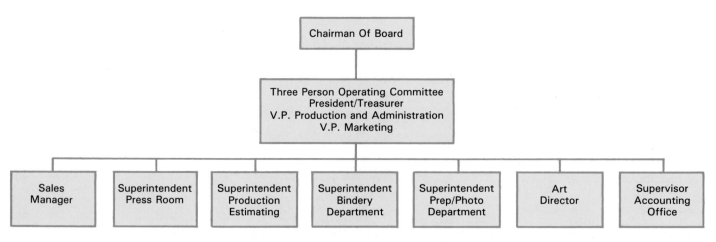

ORGANIZATION CHART
For Company with 50 Employees

Fig. 2-6. This is an organizational chart for a slightly larger company.

ORGANIZATION CHART
For Company with 68 Employees

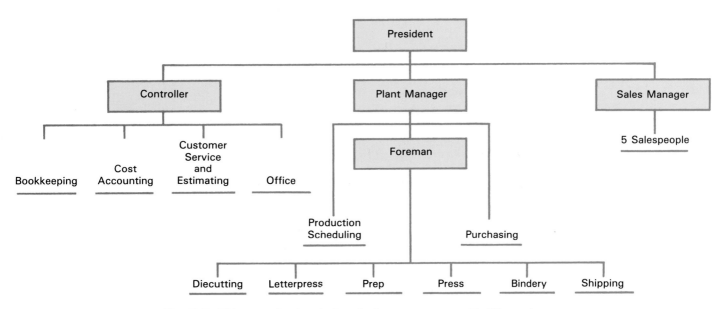

Fig. 2-7. This organizational chart is for a company with 68 employees.

ORGANIZATION CHART
For Plant with 170 Employees

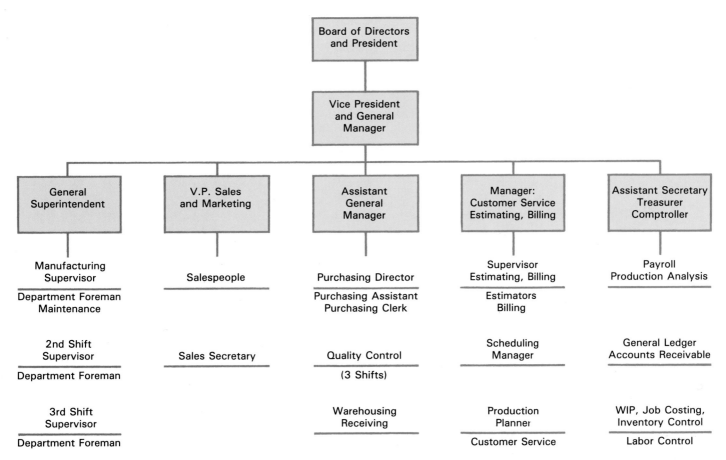

Fig. 2-8. Compare the added positions for this large graphic communications company. Trace the flow of responsibility through each area.

roles are responsible for areas within the industry. Understanding the role of each person in a management position is important. Study the charts carefully!

MANAGEMENT

The people in *management* are the leaders of a company. They are essential and affect the total organization. Part of being a good manager involves being able to get work done through other people. It also requires excellent organizational abilities, Fig. 2-9.

Management must work with other employees as a "team" to accomplish the objectives of the company. Communication, cooperation, and understanding between departments are essential for a happy, productive, constantly improving work force. Management is an important controlling factor over whether the job gets done right, and on deadline.

Some of the people on this team are: executive officers, plant managers, plant superintendents, managing editors, production managers, controllers, sales managers, supervisors, estimators, and planners.

The *Executive Officer* of the company, sometimes termed *President,* is the top administrator. He or she is considered to be the policy maker and overseer of the total operation. This person must employ good key personnel to have an effective and efficient company.

The basic characteristics important to the "management team" include the following:
1. Be able to make logical decisions.
2. Be able to get work done through others.
3. Be people oriented.
4. Be able to motivate personnel.
5. Apply factual information and not opinions.
6. Act as a mature, fair individual.

The roles of top level management were identified by the Graphic Arts Technical Foundation. The aspects of graphic communications that management must be concerned with are identified as:

1. Increased specialization of production equipment.
2. High investment requirements for new equipment.
3. Rising costs of materials and energy.
4. Shortages or lead times for critical materials.
5. Rapid introduction of new technology.
6. High interest rates for capital equipment purchases and short-term borrowing.
7. Excess production capacity.
8. Slow real growth in most market areas.
9. Threat of increased international competition for products.
10. Increase importance of government regulations in manpower, financial, and operational aspects of business.

Typically, the management personnel "wear many hats." At times, the executive officer can be the chief financial officer and also have responsibilities relating to sales. The mix of responsibilities appears to be common to the industry.

TECHNICAL SKILLS CAREERS

Employment within the graphic communications industry has two main categories: the production personnel with high technical skills and personnel having support roles—creative, and various management levels. Career opportunities are available for both men and women, Fig. 2-10. Most positions have an average wage scale with good benefits. The

Fig. 2-10. Technical skills are vital in most areas of graphic communications. Here technical person is operating a gravure cylinder engraving system. (Hell)

Fig. 2-9. The Chief Executive Officer (CEO) is the highest ranking manager in a company.

effects of the economy is not as evident as in many other industries because demand for printed material is usually constant. Most facilities have a comfortable working environment.

Pasteup artist

Whenever a printing process requires photoconversion, someone must place all of the elements in position. He or she must follow what the designer has indicated on the comprehensive. Pasting up all of the copy and pictorial material on a base sheet is the job of the *pasteup artist.*

Drafting techniques and freehand drawing may also be required by the pasteup person. Being precise, accurate, and neat are essential to this position. Look at Fig. 2-11.

Fig. 2-11. Layout artist must organize elements of publication on layout sheet. This is a demanding position that requires considerable talent.

Process camera operator

The *process camera operator* must take visual images and transfer them onto light sensitive materials. Called *film intermediates,* these films are used to make the final film for platemaking. Knowledge of lighting, optics, calculations, chemical reactions, as well as process camera operations are basic requirements.

The duties range from working with black and white line work, black and white halftones, special effects, diffusion transfer, and color separations. Some plants require specialists in each area, but many plants require the operator to be highly diversified.

A working knowledge of mathematics is preferred as well as a basic understanding of physics, chemistry, and other graphic communications processes. See Fig. 2-12.

Scanner operator

Many process camera operators move to the *scanner* as a means of making film intermediates. Discussed in Chapter 1, this electronic device is highly sophisticated. Most scanners use a laser to create the film intermediates and color separations. The classification of this operator often is

Fig. 2-12. Process camera operator must know lighting, optics, exposure calculations, chemicals, and basic methods for using camera. (Lehigh Press)

Fig. 2-13. Scanner operator is making transparency into color separations. This position requires specialized training. (Lehigh Press)

signified as a technician, suggesting a higher knowledge of mathematics and science. Look at Fig. 2-13.

Typesetter

The *typesetter* usually inputs manuscript or copy on a phototypesetting machine. This person must also be able to use and maintain the processing or developing equipment. When keystroking, high manual dexterity is an essential talent. Generally, being a good typist and being able to use a personal computer would provide excellent experience for

Fig. 2-14. Typesetter must have manual dexterity and knowledge of computerized typesetting equipment. (Information International)

Fig. 2-15. Stripper organizes films so they can be made into printing plates. As in layout, this requires using drafting type equipment. (Lehigh Press)

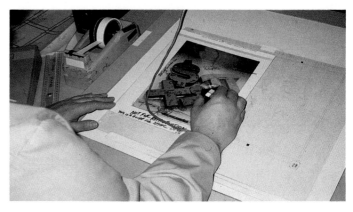

Fig. 2-16. Some facilities have electronic stripping equipment. Images are converted into digital or computer data. Then, images can be organized, masked, or sized on monitor. This saves time and energy.

becoming a typesetter. A knowledge of photography, darkroom procedures, and typographic principles may also be desirable. See Fig. 2-14.

Makeup person, stripper, opaquer

Arranging the film images into position is the job of the *makeup person* in relief printing and the *stripper* in lithographic shops. This individual must have good visual perception. Drafting knowledge and proper use of drafting tools is essential for the stripper, Fig. 2-15.

The *opaquer* retouches imperfections in films but also opaques out unwanted images. Patience is essential. As shown in Fig. 2-16, some companies have electronic or computerized stripping experts.

Platemaker

Several classifications of platemakers are found in the graphic communications industry. The *planographic* (litho) *platemaker* uses the flat (negatives located on a sheet by stripper) to place the image on a plate (image carrier). The plate is exposed when light passes through the clear areas

of the negative or positive and an image is developed on the image carrier or plate. The platemaker may develop the carrier by hand or with an automatic plate processor. A basic understanding of how to work with chemicals would be helpful.

A *photoengraver* makes plates used to print by the relief (letterpress) process. Application of mathematics and chemistry are definite needs.

A *relief platemaker* makes duplicates of originals. These image carriers (plates) are made from metal, plastic, rubber, etc. You must have knowledge of how materials react to heat, pressure, and time. Understanding other graphic processes is also suggested.

Pressroom personnel

Pressroom personnel are needed to transfer the plate image to a substrate (paper, plastic, etc.). The number of people and training involved depends on the type and size of the press. Some of the presses are small and simple to operate, but many are very complex and require extensive technical knowledge. Look at Fig. 2-17.

Fig. 2-17. Press operators must setup, run, and maintain complex printing presses. A mechanical aptitude and knowledge of ink, paper, and solutions are important.

Controlling ink, solutions, and paper are some of the basic activities. Quality control is imperative. All of the efforts must be coordinated to produce a quality product.

A knowledge of paper, ink, and press operations are essential requirements. Mechanical aptitude is also desirable to pressroom personnel.

Helpers, working under the experienced press operators, are common on many of the large presses. The small duplicator requires an individual that is capable of doing all of the tasks necessary to complete a job.

Some of the activities common to the operator of a lithographic press are: positioning plates, filling ink fountain, filling the water fountain, loading stock, controlling flow of ink and fountain solution, speed control, and inspecting finished sheet. Refer to Fig. 2-18.

The *web lithographic press person* must set up a press using huge rolls of paper rather than sheets of stock. Press size and the degree of complexity both vary. Deluxe models print on both sides of the stock, fold and then deliver a finished product with great speed.

The *letterpress press person* operates a smaller type press. Its products are common to job shop printing: letterheads, forms, cards, and envelopes.

The *cylinder press operator* sets up and controls a machine which is capable of printing from relief images at a higher rate of speed.

The *rotary press person* operates a large press commonly found in relief newspaper plants. The press is capable of running at high speeds. A team of people is necessary to do a variety of tasks.

One example of the *intaglio press operator* is the gravure press. The press operates at a very rapid speed and usually has a crew assigned to specific responsibilities. Most runs are very long.

Screen presses have a configuration uncommon to the other processes. The operator must set up the press to print on a variety of materials. Knowledge of inks, screens, and image carriers is essential.

In all processes, the press person is responsible for the quality of the printed product.

Bindery and finishing personnel

Some persons are responsible for cutting stock to size for the press or cutting the stock after it has been printed. The controls on many of the newer pieces of cutting equipment are very sophisticated.

Setting up the machine requires preciseness and high mechanical aptitude. Physical strength is sometimes a necessity. All operations require a high degree of accuracy.

Operators of folding machines must have a knowledge of slitting, perforating, and folding techniques. Again, accuracy is essential. Mechanical ability must be a high priority, Fig. 2-19.

Fig. 2-18. Press operators are checking run of printed product. (USA Today)

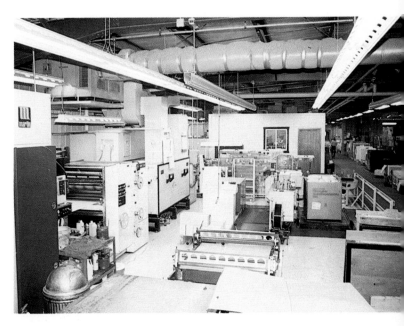

Fig. 2-19. Bindery and finishing personnel must operate and maintain various types of complex equipment.

Gathering and collating machines require operators and setup personnel who can do accurate work. Mechanical ability is also a basic requirement.

A wide variety of equipment is found in the bindery and finishing department. Many skills are highly technical, such as: die cutting, embossing, foiling, printing, etc. All require a high degree of mechanical ability and an ability to work in a precise manner.

POSITIONS THAT SUPPORT PRODUCTION

Creative persons are needed in many roles within the company. More specifically, a special talent is necessary for photographers, illustrators, designers, writers, and editors working to produce materials to be used by the printer.

Photographer

When a client asks for a halftone to be in a publication, the *photographer* may be called upon to take a high quality photograph. The photographer must create the graphic outcome, based on the stated objective. Getting the exact composition and knowing how it will look in the publication is a part of the plan. A working knowledge of camera equipment is expected of the photographer.

Many photographers work independently while others are employed by newspaper and magazine publishers. Agencies also employ photographers.

Designers

Artists or *graphic designers* are the people responsible for planning printed pieces. Creative talents are imperative. Expressing an idea visually is the primary role of this position. See Fig. 2-20.

Fig. 2-20. Designers set up guidelines or style for product. They must be very creative so that the results accomplish the designated goals.

Some designers are media specialized and cover only one phase of the design function. These people are creative individuals. Most of the activities require neatness and accuracy. A basic knowledge of each process is also very important.

Copywriter

As the name implies, the *copywriter* generates the manuscript or copy as well as other material to be printed. A love for creative writing, with a thorough knowledge of the language is imperative, Fig. 2-21. A willingness to write

Fig. 2-21. A copywriter must generate words to be used in a printed product. Advertisement copy and copy for a magazine are two examples.

on a wide variety of topics is usually needed. Many times the copywriter is not employed by the printer, but by an agency or other business firm.

Editor

The *editor* prepares the written material and illustrations for publication. This person will revise, rewrite, and check for accuracy. Copy editing includes sequencing, marking for style, and making everything within the manuscript consistent. All aspects of the manuscript are checked by the editing staff. A command of the English language is essential. Sometimes technical expertise is also needed.

Publishers of books, magazines, and newspapers commonly employ editing personnel. It is also possible for a person to offer services as a freelance editor.

Engineers

Engineers are needed to improve industrial processes. Positions are often production oriented and provide quality assurance. Most facilities need people with expertise in the area of chemistry.

Technical positions to support the engineer are also needed. Very often, four or five people are hired to support the activities of the scientist and engineer. This is also very true of the paper and pulp industry since much of the research is maintained within the plant.

Other employment categories

Under the heading of management, there are other job titles besides those already discussed.

Owner of facility

An *owner* of a printing facility should have business-management training. A thorough knowledge of printing is also very helpful. The depth of technical knowledge required depends on the type of operation.

As an owner of a small facility, no matter what the process, a total knowledge is very beneficial. Getting work done through other people is the key; therefore, a strong interest in supervision is imperative. Refer to Fig. 2-22.

Fig. 2-22. An owner of a facility usually has the same responsibilities as an executive officer or president of a company. Overseeing complete operation and getting work done through others is vital.

Plant manager

The *plant manager* is responsible for the manufacturing plan of the firm. A product must be produced within a time limit, at the lowest possible cost, and with enough quality to keep the customer happy. Another critical concern to the plant manager is the safety and health of all employees. Analyzing results and understanding people are also important.

Plant superintendent

The *plant superintendent* directs all manufacturing operations of the company and also directs the first line of

supervisors. This person must make sure all equipment is working efficiently and kept in good condition. This is a high pressure position requiring patience, but direct control.

Production manager

The *production manager* is a liaison type person—one who is capable of having close communication with sales and production personnel. The production manager is in charge of cost estimates, job entry, job planning, and scheduling. Keeping accurate records and getting along with others is essential, Fig. 2-23.

Fig. 2-23. Production manager must keep track of product as each process is completed. Here production manager is checking inventories on computer. (Screaming Color—Chapter One)

Production scheduler

The *production scheduler* sets up time tables for all jobs in an efficient and effective manner. After the job is in production, each phase must be recorded so that the product can be traced at any time during the production. Being able to plan and understand capabilities of equipment and personnel are important. Computer applications must also be understood.

Customer service representatives

A *customer service representative* is the liaison person between the customer, management, and sales force. A knowledge of the job schedule and job progress are essential. Understanding the operation of the firm is also imperative. Being able to meet and communicate with personnel helps to be successful in this position.

Estimator

The *estimator* accurately calculates the cost of a job. These estimates are used to bid or price a job. Understanding all of the operations of the plant is essential. Precise calculations are required as the figures used will relate to the technical capabilities of the various operations as well as the cost of materials. Business and technical interests are advantageous. See Fig. 2-24.

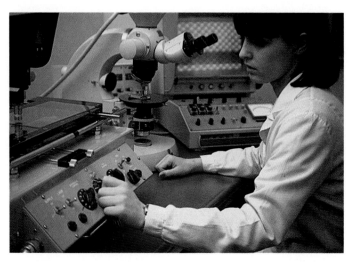

Fig. 2-25. Quality control supervisor must make sure every aspect of production is within specifications.

Fig. 2-24. The estimator fills in all the information that will be considered when pricing a job.

Controller

A *controller* has the responsibility of all aspects relating to the financial operation of the company. He or she must assure that the company operates using sound methods and practices. Contact with financial institutions, as well as preparing budgets, forecasts, analyses, reports, and statements are functions of this office. Working with mathematics and a thorough knowledge of accounting practices are essential.

EDP supervisor

The *EDP supervisor* is in charge of all the Electronic Data Processing (EDP) functions of the firm. Wherever data processing is needed in the plant, this supervisor should know how to get the best results. Computer language is a basic requirement. However, application knowledge is also necessary to get things done in a more efficient way.

Quality control supervisor

A *quality control supervisor* sets standards for production and the finished product. The job requires constant sampling to assure consistent quality and to reduce waste or spoilage. Knowledge of control devices, as a means to measure quality, is basic to the position, Fig. 2-25.

Department supervisor

A *department supervisor* or foreman may be assigned for each area in larger facilities. Supervising personnel in each department is a major responsibility. The person should be totally familiar with the equipment. He or she may be

Fig. 2-26. Sales representatives must know processes and be able to work with customers.

responsible for training all personnel within the department, especially new employees. Observing, directing, and checking work in process are common requirements.

Sales manager

The *sales manager* is responsible for establishing a profitable sales administration. Supervising sales activities, customer relations, budgeting, setting sales quotas, setting profit margins, and sales service are a few responsibilities. This person must be able to leave a favorable impression when meeting people and have a good business sense.

Sales representative

A *sales representative* position requires basic sales techniques, but it also requires a knowledge of printing processes. In a way, a sales representative must be an advisor; the customer should be able to trust the sales representative. The representative must be able to get the most for the customer's investment, Fig. 2-26. Meeting and being accepted by people is a prime prerequisite for this position. Being ambitious, highly organized, and creating a good impression are contributors to success.

PREPARING FOR A CAREER

With changes in technology, there will be resulting changes in career positions. Many of the craft jobs will require greater technical skills. Many positions will experience a change to a technician level while others might need technologists.

What are the entry levels of the various jobs within the industry? Most of the skill areas require a basic education or vocational training. The apprenticeship educational plan is one entry method. In union shops, it is the only means of becoming a journeyman (experienced male or female worker). Under this plan, the employee is a registered apprentice for a designated period of time (usually four to six years). An agreement is signed that the apprentice will receive classroom training and on-the-job training in specific skill areas.

Formal training is available in private and/or public schools. This is generally identified as vocational education when specific skills are being developed for tasks within an area of the industry.

Since many of the areas are requiring a higher degree of skill training, the community college often fulfills this need. Personnel in the skill areas should be prepared and willing to change or take advanced training to stay with the company.

Many of today's plants have had a problem created by inbreeding among management personnel. Where this happens, it tends to perpetuate past practices and tends to stifle new approaches. The trends in progressive companies have changed and management personnel are hired from the ranks of university or college graduates.

Education or teaching opportunities require a college degree from a recognized institution with accreditation credentials. The graduate must be assured that a teaching certificate is available upon graduation.

The technologist, researcher, and engineer are graduates of colleges or universities, with varying talents or expertise depending on the objectives established by the program. The person planning to attend a higher education institution should use great care to make sure the program is capable of preparing them for actual jobs in industry.

The outlook is very good for men and women in the graphic communications industry at all levels of career entry. New technology will affect all areas. Plan for change, and try to obtain a broad knowledge of products and processes.

KNOW THESE TERMS

Creative people, Skilled people, Managerial, Scientists, Technical people, Facsimile transmission, Digitized image, Robotics, Micro imaging, Agency, Quick printing, Specialty printing, Composing, Manufacturers, Pasteup artist, Process camera operator, Scanner operator, Typesetter, Stripper, Platemaker, Pressroom personnel, Copywriter, Editor, Engineer, Plant manager, Plant superintendent, Production manager, Production scheduler, Service representative, Estimator, Controller, Sales manager, EDP supervisor, Quality control supervisor, Department supervisor, Sales representative.

REVIEW QUESTIONS—CHAPTER 2

1. _____ _____ is one of the most important criteria when selecting a career.
2. Explain the five major categories of workers.
3. Why would a basic knowledge of electronics be helpful to a career in graphic communications?
4. _____ involves the use of machines to do repetitive tasks.
5. What does the term "laser" stand for?
6. The following is NOT an example of a service company.
   a. Advertising agency.
   b. Quick printer.
   c. Pressroom.
   d. Specialty shop.
7. List six characteristics important to the management team.
8. What are some of the duties of the pasteup artist?
9. A _____ _____ uses a laser-equipped device to produce film intermediates.
10. This person must touch up imperfections in film.
    a. Layout artist.
    b. Opaquer.
    c. Platemaker.
    d. Helper.
11. In your own words, what are the tasks of the editor?
12. The _____ _____ is responsible for the manufacturing done by the firm.
13. The production manager is a _____ type person who has close _____ with sales and production.
14. What does EDP represent?
15. What does it take to be a good sales representative?

SUGGESTED ACTIVITIES

1. Visit a graphic communications firm and list the classifications of jobs in the plant.
2. Contact local organizations (National Association of Printers and Lithographers, Printing Industries of America, Graphic Arts Technical Foundation, International Club of Printing House Craftsmen, International Graphic Arts Education Association, Litho Club, etc.) to find out what opportunities are available in the local, regional, or national area of the country.
3. Visit a facility and diagram the organizational plan.
4. Write the job specifications for a specific job in a local plant.
5. Explain the qualifications and duties of a graphic communications career of your choice.

Safety is extremely important in graphic communications. This operator is positioning knives in a rotary cutter. (Sequa Corp.)

Chapter 3

SAFETY AND HEALTH

After studying this chapter, you will be able to:
- Describe the importance of machine guards and personal protection.
- Explain the proper plans for fire prevention within the plant.
- Identify the correct handling and storage of chemicals and other materials.
- Summarize basic safety procedures.
- Describe proper noise control in the plant.

Providing safe and healthy working conditions in today's graphic communications industry is essential. This chapter will identify basic safety and health standards. Later chapters describe specific safety rules for specialized situations.

When a new structure is being considered, it is imperative that the designer incorporate proper safety standards. It is equally important that the workers in an existing graphic communications facility have knowledge of basic safety rules. Because of the wide variety of processes, there is always potential for injury or death when on the job. It is up to you to keep the work area safe; so study carefully!

SAFETY AND HEALTH PROGRAM

A health and safety program is an effective method of providing a safe working environment. The purpose of such a program is to recognize, evaluate, and control potential hazards in the workplace.

Many of the hazards found in the graphic communications industry will be identified in this chapter but others may be found in other printed sources (equipment instructions, manuals, labels, etc.). Unsafe walking surfaces, unguarded machinery, ungrounded electrical equipment, improper lifting methods, air contaminants, noise, and chemicals are all potential hazards.

To insure the success and progress of the safety program, management leadership is imperative. The person assigned the responsibility for safety and health of the plant must be delegated the authority to carry out the assigned program. Everyone in the establishment must be made aware of the plan. A safe operation depends largely upon all plant personnel being properly informed and aware of potential hazards. See Fig. 3-1.

Fig. 3-1. A graphic communications facility can be a very safe and enjoyable place to work. However, if safety rules are not followed, it can be very dangerous! (Variquick)

THE INDUSTRY AND ITS HAZARDS

Personnel in the graphic communications industry may be confronted with numerous hazards in the course of performing their work. These hazards include those of a mechanical, electrical, chemical, or flammable nature. While this industry has many safety and health problems common to other industries, recognition and control of those hazards with the greatest potential for injury or illness will be emphasized.

MECHANICAL HAZARDS

Many on-the-job physical injuries are the result of mechanical hazards. These hazards can be controlled if:
1. The machines are properly guarded.
2. Each person uses personal protective equipment.
3. Devices are properly locked out.
4. Everyone handles materials in a safe way.

Machine guarding

The variety and uses of machinery in the industry poses particular hazards from reciprocating, rotating, pinch-point, and shear action. These actions are shown in Fig. 3-2. Having proper guards on equipment is of utmost importance for the operator's protection.

Reciprocating and rotating motions create hazards in two general areas—at the point of operation (where work is being done) and at the points where power or motion is being transmitted from one part to another.

Any rotating part is dangerous. Loose clothing, hair, and even skin contact can be disastrous. The severity of injury is often very high, Fig. 3-3.

Typical examples of common rotating mechanisms are: spindles, flywheels, horizontal or vertical shafts, cams, and collars. Whenever something projects from the rotating unit, it becomes even more dangerous, Fig. 3-4. Extreme care must be taken when working in an area where rotating units exist, even though they are properly guarded.

Machine guarding is needed wherever hazardous machine parts are within reach of the operator. Make sure guards are in place over: belts, chains, flywheels, cutters, pulleys,

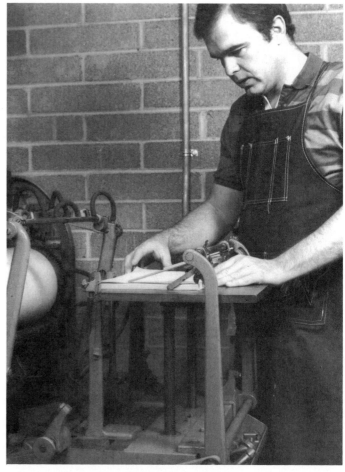

Fig. 3-3. Always dress properly for work. Note how press operator has removed all rings, his watch, and is wearing an apron to keep clothing out of press.

shafting, fasteners, punches, drills, clamps, gears, rollers, cylinders, shears, presses, and all other points of operation.

Machine guarding is planned to protect parts of the human body from being cut, squashed, or hit by flying fragments. Most of the machines in the graphic communications industry require some type of guarding. If a guard is in place, do NOT remove it to complete an operation. Refer to Fig. 3-5.

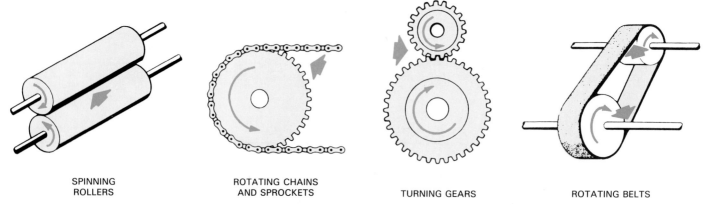

SPINNING ROLLERS ROTATING CHAINS AND SPROCKETS TURNING GEARS ROTATING BELTS

Fig. 3-2. These are four types of mechanical hazards you will find in a graphic communications facility. All can cause serious injury.

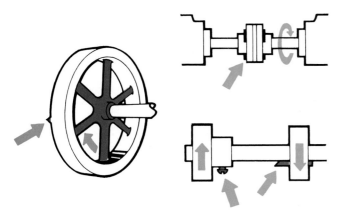

Fig. 3-4. Rotating objects pose a constant danger on presses and other equipment. They can cause serious cuts, can wrap clothing around shafts, and pull you into equipment.

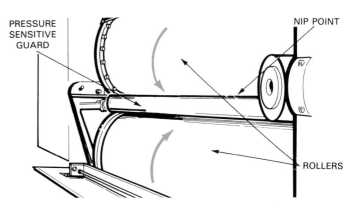

Fig. 3-6. Nip point occurs where two rollers come together. Rollers produce tremendous pulling and crushing force that can cause permanent disability. This press has pressure sensitive guard that shuts off if anything is pulled into nip point.

As illustrated earlier, *nip points* exist where two cylinders meet or come close to one another. Two gears would be another example. Many guards are of the pressure-sensitive type which automatically stop the movement of the machine when an object is wedged between the guard and the cylinder. See Fig. 3-6.

Barrier guards are another type of guard which keep you out of the operation area but can be hinged or removed. When the guard is moved out of position, the machine will not run. The power is cut off.

Metal and plastic are two materials commonly used as guard materials. Remember, just because a machine or press

Fig. 3-5. Always keep guards and covers in position when operating a press or other type of equipment. Guards primarily protect you from injury but they also keep objects from entering and damaging the press. Covers perform same general function.
(Heidelberg Harris)

looks small, this does not mean that its power cannot cause a serious injury. Without a guard, the operator's clothing could easily be caught and pulled into the nip point. Be careful to avoid long hair that might get drawn into nip points. Use a cap or head band with a tie back when needed.

Cleaning and maintaining equipment should be accomplished while the machine is NOT in motion. This is true unless the unit is totally automated and does not require human assistance for maintenance.

The guillotine paper cutter, for instance, requires a specialized type of machine guarding. A typical safety device would disallow cutting until the pressure clamp is in position or if a light beam is blocked by some object, such as a hand, Fig. 3-7. Another typical control device on the paper cutter requires that both hands of the operator must be on the operating controls, Fig. 3-8. An automatic cutter must also have a non-repeat feature.

Fig. 3-7. Operator is using large cutter to cut sheets to size. If cutter can slice through thick stack of paper like through butter, think what it would do to fingers, hands, or arms.

Fig. 3-8. Note how this cutter has two controls buttons. Both buttons must be pressed simultaneously for blade to lower. This assures that hands are out of the way when cutting.

The paper cutter knife is very sharp and all precautions should be taken to avoid injury when cutting stock or handling the blade. Follow suggested safety procedures.

When operating a machine, make it a habit not to reach for a jammed piece of paper, or to rely on an interlock when working on a piece of equipment. Make sure the POWER IS OFF at the main switch!

It is not worth the risk to yourself or other people to use equipment when guards are missing, broken, or out of adjustment.

Personal protection

Besides making sure that machines are properly guarded, there are steps that everyone must take to protect themselves from injuries.

While working with machinery, NEVER wear watches, rings, ties, medallions, bracelets, scarves, and loose clothing. Long hair can also be a problem. A rag partially tucked in a pocket and hanging loose is a poor practice.

If you are operating the press, make sure everyone is away from moving parts. Sometimes, on large pieces of equipment, sounding devices might be the indicators.

As assistant should be with you when cleaning or running a press. If you were to get caught, the assistant could turn off the press. This applies to many types of power machines.

Eye protection should be worn whenever operating a saw, grinder, or any machine which could cause material to fly and strike you or other shopworkers.

Lockout devices

Many injuries could have been avoided if the power would have been turned off. When someone is working on a piece of equipment, the power should be cut off. This is what is meant by *lockout devices;* they are power lockout devices, as shown in Fig. 3-9.

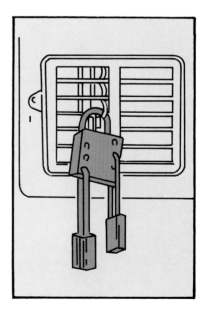

Fig. 3-9. Lockout devices are used to prevent accidental operation of machines.

When a worker finds a locked or tagged power box, it means that no attempt should be made to restore the power until everything is checked.

Many graphic communications pieces of equipment have flip covers which prevent either the run, reverse, or inch button to be accidentally pressed. It is imperative that the covers on the run and/or reverse buttons be flipped shut during gumming a plate, blanket work, or any other operation which requires the press to be inched.

Materials handling

Too often a person lifts a heavy load without seeking assistance from another person or without using some mechanical device. Whenever an object is lifted, keep your knees bent and keep your back straight. Leaning over is NOT a good practice while lifting.

Certain operations require the feet to be protected by wearing safety shoes. Press and bindery operations and storage areas are typical work areas that require foot protection.

Cuts from sharp materials are common injuries. Gloves of various types should be considered to protect your hands. Handling chemicals also requires special attention. Not all gloves are satisfactory for every job. Choose the ones that will give you the best possible protection and freedom of hand movement.

Spillage is a possibility; therefore, the action to be taken after a spill should be known by the person handling the material.

Some materials are banded with metal strapping. When cut, the metal strapping can spring and actually act as a weapon. Extreme care and proper protective devices are essential.

Compressed air

Compressed air should NEVER be used to clean off clothes, or to do general cleanup work. An air nozzle could force air through the skin and into the blood stream. This could cause death. Compressed air could also stir up paper dust that could cause a safety problem.

If an air source is used for any acceptable purpose, the pressure at the nozzle should not exceed 30 psi (pounds per square inch) or 207 kPa (kilopascals).

FIRE PREVENTION

Most graphic communications facilities use flammable and combustible materials. Fire prevention is a very important part of a plant safety program.

It is possible that paper dust or anti-setoff powders may explode if concentrated where a spark might ignite the mixture.

Solvent vapors are another source of possible danger. Prevent spillage and when pouring, make sure the area is properly vented and an ignition source is NOT present.

Ink and solvent-soaked rags, that are to be stored overnight, must be placed in a safety can, Fig. 3-10. The vapors will then be trapped inside the container. Daily emptying

Fig. 3-10. An enclosed safety can should be used to dispose of flammable rags or towels. Empty the can regularly.

of the safety cans is a requirement. Do not store oily or ink-soaked rags in a container that does not meet safety regulations. Proper grounding and bonding of equipment is essential in solvent transfer operations to prevent possible sparks.

Some precautions are:
1. Use a vacuum to pick up dust rather than blowing off dust.
2. Report leaking solvent containers.
3. Wipe up solvent and oil spills.
4. Make sure flame arrestors are intact.
5. Make sure every solvent or flammable material is properly labeled.
6. Solvents are NOT to be dumped in the drains.
7. Solvent drains must be bonded and grounded.
8. Always use a safety can when transferring small amounts of solvent.
9. Used solvents must be stored and disposed of in a manner meeting local and national standards.

Choose the proper solvent to clean machines. Remember that the vapors could be an immediate health hazard.

Know where your fire extinguishers are located and how to use them. Proper operation of a fire extinguisher is needed to prevent the spread of flames or to put out a fire quickly and efficiently. During a fire, a minute of time can be a lifetime! See Fig. 3-11.

CHEMICAL HAZARDS

The chemicals used in the industry are commonly classified in four categories:
1. Organic solvents.
2. Platemaking chemicals.
3. Ink mists and gases.
4. Fumes and dust.

CLASS A: USE ON WOOD, PAPER, ETC.
CLASS B: USE ON OIL, GAS, GREASE, ETC.
CLASS C: USE ON ELECTRICAL EQUIPMENT.

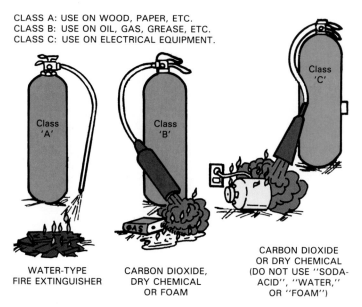

Class 'A'

Class 'B'

Class 'C'

WATER-TYPE
FIRE EXTINGUISHER

CARBON DIOXIDE,
DRY CHEMICAL
OR FOAM

CARBON DIOXIDE
OR DRY CHEMICAL
(DO NOT USE "SODA-
ACID," "WATER,"
OR "FOAM")

Fig. 3-11. Study classes or types of fire extinguishers.
(Cummins)

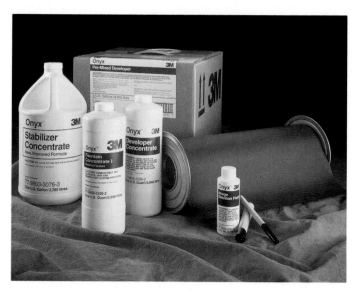

Fig. 3-13. All containers should be labeled. Always read labels
carefully before using chemicals. Note safety warnings and
actions to take in an emergency. (3M Company)

Your first line of defense is to know the kind of chemical and the hazards involved, Fig. 3-12. The labels inform you of the handling procedures as well as the health hazards. However, additional information is sometimes necessary. Look at Fig. 3-13.

The manufacturer or supplier should be able to supply you with specific information. Look for the technical names of the chemicals as well as the characteristics of the product. Flammability is a typical characteristic.

Fig. 3-12. Use caution when working with the chemicals found in graphic communications. Many can be harmful. Wear safety glasses if chemicals are caustic. Wear a respirator if chemicals produce harmful fumes. (3M Company)

All personnel should be aware of the health effects of chemicals. Some of the health effects might be for a short period of time but others might be long term.

When reading any data sheet or label, look for recommendations relating to thermal conditions, ventilation instructions, and/or protective devices.

Organic solvents

Some of the most common organic solvents found in the industry are: inks, blanket and roller washes, fountain solutions, plate cleaners, platemaking chemicals, glaze removers, degreasers, and film cleaners.

Do not rely on your nose to warn you of vapors. They need to be measured to determine concentration in the air. Specialists need to be employed to measure airborne solvents and determine safe working conditions.

Some solvents are more harmful than others but the following should NOT be used in the facility: benzene, carbon tetrachloride, gasoline, chloroform, and carbon disulfide.

Breathing solvent vapors can be very harmful to your health. The following action can be helpful:
1. Keep lids and covers on cans and drums.
2. Do NOT use large quantities of solvents in one area.
3. Clean up spills immediately.
4. Place soiled rags in a safety container.
5. Exhaust presses where needed.
6. Exhaust the platemaking area.
7. Do not identify a solvent by sniffing it.
8. Wash your hands before eating.

Some vapors may require you to wear a respirator. The proper respirator must be selected by an expert in each situation.

Solvents can also be harmful to your skin or eyes. Personal protective devices must be worn in some situations. Goggles, gloves, and aprons are typical protective devices.

If a solvent is splashed in your eyes, read the label on the container. Make sure that you wash the eyes, with lids open, for at least fifteen minutes if recommended. The next step is usually treatment by a doctor.

Image carriers

The chemicals used to prepare image carriers can burn and irritate. Wear special gloves to protect against chemicals that can enter your body through the skin. Inspect gloves for pin holes before working.

Wearing an appropriate apron will keep chemicals from reaching clothing and help prevent skin contact. The operator should never touch his or her face and eyes with gloves that have been in contact with a chemical.

Contact lenses should NOT be worn when working with chemicals. The chemical can seep and collect under the lens and cause a severe burn. Face shields and splash goggles are the best form of eye and face protection.

Many of the chemicals are concentrated. When diluting, always pour acid into water. The opposite method would produce a severe chemical reaction no matter how slowly you mix the materials. NEVER add water to concentrated acid.

Food and/or beverages should never be brought into contact with chemicals. All chemical storage must be clearly labeled.

Areas should be well ventilated wherever vapor hazards are present. Vapors should be exhausted away from the operator—especially the breathing zone.

Ink mists

Sometimes ink droplets are small enough so that they can be inhaled into the lungs. These very small droplets of ink are often thrown into the air by the press rollers.

Ink mists often contain harmful pigments, polymers, plasticizers, resins, solvents, etc. Control is necessary where a relatively large amount of ink mist is produced, such as at newspaper facilities.

Gases, fumes, and dust

Gases, fumes, and dust are chemical agents commonly found in graphic communications facilities. A gas of much concern is ozone, created by carbon arcs, some antistatic devices, and now UV-ink (ultraviolet ink) curing units. Carbon monoxide is another hazardous gas.

Fumes are found where molten material might be located. Acids also give off fumes. Some of the materials used are very toxic and should be considered extremely hazardous.

Dust might be created by the anti-setoff powders used to assist in preventing setoff of inks. Another common source is paper, a source which is often overlooked.

Proper ventilation is imperative in areas where gases, fumes, and dust are the result of an operation.

NOISE

Unwanted and excessively loud sound is found in many facilities. The best way to protect against ear damage is to control the sound. Whenever those controls do not reduce the noise to an acceptable level, ear protection must be worn. Look at Fig. 3-14.

Sound levels are measured in units called *decibels* (dBA). Presently, the length of allowable time of exposure to different decibels is given in Fig. 3-15.

A dBA reading of 90 is the maximum allowable limit for an eight hour day. If the amount is greater than 90 dBA, a specific time limit is established.

If the limit of time and sound is over the permissable level, unwanted sound must be engineered out of the operation or personal hearing protection must be provided and worn.

The types of protection devices include: ear muffs, ear plugs, or moldable inserts. Excessive noise can lead to permanent hearing loss!

LIGHT HAZARDS

Light sources, common to graphic communications facilities, can be harmful. One source, ultraviolet (UV) light can be harmful to your skin and eyes. The precautionary areas would be: carbon arc, pulsed xenon, mercury vapor lamps, UV-ink curing units, and ozone lights used on anti-setoff devices. Remember that true UV-rays cannot be seen but they are harmful; so avoid their contact. See Fig. 3-16.

Infrared (IR) light and laser beams are also potentially harmful. Whenever workers are in these areas, special precautions must be taken. Ask yourself this question— what are the precautions and what are the protective devices that should be used?

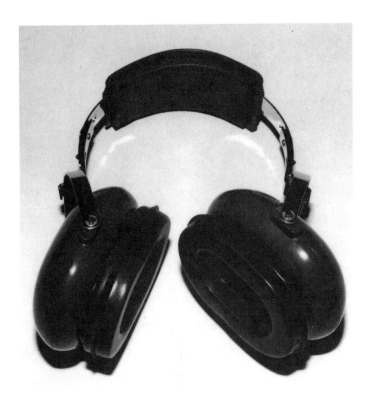

Fig. 3-14. Ear protection is often needed in bindery department. Some of the equipment can make tremendous noise that can be damaging to your hearing.

PERMISSIBLE NOISE EXPOSURES

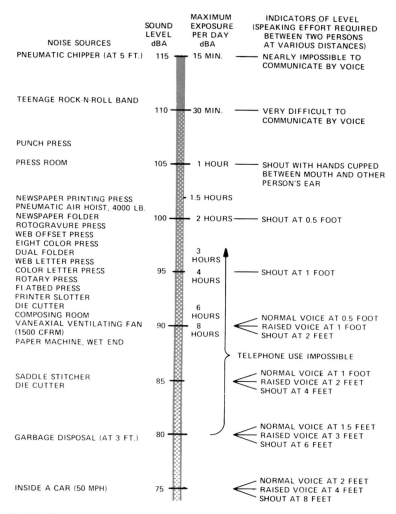

Fig. 3-15. Study this table that shows typical permissible noise exposures.

SAFETY CHECKLIST

Since safe conditions depend on a constant vigilance for possible hazards, periodic inspections are one of the most important aspects of a successful safety program.

Management will find a checklist helpful in performing a safety inspection of the facility. Fig. 3-17 shows a checklist that can be used as a way to identify problems. Then, corrective action can be taken.

GENERAL SAFETY RULES

1. Wear eye protection during any operation that could endanger your eyes. This includes working with power machinery, chemicals, air pressure, light sources, etc.
2. Keep the graphic communications facility organized. Return all tools, equipment, and supplies to their proper storage areas.
3. Never carry sharp objects in your pockets. They could easily puncture the skin.
4. Keep all guards, shields, and covers in place. They provide an important function of keeping parts of your body out of the equipment and also protect the equipment from foreign objects.
5. Ventilate the work area when needed. Turn on a ventilation fan anytime chemicals or fumes are present.
6. Never use or adjust any equipment unless properly trained. Make sure you have seen a demonstration or have supervision before using graphic communications equipment.
7. No smoking! Smoking is a serious fire hazard in a graphic communications facility. Inks, solutions, chemicals, paper, paper dust, etc., all pose a serious fire hazard.
8. Dispose of flammable materials properly. Use a safety can and empty the safety can daily.
9. Keep all walkways clear. Do not place tools or supplies in walkways because they could cause a fall.
10. Dress properly for work. Long hair can get pulled into spinning equipment; so wear a hat or tie it back. Do not wear jewelry of any kind, not even a watch, when operating equipment.

Fig. 3-16. Some types of light can be harmful to your eyes. Wear eye protection if needed. Do not look directly at bright light when working with platemakers or cameras.   (NuArc)

11. Do not stand skid pads or pallets on edge. They are heavy enough to cause serious foot or leg injury if they fall on someone.

12. Air pressure must be lowered to safe limits. Do not direct an airstream toward yourself or anyone else. Use a vacuum to clean equipment when possible.

13. Make sure you know the fire evacuations route in an emergency.

14. Know where all fire extinguishers are located and how to use them.

15. Know what to look for to prevent fires: overflowing safety container, dust buildup on equipment, opened chemicals, etc.

16. Never ride on lift trucks or fork lift platforms. Do not attempt to operate a lift or fork truck unless properly trained.

17. Stand clear when someone is operating a lift truck in your area. Be careful not to place your feet under

SAFETY INSPECTION CHECKLIST

	Satisfactory	Unsatisfactory	Not Applicable	Dangerous	Remarks
I HOUSEKEEPING					
A. Clean and orderly work area					
B. Proper materials available for housekeeping					
C. Floor holes (drains) covered					
D. Materials available for cleaning					
E. Maintenance schedule used					
F. Properly marked aisles					
G. Proper storage facilities					
H. Proper disposal systems					
I. Warnings and cautions posted					
J. Containers labeled					
K. Open aisles and fire lanes					
L. Proper handling devices					
M. Vacuming used where possible(Continued)					
II PERSONAL PROTECTIVE EQUIPMENT					
A. Eye protection					
B. Foot protection					
C. Head protection					
D. Protective clothing					
E. Ear protection					
F. Respiratory equipment					
III ADMINISTRATION					
A. Safety program					
1. Education-safety personnel					
2. Incentives					
B. Procedures					
1. Recordkeeping					
2. Accident and injury handling					
3. Posting					
C. Job hazard analysis					

(Continued)

Fig. 3-17. This is a safety checklist. Read through it and note types of things to look for when evaluating condition of workplace.

	Satisfactory	Unsatisfactory	Not Applicable	Dangerous	
IV EQUIPMENT/MACHINERY					
A. Fixed guarding					
B. Movable guarding					
C. Equipment placement					
D. Maintenance					
E. Mechanical controls					
F. Proper enclosure					
V ELECTRICAL					
A. Grounding					
B. Wiring					
C. Circuits identified					
D. Switch location					
E. Extension cords					
F. Portable electrical equipment					
VI CHEMICALS					
A. Storage					
B. Ventilation					
C. Proper identification					
D. Handling devices					
E. Clean up methods					
F. Disposal					
VII FIRE PROTECTION					
A. Flammable materials					
1. Safe storage (cabinet)					
2. Proper labeling					
3. Proper containers					
4. Disposal of rags					
B. Fire equipment					
1. Fire extinguishers					
a. Right type for location					
b. Clearly visible					
2. Automatic sprinkler					
3. Blankets (same as fire extinguishers)					
4. Smoke detectors					
5. Flame and fume arrestors					
6. Proper trash disposal					
C. Fire drills					
1. Proper exit signs					
2. Availability of exits					
3. Dissemination of exit information					
4. Education of employees					
D. Periodic checking					
VIII FIRST AID					
A. First aid facility provided					
B. Qualified first aid personnel					
1. Nurse provided					
2. First aid training available					

Fig. 3-17. Continued.

a load when being lowered by a lift truck.
18. Use hand rails or hand holds when going up or down a press.
19. Never turn a press on unless you are absolutely sure everything is ready. No one else should be near the press. Tools must be off the press and all mechanisms must be set correctly.
20. Keep your hands clear when running a press. Do not try to grab paper, lubricate, or do anything that places your hands near the rollers and nip point. All press guards must be in place.
21. Be careful when handling chemicals. Read all labels.
22. Do not pour chemicals down a drain or sewer. They must be disposed of properly to protect our environment.
23. Wear a respirator when working with hazardous chemicals that could be in the air.
24. Always work and act like a professional when in a graphic communications facility. A "joker" is an accident just waiting to happen!
25. If you are NOT sure about a safety rule or procedure, ask your instructor.

ENVIRONMENTAL COMPLIANCE

Most of the topics discussed in this chapter have been related to the safety and health of the individual worker, and were mandated by the Occupational Safety and Health Act (OSHA). The following information is also related to the health of people, but is mandated by the Environmental Protection Agency under the Clean Air Act Amendments of 1990 (CAAA). This Act has a significant impact on printers. The Clean Air Act Amendments are divided into eleven titles. Not all of the Titles affect the printing industry directly, however.

Title I is concerned with reducing the use of volatile organic compounds (VOCs). This means that choosing the right press wash and other chemicals is essential to run an environmentally safe but productive facility. If the regulations are not followed, the plant could face stiff fines. EPA is responsible for developing Control Technology Guidelines (CTGs). Some of these have been specified.

The Air Toxics Provisions of Title III will have significant effect on the printing industry. The Title lists 189 regulated chemicals; many of these are found in today's plants. The Title requires sources to install the best available air pollution devices or Maximum Achievable Control Technology (MACT). MACT guidelines are established by EPA for the Printing/Publishing and Packaging Industry category.

Under Title V, each state must establish permitting rules for all major sources of VOCs and air toxics. This will have

a major impact on the printing and converting industries.

These amendments are very complicated. For information, contact the federal EPA or the appropriate state agency.

KNOW THESE TERMS

Health program, Machine guard, Nip point, Cutter knife, Eye protection, Power lockout device, Compressed air pressure, Safety can, Organic solvents, Respirator, Ink mist, Decibels, UV-light, IR-light, Air toxics, Volatile organic compounds, Environmental Protection Agency, Occupational Safety and Health Act.

REVIEW QUESTIONS—CHAPTER 3

1. What are the four types of hazards found in graphic communications?
2. Machine guarding protects people from _____, _____, _____-_____, and _____ action.
3. This dangerous condition exists where two cylinders meet or come close to one another.
   a. Shear point.
   b. Rip point.
   c. Nip point.
   d. Cut point.
4. Equipment cleaning and maintenance is commonly done with the equipment in operation. True or false?
5. In your own words, how should you dress when operating machinery in a graphic communications facility?
6. When lifting heavy objects, lift with your legs and not your back. True or false?
7. When using compressed air, air pressure at the nozzle should NOT exceed _____ psi or _____ kPa.
8. During a fire, a _____ of time can be a _____.
9. Inks, blanket wash, fountain solutions, and plate cleaners would be examples of:
   a. Inorganic solutions.
   b. Organic solutions.
   c. Tetrachlorides.
   d. Benzenes.
10. A dBA reading of _____ is the maximum allowable limit for an 8 hour day without ear protection.

SUGGESTED ACTIVITIES

1. Using the checklist in this chapter, visit a plant and inspect its condition. Do this after getting permission and without interfering with production.
2. Make a safety checklist for a specific piece of machinery.
3. Seek information on the CTGs of lithographic, flexographic, and gravure printing.

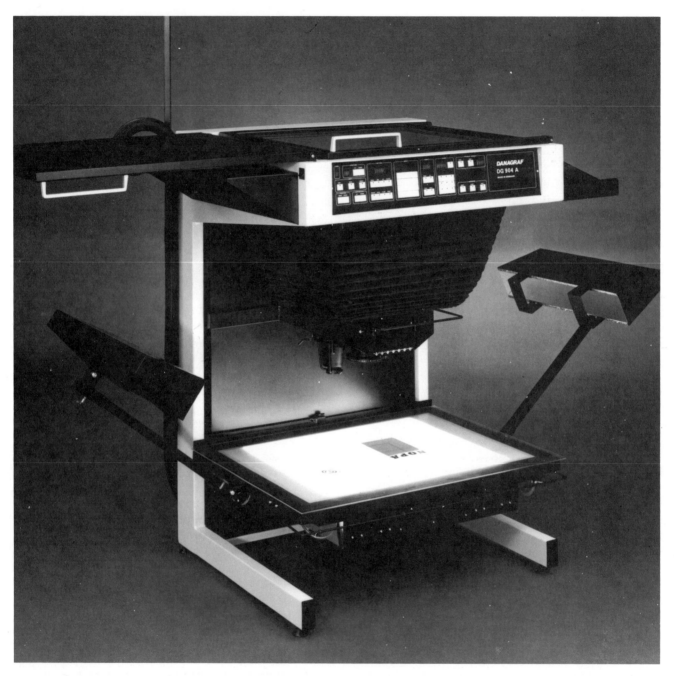

Measurements are used in almost all aspects of graphic communications. One example, numerous measurements might be made or applied when operating a process camera: enlargement or reduction measurements, exposure measurements, lens opening measurements, etc. (Danagraf)

Chapter 4

MEASUREMENT

After studying this chapter, you will be able to:

- Compare conventional and metric systems of measurement.
- Summarize the printer's system of measurement.
- Convert from one system to another.
- Explain basic paper sizes and weights.
- Summarize envelope sizes or measurements.
- Summarize screen ruling and tint measurements.
- Explain ink measurements.
- Describe other measurement terms found in graphic communications.
- Explain the use of specialized measuring tools and equipment.

This chapter will summarize how measurement is vital to the graphic communications industry. It will start out by comparing conventional and metric systems. It will then review the point and pica system. Coverage will also be given to paper size, paper weight, envelope sizes, screen ruling, tint percentage, and special measuring tools.

This chapter will prepare you for many later chapters that refer to measurement. Measurement is used in almost every aspect of graphic reproduction. Study this chapter carefully.

In a report to Congress in 1821, John Quincy Adams wrote: "Weights and measures may be ranked among the necessaries of life to every individual of human society. They enter into the economical arrangements and daily concerns of every family. They are necessary to every occupation of human industry, to the distribution and security of every species of property, to every transaction of trade and commerce, to the studies of the philosopher, to the navigation of the mariner, to the marches of the soldier, to all the exchanges of peace, and all the operations of war. The knowledge of them, as in established use, is among the first elements of education, and is often learned by those who learn nothing else, not even to read and write. This knowledge is riveted in the memory by the habitual application of it to the employments of people throughout life."

MEASUREMENT PRINCIPLES

Some of the first measuring terms referred to parts of the human body. For instance, the distance spanned with four fingers was known as four digits, while the hand was a common measuring tool, about four inches. This term is still used today to give the height measurement of a horse.

The forearm is remembered as a cubit or six palms and the length of a person's foot as the distance of one foot.

Early means of finding the weight or volume of one container or another was based on the grain or seed most common to the area. This became the standard. A grain of wheat would be a typical example.

The word "carat" (unit to measure gems) was from the carob seed which was the standard.

As societies changed, a more sophisticated system evolved to give accurate and consistent measurement. The measuring systems used were for specific purposes in various parts of the country. International trading was very limited so there was not too much demand for standardization.

By the 19th Century, the English system of weights and measures was estblished in many parts of the world, including the American colonies.

The Constitution of the United States, ratified in 1790, gave power to Congress to have uniform standards for weights and measures. Today, the National Bureau of Standards assures uniformity.

Fig. 4-1 gives the most common conventional measurements. Note how each compares to its metric equivalent and to typical uses in graphic communications.

METRIC SYSTEM

Ninety percent of the world population uses the metric system. The United States is part of the 10 percent that presently uses the U.S. Customary or English system. The metric system is not fully understood by many of the nation's graphic communications customers and employees.

An orderly transition has been indicated by legislation passed in 1975. This means that many of the tasks performed by employees will require some knowledge of the metric system.

The metric system, as a worldwide coordinated measurement system, was recognized over 300 years ago. In 1790, the metric system was established when the National Assembly of France requested the French Academy of Sciences to "deduce an invariable standard for all measures

APPROXIMATE EQUIVALENTS			
UNIT	**CUSTOMARY**	**METRIC**	**USE**
Length	inch (in) _____millimeter (mm) feet (ft) _____meter (m) yard (yd) _____meter (m) mile (mi) _____kilometer (km)		Paper, wrapping material, plates, wire rolls, scales, press calibration Covers, tapes, binders
Pressure	pounds per square inch (psi) _____kilopascal (kPa)		Web press ink pressure, air pressure, vacuum
Power	horsepower (hp) _____kilowatt (kw)		Electric motor rating
Torque	pound-feet (lb-ft)_____Newton-meter (N·m)		Bolt tightening
Volume or Capacity	fluid ounces (oz) _____milliliters (ml) quart (qt) _____liter (L) cubic inch (in³) _____cubic centimeter (cc)		Ink, oil Plate chemicals Storage, shipping
Mass or weight	ounce (oz)_____gram (g) pound (lb) _____kilogram (kg)		Postage, padding cement, chemicals Shipping, supplies
Speed	Feet per second _____meters per second miles per hour (mph) _____kilometers per hour (km/h) revolutions per minute (rpm) _____revolutions per minute (rpm)		Web press speed
Application rates	fluid ounce per square foot (fl-oz/ft²) _____ Ounces per square feet (oz/ft²) _____	milliliters per square meter (ml/m²) Grams per square meter (g/m²)	Applying materials, ink coverage, estimating

Fig. 4-1. Compare customary and metric equivalents given in this chart. Also note common uses for each measurement.

and weights." The academy appointed the commission and it came up with a simple and scientific system.

The *metric system* is a "base-10" or "decimal" system. The commission assigned the name meter to the unit of length, the name gram to the unit of mass, and the name liter to the unit of fluid capacity.

As with many new systems, enthusiasm was not evident. With time, however, adoption occurred steadily from one nation to another.

Since 1866, the United States made it lawful to employ the weights and measures of the metric system in all contracts, dealings, or court proceedings. On December 23, 1975, President Ford signed into law the Metric Conversion Act, which established, for the first time, a national policy to coordinate America's changeover to metric.

SI metric system

The International System of Units, abbreviated SI, is a modernized version of the metric system established by international agreement. The system is built upon a foundation of seven base units.
1. Length = Meter (m)
2. Mass = Kilogram (kg)
3. Time = Second (s)
4. Electric current = Ampere (A)
5. Temperature = Kelvin (°K) or Celsius (°C)
6. Amount of substance = Mole (mol)
7. Luminous intensity = Candela (cd)

Converting to the metric system will not change all units of measure. Time will continue to be in hours, minutes, and seconds. Electric power will be measured in watts and the monetary system will remain as it is now.

The metric system is very simple but initially, the units of the metric system may sound strange.

The following are essential for everyday use:
1. Kilometer, meter, centimeter, and millimeter for expressing length and distance.
2. Liter and milliliter for capacity or volume.
3. Kilogram, gram, and metric ton for weight (mass).
4. Degree Celsius for temperature.
5. Kilopascal for pressure.
6. Hectare for area.

Throughout the study of the metric system, it is evident that each quantity has its own unit of measurement and no unit reflects more than one quantity.

Metric prefixes

Computations are simpler when using the metric system because multiples of the metric units are related to each other by the factor ten (10). *Prefixes* indicate multiples or submultiples of these units. This is shown in Fig. 4-2.

Temperature measurements do not commonly use prefixes. Temperature is given in degrees Celsius and experience is the best learning device. Some common equivalent temperatures are shown in Fig. 4-3.

Rules of metric notation

Remember these metric rules of notation:
1. Symbols are NOT capitalized unless the unit is a proper name (mm).

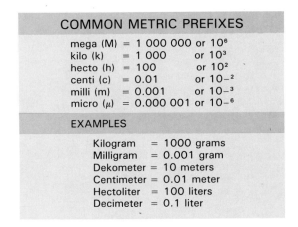

COMMON METRIC PREFIXES

mega (M)	= 1 000 000	or 10⁶
kilo (k)	= 1 000	or 10³
hecto (h)	= 100	or 10²
centi (c)	= 0.01	or 10⁻²
milli (m)	= 0.001	or 10⁻³
micro (μ)	= 0.000 001	or 10⁻⁶

COMMON METRIC PREFIXES

mega (M)	= 1 000 000	or 10^6
kilo (k)	= 1 000	or 10^3
hecto (h)	= 100	or 10^2
centi (c)	= 0.01	or 10^{-2}
milli (m)	= 0.001	or 10^{-3}
micro (μ)	= 0.000 001	or 10^{-6}

EXAMPLES

Kilogram	= 1000 grams
Milligram	= 0.001 gram
Dekometer	= 10 meters
Centimeter	= 0.01 meter
Hectoliter	= 100 liters
Decimeter	= 0.1 liter

Fig. 4-2. These are common metric prefixes. Study them carefully.

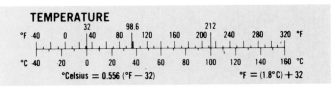

TEMPERATURE

$$°Celsius = 0.556 (°F - 32)$$
$$°F = (1.8 °C) + 32$$

Fig. 4-3. Scale compares temperature in Fahrenheit and Celsius.

2. Symbols are NOT followed by periods (mm).

3. Symbols are NOT followed by an "s" for plural (10 g).

4. A space separates the numerals from the unit symbols (2 mm).

5. Spaces, NOT commas, are used to separate large numbers into groups of three digits (21 210 km).

6. A zero precedes the decimal point if the number is less than one (0.11 g).

7. Liter and meter can be spelled either with an -re or -er ending.

As changeover takes place within the graphic communications industry, metric measurement will be more commonly used in job related tasks.

Metric conversion

In graphic communications, it is sometimes necessary to change or convert from one value to another. For instance, if a chemical value is given in liters and the equipment gives mixture ratios in quarts, you would have to convert to the same system.

A *conversion chart* can be used to change from metric to customary or customary to metric. One is given in Fig. 4-4. Note how a multiplier is used to convert values. Simply multiply the known value by the multiplier to convert over to the other system.

METRIC/U.S. CUSTOMARY UNIT EQUIVALENTS

Multiply:	by:	to get:	Multiply:	by:	to get:
LINEAR					
inches	X 25.4	= millimeters(mm)	X 0.0397	= inches
feet	X 0.3048	= meters(m)	X 3.281	= feet
yards	X 0.9144	= meters(m)	X 1.0936	= yards
miles	X 1.6093	= kilometers(km)	X 0.6214	= miles
inches	X 2.54	= centimeters(cm)	X 0.3937	= inches
microinches	X 0.0254	= micrometers(μm)	X 39.37	= microinches
AREA					
inches²	X 645.16	= millimeters²(mm²)	X 0.00155	= inches²
inches²	X 6.452	= centimeters²(cm²)	X 0.155	= inches²
feet²	X 0.0929	= meters²(m²)	X 10.764	= feet²
yards²	X 0.8361	= meters²(m²)	X 1.196	= yards²
acres	X 0.4047	= hectares(10⁴m²) (ha)	X 2.471	= acres
miles²	X 2.590	= kilometers²(km²)	X 0.3861	= miles²
VOLUME					
inches³	X 16387	= millimeters³(mm³)	X 0.000061	= inches³
inches³	X 16.387	= centimeters³(cm³)	X 0.06102	= inches³
inches³	X 0.01639	= liters(L)	X 61.024	= inches³
quarts	X 0.94635	= liters(L)	X 1.0567	= quarts
gallons	X 3.7854	= liters(L)	X 0.2642	= gallons
feet³	X 28.317	= liters(L)	X 0.03531	= feet³
feet³	X 0.02832	= meters³(m³)	X 35.315	= feet³
fluid oz	X 29.57	= milliliters(mL)	X 0.03381	= fluid oz
yards³	X 0.7646	= meters³(m³)	X 1.3080	= yards³
teaspoons	X 4.929	= milliliters(mL)	X 0.2029	= teaspoons
cups	X 0.2366	= liters(L)	X 4.227	= cups
MASS					
ounces(av)	X 28.35	= grams(g)	X 0.03527	= ounces(av)
pounds(av)	X 0.4536	= kilograms(kg)	X 2.2046	= pounds(av)
tons(2000 lb)	X 907.18	= kilograms(kg)	X 0.001102	= tons(2000 lb)
tons(2000 lb)	X 0.90718	= metric tons(t)	X 1.1023	= tons(2000 lb)
FORCE					
ounces-f(av)	X 0.278	= newtons(N)	X 3.597	= ounces-f(av)
pounds-f(av)	X 4.448	= newtons(N)	X 0.2248	= pounds-f(av)
kilograms-f	X 9.807	= newtons(N)	X 0.10197	= kilograms-f
ENERGY OR WORK (watt-second = joule = newton-meter)					
foot-pounds	X 1.3558	= joules(J)	X 0.7376	= foot-pounds
calories	X 4.187	= joules(J)	X 0.2388	= calories
Btu	X 1055	= joules(J)	X 0.000948	= Btu
watt-hours	X 3600	= joules(J)	X 0.0002778	= watt-hours
kilowatt-hrs	X 3.600	= megajoules(MJ)	X 0.2778	= kilowatt-hrs
LIGHT					
footcandles	X 10.76	= lumens/meter²		
		(lm/m²)	X 0.0929	= footcandles
PRESSURE OR STRESS (newton/sq meter = pascal)					
inches Hg(60 °F)	X 3.377	= kilopascals (kPa)	X 0.2961	= inches Hg
pounds/sq in	X 6.895	= kilopascals (kPa)	X 0.145	= pounds/sq in
inches H₂0(60 °F)	X 0.2488	= kilopascals (kPa)	X 4.0193	= inches H₂0
bars	X 100	= kilopascals (kPa)	X 0.01	= bars
pounds/sq ft	X 47.88	= pascals (Pa)	X 0.02088	= pounds/sq ft
POWER					
horsepower	X 0.746	= kilowatts (kW)	X 1.34	= horsepower
ft-lbf/min	X 0.0226	= watts(W)	X 44.25	= ft-lbf/min
TORQUE					
pound-inches	X 0.11298	= newton-meters(N-m)	X 8.851	= pound-inches
pound-feet	X 1.3558	= newton-meters(N)m	X 0.7376	= pound-feet
VELOCITY					
miles/hour	X 1.6093	= kilometers/hour(km/h)	X 0.6214	= miles/hour
feet/sec	X 0.3048	= meters/sec(m/s)	X 3.281	= feet/sec
kilometers/hr	X 0.27778	= meters/sec(m/s)	X 3.600	= kilometers/hr
miles/hour	X 0.4470	= meters/sec(m/s)	X 2.237	= miles/hour
TEMPERATURE					
(°Fahrenheit −32) X 1.8 = °Celsius					
(°Celsius X 1.8) + 32 = °Fahrenheit					

Fig. 4-4. This conversion chart can be used to change from customary to metric and from metric to customary values.

A conversion rule is another easy way of changing from one system to another. However, it is not as accurate as a conversion chart. See Fig. 24-5.

PRINTER'S SYSTEM OF MEASUREMENT

The units of measurement used in printing in most English speaking countries is the point and the pica. This is commonly referred to as the *point system*. It is mainly used in the typesetting area as type sizes are designated in points.

Line lengths are given in picas and points. The width and height of a form is also designated by picas and points.

Point and pica

The *point* is the smaller unit and it measures approximately 1/72 of an inch. It is also commonly expressed as .0138 inch. Approximately 72 points equal one inch.

The *pica* is approximately 1/6 of an inch and it is used for linear measurements of type. Type page sizes and margins are given in picas. Twelve points equal a pica and approximately six picas equal one inch.

Note! Refer to the index for more information on points and picas.

Type rules

The printers' measuring rule is called a *line gauge*. It also has other names such as: type gauge, type rule, and pica stick. Good line gauges are made of steel or other metal. They usually measure up to 72 picas. One edge usually has inches and the other edge picas and *non-pareils* (half of a pica). See Fig. 4-6.

American point system

The *American point system* has not always existed. When metal type was first cast, the measurement for each type founder was his or her own choosing. Using different foun-

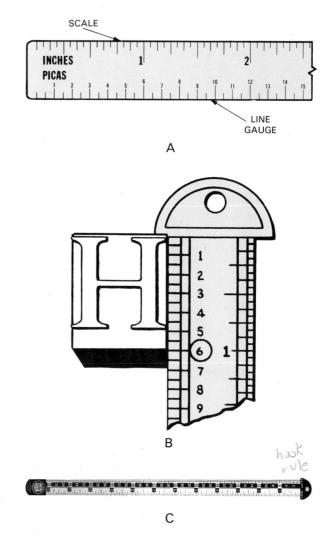

Fig. 4-6. Line gauge commonly has inch scale and pica scale for checking type size and line length. A—Line gauge with inches and picas. B—Line gauge is being used to check size of type. C—Actual line gauge.

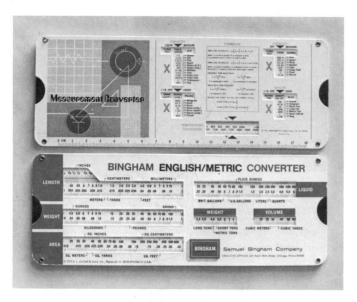

Fig. 4-5. This is a slide type converter. It is quick but not quite as accurate as a conversion table.

dries as sources was not practical. Most printers were committed to one foundry and their type styles. This went on for nearly 200 years.

In 1737, a Frenchman, by the name of Pierre-Simon Fournier, devised a standard for type measurement. The smallest unit in the system was strongly resisted and finally a royal decree by King Lewis XV was put into effect. The reason for the King making the decree was that he was very interested in printing. This forced the foundries to use a standard size.

The Fournier point was later modified by another French family. This printing family was known as the Didots. The new system conformed to the French inch. The Didot point is .0148 inches and is still used in Europe.

The United States adopted the American point system in 1886. The system used in Europe was the pattern for the American point system. As stated earlier, the two units under the system were the point and the pica. As a result, the measuring system had uniformity and purchasing type from many sources was made possible.

Until the point system, type sizes were called by name:
1. Diamond   = 4 1/2-point.
2. Agate   = 5 1/2-point.
3. Minion   = 7-point.
4. Brevier   = 8-point.
5. Long primer = 10-point.
6. Pica   = 12-point.
7. Great primer = 18-point.
8. Canon   = 48-point.

The *Agate*, referring to a book binder's burnisher or 5 1/2-point, is one of the only terms in use today. The pica became the term used to designate the largest unit of the point system.

Type height

Differences in type height (hot type thickness) caused the same problems that existed with type size. The distance from the base to the printing surface varied from printer to printer. This difference made it almost impossible to have an even printed image. This measurement was very important. Finally, a standard was established and is .918 inches. This type height designation is common to the United States, Canada, England, and most of Latin America.

Metric type size

The metric system can be used to denote the size of type. For example, millimeters can be used to give the equivalent size for either *pica point* (English-American system) or *Didot point* (European system) sizes. One pica point equals 0.351 mm. One Didot point equals 0.376 mm.

In Fig. 4-7, compare the metric, pica, and Didot systems. Note the differences in the measuring systems. The Didot

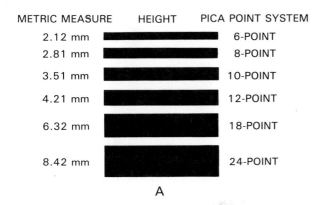

METRIC MEASURE	HEIGHT	PICA POINT SYSTEM
2.12 mm		6-POINT
2.81 mm		8-POINT
3.51 mm		10-POINT
4.21 mm		12-POINT
6.32 mm		18-POINT
8.42 mm		24-POINT

A

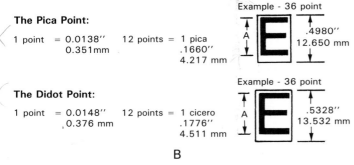

The Pica Point:

1 point = 0.0138″ 12 points = 1 pica
          0.351mm   .1660″
                               4.217 mm

Example - 36 point
.4980″
12.650 mm

The Didot Point:

1 point = 0.0148″ 12 points = 1 cicero
          0.376mm   .1776″
                               4.511 mm

Example - 36 point
.5328″
13.532 mm

B

Fig. 4-7. A—Note examples of point and metric sizes of type. B—Compare point, Didot, and millimeter sizes of type.

point is slightly larger than the pica. This is the reason that the metric equivalent can be given with the more conventional size.

Remember that the point and metric size of the letter is usually NOT a measurement from the top to the bottom of the letter itself. The point size also includes CLEARANCE SPACE above and below the letter for line spacing.

Since different type styles have different clearance spacing above and below the letter shape, it is difficult to measure the actual point size. Some typographers can identify a point size on sight. Others use a type size indicator. An easy way to tell type size, and the most sure way, is to refer to a type catalog. It will give examples of the specific type style and their point and metric sizes.

Fig. 4-8 shows two type styles that are both 24-point. However, their body size or clearance space is different. This could make point size identification difficult without typographical experience or a type catalog.

Note! With dry transfer letters, the type size in millimeters may denote the body size of the letters. It may not include clearance space above and below the letters. Refer to the catalog instructions if in doubt.

d-system

As mentioned, the point and the pica are the common measurements used today. However, new methods, based on fractions of a millimeter, are being considered. The adoption has not taken place and it appears that the present system will be used for some time.

S.J. Heden of Stockholm, Sweden, proposed a *d-system* in 1969. The Heden system proposed a unit called "d" for TYPE SIZE measurement. One "d" is defined as 0.1 millimeter. All of the necessary specifications such as type size, body size, line spacing, and width of margins would be designated by the unit "d." A two-number code would indicate the type size. The first number gives the mainstroke size; the second number would be the body size. For instance, the symbol 35/48 would indicate that the MAINSTROKE is 3.5 mm and the BODY SIZE is 4.8 mm.

"d"	Point Size
1. 35/48	14
2. 45/60	18
3. 60/75	24
4. 70/100	30
5. 90/130	36

The outcome of this attempt at standardization remains unknown, more than twenty years after introduction.

PAPER AND ENVELOPE SIZES

Presently *paper sizes* are still designated by inches as length and width dimensions. See Fig. 4-9. Metric measurement is also suggested for paper and sheet sizes. Again, metric is a possibility in the future.

The basic size is not the same for all kinds of paper:
1. Writing papers (bond, mimeo, etc.), 17 x 22 in.
2. Book (text, offset, etc.), 25 x 38 in.
3. Cover, 20 x 26 in.

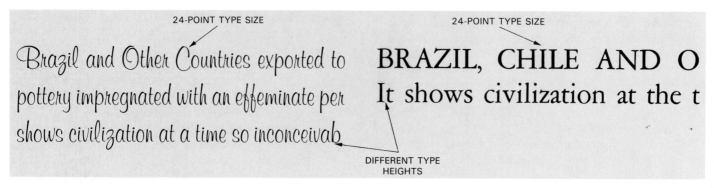

24-POINT TYPE SIZE

24-POINT TYPE SIZE

Brazil and Other Countries exported to pottery impregnated with an effeminate per shows civilization at a time so inconceivab

BRAZIL, CHILE AND O
It shows civilization at the t

DIFFERENT TYPE HEIGHTS

Fig. 4-8. Same point size designation does not always mean that actual size of letters is same height. This can make type size identification "tricky."

4. Index bristol, 25 1/2 x 30 1/2 in.
5. Newsprint, 24 x 36 in.

Envelopes

Envelopes are usually ordered from an envelope company. Each style has a special use. No. 9 for example, is for business use and measures 3 7/8 x 8 7/8 in. Window envelopes are the same size as the official envelope. Generally, they are used for invoices or statements.

The booklet envelopes are most often used for direct mail. Some of the advertising materials that come to your house in the mail use this envelope.

A common type used for wedding announcements and invitations or for other formal occasions is called baronial. A No. 6 baronial would measure 5 x 6 in.

Open-end envelopes, being larger, are used for mailing reports, pamphlets, magazines, and other similar material. A common size is 9 x 12 in. or 8 3/4 x 11 1/4 in.

ISO sizes

The International Organization for Standardization (ISO) has agreed upon the basic sizes of paper and envelopes. They are known as the ISO series. They consist of:

1. A-sizes to be used for general printing.
2. B-sizes for posters.
3. C-sizes for envelopes and cards.

The A and B metric paper sizes are rectangular. Their sizes are based on the ratio of the two sides having the proportion of one to the square root of two (1:1.416).

As shown in Fig. 4-10, the ISO-A size of paper is based on the area of one square meter. Looking over the sizes, it is clear that each cut reduces the size of the sheet by fifty percent of the previous size—A2 would double the size of the A3 size. Each ISO measurement is given in the chart in Fig. 4-11.

The A and B metric paper sizes have been considered to be trimmed sizes. However, series have been added for normal trims, bleed work, or extra trims, Fig. 4-12.

The B-series sizes are between the A-series. Looking at the BO-size, Fig. 4-13, the measure is 1000 x 144 mm which clearly identifies the ratio stated earlier. A comparison of the A, B, and C-series is found in Fig. 4-14.

Postcards, folders, and envelopes are associated with the C-series. A-series sheets are compatible with the C-series

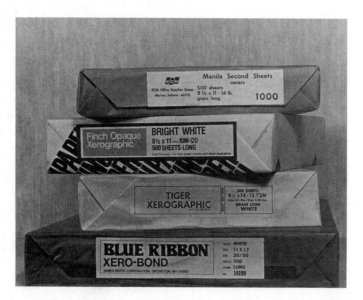

Fig. 4-9. Paper normally comes in customary sizes, like these. A ream is usually 500 sheets. Note information given on labels.

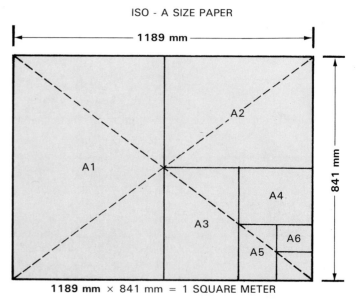

ISO - A SIZE PAPER

1189 mm

841 mm

1189 mm × 841 mm = 1 SQUARE METER

Fig. 4-10. This is a metric A-size paper.

ISO-sizes	METRIC-millimeters	CUSTOMARY-inches
2A	1189 x 1682	46.81 x 66.22
A0	841 x 1189	33.11 x 46.81
A1	594 x 841	23.39 x 33.11
A2	420 x 594	16.54 x 23.39
A3	297 x 420	11.69 x 16.54
A4	210 x 297	8.27 x 11.69
A5	148 x 210	5.83 x 8.27
A6	105 x 148	4.13 x 5.83
A7	74 x 105	2.91 x 4.13
A8	52 x 74	2.05 x 2.91
A9	37 x 52	1.46 x 2.05
A10	26 x 37	1.02 x 1.46

Fig. 4-11. Compare ISO sizes in millimeters and inches.

SIZES FOR NORMAL TRIMS		
ISO-size	METRIC-millimeters	CUSTOMARY-inches
RA0	860 x 1220	33.66 x 48.03
RA1	610 x 860	24.02 x 33.86
RA2	430 x 610	16.93 x 24.02
SIZES FOR BLEED WORK OR EXTRA TRIMS		
ISO-size	METRIC-millimeters	CUSTOMARY-inches
SRA0	900 x 1280	35.43 x 50.39
SRA1	640 x 900	25.20 x 35.43
SRA2	450 x 640	17.72 x 25.20

Fig. 4-12. Sizes for normal, trims, bleed work, or extra trims
are shown.
(Center for Metric Education, Western Michigan University)

ISO-sizes	METRIC-millimeters	CUSTOMARY-inches
B0	1000 x 1414	39.37 x 55.67
B1	707 x 1000	27.83 x 39.37
B2	500 x 707	19.68 x 27.83
B3	353 x 500	13.90 x 19.68
B4	250 x 353	9.84 x 13.90
B5	176 x 250	6.93 x 9.84
B6	125 x 176	4.92 x 6.93
B7	88 x 125	3.46 x 4.92
B8	62 x 88	2.44 x 3.46
B9	44 x 62	1.73 x 2.44
B10	31 x 44	1.22 x 1.73

Fig. 4-13. This shows B-series size paper.
(Center for Metric Education, Western Michigan University)

envelopes as shown in Fig. 4-15. One size envelope designated as DL (DIN Lang) is not derived from B or C-series sizes.

The International Standards Organization has recommended the following sizes:

1. C3 = 324 × 458 mm.
2. B4 = 250 × 353 mm.
3. C4 = 229 × 324 mm.

RELATIONSHIP BETWEEN A, B, AND C-SIZE PAPER

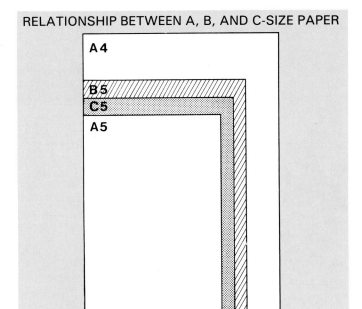

Fig. 4-14. Compare A, B, and C-series sizes of paper.

4. B5 = 176 × 250 mm.
5. C5 = 162 × 229 mm.
6. B6/C4 = 125 × 324 mm.
7. B6 = 125 × 176 mm.
8. C6 = 114 × 162 mm.
9. DL = 110 × 220 mm.
10. C7/7 = 81 × 162 mm.
11. C7 = 81 × 114 mm.

Present postal regulations must be reviewed. Sizes must comply with regulations so that additional funds are not needed to cover mail deliveries, Fig. 4-16.

Standardization appears more likely since automation has established size limitations for efficient postage equipment operation.

PAPER WEIGHT

Most papers are known by their basic weight which refers to the number of pounds in a ream of paper cut to its basic size. A ream of paper is generally considered to be 500 sheets. In a few instances, it might be 480 sheets, Fig. 4-17.

Usually, paper is referred to by its ream weight, such as 20 lb. bond or 70 lb. book. *Twenty-pound bond* means that 500 sheets of 17 x 22 in. writing paper will weigh 20 lbs. If an "M" appears after the weight, it means that now the weight refers to 1000 sheets. An example is: 25 x 38—140M. This means that 1000 sheets of 25 x 38 in. book paper will weigh 140 lb.

Each kind (grade) of paper has many sizes and weights. The categories—book, writing, cover, index, Bristol, tag, and newsprint—are commonly called the *kinds* or *grades* of paper. Each has special characteristics and common uses. How you intend to use them will determine what kind you will buy. The printer should know about paper but a reliable paper salesperson can be a great help.

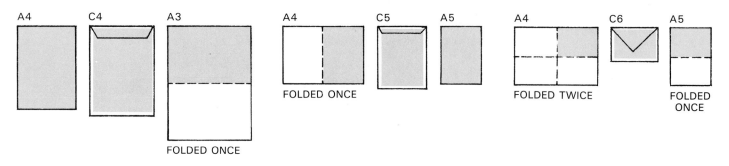

Fig. 4-15. This shows C-series envelopes and A-series sheets of paper.

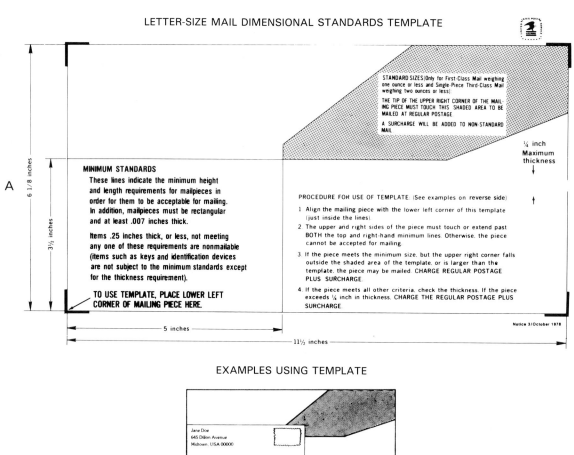

LETTER-SIZE MAIL DIMENSIONAL STANDARDS TEMPLATE

STANDARD SIZES (Only for First-Class Mail weighing one ounce or less and Single-Piece Third-Class Mail weighing two ounces or less).

THE TIP OF THE UPPER RIGHT CORNER OF THE MAILING PIECE MUST TOUCH THIS SHADED AREA TO BE MAILED AT REGULAR POSTAGE

A SURCHARGE WILL BE ADDED TO NON-STANDARD MAIL

¼ inch Maximum thickness

MINIMUM STANDARDS

These lines indicate the minimum height and length requirements for mailpieces in order for them to be acceptable for mailing. In addition, mailpieces must be rectangular and at least .007 inches thick.

Items .25 inches thick, or less, not meeting any one of these requirements are nonmailable (items such as keys and identification devices are not subject to the minimum standards except for the thickness requirement).

TO USE TEMPLATE, PLACE LOWER LEFT CORNER OF MAILING PIECE HERE.

PROCEDURE FOR USE OF TEMPLATE: (See examples on reverse side)

1. Align the mailing piece with the lower left corner of this template (just inside the lines).
2. The upper and right sides of the piece must touch or extend past BOTH the top and right-hand minimum lines. Otherwise, the piece cannot be accepted for mailing.
3. If the piece meets the minimum size, but the upper right corner falls outside the shaded area of the template, or is larger than the template, the piece may be mailed. CHARGE REGULAR POSTAGE PLUS SURCHARGE.
4. If the piece meets all other criteria, check the thickness. If the piece exceeds ¼ inch in thickness, CHARGE THE REGULAR POSTAGE PLUS SURCHARGE.

Notice 3/October 1978

A — 6 1/8 inches — 3½ inches — 5 inches — 11½ inches

EXAMPLES USING TEMPLATE

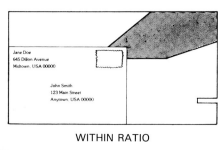

WITHIN RATIO

B

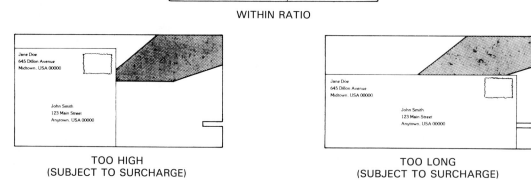

TOO HIGH
(SUBJECT TO SURCHARGE)

TOO LONG
(SUBJECT TO SURCHARGE)

Fig. 4-16. Study both sides of this template for letter sizes. It is used to determine if letter size is acceptable for normal handling by post office. A—Letter size mail dimensional standard template. B—Using template as a guide.

TYPICAL WEIGHTS (1000 SHEETS) AND SIZES AVAILABLE IN THESE WEIGHTS		
BOOK	25 x 38	60 —70 —80 —90 —100 —120 —140 —160, ETC.
WRITING	17 x 22	26 —32 —40 —48 —56 —64, ETC.
INDEX BRISTOL	25½ x 30½	117 —144 —182 —222 —286
COVER	20 x 26	100 —120 —130 —160 —180, ETC.

Fig. 4-17. This table shows standard sizes and weights of paper. Study them!

The Technical Association for Paper and Pulp Industry preferred to express the metric weight per unit area as grams per square meter (g/²). Converting customary sizes and weights of 500 sheets (t) to the metric grams per square meter (m) is shown in Fig. 4-18.

A coated book stock would be expressed as 100 g/m². A good writing paper would be listed as 85 g/m². This times 0.2666 would equal 22.610 which is the weight of a writing paper, commonly referred to as *bond*.

CONVERSION FACTORS FOR REAM WEIGHTS			
KIND OF PAPER	CUSTOMARY SIZE IN INCHES	A (m to t)	B (t to m)
Writing	12 x 22	0.266	3.760
Cover	20 x 26	0.370	2.704
Cardboard	22 x 28	0.438	2.282
News	24 x 36	0.614	1.627
Book	25 x 38	0.675	1.480

Fig. 4-18. These are conversion factors for changing from customary to metric weights of paper.

Paper caliper

Various types of caliper devices are available for measuring paper thickness. Whatever device is used, it must have an anvil. The diameter of the base is such that it will not crush the stock beyond the allowable limits.

The *paper caliper* or *micrometer* is a very accurate means of measuring the thickness of paper. It can also be used to determine the thickness of a printing plate. See Fig. 4-19.

PHOTOCONVERSION MEASUREMENT

Conventional film sizes vary: 2 1/4 by 2 1/4 inch, 4 by 5 inch, 8 by 10 inch, etc. Photographic film in use today also has metric measurements. For example, 8 mm, 16 mm, 35 mm, and 70 mm film is used in film production. Graphic communications film and paper, if accepted, would use the sizes commonly found in the A-series paper measurements.

It has been proposed that typesetting equipment use the following widths: 35, 70, 100, 150, 200, 250, 280, and 300 mm. The lengths that have been proposed for film and paper will be 7.5, 15, and 20 meters.

Screen rulings

Halftone photography *screen rulings,* discussed in Chapter One, presently uses lines per inch but metric measurement would be lines per cm. As in the customary measurement, the screen rulings below 75 are considered to be COARSE while above 133 is considered FINE. As shown in Fig. 4-20, the larger the screen number, the finer the screen. The corresponding metric screen rulings would have the same referral.

To make this comparison, the lines per inch is divided by 2.54 which would equal the lines per cm. The lines per cm multiplied by 2.54 would equal the lines per inch.

A typical comparison of screen rulings is in Fig. 4-21.

A *screen scale* or sometimes called *star scale* or *screen angle indicator,* can be used to find out what screen is used in a halftone. One is pictured in Fig. 4-22. When the scale is placed over the screened photo and slowly rotated, a star will appear on the scale. The numbers next to the star will equal the screen ruling number.

Screen angle measurement

Screen angles are measured in degrees. Fig. 4-23 shows a scale giving the screen angles for each color separation.

Discussed in Chapter One, to print four-color, a color separation must be made for each primary color. To print properly, each separation must have the correct screen angle.

From the illustration, note that black normally uses a 45 degree screen, magenta uses 75 degrees, yellow uses 90 degrees, and cyan uses a 105 degree screen angle. The line

Fig. 4-19. This paper caliper or micrometer will accurately check paper thickness.

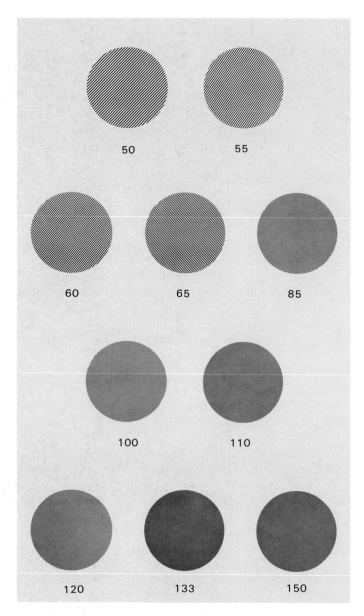

Fig. 4-20. These are samples of screen rulings. Note that the larger the screen number, the finer the screen. Screens are used to change continuous tone photographs into dotted halftones for printing.

CUSTOMARY SCREEN RULINGS PER INCH	METRIC SCREEN RULINGS PER CENTIMETER
50	20
65	26
75	30
100	40
120	48
133	54
150	60
175	70
200	80

Fig. 4-21. Note approximate comparison of screen rulings for customary and metric screens.

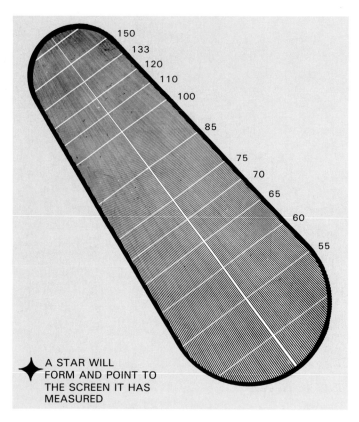

Fig. 4-22. This star scale or screen scale can be used to determine screen ruling size. Lay transparent scale over screen and rotate it slowly until star forms. The number next to center of star equals screen size.

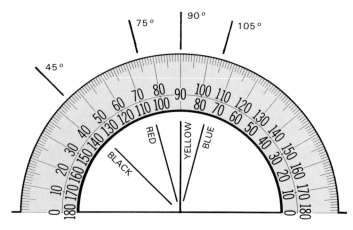

Fig. 4-23. Screen angles must be correct to prevent an unwanted Moire dot pattern on the printed page. Note normal angles for each color separation.

patterns on each screen would have this angle relationship to prevent a moire pattern (unwanted dot pattern).

Tint percentages

A *screen tint* is measured by a percentage. It is a hard dot screen that will produce even spaced dots that represent tone values of a solid color.

For example, a 10 percent tint would generally have 90 percent less ink deposited on the paper than an image printed

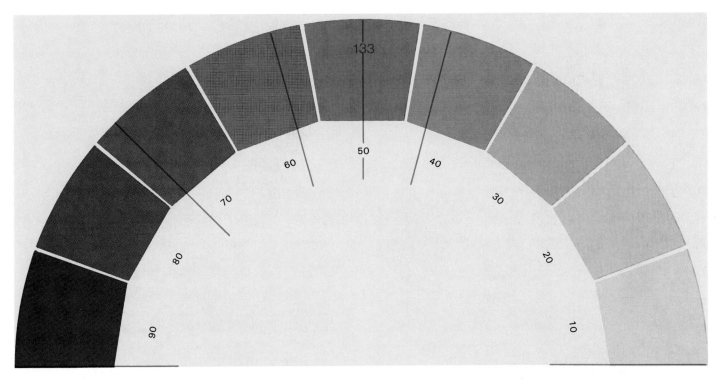

Fig. 4-24. Here are samples of screen tint percentages. Note that a larger screen percentage denotes a darker screen and vice versa.

without a screen tint. It would print very light. A 90 percent tint would have 10 percent less ink and would print dark. This is illustrated in Fig. 4-24.

Gray scale

A *gray scale* is a continuous tone wedge with different shades of gray for gauging film exposure and development during chemical processing. One is pictured in Fig. 4-25.

Densitometer

The *densitometer* is used to give a measure of density or darkness, Fig. 4-26. Two types are commonly used in an industrial environment. One is reflection while the other is transmission.

The *reflection densitometer* is used to give a reflected light measurement which indicates the tone values of printed materials or photographic prints. The *transmission densitometer* is for measuring light passing through a material.

Using photographic prints, as an example, the measurements are taken to identify the lightest areas and darkest areas of the print or any other areas used to calculate exposures.

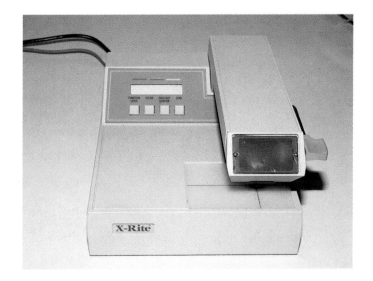

Fig. 4-26. A densitometer can accurately measure darkness or lightness of image. For example, the densitometer will measure lightest and darkest shades on a photograph. These readings are used to calculate the proper exposure for making a halftone screen or plate.

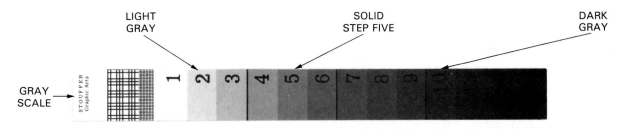

Fig. 4-25. Gray scale is used to measure film exposure and development. This is detailed in later chapters.

The density measurement given is defined as the log of the reciprocal of light reflection or transmission. The formula is stated as:

$$D = \log_{10}\frac{1}{R} \text{ or } D = \log_{10}\frac{1}{T}$$

D = Density, R = Reflection, T = Transmission

The example is that of a transmission densitometer that gives the tone range or contrast of a negative or positive.

INK MEASUREMENT

Much of the formulations relating to ink manufacturing has been in common use by the scientist, chemist, or physicist. The metric standards have been observed in Europe and most recently in Britain while we frequently use our conventional system.

It appears that ink should be sold by metric volume with the smallest requirement being a 500 and/or 100 milliliter container size. The most common container sizes would be 25, 20, 10, 5, 2.5, and one liter. Although the above is used in Britain, ink manufacturer's are using the kilogram as the unit of measurement. The greatest problem is the fact that all inks do not have the same specific gravity (weight per volume or density).

Not only the ink manufacturer, but the manufacturers of paint, adhesives, oils, and chemicals would benefit from the uniform container size.

Ink film thickness gauge

The *ink film thickness gauge* is a measuring device to indicate the thickness of the ink film on the press. The measurement is taken on the steel roller of the ink train of the press. Extreme care must be taken while taking the measurement, Fig. 4-27.

The gauge is a means of checking the amount of ink carried by the press rollers. The center eccentric circle is the measuring device. Where the ink no longer appears in the eccentric circle is the point for reading the markings on the gauge. The ink film gauge measurements are in mils.

Ink fineness gauge

The two channels on the *ink fineness gauge* are graduated to measure the pigment particle size in ink. When ink is drawn over the calibrated areas, scratch patterns will appear in the zones to identify if a finer grind of ink is needed. This measuring device is machined to a very high degree of accuracy and is commonly found in an ink manufacturing firm. Look at Fig. 4-28.

pH METER

In general terms, pH is the value which identifies the alkalinity or acidity of a solution. Therefore, a *pH meter* measures the acidity or alkalinity of a solution (press fountain solution for example). The scale ranges from 0 to 14 with 7 being neutral. All figures on the smaller side of 7 are ACID while the higher figures are ALKALINE.

The pH scale is *logarithmically calculated*. This means a change from one figure to another is ten times more acid or alkaline. Changing by two numbers would be a change of 100. Reading a pH value accurately is essential for quality control. Fountain solutions, plate coatings, papers, etc. all have pH factors. Fig. 4-29 shows a pH meter.

PRESS SPEED MEASUREMENT

Impressions per hour, abbreviated iph, is the most common method of determining press speed. It indicates the number of plate images that are printed on the substrate in one hour of time.

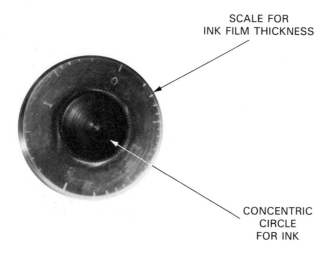

SCALE FOR INK FILM THICKNESS

CONCENTRIC CIRCLE FOR INK

Fig. 4-27. This is an ink film thickness gauge. It uses a curved or eccentric disc. The disc is placed on wet ink. Only a portion of disc will touch and pick up ink. The point where the ink stops touching the disc shows ink film thickness. Note numbers that equal mils.

Fig. 4-28. Ink fineness gauge will measure ink grain or pigment size. This tool is needed when formulating ink, for example.

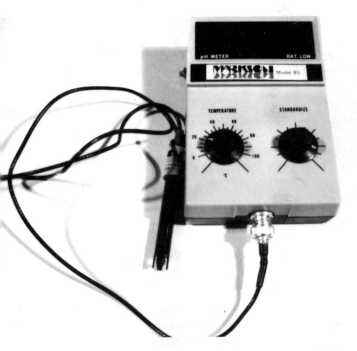

Fig. 4-29. This pH meter will measure acidity or alkalinity of a solution. Readings range from zero which is most acid, to 14 which is most alkaline. Probe is simply inserted into solution to make reading. Note dial for correcting for temperature.

A web press is very fast and may be able to make 15,000 to 20,000 impressions-per-hour. A slower sheet-fed press might be capable of printing 7,500 to 10,000 images or sheets an hour. This can vary with exact press design however.

Feet per second, abbreviated f/s, can be used to denote the speed of a web press. It refers to how fast the long ribbon of paper is moving through the press. The speed of a sheet-fed press can also be given as *sheets-per-hour* (sph).

NOISE MEASUREMENT

Decibels are a measure of the noise level in a facility. Abbreviated dBA, decibels are often measured around loud equipment to make sure the noise is not severe enough to cause ear injury.

Discussed in the chapter on safety, there are safe and unsafe limits for exposure to noise. For example, an exposure to a reading of 90 dBA is maximum for an eight-hour day. Anything louder would require ear protection. A decibel meter is used to measure noise levels.

CYLINDER PACKING GAUGE

Detailed in later chapters, *cylinder packing* is material (usually paper) placed on the press cylinder so that the plate touches the substrate with enough pressure to transfer a good image.

A *cylinder packing gauge* is used to accurately calculate the distance needed to bring the press cylinder to the diameter needed for an excellent image transfer. The *bearer* (outer ring or flange on press cylinder) is the reference point. The thickness needed to bring the blanket to bearer height

and the extra thickness needed to give the right plate pressure is imperative for good reproduction of images. This is a valuable measuring device to determine proper packing thickness, Fig. 4-30.

BLANKET THICKNESS GAUGE

A *press blanket* is a resilient material used to cover the blanket cylinder on a printing press that transfers the plate image to the substrate, such as paper. It must be perfectly uniform to produce a quality image.

Fig. 4-30. This is a cylinder packing gauge. It is used when setting up a printing press before a run. It will measure height of cylinder compared to its bearers.

The *blanket thickness gauge* is designed to allow you to measure the thickness over the entire surface of the press blanket. Low spots may develop and the gauge is an accurate way to check for this problem.

A micrometer can be used to measure the thickness of a blanket, but it will only measure the very edge of the blanket. Low spots may develop near the middle of the blanket and a thickness gauge is the best way of checking for irregularities. One is pictured in Fig. 4-31.

HARDNESS TESTER

A *hardness tester,* also called a *durometer,* is a measuring device used to check the hardness of materials such as: rubber and plastic rollers, blankets, or any resilient materials. It is important to know the hardness of various

Fig. 4-31. This blanket thickness gauge will accurately check all areas of a press blanket for any difference in thickness. Blanket thickness must be uniform for press to produce good image on substrate.

Fig. 4-32. Hardness tester will quickly measure hardness or softness of different materials. Dial shows how far pointed plunger indents into material and this can be used to find hardness.

materials. Rollers that are too hard or too soft can be troublesome to the press operator, Fig. 4-32.

The durometer is pressed against the surface of the material being measured. The probe indents the surface and the amount of indention is indicated on the dial. The reading is the relative hardness or softness of the material. Rollers, blankets, etc. have various recommended durometer readings for a variety of press sizes.

METRIC EQUIPMENT MEASUREMENT

Many of today's printing press and paper making systems are produced with metric specifications. An example is the Heidelberg Company which manufactures equipment requiring metric tools to make many of the adjustments. The manufacturer often gives the total specifications for floor space in both metric and customary dimensions.

Since metric conversion is a voluntary participation program, a coordinated effort by manufacturers appears to be the most practical approach applied to new equipment. It is imperative that the cost be kept minimal. In many cases, the changeover would appear to be very feasible as equipment becomes obsolete.

OTHER MEASUREMENTS

Other measurements, besides those discussed in this chapter, are found thoughout all areas of graphic communications. Refer to the index for more information as needed. Special measurements are covered in the chapters where they apply.

KNOW THESE TERMS

Metric system, Meter, Kilogram, Kelvin, Mole, Candela, Celcius, Milliliter, Millimeter, Meter, Metric prefix, Metric conversion, Conversion chart, Point, Pica, Line guage, "d" system, Paper sizes, Envelope sizes, ISO series, Paper weight, Paper caliper, Film sizes, Screen rulings, Screen tint percentage, Screen or star scale, Screen angles, Gray scale, Densitometer, Ink film thickness gauge, Ink fineness gauge,

pH meter, iph, sph, Decibels, Cylinder packing gauge, Blanket thickness gauge, Hardness tester.

REVIEW QUESTIONS — CHAPTER 4

1. Some of the first measuring terms referred to parts of the _____ _____.
2. _____ percent of the world population uses the metric system.
3. In the metric system, the meter would express _____; the liter would express _____ or _____; grams would express _____ or _____; pressure would be in _____; and area in _____.
4. Which of the following is an INCORRECT metric notation?
   a. 33 mm.
   b. 0.39 km.
   c. 34,000 km.
   d. 42 kPa.
5. Explain and use six metric prefixes.
6. Convert the following values.
   a. One inch = _____ mm.
   b. 12 m = _____ yards.
   c. 10 quarts = _____ liters.
   d. 12 milliliters = _____ fluid oz.
   e. 400 pounds = _____ kilograms.
   f. 25 meters/sec. = _____ feet/sec.
   g. 68 °F = _____ °C.
7. A point measures approximately _____ of an inch.
8. The pica is approximately _____ of an inch.
9. Explain the ISO sizes of paper and envelopes.
10. What is the basic weight of paper?
11. Both conventional and metric sizes are used for film. True or false?
12. Screen rulings below 75 are considered _____ while rulings above 133 are considered _____.
13. A 10 percent tint would have _____ ink deposited on the paper than a 20 percent tint.
14. Why must each color screen angle be set differently?
15. The _____ is used to measure the darkness or density of an image.

SUGGESTED ACTIVITIES

1. Choose ten items commonly found in presswork that have specifications. Look at the customary quantity and convert it to the metric quantity.
2. The following items are needed by the personnel in two graphic communication departments:
   a. 3 containers of opaque, 4 oz. each.
   b. 4 rolls of litho ruby tape, 1/4 inch wide.
   c. 4 pints of rubber cement.
   d. 2 lbs. of magenta ink.
   e. 20 reams of 8 1/2 inch x 11 inch, 20 lb., white writing paper.
   f. 5 gallons of blanket/roller wash.
   Write a requisition using the metric system to order the above mentioned items.

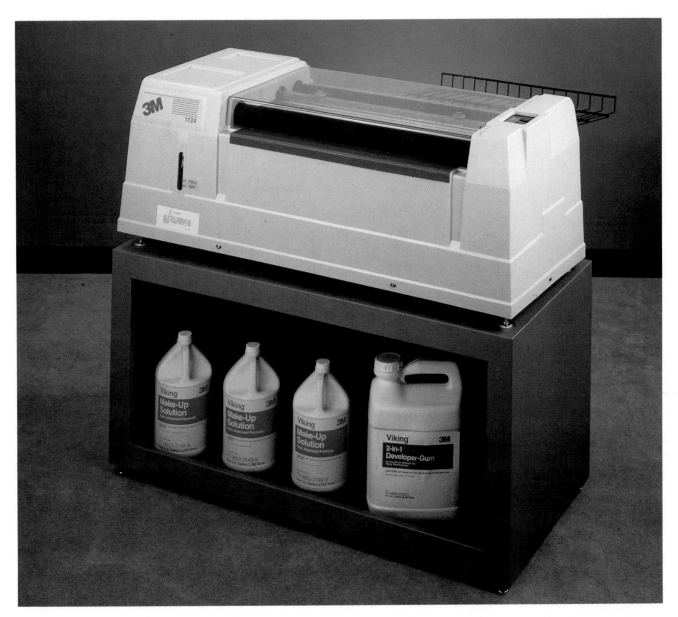

Accurate measurement is important when mixing chemicals for various aspects of graphic communications. It is critical that all chemicals used to process proofs, films, photos, and plates are mixed in correct proportions. (3M Company)

Electronics has caused tremendous change in how type is produced. The typographer can now select from a greater variety of type styles and more easily alter the type to more efficiently meet the needs of the job. Desktop publishing is one example that allows text and other images to be organized, sized, and placed on a monitor screen for evaluation before making a hard copy. This chapter will introduce you to the important ''role a typeface plays'' in the printing industry. Chapter 12 summarizes electronic production.   (Camex)

Chapter 5

TYPEFACES

After studying this chapter, you will be able to:
- Explain the development of type styles throughout the world.
- Identify the nomenclature of a typeface.
- Identify basic typeface classifications and a style of type in each classification.
- Explain the difference between a family, series, and font of type.
- Identify the common type sizes and units used in typography.
- List and explain the factors that contribute to the legibility of type.
- Summarize how computerized typesetting has increased the capabilities of typography.

This chapter introduces the role typefaces play in producing printed images. Typefaces are important, not only to the communication of thoughts, but to the overall appearance or aesthetic characteristics of the printed image.

Study this chapter carefully because it will prepare you for information given in many other chapters.

TYPEFACES

Typefaces are the visual symbols seen as printed images on a substrate (printing surface). *Characters* is another term used to identify all of the visual symbols used to compose a printed page. The assortment of images such as letters, figures, punctuation marks, and assorted symbols (dollar signs, ampersands, etc.) make up the characters necessary to put words into print.

Orderliness in graphic communications has been evident throughout history. Just as every person has a name, every typeface has a name. It would be very difficult to describe typefaces without names, just as it would be difficult to describe each human being. There are several thousand typefaces in use and available to the producer of printed products.

Typography

The *typographer* (print designer) must determine how the manuscript should be expressed in type as well as other details of reproduction and physical format. Typographic proficiency is essential since *typography* is the art of expressing ideas in type form. The typographer must decide which type style best represents the needs of a specific printed product.

For example, if the typographer is selecting a typeface used in an advertisement for a new "state of the art" electronic device, he or she would NOT select an older looking type style with fancy, curly letters. A more modern, "clean looking" type would be more appropriate and representative.

Typeface terminology

Our alphabet only has 26 letters. However, since there are thousands of alphabet types, it is important to be able to differentiate and select the correct typeface for the job. To do this, you must understand the basic terms relating to type and know how they affect the printed image.

The fundamental terms relating to a typeface are shown in Fig. 5-1. They include:
1. UPPERCASE (capital or larger letters, abbreviated "caps").
2. LOWERCASE (smaller, body letters, abbreviated "lc").
3. BODY HEIGHT (also called X-height, distance from top to bottom of lower case letters, not including ascenders and descenders), Fig. 5-1.
4. ASCENDER (part of letter that extends ABOVE body or X-height letters).
5. DESCENDER (part of letter that extends BELOW body or X-height letters).
6. BASE LINE (imaginary line drawn along BOTTOM of body height letters), Fig. 5-1.
7. WAIST LINE (imaginary line drawn along TOP of body height letters).
8. COUNTER (nonprinting areas around characters and inside loops of letters).
9. POINT (measurement of type size), Fig. 5-1.
   The basic terms relating to specific characters are:
1. HAIRLINE (thinner line or element of character). Fig. 5-2 gives an example.
2. STEM (vertical part of character).
3. STROKE (refers to thickness of line forming character element).

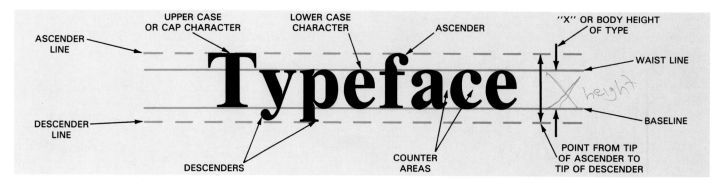

Fig. 5-1. Study basic terms relating to type.

4. STRESS (refers to slant or tilt of character).
5. SERIF (short finish off strokes or thickened tips at top and bottom of character), Fig. 5-2.
6. SET-WIDTH (distance from right to left sides of character).

You should now have a general understanding of the terms just explained and illustrated. Review these terms if needed. Later sections of this chapter, and other chapters, will discuss them in more detail. You will learn how these typeface components and characteristics can be used to alter the form and function of words, sentences, and the general "look" of the printed image.

TYPE STYLE DEVELOPMENT

Through the years, humans have strived to perfect the art of making written or printed images. The scribes of medieval Europe produced hundreds of beautiful and masterful letter forms as they hand printed book pages. The scribes made each letter into an "art form" and developed very beautiful lettering. Throughout Europe, the style of letters varied from area to area.

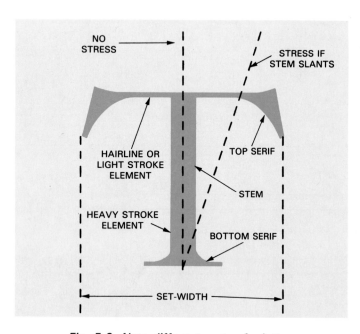

Fig. 5-2. Note different parts of a letter.

Black letter

The *black letter* had it's beginning in Germany, France, and Holland. This letter style was used as the basis for development of what is known today as *Old English*. Fig. 5-3 shows this typestyle.

The black letter prevailed long after the invention of printing but with many variations. The manuscript style common to a locality or geographic area was the imitated style used by the printer. The more delicate and lighter type style was developed in Italy and was the forerunner of the Roman letter.

𝕲𝖗𝖆𝖕𝖍𝖎𝖈 𝕬𝖗𝖙𝖘 𝕯𝖎𝖘𝖕𝖑𝖆𝖞 𝖔𝖋 𝕱𝖎𝖓𝖊 𝕻𝖗𝖎𝖓𝖙𝖎𝖓𝖌 𝕽𝖊𝖛𝖊𝖆𝖑𝖘
𝕾𝖐𝖎𝖑𝖋𝖚𝖑 𝕬𝖗𝖗𝖆𝖓𝖌𝖊𝖒𝖊𝖓𝖙 𝖔𝖋 𝕿𝖞𝖕𝖊

Fig. 5-3. Old English was a style developed from black letter. (ATF)

German black letter

As the art of printing developed, changes in type styles also increased. This was especially true in Italy as many of the German printers migrated to Italy. The German black letter influence was very evident but type styles started to lean toward the Roman. Several books were printed using the *Subiaco face* which actually was the name of the town where the printing was done.

Jenson

At this time, a major figure in the development of type styles was Nicolas Jenson. He was a Frenchman and a master engraver for the French government. History states that he was sent to Mainz, Germany. There he learned the new craft of printing but never returned to France.

Jenson is credited with designing and cutting the Roman letter that appeared in printed pieces of 1469 and 1470. These designs were the models used by type designers for hundreds of years. Jenson developed Roman lowercase letters that would merge readily into word forms. This was significant since even today we recognize words by their shape. Nicolas Jenson is credited with printing about 150 books during his ten years in Italy, Fig. 5-4.

Jenson followed the traditions of the manuscript writer in going to original Roman sources for his capitals. His lowercase letters, when enlarged, revealed the feeling of the pen drawn letter on a parchment surface. Each letter could be considered independently, yet they merged into the identity of the word.

The true character of Jenson's style has been reproduced in the *Centaur* type of today. Centaur was issued in the United States in 1914.

Other designers produced type styles in Italy, as the country was the model for all of Europe. The craft was at a very high level during this era.

The black letter, Roman, and Italic type styles were used universally in Europe for two centuries. For a time, the black letter was dominant in Germany and the Roman letter dominated in Italy. Eventually however, the Roman letter became the principal letter style used in all countries except Germany.

ABCDEFGHIJKLMNOPQR
STUVWXYZ
abcdefghijklmnopqrstuvwxyz

Fig. 5-4. This is Jenson type as known today. He modified Roman so that it would more readily form words.

Modern typefaces

The early type styles were adapted from the early pen or hand drawn manuscript letters. However, later typecutters copied from those styles that already existed. The emphasis now changed to producing *modern* type that could be produced easily by copying, rather than working from original sources. Aesthetics no longer became an important design factor. Imitation was the "order of the day" and types became thinner and lines became much sharper.

The quality of type design declined during the early 1700s throughout Europe and England and continued through the 19th century. The decline was reflected in the poorly printed books of the era.

Morris. In 1890, as a result of this decline, William Morris, an English architect, artist, and poet, set out to demonstrate that books could again be beautiful. His interest brought about the revival of early typefaces, which are the basis for many of the present-day typefaces used in book publication.

Garamond. Claude Garamond, a French printer, was influenced by Jenson but designed a more elegant and refined typeface that was typically French. This took place in the 1540s and is the face known today as Garamond, Fig. 5-5.

BRAZIL, CHILE AND OTHER
It shows civilization at the time so

Fig. 5-5. Today's Garamond type is faithful to the original style. (ATF)

The design was revived in 1919 and 1920 in the United States. The designer made a light lined, more open design that would print more clearly.

Janson. Janson is a recutting of a face issued in about the year 1675 by Anton Janson. Janson, a type founder, modified the manuscript letter by lightening the lines for better printing on a rough surface stock.

Caslon. William Caslon issued his famous typeface in England in about the year 1722. Caslon's typeface was an immediate success. The design by Caslon continued the trend toward lighter lines and more open design for better printing.

As a type founder, his design was intended to be preserved by forcing the type into the rough surface of the paper. This was very similar to stamping an image in leather, Fig. 5-6.

Baskerville. Baskerville is another famous type style name. John Baskerville marks the start of the transition, from letter design based on manuscript models, to letters designed solely for printing. Baskerville experimented in England with type and paper from 1750 to 1758. Baskerville established a paper mill, type foundry, and printing office in Birmingham, England.

The principle of fitting type, paper, ink, and presswork was Baskerville's idea and was the basis of today's planning of a printed job. This type style is shown in Fig. 5-7.

Bodoni. Another type style was designed by Giambattista Bodoni who was an Italian printer. Bodoni is considered to be a modern typeface. This typeface has extreme differences between the light and heavy elements.

The present-day Bodoni typefaces were issued in the United States in 1911, Fig. 5-8. The Bodoni Book typeface is like Bodoni's earlier period when contrast was less pronounced.

Six Roman faces have been reviewed. They are representative of the basic book faces showing the three classes of roman type designs: Oldstyle, Transitional, and Modern, as thought of today.

AT BRAZIL AND OTHER
It shows civilization at a time so
remote that it is doubtful whether

Fig. 5-6. Caslon face of today is considered a classic. (ATF)

CHESS-KNIGHT
After an apprentice

Fig. 5-7. Baskerville reflected a new trend in type design.

SOME KNIGHTS OF
After an apprentice as

Fig. 5-8. Bodoni is a modern typeface. (ATF)

The ROUGH PAPERS commonly required the four Oldstyle faces, from Jenson through Caslon, while Baskerville was a transitional typeface and was associated with SMOOTH PAPERS. Bodoni is the modern typeface, and to the designer, is considered to have the feeling of mechanical precision.

Contemporary typefaces

Contemporary typefaces are primarily the contributions of the 20th century.

First, there are the recutting of the basic book faces of the early printers. Second, there are the modifications of the basic book faces made for newspapers. Third, there are the many new display faces. Parallel to the issuance of new faces was the rapid growth of advertising and commercial printing during the first half of this century.

Thousands of faces are in existence. This number seems large but it is much like the carpenter who has a large chest of tools. So it is true of the typographer who chooses the correct typeface for the specific job. For this reason, *type catalogs,* showing numerous typefaces, are used to easily select a specific typeface. See Fig. 5-9.

Sometimes, a typeface will look similar yet have a different name. It is possible that the designer changed the type slightly and gave the style a new name since typefaces are NOT subject to copyright. For this reason, classifications have been given by their style characteristics, rather than to rely on broader names only.

RELIEF TYPE NOMENCLATURE

With *relief* or *hot type* printing, the face of the type and its surface receive ink. An impression transfers the ink to the substrate or printing surface. The names and parts of type used in relief printing are shown in Figs. 5-10 and 5-11.

The *height* of type is .918 inches (23.32 mm) when measured from the bottom of the character to the *face* or printing surface. This varies in some parts of the world but this measurement is common in North America.

Typeface elements

Discussed earlier, three elements make up the printing surface of a character. They are the heavy elements, light elements, and serifs.

Fig. 5-9. This is a sample page from a typical typeface catalog. It can be used when selecting a typeface.

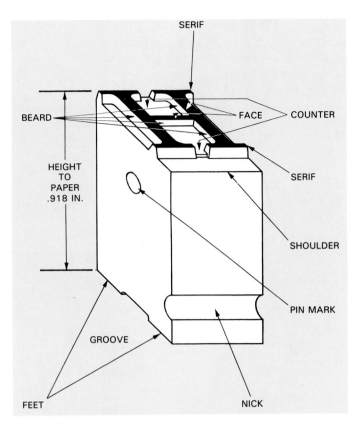

Fig. 5-10. Study nomenclature of hot type.

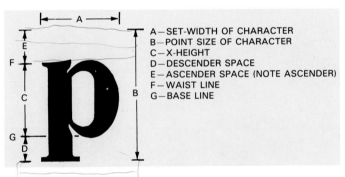

A—SET-WIDTH OF CHARACTER
B—POINT SIZE OF CHARACTER
C—X-HEIGHT
D—DESCENDER SPACE
E—ASCENDER SPACE (NOTE ASCENDER)
F—WAIST LINE
G—BASE LINE

Fig. 5-11. Study nomenclature of character face.

The *heavy elements* of the type character give identify while the *light elements* tie together. Look at Fig. 5-12.

The curves of the characters should vary to emphasize difference or unlikeness of the letters and to neutralize the vertical thrusts of the letters.

Serifs help the reader to mark the ends of the letter stroke, Fig. 5-13. The serifs found on the BOTTOM of letters imply

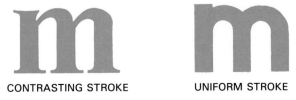

CONTRASTING STROKE   UNIFORM STROKE

Fig. 5-12. A contrasting stroke makes differences in letter shape more pronounced. Uniform stroke has same thickness.

the horizontal base line. This helps to hold the letters together to form words. The TOP serifs contribute to the unlikeness of the letter and help readability. See Fig. 5-14.

The ascenders are identifiers and also assist in the recognition of a word, Fig. 5-14. Some typefaces do not have all of the elements which have been identified.

A type classification that does not have element variation or finishing off strokes is called sans serif, Fig. 5-13. *Sans serif* means that the type style does NOT have serifs.

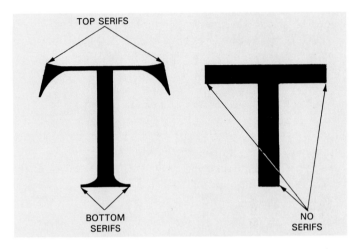

Fig. 5-13. Serifs are thickened strokes at tips of letter. Sans serif type does not use serifs.

TYPEFACE CLASSIFICATIONS

The number of typeface classifications is not totally agreed upon as some experts will list more classifications than others. For the purpose of this book, eight classifications will be identified by design, Fig. 5-15. They are:
1. Roman (Oldstyle, Transitional, and Modern).
2. Sans Serif.
3. Square Serif.
4. Text or Black letter.
5. Cursive or Script.
6. Occasional, Decorative, or Novelty.
7. Italic (variation of other classifications).
8. Dot Matrix.

Roman

Discussed briefly, the *roman type styles* are numerous in number and are the most widely used. The characteristic commonly associated with the Roman face is the contrast that exists between the heavy and light elements. One other prominent characteristic is the use of the finishing off lines or serifs.

Three patterns are common to the Roman letter form of the scribes. They are: Oldstyle face, Transitional face, and Modern face. These are shown in Fig. 5-16.

Oldstyle Roman. The *Oldstyle Roman* typefaces have a more rugged appearance, with the printing area unsymmetrical, Fig. 5-17. The fillets of the serifs are curved. Oldstyle letters look better as words; therefore, Caslon and

Readability

Fig. 5-14. Tops of ascenders are critical to readability. Cover top half of word and try to read it. Then cover bottom half and read. Note how you can determine word with ascenders.

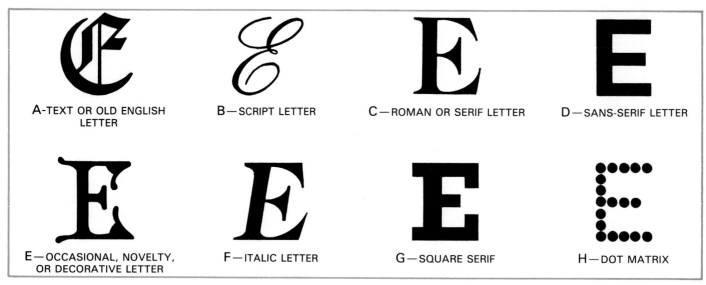

A—TEXT OR OLD ENGLISH LETTER

B—SCRIPT LETTER

C—ROMAN OR SERIF LETTER

D—SANS-SERIF LETTER

E—OCCASIONAL, NOVELTY, OR DECORATIVE LETTER

F—ITALIC LETTER

G—SQUARE SERIF

H—DOT MATRIX

Fig. 5-15. These are modern classifications of type. Study them!

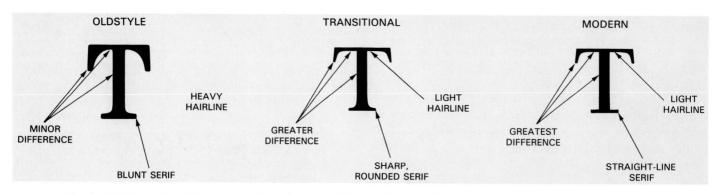

OLDSTYLE — MINOR DIFFERENCE — HEAVY HAIRLINE — BLUNT SERIF

TRANSITIONAL — GREATER DIFFERENCE — LIGHT HAIRLINE — SHARP, ROUNDED SERIF

MODERN — GREATEST DIFFERENCE — LIGHT HAIRLINE — STRAIGHT-LINE SERIF

Fig. 5-16. Note three Roman typeface designs: Oldstyle, Transitional, and Modern. Study their differences.

Garamond were used for expressing thoughts or ideas. This is the reason Oldstyle typefaces were used for book text matter.

Transitional Roman. The *Transitional Roman* face is a remodeling of the Oldstyle typeface. Greater contrast was evident between the heavy and light elements. The characters were also wider. John Baskerville improved on the Caslon typeface and it became the first typeface used to print on smooth paper, Fig. 5-18. The Oldstyle characters printed into the paper rather than on the stock.

Modern Roman. Another development was the designing of a Modern Roman typeface. The most distinguishing feature of the *Modern Roman* typeface, design by Bodoni in 1789, was the extreme contrast between the very thin, light

JADE VARIES A SHADE
It is used on jewelry or with

Fig. 5-17. Garamond is a typical example of an Oldstyle Roman face. (ATF)

THE EARLIEST PRINTER
They instructed a blacksmith
to make the frames or chases

Fig. 5-18. Baskerville typeface is an example of Transitional Roman. (ATF) elements and heavy elements. The Bodoni typeface, Fig. 5-19, has long ascenders and descenders and the serifs are not bracketed.

Sans serif

The *sans serif* classification tends to have a monotone appearance. This means the heavy and light elements have approximately the same thickness. "Sans" in French means without. Thus, the classification sans serif is for typefaces WITHOUT SERIFS, Fig. 5-20. This classification is second only to Roman in popularity today. Some of the faces being designed have slight variations between the elements.

Form follows function

THE EARLY PRINTER
They instructed the local

Fig. 5-19. This is an example of Modern Roman designed by Bodoni. Note contrast between thin and light elements. (ATF)

Franklyn Con 14

Frank Con 24

Futura 14 pt

Futura 24 pt

Fig. 5-20. Many sans serif type styles are in use today. Franklyn and Futura are typical examples. Note lack of serifs.

Square serif

Square serif typefaces are similar to sans serif but finishing off strokes are added. The shape of the finishing off strokes is square or blocked and has the same mass as the main portion of the letter face, Fig. 5-21.

Most square serif type styles have approximately the same weight with very little contrast. These typefaces have contemporary styling and are most often used as display or headlines.

Very seldom is square serif used for straight matter composition or text of a page because it is not as easy to read as type with serifs.

Text (black) letter

The *text face* or *black letter* resembles the calligraphy of German monks of Gutenberg's time, Fig. 5-22. The classification is common to specific occasions. Typical examples are: certificates, wedding and graduation announcements, religious materials, diplomas, and documents.

THE EARLY PRINTER
They instructed some of

Fig. 5-21. Stymie is an example of a square serif typeface.

Fig. 5-22. Old English is one of the typefaces common to text classification. (ATF)

A text face in all caps is very difficult to read, therefore, the use of lowercase and capital letters is recommended when setting copy. Reading difficulty of all upper case text is shown in Fig. 5-23.

Cursive (script)

Cursive or *script* typefaces are designed to simulate handwriting. Cursive type is NOT JOINED, while script faces appear to be JOINED, Fig. 5-24. This typeface classification is used primarily for special effects, announcements, invitations, and letter heads. Very seldom will it be used for setting a printed page or body copy. The contrast of characters varies with the typeface design.

Never in all caps — hard to read.

Fig. 5-23. Text typefaces are very difficult to read when set in all capital letters.

Where to look for your rain=beau

for the one man in ten who

Orders regularly entered, verbal

A

Good neighbors to the North of us

Limited Time Only

Remember the sounds of San Francisco

B

Fig. 5-24. A—Script letters are often joined. B—Cursive styles are not joined.

it's DAYLIGHT

Fig. 5-25. Decorative typefaces are intended to draw your attention. White inside open letters implies light or daylight.

Italic

Historically, *italic* is a separate classification and is a slanted version of the upright letter. Most Roman and sans serif faces have a companion italic (slanted version) of the same design, Fig. 5-26. Italic is often used to express emphasis, for titles, for foreign words, technical terms being defined, some quotations, and poetry.

Look at Fig. 5-27. Compare the typeface classifications just explained.

Dot matrix   *[handwritten: invented after computer.]*

Dot matrix is a modern term referring to characters formed by a series of small dots, Fig. 5-15H. Although not usually classified as a type style, it is a typeface commonly seen in today's business environment. Many printers for computers and typesetting equipment produce a dot matrix style. *[handwritten: Very poor quality, but accepted]*

Reverse type

Reverse type is usually white characters on a solid black or color background. This is done occasionally and can be done to stress the importance of the message or information given in the copy. A small newspaper advertisement might be reversed to make it stand out on the page and be noticed.

Typos

Typo is a nickname for a typographical error. It refers to a misspelled word. It is the job of the editor, proofreaders, and typesetter to prevent and correct typos.

Occasional, decorative, and novelty   *[handwritten: only for titles]*

Occasional, *Decorative*, and *Novelty* are all terms commonly used to denote a typeface classification that cannot be defined with specific features. The primary intent is to command attention, Fig. 5-25. The face must be carefully chosen to express the mood or relate to a specific appearance for an occasion. These faces are NOT intended to be used as a printed page or body copy. They are used when something "different" is required. Each style has an individuality and is suited for a special situation. *[handwritten: Can be flamboyant]*

Caslon Oldstyle Italic No. 471
Series Number 51
Characters in complete font
A B C D E F G H I J J K L M N
O P Q R S T T U V W X Y Z &
$ 1 2 3 4 5 6 7 8 9 0
a b c d e f g h i j k l m n o p q
r s t u v w x y z . , - ' : ; ! ?)
fi ff fl ffi ffl &
Qu QU 6 to 14 pt. only

Caslon Oldstyle No. 471
Series Number 50
Characters in complete font
A B C D E F G H I J K L M N
O P Q R S T U V W X Y Z &
$ 1 2 3 4 5 6 7 8 9 0
a b c d e f g h i j k l m n o p q
r s t u v w x y z . , - : ; ! ? ')]
fi ff fl ffi ffl &
Qu QU 6 to 18 pt. only

Fig. 5-26. An Italic face is a companion of a Roman or sans serif typeface.

This is a Roman image.

This is a Sans-serif image.

This is a Roman Italic image.

This is a Square-serif image.

This is a Text image.

This is a Script image.

This is a Decorative Image.

Fig. 5-27. These are examples of common typefaces. Memorize them!

FAMILIES, SERIES, AND FONTS

The typeface classifications discussed so far have been identified according to styles and uses. Another form of grouping is by a specific name or style of type. The term associated with a given style is called *family*, Fig. 5-28.

Family

A *typeface family* consists of the variations of one style of type. The characteristics of the design elements of the characters sets one family apart from another. Even though some typefaces are very similar, this does not make them part of the family.

As an example, Bodoni is a family and Caslon is also a family, even though their design is very similar. Refer back to Figs. 5-4 and 5-6.

Every variation of the designated typeface style becomes a part of that family. Resource knowledge relating to character widths and weights of the family are important to the personnel working with type.

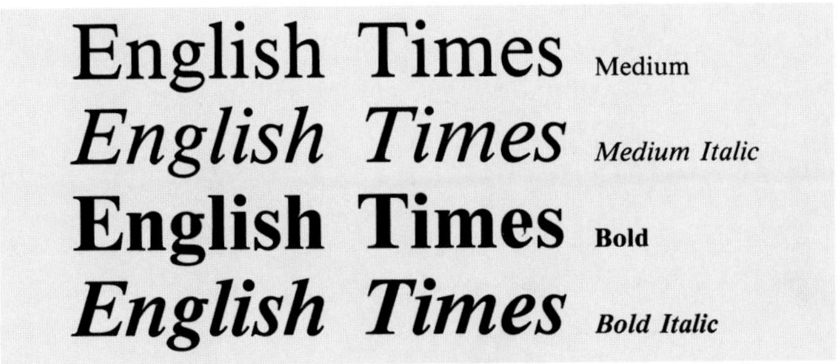

English Times Medium

English Times Medium Italic

English Times Bold

English Times Bold Italic

Fig. 5-28. This is an example of a type family. Family is same face with different weights, stresses, etc.

Widths

Some typefaces are designed to include variations in type style. The variations include the normal width as well as condensed, extra condensed, and expanded widths. Examples of variations are found in Fig. 5-29.

The *condensed typefaces* are intended to get more words in less space. They are used rather than going to a smaller typeface. *Expanded faces,* also called *extended,* fill more space without going to a larger point size.

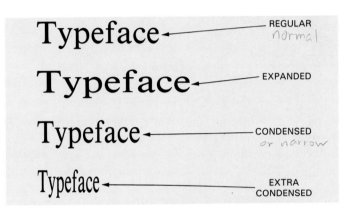

Typeface ← REGULAR normal

Typeface ← EXPANDED

Typeface ← CONDENSED or narrow

Typeface ← EXTRA CONDENSED

Fig. 5-29. Note examples of regular, expanded, condensed, and extra condensed type.

Weights Thickness

The *weight* of the letter refers to the image area. The readable image might have a lightface, medium, bold, or extra bold printing surface. With these weights, it is possible to vary the contrast for words or lines of type without changing the size. An example of varying typeface weights is found in Fig. 5-30.

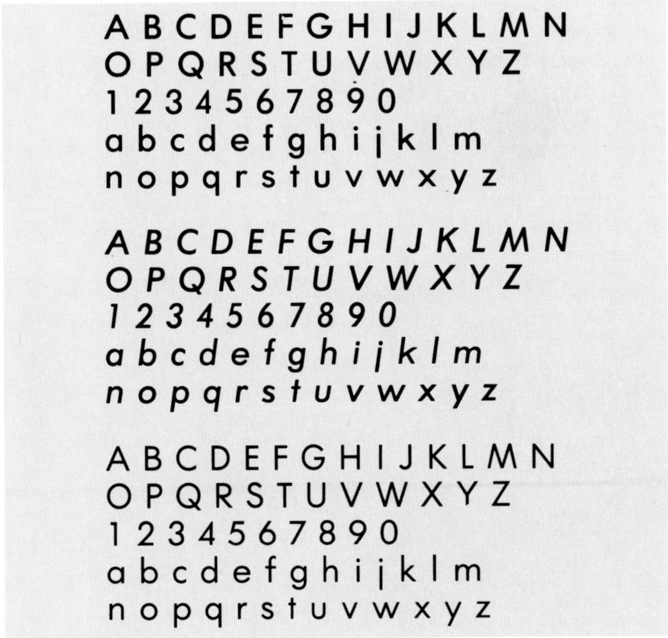

define as : light, normal, bold

A B C D E F G H I J K L M N
O P Q R S T U V W X Y Z
1 2 3 4 5 6 7 8 9 0
a b c d e f g h i j k l m
n o p q r s t u v w x y z

A B C D E F G H I J K L M N
O P Q R S T U V W X Y Z
1 2 3 4 5 6 7 8 9 0
a b c d e f g h i j k l m
n o p q r s t u v w x y z

A B C D E F G H I J K L M N
O P Q R S T U V W X Y Z
1 2 3 4 5 6 7 8 9 0
a b c d e f g h i j k l m
n o p q r s t u v w x y z

Fig. 5-30. Some type styles have a variety of letter weights or image areas.

Typeface series

A *typeface series* is a wide range of different sizes of each typeface in a family, Fig. 5-31. The common sizes used in letterpress printing are 6, 8, 10, 12, 14, 18, 24, 36, 48, 60, and 72 points. Most of the type sizes over 96 points require special equipment or are made of wood and not metal, Fig. 5-32. Not all typefaces are available in all sizes, however.

Electronic photocomposition equipment has also made it possible to have typeface sizes that are not common to the relief process. Additional sizes such as 7, 9, and 11 point can be generated with today's electronic typesetting equipment.

Type font

A *font* consists of the letters (caps and lower case), figures, and punctuation marks that are of one size and style of type. See Fig. 5-33.

The different kinds and total number of characters per font differ with the specific composing system. Hot metal composing machines did not always have the same number of characters when compared to phototypesetting machines. Fonts are designated by point sizes.

The printer's system of measurement has 12 points per pica and approximately six picas per inch. This system of measurement is used by printers and related areas of the industry.

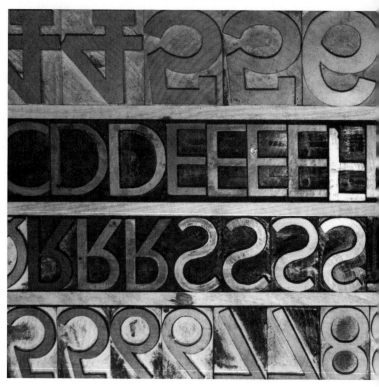

Fig. 5-32. Typefaces over 96-points are usually made of wood if to be used for letterpress printing.

8 Point Spartan Medium

10 Point Spartan Medium

12 Point Spartan Medium

18 Point Spartan Medium

24 Point Spartan Medium

36 Point Spartan Medium

48 Point Spartan Med

72 Point Spart

Fig. 5-31. A typeface series is a full range of sizes of one typeface.

24 POINT FONT

Fig. 5-33. A typical font consists of a full assortment of characters for one size typeface.

It is possible that some fonts carry ligatures. *Ligatures* are combinations such as: fi, ff, fl, ffi, and ffl. Other fonts might include *small caps* which are capital letters smaller than the normal caps of the font.

Special characters

Special characters are known as *pi characters* in phototypesetting, Fig. 5-34A. In metal typesetting, special characters are called *sorts*, Fig. 5-34B.

Metal or phototypesetting composition can be done with more than one font. With this capability, it is possible to have characters from more than one font and one of these might contain pi symbols.

TYPE AND TYPESETTING MEASUREMENTS

The units of measurement expressed earlier are unique to the graphic communications industry. The two principal measurements are the point and the pica.

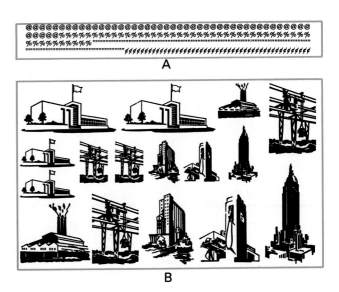

Fig. 5-34. A—Typical pi character found in phototypesetting fonts. B—Sorts font common to metal typesetting.

A *point* is equal to 0.0138 inch. A *pica* is equal to 0.166 inch. Also, TWELVE POINTS equal a pica and SIX PICAS almost equals an inch (0.996 in.).

The *body size* of type, based on height of lower case "x", is expressed in points while *line lengths* and *composition depth* is measured in picas.

Type sizes that range from four-point through 12-point are usually referred to as *text* or *body type*. Sizes above 12-point are referred to as *display type* sizes. Various sizes are shown in Fig. 5-35.

The size of type is difficult to distinguish when in print because not all styles of type have the same body dimensions. One type style might appear larger or smaller, yet both might be the same point typefaces. This is illustrated in Fig. 5-36. Note the difference.

The em

The square of any size of type is called an *em*. For example, the measurement of a 12-point type would measure 12 points wide and 12 points high. Metal type used the term *em quad* which meant that a square of the type size used was a blank (nonprinting) body. The em quad was often used as the blank for the indention of a paragraph.

Every font also has spaces (part of an em quad) used between words. An *en quad* is half of an em quad. Refer to Fig. 5-37.

This is 5 point type
This is 6 point type
This is 7 point type
This is 8 point type
This is 9 point type
This is 9.5 point type
This is 10 point type
This is 11 point type
This is 12 point type
This is 14 point type
This is 18 point type
This is 24 point type
This is 30 point
Thirty-six point
48 point
54 point
60 point
72 point

Fig. 5-35. This is an example of various common type sizes. Read through them several times while noting their size.

THE EARLY PRINTER
They instructed the local

THE EARLY PRINTERS
THEY instructed some local

Fig. 5-36. Not all typeface styles have same image size yet they may be same point size.

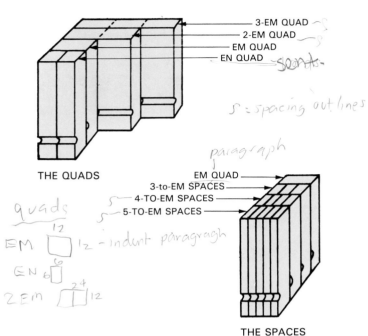

THE QUADS

- 3-EM QUAD
- 2-EM QUAD
- EM QUAD
- EN QUAD

EM QUAD
- 3-to-EM SPACES
- 4-TO-EM SPACES
- 5-TO-EM SPACES

THE SPACES

Fig. 5-37. Common spaces found in a font of type range from em quad to a thin space.

The unit

The *unit* is the splitting of the em into widths. The units per em will vary with the phototypesetting machine. The most common ones are the 18-unit count and 54-unit count, Fig. 5-38. The typefaces used in phototypesetting are given assigned unit widths although a very small amount of space is allowed on each side. When the characters are composed, they will not touch.

Set size

As you learned, *point size* refers to the HEIGHT of the type. *Set size,* or just *set,* refers to the WIDTH of the characters. Electronic composition has made width changes of words and characters easy.

It is possible to electronically expand or condense characters on the face of the monitor or visual display terminal, Fig. 5-39. The height is not changed but it is possible to expand or condense the typeface. The width of the character is changed without changing the original spacing.

For example, 12-point type with a 12-set would be normal. If 12-point is programmed 8-set, the type would be condensed. If 12-point is programmed for a 14-set, the type would be expanded. This can be done very quickly and efficiently with the "press of a button" on modern computerized typesetting equipment.

Figs. 5-40 and 5-41 give examples of type with altered set sizes. Study their differences.

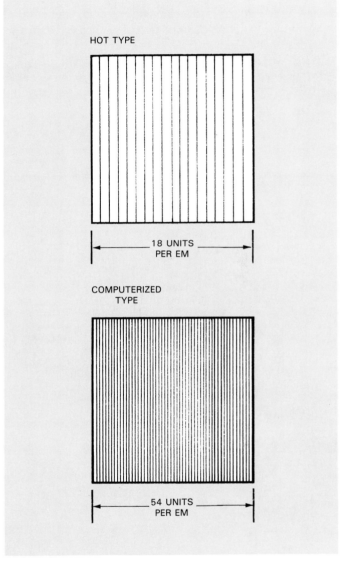

HOT TYPE

18 UNITS
PER EM

COMPUTERIZED
TYPE

54 UNITS
PER EM

Fig. 5-38. The em is divided into eighteen units with hot type and frequently 54 units with computerized typesetting.

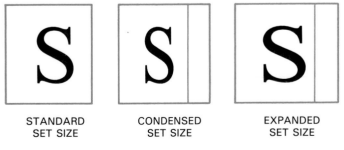

STANDARD
SET SIZE

CONDENSED
SET SIZE

EXPANDED
SET SIZE

Fig. 5-39. Set size is modern term that refers to width of characters. Computerized typesetting allows letters to be condensed or expanded with a "press of a button."

A letter may also be assigned nine units or 9-set with one kind of typeface. The same letter may be ten units or 10-set with another style of type.

Letterspacing and word spacing

Letterspacing refers to a change of space between letters, Fig. 5-42. *Wordspacing* means that the space varies between words, Fig. 5-43. When the designer has the capability of using phototypesetting, changing the letterspace is a distinct advantage. Increasing or decreasing the space between letters and words can increase the legibility of type. It is also possible to increase or decrease the amount of copy in allocated space for copyfitting by altering the letterspacing or the wordspacing.

If other than normal letterspacing is used, it is expressed as *loose-set* (large spacing) or *tight-set* (small spacing). Spacing is expressed in units but each machine has varying capabilities. Full units and half units are very common. *Plus units* (loose set) and *minus units* (tight set) are needed to give the designer freedom to change the spacing that best fits the style.

Character compensation is another term that refers to the REDUCTION of space between characters. It is used to tight-set copy.

Justifying type

Justifying refers to changing the space to make all of the lines of copy equal in width. Justification is done automatically with modern typesetting equipment.

Widow

A *widow* is a very short line, a word, or part of a word at the end of a paragraph. The rest of the line for type is empty. The line will usually be lengthened or the previous

THIS IS 12 POINT WITH 12 SET.

THIS IS 12 POINT WITH 8 SET.

THIS IS 12 POINT WITH 14 SET.

Fig. 5-40. Note difference when 12-point type has different set size.

A typesetter can generate expanded or condensed type by using a different set size. A set size GREATER than the point size results in expanded type. A set size LESS than the point size results in condensed type.

CHARACTER WIDTH STANDARD

A typesetter can generate expanded or condensed type by using a different set size. A set size GREATER than the point size results in expanded type. A set size LESS than the point size results in condensed type.

CHARACTER WIDTH CONDENSED

A typesetter can generate expanded or condensed type by using a different set size. A set size GREATER than the point size value results in expanded type. A set size LESS than the point size results in condensed type.

CHARACTER WIDTH EXPANDED

Fig. 5-41. These are examples of computer typeset body copy that has been condensed and expanded by changing set size.

A. Letterspace changes distance between characters.
B. Letterspace changes distance between characters.
C. Letterspace changes distance between characters.

Fig. 5-42. Letterspacing, as you can see, alters amount of space between each character or letter. A—Loose letterspace. B—Normal letterspace. C—Tight letterspace.

A. Wordspace changes distance or space between words.
B. Wordspace changes distance or space between words.
C. Wordspace changes distance or space between words.

Fig. 5-43. Wordspacing changes space between complete words. A—Tight wordspace. B—Normal wordspace. C—Loose wordspace.

line will be shortened to eliminate the widow. Words must usually be added or deleted by the editor to remove the widow. ←(This is a widow!)

Kerning

Kerning is a typesetting term that refers to the closing up of space between certain characters in the alphabet. It is generally done to improve the appearance and readability of the word. Kerning is normally done on letters that are top or bottom heavy.

For example, the letter "T" is top heavy and the space between the next letter can be too wide. Kerning could be done to make the next letter closer to the "T" for better appearance. This is shown in Fig. 5-44.

Fig. 5-45 illustrates many of the characters that could require kerning.

LEGIBILITY FACTORS

Legibility, sometimes termed *readability,* is a measurement of how difficult or easy it is to read printed matter. It can be a very critical aspect when selecting a typeface.

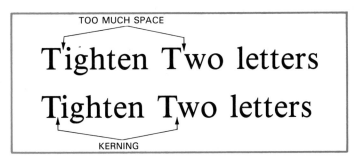

Fig. 5-44. Kerning is similar to letterspacing but only changes space between specific letters to improve appearance and readability.

To Wa Va PA y.
To Wa Va PA y.
v. p, ay VA AT
v. p, ay VA AT
AW LT Yo Fr Fo
AW LT Yo Fr Fo
ya xe te we ro
ya xe te we ro

Fig. 5-45. These are typical examples of letter combinations that require kerning. (Compugraphic)

Remember! The major consideration when selecting a typeface is PURPOSE. If content is the main purpose, legibility of the printed page should be the aim in selecting a typeface. If appearance is the main purpose, as when designing an advertisement, then aesthetic characteristics of the type can be equally important.

The type you are now reading is what a printer calls *straight matter.* Examples are: books, magazines, newspapers, and pamphlets.

Legibility of the straight matter is the result of a combination of TYPE, PAPER, and INK. When properly done, the printed matter is less tiring to the eyes. Many printed pieces will have thousands of readers of varying ages and physical conditions. This makes legibility of straight matter a priority!

Physical factors that contribute to legibility in the printed page are: visibility, letter forms, size, line width, leading, and definition.

Visibility

Visibility results from the contrast of the typeface against the light reflected by the paper. This is due to the brightness of the paper, the smoothness of the paper, and the opacity of the paper.

The term whiteness is NOT used because *brightness* is a property of both white and colored papers. The brightness of paper varies greatly. The smoother the paper, the more light it reflects, therefore, paper smoothness also affects visibility of the images.

An *opaque paper* does NOT allow print from the opposite side to show through the paper. Look at Fig. 5-46.

The term ink darkness is used because both black and colored inks have degrees of darkness. *Ink darkness* depends on the covering power of the ink. A complete coverage hides the surface of the paper.

The thicker the elements of the letters, the more ink that will be deposited on the paper for contrast. As type size decreases, this factor gains in importance.

Letter forms

Most straight matter is made up of 99 percent lower case letters. The range of acceptable variation is very narrow. Readers are accustomed to the basic letter forms. The Roman letter form was the "tried and true" classification. Today, the sans serif classification has become a familiar form. Capital letters are used sparingly because they do not form distinctive word shapes.

The more unlike or dissimilar the letters, the more certain their identity. For example, c, e, and o should be as different as possible. Since numerals are read as separate digits, they must also be dissimilar.

Letter forms that merge readily into words and phrases contribute to legibility. This means that the letter elements must relate to each other. The thick elements of a Roman letter give identity while the thin elements tie them together.

The distribution of white space in and between letters should be uniform to help shape the letters into words. Whenever letters have serifs, the intent is to aid the eye to

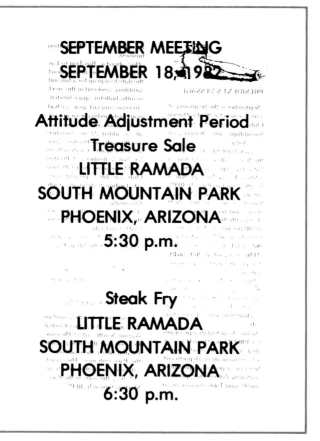

Fig. 5-46. Showthrough will reduce the brightness of the paper. Note how paper is not opaque and printed matter on back is showing through paper.

6 point — 6-248　　　　　　　1 point leaded

This Linotype method of copy-fitting is based on character count. System s that rely upon average word count to a given area seldom are accurate. Even character count calculations, although much more accurate than w ord count methods, should be recognized as approximate, or average, be cause of the influence of inevitable variables in copy. Obviously the sty le of writing has a bearing upon any copy-fitting problem. Scientific wo rks may contrast markedly with newspaper writing; the ratio of caps to lower-case bears upon statistics; short measures and run-arounds influen ce results. How is one to assess and evaluate a type face in terms of its es thetic design? Why do the pace-makers in the art of printing rave over a specific face of type? What do they see in it? Why is it so superlatively *pleasant to their eyes? Good design is always practical design. And what they see in a good type design is, partly, its excellent practical fitness to perform its work. It has a "heft" and balance in all of its parts just right*

8 point — 8-248　　　　　　　1 point leaded

This Linotype method of copy-fitting is based on character co unt. Systems that rely upon average word count to a given ar ea seldom are accurate. Even character count calculations, alth ough much more accurate than word count methods, should b e recognized as approximate, or average, because of the influe nce of inevitable variables in copy. Obviously the style of wri ting has a bearing upon any copy-fitting problem. Scientific w orks may contrast markedly with newspaper writing; the ratio of caps to lower-case bears upon statistics; short measures and run-arounds influence results. How is one to assess and evalu ate a type face in terms of its esthetic design? Why do the pa *ce-makers in the art of printing rave over a specific face of typ e? What do they see in it? Why is it so superlatively pleasant to their eyes? Good design is always practical design. And wh*

10 point — 10-248　　　　　　　1 point leaded

This Linotype method of copy-fitting is based on chara cter count. Systems that rely upon average word count to a given area seldom are accurate. Even character cou nt calculations, although much more accurate than wo rd count methods, should be recognized as approximat e, or average, because of the influence of inevitable var iables in copy. Obviously the style of writing has a be aring upon any copy-fitting problem. Scientific works may contrast markedly with newspaper writing; the ra tio of caps to lower-case bears upon statistics; short me asures and run-arounds influence results. How is one to *assess and evaluate a type face in terms of its esthetic d esign? Why do the pace-makers in the art of printing r ave over a specific face of type? What do they see in it?*

Fig. 5-47. Small type sizes below ten point are very difficult to read for the average person.

mark the terminals or finishing marks of the letter elements. Serifs also make the letters more different for easy reading.

Size

The ability to read copy, as it relates to type sizes, increases dramatically up to ten-point type. This increase flattens out with larger type sizes. The ten-point type is a norm for comfortable reading by young and middle age adults. A variety of type sizes are shown in Fig. 5-47.

The x-height of the font also contributes to legibility. A low x-height alignment would increase the size of the letters but decrease the size of the ascenders and descenders.

Line width, eye span

Line width, also called *line length,* is the distance from the right and left sides of a line or body of copy. It is usually measured in picas.

Eye span is the width people can see with one fixation (sweep or adjustment) of the eye muscles. Generally, it is agreed that the normal eye span is about an alphabet and a half with body copy. This will vary with typeface classification and size, however.

When the width of the line corresponds to the eye span of the reader, the physical task of reading is made easier. Longer lengths would require extra physical effort when reading: the more eye fixations per line, the more effort re-

quired. Horizontal travel of the eye is considered more tiring than moving from one line to the next.

Line spacing (leading)

Line spacing, also called *leading,* determines the distance separating each line of copy. It is measured in points from one line to the next. See Fig. 5-48.

Set solid means that line spacing is equal to the size of the type. For example, if the typeface is 12-point and there is no extra line spacing, it is written 12/12 and would be set solid. The typeface point size is normally written BEFORE the line spacing. *12 pt. type has 14 pt leading*

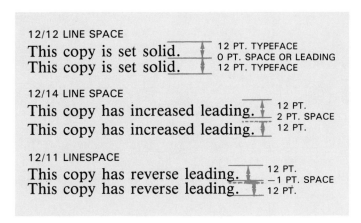

Fig. 5-48. Linespacing or leading controls how much space separates one line of copy from another.

Letter Tracking Very Tight
Letter Tracking Tight
Letter Tracking Normal
Letter Tracking Loose
Letter Tracking Very Loose

Fig. 5-49. Letter tracking allows letter spacing and word spacing to be varied simultaneously.

Letter Tracking Normal with
80% Horizontal Scaling

Letter Tracking Normal with
100% Horizontal Scaling

Letter Tracking Normal with
120% Horizontal Scaling

Fig. 5-50. Letter width can be increased or decreased with horizontal scaling.

When a column of type is set using 10-point and the customer wants more space between the lines, someone has to determine the amount of line space. The printer may, for instance, inform the customers that 10-point type will be used with 12 points of leading. The specifications will be written as 10/12 which means two points are to be added between the lines. Refer to Fig. 5-48. This terminology originated with metal typesetting and continues to be used today with computerized typesetting processes.

Many of today's typesetting machines have the capability of reducing spacing below the type size. When reducing the interline spacing, it is called *reverse leading, minus leading,* or *back leading.* The specification might be written as 10/9. This example means the space between lines is to be reduced by one point.

Proper leading between lines aids the eye to readily separate one line from another. The white space gives the eye better access to the tops of the lowercase letters. As stated earlier, the top halves of letters are the most unlike portions and they contribute most to word identity.

Leading also unites a line horizontally. Close word spacing will help to achieve unity in the line. Visibility is increased when extra leading is used on paper with low brightness. Leading lightens the tone of the page and the resulting increased visibility tends to make the type seem larger.

It is also possible to copyfit into a designated area by changing leading. By increasing leading, the copy will take up more space or area. Decreasing leading does just the opposite.

Tracking

Tracking is a feature of computer programs that allows you to control the letter and word spacing together. As discussed above, these two spacing measurements work in conjunction with one another. The common choices for tracking are very tight, tight, normal, loose, and very loose. See Fig. 5-49.

Horizontal scaling of letters is an option offered in some computer packages. This is *not* a form of letter spacing. The actual widths of the characters are changed; the proportion of character to space is not. See Fig. 5-50.

Definition

Definition refers to the sharpness or distinction of the printed images. Sharply defined letter forms are essential for easier reading. Top quality pressmanship contributes to sharp images on the page.

The relationship between the typeface and paper is very important. A small type size requires a smoother paper for good definition.

Special consideration must be given when placing typed images on a screen background because poor definition results, Fig. 5-51. The same principle applies when the background for type is a halftone image—clouds or foliage for example.

Legibility is very much like a "cake." It is the result of combining the right ingredients. The "ingredients" are all of the topics just discussed. Very often, selection of the ingredients is based on what is available. Many variables must be considered and then adjustments must be made to produce a successful product.

TYPEFACES FOR DISPLAY

Display type is intended to draw attention and to help convey the message. Because of the importance of the thought and to direct attention to it, display lines are larger in size. Generally, the smallest typeface size used in display is 14-point.

The position of the display line also gives it prominence. The words of that line supply the rhetoric (language and theme) of the printed page. Therefore, it is sometimes necessary to keep a complete thought in one line. This is shown in Fig. 5-52.

Different weights of type can be used for emphasis by contrast. Different sizes show the relationship between princi-

Fig. 5-51. *Selecting proper typeface for placement on a screen pattern is very important to legibility.*

Groups ponder suit over animal sales

By Tonia Twichell
Staff writer

Animal-protection groups are considering legal action if the Maricopa County Attorney's Office enforces its decision that the

clients several options in litigation and in changing the law.

"We do feel the policy allowing the ban to be adopted in October still is sound legally and otherwise," he said.

Fig. 5-52. *Headlines of a newspaper are an example of display type. Note how major thought, "groups ponder suit," is on first line. Secondary thought is on second line. This is commonly done in newspapers.*

ple and subordinate thoughts. Selection becomes very important as the typeface must fit the intended use.

KNOW THESE TERMS

Typeface, Typographer, Typography, Body height, Ascender, Descender, Base line, Waist line, Counter, Point, Hairline, Stem, Stroke, Stress, Serif, Set-width, Black letter, Old English, Roman letter, Sans serif, Square serif, Cursive, Decorative, Italic, Family, Condensed, Expanded, Weight, Series, Font, pi, Point, Pica, em, Unit, Letter spacing, Justification, Word spacing, Character compensation, Set size, Kerning, Legibility, Readability, Straight matter, Visibility, Line width, Leading, Definition, Display type, Tracking.

REVIEW QUESTIONS—CHAPTER 5

1. _____ is the art of expressing ideas in type form.
2. Define the term "body height."
3. An ascender extends _____ and a descender _____ the x-height letters.
4. What is the base line?
5. Explain the six basic parts of a letter or character.
6. The _____ _____ was used as the foundation for development of Old English.
7. Who was credited with designing and cutting the Roman letter?
8. Summarize four examples of modern typefaces.
9. Rough papers commonly required the four _____ typefaces while smooth papers required a transitional typeface, like _____.
10. What is the difference between serif and sans serif?
11. List and explain the eight basic typeface classifications.
12. A typeface _____ consists of the variation of one style of type.
13. A _____ consists of the letters, figures, and punctuation marks that are of one size and style.
14. What does 12/10 mean as concerned with set size?
15. This refers to the change of distance between words in a line of copy.
    a. Letter spacing.
    b. Justify.
    c. Kerning.
    d. Word spacing.
16. _____ refers to changing the distance between some letters of a word to improve appearance.
17. In your own words, how can a typographer increase legibility?
18. _____ refers to the sharpness or distinction of the printed image.
19. _____ _____ is intended to draw attention and to help convey the message; it is very large type.
20. This means that the line spacing dimension is equal to the size of the type.
    a. Reverse leading.
    b. Back leading.
    c. Set solid.
    d. Set same.

SUGGESTED ACTIVITIES

1. Select a typeface catalog and identify three Roman, three sans serif, and three occasional typefaces.
2. Select a Roman face for each of the three patterns: Oldstyle, Transitional, and Modern.
3. Evaluate the legibility of a gradeschool textbook and a college text.

Chapter 6

DESIGN

After studying this chapter, you will be able to:
- Summarize the role of the graphic designer.
- Define the term "graphic design."
- List and explain the elements of design.
- Utilize the principles of design.
- Design a graphic product to meet a specific need.

In graphic communications, *design* refers to the use of proper methods to produce both an artistic and a functional product. This requires the skillful use of several design elements and principles.

This chapter will summarize these design elements and principles. This should make you more capable of contributing to and evaluating the design of a product when employed in a graphic communications facility.

THE GRAPHIC DESIGNER

The role of the graphic designer varies greatly within the industry. This is due to the overlapping duties being performed in modern graphic communications facilities, Fig. 6-1.

Today's graphic designer might be an artist and prepare the artwork necessary for a portion of a product. This could include the freehand sketches, technical art, lettering, and calligraphy. Too often, the graphic designer has very little knowledge of the graphic reproduction processes. Yet, in some cases, it is possible for the graphic designer to also be responsible for the paste-up of the camera-ready copy. This illustrates that layout design personnel are very difficult to clearly define.

A pure *designer* would create the art images needed for the layout person. Many companies do not have the luxury of hiring people for specific skills. The designer, in many companies, takes the ideas and converts them into layouts of various stages.

Once the layout design is approved by the client, the elements are gathered and pasted up by the same person that created the design. The designer and layout person can be the same person, Fig. 6-2.

The designer initially must visually express an idea. The idea then becomes the layout and is developed into the final product.

Fig. 6-1. Graphic artist must properly use elements and principles of design to produce a pleasing product. (Screaming Color-Chapter One)

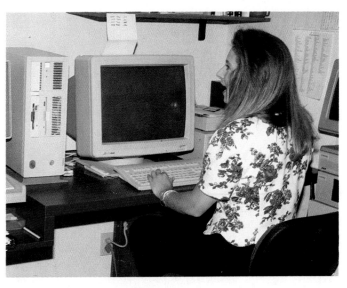

Fig. 6-2. The computer is a valuable tool for the designer or layout person.

Planning and organizing are essential to have an efficient operation. The small printing facility, from the financial standpoint, often cannot afford to employ a person to perform the design task. Therefore, designing is left to the plant personnel who may have little design knowledge. Yet, they are required to design and complete layouts in an acceptable manner, Fig. 6-3.

A definite need exists to apply basic design fundamentals. Design is an accumulation of many factors which help solve the problem of producing an image that is artistic, yet practical.

ELEMENTS OF DESIGN

The basis for most graphic design is typography. This involves the selection and arrangement of visual images (words and illustrations) to make a pleasing presentation. These visual images have impact upon the viewer; therefore, it is essential to develop a good layout of visual materials. To succeed as a graphic designer, you must apply the fundamentals of design.

The basic *design elements* are: lines, shapes, mass, texture, and color.

Lines

The first design element, *lines,* can take many different forms. Sometimes, the lines are loose and free or they can be straight and sharp, Fig. 6-4. Repetition of lines also creates patterns and this adds an emotional impact to the visual image. Lines can be used to give the printed image a "personality."

Lines can also be used as forms of a "universal language" in communication. In this instance, the lines are used to create a message. Arrows and other symbols are an example of this visual form, Fig. 6-5.

Fig. 6-4. Lines can be used to denote a specific meaning. Top would imply a free spirit. Bottom would imply a more strict or disciplined theme.

Fig. 6-3. Graphic artist is selecting type from catalog as she designs printed product.

Fig. 6-5. Symbols can be used as a form of universal language. What do these symbols mean to you?

Lines are often used to enhance or change the value of type styles. As shown earlier, lines can be very harsh or they might be very delicate. They play a very important role in planning a layout for effective communication.

Shape

Shape is a design element or form concerned with specific areas of space. Many times, shape is defined by a line. The three basic shapes are the square, circle, and triangle, Fig. 6-6.

A psychological meaning has been associated with each of these shapes. As shown in Fig. 6-7, these include:

1. The attitude related to the *triangle* is one of CONFLICTS or action.
2. The *circle* gives a feeling of PROTECTION or infinity.
3. The *square* reflects an attitude of HONESTY or equality.

Mass

Mass adds a sense of volume to shapes that are commonly found in visual presentations. The mass or solid, plus the shape, tend to give relationship with other elements, Fig. 6-8.

Different shapes of varying intensities or "weights," can be used to emphasize or de-emphasize type styles or implica-

Fig. 6-6. The square, circle, and triangle are basic shapes. They can be used to produce a desired effect.

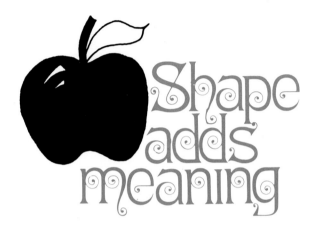

Fig. 6-8. Shape can be used to add meaning to a graphic image.

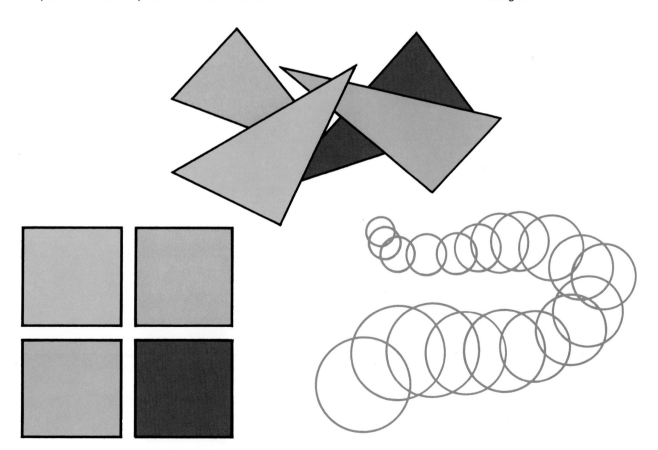

Fig. 6-7. Note psychological implications from each of these shapes. One shows organization, another motion, and the other aggression. Can you find each?

tions, Fig. 6-9. Physical forms are made by combining the three basic shapes, Fig. 6-10.

Texture

When we try to measure *texture,* the first reaction is to touch the surface. In graphic communications, this element is usually visual and no reaction would be received through the sense of touch. See Fig. 6-11.

Texture is considered when the visual images reflect the meaning of lines, as shown in Fig. 6-12, or when mass forms images that give shape and reflect a special technique. Refer to Fig. 6-13.

Texture in typography will vary and will depend upon the structure and weight of the individual letters, the amount of space between lines, and the amount of mass in a certain space.

Actual texture can be produced by embossing. A shape or irregular surface is pressed into the substrate.

Fig. 6-11. Note how lines have been used to give a surface variation and a feeling of texture.

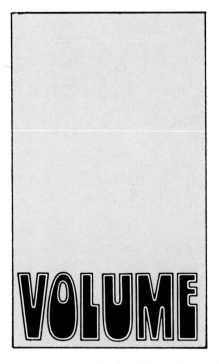

Fig. 6-9. Emphasis can be obtained by varying weight of type or other images.

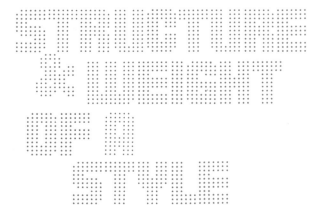

Fig. 6-12. Mass and space can also produce a texture.

Fig. 6-10. Combining shapes can be used to create a physical form.

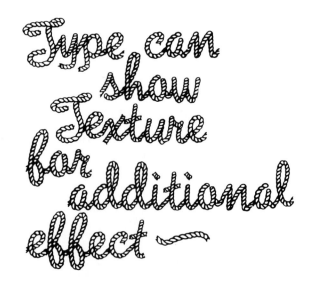

Fig. 6-13. Here lines have been added to type to produce an unusual effect resembling rope.

Color

Color is an important element to be considered when planning or designing a printed product. It can draw attention and have a strong emotional and psychological impact on the reader. Color also has traditional and symbolic meanings. It is essential that you have a basic understanding of this element.

Color moods. *Yellow, orange,* and *red* are considered to be "warm" colors and also often denote aggression, excitement, and danger. Red is considered the most active of these three. *Blue, green,* and *violet* are considered to be "cool" colors and are associated with nature and passiveness. Experiments with animals exposed to different colors have shown that there are different emotional reactions to different colors.

Color should be used to add interest and to reduce boredom. A small amount of color can eliminate the possibility of having a monotonous page.

Color wheel. The *color wheel* is a tool that can help to understand the basics of color. The color wheel provides a means of identifying color in a consistent manner.

Primary and secondary colors. The color wheel is based on three primary colors from which all other colors can be made. The *three primary colors* are: red, yellow, and blue. Mixing any two of these colors will produce a secondary color. The *secondary colors* are: green, orange, and violet. Fig. 6-14 gives a simple color wheel.

Complementary colors. *Complementary colors* are those colors that are across from each other on the color wheel. Red and green, orange and blue, yellow and violet are complementary colors, Fig. 6-15.

Different values (shades and tints) of a color may be obtained by adding white or black to a color. Also, a color takes on a different intensity when its complement is added. For example, when green is mixed with red, it will produce a *brown*. Amazing effects may be obtained not only through mixing colors, but by arranging colors in a layout so they have a direct effect on each other.

Note! Color theory is discussed in detail in Chapter 15. Refer to this chapter if needed for more information.

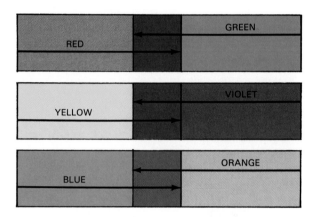

Fig. 6-15. *Complementary colors are those that are across from each other on color wheel.*

PRINCIPLES OF DESIGN

When designing a printed product, many ideas are generated. To make the images have a pleasing relationship, design principles must be applied to sort out or select the right ideas.

The basic *design principles* include: balance, contrast, unity, rhythm, and proportion.

Balance

Balance has one of the most important psychological and physical influences on human perception. Consciously and unconsciously, people have a basic need for balance.

Often, this principle is illustrated by equal balance on a scale, as illustrated in Fig. 6-16A and B. Visually, a judg-

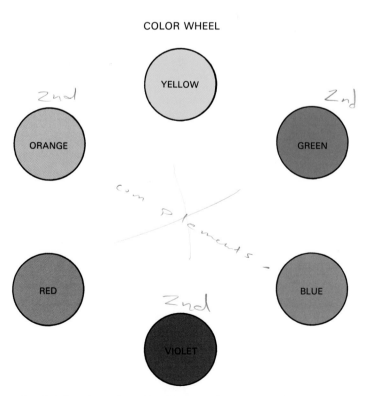

Fig. 6-14. *The color wheel is based on three primary colors from which all other colors can be made.*

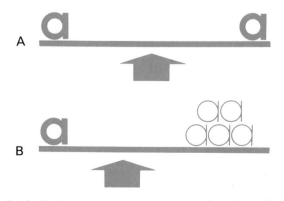

Fig. 6-16. *Balance is important to printed product. A—Even balance implies a formal presentation. B—Uneven balance is more informal or casual.*

ment can be made by the value of each image. The type of balance in A is symmetrical and it is called FORMAL. The second type in B is asymmetrical and is called INFORMAL.

Formal balance is achieved when all of the elements on a page are of equal weight and are placed symmetrically on the page.

Informal balance may be achieved by changing the value, size, and location of unequal elements on a page. The use of various colors and intensities of a single color can also be factors used in achieving balance.

As an example, two squares of differing values (such as pink and dark red), but of equal size, will appear to be unequal in size when placed side by side.

It is of great importance to consider the layout as a whole when balancing the elements. Look at Fig. 6-17.

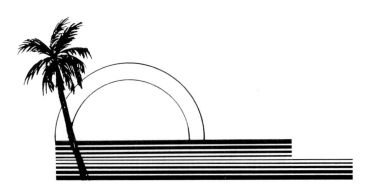

Fig. 6-17. Total layout should have balance in most instances. An unbalanced layout can be used however to attract attention or imply leisure, for example.

Contrast

The variations of elements in the printed product are the result of *contrast*. Meaning is also given to the design when using contrast. Thick lines might have little meaning by themselves. Adding thin lines, however, could enhance the design and eliminate monotony. This is illustrated in Fig. 6-18.

Typestyles can be contrasted with one another to add legibility and design variation. Some useful contrasts are: round and straight, ornate and plain, and broad and nar-

row. An example of contrast, a tall tree looks much taller if it is standing on a flat plane, as in Fig. 6-19.

The relationship between the unprinted area, and the printed area, can also be enhanced through the use of contrast, Fig. 6-20.

Care must be taken when combining contrasting elements so that the uniform effect of the total design remains unaffected. A page of many contrasting elements might lead to confusion, Fig. 6-21.

Control or maintain balance so that one, primary element dominates the layout. This principle can be used to keep the attention of the reader and keep the reader's interest moving from one element to another.

Unity

Unity is the proper balance of all elements so that a pleasing whole results and the image is viewed as one piece. Every element must create a harmonious image. The placement of these images becomes very important. The design can move and manipulate to create an interesting and easy to

Fig. 6-19. Height of image can be made to look taller if placed on flat plane. Mass on each side of tree would make tree seem shorter.

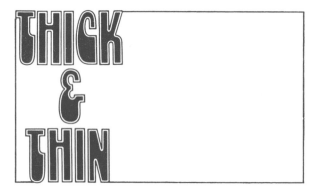

Fig. 6-18. A variation of mass will add contrast to eliminate monotony and to attract attention to section of page. Eye is pulled to area with most mass first.

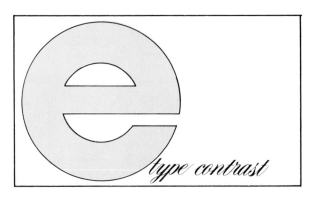

Fig. 6-20. White space is just as important as printed areas. White space around printed area will attract attention to printed matter.

Fig. 6-21. Too much of a change or excess contrast may be undesirable. These images might look more appropriate if heavy arrows were matched with heavy type and light lines were matched with light type.

comprehend combination of elements. Choosing type styles is also important to unity, Fig. 6-22.

To achieve a unified design, the layout must be constantly viewed as a whole and not as separate elements. This principle is also called *harmony,* Fig. 6-23.

Rhythm

The movement of the eye is often determined by the shapes used in the image. The square reflects the horizontal and vertical. The triangle reflects the diagonal, and the circle reflects the curve.

When the elements have been properly used to create movement and direction, the layout has *rhythm,* Fig. 6-24. Rhythm can also be achieved through the use of pattern and repetition. Patterns can be used in contrast with an element to create an effective design, Fig. 6-25.

Fig. 6-23. All of the elements should be organized into a pleasing whole. Stand back from the image and look at it. This will let you see the image as a whole.

Fig. 6-22. You must select the type style that matches the subject of the print job. Small dots forming type would imply stars in sky.

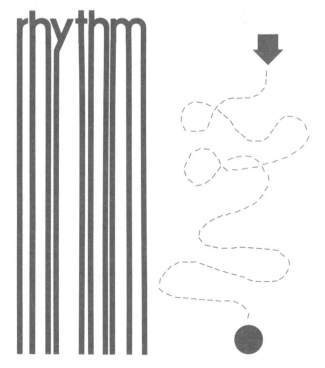

Fig. 6-24. Elements can be added to imply motion or movement. If subject is appropriate, this can be a useful device.

93

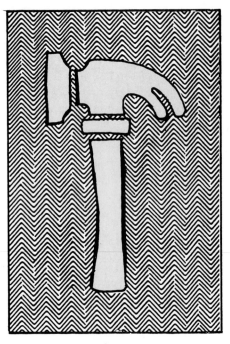

Fig. 6-25. *Image can be made to have rhythm by keeping lines and shapes related.*

Proportion

Proportion refers to the relationship between elements on a page. Proportion helps to achieve balance and unity in a layout. All elements should be used in pleasing proportion to each other. Refer to Fig. 6-26.

When using type styles, it is important that they be in proportion to the other elements on the page, Fig. 6-27. Pro-

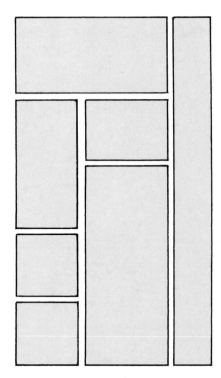

Fig. 6-26. *Size of all images should be in proportion so that the result has unity.*

Fig. 6-27. *The size of type is critical. Most important thoughts would be largest. Other images must be comparable to type size.*

portion is a means of developing an aesthetically pleasing relationship between each of the elements used in the layout.

A basic knowledge of the design elements and principles can be of great assistance to customers and printers. This knowledge will give you a greater appreciation of personal preferences and be able to realistically reflect change when needed.

KNOW THESE TERMS

Design, Graphic Designer, Design elements, Line, Shape, Mass, Texture, Color, Color moods, Color wheel, Primary color, Secondary color, Complementary color, Design principle, Balance, Formal balance, Informal balance, Contrast, Unity, Rhythm, Proportion.

REVIEW QUESTIONS—CHAPTER 6

1. In graphic communications, design refers to the use of proper methods to produce both an _____ and a _____ product.
2. In your own words, what is the role of the graphic designer?
3. The following is NOT an element of design:
   a. Shape.
   b. Texture.
   c. Mass.
   d. Beauty.
4. Explain the attitudes attributed to the three basic shapes.
5. _____ or _____ can be used to emphasize or de-emphasize type styles.
6. Texture can be produced by lines that form images or by embossing. True or false?
7. Explain color moods.
8. The _____ is a tool that can help you understand the basics of color.
9. What are complementary colors?
10. In your own words, explain the principles of design: balance, contrast, unity, rhythm, and proportion.

SUGGESTED ACTIVITIES

1. Evaluate the design of five advertisements in a newspaper.
2. Design a good and a bad advertisement.
3. Compare different kinds of printed matter from a design viewpoint. Explain why different principles might have been used in each.

Chapter 7

COPYFITTING, SPECIFICATIONS

After studying this chapter, you will be able to:
* Identify the measurement units common to the graphic communications industry.
* Copyfit using both extremely accurate and rough procedures.
* Explain the various systems used in copyfitting.
* Describe the electronic systems used by industry for copyfitting.
* Define basic terms relating to electronic or computerized copyfitting.
* Summarize the advantages of desktop publishing or pagination systems.

Copyfitting, as the name implies, is the fitting of copy or text into a specific amount of space. This can be done by altering type size, leading, line length, letter spacing, etc. Copyfitting can also involve estimating the amount of space needed for a certain amount of manuscript. As you will learn, computerized typesetting equipment is changing copyfitting techniques, Fig. 7-1.

Fig. 7-1. Modern computerized typesetting equipment is changing how text is copyfit. Computers can now change type size, leading, letterspacing, wordspacing, line length, and other parameters at the ''press of a button.''

This chapter will summarize the many techniques used to copyfit in graphic communications. Also, the last section of the chapter will briefly explain how specifications are important to producing a printed image.

REVIEW OF MEASUREMENT

The system of measurement used in graphic communications is unique to the industry. As discussed in Chapter 4, the measurement system common to all composing activities is called the *point system.* Its basic unit is the point.

In America, the point is .01383 in. or approximately 1/72 of an inch. The calculations in points are used to measure or indicate type sizes, spacing materials, and type form dimensions.

The inch is normally used to designate paper sizes, page size, and dimensions of pictures. Although metric sizes are sometimes used to designate the size of paper and film, metrics has not progressed to the stage expected. Metric measurement, however, will be discussed in this chapter.

It is imperative that all personnel in graphic communications fully understand the point system. For this reason, a brief review will be given.

POINTS AND PICAS

The point is the smallest unit of measurement; pica is the largest. The simplest presentation of the point/pica system is:
1. 12 points = one pica.
2. Six picas = approximately one inch (.996).
3. Six picas are .004 less than an inch.
4. 72 picas = approximately 12 inches (three points shorter than one foot).

For more information on points and picas, refer to the text index. This topic is discussed in other chapters.

Type forms

Fine length measurements of copy are given in picas and points. It is very possible that just a pica measure is needed. Commonly, the width and height of a type form or body of copy would be stated as 20 x 24 picas for example. The

FIRST figure is the *width* and the SECOND is the *height,* sometimes called *length.* The sizes of margins and the distance between columns can also be stated in picas.

Composition area measurements are also given as ems. An *em quad* is the square of any size of type being set. A 12-point em is an area 12 points wide and 12 points high, Fig. 7-2. The *unit* is a fraction of the width of an em.

The point is also used to designate the space between lines when additional space is needed. If 10-point type is used and additional space is unnecessary, it is said to be *set solid.*

Adding space is indicated by the term *leading.* Two points of leading would mean an additional two points are placed between each line. When composing type, the designation for a line of 10-point type with two points of leading would be 10/12 (10-point type and 2 points of extra line spacing).

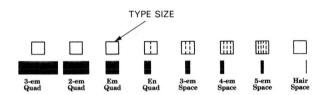

Fig. 7-2. Em quad is square of any type size.

COPYFITTING

Copyfitting, as mentioned, is the planned fitting together of copy, illustrations, and the area on the substrate. The planner or designer of graphic communications products is heavily involved in copyfitting. Without an organized system to determine the space available and amount of needed copy, unnecessary costs could occur. Resetting text, because the copy did not fit in a designated area, is very costly.

If the amount of copy is greater than the space allocated, the total design is affected. The layout artist often identifies the style of type and type size. When this occurs, without a basic copyfitting knowledge, problems are very possible.

Before images are generated, it is important to know:
1. What space is available.
2. The line length.
3. The type size.
4. Typeface style.
5. What size type will fit if the copy and space are known or what size type will fit if the copy and space are designated.

Copyfitting can be a rough estimate or it can be extremely accurate. Newspapers cannot afford to have a complicated system. Most newspaper articles are written so that they can be cut near the end without changing their meaning. The most simple system used by newspapers is the words-per-column/inch method.

Each typewriter style can be converted to the number of lines that equal an inch. When using the VDT (Visual Display Terminal), the display lends itself to editing of copy to fit into a given area. Newspapers also use the unit counting system for display lines. This was explained earlier.

Three systems are commonly used for fitting body type: word count, square-inch, and character count. Of the three systems, the character count is the most accurate and appears to be the system most commonly used in printing facilities.

WORD COUNT SYSTEM

The *word count system* uses the following estimations as a guide:
1. An em is the SQUARE of any size of type.
2. Three ems equal ONE WORD if the type size is 10-point or smaller.
3. Two and one-half ems equal ONE WORD if the type size is 11-point or LARGER.

Not all words are the same length but this will average out if applied. When a condensed or extended typeface is used, the system is NOT usable.

Word count copyfitting

If the type size and the length of the line to be composed are know, but the SPACE is to be found, use the following procedure:
1. Determine the number of words in the copy. Usually, it is not necessary to count all of the copy. Count the number of words in at least six lines and average the figure. If 60 words are in six lines, for example, the average would be ten. That figure should be multiplied by the number of lines in the copy.
2. Find the number of ems in each line. An em is the square of any size of type; therefore, the type size (in points) is divided into the line length, which is also given in points. If ten point type is used and the line length is 360 points, the number of ems is 36.
3. Determine how many words are in each line. In this case, we have selected ten point type which has three ems per word. Three ems is divided into the ems per line (36) and the answer is twelve.
4. To find the number of composed lines, divide the number of words within the copy.
5. The depth is found by multiplying the number of lines times the type size. This answer is in points. It might be necessary for you to convert it to picas, inches, or centimeters.

Sometimes, the designer provides a layout. It will specify a certain amount of space for copy. You would then need to find the AMOUNT OF COPY necessary to fill the space.
1. Select a type size and the leading (space between lines of type). Lay your copyfitter's or printer's scale over the layout to find out how many lines of a certain size and leading are needed to fill the space. Your rule typically will have scales for sizes from 8-point through 12-point. Smaller and larger sizes are found on some scales. You simply pick the scale for your point size and leading (10/12 = 12-point scale for example) and measure the depth on that scale.
2. Measure the width of the copy area to find the length of the line. Convert your line length to points.

3. To find the ems per line, divide the type size into the number of points in the line width.
4. The average word will take up about three ems of space when type is 10-point or smaller as stated earlier. Thus, to find the number of words, divide the number of ems in the line by three. This will tell you how many words are needed for each line.
5. Multiply the word count for one line by the number of lines in the copy space. This will give you the approximate number of words needed to fill the space designated by the artist.

If you have samples of the type you plan to use, there is a better method of finding amount of copy needed to fill the space.

1. Count the characters of five lines of type in the length of line designated. Take an average of the five. This is the average number of characters needed to fill one line.
2. As before, find the number of lines needed using the proper scale on the copyfitter's scale.
3. Have the copy written line-for-line to the same number of characters per line.
4. Type the same number of lines found through your calculations. This will give the number of words needed to fill the area specified by the layout artist.

Frequently, the copy has been given to the layout designer and also the size of the space has been designated, but the TYPE SIZE must be determined by the layout person. If this is the case:

1. Select a type size that would appear appropriate for the area and function of the copy.
2. Next, determine the number of words in the known area. The answer will indicate if the type size is too large or too small.
3. If the number of words in the area is smaller than the number of written words, the type size is too large. If the figure is larger than the number of words in the copy, the type size is too small.

This is a trial and error method. If the copy does not fit, select another type size and go through the same procedure.

Square-inch system

The *square-inch system* is another way of fitting type into a space. One of its greatest drawbacks is that it does NOT account for the various shapes of letters in different styles of type. Many times it is used because of its simplicity. For example, advertising copy, having plenty of white space, might use this system.

The table in Fig. 7-3 can be used to solve your common copy-fitting problems with the square-inch system.

For example, if given a space of 4 × 6 inches, how many words are needed to fill this area? The basic steps would be:
1. Find the number of square inches available (4 × 6 = 24).
2. Select size of type (12-point, leaded two points).
3. Find words per square inch (Table shows that eleven words will fit to one square inch).
4. Find the number of words that will fit in the space. Number of words per square inch times total number of square inches equals words needed. (11 × 24 = 264 words needed in this example).

It is possible that the words are written and you must find out what size of type will fit in the space.

The following steps are suggested:
1. Find the area (4 × 6 = 24).
2. Find the words in each square inch. Divide square inches of area into number of words (265 ÷ 24 = 11 words per square inch).

Looking at the table, Fig. 7-3, the typesize answer would be twelve (12) if leaded two points.

CHARACTER COUNT SYSTEM

The character count system is the most commonly used and the most accurate for fitting copy. Prior systems used words as the measurement and not the characters.

Character counting refers to counting any letter, figure, space, or punctuation used in the copy. The system does NOT allow for letter width variations but layout artists have found the method to be very satisfactory for magazine copy and advertisements. Designers of brochures, promotional materials, and financial report use this method.

With character count, each type design has a designated count for its size. This is illustrated by three type styles of the same size in Fig. 7-4.

Copy should be typewritten on 8 1/2 x 11 inch sheets of bond paper. This is needed to determine the number of characters in the copy. As stated earlier, all letters, figures,

SQUARE-INCH TABLE		
Type Size in Points	Number of Words Per Square Inch If Set Solid	Number of Words Per Square Inch If Leaded Two Points
6	47	34
7	38	27
8	32	23
9	27	20
10	21	16
11	17	14
12	14	11

Fig. 7-3. Table can be used to copyfit using square-inch system.

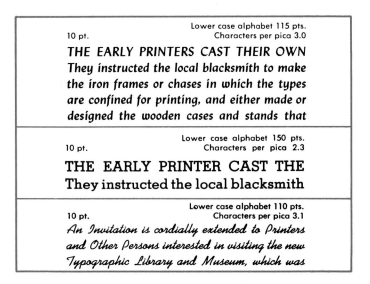

10 pt.	Lower case alphabet 115 pts. Characters per pica 3.0

THE EARLY PRINTERS CAST THEIR OWN
They instructed the local blacksmith to make the iron frames or chases in which the types are confined for printing, and either made or designed the wooden cases and stands that

10 pt.	Lower case alphabet 150 pts. Characters per pica 2.3

THE EARLY PRINTER CAST THE
They instructed the local blacksmith

10 pt.	Lower case alphabet 110 pts. Characters per pica 3.1

An Invitation is cordially extended to Printers and Other Persons interested in visiting the new Typographic Library and Museum, which was

Fig. 7-4. All three type styles of same size require varying space.

PICA TYPE

If you wish this evaluation to be confidential (you will not have access to this evaluation), you must sign and date the following waiver:

ELITE TYPE

If you wish this evaluation to be confidential (you will not have access to this evaluation), you must sign and date the following waiver:

Fig. 7-5. Two types produced by typewriters are classified as pica and elite.

spaces, and punctuation marks (points) ARE COUNTED as characters.

There are two standard typewriters: pica and elite, Fig. 7-5. Copy that is pica type size will have ten characters per inch. Elite will have twelve characters per inch.

Various ways are used to measure typewritten copy. Two of the most often used methods will be shown.

Average character count

The *average character count* method is not as accurate because it uses the typical number of characters per line. A vertical line is drawn through the typed copy where the AVERAGE LINE LENGTH is determined, Fig. 7-6.

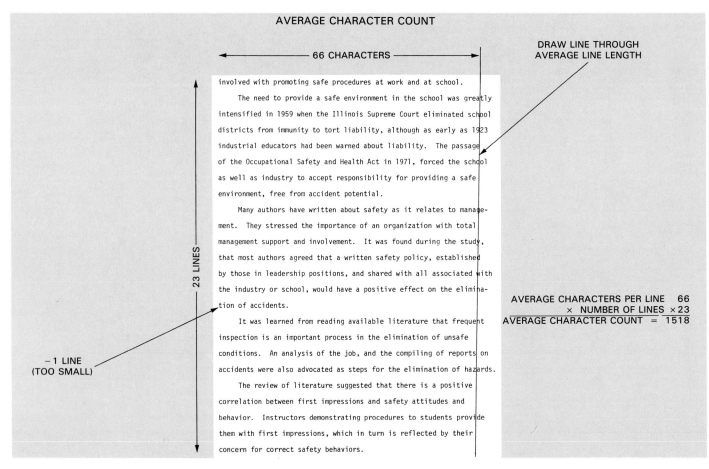

AVERAGE CHARACTER COUNT

66 CHARACTERS

DRAW LINE THROUGH AVERAGE LINE LENGTH

23 LINES

involved with promoting safe procedures at work and at school.

The need to provide a safe environment in the school was greatly intensified in 1959 when the Illinois Supreme Court eliminated school districts from immunity to tort liability, although as early as 1923 industrial educators had been warned about liability. The passage of the Occupational Safety and Health Act in 1971, forced the school as well as industry to accept responsibility for providing a safe environment, free from accident potential.

Many authors have written about safety as it relates to management. They stressed the importance of an organization with total management support and involvement. It was found during the study, that most authors agreed that a written safety policy, established by those in leadership positions, and shared with all associated with the industry or school, would have a positive effect on the elimination of accidents.

It was learned from reading available literature that frequent inspection is an important process in the elimination of unsafe conditions. An analysis of the job, and the compiling of reports on accidents were also advocated as steps for the elimination of hazards.

The review of literature suggested that there is a positive correlation between first impressions and safety attitudes and behavior. Instructors demonstrating procedures to students provide them with first impressions, which in turn is reflected by their concern for correct safety behaviors.

−1 LINE (TOO SMALL)

AVERAGE CHARACTERS PER LINE 66
× NUMBER OF LINES ×23
AVERAGE CHARACTER COUNT = 1518

Fig. 7-6. Average character count will give good estimate of the amount of space needed for typewritten page. Draw a verticle line through the average length of all lines. Count the characters in a full line. Count number of lines. Drop any widows or very short lines. Multiply number of lines by number of characters per line.

The number of characters to the left of the line, multiplied by the number of lines, will give a close estimate of the number of characters on the typewritten page.

Accurate character count

If a more accurate count is necessary, draw a vertical line at the end of the SHORTEST LINE in the typewritten copy. Measure the line to determine the number of characters in the line. The proper scale must be selected (pica or elite), Fig. 7-7. After checking the count, multiply the number of characters times the number of lines. This total represents the number of characters to the left of the vertical line. Next,

count the number of characters to the right of the line. The total of the right-hand characters must be added to the total on the left-hand side of the line, Fig. 7-8. This total gives a very accurate number of characters making up the manuscript copy.

Note! Short lines at the end of a paragraph can be considered as full lines and you will still have a good count.

Determining space needed for a manuscript

A common way of finding the amount of space a manuscript will occupy is called the *"characters per pica"* method. Printers or type catalogs provide tables giving how

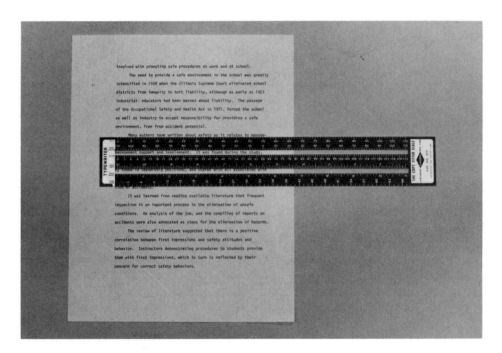

Fig. 7-7. Printer's rule will quickly let you find number of characters per line.

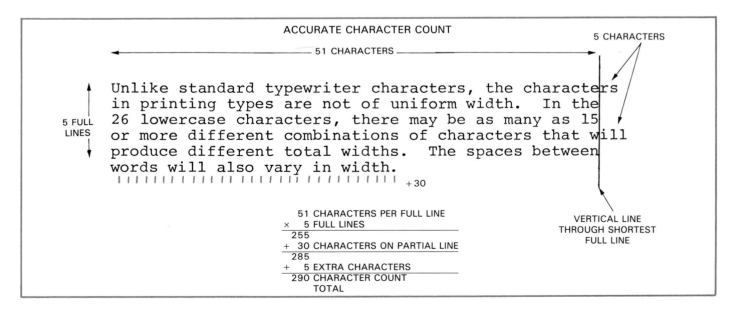

Fig. 7-8. To do an accurate character count, draw a vertical line through shortest full line. Count characters from left side to vertical line. Count full lines and multiply by number of characters. Count and add any partial lines. Then, add in the extra characters to right of vertical line.

14 pt.
Lower case alphabet 157 pts.
Characters per pica 2.2

THE EARLY PRINTERS CAST THE
They instructed some local black

12 pt.
Lower case alphabet 136 pts.
Characters per pica 2.5

THE EARLY PRINTER CAST THE TYPE
They instructed some local blacksmith

10 pt.
Lower case alphabet 117 pts.
Characters per pica 2.9

THE EARLY PRINTERS CAST THEIR TYPES
They instructed the local blacksmith to make
the iron frames or chases in which the types

8 pt.
Lower case alphabet 93 pts.
Characters per pica 3.7

THE EARLY PRINTERS CAST THEIR OWN TYPES AND
They instructed some local blacksmith to make the iron
frames or chases in which the types are confined for

6 pt.
Lower case alphabet 88 pts.
Characters per pica 3.8

THE EARLY PRINTERS CAST THEIR OWN TYPES, MADE INK
They instructed some local blacksmith to make the iron frames
or chases in which the types are confined for printing, and
either made or designed the wooden cases and stands that

Fig. 7-9. Note how catalog sometimes gives characters per pica for specific type.

many characters of a specific type style and size will fit in one pica of length. See Fig. 7-9.

Charts are also available showing the number of characters in lines of different lengths. As shown in Fig. 7-10, the lengths are given in picas.

To see how this system works, suppose that you wish to set type in 10-point sans serif face with a line width of 18 picas. Use the following procedure:

1. Count the number of characters in the typed manuscript using the appropriate scale or by counting the characters and spaces in one line. Since typewritten lines are not always the same lengths, find an average between the longest and the shortest lines. Let us assume that the manuscript has 310 characters.
2. By referring to the chart in Fig. 7-9, find the number of 10-point characters that will fill one pica of space.
   Multiply that figure (2.9) by the line length to find number of characters in a 18-pica line:
   $$2.9 \times 18 = 52.2 \text{ characters per typeset line}$$
3. Find the number of typeset lines by dividing the characters per line into the number of characters in the manuscript:

$$310 \div 52.2 = 5.93 \text{ or } 6 \text{ typeset lines}$$

4. To find the total depth of the typeset material set solid, multiply the point size by the number of typeset lines:
   $$10 \times 6 = 60 \text{ points}$$
5. Change the answer from points to picas by dividing:
   $$12 \text{ points} = 1 \text{ pica}$$
   60 points divided by 12 points = 5 picas depth

This example was for solid set type. If spacing between lines is added, the amount of spacing must be added to the type size. Your calculations must be based on the type size plus the leading.

If you are working on a large manuscript for a textbook, you can estimate the general size of the book. If you know column width, type size, number of illustrations, and size of illustrations, you should be able to find a typical divisor for typed pages and illustrations. Another book using the same general format can also be used to estimate manuscript size.

For example, this book uses 10-point type with 2-points leading and a 3 1/2 inch column width. With this format, you can divide the number of typed pages by four to get about one page of typeset copy. Since most of the illustrations are one column, you can also divide them by four to get approximately one full page in the textbook.

For example, if the author's manuscript has 1000 typed pages that are double-spaced, divide by four with this book style. This will give you approximately 250 pages of copy after typesetting. With this book style, if there are 500 illustrations, again divide by four and there would be 125 pages of illustrations.

Add all of the copy to the illustrations (250 plus 125) to get an estimate of 375 pages for the printed textbook. This is a very rough estimate but can be useful in the book publishing field. Use the word or character count system of a typical typed page to get a more accurate divisor if needed.

Characters to fill a space

Frequently, the designer has designated a given space and filling that space depends on the amount of written copy. To calculate the number of characters to fill a space, use the following steps:

1. Measure the length of each line in picas. For instance, the line gauge might indicate that it is 15 picas.
2. Assume the type to be used is 10-point Times Roman and has 2.80 characters per pica. Multiplying the two (15 picas × 2.80) gives us a total of 42 characters in each line. If a decimal appears, round it off to the nearest whole number.
3. Measure depth of the copy. In this example, it is seven

CHARACTER COUNT PER LINE

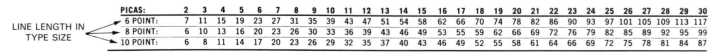

	PICAS:	2	3	4	5	6	7	8	9	10	11	12	13	14	15	16	17	18	19	20	21	22	23	24	25	26	27	28	29	30
LINE LENGTH IN TYPE SIZE	6 POINT:	7	11	15	19	23	27	31	35	39	43	47	51	54	58	62	66	70	74	78	82	86	90	93	97	101	105	109	113	117
	8 POINT:	6	10	13	16	20	23	26	30	33	36	39	43	46	49	53	55	59	62	66	69	72	76	79	82	85	89	92	95	99
	10 POINT:	6	8	11	14	17	20	23	26	29	32	35	37	40	43	46	49	52	55	58	61	64	66	69	72	75	78	81	84	87

Fig. 7-10. Chart gives line lengths for sizes and style of type in picas and also gives character count for that length.

picas. To find the number of points, multiply picas times the points in one pica. The total is 84 (7 × 12 = 84).

4. Divide the line height (10-point type) plus the leading (+2) into the depth (84 points). Seven lines (84 ÷ 12 = 7) will fit in the area designated for the copy.

5. The copy to be written is determined by multiplying the number of lines (7) times the characters per line (42). The number of characters required to fill the area is 294 (7 × 42 = 294). This is the total number of characters needed to fill the designated area.

Type size to fit space and manuscript

Whenever the amount of space is designated as well as the manuscript copy, the type size can be selected to fill the space. Use these basic steps:

1. Using the same manuscript and space as in the last problem, find the number of characters in the manuscript copy. Total characters equal 310 in this example.

2. Measure the space allocated for the depth of the copy. The measurement is in picas. Convert the picas to points. Multiply the number of picas by 12 points—12 points equal 1 pica (7 × 12 = 84). Total number of points equal 84.

3. The next step is to find how many lines can be placed in the designated depth for several sizes of type. If leading is to be included, add it to the type size. The number of points in the copy depth is 84. Divide this number by the points per line.

   a. 84 divided by 8 = number of lines for depth of copy 11.
   b. 84 divided by 10 = number of lines for depth of copy 9.
   c. 84 divided by 12 = number of lines for depth of copy 7.

   The 8, 10, and 12 represents the points for each line. If a fraction results, round it out to the next full number.

4. The line length of the designated space is 18 picas.

5. The procedure to find the number of characters per pica has been explained earlier. Number of characters per pica (2.80 × line length (18) equals 50.4.

6. The total number of characters per manuscript is 310. Divide that number by the average number of characters per line. This will give the total number of lines for the size estimated (310 ÷ 50.4 = 6.15)

7. If the number is larger than the allowed number of lines, rework the procedure with a smaller line depth size (solid or leaded) or vice versa.

ELECTRONIC COPYFITTING

The various techniques of copyfitting just explained are being rapidly replaced or supplemented with the capabilities of computers and electronic typesetting equipment. In some situations, the computer and the visual display terminal are excellent devices for fitting copy to the required space on the layout.

Desktop publishing systems, detailed later, will even allow you to fit copy and art while still on the visual display screen.

Parameter line

The *parameter line* is a list of programmed specifications for the text or copy on a computerized typesetting screen. It can be given at the top, side, or even bottom of the monitor. This allows the typesetter to constantly review information concerning type size, line spacing, font selection, line length, and depth of copy.

Since parameters or specs can be changed so easily with modern phototypesetting equipment, this has made it much easier to copyfit more precisely. A parameter line is shown in Fig. 7-11.

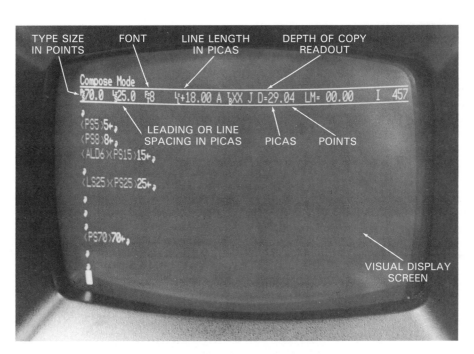

Fig. 7-11. *Display screen of most computer controlled typesetting machines will give readout of programmed specs on a parameter line. This can be useful when copyfitting.*

Depth of copy display

The *depth of copy* display is typically a number representing the number of picas and points the copy will take up when in finished form. This display is constantly updated as the typesetter inputs each line of copy. See Fig. 7-11.

For example, if the visual display terminal shows a 127.02, the typesetter would know that the copy is running 127 picas and 2 points deep. If he or she knows that the layout will only allow for 125 picas of depth, the amount of space used can be reduced by condensing the characters or by reducing leading. If more copy is needed to fill the space, the copy can be expanded or leading can be increased.

By changing the depth of copy before layout, it can save the editors or layout people from having to cut lines or words or rewriting the copy. It also saves the typesetter from having to reset after it is discovered that the copy will not fit the layout. This saves time and money.

Type size display

The *type size display* on a typesetting terminal screen may also be given on the parameter line. An abbreviation, "ps" for example, will denote that the number is the point size. This is pictured in Fig. 7-11.

With modern phototypesetting equipment, it is very easy to change point size. In fact, if the typesetter is working on a job, type size can quickly be changed to aid copyfitting. For example, if advertisement copy is running too long, type size can be reduced on one section of the ad to make it fit in the designated space.

Line spacing display

The *line spacing display,* also called *leading display,* is a readout for the distance between lines. It is also given as points on most systems. Again, an abbreviation, "ls" in this example, will denote this readout.

Line spacing, as mentioned earlier, can be changed to aid copyfitting. An experienced typesetter can modify line spacing in some jobs to make the copy and space match perfectly.

Line length display

The *line length display* is simply the length of the line in picas. Usually abbreviated "LL" on the terminal screen, it gives the typesetter constant feedback when trying to make line length changes for difficult typesetting tasks.

Indent program

The *indent program* allows the typesetter to preset the parameters for indenting copy. Once programmed, the computer will "remember" the amount of indent for future reference and use. The editor or designer must give the typesetter the specifications for the indents on the copy, as shown in Fig. 7-12. Then the output from the typesetting equipment will be indented properly.

Cut program

A *cut* is an opened area with no copy or a set of modified lines that occur in electronically typeset copy. An example is pictured in Fig. 7-13. The cut program is commonly used

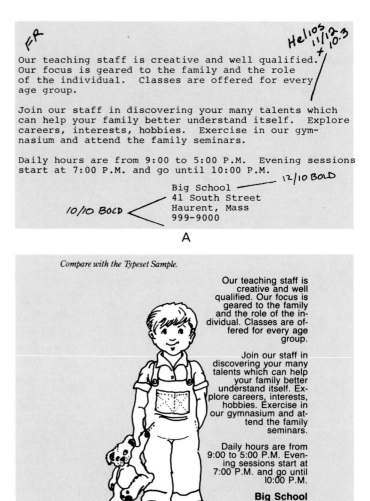

Fig. 7-12. Indent program allows typesetter to move copy over for special needs. A—Marked manuscript gives specs. B—Finished product. (Compugraphic)

when copy must fit around an illustration, as in an advertisement. This is similar to the indent program.

A *cut program* allows the typesetter to determine the depth where the copy will be cut, to specify the margin the copy will be cut from, and to define the width and depth of the cut or open area. After the cut has been made, the computer will automatically return to the previous line measure.

Other information

Other information relating to electronic copyfitting is given in other locations in this book, under pagination or desktop publishing for example. Use the text index to find more information as needed.

SPECIFICATIONS

Specifications give information relating to type style, size, column width, color use, page organization, and other facts pertaining to a printed product. Specifications provide essential guidelines for typesetting, copyfitting, and layout.

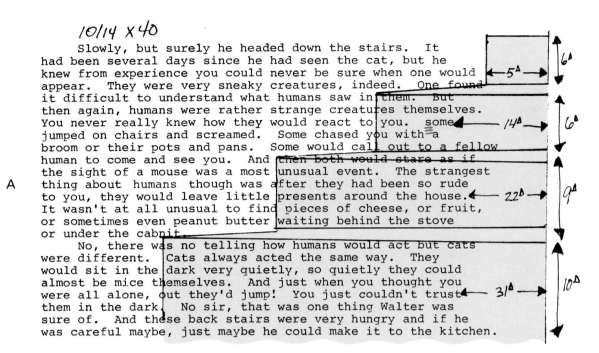

10/14 × 40

A

Slowly, but surely he headed down the stairs. It had been several days since he had seen the cat, but he knew from experience you could never be sure when one would appear. They were very sneaky creatures, indeed. One found it difficult to understand what humans saw in them. But then again, humans were rather strange creatures themselves. You never really knew how they would react to you. Some jumped on chairs and screamed. Some chased you with a broom or their pots and pans. Some would call out to a fellow human to come and see you. And then both would stare as if the sight of a mouse was a most unusual event. The strangest thing about humans though was after they had been so rude to you, they would leave little presents around the house. It wasn't at all unusual to find pieces of cheese, or fruit, or sometimes even peanut butter waiting behind the stove or under the cabnit.

No, there was no telling how humans would act but cats were different. Cats always acted the same way. They would sit in the dark very quietly, so quietly they could almost be mice themselves. And just when you thought you were all alone, out they'd jump! You just couldn't trust them in the dark. No sir, that was one thing Walter was sure of. And these back stairs were very hungry and if he was careful maybe, just maybe he could make it to the kitchen.

Compare with the Typeset Sample.

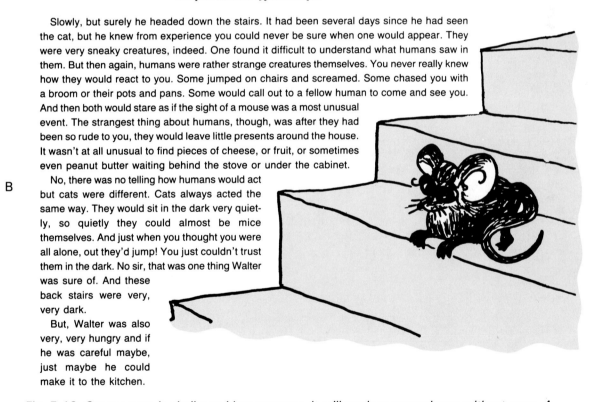

B

Slowly, but surely he headed down the stairs. It had been several days since he had seen the cat, but he knew from experience you could never be sure when one would appear. They were very sneaky creatures, indeed. One found it difficult to understand what humans saw in them. But then again, humans were rather strange creatures themselves. You never really knew how they would react to you. Some jumped on chairs and screamed. Some chased you with a broom or their pots and pans. Some would call out to a fellow human to come and see you. And then both would stare as if the sight of a mouse was a most unusual event. The strangest thing about humans, though, was after they had been so rude to you, they would leave little presents around the house. It wasn't at all unusual to find pieces of cheese, or fruit, or sometimes even peanut butter waiting behind the stove or under the cabinet.

No, there was no telling how humans would act but cats were different. Cats always acted the same way. They would sit in the dark very quietly, so quietly they could almost be mice themselves. And just when you thought you were all alone, out they'd jump! You just couldn't trust them in the dark. No sir, that was one thing Walter was sure of. And these back stairs were very, very dark.

But, Walter was also very, very hungry and if he was careful maybe, just maybe he could make it to the kitchen.

Fig. 7-13. Cut program is similar to ident program. It will produce opened area without copy. A—Marked manuscript with type sizes. B—Finished product with cut. (Compugraphic)

Refer to Figs. 7-12 and 7-13. Note how the marked manuscript has specs for type size and type style. Note how these specs were converted into typeset pages.

A *spec sheet,* sometimes called *style sheet,* is a summary of how to produce the layout or product. It is filled out before beginning production of a job. One is shown in Fig. 7-14 for this textbook. Study how these specs were used by typesetting and layout to produce several pages.

Specifications are also used during printing, binding, and finishing, Fig. 7-15. Refer to the textbook index for more coverage of this topic.

DESKTOP PUBLISHING

A *desktop publishing system* normally uses a personal computer, an interface unit, and a laser printer to organize

STYLE SHEET

Working title: _GRAPHIC COMMUNICATIONS_

Author: _PRUST_

_X_ Text _____ Workbook _____ I.G. _____ Test Masters

Copyright 19 _89_ Library of Congress Catalog Card Number _____

ISBN 0-87006-_____ Print Code _____ - _____ - _____

Projected level of audience: _____ grade

Estimated number of pages: _500_ Page size _8½_ x _11_ inches

Number of columns: _2_ Column width: _3½_ inches Margins: _DIESEL SHEET_

_____ _X_ Justified _____ Ragged Right _____ Ragged Left

	Type Style	Point Size	Leading Space
Chapter titles	UN BOLD CAPS	24	
Objectives	UN MED. BULLETS	10	12 SEE HOUSING
Body copy	E.T.	10	12
Sideheads/Centerheads	UN BOLD ITALIC CAPS	11	
Subheads	UN BOLD ITALIC C&L.C.	11	
Sub-subheads	E.T. BOLD ITALIC RUN IN	10	
Captions	UN MED ITALIC	9	12
Photo credit lines	UN MID CAP	5	
End of chapter material	UN BOLD CENTER HEADS	10	12
Call outs	7 UN MED CAPS (LINE) PHOTOS 8 UN MED CAPS.		
Glossary	E.T. WITH BOLD WORDS (RUN IN) 10		12
Index	E.T. SIZE TO COME LATER		

Four color usage: _2 FORMS_ Second color: _BLUE_

Halftones: _BLACK_ Duotones: _ONLY WHEN COVERING DUOTONES_

Line Art: _BLACK & 2ND COLOR_

Use of colored type: _____

Use of tint blocks: _BLUE_

Cover design concept: _TO COME_

Chapter opening design: _ALL START ON_

_____ _X_ Right-hand page _____ Left-hand page _____ Either

Part page design: _____

Chart design: _TO FOLLOW EXISTING TECH STYLE (8 PT MID BODY) (8 PT._

Folio location: _BOTTOM LEFT & RIGHT_ _BOLD HEADS) TITLE 10 UN_

Additional art considerations: _SAFTY TO BE INDENTED_ _MED CAPS_

WITH COLOR BAR DOWN SIDE - SAFTY COL TO BE 3½ WIDE

Fig. 7-14. This is an example of style sheet or spec sheet. Note how it gives typesetter and other personnel important information for producing product. Compare specs to actual type used in this book. Especially, note type sizes for body copy, side heads, captions, etc.

PRINTING SPECIFICATIONS

| ☐ Early budget | ☐ Late budget | ☐ Based on specs | ☐ Based on art |

Company _____ Contact _____
Address _____
Phone _____ Fax _____
Project Title _____
Description _____

Date _____
Date prices required _____
Release date _____
Delivery date _____

Quantities _____
_____
☐ Overs up to _____%
☐ Unders up to _____%
☐ No overs /unders

Page count | ☐ Plus cover, no. pages ___ ☐ Self cover | **Proofs:** ☐ Blueline ☐ Colorkey ☐ Matchprint ☐ Other ☐ Press check | **No:** ___ ___ ___ ___ ___ | ☐ New project ☐ Exact reprint ☐ Reprint w/changes

Flat size | **Finished size**

Paper

Form	# of Pages	Color	Basis Weight	Specify Cover or Book Weight	Name or Grade	Finish
Single Sheet						
Cover						
Fly						
Text 1						
Text 2						

Preparation

Electronic Prepress Output
Type of output _____
Software used and version no. _____
Fonts: _____

Disk Format ☐ Single pages ☐ Readers spreads ☐ Printers spreads

Customer Furnish
☐ Complete camera ready art
☐ Windows on art for images
☐ Flapped for colors and screens
☐ Key lined for color break
☐ Masks furnished for outlines
☐ Composite negs. in ____ pg spreads

Maps charts: No. ___ Size ___ | No. ___ Size ___ | No. ___ Size ___
Line strip-ins: No. ___ Size ___ | No. ___ Size ___ | No. ___ Size ___

Half-tones: No. ___ Size ___ Outline ___ | No. ___ Size ___ Outline ___ | No. ___ Size ___ Outline ___
Duo-tones: No. ___ Size ___ Outline ___ | No. ___ Size ___ Outline ___ | No. ___ Size ___ Outline ___

Screens: No. ___ Size ___ | No. ___ Size ___ | No. ___ Size ___
Reverses: No. ___ Size ___ | No. ___ Size ___ | No. ___ Size ___

Color Seps.

	Original size	Finished size	Trans.	Refl	Scan	Cam.	Outline	Crossover	Scan to file	Lo/Hi Res.
No. ___	___ x ___ To	___ x ___	☐	☐	☐	☐	☐	☐	☐	☐
No. ___	___ x ___ To	___ x ___	☐	☐	☐	☐	☐	☐	☐	☐
No. ___	___ x ___ To	___ x ___	☐	☐	☐	☐	☐	☐	☐	☐
No. ___	___ x ___ To	___ x ___	☐	☐	☐	☐	☐	☐	☐	☐
No. ___	___ x ___ To	___ x ___	☐	☐	☐	☐	☐	☐	☐	☐

Press

Cover ___ out ___ in ___ % Coverage ___	Fly ___ Side 1 ___ Side 2 ___ % Coverage ___	Text 1 ___ Side 1 ___ Side 2 ___ % Coverage ___	Text 1 ___ Side 1 ___ Side 2 ___ % Coverage ___
Varnish ☐ dry ☐ wet ☐ spot ☐ overall	Varnish ☐ dry ☐ wet ☐ spot ☐ overall	Varnish ☐ dry ☐ wet ☐ spot ☐ overall	Varnish ☐ dry ☐ wet ☐ spot ☐ overall
Solids ☐ yes ☐ no	Solids ☐ yes ☐ no	Solids ☐ yes ☐ no	Solids ☐ yes ☐ no
Bleeds ☐ yes ☐ no	Bleeds ☐ yes ☐ no	Bleeds ☐ yes ☐ no	Bleeds ☐ yes ☐ no
Coating ☐ aqueous	Coating ☐ aqueous	Coating ☐ aqueous	Coating ☐ aqueous
Coating ☐ UV ☐ spot ☐ overall	Coating ☐ UV ☐ spot ☐ overall	Coating ☐ UV ☐ spot ☐ overall	Coating ☐ UV ☐ spot ☐ overall

Bindery

☐ Soft fold   Fold to ___ x ___   No. of folds ___   ☐ Letter fold   ☐ Accordian   ☐ Round corner   ☐ Remoistenable gum
☐ Saddle stitch   ☐ Double saddle   ☐ Side stitch & tape   ☐ Perfect bind   ☐ Case bind   ☐ Spiral   ☐ Wire-O   ☐ GBC
☐ Perforate ___   ☐ Die Cut   ☐ Collate
☐ Drill ___   ☐ Emboss/size ___   ☐ Shrink wrap
☐ Score ___   ☐ Deboss/size ___   ☐ Mail ☐ Label ☐ Ink jet
☐ Glue pockets/size ___ No. ___   ☐ Foil stamp/size ___   ☐ Cust. supplies: ___
☐ Pockets no glue/size ___ No. ___   ☐ Trim only ___ x ___   ☐ Other ___

Shipping

Special packing _____
_____
(Bulk pack in cartons unless otherwise specified.)
No. of samples required _____
F.O.B. point _____ No. of local deliveries _____
Delivery date _____

Pricing

Vendor _____ Contact _____ Phone _____
Quantity _____ Estimated price _____
_____   _____
_____   _____

Fig. 7-15. This is a sample spec sheet used by a printer.   (Communications and Graphic Arts Leadership Council)

both copy and art on a page. It provides a fast and efficient way of copyfitting and completing layout on a computer screen. See Fig. 7-16.

Desktop publishing systems vary from one model to the next. However, most allow you to program in specifications, typeset, move copy, make simple line drawings, insert art, and finalize layout on a small personal computer. Fig. 7-17

shows an example of layout and copyfitting done on a computer. The images were generated on a laser printer.

The term "desktop" was derived from the system being very small and fitting on top of an office desk.

Note! Chapter 12 covers desktop publishing in more detail. Refer to this chapter if needed.

KNOW THESE TERMS

Point, Pica, Metric type size, Type height, Em quad, Leading, Copyfitting, Word count, Copyfitter's scale, Square-inch system, Character count system, Average character count, Accurate character count, Electronic copyfitting, Indent program, Cut program, Specifications, Spec sheet, Desktop publishing.

REVIEW QUESTIONS—CHAPTER 7

1. What are the two units of measurement unique to the graphic communications industry?
2. Six picas equals approximately one _____.
3. Paper sizes are designated by picas. True or false?
4. What is an em quad?
5. What does the term 10/12 mean?
6. _____ is the planned fitting together of copy, illustrations, and the art on the substrate.
7. _____ ems equal one _____ if the type size is _____ or smaller.
8. This is the largest drawback to the square-inch method of fitting type into a space.
   a. Many systems are metric.
   b. Copy can be rectangular in shape.
   c. Does not account for letter shapes.
   d. It requires very complex math.
9. How many words would be needed to fill a space 4 by 10 inches using 10-point type, set solid? Use the square-inch system.
10. In your own words, how do you do average character count?
11. Typically, if the top of the screen on a modern typesetting machine reads 151.06, what would this mean?
12. What does a cut program allow?

SUGGESTED ACTIVITIES

1. Visit a plant and find out what system of copyfitting is used during production.
2. Select a sample of a typewritten manuscript and determine what size type could be used to fit in an area of 4 x 5 inches.
3. Observe the use of phototypesetting equipment and how it can be used to help copyfit.

Fig. 7-16. *Desktop publishing system uses personal computer, interface unit, and usually laser printer to produce layout. Note how operator has both copy, line art, and hole for photos on screen. This serves as quick method of copyfitting and doing layout.*

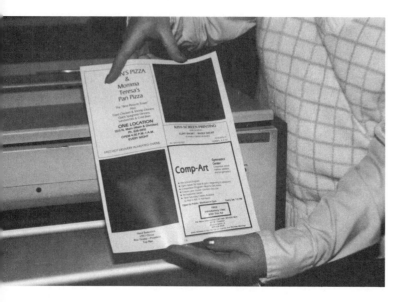

Fig. 7-17. *Here is a sample of finished layout done on desktop publishing system.*

Chapter 8

RELIEF COMPOSITION

After studying this chapter, you will be able to:
- Identify the techniques associated with relief type composition.
- Identify the materials commonly used to make relief images.
- List and explain the common spacing materials used when setting type.
- Explain the basic process used to produce slugs of type.
- Explain the proofing process used to produce copy for correction and/or reproduction.

Relief printing, also termed *letterpress, hot type, foundry type,* and *flexography,* prints from a raised surface. The nonimage area is recessed or relieved below the printing surface. The raised, inked image is pressed against the substrate to reproduce the image.

This chapter will summarize how to compose (set) metal type by hand. By learning how to hand-set relief type, you will learn about concepts (leading, proofing, registration, etc.) that relate to more modern printing methods. Some coverage will also be given to modern flexographic type relief printing.

Note! For more information on relief printing methods, refer to the text index. This topic is discussed in several other chapters.

RELIEF TYPE

Relief type, as mentioned, has the shape of the image above the nonprinting surface. A soft roller places ink on the raised image. Then the inked image is pushed against the substrate for reproduction. This process is repeated for each sheet.

Fig. 8-1 illustrates the principle of relief type. Note how the ink is deposited on the top surface. The recessed or relieved surface does not hold ink. Ink is deposited on the paper to form a graphic image.

Relief or letter press printing dates back many years. Records show that the Chinese used wooden relief type as early as the mid 800's.

The first movable metal type is said to have been developed by Johann Gutenberg in Mainz, Germany, in 1450. It is generally accepted that he printed the 42-line Bible. This was a tremendous accomplishment. See Fig. 8-2.

Before the invention of movable metal type, the image had to be carved by hand into wood or soft metal. This was a long and tedious process. Now, with movable metal type available, multiple copies could be more easily printed.

The art of printing spread to cities throughout Europe. In America, the first press was established at Harvard Academy in 1639. Stephen Daye, and his son, Matthew, worked for the Reverend Jose Glover who brought the printing press to America.

The first regularly published American newspaper was published in Boston by John Campbell, in 1704. Just as it occurred many years earlier in Europe, printing was now taking place in British North America.

Some of the early American printers were:
1. Stephen Daye, Cambridge, MA — 1639.
2. Marmoduke Johnson, Boston, MA — 1660.
3. William Bradford, Philadelphia, PA — 1685.
4. James Franklin, Boston, MA — 1717.
5. Benjamin Franklin, Philadelphia, PA — 1728.

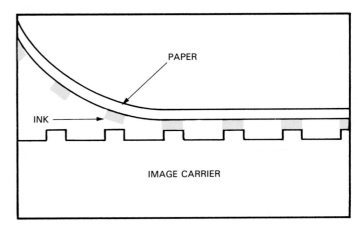

Fig. 8-1. Image that receives ink is in relief. Note how plate or image carrier deposits ink on paper or substrate.
(A.B. Dick Co.)

107

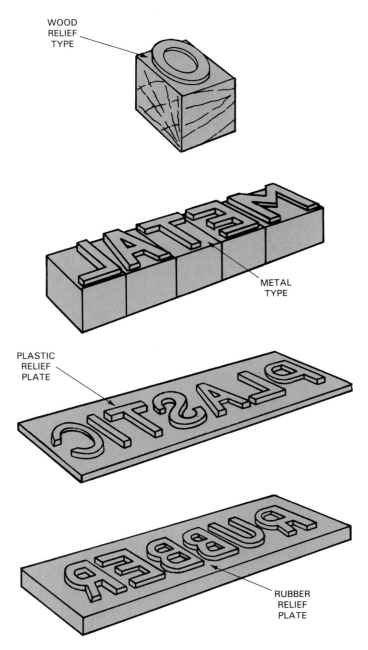

Fig. 8-2. *This copy of a page of the Bible was printed by equipment found in the Gutenberg Museum.*

Fig. 8-3. *Study four kinds of material used to print in relief.*

Relief type composition

The term *composition* generally refers to the production and organization of all images to be printed. However, in graphic communications, composition can also mean setting type or words, not line art or photographs. The *typesetter* or *compositor* is the person who sets the type.

The typesetter first makes the *galley proofs* which are the first draft of the printing job. They are used to proofread and check for errors.

The *reproduction proofs* are made by the typesetter by fixing any errors found in the gallery proofs. They are used to make the final printed product.

Relief type materials

Relief type can be made of different materials: wood, metal, rubber, plastic. This is shown in Fig. 8-3.

Wood type. *Wood type* is used to print very large type sizes using the relief process. Wood type is sometimes used for making large posters for example. Wood type is lighter than metal type and is well suited for large point size characters. With computerized phototypesetting, wood type is seldom used in print jobs today.

Fig. 8-4A shows typical wood characters. The face of the type is the polished end grain of the wood. Note that wood type is relatively soft and can be easily damaged.

Metal type. *Metal type* was once used to produce written words for printing reproduction. It is commonly termed HOT METAL COMPOSITION, or HOT TYPE, because is was produced by pouring hot, molten metal into a MATRIX (mold) to form the characters of the printed words. See Fig. 8-4B. Metal type has also been replaced by phototype.

Rubber type. *Rubber type* can also be used to make images in relief. Commonly termed a *rubber stamp,* it is another way relief printing can be used in today's market.

Plastic type. *Plastic type* is the most modern method of utilizing the relief printing process. Also termed *flexography* because the plate is flexible, it uses modern techniques to produce a one-piece plastic plate with a raised image surface. It is used to print some newspapers and other long run jobs quickly and efficiently. Look at Fig. 8-4C.

First and second generation images

A *first generation image* is the original. Hot type that is formed by pouring molten metal into a mold would be an example of a first generation image.

A *second generation image* is NOT an original, but is a copy of the original. An intermediate step has been used to produce the type for printing. Long runs, that can wear out the original image, use a second generation plate. Then, if the image wears out during the run, the original first generation image can be used to make another second generation image for continuing the same press run.

Metal relief type classifications

The kinds of *metal relief type* are: foundry type, bars of metal (slugs), single character machine composition, and special relief materials. All of these have a common factor. They must be read upside down from left to right, Fig. 8-5.

In order to print properly, metal relief characters must be of uniform height, aligned, assembled in a desired length and width, and locked up in a frame.

The metal frame that holds the type is called a *chase*. It supports the type when positioned in the printing press.

The first method of composition to be discussed is called hand-set type. The kind of type used for this method is foundry type.

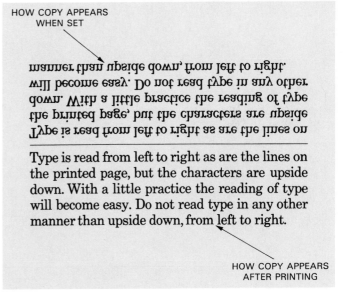

Fig. 8-5. In relief type composition, composed type is read upside down and from left to right.

FOUNDRY TYPE

Foundry type is an assortment of individually cast characters. The characters are chosen to make up words of the manuscript.

The metal used in the type is mainly lead, tin, and antimony. Lead is the major ingredient but it is very soft. The antimony is added to give hardness and fluidity. Tin gives the type its toughness and counteracts shrinkage.

The set of characters in one size and series is called a *font*. It is made up of capital letters, lower case letters, figures, and points (punctuation marks). A typical font is in Fig. 8-6.

Parts of foundry type

The typical parts of a piece of foundry type are: face counter, serif, neck or beard, shoulder, nick, groove, feet, heavy element, light element, and pin mark.

The *face* is the raised surface and the printing image. The ink is usually rolled on this surface. When the surface comes in contact with the substrate, the ink is transferred from the face of the type onto the surface of the stock, Fig. 8-7.

The *serif* is a finishing off line at the ends of unconnected elements. The serif shapes will change with type styles. This gives the face an identity. When type does NOT have serifs, it is called sans serif.

The term *neck* or *beard* is the distance between the body and face of the piece of type. This distance is necessary to eliminate the possibility of other areas being inked and becoming an unwanted image on the stock.

The *counter* is the surface of the recessed area within and around the face.

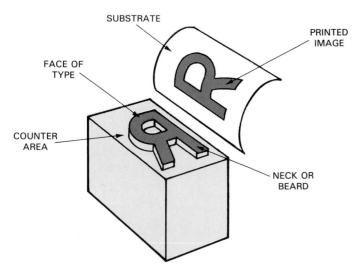

Fig. 8-6. Foundry type can be purchased as a complete font.

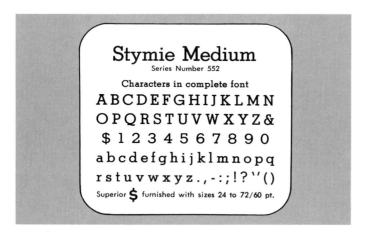

Fig. 8-7. The surface of the raised image is first inked. As it comes in contact with the stock, an image remains on the surface of the paper or substrate.

The *shoulder* is the area which extends below the base of the character. This distance will vary depending on the type style. The reason for a shoulder is the space needed for type styles and characters that have decending strokes. Letters which commonly have these strokes are g, j, p, q, and y.

The *nick* indicates the correct direction to set the metal foundry type. All of the nicks must line up when type is set. This is shown in Fig. 8-8. Type styles can have more than one nick. The nick is a guide for the compositor.

The *feet* are two areas on which the type stands. They are separated by a groove. The groove is formed by a cutting tool that removes the sprue or rough edge formed as the type is cast in a mold.

A *pin mark* is found on the side of foundry type. This mark is left by the device which removes the type from the mold. The mark identifies the foundry.

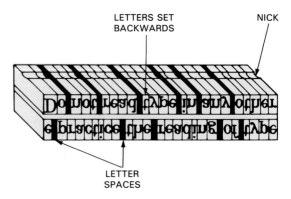

Fig. 8-8. Nicks must line up when type is set. (A.B. Dick Co.)

Dimensions of foundry type

Accuracy is essential and the dimensions of foundry type can be accurate to ten-thousandths of an inch or thousandths of a millimeter in all dimensions. Three foundry type dimensions are shown in Fig. 8-9.

The *height* of type in North America is uniform. The distance from the base of the type to the face is .918 inches and is stated as the *height-to-paper*.

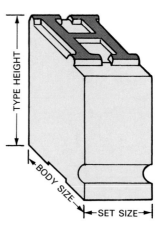

Fig. 8-9. These three dimensions are commonly associated with foundry type.

The *body size* is the distance between the front and back of the piece of type. The common foundry body type sizes are: 6, 8, 10, 12, 18, 24, 36, 48, 60, and 72 point.

The *set size* refers to the width of the piece of foundry type. This will vary with the letters, figures, and points of a font of type.

Type storage

A complete font is distributed and stored in a case. The most common case found in use is the *California Job Case*, Fig. 8-10. the case is made up of many compartments. Each compartment stores a designated letter, figure, point, or space.

The California Job Case is divided into THREE major sections. The section on the right is mainly for the capital letters. They are in alphabetical order except for the "J" and "U." The "J" and the "U" were added to the alphabet; therefore, they appear at the end, Fig. 8-10.

The lower case letters are found in the left and center compartments. These letters are NOT in alphabetical order. The larger compartments contain the letters that are most frequently used. the largest compartment is reserved for the lower case "e," as it is the most used letter. The figures are found at the top of the middle section while the points are found at various locations.

Other types of cases are also available. The *News Case* is one such example. It has one area for the capital letters in the same order as the right section of the California Job Case. The other area in the News Case is called the lower case and is organized like the left and center sections of the California Job Case.

Another type of case holds only capital letters. These can be divided into two to four sections with each section able to store all of the capital letters of a font of type.

Spacing material

The case also stores spacing materials. One type of spacing material is used to separate letters and words. These pieces of type, less than type high, are known as *quads* and *spaces*. They are used to separate words, making indentations, centering lines, and quad out lines, Fig. 8-11.

An *em quad* is the square of any size of type, while the *en quad* is half of the em quad. The en quad is usually used to separate words that are set in all caps.

The 3-em space is the common space used between words when composing type as caps and lower case. It takes approximately three of the three-em spaces to make an em quad. The other spaces are 4 and 5-em. They are approximately 1/4 and 1/5 of the em quad.

Thin spaces are available as copper (1/2-point) and brass (1-point) spaces. Any word or letter spacing materials as large or larger than an en are called quads.

Leads and slugs

The spacing materials used to separate lines are called *leads* and *slugs*. The most common lead thickness is two-points but one-point and three-point are also available. The most common size slug is six-points, but 12-point is also available. An example of a two-point lead and a six-point slug is shown in Fig. 8-12.

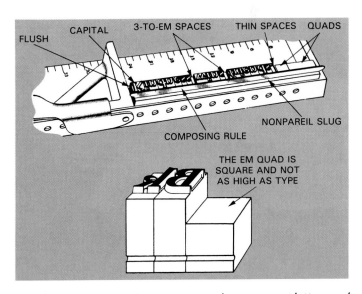

Fig. 8-11. *Quads and spaces are used to space out letters and words of a line of set type.* (American Type Founders)

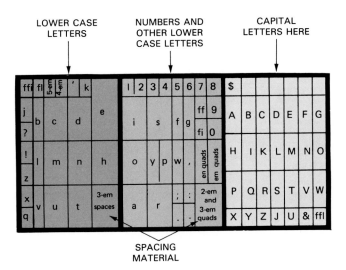

Fig. 8-10. *The California Job Case stores type and necessary word spacing material. Note three sections and locations of letters, numbers, and spacing material.*

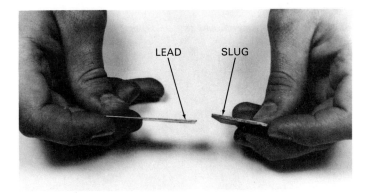

Fig. 8-12. *The slug is thicker than the lead. They are used for line spacing material.*

Furniture

Furniture, made of metal, plastic, or wood, is used to fill areas of space in and around type forms in the chase. Look at Fig. 8-13.

Typically, the widths of furniture available are: 2, 3, 4, 5, 6, 8, and 10 picas. The minimum length is usually 10 picas. The length of 60 picas is also common although furniture can be purchased longer. A typical furniture font is shown in Fig. 8-14.

Wood furniture is used to fill out the area around a form so that the form can be locked up in a chase, Fig. 8-15. The 4-pica width is nearly square, therefore; one side is grooved. The grooved side should be positioned UP to make the spacing correct.

Wood furniture has some give or flexibility. Whenever a close register is necessary, use metal furniture.

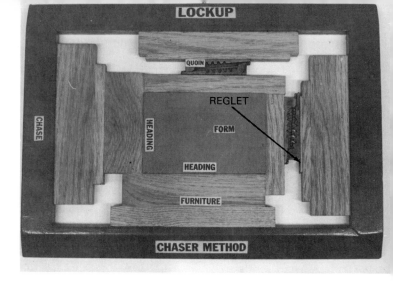

Fig. 8-15. The space around a type form must be filled in with furniture. Note names of parts.

Reglets

Another spacing material, similar to the lead and the slug, is the reglet. *Reglets* are narrow strips of wood used to fill out small spaces. Metal touching metal tends to slip. The reglets, when placed on each side of the quoins, eliminates the possibility of damaging the furniture. The pressure of the quoin tends to indent the wood.

Reglets are available in 6 and 12-point thickness and are stored in a rack shown in Fig. 8-14. The lengths are from 10 picas to 60 picas with increments of one pica.

TYPESETTING PROCESSES

Various methods are used to set type for the relief printing process. The first to be discussed is the hand composition of foundry type. The second will be machine composition using line casting of type and individual character composition. Other chapters explain more modern techniques of making plastic relief plates.

Hand composition

Hand-set composition of metal type is done by a compositor using individual characters. The job case is placed on the *bank* (compositor's work station), Fig. 8-16. The case must be supported by the lip of the bank.

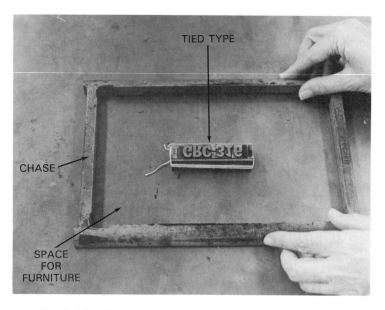

Fig. 8-13. Chase is used to hold type on press when printing. However, furniture is needed to hold type in chase.

Fig. 8-14. Furniture is made of wood or metal and used to fill in or around type forms. This is a typical font of furniture.

Fig. 8-16. The job case is placed on the compositors work station, called a bank.

Each character is picked from the case and placed in a composing stick, Fig. 8-17. The *composing stick* holds the characters and has a movable knee that can be set to the determined line length.

The composing stick is held in the left hand, as in Fig. 8-17. A slug is chosen and placed in the stick. The length corresponds to the line length. The slug is placed upright next to the closed side of the stick.

Type is set from left to right, with the nick of the type toward the open end of the stick. As each piece of type is positioned in the stick, the thumb is used to place pressure on the characters. This eliminates the possibility of spilling the type. Spilled type is known as *pied type*.

The composed type appears upside down. This reverse is necessary so that the characters read correctly when printed on paper.

Approximately two thirds of the stick is filled with type before removing it and placing it in a galley, Fig. 8-18. If the whole stick is used, sometimes the excessive pressure will spring the knee of the stick.

Place the composing stick in a galley, Fig. 8-19. The *galley* is a three-sided metal tray for storing type forms.

The type is removed from the stick by gripping the type head with the thumb and first finger. The second fingers are placed on each end of the form. Push the type from the stick using the thumb. Grip the form firmly.

If properly set, the form should lift together, as shown in Fig. 8-20. Place the form in the lower left, closed end of the galley. The galley should be positioned on the sloping bank, Fig. 8-21.

Continue this process until the whole form is set. Check your work carefully as you set the type and do not "pi" the characters when placing them in the galley.

Tying the form

The form is *tied* to prevent it from being pied or spilled while handling. A cord is wrapped around the form and overlapped on the first wrap. Make sure the form is firmly

Fig. 8-19. A compositor sets lines of type in the stick until approximately two thirds of the stick is used. The composed type is then placed in the galley.

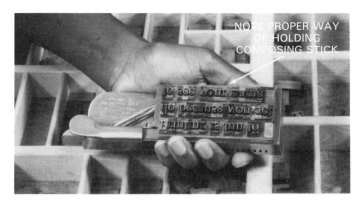

Fig. 8-17. The composing stick is used to hold the type while it is being set by hand.

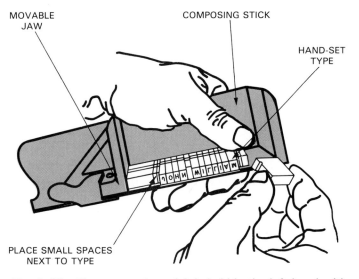

MOVABLE JAW

COMPOSING STICK

HAND-SET TYPE

PLACE SMALL SPACES NEXT TO TYPE

Fig. 8-18. The composing stick is held in the left hand with the thumb holding the last character.

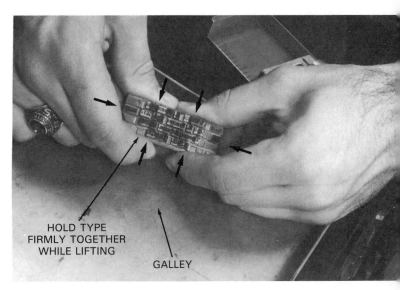

HOLD TYPE FIRMLY TOGETHER WHILE LIFTING

GALLEY

Fig. 8-20. Firmly grip the type form and place it on the galley.

Fig. 8-21. The form has less chance of falling over if placed in the galley on the slanted bank.

wrapped several times. The loose end is wedged underneath the strands of cord, as in Fig. 8-22. This will securely hold the form in place.

Knots are NOT used to lock the cord in place. A make-up rule is an excellent tool to push the cord under the strands of cord, Fig. 8-23. Tied up forms must be handled carefully even though they are securely wrapped.

WRAP STRING AROUND SEVERAL TIMES

Fig. 8-22. The cord is wrapped around form and secured by tucking loose end under strands of cord.

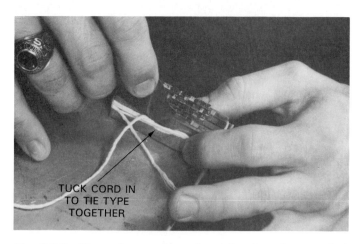

TUCK CORD IN TO TIE TYPE TOGETHER

Fig. 8-23. The make-up rule works well to force loose end of cord underneath wrapped cord.

Proofing and correcting type matter

When the form is complete, a *proof* is taken by making a print of the set type. This proof is used to check for mistakes. If a word is mispelled or spaced improperly, it must be corrected. Proofs are first made for correction. When necessary, proofs are also pulled for the reproduction of the material.

Proofs for correction

Proofs submitted to in-plant personnel are known as *office proofs*. When they are submitted outside of the plant, they are read by the customer or the author. The people that read the proof have the responsibility of seeing that all material is correct. The checked proof is initialed and dated by the proofreader.

If a proof has few errors, it is called a *clean proof*. If a proof has many errors, it is called a *dirty proof*. Dirty proofs often need a *revised proof* (second proof). This means they must be submitted again for approval after making the corrections.

Proofs for reproduction

Proofs for reproduction are generally called *repro proofs*. Repro proofs are used to make plates for letterpress, offset, gravure, and screen process printing.

These proofs must have the quality expected in the final printed product. This means that the proof must have excellent ink coverage and a high quality impression. Refer to Fig. 8-24.

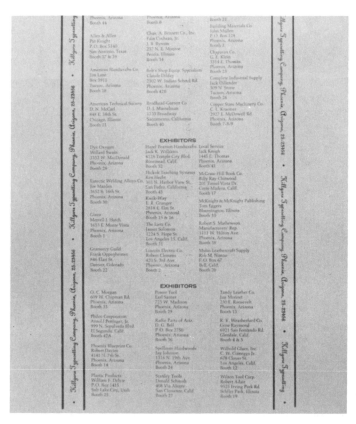

Fig. 8-24. A repro proof must be free of all flaws.

Pulling a proof

To *pull a proof,* the type form remains in the galley and the galley is placed on the bed of a proof press. This is pictured in Fig. 8-25. The open end of the galley should face the cylinder of the proof press. The force of movement then has less chance of shifting the type.

The type must be standing on its feet. The typeface must be parallel with the bed of the press. The proof press must be properly packed around the cylinder. Generally, the *packing* (paper spacing material that determines printing pressure) should be hard and firm. Too much packing will cause a type indentation into the surface of the paper. Too little packing will produce a weak impression. Always follow manufacturer's specifications.

Once the form is ready, it is inked with a brayer (hand roller), Fig. 8-26. The ink plate of the proof press can be the ink source for the brayer. An even ink film on the type form is necessary.

If a correction proof is desired, newsprint is used as the substrate for the proof. A properly prepared proof press will allow for a single sheet of newsprint. The newsprint is placed over the inked type form. Place the paper on the form carefully to eliminate letter slur, Fig. 8-27.

The cylinder of the press moves over the form or the bed moves while the cylinder turns. The pressure causes the ink to be transferred to the sheet.

The sheet is removed and sent to the proofreader. Using proofreader's marks, the proofreader makes the necessary corrections. These marks are explained in Chapter 11.

Some proof presses hold the stock while it receives the images. In most cases, these presses are used for repro proofs since the final copy must be flawless.

The paper used for repro proofs is generally a very smooth matte finished stock. Sometimes, transparent proofs are requested. This type of proof requires a special type of press. A transparent material commonly used for this type of proof is acetate.

The ink on the type must be cleaned off with a safe ink solvent using a rag. The rag must be placed in a special storage container to prevent a fire hazard.

Fig. 8-25. Proof press is used to pull a proof of type form.

Distribution of type

If the form is to be used for relief printing, the next step would be to lock up the form for printing. This procedure is discussed in Chapter 23.

Once the form has been printed, the individual type characters must be distributed. *Distribution* is the process of correctly placing the characters and spacing back into the case or cases.

The type is left in the galley and the string is removed. Grip several lines of type between the thumb and first finger. Press in from the sides with the second finger, Fig. 8-28.

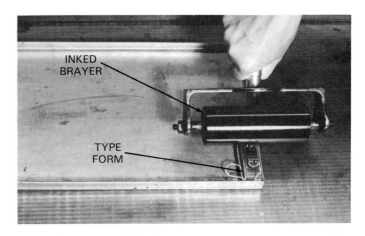

Fig. 8-26. Brayer is used to ink the type form for proof.

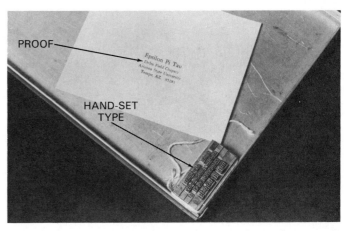

Fig. 8-27. A correction type proof uses newsprint to review image.

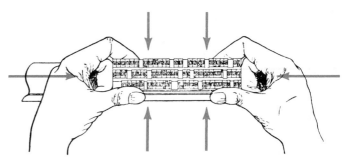

Fig. 8-28. This is the proper way to lift several lines of type when distributing back into case. (American Type Founders)

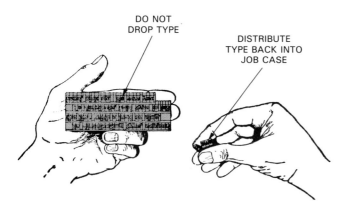

Fig. 8-29. The lines of type are supported by the left hand. Carefully return each letter to correct compartment in case. (American Type Founders)

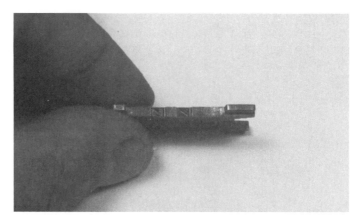

Fig. 8-30. Matrix is made of brass. It has mold area that creates a character when filled with molten metal.

Fig. 8-31. This slug of line material was cast by the Ludlow machine.

The type is transferred to the left hand. The nicks are up with the thumb and second finger holding each end. The first finger supports the lines of type, as in Fig. 8-29.

Several characters are removed from the right end of the first line by the thumb and first finger of the right hand. Each character or space is placed in the proper compartment of the case. Always start on the right side of each line. Continue until all materials have been distributed. Setting and distributing type is a slow process.

Care must always be considered to make sure the right size and style of type is distributed in the right case compartment.

This system of setting type was very prevalent years ago, but today it has become very uncommon. To truly understand typography, hand setting of type is an excellent learning experience. The knowledge gained from the experience can be transferred to today's technology.

Line casting machines

As with hand-set type, hot metal type setting machines are seldom used today. They have become the "iron horses" of the past.

Phototypesetting equipment has replaced metal line casting machines. Two kinds of type-casting machines were found in industry. They are: slug casting and individual type casting machines.

Slug casting machines

The most common type of line casting machine is called the Linotype. A few machines can still be found in the industry, but again phototypesetting has replaced them.

The circulating matrix was a major breakthrough in machine metal composition. Each *matrix*, Fig. 8-30, is used over and over to cast images as a single line of type. A cast line or *slug* is shown in Fig. 8-31. The metal used in a slug is an alloy of lead, tin, and antimony. Small amounts of other metals are also found in the slugs.

The original Linotype or Intertype machines are hand-keyboarded with new lines being cast one after another.

Each matrix is stored in the channel of a magazine of the machine, Fig. 8-32. Whenever the operator strikes a key on

Fig. 8-32. This is an old line casting machine. Magazine at top of machine stores matrices or molds for characters. As keyboard is pressed, correct matrix drops down into position. Molten metal then fills matrix to form relief type in metal.

the keyboard, a matrix is released from the magazine and drops down a guide to the assembly area.

After each word, or whenever a space is needed, a spaceband is dropped between the matrices. The spacebands are wedge-shaped devices that spread open as pressure is applied from the bottom. Once the line length is full, the matrices and spacebands are transferred to the casting position. Molten metal is forced into the die and slug area. The slug is automatically trimmed, forced out of the mold, and positioned in a galley.

> Care must be taken because the slugs are very hot. Do not allow any moisture to come in contact with the molten metal. The metal could explode and result in an injury.

The matrices are removed and transferred to a distribution system which returns each matrix to its proper channel in the magazine. The spacebands are also transferred to the proper location in the machine. The matrices and spacebands are then ready to be used again.

This machine requires daily maintenance and care. It is suggested that further information is found in the operator's manual for the specific machine.

The cast lines have the same height as foundry type which is .918 inch. Once all of the lines are set, the procedure for proofing is the same as that for hand-set type, described earlier. Since all lines are solid, the possibility of "pied type" is greatly reduced. The method of supporting the form in a galley is often magnets or galley locks.

Another line casting machine is called a Ludlow. It can cast small sizes of type but the machine's main purpose is to set larger sizes of type. Each matrix must be distributed and placed in a case designed for storage of the large mats after casting the display line.

A machine that is capable of casting a letter at a time is called the Monotype. This system requires two machines: one is the keyboard, while the other is the metal caster.

The operator energizes the keys on the keyboard which in turn causes the machine to make a punched tape. The punched holes in the paper tape are codes which, when placed in the caster, actuates the casting unit.

Each letter is cast in the designated order to form a line of type. The characters are not attached to each other. The surface or face of each image can be used directly to print images by the relief (letterpress) process.

In some cases, the cast material unit will be used to make a repro proof or another mat to act as an intermediate for another type of image carrier.

MORE INFORMATION

More information on more modern methods of using relief printing can be found in several other textbook chapters. Refer to the index to find information on flexography, mechanical engraving, photomechanical relief plates, rubber stamps, etc.

KNOW THESE TERMS

Relief, Hot type, Letterpress, Flexography, Composition, Compositor, Galley proofs, Reproduction proofs, Wood type, Metal type, Plastic type plates, Rubber type plates, First generation, Second generation, Foundry type, Neck, Counter, Nick, California Job Case, Spacing material, Leads, Slugs, Furniture, Reglets, Hand composition, Pied, Composing stick, Tied, Proof, Dirty proof, Clean proof, Distribution, Line casting machine, Slug casting machine.

REVIEW QUESTIONS—CHAPTER 8

1. What are some other names for relief printing?
2. How does relief type reproduce an image on paper?
3. These are the rough or first drafts of the printing job.
   a. Reproduction proofs.
   b. Galley proofs.
   c. First generation proofs.
   d. Second generation proofs.
4. The relief printing process is very old and is never used in today's graphic communications industry. True or false?
5. _____ _____ is an assortment of individually cast, metal characters used for relief printing.
6. List eight parts of a piece of type.
7. The _____ _____ _____ is the most common method for storing foundry type.
8. The spacing materials used to separate lines are called _____ and _____.
9. What is furniture?
10. How do you hand-set type and pull a proof?

Cold composition refers to numerous ways of setting type other than hot or molten metal composition. Computers have revolutionized composition. This is a workstation used to prepare line graphics for combining with photoset type.   (Screen - USA)

Chapter 9

COLD COMPOSITION

After studying this chapter, you will be able to:
- Identify the techniques associated with cold type composition.
- Explain the role of display and text composition systems.
- Describe the methods common to photolettering techniques.
- Explain the concept of phototext composition.
- List and explain the keyboard functions necessary for the generation of text.
- Identify and explain the input systems associated with photocomposing services.
- List and explain the image store devices commonly used for typesetting systems.
- Explain the output systems common to the industry.
- Summarize the operation of computer-controlled typesetting equipment.

The means by which images are created can be very simple or very complex. Today's technology has created sophisticated systems. High technology, especially relating to electronics and lasers, is becoming more evident at every stage of graphic communications. Although this technology is common in many phases of industry, none is more apparent than in the area of composition.

Cold type composition consists of many techniques and includes everything but hot metal composition. This chapter will include the methods commonly associated with cold type composition.

The method of creating images is called *character* or *image generation.* It is common to all of the printing processes. In cold type composition, generating typefaces or symbols is for the purpose of graphic reproduction by photographic means.

Several methods will be discussed in this chapter. They are: hand techniques, preprinted materials, strike-on composition, photo display, phototypesetting, and electronic composition.

HAND COMPOSITION TECHNIQUES

With some jobs, *hand composition,* using a pen, brush, template, clip art, or transfer letters, is utilized to manually generate the copy. This technique is limited to special situations, such as: display type, advertisements, posters, billboards, letterheads, etc. Hand composition is usually needed when the phototypesetting equipment cannot produce the correct type style or a large enough type size.

Hand lettering

One form of image development is *hand lettering.* The graphic designer uses a pen and/or brush to produce freehand images. These images are often created oversized. This allows for reduction during the photoconversion process. REDUCING the images tends to reduce the visibility of any human error. This also tends to sharpen the images.

Numerous letter forms are available today, but special designs can be difficult to find. The graphic designer then creates specific images for specific needs by hand, Fig. 9-1.

Special types of lettering and drawing pens are available to produce freehand lettering. The styles from several companies are similar. The shapes and tip sizes of the pens vary. The most common styles are: square, round, flat, and oval. Refer to Fig. 9-2.

Fig. 9-1. Hand composition involves using artist or drafting equipment to produce camera-ready images.

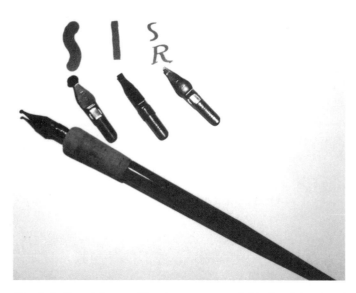

Fig. 9-2. Special pens, like these, are available for doing hand composition.

Templates

Another form of lettering is done with the assistance of a *template* which is a guide of a desired shape or letter. Some of the templates and *scribers* (tool for following template) are for one size and style of characters, Fig. 9-3.

The template and scriber shown in Fig. 9-4 allows a variety of character heights. They also allow for changing the slant of the letter or figure.

The template has the letter style cut into the template material. This directs the pen and allows the pen to deposit ink on the sheet of paper as the pen follows the letter or figure pattern. If they are outline characters, the inside of the character can be filled in with a brush or another type of inking device.

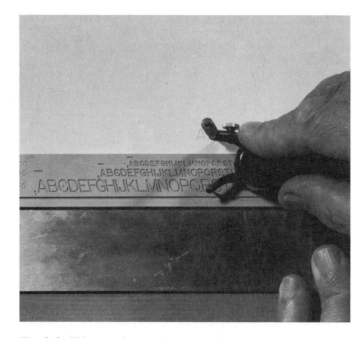

Fig. 9-3. This template and scriber will draw one size and style of type.

Templates are also available that have the letter as a pattern in the template, Fig. 9-5. The inking device follows the contour of the letter, figure, or other symbol.

Whatever type of hand lettering device is used, quality work is very important. Your tools and work area must be kept clean.

The paper also contributes to the quality of the finished image. Paper that leaves a ragged inked edge is NOT satisfactory. Most paper that absorbs ink will leave an uneven edge. A hard, smooth surface is preferable. With hard, smooth paper, the line quality will be sharper.

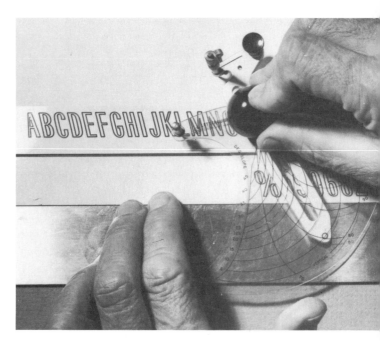

Fig. 9-4. A variety of character sizes and slants can be produced with this type template and scriber.

Fig. 9-5. Some templates have the letter patterns formed in the template.

PREPRINTED ART AND TYPE

Many types of *preprinted materials* or camera ready images are available from many sources. These companies prepare a wide assortment of illustrations to be transferred or pasted-up as camera-ready images.

Clip art

One form of preprinted material is clip art. *Clip art* is preprinted artwork that is to be cut and pasted-up to complete the mechanical. The preprinted artwork is normally cut from the book. See Fig. 9-6.

Clip art material is commonly used during seasonal activities. Thanksgiving and Christmas are typical examples when clip art would be timesaving. Many of the pieces of artwork are very appropriate for advertising layouts. They save the artist from having to draw Christmas trees, wreaths, turkeys, and other common images.

The artwork must be high quality and the density of the image such that it will reproduce properly. The most common form of clip art has black images on a white background.

Some of the clip art is also available as separations for color printing, Fig. 9-7. Four-color clip art can be very efficient if the artwork is appropriate to the situation.

Suppliers make this type of material available and sell it outright or have the service available as a subscriber. The advantage to the subscriber service is that most of the clip art is continually updated and it is free of a copyright.

A typical clip art service catalog is shown in Fig. 9-6. Many occasional types of material are available. Care must be taken so that images will not show major imperfections when enlarged.

Camera-ready art is also available from companies on a one time basis. These prepared images are often printed and organized or grouped as specific themes, Fig. 9-8.

Dry transfer

Dry transfer sheets are a form of pressure sensitive material available to create images. Purchasing transfer sheets of letters and/or figures is an inexpensive way of producing professional, camera-ready copy. Each sheet

Fig. 9-8. Special themes for preprinted material are available.

Fig. 9-6. These clip art books contain images that can be used quickly and efficiently. They save the time normally taken to hand draw the images.

Fig. 9-7. This is an example of clip art for multicolor printing. Each image is a color separation and can be used to make a plate for a primary color. Note how intended color for each image is printed near the border of the picture.

consists of a complete alphabet with a scheme of letters for each style. The most commonly used letters (A, O, E, etc.) usually have more characters per sheet than less used letters (X, Y, Z, etc.). The sizes and styles of type available are numerous. See Fig. 9-9.

Each letter is placed in position and *burnished* (rubbed) down, as shown in Fig. 9-10. *Burnishing* is accomplished with a smooth wood, plastic, or metal tool with a round tip. When properly burnished, the dry transfer image will adhere to the base sheet.

Care must be taken to place each image in exact position. The image can be removed if a mistake is made, but the process is slow.

Transfer sheets are generally used for large, display type. The sheet that holds the type is usually a 10 x 14 inch base sheet. The base is made of transparent or translucent material.

Proper storage and handling of the sheets is required because folding or scratching could ruin the transfer images. Close inspection is necessary to detect a crack or break in the images. Most of these materials have a shelf life. The adhesive can dry out and not stick.

The images on the transfer sheets are available in black or white. The most common type is the black transfer image.

Dry transfer sheets are also available to create borders and other decorative artwork. This is a very inexpensive way when a limited number of camera-ready images are needed of a decorative nature. Look at Fig. 9-11.

It is also possible for you to make your own rub off letters using a special image transfer system. A negative is needed of the desired alphabet or any other image to be transferred. The negative is then placed in contact with the transfer material and exposed to ultraviolet light.

After exposure, the material is developed and rinsed with cool water (around 20 °C), dried, and then transferred. Images should not be exposed to light for an extended period of time. Therefore, the transfer material should be stored with a protective liner in place. Once the image is exposed, developed, and transferred, it is not affected by light.

Fig. 9-9. These are examples of dry transfer letters. They are available in many styles and sizes of type. They will produce high quality words for special situations.

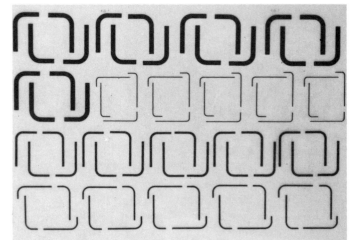

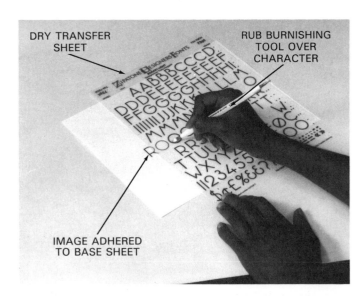

Fig. 9-10. To use dry transfer letters, position the letter carefully. Then, burnish or rub the letter to adhere it to the base sheet.

Fig. 9-11. This is an example of borders and arrows in dry transfer. They save time during layout and produce quality images.

Other pressure sensitive materials have an adhesive back. The images are removed from the carrier. Once removed from the plastic or other type base sheet, the image is very carefully positioned on the mechanical, Fig. 9-12.

Shading material is also available, Fig. 9-13. The material is positioned and cut. This allows for the removal of the unwanted areas. The desired surface is rubbed or rolled to assure that it is properly adhered.

Fig. 9-14. This is an example of an older strike-on system. It works like a typewriter to produce copy for reproduction.

A limitation with the strike-on system is that the typefaces are only in small text sizes. The smallest is 6-point generally, while the largest type is usually only 12-point. If a larger type size is needed, it is difficult to change type size. The copy must be enlarged photographically using a process camera. This is time consuming and costly. It can also reduce the sharpness of the characters.

When using a strike-on direct impression unit, the substrate which receives the image must be smooth—typically high quality, white stock with a matte finish.

The ribbon is generally a one-time, plastic-base type that will give a sharp, well defined image. Cleanliness must always be considered as an essential element of copy presentation.

Most strike-on systems are *proportionally spaced* which means the characters have different widths or horizontal sizes. For example, a letter "i" would not take up as much space as the capital letter "B" in a word. Proportional spacing sets the characters the correct distance apart depending upon the shape of the letters. This increases the complexity of the machine considerably, especially since they are primarily mechanical. Most typewriters are NOT proportionally spaced.

The *semiautomatic strike-on system* requires that the operator set the line to a length within the justification range. Once it is set, the word spacing can be determined to make the line justified. The second typing would be justified by the machine.

The *automatic strike-on system* requires the operator to type the copy only once. The typing unit places the copy on magnetic tape. The operator need not be concerned with the style of type, the correct line spacing, line length, or the justification mode.

The tape is fed into a second unit which automatically types the second copy. The specifications are established by the operator and the machine types according to the commands. An automatic strike-on system is shown in Fig. 9-14.

Fig. 9-12. Here artist is positioning pressure sensitive image.

Fig. 9-13. Shading material can be cut to the desired shape.

STRIKE-ON COMPOSITION

The simplest piece of equipment which demonstrates the concept of *strike-on composition* is the typewriter. It is a direct impression method of placing an image on paper. The letter or image strikes the paper. The image is produced on the paper by placing a ribbon between the image and the stock. The impact deposits the ribbon material and creates camera-ready copy. See Fig. 9-14.

Two types of magnetic tapes are in use; one is the reel to reel and the other is the cassette. The reel to reel is not a system commonly used for phototypesetting but it is used to store information. Parts lists and directories are common examples. Searching for information on the tapes is very rapid.

Instead of magnetic tape, some older systems use a paper tape. The *paper tape* uses a series of holes to store information for the typesetter, Fig. 9-15. When the copy is typed, a *paper punch* mechanism forces holes in the ribbon of paper forming a code that represents the copy, Fig. 9-16. The punched tape can then be fed through a *reader* that translates the codes to allow the machine to produce strike-on copy.

Fig. 9-15. Paper tape was once used to store typeset data. It has been replaced by magnetic disks.

Fig. 9-16. Punch would force holes in paper tape to form code representing typeset material. Tape could then be fed through reader to operate typesetting equipment.

The width of paper tape varies but most range from 3/4 of an inch to one inch. The specific tape widths are identified by levels. They are listed as six, seven, and eight levels. This figure represents the number of punched holes that can be made across the tape. A 6-level tape would have a maximum of six holes punched across the tape. The six level tape is the old TTS (Teletypesetting) code. Many newspapers used to use this code as a base.

The six level tape has the possibility of 64 variations. If an eight level tape were used, the variations would jump from 64 to 256 variations.

The eight level tape was used as a standard computer tape. Whenever phototypesetters or other component systems use a tape to drive the system, it is important that the tape be compatible with all of the components.

Very few facilities still have strike-on or paper tape systems. They have been replaced by more modern electronic systems.

PHOTOCOMPOSITION

Photocomposition is the generation of type using photographic paper or film exposed to light. This system of generating copy is changing rapidly.

Several methods of photographically composing images are found in the graphic communications industry. The first method is concerned with the equipment that generates large, display type. The second is the equipment used to set body copy or text and is a combination of the two methods.

Photo display composition

Various kinds of photo display units are available today. Some of the units are very simple while others are very complex. The simplest device uses the contact method.

Contact method means that a negative or positive are in direct contact with the photographic paper and a light source. They are exposed to light for a designated period of time. The light strikes the light sensitive paper through the clear area of the film. The image is processed and the results are representative of quality images, photographically prepared. This method, since it is contact, produces an image size equal to the master negative or positive.

Strip printer

One of the least expensive devices is the strip printer. Each image must be positioned by hand. The light source is over the paper and the negative, Fig. 9-17.

The strip printer's film strip has one font and size of type on each strip. The font is moved through the composing unit and photographed one image at a time. The results are satisfactory. This system could be used where volume is not a prime consideration.

The location of the strip printing machine must be in subdued light. Sources of unwanted light might create exposure problems.

Several more machines, with the same concept are available, Fig. 9-18. Refinements have gradually allowed for faster machine operation. The light sensitive stock is usual-

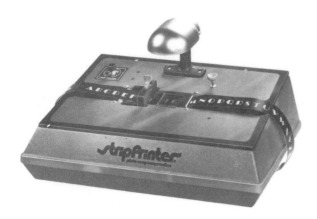

Fig. 9-17. A strip printer is a typical example of the contact method of display composition. Film strip is shifted to position the correct letter over opening. When light is activated, image is burned on film or photopaper inside machine. Next letter could then be positioned and burned.

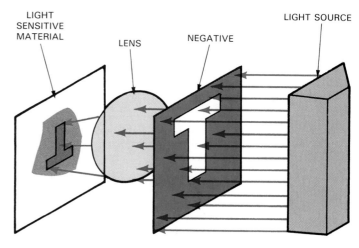

Fig. 9-19. This shows basic principle of projection photocomposition. Light is projected through transparent image and onto light-sensitive material.

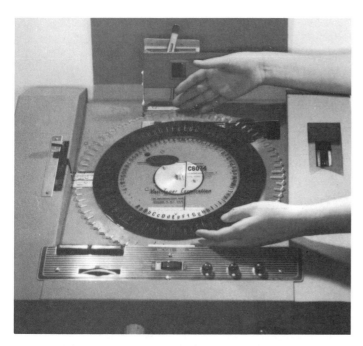

Fig. 9-18. This machine uses a disk to hold character images. Disk is turned until correct letter is positioned. Then, machine is activated to expose letter onto film or photopaper.

ly 35 mm wide. It is processed automatically. The exposure area in the machine is considered to be the "darkroom" of the composer. Do not lift the hinged door in the back as this will allow the light to expose the photographic paper.

The developing or processing chemicals may only be stored for a short period of time. When exhausted, dump the chemicals in a container designed for that purpose. Wash the processing unit with cold water regularly. Follow the manufacturer's instructions.

Phototypositor

Another display type composing machine is the *phototypositor,* Fig. 9-19. The phototypositor also uses a filmstrip. Some of these machines have much more versatility than

the disk machines because they can create images of different sizes. Some, with special lenses, can distort, condense, extend, and create other unusual shapes.

Again, continuously fed, light sensitive photopaper is the most common form of image base. If operated properly, the images are high quality and can be used for various image preparation techniques.

The phototypositor is a machine sometimes found in a graphic design type of studio. Generally, these machines are not high-volume units, and their use is becoming very limited.

Projection method

The *projection method* still has a film strip or disk, but the light source passes through the master, through a LENS, and onto the photographic paper. The projection method allows for the enlargement of the type font to designated sizes. The sizes vary with the model of the equipment.

The typical steps, to set a given number of words, without any special composing requirements, are as follows:
1. Select style and size of type.
2. Make sure cassette (film enclosure) is in place.
3. Turn on machine.
4. Type; observe as displayed.
5. Send; copy is now being positioned on 35mm photographic paper.
6. End take; Move photographic paper after exposure so that the last letter or word is not cut off.
7. Cut photographic paper.
8. Remove *cassette* (enclosure for film).
9. Process film.

The processed film should be dense with images of excellent quality. Inspect the images closely for problems.

Combination composing equipment

Most of today's equipment is capable of composing display lines as well as text. The capabilities of machines vary greatly. For this reason, it is imperative that a close review of objectives and outcomes be clearly identified before purchasing equipment.

PHOTOTEXT COMPOSITION (PHOTOTYPESETTING)

Phototext composition or *phototypesetting* also uses a light sensitive paper or film and a light source to set copy. Also termed *computerized typesetting,* it is a widely used method of setting text.

There are several variations of phototypesetting equipment. Many shine a light through a permanent character image (disk, strip, drum, or matrix image) to expose the image on the photopaper or film. Others use a CRT (cathode ray tube) or a *laser* (intense light beam) to burn the image into the photographic paper or film.

The number of photocomposing machines has increased very rapidly during the last few years. Choosing the right system has become complicated. Many of the manufacturers have an excellent product that will fit a variety of needs. Technological changes have added typesetting capabilities that are needed by some composing departments.

A concern of many graphic communications departments should be adaptability. When equipment can be expanded or updated with technical advances, it will decrease equipment obsolescence and save revenue.

Phototypesetting equipment is changing rapidly. To keep informed, you should read journals, attend workshops, as well as seek information from specific vendors.

Components of phototypesetting equipment

Although specific designs vary, there are several components typical to modern phototypesetting equipment. Illustrated in Fig. 9-20, these parts include:
1. KEYBOARD (typewriter style key input with extra keys for programming in specifications and altering copy).
2. VIDEO DISPLAY SCREEN (picture tube or monitor for showing words that have been keystroked and also other copy information).
3. COMPUTER CONTROL UNIT (computer "brain" that temporarily stores data from keypad; also feeds data to, and controls disk drive, proof printer, and image generator).
4. DISK DRIVE (magnetically deposits data on disks for storing typeset material), Fig. 9-20.
5. PROOF PRINTER (low quality printer for making hard copy printouts for proofreading typeset material).
6. IMAGE GENERATOR (device that uses light source to deposit copy on photographic paper or film).
7. FILM CASSETTE (enclosed box or "portable darkroom" that holds photopaper or film before being processed in image generator or developer).
8. DEVELOPER (mechanism for moving photographic paper or film through chemicals that develop copy image and make image permanent).
9. OPTICAL CHARACTER READER (sometimes used to convert typewriter copy into computer data, eliminates manual keystroking of copy by typesetter).

Computer typesetting terminology

There are many unique terms that pertain to the operation of computerized phototypesetting equipment. It is important that you understand these commonly used terms. Several of these include:

On-line. When a piece of computerized equipment is *on-line,* it can communicate directly with other units or pieces of equipment without human assistance.

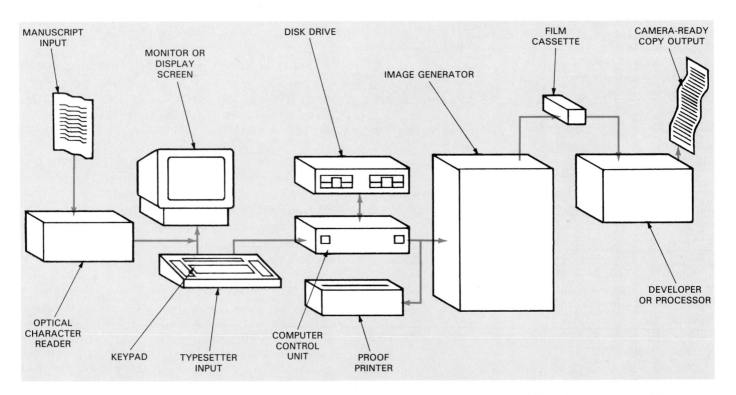

Fig. 9-20. Study the basic parts of a typical phototypesetting station. Input is on left and output is on right.

Off-line. A piece of computerized equipment which cannot communicate directly with another is considered to be *off-line.*

Input system. A device which provides information to a machine or computer to make it perform is called an *input system.*

Output system. The end product produced by a machine or a system (galley for instance) is accomplished by the *output system.*

Storage system. Any device capable of storing computer data that can be called back when needed is a *storage system.*

Transfer system. By instructions, the switch control or *transfer system* can go from one mode to another. It also has the ability to write, copy, exchange, record, or store data.

Developing system. The process of changing a latent image on various substrates to a visible image is the *developing system,* also called *processor.*

Edit mode. The *edit mode* is for changing or rearranging text material, which may include many features such as: change, merge, insert, delete, etc.

Compose mode. The process of setting display and text material is done in the *compose mode.*

Buffer. A computer compensating device which provides temporary storage when differences in data handling rates occur is called a *buffer.*

Analog signals. *Analog signals* represent a variable (voltage for example) which has a continuous or gradual range of numeric quantities used by a computer.

Digital signals. *Digital signals* are discrete integral numbers or on/off conditions to represent quantities that occur in computer data.

File management. *File management* is a unit of stored and retrieved data; keeping track of the file locations as well as the files that are not used.

Hyphenation routine. *Hyphenation routine* is a determination of the correct breaking points for words at the end of a line. In this routine, the computer can search for words in a dictionary, look for suffixes and prefixes, and scan for other probabilities for automatic hyphenation of words.

Direct input. An example of *direct input* is when the keyboard inputs the information directly to the image unit for output. The keyboard cannot stand alone.

Floppy disk. A *floppy disk,* mentioned briefly, is a very thin flexible magnetic disk used to store computer data and programs. It is enclosed in a protective envelope.

Hard disk. A *hard disk* is capable of storing a greater amount of computer data than a floppy disk. It is permanently housed in its drive unit.

Binary system. The *binary system* is the "language" of a computer and has two alternatives such as yes and no or on-off. As a numbering system, it has two as its base and uses only zero and one.

Front end. The *front end* is the information handling portion of any machine or system.

Control signal. The *control signal* regulates function of the machine. If a flag (code) appears, this denotes that a control signal follows.

Software. The programs on disks that direct the computer to perform designated functions are called *software.*

Hardware. The mechanical and electronic devices that make up the machine are termed *hardware.*

Cathode ray tube (CRT). An electronic tube that shows images on the flat end of the tube is called a *cathode ray tube, CRT, monitor,* or *visual display screen.*

Fiber optics. When a small diameter strand or thread-like glass or plastic is used to transmit lights, it is called *fiber optics.*

Laser. The letters *"LASER"* stands for Light Amplification by Stimulated Emission of Radiation. A very narrow beam of monochromatic, coherent light is produced.

Cursor. The *cursor* is a spot of light on the screen of the terminal or CRT which indicates where the next entry will take place.

Scrolling. *Scrolling* involves moving the lines on the display screen forward (upward) or backward (down).

Block. Words considered to be a unit and are stored as a group or page of a book could be considered to be a *block.*

Mouse. A *mouse* is a moveable handset used to quickly locate and/or reposition material on the screen.

Temporary memory. *Temporary memory* usually refers to the short term memory produced by the electronic or integrated circuits in the computer itself. This data is lost when the system is turned off.

Permanent memory. *Permanent memory* normally refers to data placed on disk storage so that data can be kept for long periods of time.

File. A *file* is temporary or permanent memory in the computer listed under a designated name.

Page. A *page* is a numbered portion or section of a file.

There are many other terms that relate to computerized type. Refer to the equipment manual for help as needed.

Computer binary code

The *binary code* is a computer-related numbering system using zero and one as its only digits or numbers. It is the system used to allow computers to store and utilize data. A basic understanding of the binary numbering system is helpful if you plan to work around modern graphic communications equipment.

A *bit* is one binary number, either a zero or a one. It is the basic or smallest piece of data used by the computer.

A *byte* is a group of eight adjacent bits and it used to store or transfer computer data. The eight bits, depending upon their sequence and content, control the information (character or number) in the computer data.

The computer's binary code system provides two possible codes—a yes (voltage pulse) or a no (no voltage pulse). If we substitute a magnetic charge on a floppy disk to mean a yes (voltage charge) and the lack of a charge to mean a no, we have the potential for storing information in a computer.

A complex system of thousands of yes or no replies can be produced. In this way, a computer can store and manipulate characters, words, sentences, and other data in binary code.

Input systems (keyboards)

The keyboard is the most common type of input device for putting information into the typesetting device, Fig. 9-21. The typical typewriter keyboard is the most common layout and it is known as the *"qwerty" keyboard*. The name comes from the top row of alphabet keys which spell "qwerty." See Fig. 9-22.

Special keyboards are available for specialized jobs but most input systems will have typewriter style keys and extra function keys. This is also true of direct entry, disk, or tape input systems. The keyboards can be directly attached to the composing unit or can be a separate unit from the other parts of the machine, Fig. 9-23.

Fig. 9-24 shows an older style phototypesetting station. Note that the keyboard is an integral part of the machine. Modern systems have a separate keyboard and a full monitor. This system only shows a few characters at a time which makes copy changes more difficult. Also note the depth of copy display for copyfitting.

Fig. 9-22. Typewriter keyboard is often nicknamed "qwerty" keyboard because letters spell qwerty. This is the most common type of keyboard.

Fig. 9-23. Modern typesetting equipment has separate keyboard and a full screen for viewing input. Copy can be placed adjacent to screen for easy eye movement from copy to video screen.

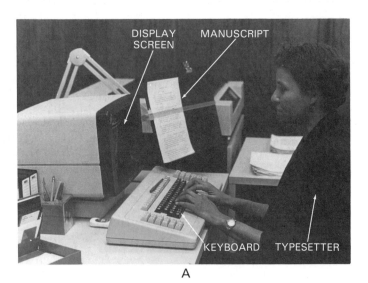

A

B

Fig. 9-21. A—Typesetter is keystroking manuscript using keyboard. B—Note basic components for inputing data into phototype equipment.

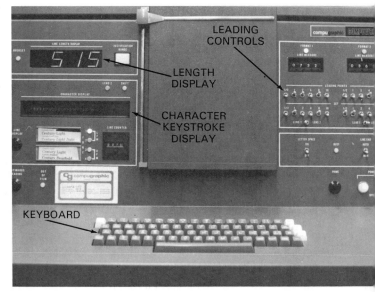

Fig. 9-24. This is an older direct input system. It does not have full video screen and keyboard is part of housing.

Function keys

Function keys, also called *control keys,* are additional keys used by the typesetter to program in data concerning the text material and file management. Function keys are found at the top or sides of the typical keyboard. The qwerty keyboard alone cannot input enough data so the computer can do typesetting type tasks.

Standardization has not taken place as far as function key designations. The basic function or purpose may be the same but the location and symbol might vary from one manufacturer to another. A typical keyboard is found in Fig. 9-25.

There are sometimes two function keypads: editing keypad and file keypad.

Editing keypad

The *editing keypad,* found on some systems, is for doing editorial tasks: moving cursor, scrolling up or down copy, deleting copy within the *opened* (current) file. Some of the more commonly used editing keys are:

1. The *define key* is used with block key to define blocks of copy for manipulation, Fig. 9-26.
2. *Delete keys* can be used in conjunction with the cursor to drop letters, words, lines, and blocks of copy.
3. *Insert key,* the opposite of delete, is for placing copy into a defined location, Fig. 9-26.
4. *Scroll keys* are for moving copy up or down on screen. *Scroll up* would move copy toward end of page. *Scroll down* would move copy toward beginning or start of page.
5. The *arrow keys* move the cursor in the direction of the arrow head. Pressing a key once will move cursor one letter space. Holding an arrow key will make cursor move constantly in direction of the arrow. See Fig. 9-26.
6. The *limit key* can be used in conjunction with cursor movement and scroll keys to rapidly jump to the limit of the cursor direction.

7. The *clear memory key* will erase data in short term storage. This key would be used after placing data in permanent disk storage, Fig. 9-26.
8. An *abort key* can be provided to cancel various system commands and functions. It removes commands from screen and returns data to memory.

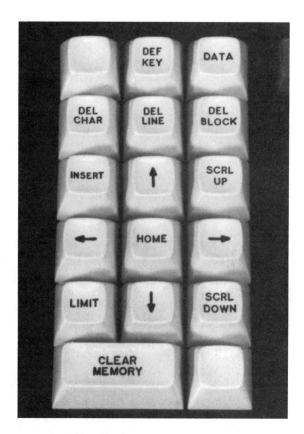

Fig. 9-26. This is a typical editing keypad. It is used by typesetter to move cursor, change wording, and do other kinds of editorial functions. Study key names.

Fig. 9-25. This is a keyboard for an electronic imaging system. Note extra keys.

File keypad

The *file keypad* used on some systems, controls major functions: moving files, loading fonts, operating image generator and disk drive, etc. Although specific keys vary with the system, you should have a general understanding of typical file management keys.

1. The *system command key* is used to load fonts, unload fonts, and other similar tasks, Fig. 9-27.
2. The *queue key* works with the file names and function keys to transfer data to the proof printer, image generator, etc.
3. The *display key* is to show disk index data, fonts, and queues.
4. The *insert key* transfers data from screen memory to the addressed file and page.
5. The *delete key* removes addressed page of open file from disk and screen memory, Fig. 9-27.
6. The *next page key* moves to the following page in the addressed file.
7. The *replace page key* sends all data in screen memory to disk memory and replaces existing disk memory. Next page is then displayed on screen.
8. The *previous page key* calls the preceding page to the screen.
9. The *call page key* opens the file and calls first page to screen, Fig. 9-27.
10. The *merge key* is used to load a page from disk to the screen and insert it at cursor location.
11. The *secondary file key* communicates with another file to transfer page to screen. It can be used to send page or block from current file to another file.
12. The *new file key* is to program in new file on disk.
13. The *append key* inserts data before cursor to end of current file.
14. The *close file key* is for ending the current file to open another file.
15. The *compose key* makes system scan page to update parameters.
16. The *execute key* signifys completion of file management and other functions.

Again, remember that these are typical examples of the keys found on some computer typesetting equipment. Key names can vary and so can their exact function. Always refer to the equipment manual for exact details.

Direct input

Direct input devices are numerous in terms of available models. The least complex machines are the table type variety. They have limited text composition capabilities.

The *direct input system* takes the image directly from the keyboard to the system that places the image on photographic paper or film. A typical direct input device is shown in Fig. 9-24. The keyboard is an integral part of this machine.

Video display screen

The *video display screen* is a television-type picture tube for showing copy and other related information. Also called a *monitor,* CRT (cathode ray tube), etc., it allows the typesetter to view copy as it is set and to verify the parameters programmed into the computer.

The term video display screen should NOT be confused with video display terminal. The *video display terminal* (VDT) includes the video display screen, the keyboard, and the disk drive. These components are needed by the typesetter to operate the system, Fig. 9-28.

The terminal screen is usually a 12 inch CRT that displays between 15 and 25 lines of data. Some of these lines may be status lines for giving type size, line length, leading, font, etc. The remaining lines are for showing typeset copy.

The screen can have approximately 64 characters maximum per line and 256 alphanumeric characters or function symbols for display. *Alphanumeric* means letters and numbers.

The screen or CRT operates on the principle shown in Fig. 9-29. An electron gun directs a beam of light across and

Fig. 9-27. This is a typical file management keypad. It is for moving files into disk storage, etc.

Fig. 9-28. The typesetter uses a video display terminal to operate the typesetting system. (Covalent Systems)

against the back of the screen. The beam makes a phosphor coating on the surface of the screen glow. This produces a white image wherever the electron beam scans and strikes the picture tube. The electronic circuitry in the typesetting equipment directs the electron gun to scan across the screen 60 times per second. This is fast enough to produce images of letters and numbers on the screen.

On older systems, the specific typeface or font programmed into the system is not shown on the screen. It displays only a standard display face. Only when the image generator and processor (developer) produces the galley will the actual font and type size be shown.

The *cursor* on the screen shows the typesetter where the next insertion or modification of copy will take place. As the typesetters read the manuscript at eye level, the material can be quickly typed into the machine.

The VDT has excellent features from the standpoint of flexibility, editing, and verification. It is one of the most rapid and accurate methods of setting copy.

When considering an electronic system, the characteristics of the equipment must be determined. Some of the more important characteristics are: character set, pi characters, type styles, point size capability, line length, leading, copy make-up, type of copy, specification standards, serviceability, keyboarding speed, correction capabilities, and verification.

Control unit (computer)

The *control unit* or *computer* for modern phototypesetting equipment acts as the "brain" to monitor inputs and control outputs. Refer to Fig. 9-30.

As the typesetter inputs data, the computer (control unit) converts the keyboard signals into electrical signals. The complex electronic circuits in the computer analyze and store this electrical-electronic data. Preprogrammed circuits can then produce outputs to correspond to the typed inputs.

After the short term memory is full or when the copy is finished being set, the small control keypad can be used to

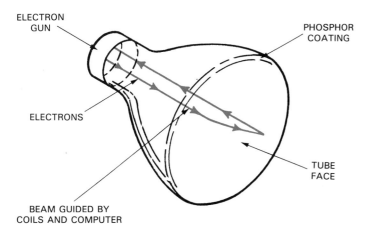

Fig. 9-29. Video display screen is a cathode ray tube. Electron gun directs beam of light against face of screen. Phosphor coating on screen glows when struck by beam. Computer circuitry makes electron beam scan across screen so fast that we see glowing, stationary images.

Fig. 9-30. Control unit or computer for phototypesetting equipment directs data through system. It can direct data to proof printer for hard copy output, to disk drive for permanent storage, or to image generator for camera-ready copy.

send the data into long term memory by activating the disk drive. Or, the copy data could be sent to the proof printer for a hard copy to do proofreading.

After proofing, the typesetter can correct any mistakes or include any modifications in text. The copy is then ready for output. The control unit is then used, in conjunction with the control keypad, to send the copy data to the image generator.

Magnetic disk storage

Magnetic disk storage refers to placing computer digital signals on a "floppy" or "hard" disk. The electrical signals from the system controller are converted into magnetized areas on the disk. Look at Fig. 9-31.

Most systems use magnetic or disk storage to supplement temporary storage provided by the computer circuitry. Either floppy or hard disks can be used to *"boot up"* (turn on and prepare computer) or *"run"* (operate) the program.

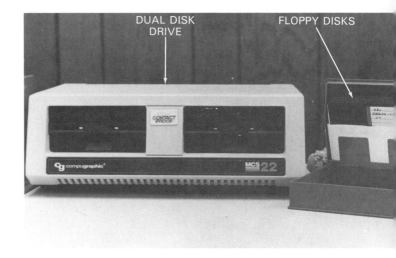

Fig. 9-32. This is a dual disk drive, as commonly used with phototypesetting equipment. Note floppy disks in storage box on right.

Fig. 9-31. Magnetic disks for data storage, in the common 5 1/4 inch and 3 1/2 inch sizes. The smaller disk, even though it has a rigid shell, is still commonly referred to as a ''floppy disk.''

Disk drive

The *disk drive* holds and writes to or reads from the magnetic disks, Fig. 9-32. The floppy disk is inserted into the front slot on the disk drive. When being loaded, electrical signals from the controller are fed into the disk drive. The disk drive then spins the disk and a magnetic head (similar to a record-play head in a cassette recording tape deck) magnetizes (writes) tiny areas on the disk as it spins past the head. The magnetized areas correspond to the computer data input and typeset material, and can be later read.

The disk drive is sometimes in the same housing as the display screen. This varies with the manufacturer.

A *single disk drive* can only hold and operate one disk at a time. It is seldom used with typesetting equipment but is often found in home computers or word processors.

A *dual disk drive* can hold and operate two magnetic disks simultaneously. This allows two typesetters to work off the same drive and controller. A dual disk drive also allows you to copy another floppy disk. It will also let the typesetter input copy onto one disk while the other disk is outputting to the proof printer or the image generator.

Floppy disks

A *floppy disk* is a thin plastic circle coated with a magnetic material. The read/write (magnetic) heads in the disk drive arrange the magnetic charge on the disk to store data. The amount of data that can be stored on a floppy disk has risen dramatically, up to 2 million bytes of information. See Fig. 9-31.

Today, common disk sizes are 5 1/4 inch and 3 1/2 inch. Eight inch disks were once used, but are now almost phased out. Both the 8 inch and 5 1/4 inch disks have a square protective cover or jacket made of a thin, flexible plastic. The 3 1/2 inch disk has a square cover of rigid plastic, which provides better protection. There are two openings in the protective covers: a center hole or hub and a slit that exposes the magnetic coating of the disk. The hub is used by the disk drive to spin the disk at high speed inside the protective jacket. The slit gives the disk drive's head access to the disk to read or write informatiton. On 8 inch and 5 1/4 inch disks, this slit is always open. The 3 1/2 inch disk has a spring-loaded slide that covers the slit when the disk is out of the drive.

The disk surface contains magnetic tracks that hold the data (typeset material) encoded as *files*. Since files vary in length (one may contain a single typewritten page, another an entire chapter of a book), the number of files that will fit on a disk will also vary. Each file has a *filename* that is used to "call it up" for changes or processing.

The magnetic disk is relatively low in cost, takes up little storage space, and allows rapid access to data. It permits the operator to easily correct or add to the contents of any file. The major drawback is lack of complete standardization—disks used in one system are not always capable of being used in a different system.

Hard disk drive

The *hard disk drive* operates on the same principle as the floppy disk, but can hold more data. It contains several rigid aluminum disks coated with a magnetic material. Tracks are packed more densely on a hard disk than a floppy, so they can hold much more information. A hard disk will also store and recall data much faster than a floppy disk.

The hard disk drive is a single enclosed unit. The rigid aluminum disks are permanently installed; they cannot be removed from the drive like a floppy disk can from its drive. Hard disk drives are available in a large number of different capacities, holding a hundred times or more the amount of data that can be stored on a floppy disk.

Disk data

There are three common types of data or uses for magnetic disks. They can be used for programming the system, for programming in the font, or for file storage.

For example, a *programming disk* is normally installed first to "boot up" the system. This readies the computer circuits to handle the typeset material properly.

The *font disk* is then installed to determine the typeface for the job. Several different fonts can be included on one floppy disk. See Fig. 9-33.

The *file disk* is installed next to serve as long term storage of data. When the computer's short term memory circuitry is full, the controller can transfer this temporary data into the disk drive. It can then be permanently stored on the disk even if power to the system is shut off or the disk is removed from its drive.

Fig. 9-33. Operator is "booting up" system by inserting disk. This will ready system for image input.

Proofing programs

Many *proofing programs* are available today to detect errors in spelling, punctuation, hyphenation, and style. Each program can do very specific tasks, such as detecting incorrect, extra, or missing punctuation; misspelled words, incorrect hyphenation or positioning of a hyphen, incorrect abbreviations, missing capitalization at sentence beginning (arizona), incorrect capitalization at sentence beginning (ARizona), and doubled words. This is a small sample of what proofing programs can do to increase typesetting efficiency.

Proof printer

The *proof printer* will output a rough copy for checking the typeset material. The printer is often a low quality image, dot matrix printer, like in Fig. 9-34A.

The printer helps save money because it prints on inexpensive paper and not expensive photographic paper or film. When changes are made, they can be altered on the screen and not on the expensive galley sheet material.

The proof printer can be considered as part of the output system. However, since its copy is NOT camera-ready, most experts agree the galleys, that are reproduction quality, provide the output.

OUTPUT SYSTEM

The *output system* for phototypesetting equipment is completed by the image generator and the processor. They ready the copy for layout, platemaking, and reproduction on a press.

Image generator (phototype machine)

The *image generator,* also termed *phototype machine,* uses a light source to expose the copy onto photopaper or

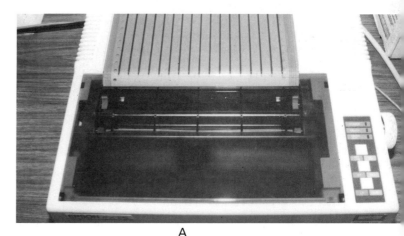

A

B

Fig. 9-34. Proof printers. A—A dot matrix printer for quick, low-quality images printed on inexpensive paper. B—A digital proofer provides better quality, more precise proofs. (Screen-USA)

film. Several different methods can be used to "burn" the image onto the paper or film. One type of image generator is shown in Fig. 9-35.

Fig. 9-36 shows the various principles used by an image generator. Some use a character set with negative shapes for each character. Others use a CRT or a laser, without a character set, to precisely shape each character.

Master character set is the name given to the original type images used to reproduce copy, Fig. 9-37. The character set will be a specific font and can be enlarged, reduced, expanded, or condensed using the keyboard input. The character set moves the correct letter into position to form words typeset at the keypad. See Fig. 9-37A.

The *laser image generator* is a comparatively new process that is becoming very common. A computer operates the laser and directs the light beam to form the letters of the alphabet, numbers, etc. The laser beam is so small, and the computer so accurate, that very precise characters are formed rapidly. Refer to Fig. 9-37B.

The CRT (cathode ray tube) is another method of forming type, Fig. 9-37C. The CRT, which is like a television picture tube, forms the letters of the copy. The light from the tube burns the image into the photographic paper or film.

Unlike the character set method, each letter is scanned and formed by a pulsing light. The computer controls the movement and pulsing of the light source to precisely form the shape of each letter. This is shown in Fig. 9-38.

The images made by this machine are placed on photographic film or paper in positive form. It is possible, when using film, to expose the film through the back. This allows for very accurate emulsion-to-emulsion exposure. Of the two, photographic paper is the most used, however.

The latest image generator models have the capability of setting wrong-reading images on the screen. The type of phototypesetting film for various operations must be carefully checked.

PHOTOTYPESETTING PAPER

Phototypesetting paper turns black when exposed to light and then processed or developed. The grades of paper vary with the manufacturer. Two types are prevelant: stabilization paper and resin-coated paper.

Photopaper costs less than film and is more practical for most printing jobs. The paper is very hard and smooth but you can still write or mark on it with a pencil or pen. This allows for easy final correction before making the printing plates.

Stabilization paper

Stabilization photopaper is the least expensive. It is a high contrast, orthochromatic (reacts to all light colors but red), rapid, projection-speed paper. The base is made of fiber and is considered to be lightweight. The surface brightness will vary with the manufacturer. See Fig. 9-39.

The specific needs of the job will determine proper paper selection. Machines that use a xenon flash or CRT exposure find the paper very acceptable. The emulsion consists of silver halides and a developing agent.

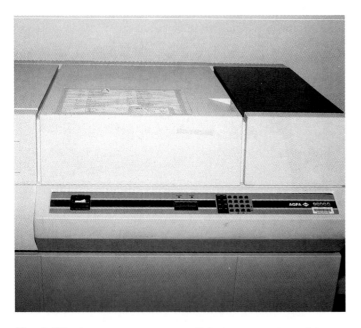

Fig. 9-35. Image generator uses light source to deposit image on film or photopaper.

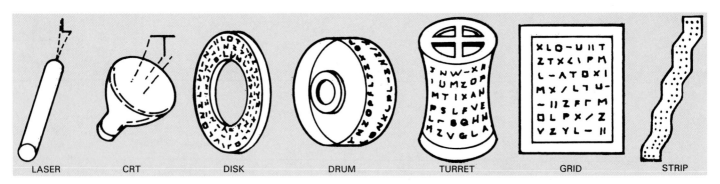

Fig. 9-36. These are the common methods that an image generator can use to produce type. Disk, drum, turret, grid, and strip have permanent character images. Light shines through transparent character to expose image on film or photopaper. Laser and CRT use light source, without permanent character image, to produce shape of characters. Computer circuitry directs light source to form letter shape.

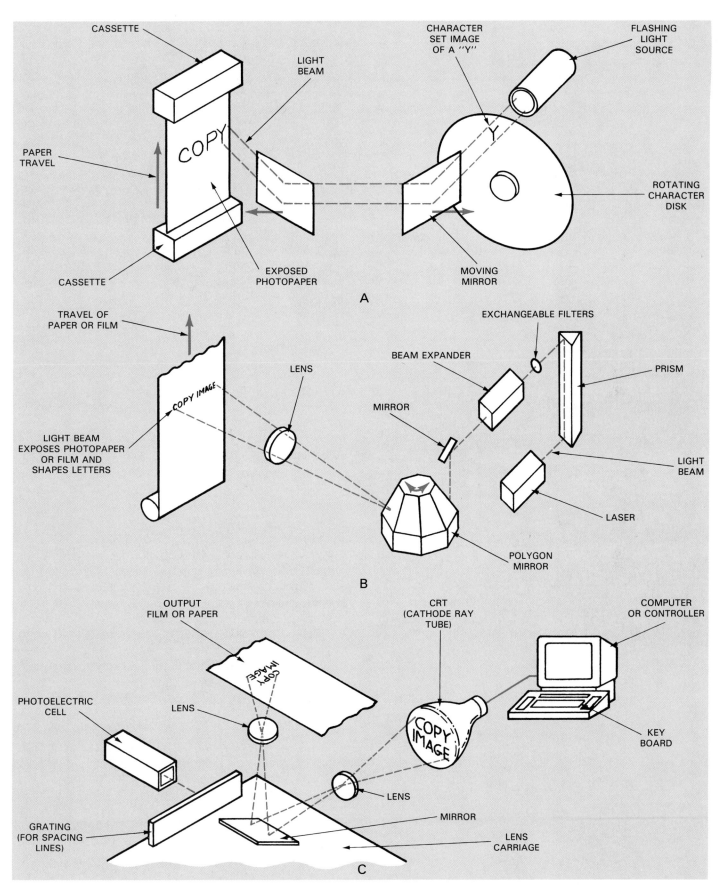

Fig. 9-37. *Typical principles used inside image generators. A—With character set, light shines through letter and is reflected onto film or photopaper. Character set shifts or moves to expose correct letters to form words and sentences. B—Laser typesetter directs beam of light to shape and burn each letter onto film or photopaper. A character set is not used. C—CRT image generator forms letter shapes on cathode ray tube. This burns image onto film or photopaper.*

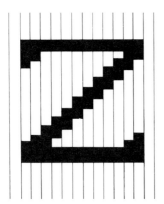

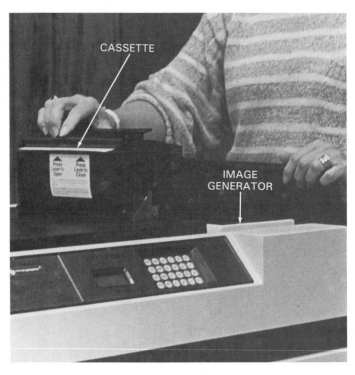

Fig. 9-38. CRT and laser image generators form letter or character shapes by scanning light beam from side to side.

Fig. 9-39. Photopaper and film have a shelf life and must be used before expiration date for good results.

Fig. 9-40. Typesetter is removing photopaper cassette from image generator. It is then placed in processor to develop latent image.

Once the paper has been exposed, it must be developed or processed, Fig. 9-40. This is commonly called the *stabilization process.* The paper must be handled in a darkroom environment compatible with the sensitivity of the emulsion.

Stabilization papers are not intended to be stored for long periods of time. It is possible, with care, to keep the processed paper for a couple of weeks. Discoloration is one of the factors that will create poor quality in the final photoconversion process. Old photopaper can turn dark in spots after processing and layout. This can ruin the printed product.

Resin-coated paper

Resin-coated photopaper, abbreviated RC, is more costly, but it also has a longer storage life than stabilization paper. It is a rapid, projection-speed, high contrast, orthochromatic, resin-coated base paper. This paper is also considered to be lightweight. Xenon flash or cathode ray tube exposure type machines also use RC paper. Look at Fig. 9-39.

Several factors are associated with this paper: wide development latitude, very white background, and high image density. The paper does not curl, which is a plus factor when pasting up the galley. The stability of the paper is good. Surface glare and background discoloration are minimum.

Resin-coated paper, as with stabilization paper, must be handled in an environment compatible with the orthochromatic sensitive coating on the stock. This means that you CANNOT work with this paper in regular room light.

PROCESSOR (DEVELOPER)

The *processor,* also called *developer,* uses chemicals to make the latent image on the photopaper or film visible and permanent. The cassette is removed from the image generator and mounted on the processor. The processor automatically feeds the exposed paper to develop the paper or film, as you would a photograph, Figs. 9-41 and 9-42.

A typical stabilization developing machine uses two-stage processing. The first chemical is an activator which is an alkaline solution to develop the image. The second solution neutralizes the alkaline activator and is called a stabilizer. Refer to Fig. 9-43A.

When the paper comes out of the bath, it is damp and the surface is sticky. It must be dry before another surface can touch the image side of the paper.

Three-stage processors are also available. This type processes, fixes, and washes the phototypesetting paper. As with the other processor, the paper is damp and slightly sticky. See Fig. 9-43B.

Fig. 9-41. *Processor chemically treats photopaper or film as you would a photograph. Cassette is installed in processor. Processor then pulls photopaper sheet through chemicals for automatic developing.*

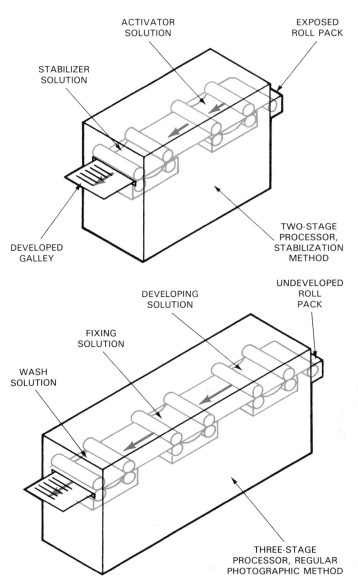

Fig. 9-43. *Study two-stage and three-stage processors. Exposed film or roll pack is automatically fed through machine and is dipped into chemicals.*

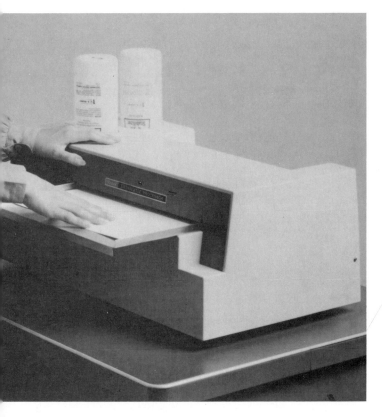

Fig. 9-42. *This is a smaller, less expensive processor. It develops and stabilizes photopaper. (Eastman Kodak Co.)*

Chemical replenishment must be done at regular intervals to produce high quality images. Quality checks are necessary at all times. The density of the image can be checked by using a reflection densitometer. For this purpose, a solid area, such as a large dot, should be a part of the photographic image. A standard should be known and maintained.

Processing of resin-coated papers differs from stabilization paper. The steps used to process RC paper is the same as phototypesetting film. In order to process the exposed RC paper, the paper must go through a series of baths. They include: developing bath, fixing bath, washing, and sometimes drying.

Again, replenishment of the chemicals is imperative to assure high quality results. The developer must be kept at the proper strength. It is also important to maintain the proper solution temperature and to use the correct type of chemicals. This information is available from the manufacturer of the equipment.

This processing equipment is very expensive and requires proper maintenance to assure good operation and long service life. See Fig. 9-44.

Rapid access systems are becoming very popular as processing units. The main reason is the reduced processing time. These systems are more compact. The amount of chemicals needed in the processing units has been reduced and the system operates with higher solution temperature. This type processor turns out dry galleys in approximately two minutes.

Optical character recognition

Optical character recognition, abbreviated OCR, is a system that can scan and convert typewriter copy into computer data. This eliminates the need to hand keystroke or typeset copy manually. This provides a very fast method of inputting text into the computer or typesetting equipment. See Fig. 9-45.

Often called *optical character readers,* modern machines are capable of reading almost any typewriter copy. Machines can read and input a full typed page in less than 30 seconds. This is typically ten times faster than manually typing the copy on a keyboard, Fig. 9-46.

The typed material must be "clean" because hand-written copy cannot be read and scanned by most machines. However, the reader can input the copy into the word processor or typesetting equipment, then the editor or typesetter can make the marked changes on the manuscript more easily using the display screen, cursor, and editing keypad.

Today's optical character readers will automatically feed in and read a stack of typed manuscript. For example, one machine will automatically read up to 50 sheets of text without operator assistance. Any problems with the copy will be flagged (coded) by the machine so the editor or typesetter can check and correct any troubles.

Some optical character readers will also scan and pickup drawings, graphs, etc. These images can also be converted into computer data for display on the screen or for output onto photographic paper or film.

Depending upon the make of the reader, it can be compatible with a personal computer, desktop publishing system, or computerized typesetting equipment.

Fig. 9-44. Typesetter is removing galley sheet from processor. Note how latent image is now visible and permanent. (Holland Printing)

Fig. 9-45. Optical character reader or automatic data entry system can reduce work load of typesetters. It will read typed pages and convert them into computer data. Then, copy changes can be made on video display screen instead of on typed manuscript. (CompuScan)

Fig. 9-46. Operator is using optical character reader. It will automatically typeset a full page in less than 30 seconds which is many times faster than the best typesetter. It will also read almost any typewriter face. Problems are coded so data can be checked and corrected easily. (CompuScan)

KNOW THESE TERMS

Character generation, Hand composition, Letter template, Scriber, Preprinted materials, Clip art, Dry transfer sheets, Burnish, Strike-on composition, Paper tape, Paper punch, Reader, Photocomposition, Contact method, Strip printer, Phototypositor, Keypad, Video display terminal, Computer control unit, Disk drive, Proof printer,

Image generator, Film or paper cassette, Developer or processor, Optical character reader, On-line, Off-line, Input system, Output system, Storage system, Transfer system, Edit mode, Compose mode, Buffer, Analog signals, Digital signals, File management, Hyphenation routine, Direct input, Floppy disk, Hard disk, Binary system, Front end, Control signal, Software, Hardware, CRT, Fiber optics, Laser, Cursor, Scrolling, Block, Mouse, Temporary memory, Permanent memory, File, Page, Qwerty keyboard, Function keypads, Editing keypad, Define key, Delete key, Insert key, Scroll key, Arrow keys, Limit key, Clear key, Abort key, File keypad, Command key, Queue key, Display key, Insert key, Page keys, Merge key, File keys, Compose key, Execute key, Alphanumeric, Magnetic disk storage, Dual disk drive, Programming disk, Font disk, File disk, Proofing program, Master character set, Laser image generator, CRT image generator, Photopaper, Stabilization paper, Resin-coated paper.

REVIEW QUESTIONS—CHAPTER 9

1. _____ _____ involves using a pen, brush, template, clip art, or transfer letters to manually generate copy.
2. How do you burnish dry transfer sheets?
3. Strike-on composition is relatively new and is the most common method of setting type. True or false?
4. Explain proportionally spaced type.
5. _____ is the generation of type using photographic paper or film exposed to light.
6. How does a phototypositor work?
7. Summarize three principles used in phototype equipment so that images can be produced.
8. List and explain the nine basic components of phototypesetting equipment.
9. This is a temporary storage device for computer data when differences in data handling rates occur.
   a. Analog device.   c. Transfer device.
   b. File device.   d. Buffer device.
10. The _____ _____ is the information handling portion of any machine or system.
11. Explain the difference between computer software and hardware.
12. When a small diameter thread of plastic or glass is used to transmit light or data, it is called _____ _____.
13. What is a cursor and how is it used?
14. Explain the difference between permanent and temporary memory in a computer or in modern phototypesetting equipment.
15. _____ _____, also called _____ _____, are additional keys used by typesetter to program in data concerning text material and file management.
16. Summarize the function of five editing keys and five file management keys on a typical computer-controlled phototypesetting keyboard.
17. What is the function of the control unit on modern phototypesetting equipment?
18. Describe the advantages of a dual disk drive over a single disk drive.
19. A floppy disk and a hard disk will fit into and run on the same drive by inserting either into the front slot on the machine. True or false?
20. In your own words, explain the operation of modern image generators and processors.

SUGGESTED ACTIVITIES

1. Purchase some transfer letters and use them to produce your own letterhead stationary.
2. Visit a printing facility that has its own typesetting equipment. Observe the typesetter using the equipment.
3. When visiting a facility, list the types of equipment they have for setting type.
4. Use the manual to operate computer typesetting equipment. Set different types of jobs.
5. Subscribe to printing magazines and read about the lastest changes in equipment.

Computers can also be used to do layout. With desktop publishing systems, you can set type, draw illustrations, make charts, and then size and organize everything on the layout page shown on the display screen. More and more electronic layout should be seen in the future. Chapter 12 details electronic production.

Chapter 10

LAYOUT

After studying this chapter, you will be able to:
- Identify the elements of printed communication.
- Explain the role of the layout person.
- Describe the steps for producing a layout sheet.
- Identify the stages of the layout process.
- Summarize the tools and equipment used by layout personnel.

This chapter will explain the process of doing layout or preparing a mechanical. The *mechanical,* also called *paste-up* or *layout sheet,* is completed by placing the galleys (camera-ready copy from typesetting), line art, and other images on a base sheet. The mechanical must also leave space for photographs. Photos are not placed on the mechanical because they must be screened and then attached to the flat.

The *flat* is the assembled photographed negatives or positives of the mechanical or layout sheet. It is used to make the printing plate. The plate is then used on the press to run large quantities of the layout images.

LAYOUT ELEMENTS

Layout is the arrangement of printing elements on a base sheet. The *elements or components* of printed communication are:
1. Text or body type.
2. Display type.
3. Illustrations.
4. White space.

The arrangements of these elements must be pleasing to the eye and easy to read. The layout person or designer puts the elements together to make a composition. The layout person plays a very important role in planning each job. The solutions to layout problems are endless.

If the same elements were given to several designers, it is very probable that three different layouts would be submitted. Which one is the best? If all have applied good principles of design, it might be impossible to say one is better than another. Sometimes, it comes down to the simple statement, "I like this one."

Remember the finished layout must include sound principles of design. Design was fully explained in Chapter 6.

Remember! The major objective of the layout is that the printed material must be seen and read. You must consider each element as it relates independently and also as it relates to the total job.

Text type

The first element, *text type,* must be chosen to reflect the intent of the message. The straight matter must be very legible and relate to the topic. Typically, a very modern topic would NOT use an Oldstyle typeface, Fig. 10-1.

Type blocks need appropriate "elbow room." White space can be as important as the type itself.

Usually, the text is not the focal point or attention. The straight matter will contain a message that will expand upon the other elements. Because of this need, all elements are positioned in a logical progression of importance. Some elements will be primary while other elements become secondary in meeting the layout objectives.

Fig. 10-1. Layout requires much thought and planning. Even selecting a typeface is important because it should correspond to topic of printed piece.

Display type

Display type is intended to draw attention. The headline of a newspaper is a typical example of display type, Fig. 10-2. The display line creates a message. If the headline creates interest, the reader will proceed to the text type.

The display line in an ad leads the reader to other information. After reading the display material, the person must be satisfied or directed to do further reading in the text.

The style of display type is very influential because it helps convey the message. Some type styles can be very dramatic, Fig. 10-3. In this case, the topic and style must be compatible. Fine line display type is usually NOT appropriate when used with other heavy mass images and vice versa.

Some type styles are directional and lead the eye of the reader. Sometimes, the designer organizes the display line for an ad using hand-lettering display type.

Choosing a display typeface is very important. The display must be distinctive and appropriate. To properly select a typeface, the objective of the job must be fully understood by the layout person or designer.

Illustrations

For the purpose of discussion, *illustrations* include: ornamentation, photographs, and artwork (line art). Illustrations are common in most printed materials. For example, ads might include illustrations of the product.

The language of a photograph can be very revealing, Fig. 10-4. An old saying—"A picture is worth a thousand words," applies to many printed pieces. Pictorial images are a very strong way of conveying a message, Fig. 10-5. They add another dimension to increase understanding as well as interest in the product.

White space

White space includes areas void of printed images. Filling up every available space will usually not produce good results. Utilizing all of the space can be a negative factor.

Tech Foundation Reprinting 'Web Offset Press Trouble' Textbook

The third edition of "Web Offset Press Troubles," published by the Graphic Arts Technical Foundation, is being reprinted with minor corrections and updates and will soon be available to the industry.

visor of the engineering division, updated the reprint.

He also revised the third edition printed in 1979. The first edition was originally compiled by Robert F. Reed.

Fig. 10-2. The headline is one form of display type. It should draw attention to and summarize printed product.

Fig. 10-3. Display type should also summarize the message of printed piece.

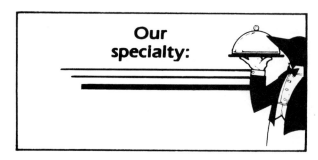

Fig. 10-4. Any illustrations can be used to quickly convey a message or theme—a picture paints a thousand words!

Fig. 10-5. An example of the power of an illustration. Note how this road sign gives directions with minimum use of words.

Line art

Line art is normally pasted down same size on the layout sheet. If needed, the original art can be reduced or enlarged using a stat camera. Then, the correct size line art can be adhered in place on the mechanical, Fig. 10-13.

Line art to be reduced or enlarged for layout must be sized, as described earlier. The layout person must denote the percent of reduction or enlargement for the camera operator. Then when the photo duplicate returns, it will fit in the layout space perfectly.

Fig. 10-13. Line copy is usually made to size and pasted down on the base sheet.

Photographs, tone copy

Photographs must be handled very carefully during layout. Their surface will scratch and mar very easily. Never write on an overlay placed on top of a photo. The pressure from the pen or pencil can indent the photo's surface. This can leave an unwanted mark or reflection during reproduction or screening on the process camera or scanner. See Fig. 10-14.

Photographs and tone materials are NOT pasted down on the layout sheet. Usually, an outline of the space for the photo is marked on the layout sheet. A figure number is assigned to the space and to the photo. Then the stripper will know where to place the screened halftone of the photo when making the flat. See Fig. 10-15.

When the line art and *tone* (shading) *material* are used together, the tone material is placed on an overlay. For instance, if the tone material is going to be used to place color in the line art, it must be cut to the shape of the art and placed in register on the overlay.

When trimming excess paper from a stat (photo of line art), it is a good practice to leave at least one-eighth of an inch trim or border. This is true for all pasted-up materials. Sometimes, when trimmed or cut too close, a shadow will be cast when shot with the process camera. The shadow line on the negative will have to be *opaqued* (covered with light stopping solution). If too close to the image, the shadow line becomes more difficult to opaque out when stripping.

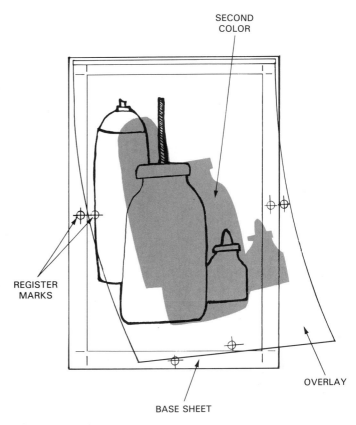

Fig. 10-14. An overlay sheet is needed when something is going to be printed in color or as a percentage of black. Note how this overlay could be adding a color or shading to the line art. Also note register marks.

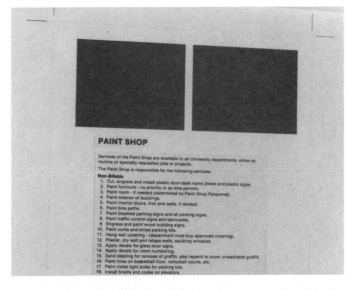

Fig. 10-15. Notice how two holes would be left for photographs. Photos have to be screened into halftones and the film is then positioned by the stripper.

Mounting

Mounting involves attaching a piece of artwork or illustration on a separate mounting board. This will protect the artwork from being bent and damaged. When mounting, leave at least a one inch margin on all sides. Protective tissue is fastened to one edge to cover the illustrative material. This cover is for protection and is not commonly used to write instructions. If it is necessary to write on the tissue, place a piece of acetate under the sheet to eliminate the possibility of ruining the artwork.

Mark-up

Marks/info given to

Mark-up involves writing directions or specs for the visual images on the layout materials. A marked-up photo is given in Fig. 10-16. Markings should be carefully placed on the border or back of mounted photos. Photographs that are NOT mounted should NOT be marked on the back. Pressure can cause marks to appear on the print side. These marks could photograph later and appear on the negative. The photo can be seriously damaged and many times, cannot be used in the job.

Never use a paper clip on a photograph! It can leave an unwanted mark or scratch on the print. Crop marks should be placed in the margin or in an area that will not be reproduced.

Information on the photos might include: job title and/or number, location in printed piece (page number), figure number if applicable, percentage enlargement or reduction, or size, and name of layout or referral person.

Sketches and drawings are marked in the same manner as photographs. They must be cropped, sized, and located. If possible, sizing and marking up for the same size change, rather than making each one a different size, will save time and money. The person operating the process camera or scanner will have fewer settings for enlarging or reducing the images. The art can be *"gang shot"* (several images reduced or enlarged at the same time).

Workmarks

Using the approved layout, the paste-up artist lays out the elements using material acceptable to the need. Corner or trim marks are always placed on the base sheet, Fig. 10-17. Center marks are usually positioned and are essential for color work, Fig. 10-18. These marks are helpful to the layout person and the stripper.

A *light blue pencil,* which will not be picked up photographically, is commonly used by the paste-up person. It can be safely used to draw the type positions, margins, etc., to assist in positioning repro proofs,

FIG. 10-16 p. 148   *REDUCE TO 5"*

Fig. 10-16. Full instructions for handling each photo must be given clearly. Space for photo must be numbered. Information on enlargement or reduction, screening, etc. must also be written out.

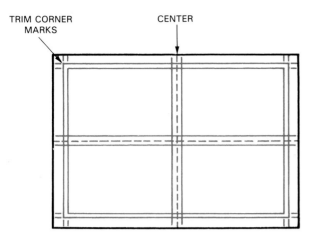

Fig. 10-17. *Some layout sheets have preprinted trim, center, and fold guide lines on them. If not, you will have to draw these reference lines on the base sheet. Trim marks show the limit of the image area or where the product will be trimmed during binding and finishing.*

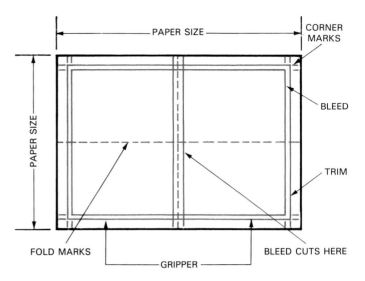

Fig. 10-19. *Bleeds, that extend off of printed page, should have 1/8 inch trim margins.*

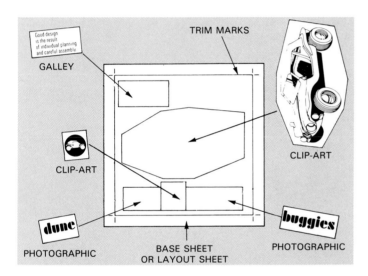

Fig. 10-18. *Instructions can be written on outside of trim marks and they will not show up on printed piece.*

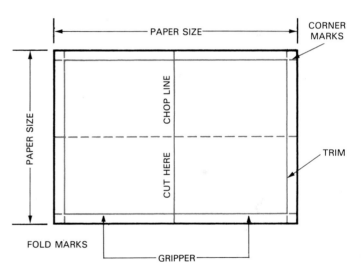

Fig. 10-20. *Workmarks are guides for layout person and printer. They must be accurate.*

photographic composition, and other elements, Fig. 10-18. Sometimes the layout sheets have location or margin lines preprinted on them.

If a pencil is used, the instructions should be given in the margin of the layout sheet.

Trim margins should usually, be one-eighth inch for marking of paste-up for bleeds. This is shown in Fig. 10-19.

A *bleed* is where an image extends out of the border. For instance, a photo of a sky scene could be bled off the top of a page in this book. Fig. 10-20 shows workmarks for a layout sheet.

LAYOUT SURFACES

The two most common working surfaces in layout are: a drafting board and a light table. The board can be made of various materials, the most common material being wood. See Fig. 10-21.

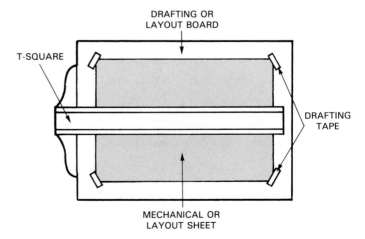

Fig. 10-21. *The layout surface, called a layout sheet or a base sheet, will hold the pasted down elements. It is usually made up on a drafting board using a T-square. Drafting tape is used to hold the base sheet in alignment on the board.*

The drawing board can be purchased in a range of sizes. Some people need the board to be portable. Others require a larger, more stable work surface. Look at Fig. 10-22A.

A light table is sometimes used in layout when backlighting is needed. For example, it will allow light to pass through two images for easier alignment or registration. The light table will also make transparencies or negatives more visible, Fig. 10-22B.

Another excellent layout surface material is a piece of clear plastic. If used on a light table, it has the advantage of allowing light to show through.

LAYOUT BASE SHEET

The *layout sheet* or *paste-up base sheet* is also very important since most of the elements are attached to its surface. A wide variety of base sheet stock is available. Some of the points to consider when selecting a layout sheet are: the surface must accept a variety of adhesives, may need to permit drawing with ink, must be reasonably stable, and must be cost efficient.

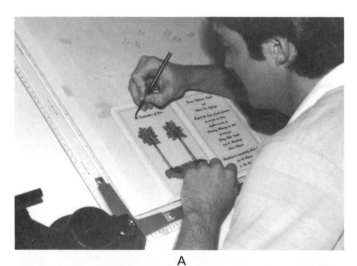

A

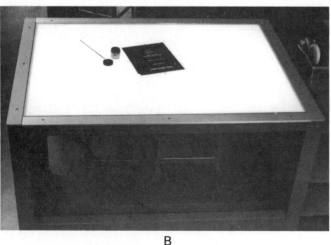

B

Fig. 10-22. A—An art board or drafting board is most commonly used work surface during layout. B—Light table is sometimes used in layout when it is desirable to see through images.

Preprinted base sheets are often used in publication work when the same type of job is done repeatedly. Many of the plants using preprinted sheets do not use a T-square. The paste-up people rely on the nonreproducing lines to be the guide for placement of images. The grid lines are often measured at intervals of one pica, Fig. 10-23.

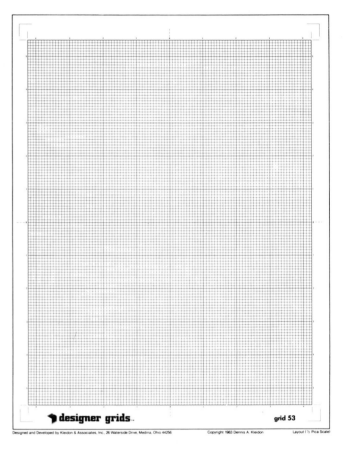

Fig. 10-23. A grid sheet is an excellent layout tool. It will allow very fast and accurate work without the use of a T-square or measuring tools. Grid lines serve as guides for positioning copy and art. They will not show when photographed.

Base materials are available in a wide range of surfaces and finishes. Mounting boards usually have a smooth nonabsorbent surface. Dull-coated, enamel paper is good for ruling and composition. Book page paste-up is often done on 110 lb. white index.

Stock is also available which has a high gloss finish. The surface accepts ink but waxed copy has a tendency to shift if not burnished properly.

When cost is a factor, 70 pound white offset paper can be used as a base sheet. This base sheet works very well on a light table. Any time the paste-ups are only used for a short period of time, paper base sheets are used.

The size of the base sheets will vary. Their size may depend on the size of the copyboard of the process camera used to photograph the finished mechanical.

Illustration board is a thick base sheet which has considerable stability. The surface is smooth and accepts media used by the paste-up artist. Illustration board is expensive, but it is often recommended when careful handling is a major factor. Some facilities will use the board when storage or re-use is required.

Thin plastic sheets are also used when preparing a mechanical. These sheets are very stable. Frosted or clear plastic sheets are often used as overlays. The overlay sheet supports all of the images which are needed for a second color, Fig. 10-24.

LAYOUT TOOLS AND EQUIPMENT

Many tools are needed for paste-up or layout. Tools should be kept in good condition and in a convenient location. The most common layout tools are: triangles, T-square, scissors, art knives, rulers, tweezers, compass/dividers, tape, ink, light blue pencils, pens, brushes, burnishers, erasers, and buffer sheets.

Pencils

The *pencil* is an essential tool for various layout tasks. Keeping a pencil sharp is essential for fine line accuracy. Even pressure and rolling the pencil as a line is drawn, will cause the lead to wear evenly, Fig. 10-25.

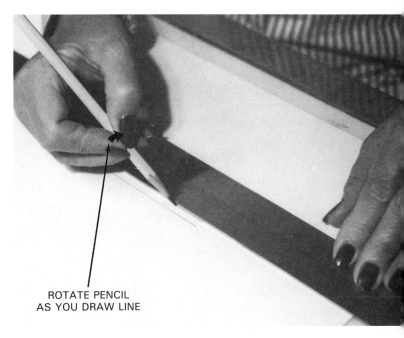

ROTATE PENCIL
AS YOU DRAW LINE

Fig. 10-25. When using a conventional pencil, keep it sharp and roll it as you draw lines. This will help keep line width equal as lead wears down.

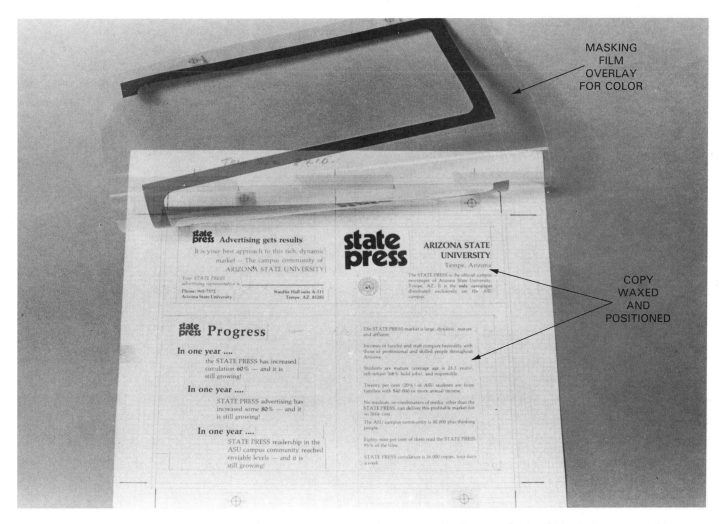

MASKING FILM OVERLAY FOR COLOR

COPY WAXED AND POSITIONED

Fig. 10-24. The overlay sheet is needed to make a plate for a second color or a shade of black. Images on this layout sheet will be printed black. Image or design on overlay will be printed in color.

non-
re-photo

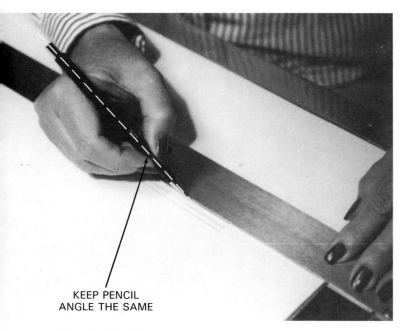

KEEP PENCIL
ANGLE THE SAME

Fig. 10-26. Mechanical pencils, with very small diameter lead, are replacing conventional pencils. They never need sharpening and produce consistent line weights.

Mechanical pencils use a small diameter lead that can be extended out of the tip as the lead wears down, Fig. 10-26. They are often recommended and used over a conventional pencil. They do not have to be sharpened and their lead is so small that you do not have as much of a problem with line thickness variation.

The lead for mechanical pencils comes in various thicknesses or diameters. For example, one popular mechanical pencil is sized metrically. The lead diameter can be given as 0.5 mm for example.

When ruling with any kind of pencil, make sure that the contact point is next to the support edge of the T-square. Also, maintain the same general pencil angle as you slide the pencil to draw a line. This will result in a straight, uniform line.

Pencil *lead hardness* is given as a letter-number designation—7B is the softest and 9H is the hardest lead. A harder lead would be good for light lines. A softer lead would produce darker, but more easily smudged, lines. Select a lead hardness that matches the task.

Mentioned briefly, a *light blue pencil,* often referred to as a *"nonrepro pencil,"* is used on the base sheet to indicate where the copy is to be placed. The lines indicate the shapes and positioning of material. Light blue lines do not reproduce. They will not appear on the platemaker's negative.

Instructions for sizing, tint screens, stripping, or make-up instructions, or any other information is written on the mechanical or tissue sheet in light blue pencil.

Sometimes, a 6H pencil is used to make fine guidelines. Since they are light gray lines, the line will drop out when photographed. The safest way is to use a light blue pencil and keep the lines sharp to make precision guidelines.

Pens

Special *pens* are used to produce very sharp images in ink during layout. They are several types used by the layout person.

The *ruling pen* has movable *nibs* (jaws) that can be set for different line weights or widths. As shown in Fig. 10-27, a thumb screw can be turned to adjust the nib width. Ink flows off the nibs to produce an inked line. This type of pen can be used to rule or draw borders. It will make good straight lines but does not draw curved lines efficiently.

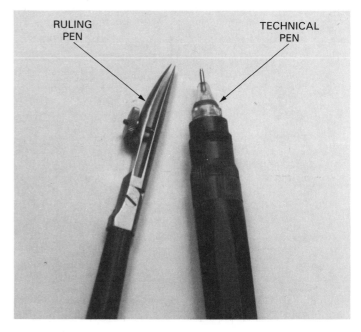

RULING
PEN

TECHNICAL
PEN

Fig. 10-27. These are the two most common ink pens used in layout. Ruling pen has adjustable nibs that can produce different line weights. Technical ink pen has precisely sized tip or nib for drawing accurate lines.

The *technical ink pen* has a set tip or nib size and is commonly used to make camera-ready illustrations and other line work, Fig. 10-28A.

Pen tip size is normally given as a numbering system: 00 being fine, No. 1 being larger, No. 2 even larger, etc. A metric equivalent is also given. For example, a 00 pen would have a 0.30 mm diameter tip, No. 2 pen would have a 0.60 mm tip. A color code on the pen's cap also shows pen size.

Fig. 10-28B shows some lines drawn with different sizes of technical ink pens. Fig. 10-28C gives pen sizes and resulting line widths.

Hold the pen as straight as possible because tilting the pen can upset ink flow and line weight. Allow ink to dry before touching because the ink will smear easily when wet.

The technical ink pen screws apart and has a small reservoir for ink, Fig. 10-29. Be careful not to spill the ink when filling the pen. Keep pens clean and handle them carefully because the tip is very delicate and easy to damage.

Today's market also has a variety of felt tipped pens. Most are NOT recommended but some have been developed specifically for making camera-ready art.

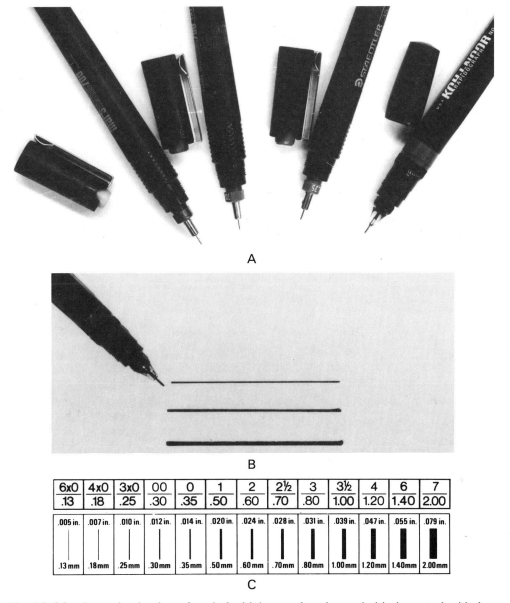

6x0	4x0	3x0	00	0	1	2	2½	3	3½	4	6	7
.13	.18	.25	.30	.35	.50	.60	.70	.80	1.00	1.20	1.40	2.00
.005 in.	.007 in.	.010 in.	.012 in.	.014 in.	.020 in.	.024 in.	.028 in.	.031 in.	.039 in.	.047 in.	.055 in.	.079 in.
.13 mm	.18 mm	.25 mm	.30 mm	.35 mm	.50 mm	.60 mm	.70 mm	.80 mm	1.00 mm	1.20 mm	1.40 mm	2.00 mm

C

Fig. 10-28. A good selection of technical ink pen sizes is needed in layout. A—Various pen sizes. B—Lines draw with varying pen sizes. C—Chart shows common pen sizes and actual line weights.

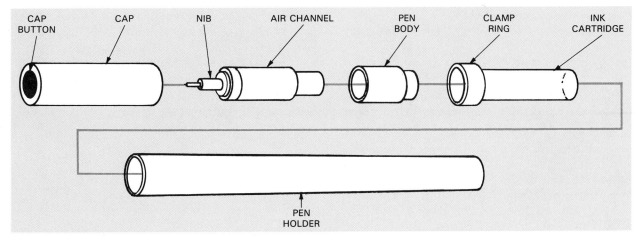

CAP BUTTON CAP NIB AIR CHANNEL PEN BODY CLAMP RING INK CARTRIDGE

PEN HOLDER

Fig. 10-29. Exploded view shows basic parts of typical technical ink pen. Pen must be maintained to make good line work.

Whichever type pen is used by the layout person, it is important to hold the device straight up and down and use even pressure to assure consistent density and width of lines.

Ink
carbon black

India ink is the most common type of ink used today. It works very well in modern technical ink pens. As shown in Fig. 10-30, a small plastic bottle of india ink will allow you to fill a technical pen easily. It has a pointed outlet so the ink can be deposited in the pen's small reservoir quickly and efficiently. Ink can also be purchased in larger jars or containers.

Whatever ink is used, it must be able to produce a very dense image. It should cover fully to produce a sharp black line.

Fig. 10-31. Brushes can be used to white out unwanted areas, to touch up photos, and to ink large areas. Various brush sizes are essential in layout.

Fig. 10-30. India ink is commonly used in technical ink pens and ruling pens. This small bottle is handy for filling small reservoir in technical ink pen.

Brushes

Brushes are commonly used to white out and touch up areas of artwork. A wide brush can be used to fill in a large area with black ink, for example. A narrow or small brush might be used to place white out on smeared black ink. Brushes can also be used to touch up or modify photographs. See Fig. 10-31.

Brush size and stiffness should match the task. Always clean brushes thoroughly after use to extend their service life.

A cotton swab can be used in place of a brush in some situations. A swab can also be used to clean excess wax off a layout sheet.

T-square

The *T-square* is commonly used to align images, to cut elements, and for ruling. It is one of the most important pieces of equipment in layout. The T-square consists of a thin straightedge blade fastened to a head, Fig. 10-32. The T-square blade should be made of thin steel and securely joined to the head.

Plastic T-square blades are NOT satisfactory when used as a guide for cutting. The blade of the knife can easily cut the plastic and ruin the blade.

When using the T-square, hold the head firmly against the left side of the drafting board. It is good practice to draw lines with the upper edge of the T-square blade, Fig. 10-33.

The technical fountain pen works well with thin bladed, steel T-squares. Some have a beveled edge so that ink will not run under the blade.

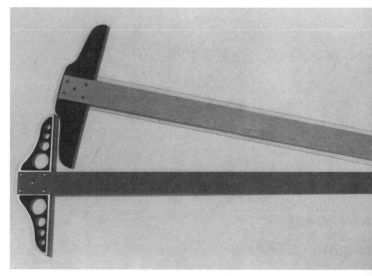

Fig. 10-32. A good T-square is vital to accurate layout work. A metal blade is much better than a plastic one. It will not be cut and ruined by art knife.

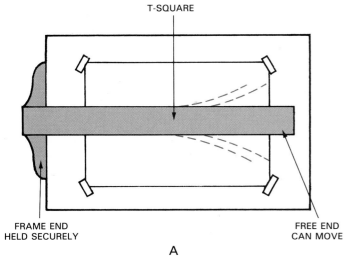

T-SQUARE

FRAME END
HELD SECURELY

FREE END
CAN MOVE

A

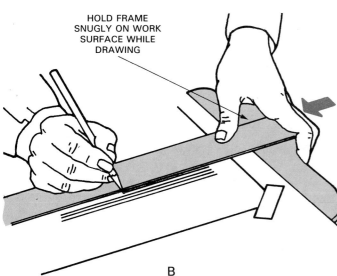

HOLD FRAME
SNUGLY ON WORK
SURFACE WHILE
DRAWING

B

Fig. 10-33. A—Always work near frame end of T-square. Other end can flex and upset accuracy. B—Press frame against layout board while drawing lines with other hand.

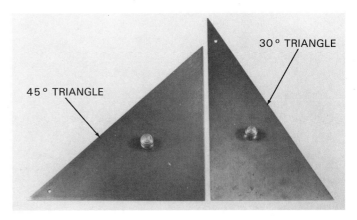

45° TRIANGLE

30° TRIANGLE

Fig. 10-34. The 30 and 45 degree triangles are the most common. They should be a size that meets the layout.

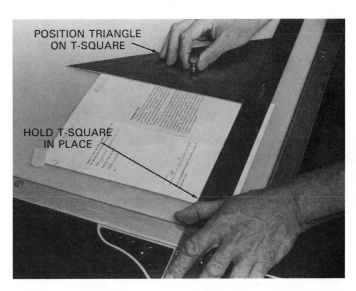

POSITION TRIANGLE
ON T-SQUARE

HOLD T-SQUARE
IN PLACE

Fig. 10-35. When using a triangle, hold T-square against drafting board and triangle against T-square. This will align triangle properly.

Always try to work near the frame end of the T-square. This will result in more accurate work. The other end of the T-square is unsupported and can flex up or down. This can cause images to be out of alignment, Fig. 10-33.

Triangles

The *triangle* is used to draw vertical and slanted lines during layout. The two most common types are the 30 degree triangle and the 45 degree triangle. This refers to the angle of the longest surface on the triangle. Look at Fig. 10-34.

Various triangle sizes are available. Select a size that matches the job. The 12 inch, 30-60-90 degree triangle is very common because it will reach all the way across a 8 1/2 by 11 inch format, Fig. 10-35.

Triangles are also available in metal or plastic. Plastic is acceptable for drawing but NOT cutting. Clear plastic can be desirable when it is helpful to be able to see through the triangle while working.

Inking triangles usually have a two-step lip on their outer edge. This raises the extreme edge of the triangle off of the

paper to help prevent ink smearing. A conventional triangle has its outer edge touching the paper and can allow ink to flow under the triangle and ruin the line. A metal triangle can have a tapered edge that serves the same purpose as a two-step edge.

An *adjustable triangle* is used to layout angles that are not included with the two common triangle configurations. It can be swiveled to produce any special angles.

To use a triangle, hold the T-square against the drafting board with one hand. Use the other hand to position the triangle against the T-square. Then hold the triangle in place while working. This should align the triangle properly. Refer to Fig. 10-36.

Rulers

Rulers are used for numerous types of measurement during layout. Many kinds of rulers are available. In most cases, the 18 inch ruler is long enough. Inch, millimeter, and pica measurements are essential. Fig. 10-37 shows several types of rulers.

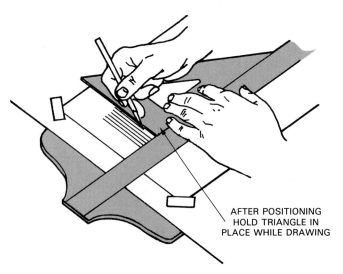

Fig. 10-36. After alignment, press down on T-square and triangle while working.

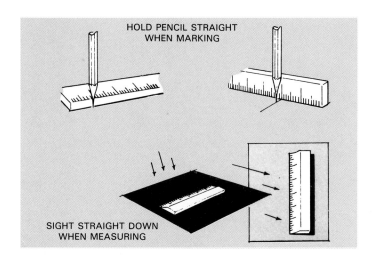

Fig. 10-38. Sight down ruler scale from top to get accurate measurements. If you sight down at an angle, your measurement will not be precise.

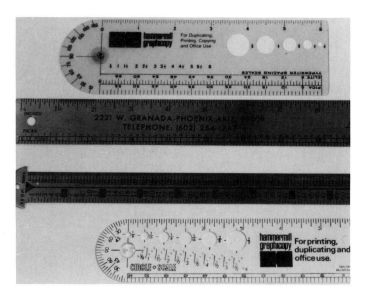

Fig. 10-37. Various types of rulers are used in layout.

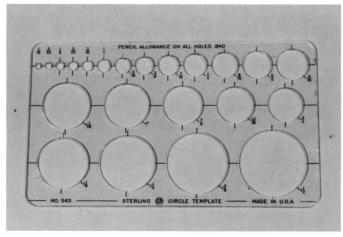

Fig. 10-39. Numerous types of templates are used in layout. This is commonly used circle template with sizes next to each hole. Others are available for ellipses, electrical circuit symbols, etc.

When measuring with a ruler, make sure you view straight down at the markings. If you sight down at an angle, an incorrect measurement can result. See Fig. 10-38.

Templates

Templates are used to draw accurate shapes. They can be used to draw circles, ellipses, and other specialized images. Fig. 10-39 shows a common circle template. Special templates are available for electrical symbols, arrows, etc. They can save time and produce excellent results.

An *inking template* has small nipples or bumps on its bottom surface. This holds the template off of the paper so that ink cannot flow under the template surface.

When using a template, position the template. Place your pen inside the template shape. Then, slowly move the pen around the template to produce the image shape. Hold the pen straight up. Tilting the pen will produce an inaccurate shape, Fig. 10-40.

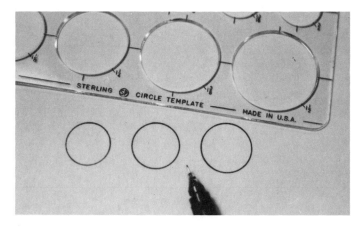

Fig. 10-40. When using a template, keep pen straight as you move pen or pencil around shape. If you tilt pen or pencil, shape will be distorted. This template has small dimples on bottom surface to keep ink from flowing under template and ruining image.

Compass, dividers

The *compass* is a device that will also draw circles. When drawing circles, you can use either a lead point or an inking point, Fig. 10-41.

It is also possible to use a swivel knife in a compass. The knife can be used to cut overlay film. See Fig. 10-42.

Dividers will measure and transfer measurements from one source to another. It might be used to check the space of an area during layout, Fig. 10-43.

Tweezers

Tweezers can be used to hold and position small elements during layout. Often, a correction has to be placed very accurately. Tweezers can help grip the small piece of copy.

Self closing, pointed tweezers are recommended. Placing pressure on the tweezers opens them. See Fig. 10-44.

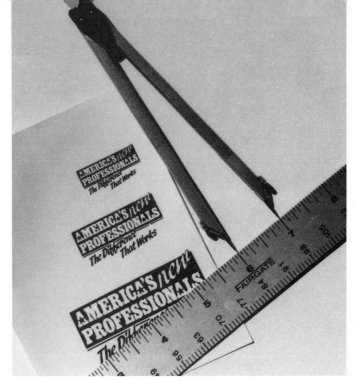

Fig. 10-43. Dividers are commonly used to transfer measurements to layout.

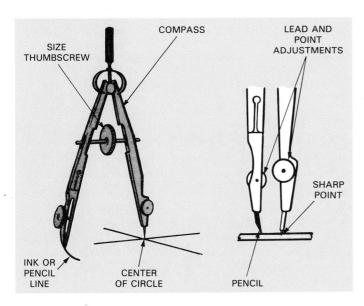

Fig. 10-41. Compass will accurately draw a circle in pencil or ink. It is handy when template sizes do not match size of circle needed.

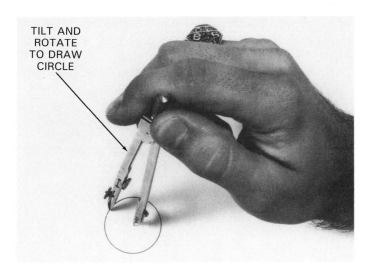

Fig. 10-42. To use compass, twirl top of compass while leaning it in the direction of rotation.

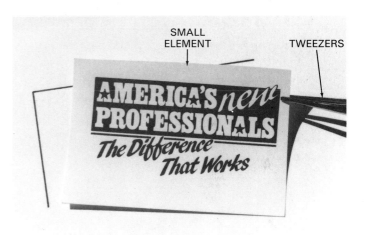

A

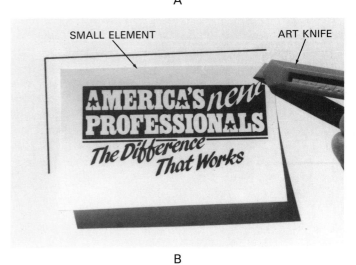

B

Fig. 10-44. A—Tweezers are handy for positioning small elements on layout sheet. B—Point of knife will also help shift and accurately position small element.

Art knives

The *art knife* is a valuable tool for making precise cuts in materials. It will produce accurate cuts of galley material, shading material, etc. The knife point can also be used to shift or position small elements during layout, Fig. 10-45.

A *swivel knife* has a cutting head that will rotate. It is handy for cutting curved or irregular shapes. The swivel knife will closely follow curves when you pull the knife around the shape, Fig. 10-46.

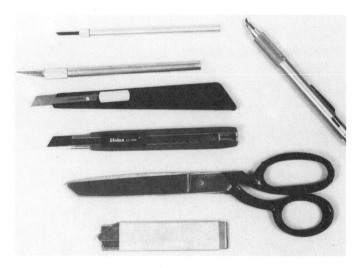

Fig. 10-45. Here are some of the cutting tools used in layout.

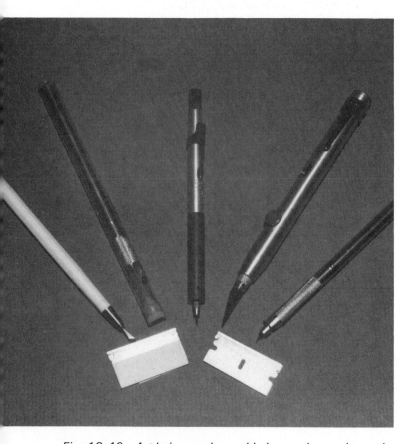

Fig. 10-46. Art knives and razor blades can be used to make very accurate cuts.

Fig. 10-47. Metal guide should be used when cutting straight lines with art knives. Slowly pull knife next to guide to make accurate cut.

Fig. 10-47 shows how to use an art knife.

DANGER! Be very careful when handling art knives. They are very sharp and can inflict deep cuts into your skin. A protective cover should be placed over the blade when the tool is not in use. Never place an unprotected knife in a drawer or storage tray. You could be cut when reaching in to get tools.

Single-edged razor blades are also used with a special holder. However, many people do not recommend their use because it is so easy to get cut. Whatever cutting device is used, use extreme care. See Fig. 10-46.

Scissors

Scissors are used in layout to make rough cuts of materials. They will not cut as accurately as an art knife. For example, scissors might be used to cut excess white space off of a stat. Refer back to Fig. 10-45.

Burnishers

The *burnisher* is used to apply firm pressure to adhere material to the base sheet. In most cases, a clean tissue or thin acetate sheet is placed over the copy before burnishing. The purpose of the sheet is to prevent damage to the art or copy.

Two types of burnisher are commonly used in layout. The first is the roller type, Fig. 10-48A. It is made of wood or plastic and allows for good even pressure. The roller is generally used to adhere larger pieces of copy or art to the base sheet.

The second type of burnisher is the beveled edge stick or rod. It can be made of plastic, wood, or metal, Fig. 10-48B. Various designs are available. An ordinary dowel rod can be beveled and polished to make an excellent burnishing tool. Look at Fig. 10-49.

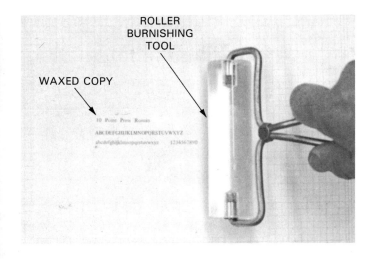

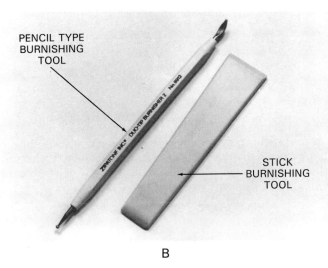

B

Fig. 10-48. Burnishing is done to make elements stick properly to layout sheet. A—Roller type burnishing tool is used for large section of copy. B—Stick or rod burnishing tool is for smaller elements.

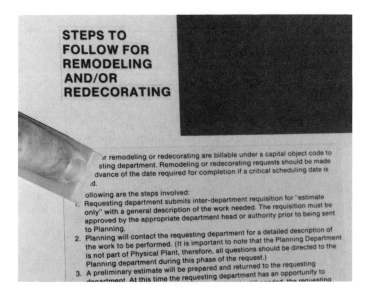

Fig. 10-49. Here layout person is using burnishing stick to bond waxed galley to base sheet. A roller could also be used for this task.

Magnifiers

Magnifiers are viewing devices for inspecting small areas on images, Fig. 10-50. The 8X and 10X magnifiers are commonly used, although other powers are available.

Whatever power is chosen, the figure represents the number of times the image is enlarged. For instance, a 10X magnifier means that the image is ten times larger than the original image.

The paste-up person commonly uses the magnifier to check alignment, dot patterns, copy, and artwork. See Fig. 10-51.

Cutters

Table model cutters are often used to trim large, unwanted areas from the material to be pasted up, Fig. 10-52. The card cutter and wheel type trimmers are needed to swiftly and accurately trim strips from galley material. Scissors are slower and less accurate.

Fig. 10-50. Magnifiers are needed for close inspection of images. They are available in different powers.

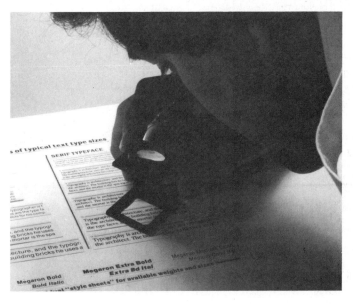

Fig. 10-51. Layout person is checking quality of type used in this job.

159

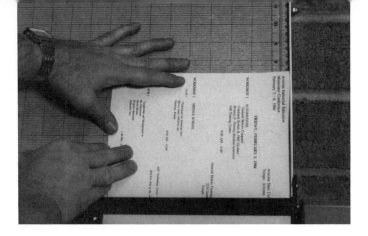

Fig. 10-52. This table top cutter is handy for quickly and accurately trimming off unwanted material from galley sheet.

Cutting boards

A *plastic cutting board* makes an excellent cutting surface. It will protect the desk or drafting table surface from damage.

> WARNING! Use extreme care when handling cutting tools. Knives, razor blades, table top cutters can all cause serious injury!

Proportion scales

Mentioned earlier, a *proportion scale* is used to calculate the percent of reduction or enlargement for images. Several are shown in Fig. 10-53.

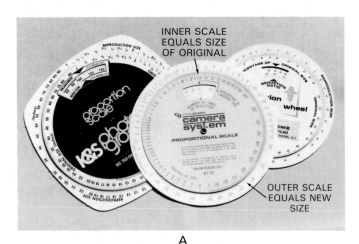

A

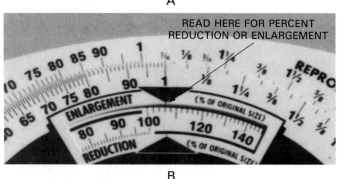

B

Fig. 10-53. A—Proportion scale is commonly used to size images for layout. Measure size of available space and image size on illustration. B—Set two scales on proportion scale to correspond to these values. Then, read percent enlargement or reduction off of other scale.

One example of using a proportion scale would be to fit a six inch image into a 3 1/2 inch wide column of space. You would use a rule to measure the image width and the column width. Then, simply rotate the wheel on the proportion scale until the correct values line up.

In this example, the original size of six would have to align with the reproduction size of 3 1/2. With these values aligned, an arrow on the wheel will point to the percent of original size or 58 percent in this case.

This percentage value would be given to the stat camera operator, process camera operator, or scanner operator. The photographically reproduced image would then fit in the space.

PASTE-UP MATERIALS

All of the elements to be positioned on the mechanical must be attached to the base sheet. The bonding materials most commonly used are: wax, rubber cement, tape, and spray adhesives.

Hot wax adhesives

A *hot wax adhesive* is the most common method of bonding elements to the layout sheets. The wax system is fast, clean, and convenient for adhering copy to the base sheet. See Fig. 10-54.

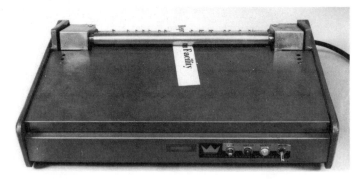

Fig. 10-54. Elements to be pasted down, copy in this example, are fed through waxing machine. It will deposit thin layer of melted wax on back of image. Image can then be adhered to base sheet easily.

A *table top waxer* melts and automatically applies the softened wax to the back of the elements. It is motorized and feeds the images through the waxing roller at a constant speed. This applies an even coating of wax to the underside of the paste-up materials. The image elements will then stick to the layout sheet when positioned and burnished.

Wax is an outstanding layout adhesive because you can move elements, even after the wax has hardened. You can lift or pull up the images without damaging them. If needed, heat will soften the wax and help free the copy. This is very useful when changing layout or making corrections.

NOTE! It is important to read the manufacturer's guide because proper wax temperature and waxer maintenance are needed for proper layout results.

Rubber cement

Rubber cement is also used as an adhesive during layout. A thin coat of rubber cement is placed on the underside of the copy using a brush. Since the total surface should be coated, it is a good idea to place scrap paper under the copy. Refer to Fig. 10-55.

Rubber cement dries quite rapidly. Placement must be done immediately after coating the copy. Slight movement is initially possible. However, once the rubber cement is set, movement is very difficult without damaging the copy.

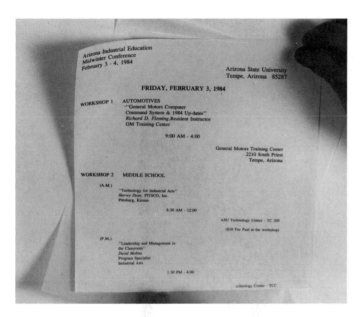

Fig. 10-55. Rubber cement can be used to adhere elements but is not as handy as wax in most instances. Place a sheet of paper under element when coating with rubber cement. Rubber cement is frequently used to mount art on illustration board.

Sometimes you should coat both surfaces (base sheet and copy) to assure greater holding power. With this method, both surfaces are allowed to partially dry before placement. Remember though, bonding is immediate and image movement is impossible without cutting the base sheet.

Using rubber cement tends to be messy. It is possible to clean semi-dry rubber cement from the sheet by rubbing or using a soft eraser when the cement has fully dried. It is also possible to take old rubber cement and roll it into a ball as a means of removal. Even though the excess cement is removed, the edges still tend to collect dirt.

Other adhesives, similar to rubber cement, are available. Some of these can be purchased in tubes or sticks. Some of the applicators are intended for spot adhering.

Read the information carefully before purchasing any adhesive to make sure that the product meets the needs of the layout task. In particular, make sure the adhesive will not distort the copy.

Spray adhesives

Spray adhesives are available but extreme care must be taken when using them. The overspray sticks to everything. A scrap piece of paper under the image is necessary. Even when using the undersheet, the spray particles tend to fall on other areas.

Controlling this overspray factor is a problem. Spray adhesives usually bond instantaneously and movement is very doubtful without damaging the copy. Placement must be accurate the first time!

Tape

Tape is commmonly used to hold the layout sheets to the drawing board or to a light table. They are also used to hinge flaps or attach overlays to the layout sheet.

Drafting tape is similar to masking tape but its adhesive is not as sticky. It can be pulled off of paper without damage. Drafting tape is commonly used for temporary holding tasks, as when holding the base sheet to the drawing board.

Transparent plastic tape is also used in layout but its adhesive is slightly more permanent. It is frequently used to bond overlays in place on the layout sheet.

White paper tape can be used in place of drafting tape in some situations. However, it is more difficult to remove and is considered more permanent.

Double-coated tape has adhesive on both sides. It is sometimes used instead of an adhesive or way to bond elements to the base sheet. This is only done when the mechanical will NOT be retained or reused. The double-coated tape will hold the elements in place while being reproduced. With most double-coated tapes, it is very difficult to remove and reposition images without damage, especially after a period of storage.

Masking film

Masking film is a material which has two layers: a plastic base and an emulsion layer. The support layer is a thicker sheet of clear plastic. The masking film is a very thin pliable plastic sheet with either ruby or amber coloring. Masking film is used to make windows, solid areas, color overlays, and dropouts during layout.

The colored layer is cut with an art knife and the unwanted material peeled off. The remaining color film is positioned on an overlay for the mechanical, Fig. 10-56. It is also possible to peel off the wanted emulsion area and attach it directly to the mechanical. This is a less common practice, however.

The purpose of a *window* is to make a clear area in the negative, Fig. 10-57A. For example, a halftone might be positioned in the window area. The reason being that a continuous tone print (photograph) cannot be treated or handled the same as line copy. This will be explained in a later chapter. By using a window and attaching the halftone, only one step is needed to put the image on a plate.

The same window results could be achieved by using black paper. A solid can be created in the same manner.

Whenever a *dropout* is called for, the shape of the dropped out area is cut on the masking film. The dropped out area might appear as a silhouette of an object. Look at Fig. 10-57B.

A masking film overlay is commonly used to produce a second color on the image. The images on the layout sheet

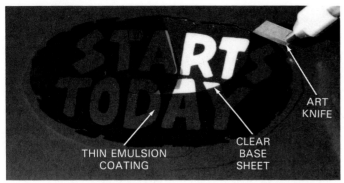

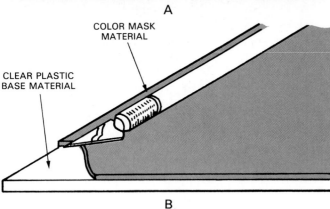

Fig. 10-56. Masking film consists of thicker sheet of clear plastic with thin layer of emulsion on top. A—Masking film can be registered over image. Then art knife can be used to cut thin emulsion away, forming a window. B—Basic construction of masking film.

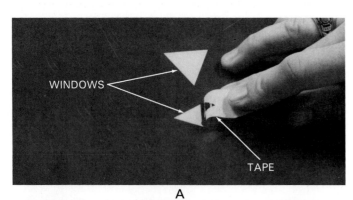

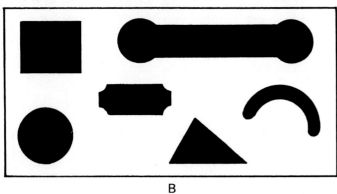

Fig. 10-57. A—After cutting out shape of image, peel emulsion off of plastic sheet. Here tape is being used to lift small piece of emulsion. B—Dropout appears as silhouette.

are printed black. The images on the film overlay are printed in a color, Fig. 10-58.

To use masking film for a second color, the film is usually taped into position on the layout sheet. Then an art knife is used to cut out the shape of the image. The area without color is peeled away. The color area remains on the clear plastic and is registered over the layout image, Fig. 10-59.

Instructions for the printer are commonly printed on the overlay. For example, the overlay might print in 70 percent red. Another overlay might print in 30 percent red.

Registering the overlay is explained later in this chapter.

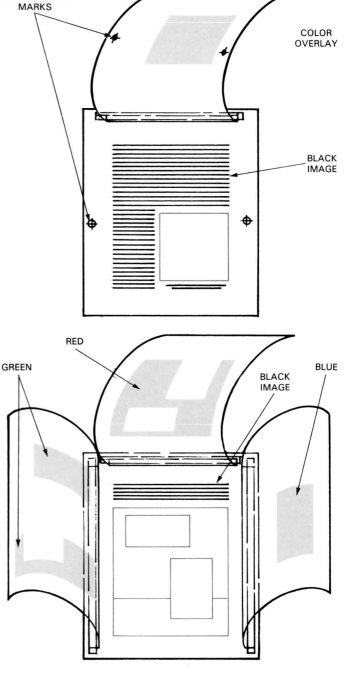

Fig. 10-58. Making film overlay is commonly used to add color to black base image. Tape is commonly used to hold overlay to top of base sheet.

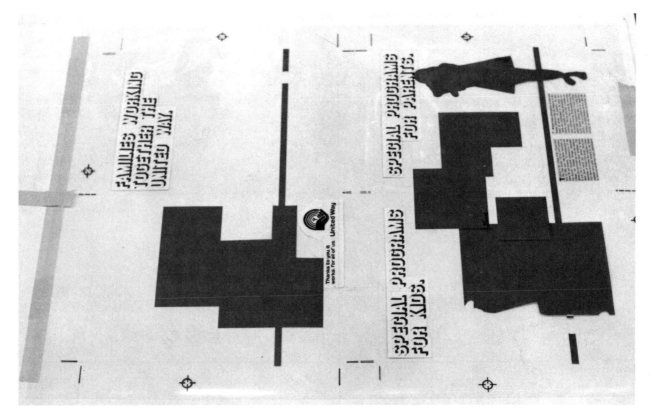

Fig. 10-59. *This is an actual layout sheet with overlays in place. Note register marks and trim marks that will be explained later in this chapter.*

Shading film

Shading film is similar to masking film but it has images on the emulsion. Fig. 10-60 gives some examples of the patterns available in shading film.

Shading film can be adhered to the layout sheet image to print black or as the same color as the layout sheet images. It can also be placed on an overlay to produce a second color.

Shading film is placed over the layout image and is cut to the desired shape. The unwanted areas are peeled away. Then the wanted image shape is burnished down. Running the image through a thermal copier tends to set the adhesive and make the emulsion stick more permanently to the base sheet.

Border material

Border material is available in roll and sheet form. It has a pressure sensitive back that bonds to the layout when burnished in place. It provides a quick and efficient method of placing a border around an image. Some examples are shown in Fig. 10-61A.

To use preprinted border material, draw blue layout lines showing the dimensions or location of the border. You can sometimes follow existing blue lines already printed on the layout sheet. Place the border tape in place along the guide line. Overlap the corners of the tape, as shown in Fig. 10-61B. Press the border firmly in position.

To make a mitered or square corner, use a sharp knife to cut each piece at 45 degrees. This technique works well

Fig. 10-60. *Shading film comes in various designs. It can be bonded directly to layout images to shade area of illustration for example. It could also be placed on overlay for second color.*

A

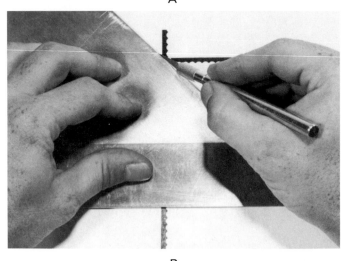

B

Fig. 10-61. A—Examples of border material. B—Preprinted border material can be handy. To make a good mitered corner, overlap border tape and cut at a 45 degree angle.

when the borders are intricate images. Straight line borders can be cut off square. See Fig. 10-61B.

A technical ink pen can be used to draw straight line borders. You must be careful to produce a clean, equal width line however.

Round corners on border tape can be produced with a technical ink pen. First use the pen to make square corners at the ends of the border tape. Then, use the same pen and a circle template to draw a circle that fits properly on the corner. Use a knife to cut the inked circle into quarters. Adhere each piece of the circle over the square corner to complete the border with rounded corners. See Fig. 10-62.

GUIDES

Guides show exact locations and dimensions for the different parts of the layout. They are very important to the preparation of a mechanical. The guides appear as trim marks, register marks, centerlines, and fold lines.

Trim marks

Trim marks are cutting guides that indicate the page size after the elements have been printed. These control devices are available as rub off or pressure sensitive images. Look at Fig. 10-63.

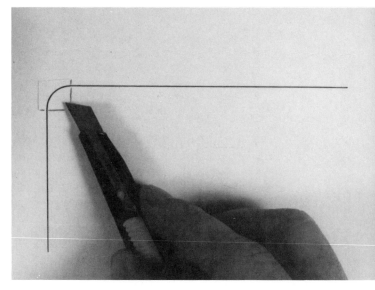

Fig. 10-62. One way to draw round border is to first draw square corner. Then draw a complete circle to fit corner. Cut circle into four equal parts or quadrants. Then adhere parts of circle over corner to form round shape.

If preprinted marks are not used, trim lines or marks must be drawn. The inked lines must be fine and drawn with accuracy. These marks are photographed and printed but are cut off during the binding-finishing process.

Register marks

Register marks are control devices that assure the proper positioning of overlays on the layout sheet. They are normally placed on a nonimage area of the layout.

As an example, if one color overlay is used with a layout sheet, register marks are placed on the outside border of the layout sheet. Then, with the overlay in exact position, another set of register marks are adhered to the overlay sheet. The layout sheet marks and the overlay marks must be directly on top of each other or in register.

The number of register marks, and their location, will vary from one facility to another. For best control, the register marks should be placed on the longest axis or on the sides with the shortest dimension. Another mark is used on the opposite side of the layout sheet. You can also place register marks on the side and bottom of the layout.

Noncritical register can be used when all copy does not need extremely accurate alignment. For example, this can be used when images are next to each other but are printed in different colors. One image is not placed on top of the other. Look at Fig. 10-64.

Lap-register is used to eliminate the possibility of the stock showing through, one color overlaps another. This is shown in Fig. 10-65.

Hairline or *tight register* refers to registration that must be very accurate. Color registration is usually critical and would require tight register. See Fig. 10-66.

The term *out-of-register* refers to images that are NOT aligned properly. This could be due to layout error or misalignment at the printing facility, Fig. 10-67.

Layout

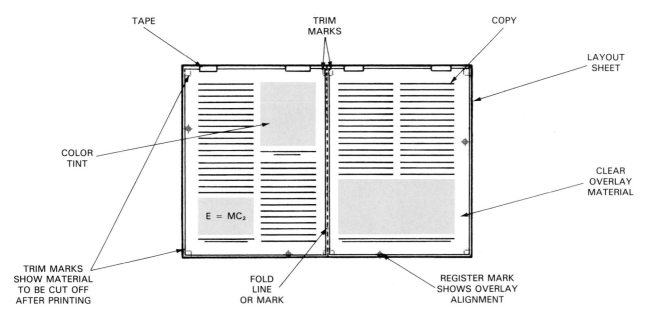

Fig. 10-63. Study the various types of guides used on layout sheet. Register marks align overlays. Trim marks show where paper will be trimmed during binding and finishing operations. Fold line shows where page will be folded during binding and finishing.

Fig. 10-64. This is an example of loose register.

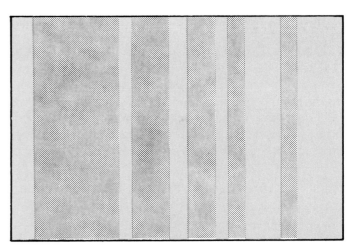

Fig. 10-66. Very accurate register is sometimes called hairline register.

Fig. 10-65. At times, specs may call for overlapping of images to assure that stock does not show through.

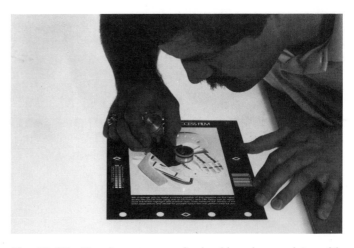

Fig. 10-67. Here layout person is checking close register with magnifier.

Centerlines or fold lines

Centerlines and *fold lines* are used to position images on a single page or to locate a fold line for more than one page. The symbol ℄ (centerline) is often used to inform the person doing the paste-up. Refer to Fig. 10-63.

As mentioned earlier, other control marks might be required by the department within the plant. The marks might also vary. The important factor is that the lines must be uniform and have the quality necessary to create an image on the negative or positive.

ASSEMBLING THE MECHANICAL

This section of the chapter will summarize all of the information you have just learned.

As discussed, a *mechanical* is a pasted-up version of the final printed piece or the camera-ready copy. The camera-ready copy is ready for photomechanical techniques that convert it to film. The term "mechanical" comes from the word photomechanical (photographic and hand assembly).

As you learned, the mechanical is made up of many elements. This would include all line work such as: illustrations, type, and any other artwork which has high contrast, single tonal value. If all of the elements are to be printed as one color, it is often possible to have one mechanical but it would not include any continuous tone materials.

An example of *continuous tone material* would be black and white or color photographs. They would require an additional photomechanical technique discussed later.

The mechanical can be prepared with all elements pasted in place or submitted as a mechanical plus separate art. The positions for the separate art are located on the mechanical as *strip-ins*. The correct location is indicated on the mechanical.

Good paste-ups

The person doing the mechanical is often an employee of the printing firm, publisher, or is an outside person directed by the customer.

A good paste-up will eliminate many of the unnecessary film handlings during platemaking operations. The copy should be of equal density. Exact positioning of elements is essential. The instructions must be written in a very concise and clear manner and cleanliness must be stressed.

A good paste-up eliminates many of the costly problems that can occur at a later stage of production.

Collecting elements

Before paste-up, it is important to collect all of the various elements. Gathering all of the photos, illustrations, display lines, and body copy contributes to an efficient operation. It is a good idea to check and see that all the elements can be positioned according to the layout. Incorrect material must be given immediate attention.

Attaching elements

Since the mechanical becomes the original for photomechanical production, all of the elements must be made ready for a single shot by the process or copy camera. It is also possible that more than one shot is necessary when overlays are used.

Typical steps in assembling the mechanical are as follows:

1. Before beginning the mechanical, make sure the layout has been approved by an authorized person.
2. The size of the layout must be identified and check all job specifications.
3. Lay out the job on the base sheet. Make sure the base sheet is large enough to provide margins for control marks and instructions. Actual size is preferable. Outline the size, using a T-square, triangle, and a pencil if needed. Measurements are critical.
4. The guidelines and the control marks must be carefully positioned. Include: register marks, trim marks, bleed marks, fold lines, and image lines as needed. Register marks, trim marks and bleed marks must be thin and sharp. The fold lines and image lines are often made with a nonreproducing pen or pencil. Preciseness is very important.
5. The layout person is responsible for making any irregular shapes. This would also include the positioning of borders and other line materials.
6. Trim the line image materials. The repros, photo copy, clip art, and other images should be trimmed to leave a margin of about 1/8 of an inch from the image area. Scissors, a cutter, knife, and razor blade are common tools to trim material.
7. All repro proofs, photocomposed material, lettering, line art, and diffusion transfer must be pasted on the base sheet. The elements are adhered with rubber cement, wax, or tape, as stated earlier.
8. Care must be taken to spray the surface of some proofs and artwork to assure the surface will not smudge. Spray fixatives are commonly found and used in the industry.
9. Excessive adhering material must be cleaned from the mechanical. Dirty mechanical art cannot be accepted by the industry.
10. Preparing a window is another important step. When halftones are to be placed on a page, one way is to cut masking film the exact size of the desired halftone area. This area will appear clear, and the halftone negative or positive will be attached to the film if it is to be printed on the same plate. The window can also be used as the location for a screened or tinted image.
11. Separate art must be indicated on the mechanical and keyed for positive identification.
12. Whenever additional instructions are needed, a vellum or tissue sheet can be hinged to the base sheet.
13. Cover the mechanical with a paper flap. Kraft paper is the most common material.
14. The name of the source and the job number should accompany the mechanical.

Applying overlays

As discussed, the *overlay* is a transparent or translucent sheet hinged to the mechanical base sheet. The overlay sheet

is often the base for the second color material. Each additional color usually requires a separate overlay sheet.
1. Draw the guildelines necessary for the additional color.
2. Position all control marks.
3. Place the art or type on the overlay.
4. Prepare the separate or combination mechanical. A *combination* is the preparation of line art and halftone material for one plate.

Layout factors

The methods of preparing a mechanical can vary from one person to another. When the mechanical is prepared properly, few difficulties will be encountered for any of the printing processes. Keep these factors in mind:
1. Proofreading is a basic requirement.
2. Accurate sizing of all elements is critical.
3. All artwork must be clean.
4. Protect the mechanical with a paper flap.
5. Proper density of all line elements must be checked.
6. Proper tonal range of continuous tone prints must be inspected.
7. All defective material must be corrected.
8. Accurate positioning of all elements is essential.
9. Accurate registration of overlays is also essential.
10. Clearly state instructions for the job.
11. Determine if "in position" or separate art is required.

ELECTRONIC LAYOUT

Many electronic imaging systems are used today for page assembly work. It is a very efficient way to process work in the prepress area. This includes the process of image stripping and preparation of line art and graphics. The configuration shown in Fig. 10-68 consists of CPUs, image disks, and three workstations: the image workstation for stripping in the retouching pictures, the graphics workstation for processing graphics and tints, and the input-output workstation for managing input of images and output of final assembled pages. A laser printer or an image generator are common output devices. See Chapter 12.

Fig. 10-68. An electronic page layout system.
(Screen - USA)

PRODUCTION FOR PRINTING

A brief description of the techniques common to the four major printing processes will be presented in this section. These processes are: relief (letterpress), planography (lithography), intaglio (gravure), and porous printing (screen process).

Letterpress

The relief process is capable of reproducing excellent line, halftone, and color art. The printing plates are in relief and proofs of the images are easy to produce. The proofs can be cut apart and arranged in the layout requested.

The substrate to be used is limited when compared with other processes since the stock surface must be smooth.

Whenever plates are required, they are expensive. Correcting the plate is also expensive since a new plate must be made. Layout must be done properly.

Mechanical art is usually required when printing advertising material with letterpress. Line art is prepared on a base sheet, but do not include the continuous tone material as part of the mechanical. The continuous tone print is engraved separately. Sometimes, a layout is sufficient, depending on whether plates or original type are used.

The engraver informs the artist how to supply art. This knowledge is necessary if the printing requires surprinting, dropouts, or mortising.

Line work does not require special preparation. Whenever metal type is used, a proof is essential to check the copy.

A wide range of screen rulings are used in letterpress. A fine screen can produce excellent quality on very smooth stock and a quality printing unit. A 120 line screen or slightly higher is used for common magazine work. Newspapers tend to use a very coarse screen ranging from 55 to 85 line.

Lithography

A wide variety of lithographic printers are found throughout the United States. It appears that the litho process also has a wide range of quality. The lithographic process also affords the printer the opportunity to use a variety of stock. Printing on an irregular surface, as well as a smooth surface, is common within the industry.

The procedure outlined in the typical steps in assembling a mechanical should be used as a guide for lithographic art preparation. The material for many lithoplates is assembled as film negatives. Whenever a positive type plate is used, the film must also be in positive form.

Gravure

The gravure process is an excellent reproduction method for extremely long runs, such as catalogs. The press operates at very high speed.

The line work and continuous tone material is placed on a gravure cylinder as screened material. The total cylinder or gravure plate is a halftone. Once the images are etched in the plate, it is very difficult to alter them.

When preparing the line art, it must be remembered that the lines will be screened. The edges will appear irregular if they are very fine.

All type, lettering, line art, etc. must be submitted as a single mechanical. Shading films are not applicable to the gravure process. Tints must be positioned by using guidelines.

With gravure, type styles with thin lines and serifs should be used with caution. Reverse type should be chosen carefully so that the letters do not fill in.

Screen process

Screen process is a versatile method of printing on many types of surfaces. It is capable of doing line and halftone work. Some of the screen process work in the electronic field is very precise and the equipment very sophisticated. Special ink is required for screen printing.

The art work is assembled much like that for lithographic work. Laying out to size, with all of the elements in position, will generally be acceptable. Overlays are necessary for additional color work.

Halftone work must be coordinated with the printer since screen size and its relationship to dot size is essential. The techniques vary slightly when using photographic or hand-cut stencils. The artist should be aware of the techniques to be used when printing.

KNOW THESE TERMS

Mechanical, Flat, Elements, Text type, Display type, Illustrations, White space, Objectives, Thumbnail, Rough, Comprehensive, Cropping, Scaling, Tone material, Mounting, Mark-up, Workmarks, Bleed, Blue pencil, Drafting board, Light table, Base sheet, Illustration board, Mechanical pencil, Lead hardness, Ruling pen, Technical pen, Nib, India ink, Brushes, T-square, Triangle, Inking triangle, Adjustable triangle, Template, Compass, Divider, Tweezers, Art knife, Swivel knife, Burnishing, Magnifier, Cutter, Cutting board, Proportion scale, Hot wax adhesive, Rubber cement, Spray adhesive, Drafting tape, Plastic tape, White paper tape, Double-coated tape, Masking film, Window, Dropout, Shading film, Border material, Guides, Trim marks, Register marks, Noncritical register, Lap-register, Tight register, Out-of-register, Centerlines, Fold lines, Electronic layout.

REVIEW QUESTIONS—CHAPTER 10

1. What is the difference between a mechanical and a flat?
2. The following would NOT be included as a layout element.
    a. Body copy.
    b. White space.
    c. Display type.
    d. Illustrations.
    e. Registration marks.
3. _____ _____ is intended to draw attention to the printed piece.
4. In your own words, how do you use white space to produce a good layout?
5. List thirteen steps for preplanning layout properly.
6. The _____ _____ is a rapidly drawn design of the layout.
7. How do you crop a photograph?
8. Line art is normally pasted down same size on the layout sheet. True or false?
9. Why is a light blue pencil commonly used by the paste-up person?
10. A _____ _____ _____ is commonly used to make camera-ready illustrations in ink.
11. List some uses for brushes in layout.
12. In your own words, how do you use a triangle?
13. Explain two methods of positioning very small pieces of copy.
14. This tool would be used to help properly adhere waxed copy to the base sheet.
    a. Magnifier.
    b. Proportioner.
    c. Burnisher.
    d. Bonder.
15. A layout sheet has a column width of four inches. A cropped photo has an image area six inches wide. How would you use a proportioning scale to find percent reduction?
16. _____ _____ is commonly used to hold the layout sheet on the art board or light table.
17. What is masking film?
18. _____ _____ is similar to masking film but it has images on the emulsion.
19. Trim marks are _____ _____ that indicate the _____ _____ after the image has been printed.
20. In your own words, explain how to use register marks.

SUGGESTED ACTIVITIES

1. Prepare a layout for a mechanical using control marks, tints, line art, copy, and continuous tone prints.
2. Visit a lithographic plant and compare the procedures used to prepare mechanicals with the procedure listed in the text.
3. Visit an agency which prepares mechanicals for full color and pre-separated color. List the kinds of tools, equipment, and materials used by the paste-up person.
4. Write the specifications for a company newsletter. Layout the base sheet according to the plan.
5. Prepare ten thumbnail sketches for a flyer of your choice.
6. Visit a plant and list tasks performed by the graphic designer, layout person, and paste-up person.

Chapter 11

PROOFREADING

After studying this chapter, you will be able to:
- Explain the duties of a proofreader.
- Mark proof copy using standard proofreader's marks.
- Describe basic electronic copy processing.
- Summarize how corrections are made on the video display terminal.
- Describe the advantages of automatic proofreading programs.

This chapter will summarize the role of the proofreader in the graphic communications industry. It will outline the various duties of the proofreader and how they relate to the other personnel in the facility. The chapter will also introduce the use of proofreading or spelling programs and how they can be helpful in making sure the copy is typeset accurately.

PROOFREADING

Once a manuscript has been written, the copy is edited and marked before being sent to the compositor (typesetter). The compositor must follow all editing instructions and set the copy exactly as it is written.

After the copy is set, the *proofreader* must make sure that the compositor has not made errors. The *proofreading process,* in very simple terms, involves marking corrections on the copy after it has been set by the compositor.

A *proof* is any copy or art that is checked before going into print. This could be a galley set by the compositor, a printout produced by a low quality printer, or a photocopy of a layout sheet.

Proofreader's responsibilities
The common duties of a proofreader are:
1. Check that the size of type corresponds to the specifications for the job.
2. Check that the line length is the same as the marked copy.
3. Make sure the style is correct.
4. Check that the spacing between lines is the same as specified.
5. Check the spelling of all words.

6. Make sure word divisions or hyphenations are correct.
7. Where inconsistencies exist, the proofreader must make notes or contact the editor.
8. Compare the first edition (manuscript) with the new edition (typeset copy).

The original copy should be carefully checked against the typeset copy to eliminate costly mistakes on the final product. This is especially true with some typesetting methods which do not reflect today's technology.

Proofreading careers
In the larger publishing and printing facilities, people are hired with expertise in proofreading. In smaller facilities, a variety of people might have this responsibility—from a person in layout to the experienced compositor. Every printer, especially in the small plant, should be able to read proofs.

Many facilities hire people as proofreaders. Some of these include:
1. Publishing houses (books, magazines, etc.).
2. Newspapers.
3. Advertising agencies.
4. Commercial typesetting facilities.
5. Government agencies.
6. Editorial service companies.
7. Associations.
8. Public relation firms.
9. Direct mail marketing companies.
10. Any large corporation that produces printed matter for advertisements, training manuals, stockholder's reports, etc.

A proofreading position can easily lead to advancement into copy editing, supervision of other proofreaders, sales, etc.

Proofreading skills
The proofreader must be a meticulous person. He or she must be able to accurately check individual letters in words as well as look for combinations of letters. This person cannot scan but must study each word separately.

The proofreader has a very important job of making sure the final product reflects quality and professionalism. If proofreading is done poorly, the highest quality paper, the best printing methods, excellent content, and other favorable aspects of the product will be ruined.

Typos (typing errors) or specification inconsistencies will make any printed product appear amateurish and will make users of the product dissatisfied.

Copyholder

In some of the larger plants, a person will be assigned to read from the original manuscript (nicknamed *dead copy*). This person is called the *copyholder*. Sometimes, the proofreader and the copyholder take turns reading. However, the proofreader marks corrections on the proof (nicknamed *live copy*). See Fig. 11-1.

The reading of proofs takes place in a variety of locations. At times, proofreading takes place in the composing room, Fig. 11-2, or a special room designed to eliminate noise and interruptions. Very often, the proofs are read by the printing customer.

Fig. 11-1. *Proofreader must check work of typesetter. Here reader is working with an assistant. Reader follows camera-ready copy and copyholder follow original manuscript.*

Fig. 11-2. *In high volume facilities, proofing can take place in typesetting area. This extra, larger video display screen or preview screen lets reader see copy as it will appear on galley. Reader can follow copy on screen while copyholder reads manuscript out loud. Then, correction cycle is much more efficient. Galley is proofed before it comes out of processor.*

Whenever and wherever proofreading takes place, comparing the proof with the original manuscript is recommended. Many times customers concentrate on the proof and very seldom refer to the manuscript. When this takes place, it is called *"horsing"* and it is not a recommended technique of proofreading. Copy omissions, changes in wording, sentences out of sequence, and other problems can result.

COPY CORRECTION

Two methods of copy correction are common to the industry—the guideline system and the book system. Very often, a company will have a recommended office style. Having one system in an organization makes for consistency and it reduces the possibility of errors. When everyone is aware of the system, production improves.

Guideline system

When using the *guideline system,* the error is circled and a line is drawn through it. Then, a line is drawn to the margin. The line is directed to a proof mark that identifies the change to be made, Fig. 11-3.

WORKSHOP 1
AUTOMOTIVES

"General Motors Computer
Command System & 1994 Up-dates"
Richard D. Fleming Resident Instructor
GM Training Center

Fig. 11-3. *Guideline system has proofreader mark through mistake and then draw a line to border or margin. Proofing symbols are then written in margin to instruct compositor of needed alterations.*

A *"dirty proof"* means that MANY corrections must be made to correct the proof. Having many changes might require that the lines cross and are very close to each other. If the proof is dirty, the lines can become very confusing.

Book system

The *book system* is a much cleaner method of marking copy for corrections. A mark or change is made above or below the error and a symbol is placed in the margin to indicate the location or type of error, Fig. 11-4. The typesetter now knows how to correct the fault. This system is less time consuming and more efficient.

tr A new wbefed combination gravure and *wf.*
l.c. intaglio Press is now being installed at the U.
cap S. Bureau of Engraving.

Fig. 11-4. *Book system is cleaner method of marking copy. Symbols (caret to show an insertion, for example) are placed on copy where they apply. Additional symbols can be placed in margin as needed.*

PROOFREADER'S MARKS

Proofreader's marks are universally used symbols that single out and explain copy changes or errors. The symbols are used to show when something is to be taken out, added, or changed. Fig. 11-5 shows proofreader's marks.

The following is a summary of the most common proofreading or editing marks:

1. The *period symbol* is a dot with a circle around it. The circle is needed so that the period is easier to identify. Just a dot could be missed by the typesetter.
2. The *caret* is a right-side up "V" or an inverted "V" and it shows where something must be added to the copy.
3. *Punctuation symbols,* such as commas, semicolons, apostrophes, etc., are denoted with a caret over or under the punctuation mark. If the punctuation goes near the bottom of the line, the mark (comma for example) is placed under the line and vice-versa.
4. The *hyphen symbol* is usually a small line with a caret under it. Some readers use two small lines to represent a hyphen. Also, a small line with an "N" above or below it could be used for hyphen and a small line with an "M" above it is used as a *dash symbol.*
5. A *delete symbol,* for removing letters or words, is a distorted capital "S." This symbol varies slightly from person to person but consistency is helpful, Fig. 11-6.

PUNCTUATION		SPACING	
⊙	Period	#	Insert space
ˆ,	Comma	eq #	Equalize space
⊙	Colon	⌣	Close up
ˆ;	Semicolon	**STYLE OF TYPE**	
ʾ,	Apostrophe	wf	Wrong font
ˆˆ	Open quotes	lc	Lower case
ˮ	Close quotes	cap	Capitalize
=/	Hyphen	u lc	Initial cap, then lower case
ᵏ ᵐ ᵉ	Dash (show length)	sc	Small capitals
( )	Parentheses	C sc	Initial cap, then small caps
DELETE AND INSERT		rom	Set in roman
✓	Delete	ital	Set in italics
✓	Delete and close up	lf	Set in light face
see copy (out)	Insert omitted matter	bf	Set in bold face
stet	Let it stand	3	Superior character
PARAGRAPHING		3	Inferior character
¶	Paragraph	**MISCELLANEOUS**	
fl ¶	Flush paragraph	X	Broken type
1 2	Indent (show no. of ems)	☾	Invert
run in	Run in	⊥	Push down
POSITION		sp	Spell out
⌐ ¬	Move right or left	/	Shilling mark (slash)
⊓ ⊔	Raise, lower	⊙⋯	Ellipsis
ctr	Center	see l/o	See layout
fl L fl R	Flush left, right	? query	Query
═	Align horizontally		
‖	Align vertically		
⬆ ∿	Transpose		
tr #	Transpose space		

Fig. 11-5. This chart gives some commonly used proofreader's symbols. Study them carefully. If you are going to be employed in graphic communications, you should understand proofing marks. Keep in mind that these marks will vary from facility to facility.

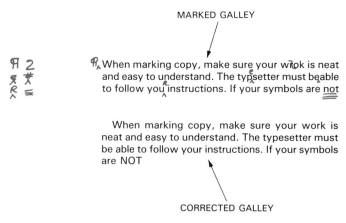

MARKED GALLEY

When marking copy, make sure your wrok is neat and easy to understand. The typesetter must be able to follow you instructions. If your symbols are not

When marking copy, make sure your work is neat and easy to understand. The typesetter must be able to follow your instructions. If your symbols are NOT

CORRECTED GALLEY

Fig. 11-6. Here is a sample of proof marks being used to correct copy problems. Note their use!

6. A *close-up symbol* is two small curves above and below the letters or words and it means remove space. For example, it would be used if the typesetter accidentally hit the space bar in the middle of a word.

7. A *stet symbol* means to "let copy stand" or ignore any denoted change in copy. It is the word "stet" written in lower case letters and the denoted correction is unnecessary. Dots may be placed under the letters or words to denote the stet symbol.

8. A *paragraph symbol* is two lines with a curve at the top. It is used to show where a sentence should start and new paragraph is to be indented.

9. A *flush symbol* is a lower case "fl" and means copy should be shifted to margin.

10. A *move* or *shift symbol* is a square with one side missing. Copy can be moved up or down and right or left with this symbol.

11. A *center symbol* means to center copy and it is denoted with half squares on each side of the copy or a lower case "ctr."

12. A *transpose symbol* means to reverse the sequence of letters or words. It is shown as a sideways or lazy "S," wavy line, or as the abbreviation "tr." An elongated "S" would be used to transpose words.

13. The *insert space symbol* is like a small tick-tack-toe board or numeral sign and it means separate or add space. This symbol might be needed if the typesetter failed to hit the space bar between two words.

14. A *lower case symbol* means change letters from capital to lower case and is given by the letters "lc."

15. The *capital symbol* means change to capital letters and is usually denoted by placing three lines under the letters. The letters "cap" in the border can also show capitalization.

16. The *italic symbol* is usually a single line under the characters.

17. A *broken type symbol* is an "X" and it means that the typeset material is defective or has been damaged in layout.

18. A *push down symbol* is an inverted "T" and it denotes that copy should be moved down.

19. A *see layout symbol* means something is wrong and you should compare the manuscript or rough with the layout. It is given by writing "see l/o."

20. A *query symbol* denotes that the editor or proofreader is not sure if something is correct. This may refer to content of material, sequence, etc. A circled question mark and the word "query" would be used to denote a possible problem.

The use of these and other proofreading marks will vary. It is important however that everyone in the same facility use the same marks. This consistency will reduce errors and increase communication as a printed product moves through each step of production. Refer to Fig. 11-7.

Fig. 11-7. When proofing, go slowly! Read slow enough so you can check each word. Ruler will help follow line. This reader is using guideline system for small job.

Proofreading and editing marks must be written clearly and should be exaggerated so they are not overlooked. When needed, you can write special notes pertaining to the marks in the border. Sometimes an extra sheet may have to be attached to the layout giving instructions for the typesetter or layout person.

AUTHOR'S ALTERATIONS

Author's alterations are changes made by the author or the customer developing the printed product. Abbreviated AA's, they can be made easier if a printout of the manuscript is sent to the author or customer before layout, Fig. 11-8.

As the product moves through production, author alterations become more expensive. After layout, alterations require resetting and rework of the layout sheets. After printing, alterations require rework by the typesetter, layout changes, and changes on the flats or "silver prints" (prepress proofs). This can be an expensive and time consuming process.

Fig. 11-8. *Computer programs are available to check for spelling and even common grammatical errors. Corrections can then be made before processing.*

USING PROOFS

The first proof is generally sent to the proofreader along with the original copy. This could represent the total job for a commercial printer or it could be a printout copy which in no way resembles the final printed piece, Fig. 11-9. In most cases, a proofreader for publications will ask for clean proofs to be submitted to the publisher, customer, or editorial department.

Once the proofreader receives the proofs, all of the corrections will be placed on ONE COPY. The corrected copy is sometimes sent to the customer or whomever is to review a marked proof.

Galley proofs for relief images are made on a proof press with the image appearing on newsprint. Hardcopy from a phototypesetter is also referred to as a galley proof.

Fig. 11-9. *Proofreader has just received proof of printed product. She is looking it over quickly to detect major problems. Camera-ready galley will also be proofed.*

Reproduction proofs are also made from relief images but are usually pulled on matte book stock. These images are sharp and can be used for camera-ready copy. Camera-ready copy is of the same quality expected in the final printed product.

Comparison proofing

Comparison proofing is done primarily to find major problems: copy deletion, incorrect sequence, copy duplication, etc. It is not recommended to check each word because all of the work is completed by one person. Generally, the reader scans quickly through the proof once to check for problems. The reader then places the proof next to the manuscript and traces along the lines of the proof with a pen to control speed. Placing a straightedge across the copy and moving it slowly down the page is also helpful.

Switching back and forth from proof to copy can be troublesome but it is acceptable for small jobs with little copy. Check the first and last words of paragraph to find missing or duplicated copy.

Remember! Always compare proof with copy. Do NOT compare the copy with the proof.

Two-person proofing

The *two-person proofing system* requires the reader to work with an assistant. This is the most common proofreading method when accuracy and speed are important. It is frequently used with larger jobs, such as this textbook for example.

As mentioned, the two people are referred to as the reader and the copyholder. The *reader* follows the camera-ready copy to check closely for errors. The *copyholder* follows the original manuscript. Usually, the two take turns reading to each other. Each word must be carefully pronounced and reading must not be too fast. The reader must have time to scan the letters of each word, check punctuation, style, and other items.

Usually, a special jargon or language is developed between the reader and copyholder. For instance, some readers pronounce each period as "peer" or each capital letter as "cap" to denote the end and beginning of sentences.

MARKING CORRECTIONS

Corrections must be accurately and clearly marked on the layout sheets. Since most galley sheets are on slick photographic paper, a colored marker or pen is commonly used to pinpoint a change. Nonreproducing blue pencil is used in the border of the layout sheet for proofing symbols and notes.

When marking copy, only mark copy that must be changed. If your work is sloppy, you might mark into a good line and ruin it. Then the typesetter will have to reset or run off the extra line unnecessarily.

The initials of the proofreader are commonly written in the lower corner of the layout sheet in blue pencil. If there are questions concerning the page, the person involved can be located for answering questions. The initials also show that the page has been proofed and is ready to be corrected. In some cases, the editor or writer will also look over the corrections and layout sheets before being returned to typesetting.

CHECKING CORRECTIONS

The editor or proofreader will have to go through and read any changes in copy after typesetting alterations. Usually, just the changes are read and not the complete job. The blue pencil marks and a new section of galley pasted down over the marked galley denote where changes have been made. One person can usually read and check the corrections. If the changes are OK, the blue pencil marks are erased.

TYPESETTING CORRECTIONS

Once the corrections are marked on the proof sheet or layout sheet, the typesetter must keystroke the changes following the proofreader's marks. With modern computerized typesetting equipment, this job is made much more efficient. Look at Fig. 11-10.

Discussed briefly in Chapter 9, the copy or manuscript is stored on magnetic floppy disks. The typesetter must refer to the file and pull up the copy to be corrected. The copy will then appear on the video display screen.

To change a letter in a word, the cursor (square dot) on the screen is shifted to the letter or letters to be changed, Fig. 11-11. To change one letter in a word, move the cursor

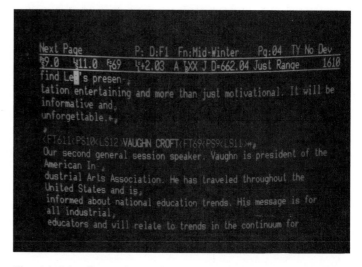

Fig. 11-11. Cursor is used to control changes in copy. It can be quickly moved over screen to location of change. By placing cursor over a letter, that letter can be deleted or changed. Cursor can also be used to define blocks of copy for moving paragraphs, dropping sentences, etc.

to that letter using the editing keypad. Then, hit the delete button and that letter will be dropped. Hit the insert button on the editing keypad and then the letter to be added to the word. On newer systems, the change can be made by merely overtyping, using the normal keyboard.

The file management keypad can then be used to define the block of copy to be changed with the new word. The block of copy can then be produced by the image generator, processed, and then sent to layout for positioning.

It is also possible to move words, paragraphs, or blocks. As an example, if two sentences are to be transposed, move the cursor to the second sentence and identify it by touching the definition key. Next, move the cursor to the beginning of the first sentence. By touching the move key, the space is opened up and the sentence inserted.

Once the system is understood, correcting of copy can be done very rapidly. Proficiency comes with practice.

Many of the visual display terminals have the capability of selecting type options. If a boldface or an italic type is needed, the key is readily available. Sometimes, this is accomplished by keys labeled UR (upper rail) or LR (lower rail). These terms were used in old line casting machines terminology and have carried over. The upper rail designation was associated with the option of boldface or italic while the lower rail was the usual choice.

The terminology might not always be the same but other keys common to the typesetting unit are: flush left, flush right, centered, em quad, en quad, return, etc. Most offices will have a list of the basic commands for the system.

All of this takes place before the copy comes out as a print or hard copy. The corrections and changes are made electronically (computer memory) or on a floppy disk. Sometimes, after the hard copy is received, a change needs to be made. Today's systems make it possible to recall the copy on the screen. The images are taken out of storage and only the mistake needs to be reset or keystroked over. The

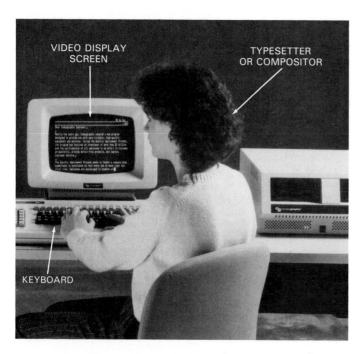

VIDEO DISPLAY SCREEN

TYPESETTER OR COMPOSITOR

KEYBOARD

Fig. 11-10. With today's computerized typesetting equipment, changes in copy are easy to make. File can be pulled up showing specific sections of copy. Changes can then be made using the keyboard. Bulk of copy does not have to be keystroked again.

correction is on the screen and the bulk of the copy does not have to be reset. Resetting good copy only increases the chance of errors slipping through the system. Calling up a file, making the correction, and outputting the corrected block can be done quickly and efficiently by a knowledgeable typesetter.

Fig. 11-12 summarizes a typical correction cycle.

Note! Electronic typesetting equipment varies greatly. Always refer to the operating manual for the specific system. The manual will describe its operation.

Refer to the index for more information on setting type, computers, typefaces, optical character readers, etc. These topics are discussed in other textbook chapters. The next chapter explains electronic production.

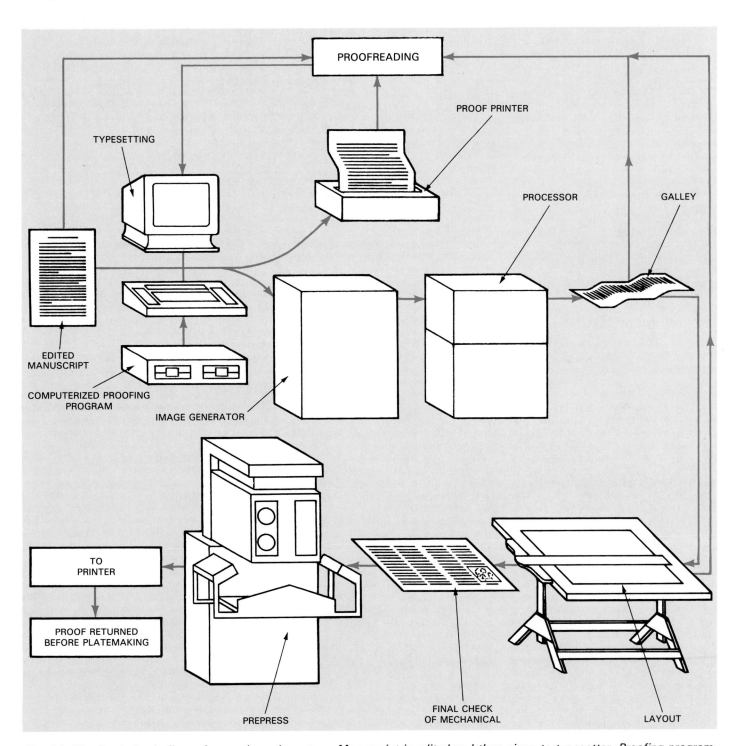

Fig. 11-12. Study basic flow of copy through system. Manuscript is edited and then given to typesetter. Proofing program can help prevent typos by producing warning signal. Hard copy can then be run off on proof printer or as a galley on photopaper. Either of these then goes to proofreader. Marked copy is then returned to typesetting and corrected. Galley is then pasted up on layout sheet and again proofed. Printer will return "silver prints" or proof sheets for a final check before going to press. This system can vary depending upon the facility and type of printed product.

PROOFING PROGRAMS

A *proofing program,* also called a *spelling program,* will automatically check the spelling of words as they are keystroked by the typesetter. A floppy disk holds computer data called a "dictionary" of thousands of words.

The proofing program compares every word that is typed into the system with the words in the program dictionary. If a word is typed incorrectly (not in dictionary), most systems will make an audible "beep" to signal a potential problem. If a word is technical or slang and it is not in the dictionary, the typesetter can ignore the sound signal.

Proofing programs can be very helpful to production speed and quality. They can greatly reduce typos and make the correction cycle much easier for everyone involved with producing the mechanicals. The proofreader must still go over the copy. However, with fewer typing errors to worry about, more effort can be given to checking style, illustration references, sequence, and other important aspects.

Proofing programs are available for modern typesetting machines, home computers, and word processors. The size of the proofing dictionary will vary. A typical proofing dictionary might contain 80,000 words. Other specialized words can be added to the program disk as needed.

KNOW THESE TERMS

Proofreader, Typos, Dead copy, Live copy, Guideline system, Book system, Proofreader's marks, Caret, Stet, Transpose, Query, Galley proof, Reproduction proof, Comparison proof, Two-person proofing, Proofing program.

REVIEW QUESTIONS—CHAPTER 11

1. The _____ or _____ must follow all editing or proofreading instructions and keystroke the copy exactly as it is written.

2. The _____ _____ involves marking corrections on the copy after it has been typeset.
3. What is a proof?
4. Explain eight responsibilities of a proofreader.
5. Name some of the facilities that hire proofreaders.
6. The original manuscript is often called the _____ _____ and the proof is called the _____ _____.
7. Explain the basic differences between the guideline and book systems of marking copy.
8. In your own words, how would a caret be used to mark copy when proofreading?
9. List and explain ten proofing symbols.
10. This system has a computerized dictionary that can check spelling as words are keystroked.
    a. Book system.
    b. Comparison system.
    c. Proofing program.
    d. Management program.

SUGGESTED ACTIVITIES

1. Type the following copy (next paragraph) on a sheet of paper. Proofread the copy and use proofreader's marks to indicate the corrections required. The manuscript would be the second paragraph.

    It is nececssary for a compositer, at have at laest an Elementery under standing of the marks to correct his or her own errors: and often the errors of others.

    It is necessary for a compositor to have at least an elementary understanding of these marks because he or she must usually correct his or her own errors and the errors of others.
2. Practice writing proofreader's marks. Make your own summary sheet of the marks in chart form.
3. Visit a facility that does proofreading. Talk with the proofreaders and study their style for marking copy.
4. Observe the use of a proofing program.

Chapter 12

ELECTRONIC PRODUCTION

After studying this chapter, you will be able to:
- Explain the process of creating images electronically.
- Describe the basic components of an Electronic Imaging system.
- Explain the advantages and disadvantages of the PC and the Macintosh for electronic imaging.
- Describe the input devices commonly associated with the capturing of data.
- Explain the software needed for electronic publishing.
- Describe the output devices commonly used for electronic publishing.
- Define and correctly use the terms unique to electronic imaging.
- Summarize the electronic imaging process.
- Explain the techniques used to prepare text and graphic images.

The process of preparing copy and film for print production has gone through many changes in recent years. The need to prepare camera-ready copy with traditional paste-up techniques, then shoot it to produce film for stripping and platemaking, has been eliminated in many printing and publishing operations. This has come about through the introduction of desktop computers and page composition software that can produce camera-ready art, film, or even plates directly from laser output devices. Many professionals in the field of graphic communications refer to this process as *desktop publishing*, Fig. 12-1, while others call it *electronic imaging,* or *electronic prepress*. There is no commonly accepted exact definition for any of these terms.

Preparing products for printing using this new technology requires the introduction of equipment, processes, and procedures that are either new or vastly different to many printing professionals. Typically, the equipment usually consists of a desktop computer and its associated peripheral devices. The process allows an individual to integrate text and graphic matter on the electronic page, using a desktop computer. This application of technology has provided many individuals and groups with the capability to prepare professional-appearing documents which, only a short time ago, would have required outside assistance.

COMPONENTS OF ELECTRONIC IMAGING SYSTEMS

Electronic imaging is a term for the use of the personal computer to create, edit, and compose text and graphics into pages for consumption by individuals, the general public, or special audiences. It requires a desktop computer, computer software, and an output device to accomplish the task.

INPUT DEVICES

There are a number of ways in which the electronic publishing system acquires data. This acquisition of information can take the form of graphics and/or text in many different file formats. The following section will describe several input devices.

Keyboard
The keyboard is the traditional way of inputting copy for an electronic imaging system. Typically, this device is used to enter text in ASCII format. It is possible to enter graphic images directly from the keyboard, although other devices also exist for this purpose and can achieve it more easily.

Mouse
Many electronic imaging systems rely extensively on input from a *mouse*, especially for user interfaces and graphics. There are a number of styles available, depending upon the user preferences and tasks being performed.

Digitizing tablet
The *digitizing tablet* is another form of input to the system where the keyboard is not needed, Fig. 12-2. The main difference between a mouse and a digitizing tablet is that the puck or mouse must be moved on top of the digitizing tablet

Fig. 12-1. This workstation has the components needed to combine text and graphic images electronically for publication. (Chapter One, Screaming Color)

177

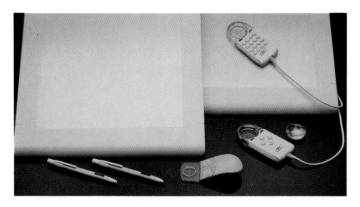

Fig. 12-2. The digitizing tablet is an input device that can be used to trace a drawing and convert it to a graphic image file. The tracing work is done with a mouse-like pointing device called a puck. (KURTA)

Fig. 12-3. The photo multiplier (PMT) scanner is an example of scanning devices that can be used to input images. (Scitex America)

to move the pointer on the system monitor. This is very useful with forms of graphics that require high precision.

Pointing device

Other forms of input tools used frequently with a digitizing tablet are called *pointing devices*, although this term has a broad definition. Cordless mice, cordless pens, pucks, and pressure-sensitive pens are all included as ways to input data into an electronic imaging system.

Scanners

The technology of these devices creates logical divisions for the discussion of this topic. These include Photo Multiplier Tube (PMT) scanners, Charge Coupled Devices (CCD) scanners, and Video Tube (VT) cameras, Fig. 12-3. Image capture using the various forms of scanning technology is discussed elsewhere in this textbook.

PLATFORM

The *platform* of an electronic imaging system is the computer that is used to operate the software; it includes the elements necessary to create, assemble, and output the page. The most popular platforms in use today are the Macintosh,

the IBM personal computer (PC) and the numerous "clones" that are compatible with the PC. See Fig. 12-4.

Macintosh

The Macintosh computer was introduced in 1984, and quickly became popular because of its ease of use and ability to generate high-quality graphic images. The Macintosh system was designed around a concept of a graphical user interface, which allowed for easy-to-understand graphic representation of computing tasks on screen. This platform was central to the development of electronic imaging, and continues to play a major role. The Macintosh system has continued to evolve in the publishing field, providing greater power to the user with each upgrade.

Some Macintosh advantages for electronic imaging include:

• The graphic interface between the operator and the computer is intuitive, with icons that represent the desired actions.

A

B

Fig. 12-4. Imaging system platforms. A—The Macintosh platform is widely used. B—IBM-compatible computers using the Windows interface have become popular for electronic production. This model has two drives with removable units for storing and transporting large electronic files. (Tandon)

- The majority of electronic imaging and graphic software on the market was developed for the Macintosh.
- Most Macintosh platforms support 32 bit color which is critical to the printer using cyan, magenta, yellow and black (CMYK) color separations.
- Software developers are required to use the same basic display and menu items, providing compatibility and continuity between software programs.
- Unlimited RAM access for the system.
- No limits on hard drive accessibility.

There are some limitations on the Macintosh, however. It has poor multi-tasking capability for such things as printing and disk file transfers, is susceptible to viruses, and is more expensive than comparable IBM-compatible computer systems.

IBM PC and compatibles

These computers are frequently referred to as the "MS-DOS computers," because of the original Microsoft operating system they used. Today, many of them have shifted to another Microsoft system, a *graphical use interface* (GUI) called Windows. This provides tremendous potential for desktop publishing to use these platforms.

The PC has some limitations for electronic imaging in terms of memory, availability of disk space, color capabilities, and operating system. There also are fewer electronic imaging programs available for the PC than for the Macintosh. To make a PC useful for electronic imaging requires the use of various peripheral devices, removing the initial price advantage these machines have over the Macintosh platform.

The PC is beginning to establish itself in the world of electronic imaging that has long been dominated by the Macintosh computer system. In some business environments where the PC is the only available platform, many users are successfully using these computers for a variety of publications. Factors contributing to the increasing competitiveness of the PC include the introduction of faster, more powerful chips; the introduction of Microsoft Windows as an easy-to-use interface; greater availability of powerful page composition software, such as QuarkXPress, and strong price and feature competition among manufacturers, resulting in greater

affordability. An important advantage for the PC is its multi-tasking capability, which allows several things (such as file retrieval and printing) to occur at the same time.

MONITORS

Most electronic imaging systems use a *WYSIWYG* ("What You See Is What You Get") display, Fig. 12-5. Some monitors are large enough to display an entire page or even two pages; others require scrolling across and up and down to see a full page displayed in actual size. In addition to type of display, other monitor issues of importance include *resolution* and *color capability*. The resolution of most electronic imaging monitors is 72 ppi (pixels per inch). This is convenient, since it corresponds to the type measurement system where 72 points is equal to one inch.

Monochrome display

This type of monitor is capable of displaying images in only one color: a pixel on the screen can either be on or off. Monochrome monitors are the least expensive to purchase and are able to provide a sharp, crisp image for lines and text. A process of *dithering* is used to display continuous tone images on the screen. A dither is a pseudo-halftone that creates the illusion of a continuous tone image by varying the pixels that are on or off in a given area. With the PC, add-on boards can be used to give greater resolution and capacity for the monitor.

Gray scale monitor

This type of monitor is capable of displaying images in 256 levels of gray. Each pixel on the monitor can have any one of 256 different gray tones, creating a display that accurately represents a continuous tone image. A gray scale monitor usually will require the addition of an internal board to the computer.

Color monitor

Color monitors are available in 8-bit and 24-bit modes. The number of bits relates to the number of colors that can be displayed on the monitor at one time. With an 8-bit monitor, any one of 256 colors can be displayed by each pixel on the monitor. This is acceptable for many applications. A 24-bit monitor is used when the need to match colors or display different shades on screen is very important. The use of 24-bit color has a price, however: the user must make a sacrifice in refresh speeds and the ability to update quickly. Some programs support 32-bit color which allows for additional color manipulation on the screen.

The color monitor uses the *additive color* theory, based upon the combination of red, green and blue (*RGB*) to form white light. This creates a problem for the desktop publisher who is trying to achieve a WYSIWYG color environment. Since colors are displayed in RGB, there is difficulty in matching the printed results of the *subtractive color* environment. In subtractive color environment, *CMYK* (cyan, magenta, yellow, black) inks are combined to remove color from the printed sheet. This means that full color representation of

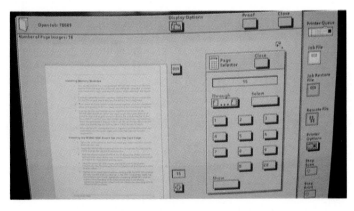

Fig. 12-5. A WYSIWYG ("What you see is what you get") display shows you, on the screen, what will appear on the printed page. The document page is displayed at the left in the same way it will appear when printed.

images on the monitor and on the printed sheet are achieved through different principles. The result is visual color discrepancies for which the designer must compensate when making color judgments using the monitor.

STORAGE DEVICES

The effort and time required to produce the file using an electronic imaging system suggests that some form of storage is required after the file is created. A number of different types of storage are available.

Floppy disks

The floppy disk is the standard medium for storage. It has limited capacity, although the capacity is continuing to increase. The floppy has relatively slow access and data transfer speeds and formatting sometimes can be a problem. The continued popularity of this medium can be attributed to its stability and relatively low price.

Hard drives

Hard drives are available as either internal or external types. Virtually all electronic imaging systems have an internal hard drive. This storage medium is also relatively inexpensive. The single most critical occurrence for a hard drive is when it becomes inoperable ("crashes"). The adage of "It isn't **if** your hard drive is going to crash, it's **when** your hard drive is going to crash" should be taken very seriously. Optimizing the drive for operational efficiency and regularly backing up the data are both considered standard operating procedures when important data is on the hard drive.

Removable cartridges

When dealing with large graphic files, removable cartridges provide the user with the option for a transportable storage medium. See Fig. 12-6. This has contributed to their popularity and made them a standard presence in electronic imaging systems. Most such cartridges have rather slow access and data transfer speeds. The drives have interface capability with many systems, although some formatting incompatibilities do exist.

Magneto-optic (M/O) storage

This form of storage is also known as "optical storage," although it is actually magnetic. Like other magnetic media, it allows data to be erased and new data written to the disk. The drive has two lasers, one to write the data onto a disk coated with magnetic material and the other to read the data back when the user retrieves the file. Data retrieval is quite slow although it is much faster than the process of writing the data to disk. The large capacity of these devices makes them an excellent choice for storing a large number of files for future use.

Photo CD

The *Photo CD* (Compact Disc) provides for large storage capacity for photographic images. A photo CD can be ordered when the new film is originally processed, and

Fig. 12-6. These are examples of cartridges used with removable cartridge storage devices.

delivered along with the slides or prints from the film. You can also have up to 100 photos (35 mm slides or negatives) put on disk. The images can be loaded into any electronic imaging computer equipment with a compatible CD-ROM drive and the necessary software. A picture from a photo CD can be used like any other scanned image. It can be edited with image-manipulation software and output.

SOFTWARE

Software used for desktop publishing is classified by the way documents are prepared. This is not much different from the way that copy for printing is traditionally prepared. The process essentially consists of preparing text and graphics, then composing pages using these elements. The classes of software for these tasks consist of *word processors*, *graphics editors*, and *page composers*.

Word processors

A word processor is used to generate the *copy*, or text, that will be formatted in the page composer in the electronic imaging process. Many word processors have the capability of providing both text and graphics formatting. However, it is generally considered better to use the word processor strictly for text entry and editing, instead of trying to create the entire publication with it. This is particularly true if the publication will require extensive text formatting and incorporation of numerous graphic elements.

Graphics editors

When a designer begins using graphics in publications, he or she must be familiar with the various graphic types that are processed using graphics editors. In the current realm of electronic imaging, these can be broadly divided into bit-mapped images and object-oriented images.

Bit-mapped images are graphics files that contain a map of *pixels* (tiny rectangular picture elements), each of which is assigned characteristics. In a simple black and white bit map, pixel characteristics are limited to "black" or "white." In these files, one bit of information is assigned to each pixel: either it is "on" (black) or "off" (white), which in turn determines where ink is placed on the paper. Graphics programs are able to also store additional information about each pixel location, providing gray scale and color data. Each of these pixels might require eight or even 32 bits of information to describe.

Another key factor of bit maps is *resolution*, measured in pixels per inch (ppi). In general, the higher the resolution, the greater the amount of memory required for storage. It is important to note that 300 dpi (dots per inch) resolution is adequate for most images. The user should avoid images larger than necessary to conserve on valuable storage capacity and output time.

Bit-mapped images are primarily used to reproduce continuous tone images (photographs); they should be avoided, if possible, in other electronic imaging work. When bit-mapped images are used for reproducing photographs, they are converted to halftone dots and placed on film for printing.

Object-oriented images are able to be defined in terms of mathematical parameters. Type and line art are examples of object-oriented page elements. A designer has greater control over these images than over bit-mapped images, because they are created with mathematical parameters instead of patterns of dots. Through use of these parameters, the designer has control over shape, placement, line width, and object pattern. Another advantage of this type of image is that the computer can store it very efficiently.

An object is characterized by *handles* that allow identification, relocation, and resizing of the object. To accomplish this, the designer selects the item with a mouse by clicking on it to make it active. Once the object-oriented image is active, any of its parameters can be changed. Because the object is defined geometrically, shapes will not break up when enlarged or reduced.

Page composers

The assembly of text and graphic images into the final page is accomplished with a page composer. Common page composition software packages include Aldus PageMaker™, Ventura Publisher™, and QuarkXPress™. Although the specific operations of the packages are somewhat different, an experienced operator can use any of them to accomplish many of the prepress production requirements interactively on a computer monitor. These programs create a code in *PostScript*™ (a page description language) that eventually is sent to an output device. That device converts the PostScript code to a bit-mapped image on paper, film or plate material.

OUTPUT DEVICES

When a file is completed by a designer using the page composer, it is sent to the output device where all elements of the page are converted into bit maps for imaging. This conversion process, called *rasterizing*, is carried out by a *Raster Image Processor (RIP)*. The RIP function as an interpreter of the PostScript language for an output device such as an imagesetter. A RIP converts both object-oriented images and bit-mapped images from the page composer into machine pixels (bit maps) at a set output resolution. The three common types of output devices are the dot matrix printer, the laser printer, and the imagesetter.

Dot matrix printer

The output quality of the dot matrix printer is generally considered to be the poorest of the three devices. Images are formed by ink dots that are applied to the paper by various means. Because of the dot structure, the images have rough edges. The number of dots per inch varies with the type of dot printer used. The resolution can vary, but 72 dots per inch is common.

Dot matrix printer output is not of the quality needed for final reproduction, but it works very well for page proofs showing the positioning of text and graphics. Printer speeds range from approximately 50 to 200 characters per second.

Laser printer

The laser printer operates much like the photocopying machine. The copying machine uses reflected light to create an image on a drum, while the laser printer uses a laser beam to polarize an image on the drum. The light produced by a laser, in general, is far more directional and powerful than any other light source, Laser printers vary in size, efficiency, and cost.

Laser printers are most often used as the output device for desktop publishing work done on a personal computer. Any material that is to be printed is sent through the computer to the printer. The laser printer uses the description of the material to construct an image of the page in its memory.

The description sent by the computer to the printer is in a page description language, such as PostScript. The laser printer has a built-in computer, usually called an engine. It understands the page description language and translates the output of the computer into a bit-mapped image for printing.

The printer takes the bit-mapped image of the page and transfers it to a light-sensitive drum, using the laser light. See Fig. 12-7. The drum of the printer holds a positive electrical charge. The laser light scans the rotating drum, emitting the

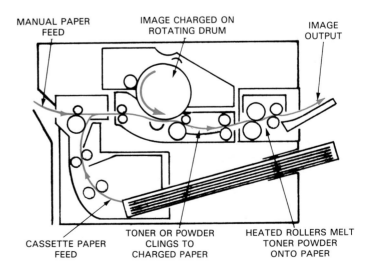

Fig. 12-7. A laser printer produces an image by a scanning technique combined with electrostatic principles. Rollers feed paper at a constant speed through the printer.

image are drawn from printer memory. Areas where the black part of the image would be are neutralized or are made more negative. This leaves the surrounding area positively charged.

As with many copying machines, a positively charged black powder (*toner*) is used to create a visible image on the paper. As the drum rotates through the toner powder, the toner is repelled by the positively charged areas and attracted to the negatively charged image dots, The toner-filled dots or groupings of dots make up the image of the page.

The paper with its toner image next passes between two heated rollers. The heat fuses (melts) the powder dots onto the paper to produce a permanent image. The finished product is placed in the receiver tray. The images created by the laser printer have high resolution. Depending upon the printer model, resolution may be as coarse as 300 dots per inch (dpi) or as fine as 1200 dpi.

Imagesetter

When high-resolution images must be output for commercial printing, an *imagesetter* is used. See Fig. 12-8. The output station consists of two parts; the RIP (raster image processor) and the imagesetter.

As noted earlier, the RIP converts the PostScript instructions into a bit-mapped image at the resolution of the selected output device. Any problems in the output are likely to occur during this phase. It becomes the responsibility of the imagesetter operator to troubleshoot these problems and fix the file prior to before again sending it to the imagesetter.

Using laser technology, the imagesetter outputs the page or color separations on the selected medium: resin-coated photographic paper, film, or plate material. To insure high quality output, especially with color separations, special attention must be given to calibration and maintenance of the imagesetter. Imagesetters are manufactured by a number of different companies. They differ in speed, precision, resolution, screening technology, and media capability.

Fig. 12-9 shows examples of output results from a dot matrix printer, a laser printer, and an imagesetter. Note the difference in the resolution.

ELECTRONIC IMAGING PROCESS

Electronic imaging, under the title "desktop publishing," had its start as a communications tool for individuals, groups

Fig. 12-8. This family of high-volume, internal-drum imagesetters is designed to meet the varying needs of commercial printers, color separators, advertising agencies, and publishers of newspapers, magazines, and catalogs. (Scitex America)

and businesses. Using personal computers and dot matrix or laser printers, the early practitioners turned out newsletters, sales flyers, instruction booklets, and similar publications.

This application of technology has not only provided advantages to groups and individuals, but has become a familiar part of the traditional printing and publishing industry as an option for preparing copy for printing. It is becoming very common for clients to deliver work to the printer on a disk as a digital file instead of the traditional camera-ready copy. This has created both new benefits and new problems for the printer. The benefits deal with increased productivity and greater responsibility on the part of the client/designer. The new problems deal with how well the new technology lends itself to the printing process, particularly when multiple color work is submitted.

Text preparation

Several options exist when preparing text for use in the electronic imaging process. The simplest would be to enter copy directly onto the page while using the page composition software. This is an acceptable method with small amounts of copy or when the copy varies significantly throughout the page such as in a newspaper ad. When a page has a large amount of text, however, it is better to create it separately using some form of word processing package. If hard copy

IMAGESETTER

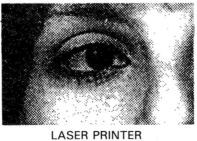
LASER PRINTER

DOT MATRIX PRINTER

Fig. 12-9. Compare reproduction of the same original image by three different output devices. An imagesetter will normally produce the most accurate reproduction. A laser printer results in reproduction close to imagesetter quality. The dot matrix produces a coarser image that is acceptable for many applications. (LowDOWN) exists, Optical Character Recognition (OCR) scanning is also a viable option.

Word processing

Word processing packages are highly efficient tools for creating and editing text. Originally designed for the business environment, they have allowed computers to replace typewriters in preparing most documents. Although word processors are intended primarily for handling text, some packages have focused on the ability to incorporate graphic images. When combining numerous graphic elements with text, however, a page composer is preferred.

Text generated with a word processor is usually stored in the American Standard Code for Information Interchange (*ASCII*) format. This is a standard code for characters using an eight-bit code combination. Each character is assigned a value between 0 to 255.

To assist in formatting the text when it is placed in a page composer, it is possible to incorporate special ASCII codes, known as *text filters*. These codes are placed in the text to identify specific attributes, such as headlines, subheads, or body text. When the text is imported into the page composer, the ASCII code is recognized and assigns the specific text attributes to that copy. This technique saves the person using the page composer many hours of formatting once the text has been placed in the document.

Many page composers also have the ability to recognize the formats of the common word processing packages on the market. This allows the page composer to recognize the text files and retain much of the formatting that was applied in the word processor. The greater the compatibility of the page composer to the word processor, the less formatting needed once the text has been incorporated into the page composer.

Graphic images

The visual images that make up the page, as distinguished from text, are collectively called graphics. See Fig. 12-10. Traditionally, these can consist of line images or continuous tone image that are converted to halftones for printing. When the page is prepared using electronic imaging, the file formats of the graphics becomes a very important consideration. This will determine how much manipulation can be done

Fig. 12-10. Graphics can be created and manipulated on screen, then merged with text files, using a page composer. (Chapter One, Screaming Color)

to the image and how well the image will be reproduced when output. In the broadest sense, all images can be classified as being either bit-mapped or object-oriented. The topic of graphic images must also address file formats and how to use these images.

FILE FORMATS

There are a number of file formats used for either bit-mapped or object-oriented images. In addition, descriptions of image placement, resolution, color, background, and a number of other important aspects of the image are contained in the file format.

Paint file

Files in this format result from programs that create a bit-mapped description of the image on the monitor of a typical electronic imaging system. The operator will use drawing tools, such as a "pencil" or "paint brush," to create strokes on the screen. These are recorded in the file as a bit map having a 72 dpi resolution, the same as the resolution of the monitor. These images should generally be avoided because of the jagged edges the image will display, even on low-resolution output devices. These images are useful, though, especially as templates that can be traced over with object-oriented editors.

PICT

PICT is a file format intended for the display of graphic images on the monitor. These images should usually be avoided for all other purposes, especially for outputting. Images in PICT format display very well, but have low resolution equal to the electronic imaging systems monitor. The result when using one of the images to output to an imagesetter is an image that is *pixelized*, (an image made up of large squares). In rare situations, this might be desirable, but is not acceptable for most publications.

TIFF

Tagged Information File Format (*TIFF*), was developed by Aldus as a graphic file format. The code was then made available to many developers to use in writing and designing their software packages. This format is actually a bit-mapped format and is accepted into many different programs.

RIFF

Although RIFF (Raster Image File Format) is not exactly the same as TIFF, it is very similar. This format was originally intended for the use with black and white continuous tone images. Files are easily converted to TIFF.

EPS

The *EPS* or EPS(F) (Encapsulated PostScript) file format is the most stable of the file formats to use in outputting to an imagesetter. It is not quite so convenient as TIFF, but will usually provide more stable results when output. This file format is an object-oriented format that has the capability of containing bit-mapped images. Because it handles both object-oriented and bit-mapped images, EPS provides a very reliable format for graphic images in the electronic imaging environment. When using this format, it is possible to display just a box with the file name rather than the image itself. This improves the refresh rate on the electronic imaging systems monitor, but makes text wrapping and sizing very difficult for the page composer. If a box appears and an image is needed, the file should be brought into an object editor and re-saved with a PICT display of the image. Another advantage of this format is the ability to save the format in either ASCII or binary code. ASCII allows a knowledgeable operator the ability to edit the PostScript code to make corrections to the image, while binary provide faster image processing.

DCS

The DCS (Desktop Color Separation) format is an extension of the EPS file format. This was developed especially for outputting a CMYK separation to an imagesetter. The format creates five parts, consisting of information for the cyan, magenta, yellow, and black separations and a PICT image. The PICT image is used for placement and positioning in the page of the document. The other four parts are linked to the document through this image. The CMYK images provide information to the imagesetter to create separate images for each of the four process color plates. This format has proven itself reliable during the film conversion process through the imagesetter.

PAGE COMPOSITION

Once the graphics and text for the composition have been created they are combined into pages. This is best accomplished with software intended for this purpose, such as QuarkXPress, Ventura Publisher, or Aldus PageMaker. Although page composers have individual differences in the way to accomplish page composition, many of the features are similar.

Page grid

The *page grid*, sometimes called a *frame*, is the basis of the page design. The margins, columns, gutters, headers and other basic page elements are established with the page grid. The page grid, along with other common elements of the publication, makes up the template.

Template

The design of a page typically will result in certain common attributes that are repeated from page to page or section to section. Attributes such as columns, margins, folios, headers, and footers, can be repeated from page to page. It is also common to have several similar formats on the same page or throughout the publication. A *template* (called a *stylesheet* in some programs) can be used to easily set up a new publication or page with similar attributes. The page geometry, typography, and other elements common to all pages are created and then saved as a template. Each time

a new page or publication is needed, the operator starts by opening the template, then customizing the page based upon the mark-up.

The main advantage of using a template or stylesheet is increased operator productivity and reduced time spent recreating the same page information.

Master page

Some page composers have what they call a *master page* contained within the template. It is possible to have several master pages stored within a template. This allows different page composition attributes throughout a publication. An example of this is ad pages in a newspaper, such as a half page, tabloid page, or full page. The publication is composed by not only positioning text and graphics, but also assigning attributes to the individual page through the master page.

FONTS

A *font* consists of all type characters of the same size and style. An example would be 12 point Helvetica Bold. Fonts used in electronic imaging are usually object-oriented, although some are based upon bit-mapped images. The significance of using object-oriented images (*outline fonts*) is that many sizes and styles are available from a single definition through manipulation of its mathematical description. This provides a great deal of flexibility, but also can produce unexpected results.

To provide for both display and output, two font descriptions are usually required: a display or screen component and an output or printer component.

Screen fonts

This is the font description used to display the text in a WYSIWYG (What You See Is What You Get) format. The limitations in accomplishing this are monitor resolution and the need for accurate font descriptions for all sizes and styles. Screen fonts are bit-mapped and thus would provide 72 dpi description to the output device.

Printer fonts

These are object-oriented image files that provide accurate outline descriptions to the output device when it is rendering the font. Without this information, a 72 dpi bit-mapping of the font would occur, causing undesirable jagged edges on the type. When printing files, the most efficient arrangement is to have the printer font residing in the output device's memory. To improve efficiency, downloading printer font information to the output device prior to printing is recommended. This improves output speed during the printing process and reduces the possibility of getting low-resolution bit-mapped font output.

Font formats

A variety of font technologies and utilities for fonts exist. The desktop computer can render fonts in three ways: Bitmap, PostScript, and TrueType™.

Every computer comes equipped with fonts designed for printing on nonPostScript output devices. These fonts are called bit-mapped fonts or just *bitmaps*. Each bitmap is an arrangement of pixels used to display on the monitor. For output, a unique description of the font is required for each size and style font selected.

PostScript fonts have two parts, a printer part and a display part. Each character consist of instructions for forming an outline of each character, which is then imaged by the printer. PostScript characters have no specific size associated with them, as do bitmaps. Therefore, if a font is selected, all sizes and style definitions of the font are available for output to either the screen or the printer.

Apple introduced TrueType outline font technology when it began marketing its new Macintosh operating system, called System 7. These fonts are variable or scalable fonts. They produce smooth characters in any size or style on both the printer and the monitor. Unlike the PostScript fonts, they consist of only one part that can be used on both devices (monitor or printer). TrueType fonts sometimes create an output problem when the PostScript output device, such as an imagesetter, cannot interpret the font shape.

Using fonts

It is vital that the fonts used by both the client and the production team are the same version, name, and manufacturer. Kerning tables, spacing defaults, and even character shapes can be different in different versions, even with the same name. Keep an updated list of all fonts on the system and provide that list to all clients. If a client wishes to use a typeface not currently in the output system, he or she must provide the complete font, screen faces, and printer drivers, to the production team. Even this, however, does not guarantee success — it is best to acquire the font and test it before using it in a final document. NOTE: In such situations, it is the client's responsibility to make sure that font use is handled in the proper legal manner as licensed by the manufacturer.

A complete list of fonts used to create a document should accompany the digital document submitted for output. This can assure consistent use of the same font for input and output. The client should be careful, when selecting a style attribute (such as bold italic), to be sure it is available as a printer font. Many raster image processors and printer drivers ignore such application commands and simply use the printer font in its manipulated version. On screen, the font will display correctly, but the attributes may not translate to the output. In general, use the actual stylized typeface whenever it is available.

HARD COPY PROOFS

Providing hard copy proofs is a vital time- and cost-saving practice. The client should supply a hard copy laser proof with each digital file. This proof must exactly match the supplied file or include specific written instructions regarding any exceptions.

Files transmitted sent by modem (telecommunications) must also be accompanied by a hard copy proof. Often this proof will be sent by facsimile, although it is not unusual to

also have the original sent to the production team via overnight courier. A proof that is faxed should be 100% size. If necessary, it can be sent in pieces (tiled).

Only under critical circumstances, and with written direction from the client indicating they will take full responsibility, should an electronic file be produced without a proof. If possible, a laser proof should be faxed to the client for approval and returned with the client's signature before outputting the file.

All art and images should be clearly marked on the proof. In general, EPS files are used as live images unless clearly marked For Position Only (FPO). It may be helpful to ask clients who use FPO images to save them in PICT format, rather than EPS, to avoid confusion. TIFF format scans should be kept in the 4/C TIFF (32 bit) mode for output. Output of RGB files can be disappointing if not converted to CMYK form before output.

ART AND IMAGES

For best reproduction, all artwork and images placed into a page layout program should be placed at 100 percent size and at the correct angle. All manipulations made to art in the page layout program increase output time and potential PostScript errors. If, for instance, the client has placed a logo created in Adobe Illustrator™ into a QuarkXPress document, then resized and rotated it, the production team should go back to the original Illustrator file. They should copy the art and save it to a new file, then size and rotate in Illustrator to match the specs in the QuarkXPress document. The new original can then be placed into the page layout program.

Resolution of continuous tone images is another issue. The quality of a scanned image will decrease as it is scaled up. As a general rule, the scanned image used at 100 percent should have a minimum ppi sampling of 1.5 to 2 times the output screen ruling (measured in lines per inch, or lpi). Finely detailed images should be sampled up to 3 times the output line screen. For example, an image that will print using a 200 line screen should have a resolution of 300 to 600 pixels per inch, depending upon the amount of detail. If the image is scaled (made larger or smaller than the original) the effective resolution is also changed.

FILE TRANSMITTAL

Consistency is the most important quality control element in the production environment. The computer does not negate the need for proper recordskeeping. All digital mechanicals should be accompanied with a transmittal form, such as the one developed by the Graphic Communication Association (GCA), that provides space for verification of all digital specifics. In addition to this form, a printed directory of the shipping disk window should be provided from the client. This verifies the existence and location of all linked files.

All elements used in the creation of a document (artwork, scans, and screen and printer fonts) should be grouped with that document. Check to see if the client has renamed artwork after importing it into the document (possibly during disk preparation). Links will not update if file names have been altered.

Disks or cartridges holding a digital file should include:

- The page layout file (in QuarkXPress, Ventura Publisher, or other page composer)
- Live EPS files to be output to film
- Live scans or images
- Original application files for any EPS file (such as the original art in Illustrator format) in case revisions are necessary.
- If QuarkXPress 3.0 or earlier versions was used, the "XPress Data" and "XPress Hyphenation" files.

Nondigital materials accompanying the digital file from a client should include:

- 100 percent size hard copy proof
- Original artwork (scanned on a desktop scanner) that is FPO in the digital layout document
- Transparencies or reflective artwork that is FPO in the digital document
- A completed transmittal form
- A printed directory of the shipping disk

All graphics in a layout should have either live electronic elements or accompanying hard copy originals.

PROGRAM FEATURES

As indicated earlier in this chapter, the programs used in electronic publishing vary in features, according to their designers' preferences and the needs of users. Some basic terms that describe images on the screen, Fig. 12-11, are common to most such software, however. Thus, the examples in this section are representative of the features of electronic imaging systems.

Toolbox

The term *toolbox* refers to an area on the screen that contains several *icons* or tools. Fig. 12-12 shows a toolbox for one type system. This toolbox is used to select tools for drawing lines, circles, squares, and for performing other functions.

Drop-down menus

Drop-down menus (sometimes called "pull-down") are handy because they will quickly show various functions. See Fig. 12-13. By moving the arrow or cursor over the **format** choice on the menu bar and pushing the mouse button, the format menu will drop down. The arrow can then be moved over the drop-down menu to select various commands.

Electronic layout page

With an electronic publishing system, the *layout page* will usually be a rectangle drawn in the center of the screen. Using the computer, you can add the desired rules and guides for the layout. You can select column widths, margins, rules to appear between columns, and other features.

After programming this layout page data, the text and art can be quickly made to align and fit in the preset columns. Fig. 12-14 shows a drop-down menu for selecting size of the displayed image. Size of an image can be increased, decreased, or made to fit in a window. The same drop-down menu is used to select the "Column Snap" feature, which quickly moves text into alignment with the present column width.

As in conventional manual layout on a drafting board, holes are frequently left for photographs. Without a

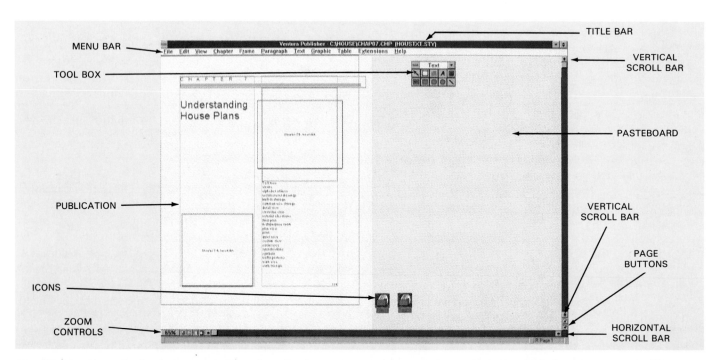

Fig. 12-11. Note the basic terms used to describe images on the screen of a typical electronic imaging system. The terms and location of areas on the screen can vary with the type of system used.

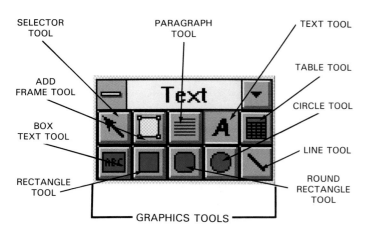

SELECTOR TOOL

PARAGRAPH TOOL

TEXT TOOL

TABLE TOOL

CIRCLE TOOL

LINE TOOL

ROUND RECTANGLE TOOL

ADD FRAME TOOL

BOX TEXT TOOL

RECTANGLE TOOL

GRAPHICS TOOLS

Fig. 12-12. This desktop system has a toolbox menu that graphically represents different commands used when working with graphics. The menu and available tools may vary with the specific system.

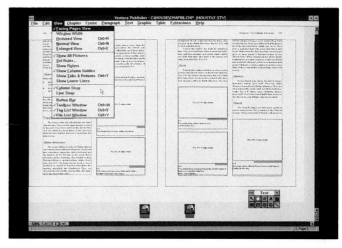

Fig. 12-14. This drop-down menu allows you to select two-page, enlarged, or reduced views, and determine whether rulers and guides should be displayed.

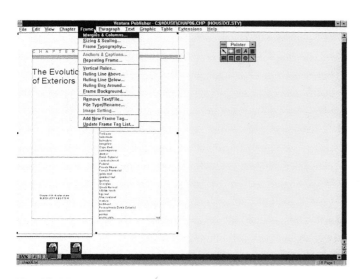

Fig. 12-13. A drop-down menu can be activated by moving arrow to the top menu bar and clicking the mouse button on the selected area. The menu will then expand down into the screen. This menu is for working with format of publication.

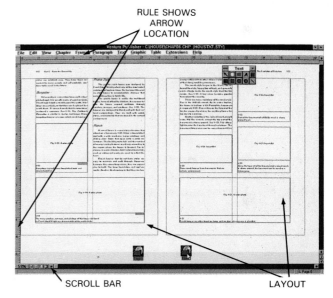

RULE SHOWS ARROW LOCATION

SCROLL BAR

LAYOUT

Fig. 12-15. This screen image shows scales for judging sizes of images and for checking exact location of arrow. The location of a box for including a photo in the layout must be precise. Scroll bars along bottom and right of screen are used to move window when layout sheet is enlarged for detail work. This can vary depending upon specific system.

sophisticated scanner and software, photos cannot be placed in the computer and on the screen. However, the space for the photo must be calculated and shown on the screen. See Fig. 12-15. Rules along the top and sides of the screen may be provided for sizing images. This is a handy feature. The *notepad* area of the screen can be used to hold images before placing them on the layout sheet.

Electronic line art

With the electronic publishing system or a separate drawing program, you can quickly generate line art on the screen. Using the correct tools, simple line drawings can be made using various line weights and designs. Fig. 12-16 shows a drop-down menu for selecting various line weights and dashed lines.

Charts, with their numerous horizontal and vertical lines, are one of the most common applications of desktop-

generated line art. A drawing program will rapidly produce perfectly aligned lines for charts. Words can then be added to the chart, as shown in Fig. 12-17.

Images can be drawn with the computer, using a drawing program. A menu for shading is shown in Fig. 12-18. Different percentages and designs can be selected. The shading can then be added to the art.

A menu for a *paint program* is pictured in Fig. 12-19. The arrow or cursor can be moved over each area to draw the specific shapes or textures. A paint program lets you quickly draw special designs or paint in special tints on line drawings. An example of a simple line drawing with special shading is given in Fig. 12-20.

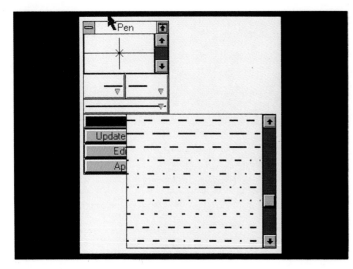

Fig. 12-16. An electronic imaging system allows you to draw lines of different types and weights.

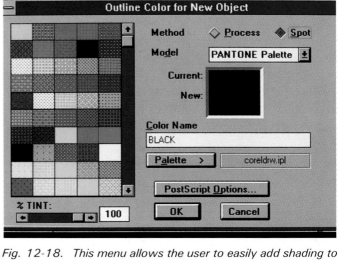

Fig. 12-18. This menu allows the user to easily add shading to images. Note different percentages and designs.

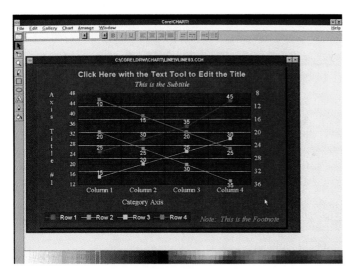

Fig. 12-17. Imaging systems are commonly used to draw charts similar to this one. It will generate perfectly straight lines in a fraction of the time it would take to draw or ink them by hand. Titles can be added to the chart to complete the job.

Fig. 12-19. This is an example of the menu for a paint program.

These are a few of the examples of electronic publishing features. Fig. 12-21 shows a flowchart (block diagram) outlining an electronic publishing system.

PURCHASING FACTORS

When planning to purchase an electronic imaging system, certain factors should be given consideration. These are some of the typical factors that should be listed for each system being considered: name of the product, price information, operating requirements (RAM, hard drive size, system version), product information (interface, characters-based, video display support), handling of documents and editing features (size of documents, capabilities, spell-checker), features relating to design (templates, clip art, rotating images, patterns, tables), fonts (type of font manager, number of typefaces), printing (printer support, separations, spot color

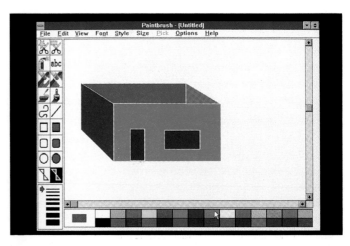

Fig. 12-20. This simple house is an example of an easily made drawing using the capabilities of a drawing program. Such programs can be used to create very complex drawings, if needed.

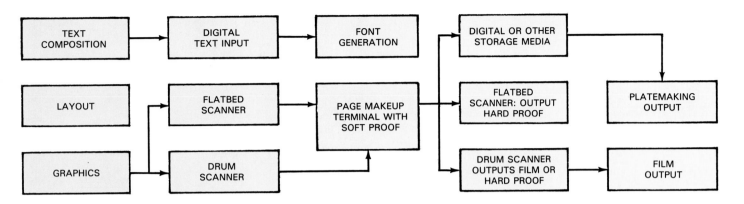

Fig. 12-21. This flowchart shows the operation of a electronic production system that can output hard proofs, film, or plates.

and full color), capabilities (imported text formats, imported graphic formats), and support the vendor or manufacturer provides after purchase.

KNOW THESE TERMS

Electronic imaging, Electronic prepress, Desktop publishing, Mouse, Digitizing tablet, Pointing devices, Platform, Graphical user interface, WYSIWYG, Resolution, Color capability, Dithering, Additive color, RGB, Subtractive color, CMYK, Photo CD, Word processors, Graphics editors, Page composers, Bit-mapped, Pixels, Object-oriented images, Handles, PostScript™, Rasterizing, Raster image processor, Toner, Imagesetter, ASCII, Text filters, PICT, TIFF, EPS, DCS, Page grid, Frame, Template, Stylesheet, Master page, Font, Bitmaps, Toolbox, Icons, Drop-down menu, Layout page, Notepad, Paint program.

REVIEW QUESTIONS—CHAPTER 12

1. Define the term "electronic production."
2. List the basic components of an electronic imaging system.
3. The term _____ refers to the program that operates the system.
4. What do the letters WYSIWYG represent?
5. How is a mouse used with an electronic imaging system?
6. What is an "icon"?
7. Define the term "resolution" in relation to an electronic imaging system.
8. What are two high quality output devices?
9. What is the main purpose of a word processing unit?
10. What is the main difference between text preparation and graphic imaging?
11. What is the main advantage of using a template?
12. On the screen of the monitor, what is the layout?
13. One size and style of type is called a _____.
14. Why would a WYSIWYG system be desired?

SUGGESTED ACTIVITIES

1. Visit a computer store and identify the equipment commonly associated with desktop (electronic) publishing systems.
2. Describe the page composition software used with each desktop system and identify its compatibility with other systems.
3. List the types of publications capable of being produced by various desktop publishing systems.
4. Visit a graphic communications (printing) facility and ask to observe the operation of an electronic imaging system.

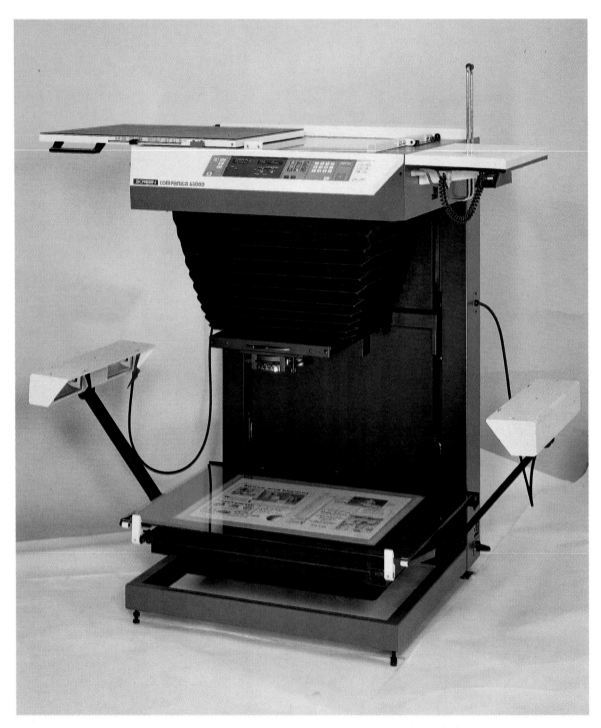

This process camera has electronic controls that automatically adjusts exposure, sizing, etc. It saves time and reduces waste of film. (Screen - USA)

Chapter 13

LINE PHOTOGRAPHY, PROCESS CAMERAS

After completing this chapter, you will be able to:
* Identify the types of films commonly used in graphic arts photography.
* Explain the differences between horizontal and vertical cameras.
* Identify the major parts of a process camera.
* Explain the basic procedure for shooting line images.
* Describe how to choose and adjust illumination.
* Summarize the capabilities of automatic exposure or computer controlled process cameras.
* Describe the operation of a camera processor.

This chapter discusses the conversion of original *line art* (line drawings and copy) to film negatives or positives, Fig. 13-1. It is concerned with the conversion of these images to high contrast intermediates (films) which can be used to produce printing plates and a final printed product.

The camera person must be competent and must be highly skilled at producing quality negatives and positives. Today's operator must have much more theoretical knowledge than in the past. Photomechanical methods require knowledge relating to physics, chemistry, and electronics. The nature of light, optics, and processing must also be fully understood.

Photomechanical methods (graphic arts photography) is common to relief, intaglio, planography, as well as screen process image carriers. Today's graphic communications facilities rely heavily on photomechanical techniques.

In the future, the importance of photoconversion might change as forecasts tend to indicate that technological advancements will eliminate the negative or positive as an intermediate. The image, using electronics, will go directly to the image carrier or plate.

ILLUMINATION

Line photography for graphic reproduction requires *illumination* (light) to cause a physical change of the film or light sensitive material, Fig. 13-2. The *illumination* or *light source* is an important aspect affecting the operation of a process camera. As you will learn, it can greatly affect the quality of the finished product. See Fig. 13-3.

Light sources

Sunlight is an excellent source of light because it contains all colors of the spectrum. However, it is not practical to use sunlight as a light source for process camerawork. Fig. 13-4 shows how light is used to expose film on a camera.

Fig. 13-1. Line art, including text and drawings that are not continuous tone, is converted to film negatives like these to produce printing plates.   (Chapter One, Screaming Color)

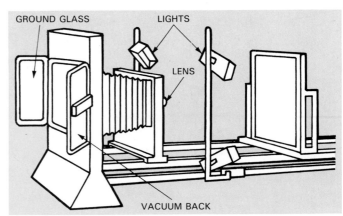

Fig. 13-2. Process camera, also called a copy camera, is simply a large, high quality camera. It has components that correspond to smaller hand-held cameras.

191

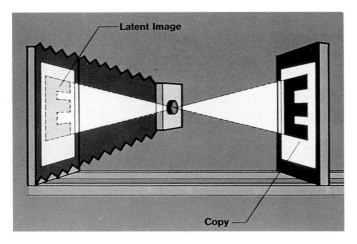

Fig. 13-3. Light strikes image and reflects into camera lens. Lens directs image onto light sensitive material or film. This exposes image on film for reproduction.

Fig. 13-4. This shows actual lights exposing image on large process camera. (Chapter One, Screaming Color)

Tungsten-filament lights are sometimes used but they are not highly recommended. Tungsten-filament lights are deficient in the blue and ultraviolet rays and are excessive in the red rays. Another drawback is that some of the tungsten evaporates at high temperature and deposits on the inside of the light bulb. The intensity of light can then be decreased. It is impossible to clean the inside surface of the light.

Quartz-iodine lamps are another type of light source. The outside material is made of quartz while the tungsten bulb is made of glass. This type of bulb is smaller and withstands a higher temperature. The color temperature of this light source is greater than the tungsten bulb.

Cleaning the quartz-iodine bulb with a soft cloth is essential. The bulb should never be touched by your hands because this will greatly reduce bulb life. Surface heat becomes greater in the touched area because of oils from your skin. This can cause rapid failure of the light bulb.

Never look directly into a light source. The rays may be harmful to your eyes as well as your skin.

Carbon-arc is another source of illumination. This is a very efficient light source with qualities close to the rays from the sun. Its use has decreased because of other available types which are cleaner and do not require special protection, as stated by Federal Health and Safety Regulations. The carbon-arc source requires proper ventilation or exhausting. It has been commonly used in photoengraving and lithographic platemaking.

Pulsed-xenon lamps are commonly found in many of today's graphic communication facilities. They are an excellent light source with spectral output close to daylight. The system is used on many process cameras today, Fig. 13-5.

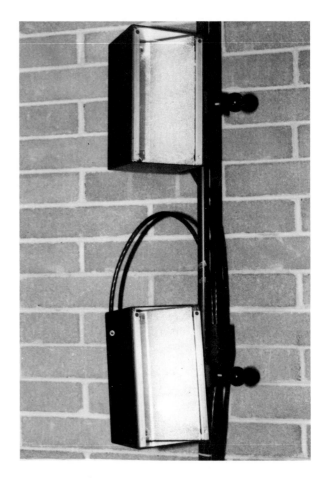

Fig. 13-5. Various types of exposure lights can be used on a process camera. You should know type and how they affect camera operation. These are commonly used pulsed-xenon lights.

Mercury-vapor lamps are high in ultraviolet radiation. They provide a good source of light for making plates and are of value to the color separation specialist. The warm-up period has been eliminated. Mercury lamps are a good means of exposing materials that require long periods of light exposure.

The intended use of the light source must be considered when selecting equipment. Proper illumination is a critical consideration. Refer to Figs. 13-6, 13-7, and 13-8.

Fig. 13-9 compares three common light sources. Note how their spectral outputs differ.

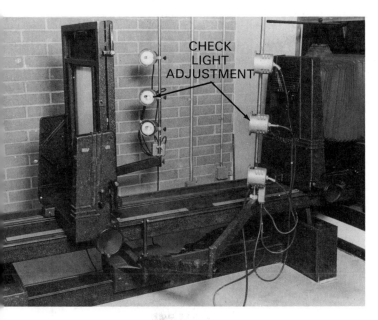

Fig. 13-6. Lights must be adjusted to the correct distance and angle. If adjusted improperly, reflections, overexposure, underexposure, and other troubles can result.

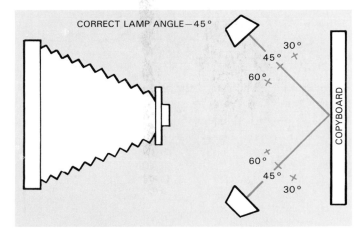

CORRECT LAMP ANGLE—45°

30°
45°
60°

COPYBOARD

60°
45°
30°

Fig. 13-7. This is a typical lamp angle adjustment for most exposures. Refer to the camera operating instructions for details however.

Controlling the light source

Whatever system is selected, the line voltage to the lights often fluctuates. Whenever the voltage changes, a different amount of light can strike the film. The final product will not be consistent when this happens. Regulators and integrators can give the necessary exposure consistency. *Regulators* will give constant voltage while *integrators* will make sure the amount of light striking the light sensitive surface will be the same. This topic is discussed later in the chapter.

Light spectrum

Light or the visible area of the electromagnetic spectrum is a very small part of the total spectrum. This area is made up of various wavelengths. Each color has a different wavelength.

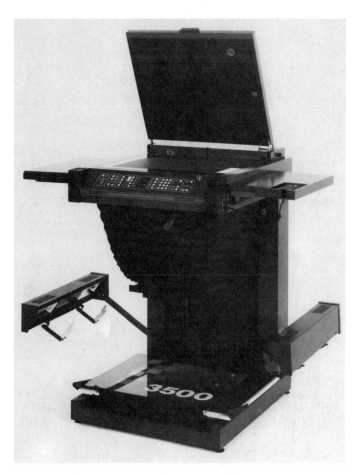

Fig. 13-8. Note that the lights on this camera are preset at about a 45 degree angle. (Agfa-Gevaert)

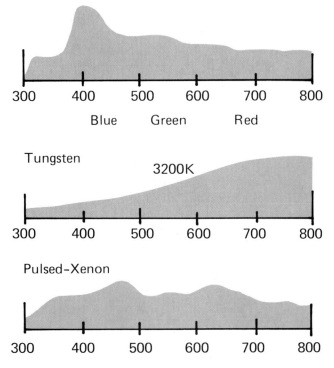

Carbon-Arc

300   400   500   600   700   800

Blue   Green   Red

Tungsten

3200K

300   400   500   600   700   800

Pulsed-Xenon

300   400   500   600   700   800

Fig. 13-9. Note differences of approximate spectral output for these light sources.

193

Gamma rays are very short, while *radio waves* are long. The visible spectrum falls between these two. These wavelengths are measured in millimicrons. One *millimicron* is equal to one billionth of a meter.

The approximate positioning for each color in the visible spectrum is shown in Fig. 13-10.

Note! Color is discussed in detail in Chapter 15.

Color temperature

The term *color temperature* refers to the method of rating the quality of a light source for color reproduction. Color temperature must be considered whenever color separations are to be prepared for full color work. The term *Kelvin* is the metric unit of temperature because it gives the necessary wide temperature range.

On the commonly used Celsius temperature scale, water freezes at about 0°C and boils at about 100°C. The "C" is defined as an interval of 1K, and the Celsius temperature 0°C is defined as 273.15K (Kelvin).

Today, most of the full color work in the industry is viewed at 5 000K. Daylight is approximately the same as 5 000K. Actual sunlight is rated at 5 400K.

Color viewers should be used in all facilities that do color work. They provide the correct color temperature for accurate color evaluation, Fig. 13-11. What is important to remember is that printed pieces will not look the same under different light sources. If a customer looks at the proof under similar circumstances, everyone will be more likely to be satisfied.

The color temperature is a very important factor to be considered whenever you are viewing color work. Tungsten and fluorescent bulbs do NOT have the same color temperature.

Fig. 13-11. Color viewing booth is essential when looking at color images. If in room light, the light may be weak in certain wavelengths and this will not give a true and dependable perception of color. A viewing booth has a light source that simulates daylight. (Chapter One, Screaming Color)

GRAPHIC ARTS CAMERAS

The camera commonly used to produce graphic images on photosensitive materials is usually called a *process camera*. Another term is the *copy camera*.

Process cameras are designed to produce single-plane images. This means that the camera photographs flat

THE ELECTROMAGNETIC SPECTRUM							
GAMMA RAYS	X-RAYS	ULTRAVIOLET LIGHT	VISIBLE LIGHT	INFRARED LIGHT	SHORT WAVE RADIO	BROAD-CAST WAVES	WIRELESS
VIOLET	INDIGO	BLUE	GREEN	YELLOW	ORANGE	RED	
SHORT WAVELENGTHS HIGH FREQUENCY					LONG WAVELENGTHS LOW FREQUENCY		

Fig. 13-10. Each color has its own wavelength or frequency. This will be discussed fully in Chapter 15. Daylight has all colors of spectrum combined.

materials. Some modern computerized cameras can also photograph three-dimensional objects, however.

The graphic arts camera must be capable of converting three types of images: line work (line drawing for example), continuous tone work (black and white photograph for example), and full color work (four-color photograph for example).

Note! This chapter is concerned with line work. The other types of images will be discussed in separate chapters. Refer to the text index as needed.

Process cameras are available in a variety of styles and sizes. Two major types of process cameras are commonly found in the industry. The first of these is a vertical camera, while the second is a horizontal camera, Fig. 13-12. As you will learn, the principle is the same but the capabilities of each varies.

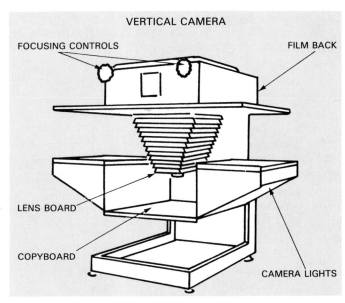

Fig. 13-13. Study the major parts of a vertical camera. (A.B. Dick Co.)

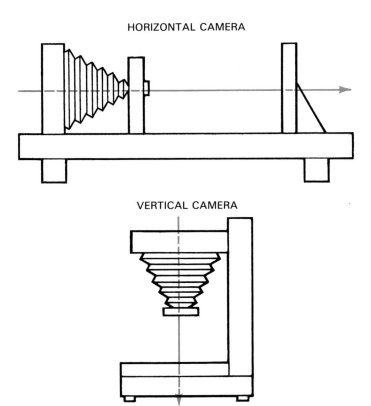

Fig. 13-12. Two major types of process cameras are horizontal and vertical. There are many variations within these two categories however.

If a special film holder is provided, it is called a *daylight camera* and can be placed in an area outside of the darkroom.

When selecting a process camera, make sure that the frame is sturdy and will withstand extended use. The structural arrangement of the shutter and timer cannot be overlooked. Easy focusing and viewing of the image must be considered as the image must be sharp and not fuzzy. Electronic controls are very desirable, Fig. 13-14.

Vertical cameras

The *vertical camera* has a vertical (up and down) viewing plane. It can also be called a *gallery camera*. Fig. 13-13 shows the basic parts of a vertical camera.

Whenever space limitations must be considered, the vertical camera becomes very functional since it is very compact. A drawback is that some cameras cannot be used in ordinary room light unless a special filmholder is used on the camera. This factor forces many facilities to place the camera in the darkroom, but allocating that space also may pose problems.

Fig. 13-14. This is a very modern vertical camera. Note electronic control panel at top. (RPS)

Enlargement and reduction of images are also important factors. Many of today's cameras are capable of enlarging to 200% or reducing to 20% of the original size. The size of the copy and film is limited with the vertical camera but it is commonly found in today's graphic communication facilities.

Horizontal cameras

The *horizontal camera* has a horizontal (side-to-side) viewing plane. It is also called the *darkroom camera* since the film is loaded in the darkroom while the rest of the camera is outside the darkroom. This allows for an efficient operation. Fig. 13-15 illustrates the parts of a horizontal camera.

There are two variations of horizontal camera: the floor type and the overhead type.

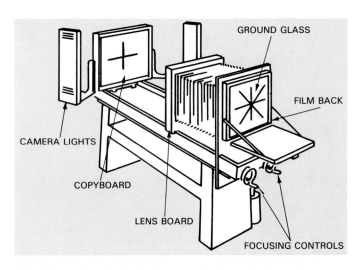

Fig. 13-15. Study the basic parts of a larger horizontal camera. (A.B. Dick Co.)

As the name implies, the *floor horizontal camera* has a large bed that mounts on the floor of the facility. The copyboard and lensboard slide on this bed, Fig. 13-16.

The *overhead horizontal camera* has the bed and copyboard attached to the overhead framework of the camera, Fig. 13-17. It allows for easy access around the copyboard and lensboard, and tends to eliminate potential vibration problems.

Process camera parts

To have a better understanding of the process camera, each major part will be identified and discussed. The parts listed are common to all types of process cameras. As shown in Figs. 13-13 and 13-15, the major parts of each camera are:
1. Frame (main supporting structure).
2. Copyboard (for mounting original image).
3. Lighting system (to expose image on film).
4. Lensboard (supports lens and bellows).
5. Film back (holds film).
6. Copyboard control (used for sizing image).
7. Lensboard control (used for adjusting camera).
8. Ground glass (viewing image before exposure).

Frame

The sturdiness of the camera is determined by the *frame,* also called *bed.* A well constructed frame is essential to eliminate the possibility of poor alignment. The copyboard, lensboard, and film back must be in perfect alignment to assure quality reproduction. Refer to Figs. 13-18 and 13-19.

Lighting system

The system of illumination or lighting, as discussed, varies from one manufacturer to another, but the manner in which they can be adjusted is of great importance. See Figs. 13-19

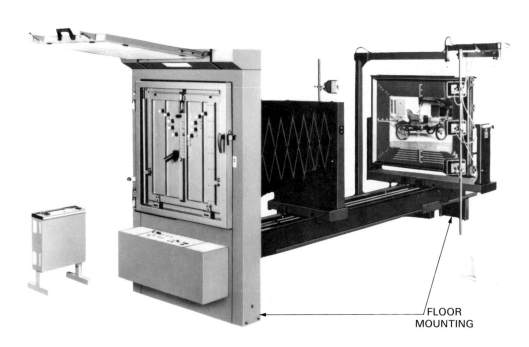

Fig. 13-16. This is a floor model horizontal camera. It bolts to floor of facility. Large frame keeps parts in alignment. (Screen - USA)

Fig. 13-17. This is an overhead model process camera. It bolts and suspends from ceiling of facility. This arrangement is needed if large equipment in other areas could cause floor to vibrate, upsetting camera operation. (Chapter One, Screaming Color)

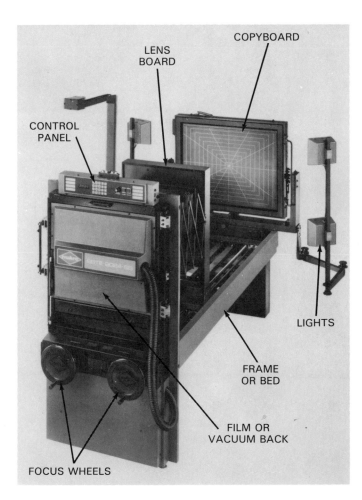

Fig. 13-18. Note components of this computer-controlled horizontal camera. (nuArc)

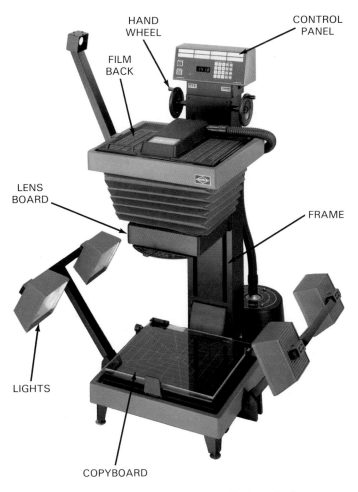

Fig. 13-19. Here is a computer-controlled vertical camera. Note part names. (nuArc)

and 13-20. They must be capable of giving off even light and be sturdy enough to take the abuse of handling. The lights must also be designed for easy positioning, Fig. 13-21.

Copyboard

The *copyboard* holds the original image while it is being shot, Fig. 13-22. The glass must be high quality to eliminate the possibility of light distortion which could cause reproduction problems. A sponge material or spring load is usually found under the glass to assure contact between the copy and the glass. The copy must have even contact with the glass. Some copyboards have a vacuum board which holds the copy in place. Refer to Fig. 13-23.

All copyboards using glass must be handled with extreme care because the glass could break, Fig. 13-24. If pins are used, make sure they are of proper height. A pin that is too high or misaligned could break the copyboard glass. HANDLE THE COPYBOARD WITH CARE!

Fig. 13-22. Original image must be positioned on copyboard properly. The copyboard glass must be high quality and perfectly clean for quality reproduction.

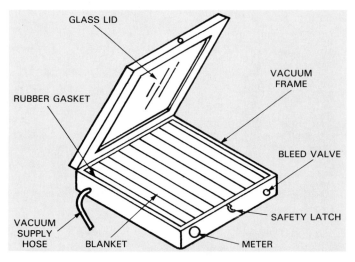

Fig. 13-23. Vacuum back assures that original image is held firmly against glass on copyboard. This principle is also used with film back. Soft blanket can also be used without vacuum back.

Fig. 13-20. Camera operators are adjusting lights and lens before making exposure. Note that they are on the outside of the darkroom. The copyboard and lens are in a daylight area.

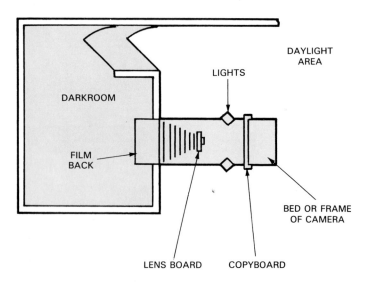

Fig. 13-21. This is a typical layout for a horizontal camera and darkroom.

Fig. 13-24. This photograph shows copyboard and lens board clearly. Note how they are supported on frame of camera.

Lensboard

The *lensboard* is the support for the lens housing, Fig. 13-20. This part should be well constructed because it holds the very expensive lens of the camera. The lens must be held in constant alignment. See Fig. 13-24.

Film back

The *film back* is the film plane and the means of supporting the film. The most common device to hold the film in position is a *vacuum back,* Fig. 13-25. Some have channels to hold various sizes of film while other backs are perforated to support the film evenly over its surface.

Fig. 13-26. Scale control like this one and other controls will vary with make and model of camera. Always follow operating manual for specific type of camera.

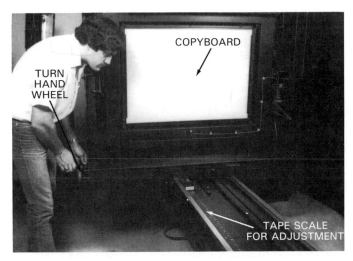

Fig. 13-27. Camera operator is adjusting position of copyboard.

Fig. 13-25. The film back, also called vacuum back, holds the film in place for the exposure. Film must be located properly and must be slightly larger than image area.

Copyboard controls

Copyboard controls are for positioning the copyboard in relation to others parts of the camera. This is essential for same size, enlarging, or reducing the copy, Fig. 13-26. Some of the sophisticated systems are computerized and automatic positioning is possible.

The lensboard must also be able to be moved to reproduce the size image specified, Fig. 13-27. The controls for the two boards are usually the same. Fig. 13-28 shows how moving the lensboards changes reproduction size. Fig. 13-29 shows a lens control.

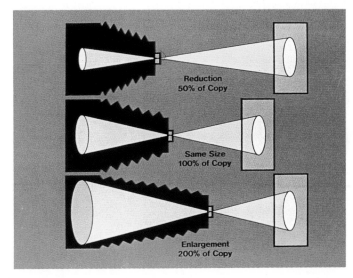

Fig. 13-28. Study how process camera can be used to enlarge or reduce size of image. Size requirements must be provided with art so camera operator can shoot images up or down correctly. (Chapter One, Screaming Color)

Fig. 13-29. Here operator is adjusting lens for correct f-stop. (Chapter One, Screaming Color)

Ground glass

The purpose of the *ground glass* is to view the copy before it is placed as a latent image on film, Fig. 13-30. The system will vary. Some swing from the top, others from the side. They position themselves in the same plane as the film. The ground glass is also used to check for proper focus of the copy, Fig. 13-31.

These are the major parts of the process camera. Many sub-parts are required but vary from camera to camera.

LIGHT SENSITIVE MATERIALS

In the simplest of terms, *light sensitive materials,* also termed film or photo paper, have a soluble protective coating on the emulsion. The *emulsion* is a light sensitive coat on a base material. An *antihalation backing* is on the other side of the base material, Fig. 13-32.

The protective coating on the emulsion helps to keep the emulsion from being scratched. The emulsion is made up of chemical compounds forming light sensitive materials.

Fig. 13-31. Another view of ground glass on a large horizontal camera.

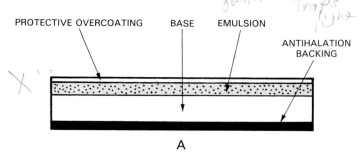

PROTECTIVE OVERCOATING   BASE   EMULSION

ANTIHALATION BACKING

A

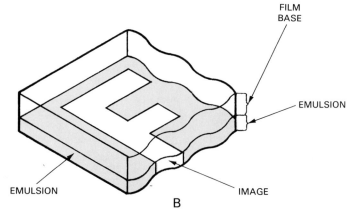

FILM BASE

EMULSION

EMULSION

IMAGE

B

Fig. 13-32. Note principle of light sensitive material or film. A—Cutaway of film. Emulsion is light sensitive material that reacts to light. Base supports emulsion. B—When light strikes emulsion, it generates latent image on emulsion. Processing or developing will make the image visible.

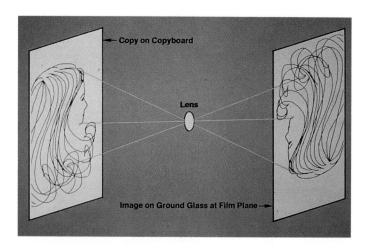

←Copy on Copyboard

Lens

Image on Ground Glass at Film Plane→

Fig. 13-30. Ground glass will let you view image that will appear on film. It will let you check focus, sizing, and location of image on film board. (Chapter One, Screaming Color)

Although silverless light sensitive materials are available, the silver compounds are most often found in industry.

Emulsion

The emulsion is usually made up of silver halides suspended in a gelatin. The compounds of silver are made up of three halides: chlorine, bromine, and iodine. The three compounds that are formed are silver chloride ($AgCl$), silver bromide ($AgBr$), and silver iodide (AgI).

The lighting used by graphic arts photography exposes the particles of silver halides. As the light strikes the emulsion, those areas are changed to black metallic silver when developed.

Two types of *intermediates* are common to graphic arts photography emulsions; they are: a negative and a positive. The *negative* appears opposite of the original while the *positive* appears the same as the original, Fig. 13-33. In the negative, the dark areas of the copy appear clear. The dark areas of the original appear dark in the positive.

The amount of darkness in the negative or positive is referred to as its *density*—its ability to hold back or block

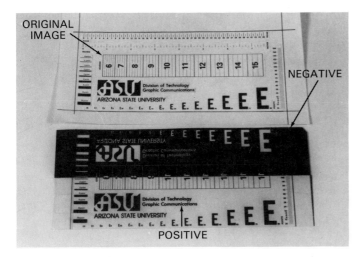

Fig. 13-33. A negative appears as the opposite of the original. A positive is like the original.

light. The density of a negative or positive is influenced by several factors. The variables are:
1. Length of exposure to light source.
2. Chemical composition.
3. Developing temperature.
4. Amount of developing time.

Conventional emulsions are generally thought of as being negative forming, but it is possible to produce positives by special treatment of the film. Making a positive from conventional emulsions is sometimes called *image reversal*. This can be done by a pretreating process from the manufacturer.

Post treatment might also produce a positive image. This means the processing steps change. Use the manufacturer's guide to produce the desired results.

An emulsion also has a *density capacity* which is the maximum density allowed by that emulsion. The range of capacity usually is from a density reading of 2.0 to 4.0 as read by a densitometer. Up to a certain point of exposure, it will continue to have greater density. Once that point has been reached, density no longer increases and the film has reached its capacity.

Measuring the effects of exposure and development is called *sensitometry* of the light sensitive materials. Generally, increased exposure increases density.

Many factors affect exposure. For example, the intensity of the light aimed on the film depends on:
1. The brightness of the camera lights.
2. The distance the lights are located from the copy.
3. Direction or angle of lights.

The image on the copy must be high quality. The quality of the lens system and the aperture of the lens are additional factors. Changing any one of these factors will affect exposure.

The density values have a logarithmic definition.

Characteristic curves

The *characteristic curve* indicates how a given material (film) reacts to light and development. As shown in Fig. 13-34, the vertical line on the chart is typically the density

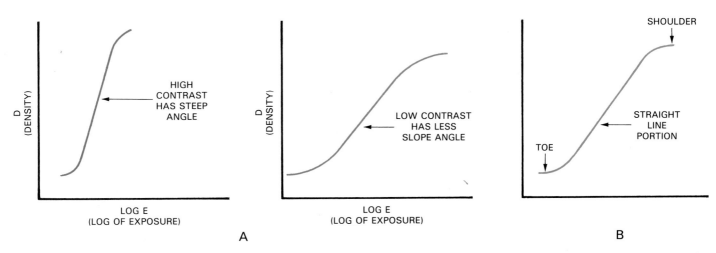

Fig. 13-34. A—Note differences in graph for low contrast and high contrast film. B—Typical characteristic curve has toe, straight line, and shoulder for light sensitive material.

The Crush starring Alicia Silverstone

(D) scale while the logarithm (LOG) of exposure is expressed on the horizontal scale. The characteristic curve of a film is given by the manufacturer of the light sensitive material. This is called the D-log-E chart, the example is typical of a negative type film. A positive-to-positive film would have the slant from left to right.

The three segments of the characteristic curve are the toe, straight line, and the shoulder.

The *toe* represents the initial response.

The *straight line* portion represents the exposure range which identifies the density that is proportional to Log E.

The *shoulder* is that portion in which more exposure would not increase the density.

The film used for line and halftone work is considered to be high contrast film. The characteristic curve for this film would be steeper than a low contrast film.

The slope of the line is called *gamma,* designated by the Greek Letter "Y". The gamma is affected by development time. The longer an exposed piece of film is developed, the higher will be its gamma.

Film emulsions do have latitude. Minor errors can take place without wasting materials. However, remember that high contrast films have less latitude than low contrast films.

Color sensitivity

Silver films are sensitive to colors of light. Silver halide emulsions are normally sensitive to ultraviolet, blue violet, and blue regions of the spectrum. Knowing what types of film to use for photoconversion is a basic requirement.

Film types

Three classifications of film are common to the graphic communications industry. They are classified as blue sensitive, orthochromatic, and panchromatic film emulsions. Each of the three are sensitive to a certain band of the electromagnetic spectrum. This is illustrated in Fig. 13-35.

The *blue sensitive films* are highly sensitive to only the blue portion of the spectrum. Sometimes, this film is referred to as "color blind." It is commonly used to copy black and white photographs.

The *orthochromatic films,* called "ortho films," are sensitive to a wider range of the spectrum but are NOT sensitive to red. Therefore, a red bulb is used as the safelight in the darkroom when handling ortho type films.

The film is commonly used to photograph black and white images but will work very satisfactorily with some filters to create color images on film. The ortho materials tend to be faster acting than the blue sensitive materials.

The color sensitivity of *panchromatic film,* often termed "pan film," is the closest to the human eye of all the commonly used film. This film will reproduce the total range of the visible spectrum. It is an ideal type of film for reproducing colored copy in monochromatic form. Pan film, however, must be handled in total darkness.

Film bases

The *base* of a film is the support for the emulsion. The two most common types are made of plastic or a special grade of paper. Most of today's graphic films use a polyester base. The *polyester base* is a very stable material and its size changes very little with relative humidity and temperature. The base has a long storage life and special handling instructions should be followed as indicated by the manufacturer.

The *acetate base* films are not as stable as the polyester bases. Humidity will affect the size of the base.

Polystyrene base film does not change size during the processing stage but temperature control is important.

Special photographic bases often have stability problems. They are subject to curl. The cost of this type of film is much less than the plastic type bases.

Another base is glass. *Glass base* films are used where a special application is required. This would include extreme dimensional stability. Glass is a very costly type of support material for film.

Prescreened film

Prescreened film is not used for line photography but would be used for halftone work (explained in the next chapter). It is a high contrast film which has a halftone dot pattern built into the film. Its main application is in the making of halftones from a continuous tone photograph without using a halftone contact screen. The dot pattern is needed so the plate can pick up ink and deposit the varying sizes on the substrate.

Rapid access film

Rapid access film is used to make negatives with the process camera. It is also used to produce contact negatives and film positives. The film is processed in rapid access chemicals. It is a very fast way to make film intermediates.

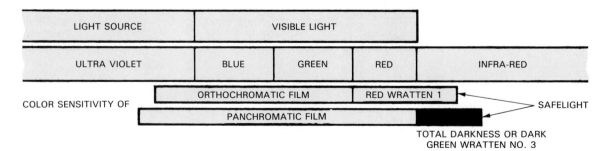

Fig. 13-35. The color sensitivity for film varies as indicated above. You must select film to correspond with requirements of job.

Contact films

Contact film is considered to be a blue sensitive film. This film has a great amount of latitude. Latitude means, in the processing cycle, slight variations have very little effect on the film reproduction. These films are used to make positives from negatives or to make negatives from film positives.

Daylight films

Some of today's films are considered to be *daylight handling,* which means the emulsion is not very sensitive to light. The film is intended to be exposed with a very high intensity light source. Most of these films are intended to be used for emulsion-to-emulsion contacting. A base-to-emulsion contact would create a poor quality reproduction.

Antihalation coating

An *antihalation coating* is a biodegradable dye coated on the back of most films to eliminate the scattering of light or reflection of light. It absorbs the light, Fig. 13-32.

Duplicating film

As the name implies, *duplicating film* will make a duplicate of the negative or positive. A duplicate negative can be made from a negative or a duplicate positive can be made from a positive.

One thing to remember is that a longer exposure, using "dupe film," will create LESS DENSITY. The film has been pre-exposed to maximum density; therefore, greater exposure causes less density.

A high intensity light source should be used when exposing regular duplicating film. A high speed duplicating film can be exposed by using a point source light on a contacting frame. A super-speed duplicating film can also be used.

USING FILTERS

Filters can be used on a process camera to photograph color line copy and convert the color image to black. Filters can also be used to drop out specific line colors and leave the area white. The resulting stat will only be black and white. Filters must be used in conjunction with recommended films to produce the desired results.

Filters fit onto the camera so that light passes through them before striking the film. They mount onto the lens assembly. Since a filter blocks out part of the light spectrum, they affect exposure. Less light can pass through the camera and onto the film. Adjustments must be made for more exposure when using a filter.

Fig. 13-36 gives a chart showing how specific filters and films can be used to *photograph as black* (hold a color as

TO PHOTOGRAPH BLACK (to hold a color) use film and filter* suggested:			Color of Copy	To PHOTOGRAPH WHITE (to drop a color) use film and filter* suggested:		
Blue-sensitive Film	Orthochromatic Film	Panchromatic Film		Blue-sensitive Film	Orthochromatic Film	Panchromatic Film
Not recommended	Orange (16) Yellow (15, 12) Green (61, 58) Yellow (9, 8)	Green (61, 58)	Magenta (process red)	No filter needed**	Can try:** Blue (47B) Magenta (30) Blue (47)	Red (25, 29)** Magenta (30) Blue (47B)
No filter needed	No filter needed or Blue (47B)	Blue (47B, 47)	Red	Not recommended	Not recommended	Red (29, 25, 23A) Orange (16)
No filter needed	Blue (47B) Magenta (30) Blue (47)	Blue (47B, 47)	Orange	Not recommended	Not recommended	Orange (16) Red (29, 25, 23A)
No filter needed	Blue (47B) Magenta (30) Blue (47)	Blue (47B, 47)	Yellow	Not recommended	Orange (16) Yellow (15, 12) Green (61, 58) Yellow (9, 8)	Red (29, 25, 23A) Orange (16) Yel (15, 12, 9, 8) Green (61, 58)
No filter needed	Blue (47B) Magenta (30) Blue (47)	Magenta (30) Red (25) Blue (47B, 47)	Green	Not recommended	Orange (16) Yellow (15, 12) Green (61, 58) Yellow (9, 8)	Green (58)
Not recommended	Not recommended	Red (25)	Cyan (process blue)	No filter needed	No filter needed	Blue (47B, 47)
Not recommended	Orange (16) Yellow (15, 12) Green (61, 58) Yellow (9, 8)	Green (58) Red (25)	Blue or Violet	No filter needed	Magenta (30) Blue (47B, 47)	Blue (47B, 47)

*Numbers are for Wratten filters. Filters are used singly. Where more than one is listed, try in order presented. Variations in color of copy may require other filters.
**To drop magenta, use pan film and a Nc 25 filter.

Fig. 13-36. Filters can be used on process camera to drop out color on an original or to change a color to black. Chart shows recommended filters and film. (Eastman Kodak)

black) or to *photograph as white* (drop color leaving white space).

Note! For more information on filters, refer to the textbook index.

DIFFUSION TRANSFER

The *diffusion transfer* process is capable of making a line positive, screened positive, or lithographic printing plate using a process camera.

A negative sheet is exposed to the image on the process camera. To transfer the image, it is contacted to a receiver material and then processed. See Fig. 13-37.

Fig. 13-38 shows a diffusion transfer processor. Fig. 13-39 shows a system for washing and drying processed diffusion transfer materials. Fig. 13-40 pictures an image leaving another type of diffusion transfer machine.

After processing, the negative and the receiver material must be in contact for approximatley 30 seconds. The two are then pulled apart, Fig. 13-41. The unexposed part of the

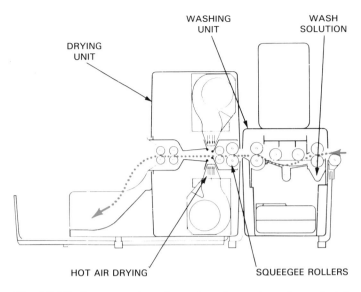

Fig. 13-39. Cutaway view shows how image transfer material is fed through washing-drying unit. Washing and drying helps keep image uniform. (Agfa-Gevaert)

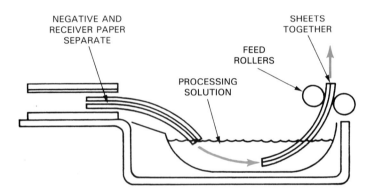

Fig. 13-37. Diffusion transfer process has image almost in contact with transfer material as two are sent through processor.

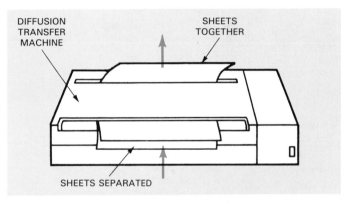

Fig. 13-40. Here you can see the finished product leaving an automatic diffusion transfer machine.

Fig. 13-38. This is a typical diffusion transfer processor. (nuArc)

Fig. 13-41. After exposure, two diffusion sheets are left in contact for approximately 30 seconds. Then, pull them apart. Emulsion side is darker than base side. Emulsion side of negative must face coated side of the receiver paper.

emulsion transfers to the receiver material. This system gives good dense copy in a positive form.

The process bypasses conventional film developing, opaquing, stripping, and film contacting usually associated with the processing steps.

The materials commonly associated with the diffusion transfer process are:

1. *Negative paper* — This is a light sensitive, camera-speed, negative material. It must be handled in red safe light.
2. *Reflex paper* — This is a light sensitive, contact speed, negative paper. It can be handled in subdued room light.
3. *Receiver paper* — This is a chemically sensitive paper designed to receive the image. It is NOT light sensitive.
4. *Transparency receiver* — This is a chemically sensitive clear receiver film to produce a positive. It is NOT light sensitive.
5. *Offset plate* — This is a chemically sensitive, metal plate made to receive the image for specific presses.
6. *Activator* — This is a chemical, in liquid form, to process the transfer material.

Exposing negative materials

To expose negative materials, the following procedure is suggested:

1. Place the emulsion side of the negative material toward the lens of the camera. The emulsion side of the negative paper is black.
2. Expose the negative material. The exact exposure time must be determined by a test exposure. The same f-stop and time for ortho type film would be a satisfactory place to begin.
3. For halftones, a diffusion transfer contact screen should be used. A main white light and a yellow flash exposure is suggested. Again, tests must be made. Remember to use red safe lights.
4. To process the material, the processor must be filled to the proper level with activator liquid.
5. Place the exposed side of the diffusion transfer paper in contact with the coated side of the receiver sheet, Fig. 13-37. The exposed material should go into the processor facing up and the receiver material goes into the processor facing down. The two sheets must travel together and be square with each other.
6. During the processing, the sheets are squeezed together after they pass through the chemicals. They exit the processor in contact. Typically, allow the two sheets to remain in contact for 30 seconds before stripping them apart. After the 30 seconds, pull them apart.
7. A quality positive should be the result. Do not stack the prints until they are thoroughly dry.

Reflex paper

A *reflex paper* is also available. This material is used for making a same size, positive proof of a completed paste up without the use of the camera. This material can be handled in subdued light. The emulsion side of this paper has a glossy appearance.

The copy is placed in the vacuum printing frame with the material to be copied, face up, toward the light source, Fig. 13-42. The reflex paper is placed over the copy with the emulsion side toward the copy. Close the frame and turn on the vacuum before exposing.

Exposure should be with a quartz lamp at about four feet (122 cm). Exact exposure times must be determined by a test. A typical example would be a 30 second exposure with a quartz light at four feet. The processing is the same as for the negative material.

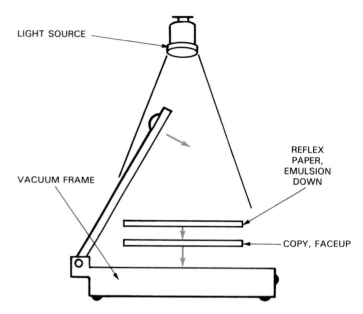

Fig. 13-42. Note correct way of exposing reflex material.

Silverless light sensitive materials

Although *silverless materials* are not that prevalent, they have a very definite place in the industry. The most used process is called *diazo*. The diazo coating, which is a diazonium salt, is exposed by ultraviolet, violet, or blue light. The image areas must absorb these light rays while the nonimage areas allow light to pass through to the diazo coating.

When this type of light sensitive material has been exposed to the copy, it must be developed. Chemical development is of two types: wet or dry. The type of development depends on the type of light sensitive materials used.

A wide variety of silverless materials are used for special purposes. Proofing is one use. Some require the use of heat to make film negatives.

Some of the films are crystal coated and have applications ranging from photography, microfilming, and lithographic platemaking. More applications are anticipated in the future.

CAMERA OPERATING PROCEDURES

For efficiency, it is imperative that you understand the basic procedures for operating a process camera. Each plant might have a suggested procedure but following a basic plan

helps eliminate the possibility of mistakes. Consistent procedures lead to a more profitable operation!

The following basic steps will be discussed: Loading the copyboard, setting for size, controlling lens opening, focusing the image, positioning the film, setting exposure time, and exposing film.

Loading the copyboard

The glass used in the copyboard should be perfectly clean, polished plate glass. The hinged frame allows the operator to place the images to be shot in position before being clamped in place, Fig. 13-43.

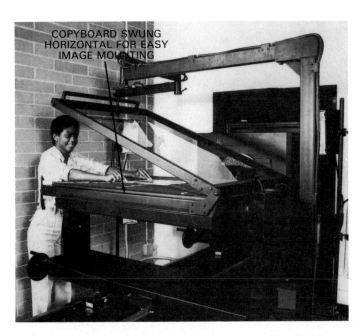

Fig. 13-43. Here camera operator is placing original image on copyboard. Note that copyboard has been swung into horizontal position while placing copy on board. After positioning image, copyboard will be swung back down in front of camera lens.

Most copyboards will accommodate various material thicknesses. Care must be taken so that a build up of materials on a small area does not create an excessive amount of pressure. This could break the glass.

The copy is placed on the copyboard so that it is readable on the ground glass. This means that the image that appears at the top of the copyboard will appear on the bottom of the ground glass when using a horizontal camera. It is also wise to position the copy in the approximate center of the copyboard.

Note! A minimal amount of copy handling eliminates the possibility of getting dirt on the copy surface.

Extreme care must be taken to make sure the copyboard is eased into position. If forced or dropped, it could shift the copyboard out of alignment. Then, not all planes would be parallel with one another and their reproduction would not be exact.

Most copyboards have a *mat* which is zoned to assist in copy placement. Check the copyboard glass for dirt because

it could create an unwanted image on the film. Most manufacturers will recommend a good graphic arts glass cleaner that will not affect the copy.

Setting light source

The lamps or light sources are often a part of the copyboard housing. The lamps are positioned approximately 30° to 45° from the copy, with a slight crossing of the highest intensity portion of the lamps. There should not be a reflection back to the lens. The distance from the copyboard is around three feet or one meter as shown in Fig. 13-44.

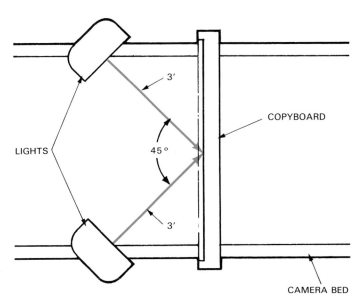

Fig. 13-44. Make sure lights are adjusted properly. They should be correct distance and at correct angle in relation to copyboard. Refer to camera operating manual if in doubt.

The lighting must be controlled to give even illumination. Do not touch the lamps when positioning the lamp housing or lamp life will be reduced.

Setting size and lens diaphragm

Not all of the finished negatives or positives will be shot the same size as the original copy. When the original copy is larger than the final work, the process is commonly called *reduction*. When the images must be increased in size, it is called *enlarging*. The process camera has this capability.

The term *scaling* is associated with enlarging or reducing copy. As explained in earlier chapters, when reducing the original size of 12 inches to 6 inches, it would be a reduction of 50%. The negative or positive would be 50% of the original size. Going from 6 to 12 would be a 200% enlargement. Percentage calculators are used to determine the reduction or enlargement.

Process cameras have various types of gauge devices to regulate the size. The *tape* is a very common method. The readings appear on a calibrated scale. Often, the tapes can be regulated from the darkroom or the copyboard end of the camera.

What is important to remember is that both tapes (copyboard and lensboard) must have the SAME READING to be in focus.

Some cameras have scales attached to the camera base. The indicators must line up with the scale markings. This is true of the lensboard as well as the copyboard.

Today's sophisticated cameras have micrometer type settings that are programmed and automatically positioned for proper focus. These types are used where extreme exactness is a requirement. The photographic lens determines the positioning of each scale for the lensboard as well as the copyboard. They are calibrated to each camera. This means that the tapes or scales are specifically designed for each process camera.

Cameras can have automatic or manually controlled diaphragm openings, Fig. 13-45. The arm, which regulates the f/stop opening, is very easy to use. If the copy is to be set at 100%, move the arm to 100% on the f/22 scale, Fig. 13-46. The size of the opening determines the amount of light that is calibrated to strike the light sensitive material.

f-Stops

The *f-stops* on process cameras generally range from f/8 to an f/90—The smaller the number, the larger the opening and the smaller the lens opening, the larger the number. Typical f-stops are: f/8, f/11, f/16, f/22, f/32, f/45, f/64, and f/90. See Fig. 13-47.

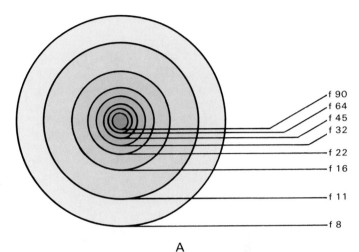

f 90
f 64
f 45
f 32
f 22
f 16
f 11
f 8

A

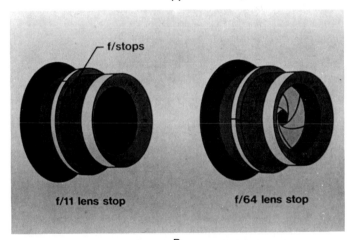

f/stops

f/11 lens stop   f/64 lens stop

B

Fig. 13-45. Operator is adjusting f-stop of process camera.

Fig. 13-46. Close-up of manually adjusted f-stop control. Note different f-stops and percentages on scale.

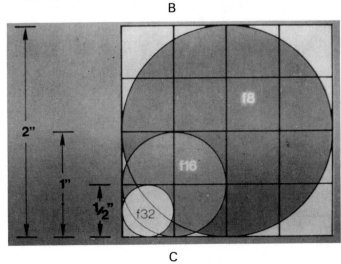

2"
1"
½"
f8
f16
f32

C

Fig. 13-47. Principle of camera lens. A—Lens opening diameter corresponds with f-stop numbers. B—Extreme examples of f-stops. C—Size relationship of a few f-stops.
(Chapter One, Screaming Color)

A process camera's best resolution is toward the middle numbers. For best results, the manufacturer usually recommends the correct f-stop. This is usually three or four times down from the largest opening. If f/8 is the largest opening, f/16 or f/22 would be the best f-stop to get the sharpest images.

Remember! The sharpness of the image is NOT toward the smallest or largest diaphragm opening but near the middle settings.

It should also be noted that for each step down in f-stop, the exposure time must be doubled. Half as much time is needed at f/8 as f/11 for the same amount of light to strike the light sensitive surface. As an example, if the exposure time is 20 seconds at f/11, at f/8 it will require 10 seconds of light exposure. This would be true of each f-stop because the time doubles when going to the larger f-stop. This is shown in Fig. 13-48.

Each successively larger number will decrease the diaphragm by one half which accounts for the exposure time changes.

Focal length

Each lens has a *focal length* which is the distance from the center of the lens housing, called the *nodal point,* to the surface that supports the film (film plane). See Fig. 13-49.

When the process camera is set at its maximum reduction, it is commonly referred to as an *infinity* setting.

The letters "FL" are used to denote focal length. The focal length of a camera is one fourth of the distance from the copyboard to the film plane when the camera is in focus and set for the same size (100%) reproduction. Much of the necessary information such as the diameter of the lens, and f-stop, and focal length are stamped on the lens barrel.

Focusing the camera

To be in *focus* or to produce a sharp image, the copyboard and lensboard must be correctly positioned. The adjustment tapes or scales must READ THE SAME. If the copy is to be reduced by 50%, each one of the scales must read 50%. The lens diaphragm must be positioned to correspond to the readings on the scales, as illustrated earlier.

In order to see the image, the ground glass must be brought into position for viewing. The ground glass is in the same plane as the film, Fig. 13-50.

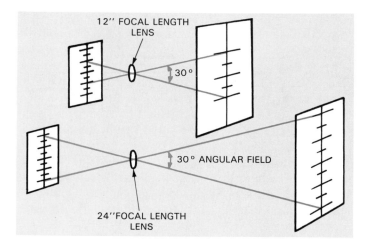

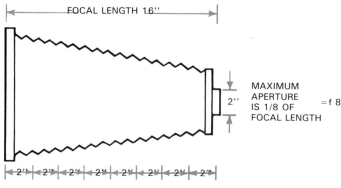

$$\text{SPEED OF LENS} = \frac{\text{FOCAL LENGTH}}{\text{DIAMETER}} \text{ or } \frac{16}{2} = f\,8$$

Fig. 13-49. Note how focal length affects camera operation. (Chapter One, Screaming Color)

The camera master controls must be turned on. The next step is to turn on the *focus switch.* This switch opens the shutter and allows light to pass through the lens. Each camera has its own shutter design. Most are made of movable metal leaves which open and close automatically when the focus switch or exposure unit is turned on.

When the focus switch has been activated, the camera lights go on and the shutter opens. The image is now visible on the ground glass. The operator often uses a magnifying glass to check the images for sharpness, Fig. 13-50.

DIAMETER OF OPENING	1 in.	8/11 in.	1/2 in.	4/11 in.	1/4 in.
F-STOP/ NUMBER	f/8	f/11	f/16	f/22	f/32
EXPOSURE TIME	10 sec = equivalent exposure	20 sec = equivalent exposure	40 sec = basic exposure	80 sec = equivalent exposure	160 sec = equivalent exposure

Fig. 13-48. Chart shows f-stop numbers with diameter of lens opening and typical amount of time needed for exposure film. Note how time becomes longer as f-stop number becomes larger.

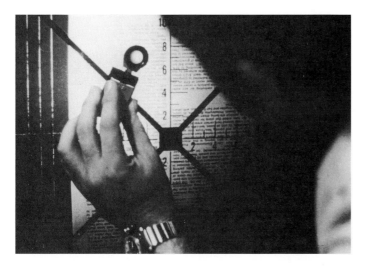

Fig. 13-50. Inspect image closely on ground glass. Image must be in focus and located properly. Magnifier makes close inspection easier.

The image area also indicates the size of film needed for photoconversion. If the critical settings are correct, the image will be the desired size and the images will be sharp.

The focus switch must be turned off before operating the camera for regular exposures to a sensitized material.

Care must also be taken to make sure that boxes of film are closed while checking the focus. Any film in the darkroom that is left out will be exposed and ruined. This constitutes waste which takes away from the profit of the business.

Return the ground glass so that the vacuum back is positioned and ready for use, as in Fig. 13-51.

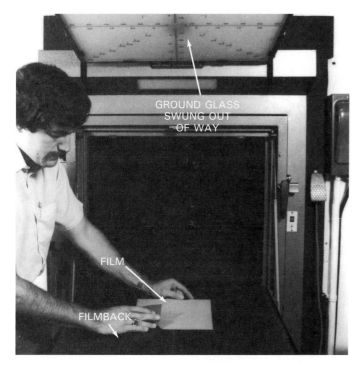

GROUND GLASS SWUNG OUT OF WAY

FILM

FILMBACK

Fig. 13-51. With safelights on in darkroom, position film in image area of camera back.

Positioning the film

Where to position film on the vacuum area must be determined. It is imperative that the film be perfectly flat on the film plane. Most camera backs have positioning indications which correspond to the copyboard markings.

In most cases, the film should be centered on the back, with the emulsion side of the film toward the lens for exposure, Fig. 13-51.

The size of the piece of film is determined by the final reproduction size. Make sure a sufficient margin exists so that the image does not extend beyond the edge of the film.

Handle the film very carefully, by the edges, so that finger marks do not appear on the film, Fig. 13-52. The emulsion of the film will also scratch very easily. Make sure the film box is closed after a piece of film has been removed.

Setting exposure time

The amount of time it takes to properly expose a piece of film is determined by the speed of the film, the illumination, copyboard distance from the lens, and the distance the film is from the lens.

The ratio of distance for the copyboard and film plane and the lens has been set by the manufacturer, while the illumination will vary from camera to camera. The lamp distance from the copyboard may also be set by the manufacturer or the camera may allow the operator to establish the lamp-to-copyboard distance.

Basic exposure for line copy

Each camera will have a best time for reproducing the camera-ready copy. This is commonly called the *basic main exposure.*

The technique recommended by the Graphic Arts Technical Foundation to prepare your settings is known as the *step-off method* or *test exposure.* Using this system, the operator places a piece of film (8 x 10) on the film plane, usually a vacuum back. All but one to two inches are covered with a material that does not allow light to pass through it, Fig. 13-52. If the masking sheet does not make good contact, tape down the edge.

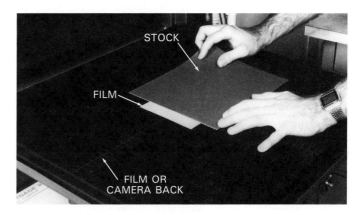

STOCK

FILM

FILM OR CAMERA BACK

Fig. 13-52. To make test exposure with step-off method, cover portion of film with light stopping stock. Make exposure and then slide stock or paper approximately one inch. Repeat this procedure. Process film and analyze result of each exposure.

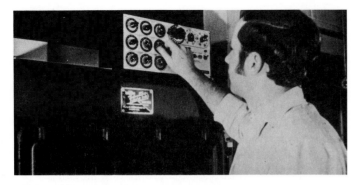

Fig. 13-53. When making test or actual exposure, make sure camera settings are correct.

Make the first exposure using a selected number of seconds or units, Fig. 13-53. Four seconds might be an acceptable starting point. After each exposure, move the mask one inch or the distance necessary to make at least five exposures on the one piece of film.

As you step the mask, each increment is increasing the same amount each time, using four as an increment. The first step will have a 20 second exposure if five steps are used. It is imperative that the copy be of excellent quality and large enough to cover the whole piece of film.

Once all of the exposures have been made, the film must be processed according to the manufacturer's recommendations. The right exposure time should give the sharpest image with high density and no filling in of the copy, Fig. 13-54.

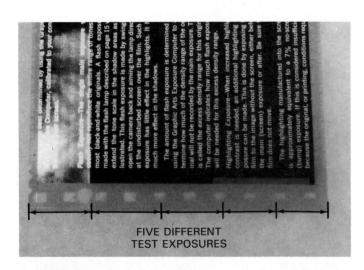

FIVE DIFFERENT
TEST EXPOSURES

Fig. 13-54. The best exposure time will produce the sharpest image on the test film. Keep track of how long each test exposure was and shoot the actual shot using this data.

Exposing film

Now that the basic main exposure has been determined for line copy, place your camera-ready material on the copyboard. A control device, called a *gray scale* should be positioned next to the copy, Fig. 13-55. Make sure the lamps are properly positioned. Double-check all settings.

Select the film size and place the film on the camera back, working only under red safelight conditions. The next step is to activate the timing unit to expose the film, Fig. 13-56. The exposed film is ready to be processed.

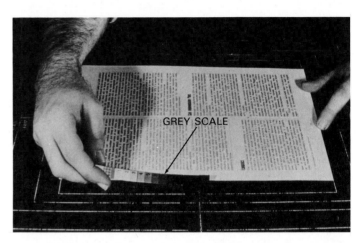

GREY SCALE

Fig. 13-55. Camera operator is placing gray scale next to film. It will help determine best exposure time or if image has been under or overexposed.

Fig. 13-56. Operator is using vertical camera to shoot line image. Exposure lights are on and have been set after using test exposure data.

Automatic devices

Many of today's cameras have automatic exposure systems. These are commonly called *exposure control units*. One of these units is called a *timer* or *exposure computer*, Fig. 13-57. This is a simple device which controls the duration of the exposure, and is a necessary device on a process camera.

A

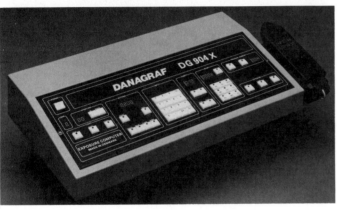

B

Fig. 13-57. A—This is a timer sometimes used to control exposure duration. B—This is a more complex exposure computer. It can be used to calculate or control size percentages, exposure, focus, screening, bump exposures, aperture settings, electronic shutter control, light integrator, density, and other functions. (Danagraf)

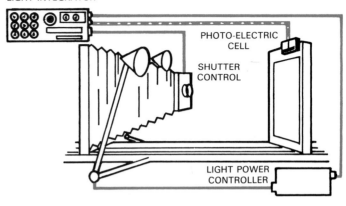

Fig. 13-58. Light integrator can regulate amount of light striking film. It can compensate or adjust for any variations in voltage, etc. that might upset exposure. Note basic parts of integrator system. (Chapter One, Screaming Color)

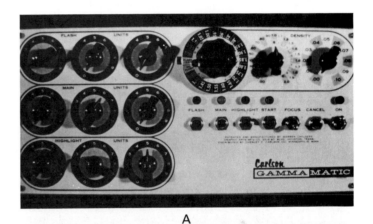

A

B

Fig. 13-59. A—Camera controls. B—Light sensing device near film back can measure actual light hitting film for precise exposure.

Even though the duration of exposure is controlled, the line voltage to the exposure lights can fluctuate. This means that the light intensity could vary and the exposure could be unequal even though the time is the same. This can cause exposure difficulties.

A device that accounts for a change in voltage to the lights is called a *light integrator,* Fig. 13-58.

An integrator assures that the same amount of light strikes the film, based on the exposure setting. This is an important device to assure a consistent amount of light strikes the film or light sensitive surface each time a shot is taken. An ordinary timer only allows for time and NOT for the amount of light. See Fig. 13-59.

Computerized exposure

Some *computerized systems* are very sophisticated and account for the exposure and density values of copy, Fig. 13-60. The computer system automatically calculates the exposure. Once the input information is plugged in, the calculations and exposure are made automatically by the computer.

Fig. 13-60. This is a modern electronically-controlled horizontal camera. Note control console at left for programming in data. It can store exposure data and reproduce the same exposure upon command. It also has a photocell that serves as a light integrator to assure consistent exposures.   (Screen - USA)

Various devices are on the market. Use the manufacturers guide to learn about the system available. An electronically controlled vertical camera is shown in Fig. 13-61.

CAMERA-PROCESSOR

A *camera-processor* combines a process camera and a developer into a single unit. One is pictured in Fig. 13-62. This unit is a daylight reproduction camera for line, screen, and continuous tone work. It is computer controlled and automatically does sizing, focusing, exposure, and processing.

Most camera-processors have an on-line scanning densitometer that checks the minimum and maximum densities of the image to assure quality reproduction. The film is usually in roll form and can be fed over the camera back and then into the processor after exposure. A developed image is fed out one end of the unit.

Fig. 13-63 shows the control panel for one brand of camera-processor. Note that control keys are provided for the lighting system, focus, processor, sizing, exposure, screen density, lens movement, copyboard movement, and other functions.

Since cameras vary, always follow the operating manual for the specific type or model. Procedures vary.

Fig. 13-61. This is a computer-controlled vertical camera. It has memory for storing main, flash, and backlighting exposure information. It also has a built-in light integrator system. (nuArc)

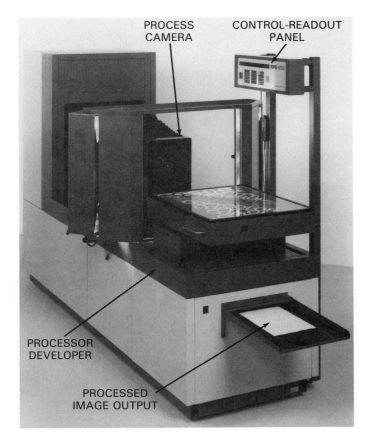

Fig. 13-62. This is a camera-processor. A horizontal camera and a film developer are combined into a single unit. A roll of light sensitive material is fed through back. After exposure, it is then automatically processed and cut into sheets. It has computer controlled sizing, focusing, exposure, and developing. It is a daylight camera and has an on-line scanning densitometer that checks minimum and maximum densities of image. (Visual Graphics Corporation)

FILM PROCESSING

Film processing or developing is covered in Chapter 17. Refer to this chapter for more information as needed.

KNOW THESE TERMS

Line art, Photomechanical, Illumination, Tungsten filament, Quartz-iodine lamp, Carbon-arc, Pulsed-xenon, Mercury vapor, Electromagnetic spectrum, Millicron, Color temperature, 5000 K, Process camera, Copy camera, Vertical camera, Horizontal camera, Floor camera, Overhead camera, Copyboard, Lensboard, Film back, Ground glass, Emulsion, Antihalation backing, Imtermediate, Negative, Positive, Image reversal, Density capacity, Sensitometry, Characteristic curve, Toe, Straight line, Shoulder, Gamma, Color sensitivity, Blue sensitive film, Ortho film, Pan film, Film base, Polyester base, Acetate base, Glass base, Prescreened film, Rapid access film, Contact film, Duplicating film, Daylight film, Filter, Dropping color, Diffusion transfer, Negative paper, Reflex paper, Receiver paper, Activator, Silverless materials, f-stop, Focal length, Nodal point, Focus, Test exposure, Exposure computer.

REVIEW QUESTIONS—CHAPTER 13

1. In the future, the importance of photomechanical methods may decrease. True or false?
2. This light source is weak in the blue and ultraviolet rays but is excessive in the red rays.
   a. Quartz-iodine lamps.
   b. Carbon-arc lamps.
   c. Mercury-vapor lamps.
   d. Tungsten-filament lamps.

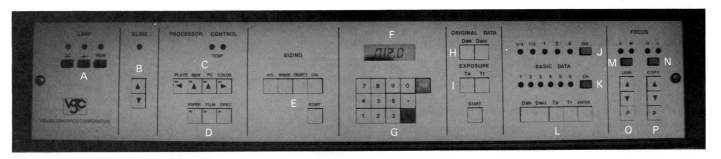

| A. Lighting System | D. Processor Speed Control | G. Keyboard for data input, calculation, and memory recall | J. Exposure Compensator | M. Automatic or Manual mode for focus |

A. Lighting System
- reflective lighting
- transparency lighting
- operator viewing

B. Slide Enlarger focus
- enlarge
- reduce

C. Processor Control mode
- platemaker
- black & white
- photocomp
- color

D. Processor Speed Control
- paper
- film
- special materials

E. Sizing Control
- manual input of % enlargement/reduction
- percentage enlargement/ reduction calculator input
- start button

F. 4-Digit LED Readout

G. Keyboard for data input, calculation, and memory recall

H. Original Data, Halftones
- enter minimum copy density
- enter maximum copy density

I. Exposure Time, Halftones
- to display main exposure time
- to display flash exposure time

J. Exposure Compensator

K. Memory Selector for up to 6 channels of stored programs

L. Basic Data Entry
- enter minimum screen density
- enter maximum screen density
- enter main exposure time
- enter flash exposure time for halftone work

M. Automatic or Manual mode for focus

N. Fast/Slow speed for separate manual drives —lensboard or copyboard

O. Forward-Back movement of lens

P. Forward-Back movement of copyboard

Fig. 13-63. Here is electronic control panel for one model camera-processor. Note that it has electronic controls for lighting, processing, sizing, memory, density, auto or manual focus, and other functions. (Visual Graphics Corporation)

3. The term _____ _____ refers to the quality of the light source.
4. Which of the following temperatures is closest to daylight.
   a. 5000K.
   b. 4000K.
   c. 6000K.
   d. 3000 K.
5. A vertical camera is commonly used for larger images than a horizontal camera. True or false?
6. List and explain eight basic parts of a process camera.
7. The amount of darkness or lightness in a negative or positive is termed its _____.
8. What are three factors that affect how much light strikes the film on a process camera?
9. The _____ _____ indicates how a given material or film will react to light and development.
10. In your own words, explain the three major types of film.
11. How can you use filters to stat colored line art and make it black and white and use filters to drop certain colors?
12. What is diffusion transfer?
13. The f-stops on a process camera ranges from _____ to _____—the smaller the f-stop number, the _____ the lens opening.
14. How do you use the step-off method to make a test exposure?
15. What is a light integrator?

SUGGESTED ACTIVITIES

1. On a four-by-six white card, place six (6) examples of image materials. Examples would be: Pencil copy, inked copy, transfer letters, a swatch of painted color other than black or red, printed material, rubylith, etc. Shoot them as line copy and inspect the results.
2. Visit various facilities and examine how process cameras are used.
3. Go to the library and read periodicals that discuss graphic arts cameras.
4. Read through the operating manuals for various process cameras.

Chapter 14

HALFTONE REPRODUCTION

After studying this chapter, you will be able to:
- Explain the principles of halftone reproduction.
- Evaluate continuous tone originals.
- Describe the role of densitometry in halftone reproduction.
- Explain and use halftone contact screens.
- Discuss non-conventional methods to reproduce halftones.

This chapter will continue your study of graphic communications by explaining how continuous tone photographs are prepared for reproduction. Unlike line art, photos consist of many different shades or densities. Since a printing press only uses one shade or density of ink, the photo must be altered into a halftone containing a dot pattern corresponding to the many shades in the photo. Then, the printing press can deposit ink on paper so that the image will appear like a continuous tone photograph.

HALFTONES

It is important for you to understand that the printing press reproduces the image on the plate with only one color and density of ink. The reproduction of high contrast copy or line copy conforms to this limitation. If the press operator is printing from a plate that has type matter and simple line illustrations, then the press sheet will have the same image printed in one uniform color and density of ink.

Halftone reproduction is the process of printing a continuous tone image, such as a photograph or painting, on the same one-color printing press. See Fig. 14-1.

The term *"halftone"* comes from the old artist hand-engraving process of breaking the image up into quarter tones, halftones, and three-quarter tones. A halftone reproduction gives the viewer an illusion of a continuous tone image when it is actually a tone pattern composed of dots that vary in size, but not density. Refer to Fig. 14-2.

Continuous tone copy is composed of tones ranging from white to black or light colors to dark colors, Fig. 14-3. You have learned from line photography that white or light colors will reflect considerable light from the copyboard, through the lens and onto the film emulsion. It is also known that

A

B

Fig. 14-1. A photograph must normally be converted into a halftone before it can be reproduced on a printing press. A— Note small dot pattern in this reproduced photo. B— Line copy does not have to be screened.

215

Fig. 14-2. *Close-up section of this halftone shows dot structure. (Chapter One, Screaming Color)*

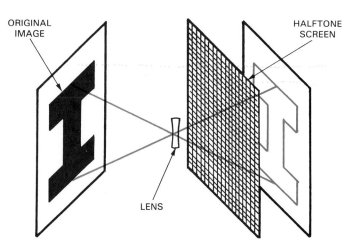

Fig. 14-4. *To convert a continuous tone photo into a halftone, a screen is placed over the film. Then, the light from the original image must pass through the dot pattern before exposing the film.*

The *halftone screen* records dots that vary in size according to the amount of light reflected from the continuous tone copy. This halftone dot structure, when printed with a uniform density of ink on the paper, creates the illusion of many different shades or tones. Look at Fig. 14-5.

CLASSIFICATIONS OF CAMERA COPY

Basically, there are two major categories of copy to be reproduced on the process camera. All forms of original copy will be either continuous tone or line work in nature. The camera person responsible for halftone reproduction should have the knowledge necessary to evaluate the copy, and further define it into one of the four copy classifications listed below:
1. Line work.
2. Mechanical shading.
3. Continuous tone.
4. Pre-screened copy.

HIGHLIGHT   SHADOW   MIDTONE

Fig. 14-3. *As you can see, a photo consists of many shades or tones.*

black or dark colors absorb light and thus reflect limited amounts of light through the lens and onto the film emulsion.

To record the other intermediate tone values in the continuous tone original, the camera operator needs a slightly more sensitive film. A halftone screen is also needed to record different size dots that represent *highlight values* (whites), *midtone values* (grays), and *shadow values* (blacks). Refer to Fig. 14-4.

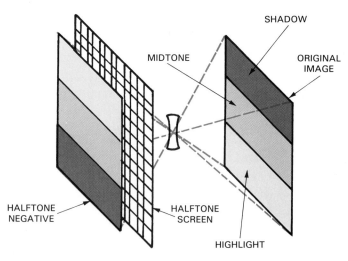

Fig. 14-5. *Here you can see how a halftone negative is the opposite image as the original.*

Linework

The first classification of camera copy is line work and it has already been defined in the preceeding chapters. Refer back to Fig. 14-1.

Mechanical shading

The second classification, known as *mechanical shading,* is considered to be a form of line work, but requires more attention because of the fine details and intricate nature of the images. Mechanical shading, like line copy, will contrast the image and non-image areas by the use of only light colors (white) and dark colors (black). Tints, textures, and some coarse or stippling airbrush techniques can also be classified as mechanical shading, Fig. 14-6.

Fig. 14-7. *Continuous tone images can be reflection copy, like the two photos, or they can be transmission copy, like the small 35 mm transparency.*

Fig. 14-6. *Tints or textures are normally classified as mechanical shading and they require more attention when being reproduced.*

Camera copy that consists of mechanical shading often requires the use of a halftone sensitive film rather than the less sensitive line film. The alignment and focus capabilities of the process camera are critical considerations. The use of a magnifiying lens on the ground glass is suggested to check for accuracy. It is further suggested that a slight reproduction enlargement of copy containing 133 lines or finer tint screen rulings be used when possible.

Continuous tone classifications

The third classification of copy, known as *continuous tone,* can be broken down into two sub-categories—reflection and transmission copy. This is pictured in Fig. 14-7.

Reflection copy includes photographs, oil paintings, chalk or charcoal renderings, and water color work. They will reflect different amounts of light from the different tone values of the original. See Fig. 14-8.

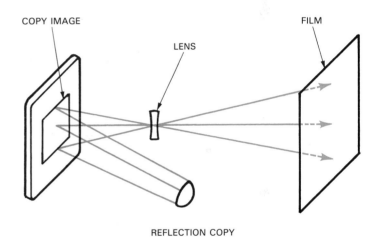

Fig. 14-8. *A—Reflection copy will reflect light and you cannot see through it. B—Transmission copy will allow light to pass through and must be handled differently on the process camera.*

Transparent or *transmission copy* includes 35mm black and white or color slides and large format transparencies. Since light will pass through the image, they will commonly require back lighting techniques on the process camera. This form of continuous tone copy will require the use of a process camera that has a semi-transparent backing on the copyboard, Fig. 14-8.

When the copyboard lights are positioned behind the transparent copy or slide, the amount of light transmitted through the different densities of the original will record image and non-image areas on the film being exposed through the process lens.

Both reflection or transmission forms of continuous tone copy will require the use of a *halftone grade film,* which is considered more sensitive and dimensionably stable than *line film.* The reproduction of continuous tone copy will also require the use of a halftone *contact screen* or *glass screen* to record the dot pattern that is needed for the printing press.

With some printing processes, such as gravure, all of the images are screened. Further information on gravure image generation will be given in a later chapter.

Continuous tone copy may consist of black and white or color images. It should be suggested that your initial experiences in halftone photography be limited to black and white photographs. Understand that the different hues or colors in a color photograph will either reflect or absorb light.

Depending on the nature of the film emulsion used, either chromatic or panchromatic film, the red lipstick on the color portrait of a woman, for example, may turn out black or gray when printed as a black and white halftone. It will take practice and experience in the evaluation of color originals to make quality black and white halftones. Fig. 14-9 shows a common method.

Prescreened images

The final classification of camera copy is *prescreened* or *preprinted* halftone images and they already contain a screen or dot pattern. This category can be treated as mechanical shading or can be re-screened into halftones by different techniques. Prescreened prints can be made in the camera or enlarger. If shot as line work, the same considerations for mechanical shading should be given.

Using a contact halftone screen is one method to make a re-screened halftone reproduction.

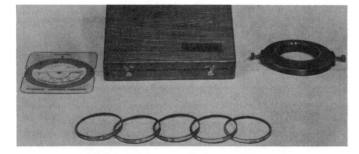

Fig. 14-9. Different types of filters can be used for converting color original into black and white.

Another method is to angle the halftone screen 30° from the original screen angle to prevent a moiré pattern. A *moiré pattern* is a visually undesirabale dot exaggerating effect when two different screen patterns are randomly positioned or superimposed. See Fig. 14-10.

A simpler method is to move the lensboard 2% to 4% out of focus from the desired reproduction percentage, in an effort to diffuse the halftone image by a soft focus technique.

Fig. 14-10. A moiré pattern, like this, will result if screen angles are not correct.

HALFTONE SCREEN PROCESS

The *halftone screen process* is the procedure of converting a continuous tone original into an uncontinuous dot structure. This conversion is made with either a crossline (glass) or contact halftone screen placed over the film. A fresh film emulsion is placed in the path of the imaging or main exposure.

The old traditional crossline screen consists of two pieces of ruled glass. The ruled glass depressions are filled with an opaque pigment and cemented together at right angles, Fig. 14-11. For black and white work, the screen was posi-

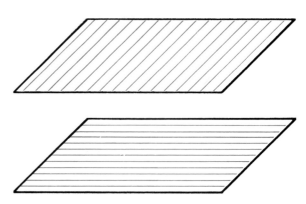

Fig. 14-11. Enlarged and separated, an older crossline screen was made of two pieces of glass with opaque lines on them.

tioned at a 45° angle so that the human eye focuses on the printed halftone in vertical or horizontal orientation, thus the rows of dots appear less obvious at 45°.

Further study on the effects of the glass crossline halftone screen can be researched using the Penumbra Theory, Pinhole Theory, or the Diffraction Theory.

For our purposes, this chapter will discuss the types of halftone contact screens currently being used in the industry. Even though the crossline screen is still being used for halftone work, more camera operators prefer to use the less expensive, simpler, and faster contact screen.

Contact screen

A *contact screen* is a series of uniform vignetted (soft) dots mounted on a flexible support base. Unlike the sharp ruled lines in the crossline screen, the *vignetted dot structure* in the contact screen is diffused or appears out of focus when magnified, Fig. 14-12.

A halftone contact screen differs from a tint screen. A *tint screen* is used in the platemaking process to create the uniform tone pattern. It contains a HARD DOT structure that is specified by a dot percentage.

The halftone contact screen is used like the name suggests, in close vacuum contact with the film emulsion. During the camera exposure, the different amounts of light reflected from the different tone values of the copy, will penetrate the vignetted dot structure of the contact screen, and record the latent image on the film.

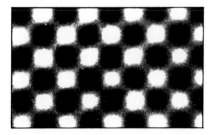

Fig. 14-12. This is an example of an enlarged area of a contact screen.

Where the highlights or white areas of the copy reflected considerable light, the dots are larger on the film. This is because the extra light passes through the fringe of the vignetted dots.

When dim light is reflected from the shadow or black portions of the copy, the dot structure will be smaller, having passed through only the transparent center of the vignetted dots.

Percent dot sizes

The *halftone dots sizes* are specified as percentages of ink density on a printed sheet. The highlight dots will usually be 5% to 10% in size, with the midtones ranging from 30% to 70%, and the shadow dots around 90% to 95%. The halftone negative will represent a reversal of the original, but the dot structure is still in reference to the positive printed image, Fig. 14-13.

Screen color

Halftone contact screens can be magenta or gray in color. Either screen may be used for reproducing black and white halftones from black and white copy. Magenta contact screens can be used in combination with magenta or yellow color compensating filters to either compress or extend the screen range. The magenta screen can be used in any photomechanical reproduction process, except direct screen color separation where the magenta dye in the screen will alter the effects of the color separation filters.

Perhaps the most commonly used contact screen is the gray contact screen. This is because the silver or gray color is neutral and will not alter the effects of color separation filters.

Negative and positive screens

Contact screens can be designated for negative or positive purposes. Usually, the *positive screen* will have a longer screen range or tone reproduction capability than the negative screen. Using different exposure techniques, it is possible to make a halftone negative with a positive screen.

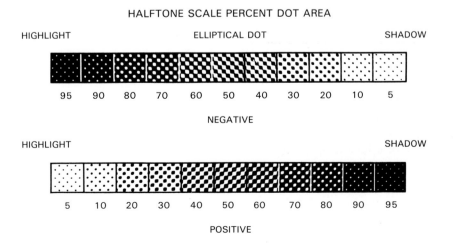

Fig. 14-13. Note how a percentage can be used to denote highlight and shadow areas of an image. A negative and a positive are opposites.

As a rule of thumb, use positive screens to reproduce positives, and a negative screen to make negatives.

Screen shapes

Most halftone contact screens are rectangular in shape, but some companies prefer a circular screen to obtain the different screen angles. When purchasing or making a circular screen, the diameter of the screen must be slightly larger than the diagonal of the largest film size to be used. Look at Fig. 14-14.

Fig. 14-14. The contact screen must be properly handled and stored.

Screen dot shapes

Halftone screens have three different dot shapes. These are square, elliptical, and round. Refer to Fig. 14-15.

The SQUARE DOT is often referred to as a *conventional dot*.

The ELLIPTICAL DOT is sometimes called the *chain dot*.

The *square dot* was the traditional dot used, and received its shape from the crossline screen. It is often the easiest to

determine dot percentage, especially in the dot etching process.

Today, the *elliptical dot* or *chain dot* structure is the most popular because it offers a smoother tone rendition in the middle tones. The comparison of the elliptical dot and square dot in a portrait of a person will visually prove this difference in the middle tones or facial tones.

The *round dot* is used primarily with high-speed web offset printing and was widely accepted in the European markets. The round dot tends to compensate for ink entrapment, plugging, and dot gain in the lighter middle tone dots.

The square and elliptical dots will join at 40% to 50% dot values for middle tones. The round dot will not form or join until 60% to 70%. Thus, the round dot is NOT as accepted in conventional printing because there is a loss of detail as compared to square and elliptical dots.

So far this chapter has discussed the use of a single dot screen. Halftone screens can have a secondary ruling in the middle tones and shadows to reproduce extremely fine details. These screens, containing a secondary ruling, are referred to as *dual-dot halftone screens*.

Selecting halftone screens

Halftone screens are selected by their *rulings* or number of lines or dots per inch, Fig. 14-16.

The ruling should be selected by the printing capabilities of the press room. Capabilities can vary.

Fig. 14-16. This is a chart for checking screen tint percentages. (Lehigh Press)

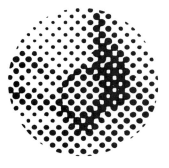

SQUARE DOT STRUCTURE   ELLIPTICAL DOT STRUCTURE   ROUND DOT STRUCTURE   DUAL-DOT SCREEN

Fig. 14-15. Note the difference in detail in the magnified image using the different dot shapes. The square and elliptical give more detail and are more commonly used. Also note dual-dot screen.

If the camera operator selects a 150 or 300 line screen for high quality work and sends it to a press room containing small offset duplicators, the efforts will probably be wasted. Furthermore, the paper that the job is to be printed on should be considered prior to screen ruling selection. Some papers will be more absorbent and will produce a dot gain.

Special screens

In addition to the normal square, elliptical, and round dot screens, special design or texture screens can be used. *Steel etch, mezzo tint, straight line, wavy line,* and *concentric circles* are just a few of the more common special effect halftone screens that can be used. These are shown in Fig. 14-17.

Handling halftone screens

The life and quality of a halftone contact screen depends upon its care and handling. Be careful to treat the contact screen like a piece of film. Protect it from dirt, scratches, processing chemicals, and finger marks.

If the contact screen has to be cleaned, remember that only x-ray screens, NOT magenta screens, can be washed. The magenta dye used to make magenta screen could run or change density unevenly.

The gray contact screen is a delicate film base that has a continuous tone emulsion on one side. To wash the gray screen, use a clean tray of water at room temperature with a neutral wetting agent, dishwashing detergent, or a commercial screen cleaner. Do NOT rub or squeegee the screen. It is recommended that the solution drain uniformly off the screen. Most developer or fixer stains will NOT wash off.

EVALUATING CONTINUOUS TONE ORIGINALS

The continuous tone original, to be used as camera copy for halftone reproduction, will contain a wide range of tones. These tones range from the whitest value, referred to as the *highlight,* through gray values referred to as the *middletones,* to the darkest black called the *shadow.* Refer to Fig. 14-18 for examples.

ROUND DOT (100)   SQUARE DOT (100)   ELLIPTICAL DOT (100)   MEZZOTINT (75)

STRAIGHT LINE (62)   SUNBURST (100)   MEZZOTINT (150)

STEEL ETCH (50)   WAVY LINE (60)   CONCENTRIC CIRCLE (60)   STEEL ENGRAVING (50)

NEW HALFTONE MADE FROM OLD HALFTONE WITH CAPROCK RE-SCREENER FILTERS

LINEN (50)   Original 100 Line Halftone   100 Line Halftone Re-Screened With 60 Line Screen   60 Line Halftone Not Re-Screened

Fig. 14-17. Note how special effects screens can be used to alter an image.   *(Caprock)*

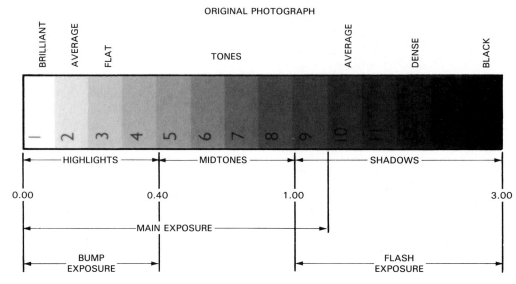

Fig. 14-18. Study example of highlights, midtones, and shadows. (©EASTMAN KODAK)

Density

The term *density* refers to the degree of blackness or the light stopping ability of an image. Density is a measurement system used in photography. A high density image would be solid or almost solid black, for example. A low density would not be solid or black, but white.

Density is given numerically — 0.00 would be white and 3.00 would be black for transmitted light. For reflected light, 2.00 would be the blackest density and 0.00 white. Near the middle of these two densities would be gray with a density value around 0.30 to 0.60. As you can see, as the density value becomes large, the image becomes darker and vice versa.

As you will learn, density can be measured with a gray scale or a densitometer.

Gray scale

The density difference between the highlight value and shadow value is known as the *photo-density range* or *copy density range,* Fig. 14-19. To determine the density of a highlight or shadow, reflection *gray scale* or *density guide* with pre-calibrated density steps will give a numerical value, but only with visual accuracy. You have to compare the example density to the image density visually.

Densitometer

A *reflection densitometer* is an electronic instrument that uses a photocell to accurately measure the amount of light reflected from or through different tone values. It is recommended that a reflection densitometer be used whenever possible, for the purposes of accuracy and consistency. See Figs. 14-20 and 14-21.

High-key and low-key

Another set of terms used to evaluate continuous tone originals are high-key illustrations and low-key illustrations. A photograph that is called *high-key* will contain the most

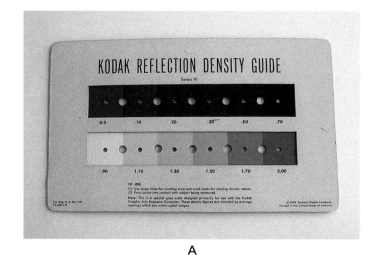

A

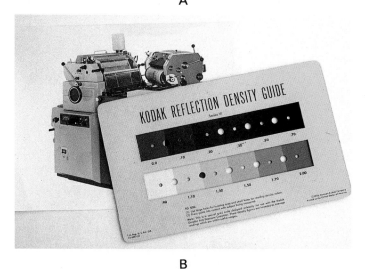

B

Fig. 14-19. A—A reflection density guide can be compared to areas on image to visually assign a density value to the shade or tone. Holes in guide let you lay guide directly over image to match up densities more accurately. B—Density guide being used to check highlights and shadow of photo.

important details in the highlights or lighter tones. A *low-key* photograph is primarily shadow tones. The important details fall between the midtones and shadows, Fig. 14-22.

Dot geometry

An important consideration for the camera person when reproducing halftones is tone reproduction or selection of

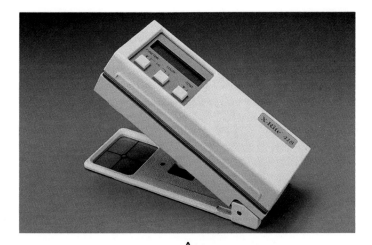

A

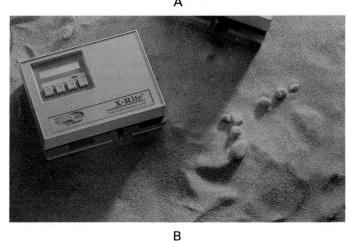

B

Fig. 14-20. Densitometers provide an accurate way of assigning density values or determining if the values have been attained. A—This is a digital color transmission/reflection densitometer. It will read the density of a photograph or the density of a negative or positive. B—These are examples of automatic strip-reading densitometers. (X-Rite, Inc.)

Fig. 14-22. A low-key illustration will have the important image area more shadow than highlight. A high-key photo will have the important image area in highlight and less important areas in shadow. Can you tell which of these is high-key and which is low-key?

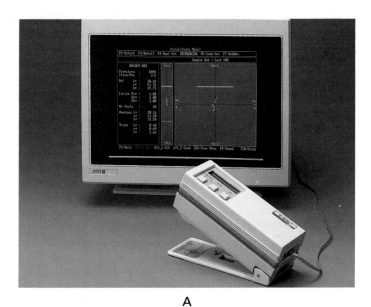

A

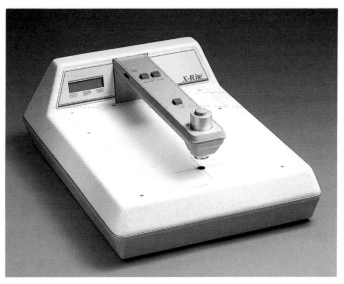

B

Fig. 14-21. Density identification systems. A—The spectro-densitometer gives very specific information. B—Digital transmission densitometer is used to measure densities of negatives and/or positives. (X-Rite, Inc.)

dot geometry. The camera person's abiltity to place the 50% midtone dot in the proper gray tone depends on his or her evaluation of the camera copy.

When reproducing high-key copy, the midtone dot placement should be closer to the shadows, so as to record the important details in the highlights. The opposite is true when reproducing low-key copy, the midtone is placed, through selected exposures, in close proximity to the highlight dot structure.

Paper absorption

Another factor controlling tone reproduction or dot sizes and location, is the type of paper surface used in the job. An absorbent paper will cause the dot sizes to increase (*dot gain*) as the ink is absorbed into the paper.

Determining halftone exposures

To determine halftone exposures for the reproduction of a continuous tone photograph, the highlight and shadow densities will have to be determined. Whether a reflection density guide or a reflection densitometer is used, the camera person should read several possible highlight and shadow locations to determine the true densities of the copy.

Spectral highlights and shadows should NOT be used in determining the copy density range. *Spectral highlights* and *shadows* may be the lightest and darkest details of the original, but are considered too small in size to be used in determining tone reproduction requirements. An example of spectral highlights could be fine white pin stripes on a piece of clothing in a portrait.

Fluorescing agents

Another consideration in evaluating the continuous tone original is whether the photographic paper contains fluorescing agents. Today, this is rare, but occasionally a camera person will receive a photograph for reproduction that has *fluorescing agents* in the paper to make the highlights more brilliant.

A black light, rich in ultra-violet light, will identify papers with fluorescing agents. Unfortunately, these whitening agents will affect your predetermined exposures and change the desired dot sizes in the halftone. A piece of W-2 mylar or any ultra-violet filtering agent placed in front of the camera lights should reduce the effects of this problem.

Tone range limitations

When accepting original copy from a client for halftone reproduction, the limitations of tone range should be explained. Most photographs will have a *reflection density range* of about 1.70. This is the difference between the highlight density value and the shadow density value in the photograph. Some professionally produced glossy prints can have a density range in excess of 2.00.

The client should be told that the printed press sheet has a density range capability of only about 1.60, using a coated stock and only one pass through the press. This concern is magnified with the use of transparent originals that have a density range capability of about 3.00. The client should

understand that the longer density ranges of the original will be compressed or reduced due to the nature of the printing process. Facsimile tone reproduction is the ultimate concern in halftone photography, but due to the total printing process limitations, some loss of detail and tonal separation will be experienced.

DENSITOMETRY

Densitometry, mentioned earlier, is the science of measuring tone or optical values with either reflection or transmission techniques. Density measurements provide quantitative information or specifications for halftones. A density value represented as a numerical value, used in halftone reproduction, is universal between different departments in a printing company, as well as between different companies.

In halftone photography, the camera person uses a *reflection densitometer* to accurately determine different tone values such as the highlight and shadows of an original. When the halftone negative has been processed, a *transmission densitometer* can be used to determine the opacity or amount of light stopping capability for different areas of the film negative.

Using densitometers

When using either reflection or transmission densitometers, certain considerations should be observed. For black and white halftone applications, the densitometer should be set for a tristimulus reading. *Tristimulus* means that the densitometer is reading through all three color separation filters and NOT one specific part of the light spectrum.

Always zero and calibrate the densitometer to manufacturer specifications before using. It is suggested that densitometers warm-up, and in a few cases, are left on around the clock. Be sure to follow manufacturer's recommendations.

Maintenance records should be kept to keep track of dates for the replacement of light sources, filters, and any other necessary components.

A block of *magnesium oxide* can be used as a white standard to internally zero a reflection densitometer. Above all else, keep your densitometer clean and treat it as a precision instrument.

Sensitometry

Sensitometry is the study and measurement of the sensitivity of photographic materials, in relationship to exposure and development. Before understanding the functions of the different exposures used in the production of a halftone, the nature of film emulsions should be identified. Primarily, a film emulsion is composed of a pure gelatin and innumerable silver halide crystals in microscopic dimensions.

Emulsion sensitivity is rated by an arbitrary numerical system known as ASA. The higher the number rating assigned to a film emulsion, the faster the film will react to a light exposure. ASA 200 film is not as fast as ASA 400 film for example.

Another characteristic of a film emulsion is the *contrast* or *density reaction* to different development techniques. The film emulsions response to different exposure and processing can be graphically plotted as a *characteristic curve*. Another name for the characteristic curve of a film emulsion is *density-log exposure curve*.

To plot a characteristic curve for a specific film emulsion, a controlled exposure is given through a transmission gray scale. This will give a uniform stepped density to the carefully processed film. The different density steps of the processed negative will be read by a transmission densitometer.

Discussed briefly in the previous chapter, the test data is then plotted on a graph with the X-axis (horizontal) representing exposure factor or original gray scale density. The Y-axis (vertical) represents the reproduced density, Fig. 14-23. The plotted density steps will form a curve shape that represents the film emulsions contrast and sensitivity to light exposure.

Hurter and Driffield. As a result, the characteristic curve is often called the *Hurter and Driffield curve*.

To determine the contrast or gamma of a specific exposed film in a specific development situation, the slope of the straight line portion of the curve is used.

The formula for determining gamma is:

$$\text{Gamma} = \frac{AY}{AX}.$$

Simply stated, the rise is the distance over the run of the straight line portion of the curve.

From Fig. 14-24, it can be shown that the steeper the slope of the curve, the higher the gamma or the more high contrast the film emulsion. Basically, the same film emulsion developed longer will yield a higher gamma or contrast than shorter development times.

The ability to identify gamma, or control the contrast by development, is beneficial in the selection of different films for specific applications.

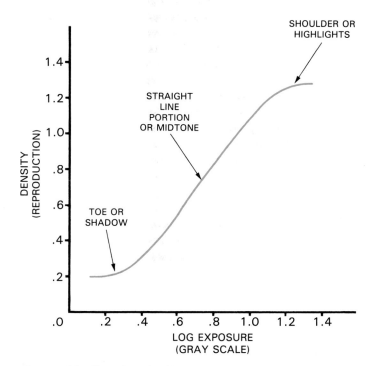

Fig. 14-23. Test data for film is plotted on graph like this one.

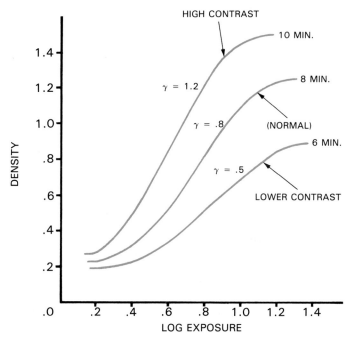

Fig. 14-24. This is an example of three gamma curves for one film emulsion.

The shape of the characteristic curve is divided into three distinct portions: the toe, the straight line portion (average gradient), and the shoulder.

The *toe portion* of the characteristic curve is the lower part of the graph and represents the shadow areas of the original. The *midsection* of the curve is identified as the *straight line portion* or average gradient, which will determine the contrast of a film by representing the midtone values of the original. The *shoulder* is the upper part of the curve and defines the highlights of an original.

Emulsion contrast

Emulsion contrast is known as *gamma*. The technique to express development contrast numerically was credited to

Base density fog

Another characteristic typical of all films is *base density fog* which relates to the density of the film's base material. To determine the base density fog of a specific film, place the unexposed film into the fixer solution. After washing and drying the film, take a reading on a transmission densitometer to identify the optical density of the film base.

Another factor that will add density to an unexposed sheet of film is *developmental fog,* sometimes referred to as *base-plus-fog*. Some developers, due to processing conditions, are unable to differentiate between exposed and unexposed silver halide crystals. Therefore, some development will affect the unexposed film emulsion and create a developmental fog problem.

To test for this, a sheet of unexposed film is processed. Then, take a reading on a transmission densitometer to identify developmental fog plus base-density-fog.

Dichroic fog is a problem affecting the film emulsion density during processing. *Dichroic fog* is a deposit of silver particles that are suspended in the developer solution and appear to leave a purplish coating on the emulsion. This is caused by the developer being contaminated with small amounts of fixer, or fixer containing carried-over developer. Using a proper stop bath and pure water wash should help prevent this problem.

HALFTONE EXPOSURES AND SCREEN RANGES

It should be stated that all effects and results in photomechanical reproduction are directly related to the laws of physics and applied mathematics. For this reason, all exposures required in halftone reproduction are predictable and the results are explainable. The typical halftone negative will require two exposures, and in some selective situations, three exposures. As you will learn, each exposure serves its own function in the successful facsimile reproduction of the original image.

MAIN EXPOSURE

The *main exposure* in halftone photography is through the camera lens using a halftone screen. Its primary purpose is to reproduce the highlight, midtone, and shadow details of the original.

The main exposure of an original photograph will reproduce only the tonal range of the contact halftone screen. This means that if the photo density range is equal to the screen range, only a main exposure is required.

Rarely will the photo range equal the screen range, thus *supplementary exposures* known as the *flash* or *bump exposures* will be needed after the main exposure.

Determining main exposure

To determine the main exposure for a specific camera, halftone screen, and type of film, the camera person will need to make a basic main exposure test. A *main exposure test* requires an exposure, usually two to three times a normal line shot of a reflection density guide or of a gray scale. See Fig. 14-25.

All variables affecting halftone results, such as flare, camera light positioning, f/stop selection, and processing techniques, must be controlled and recorded. Place the film, emulsion-side up, with the halftone contact screen emulsion-side down on top of the film. After making the estimated basic main exposure, process the film in a controlled environment. Keep the temperature, time, agitation, and chemistry exhaustion under control.

Examine the dry negative on a light table with a magnifying lens to determine highlight and shadow locations. If the highlight dot structure (10% dot) is located between the 0.00 step and the 0.30 step on the scale, your estimated exposure will become your basic main exposure. If the reflec-

Fig. 14-25. Gray scale will provide a guide when checking exposure and processing.

tion density guide or gray scales are NOT precalibrated, you will have to read the steps on a reflection densitometer to accurately determine the density of tone values.

Understand that normal highlights in an original photo will fall between 0.00 and 0.30 in density. If your test exposure does NOT contain a 10% dot between and including the 0.00 and 0.30 step, you will have to either increase or decrease the exposure and retest, Fig. 14-26.

Finding screen range

The test used to determine the basic main exposure will also identify the effective or basic screen range. If an acceptable highlight dot placement is obtained, then identify the density step where a 90% to 95% shadow dot is located.

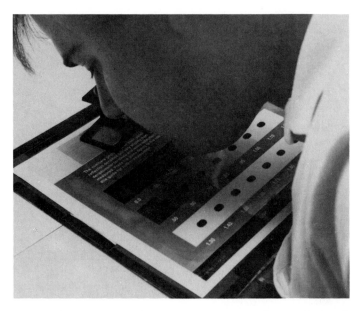

Fig. 14-26. After making your test exposure, inspect it closely so that you make most accurate camera adjustments.

The difference in density between the highlight and shadow steps will numerically determine the screen range for that specific camera, film, and processing conditions.

FLASH EXPOSURE

The *flash exposure* is considered a supplementary exposure used to form shadow details or dot structure. The flash exposure is a non-imaging, yellow, or white light exposure made through the halftone screen and the lens.

The term *non-imaging* means that the exposure affects the entire emulsion surface uniformly and does NOT record the original image or copy.

The highlight areas recorded on the film by the light reflectance from the main exposure will have little or no effect from the flash exposure. However, the shadow areas of the original, that have a density exceeding the screen range, will appear to have either a clear or latent gray dot structure on the processed film. The flash exposure will form the shadow dot structure in halftone reproductions where the copy density range exceeds the screen range.

The flash exposure, by itself, is considered to be meaningless other than its ability to expose uniform dots through the center of the vignetted screen structure. When used in conjunction with the main exposure, the flash exposure will reinforce or add supplemental exposure to shadow dots that have not received enough main exposure to become hard dots.

Determining flash exposure

The amount of flash exposure is determined by the excess density or the difference between the screen range and the copy range. Understand that too much flash exposure will alter the tone reproduction of the highlights and midtones.

It is suggested that a flash lamp be mounted about five to six feet (1.5 to 1.8 m) from the camera back. Use either a 7 1/2 or 15 watt bulb. The filter commonly used is either a safelight filter 00 or a white light diffusion filter or sheeting.

If a magenta screen is used, the flash lamp should contain a 00 safelight filter. With a gray contact screen, either light source is appropriate.

With some of the newer cameras, an internal flashing lamp is housed in the bellows section. Some vertical cameras will still require a flash exposure through the lens with white paper on the copyboard. Though this is not a conventional technique for flash exposure, it will still yield the same results.

Basic flash test

To determine the basic flash exposure for a specific film, halftone screen, and camera, a step-test exposure will be needed. The basic flash exposure will be the required amount of light needed to record an acceptable shadow dot (90% to 95%) on a fresh piece of film using a halftone contact screen.

For this test, position a piece of halftone grade film on the vacuum back, emulsion side out. Cover it with the halftone contact screen emulsion-to-emulsion. Using an opaque template or shield, make a series of step-exposures with the auxiliary flash lamp. It is important to keep the film plane stationary.

Process the test exposure using the manufacturer's time and temperature instructions furnished with the film. Using a magnification lens and a light table, inspect and select the exposure step that has the first usable 90 to 95% shadow dot. This is the basic flash exposure time, and will later be used in determining the halftone exposures for specific copy.

Bump or no-screen exposure

Another less common supplementary exposure is the bump or no-screen highlighting exposure. It has been stated that the purpose of the flash exposure is to extend the screen range capabilities to match the photo density range.

The purpose of the *bump* or *no-screen highlight exposure* is to shorten the screen range to compensate for camera copy or photos with a density range LESS THAN the screen range. Essentially, the bump exposure is a no-screen or line shot of the continuous tone camera copy. This will enhance the highlight details by REDUCING the size of dots with the additional exposure.

The bump exposure is calculated as a percentage of the main exposure, and should be between two to 15% of the time used for the main exposure.

Often, neutral density filters are used in front of the camera lens during the bump exposure due to the extremely short exposure times. *Neutral density filters* will reduce the amount of light passing through the camera lens without changing the rendition of the colors in the light spectrum. When exposure times become extremely short, the accuracy of the camera timing device can present a problem.

To determine the effect of a bump exposure for a specific reproduction situation, the basic main exposure test is given with a 10% bump exposure. After processing, magnified inspection of the film negative will identify the extent of density compression, Fig. 14-27.

Many large manufacturers provide tables to predict density changes for the differences in bump exposure percentages.

HALFTONE EXPOSURE COMPUTERS

An *exposure computer* or *calculator* should be used to determine the different exposures required to make a good halftone, or facsimile reproduction, of the original continuous tone copy. It is not uncommon to find small camera departments in the industry that determine exposure times by trial and error. However, most exposure computers or calculators are easy to use and will yield consistent and predictable results.

There are two categories of exposure determining devices, these are hand-operated dials and electronic memory devices. Depending on the extent of camera work being completed and the sophistication of equipment in the facility, either system should eliminate the guess work involved with halftone exposures.

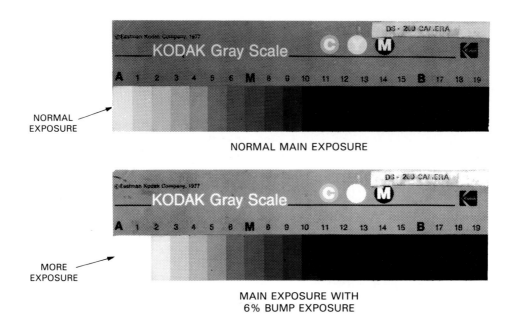

NORMAL MAIN EXPOSURE

MAIN EXPOSURE WITH
6% BUMP EXPOSURE

*Fig. 14-27. Bump exposure affects highlight areas and can
be used to enhance highlights of photo when needed.*

Hand-operated dials

The *hand-operated dials* are the least expensive and easiest to use. These devices have been in the industry for a long time. Some of the more common ones used are shown in Fig. 14-28.

Perhaps the most typical type used over the years was the Kodak Q-12 Exposure Computer. Not only would the Q-12 determine halftone exposures, but could easily be used for duo-tones and special effects, such as posterizations. The Q-15 was introduced by Kodak as a more accurate device to replace the Q-12. The Q-15 would compensate for reciprocity failure and other exposure factors, such as the effect of the flash exposure to the highlight dot structure.

The important concept to remember, when using any exposure determining dials, is that all test data must be accurate before calibrating the device. The technique used to

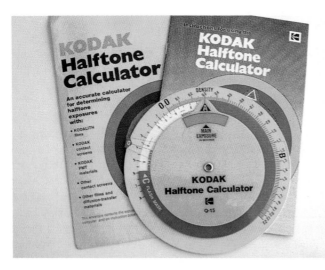

*Fig. 14-28. Hand-operated devices provide simple way of
calculating camera settings.*

determine the basic main and flash exposures should be typical of production operations.

To use these devices, rotate the dials to program the device in regards to basic main exposure, screen range, and basic flash exposure. After the dials have been set, the only data the camera person must use is the original copy highlight, shadow, and photo density range. The main exposure is directly related to the highlight of the copy. The flash exposure, if required, is relative to the photo density range in comparison to the effective screen range.

When looking at original continuous tone copy, the camera operator should be able to develop an instinct for exposure.

Simply stated, a continuous tone original that has EXTREME CONTRAST will probably require a flash exposure due to its large photo density range.

The photo that is LACKING CONTRAST will probably require little or no flash exposure because the screen range will be more comparable to the photo range.

The FLAT or POOR CONTRAST original will probably require a bump exposure to enhance the reproduction or compress the screen range to match the photo range.

Electronic memory devices

Recent technology has been responsible for the development of electronic memory devices used to determine exposure information. Fig. 14-29 shows typical examples of on-line exposure devices. Operation of these devices, after they are calibrated with test data, require only the specific density information from the original. In most cases, these units will override or act as the timing device for the process camera.

Data centers

Similar to electronic, programmable on-line timing devices are newer photomechanical data centers. These data centers

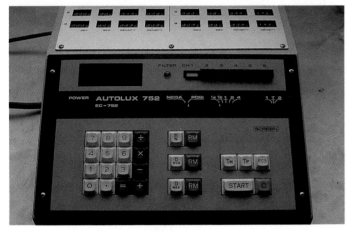

Fig. 14-29. These are two electronic memory devices that can be used when making halftones.

are separate from the camera, and will do a wide variety of exposure computations based on reproduction requirements. In addition, the programmable memory chips in these calculators will determine the placement of the midtone dot, copy sizing requirements, chemistry mixing proportions, filter selections, and a combination of other typical photomechanical functions.

Two of the more common data centers are illustrated in Fig. 14-30. Both function with the use of programmable

Fig. 14-30. This is a data center used to make calculations for halftone production.

memory chips designated to run specific programs with a minimum of input data. The data centers will do more calculations than the other devices, but will require the same test data to perform exposure calibrations.

To gain the most benefit possible from any of the electronic memory devices or data center, all reproduction variables must be controlled. It would be suggested that a calibrated densitometer, an automated film processor, and camera equipped with a light integrator be used to keep all variables constant.

Discussed in the previous chapter, a *light integrator* is a photocell attached to the copyboard that will control the camera timing device. If the voltage to the camera lights fluctuates, the photocell will adjust the length of exposure to compensate and preserve accuracy. The same amount of light will strike the film with the same exposure setting.

PRODUCTION OF A HALFTONE

To produce a halftone of an original continuous tone photograph, the camera person must first evaluate the photo density range. The highlight or whitest white of the photograph must be identified with either the use of a precalibrated reflection density guide or a reflection densitometer.

Before using the reflection densitometer, be sure to zero and calibrate it against the standard plate provided by the manufacturer. Read more than one highlight location to determine the true highlight density reading.

After recording the highlight, use the same procedure to determine the shadow density reading.

Remember! Do NOT read the spectral highlights and shadows of the photograph.

To determine the *photodensity range* simply SUBTRACT the highlight density value from the shadow density value, Fig. 14-31.

Fig. 14-31. Note how highlight and shadow density readings are used to determine photo density range.

To determine the exposure times for the halftone, select one of the exposure computers or calculators and follow the manufacturer's directions. To use the exposure computer or calculator, you will need to calibrate the exposure dials with the following test data: basic main exposure, basic flash exposure, and in some cases, the basic main exposure with a predetermined percentage of bump exposure.

After calibration and the knowledge of the effective screen range, rotate the dials or depress the calculator buttons to input your photo density information. This will ultimately calculate and produce the desired exposures.

Be sure to follow the manufacturer's instructions. The instructions in a step-by-step sequence are not as difficult as they may first appear.

After determining the proper exposures required, mount the photo on the camera copyboard with a reflection gray scale next to it. Set the copyboard and lensboard at the predetermined reproduction percentages.

The normal f/stop for halftone work is f/16, but be sure to set the f/stop for the same setting as used in the basic main exposure test. The rest of the halftone process will be completed in the darkroom.

In the darkroom, use the ground glass to determine focus, film size, and film location. See Fig. 14-32.

Place the halftone grade film emulsion-up on the vacuum back, with the halftone contact screen emulsion-down on top of the film, Fig. 14-33.

Be sure to allow adequate vacuum draw down time. In most cases, it is a good practice to use a screen roller or photo chamois to insure screen draw down is uniform, Fig. 14-34.

At this point, make the required halftone exposures. The sequence of exposures should remain consistent from halftone to halftone. It makes relatively little difference as to whether the main exposure is given first or last.

To make the main exposure, simply close the film back. Adjust the camera and actuate the camera lights through the lens.

To make a flash exposure, position the film back perpendicular to the flash lamp and expose without releasing the vacuum or halftone contact screen.

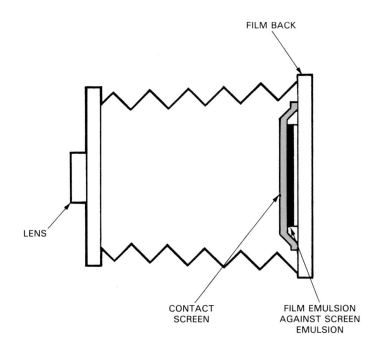

Fig. 14-33. Note how screen is placed over film on film back of process camera. This will make light from original pass through screen dot structure before striking film.

Fig. 14-34. A screen roller or a photo chamois should be used to insure that screen draws down properly.

The bump exposure is made without releasing the vacuum pressure, but carefully remove the halftone contact screen. After removing the screen, expose with the camera lights and lens for the predetermined percentage of the main exposure.

When the exposures are complete, release the vacuum pressure and place the halftone screen back into its protective folder or sleeve.

PROCESSING THE LATENT FILM IMAGE

Processing the halftone can be either completed in a stabilized automated film processor or in processing trays using hand techniques.

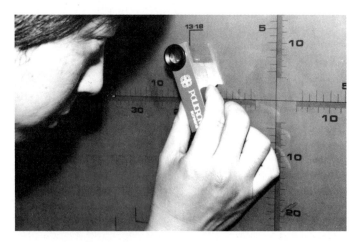

Fig. 14-32. Camera operator is using magnifier to check focus before making exposure.

If the film processor is selected, be sure to first use the appropriate *control strips* to determine if the chemistry level is stabilized.

To use *processing trays,* the camera person can use either a time and temperature method or inspection technique. Place the film with the latent or nonvisible image in a tray of fresh developer. Processing to time and temperature is the most accurate method if the basic test times prove consistent.

Inspection development

As the developer becomes exhausted by either film use or oxidation, the inspection method proves beneficial to the camera person. In the *inspection method,* the person processing the film looks for an acceptable highlight dot first, and then checks for the acceptable shadow dot in reference to the original artwork or photograph.

Still development

One advantage to processing by the inspection method is the still development technique. Still development requires a period of about 45 seconds where no agitation of the developing tray takes place. The purpose of *still development* is to allow the shadow dot structure to develop faster than the highlight dot structure.

In theory, the dense or black highlight areas of the halftone negative have spent or exhausted the developer covering that part of the emulsion, faster than the shadow areas. Without agitation, new developer would not be able to relocate.

Stop bath

After the appropriate development occurs or the time method expires, transfer the negative to the *stop bath* to stabilize the film. The negative will require approximately 15 seconds in the acid bath to neutralize the effects of the alkaline developer.

Fixing

Transfer the negative to the *fixer,* for twice the duration of time required to clear the unexposed silver particles. With fresh rapid or liquid fixer (amonium thiosulfate), the unexposed silver removal and emulsion hardening process will require about four minutes.

Washing

After fixing the film for the appropriate time, *wash* the negative in running water for ten minutes. Wash the film thoroughly. If the wash cycle does not remove the chemistry from the film emulsion, the chemistry will possibly transfer to the film dryer. Note! Chapter 17 explains film processing in detail.

EVALUATING HALFTONE NEGATIVES

Once the halftone negative has been dried, the camera person uses a light table and a magnification glass to inspect

the results. Always view the negative on the BASE or PLASTIC SIDE of the film to avoid scratches, Fig. 14-35.

Inspecting the highlight or dense areas of the negative should reveal a 5 to 10% dot structure. Remember that the dot percentage represents ink on paper or the positive image. Thus, the shadow or least dense areas of the halftone negative should be represented by a 90 to 95% dot structure, Fig. 14-36.

Fig. 14-35. Here are some examples of a good and two bad exposures. (Chapter One, Screaming Color)

Fig. 14-36. Camera operators are checking halftone images on the film after development.

If the highlight dot structure is smaller in size than the desired 5% dot, simply REDUCE the main exposure. If the dot structure was too large a percentage, the main exposure will need to be INCREASED.

The highlight dot structure of the printed halftone will look muddy or dull if the dot percentage is larger than the desired 10%. Remember that the main exposure will have the most influence in controlling the highlight dot structure.

Upon evaluation of the shadow dot structure, it should be understood that the greater the flash exposure, the LARGER the shadow dot size. This means that if the dot structure in the shadows is NOT a hard dense dot or it appears latent, the flash exposure should be INCREASED.

As the developer is used or becomes oxidated, it will tend to become high contrast in nature. This high contrast effect will be most noticeable in the development of the shadow details or dot structures. Either still development or increased flash exposure will compensate and allow for the full 90 to 95% dot structure to develop.

PRE-SCREENED DIFFUSION TRANSFER HALFTONES

Another alternative method of producing halftones is the use of the *diffusion transfer process*. This process will produce a positive halftone print on photographic paper.

The advantage to this method is that the halftone illustration can be pasted-up with the line copy, and be exposed as one line shot. The diffusion transfer or PMT (photo-mechanical-transfer) halftone should be reproduced at the desired size. This will prevent further enlargement or reduction from distorting the dot structure.

The use of a special diffusion transfer halftone contact screen will be required. Remember that diffusion transfer products react to light exposure in the opposite direction of normal film emulsions. The longer exposure of light to the diffusion transfer emulsion will result in less density. To determine the screen range and other basic exposure times, follow the same procedures as previously mentioned. The one consideration is to use a 15 to 20% highlight dot structure and a 85-90% shadow dot structure. This will produce a desired *flat reproduction* (lower contrast), as it is re-exposed in the line work process. The same exposure computers or calculators, as outlined before, will determine individual photo requirements and times.

HALFTONES USING AUTO SCREEN FILMS

The production and use of autoscreen halftone films is limited today, but should be explained. The autoscreen film is not like most normal films that have equal and uniform emulsion sensitivity.

The emulsion of an *autoscreen film* has innumerable light sensitive areas that match the ruling of a halftone screen. These light sensitive areas have the most sensitivity in the center and decrease in sensitivity much like the vignetted dot structure. Thus, the auto screen films have their own built in halftone screen, and do NOT require the use of a contact screen.

There are several advantages to this method of halftone reproduction. One such advantage is that a halftone can be created in a professional photographer's view camera while photographing still life. Without the use of a halftone contact screen, the exposure times will be shorter. The autoscreen film should yield better detail rendition without the screen interference.

HALFTONES USING RAPID ACCESS PROCESS

Rapid access films are designed to have extreme latitude in the development process. For this reason, the exposure time will remain critical but the development will be a more controlled reaction.

The rapid access process has been in use for typesetting and line work for several years. Recently, manufacturers have designed a new rapid access contact screen that will produce a hard dot for reproduction purposes. Thus, halftone reproduction will benefit from the many advantages typical to the rapid access process.

Some of the advantages of using rapid access films and chemistry are:
1. The speed and ease in processing the films—no chemicals to mix.
2. No real temperature control required for processing film in trays.
3. Total repeatability and consistency in results.
4. Economical in most operations.

SCANNER HALFTONE SCREENS

A *scanner* is a device that uses a laser to convert an image into a digital code. When in digital form, the image can be enlarged, reduced, or modified in almost any way. A continuous tone image can also be screened when on the scanner, Fig. 14-37.

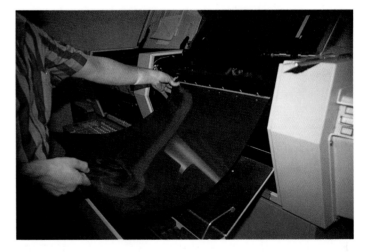

Fig. 14-37. Scanner can also be used to convert a continuous tone photo into a halftone. Either a contact screen can be placed over the film on the output drum of the scanner or a screen dot pattern can be produced digitally using a computer.

There are two general ways that a scanner can convert a continuous tone photograph into a halftone. A contact screen can be placed over the film when on the output drum of the scanner. The screen can also be produced electronically using a computer to produce a dot pattern when outputting the image onto film. Look at Fig. 14-38.

Note! Scanners are explained fully in Chapter 15. Refer to this chapter for more information on scanners.

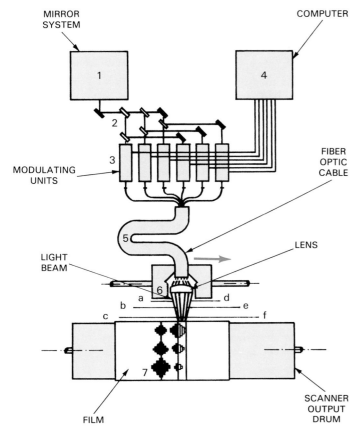

MIRROR
SYSTEM

COMPUTER

MODULATING
UNITS

FIBER
OPTIC
CABLE

LIGHT
BEAM

LENS

FILM

SCANNER
OUTPUT
DRUM

Fig. 14-38. Electronic halftone screen generation on a scanner. A mirror system (2) splits the laser beam (1) into six components of equal intensity. These reach the modulation unit (3) where a digital control signal from the halftone computer (4) selectively switches the component beams on or off, forming a halftone dot pattern. A light guide cable or fiber optic cable (5) feeds the modulated component beams (a) to (f) to the recording head (6) where a zoom lens projects the beams on to the recording drum (7) to expose the mounted film. (Hell)

KNOW THESE TERMS

Halftone, Halftone reproduction, Continuous tone, Highlights, Midtones, Shadow values, Halftone screen, Reflection copy, Transmission copy, Halftone grade film, Moiré pattern, Vignetted dot structure, Tint screen, Dot percentage, Screen shape, Density, Photo-density range, Density guide, Densitometer, High-key, Low-key, Dot gain, Reflection density range, Tristimulus reading, Emulsion sensitivity, Sensitometry, Density-log exposure curve, Gamma, Fog, Main exposure, Flash exposure, Main exposure test, Bump exposure, Neutral density filters, Exposure computer, Flat contrast, Control strip, Processing trays, Inspection method, Still development, Stop bath, Fixer, Wash, Autoscreen film, Rapid access film, Scanner screening.

REVIEW QUESTIONS—CHAPTER 14

1. Why must a continuous tone photo be converted into a halftone for printing?
2. A halftone screen is used to record different size dots that represent _____ values (whites), _____ values (grays), and _____ values (blacks).
3. What are the four classifications of camera copy?
4. _____ _____ includes photos, oil paintings, chalk or charcoal renderings, and water color work.
5. _____ or _____ copy includes 35 mm slides or large format transparencies.
6. Explain the difference between halftone grade film and line film.
7. How do you prevent a moiré pattern?
8. A _____ _____ _____ in a contact screen appears out of focus or diffused when magnified.
9. What printing process has all of the images screened?
10. Highlight dots will usually be _____ to _____ percent in size, the midtone will be _____ to _____ percent, and the shadow dots will be _____ to _____ percent.
11. In your own words, explain screen dot shapes.
12. How do you select a screen ruling?
13. The term _____ refers to the degree of blackness or light stopping ability.
14. What is the difference between a high-key and a low-key photo?
15. Most photos will have a reflection density range of about _____.
16. How do you use a densitometer?
17. The main exposure in halftone photography is through the _____ _____ using a _____ _____ over the film.
18. The _____ _____ is considered a supplementary exposure used to form shadow details.
19. What do you do when you are shooting a flat or poor contrast original?
20. What are two ways that a scanner can be used to screen a continuous tone photograph?

SUGGESTED ACTIVITIES

1. Visit a graphics facility and observe a camera operator shooting continuous tone materials.
2. Use a magnifying glass to inspect the dot structure in photos printed in this book and other publications. Note how paper, dot size, dot shape, etc. affect the image.
3. Use a process camera to shoot a black and white photo and convert it into a halftone. Experiment with different exposure times, films, screens, and development methods.

More and more presswork is four-color. It is important that you fully understand color theory before studying other aspects of the industry.   (Heidelberg Harris)

Chapter 15

COLOR THEORY AND REPRODUCTION, SCANNERS

After studying this chapter, you will be able to:
- Explain the basic principles of color and light.
- Identify the three major systems used to produce color separations.
- Describe the operation of the equipment used in color separation.
- Describe the normal screen angles for color reproductions.
- Explain the working principles of a color scanner.
- Summarize the process of ink analysis for establishing color correction.

Color plays a very important role in our daily lives. For example, our desire to view a movie or purchase a box of cereal is enhanced by color. Color can better describe a product in almost any printed piece.

As you will learn in this chapter, color reproductions are becoming more important to the printing and publishing industry. The use of color in a printed product can add credibility. The attention value of color work exceeds that of black and white reproductions.

Marketing studies have proven color to be more effective than black and white by a ratio of 8 to 1. The designer often uses the *aesthetics* (beauty) and quality of color to create a specific mood.

In the past, the use of color has been an exception in black and white publications. The high cost and difficulty of full color work restricted the use of four color process printing. With the new technological changes, industry forecasts predict color reproduction to increase approximately 10 percent a year well into the next decade.

COLOR THEORY

The theory of color reproduction is based on the simple understanding that all the necessary colors required of a reproduction are contained in the unprinted sheet of white paper, Fig. 15-1. White contains all colors of the spectrum.

When the four basic colors of process ink (yellow, magenta, cyan, and black) are overprinted, a filtering action occurs. This filtering action allows for different proportions of colored light to strike the cones of the human eye, thus stimulating different brain responses for all colors of the spectrum.

To produce a four color process reproduction of an original color image, the copy is separated photomechanically or electronically into three primary colors and black. This process is known as *color separation.*

Color separation involves the use of a color filter principle. Each color filter will separate the necessary colors of light to produce its *complementary color* or *printer.* When the separations of the primary printers and black are combined on the press sheet, the colors of light that were subtracted by the filter will then appear.

For example, the yellow printer is created by reproducing a negative film image through the use of a blue filter. The blue filter stops the red and green light images from passing and only permits the blue light image to be recorded.

When the yellow printer separation is plated in positive form and printed, the yellow ink on the white paper acts as a filter to stop the blue light from being reflected. The eye sees white paper as equal portions of red, green, and blue light. However, if the blue light is filtered by an ink film layer, the red and green light alone will represent the color yellow to the human eye, Fig. 15-2.

This principle is why the process ink pigments are considered to be *subtractive filters* and all the essential colors of a reproduction are contained in the white press sheets.

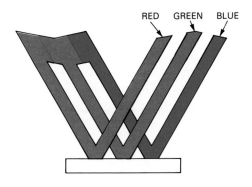

RED GREEN BLUE

Fig. 15-1. The human eye sees unprinted white paper as equal portions of red, green, and blue light. The use of process inks produces a filtering type action that results in different reproduction colors.

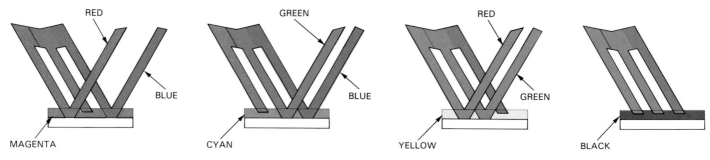

Fig. 15-2. *This shows action of colored light reflection from white paper as it passes through four primary ink layers—yellow, magenta, cyan, and black.*

Principles of color and light

The ability to see color is directly related to the cones and rods located in the retinal cells of the human eye. The sensation of color vision is primarily a result of light stimulating the bulbous cones. The cones in the eyes are receptors for *chromatic colors,* such as red, green, and blue. The cylindrical rods are functional in vision under reduced illumination, and transmit color only as various shades of gray or as *achromatic colors.*

The rods of the eye are more effective than the cones under limited light, after sunset or at dusk for example. The objects we see after dusk are silhouetted and have little color value.

Color vision results from the percentage of white light reflected from a colored object to stimulate the cones in the eye that interact with the brain.

When the human eye sees white paper, it is an equal response of the more than six million cones to red, green, and blue light. White light is made up of many colors. These colors are defined in the visible light spectrum, which is a very small portion of the electromagnetic spectrum. Only the small portion of the electromagnetic spectrum, known as the *visible light spectrum,* is of concern to the graphic arts industry.

White light can be broken down into six major colors by using a glass prism. The glass prism serves to separate the different energy wavelengths of white light to form the visible spectrum. The colors of light will always follow a certain order, as determined by their wavelengths.

1. Red = 700 nanometers.
2. Orange = 620 nanometers.
3. Yellow = 575 nanometers.
4. Green = 525 nanometers.
5. Blue = 450 nanometers.
6. Violet = 400 nanometers.

The measurement of a wavelength of light can be expressed as a nanometer. A *nanometer* is equal to one billionth of a meter. These wavelengths travel at the speed of light or at about 186,000 miles per second. When light passes through a glass prism, it slows down the different wavelengths and separates them into the different colors in the spectrum.

For the purposes of color separation, the light spectrum will be divided into three major portions: red, green, and blue. These three colors are known as the *primary additive*

colors. The three primary process ink pigments (yellow, magenta, and cyan) are known as the *primary subtractive colors.*

The three additive primary colors and the three subtractive primary colors can be arranged to form a color wheel, as shown in Fig. 15-3. In the construction of the *color wheel,* each additive primary color is opposite its complementary subtractive primary color.

When the three additive primary colors of light are added together, the result will equal *white light.* When the three pure subtractive primary colors of pigment are overlapped on the white sheet of paper, the result is *black* or the absence of color.

In theory, color reproduction should be accomplished with only three pigments of ink: yellow, magenta, and cyan. However, one of the major limitations of process color printing is the impurities in the ink pigment. With the inks available in today's pressrooms, the three primary ink

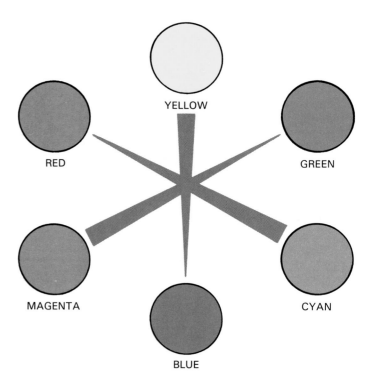

Fig. 15-3. *Color wheel shows relationship of colors. Note that each additive primary color is opposite its complementary subtractive color.*

pigments overlap to produce a dark shade of brown, NOT black. Thus, process color reproduction uses four colors of ink, the three subtractive primary pigments and a black.

Considerations for viewing color

The use of the human eye as a receiver of a color sensation is usually subject to an inherent number of errors. To accurately and consistently evaluate color reproduction, these inherent deficiencies must be isolated.

One of the main difficulties of the human eye is its inability to remember exact colors or hues.

Hue is a dimension or quality of color that distinguishes one pigment from another. Simply said, hue is the difference between a red and a blue or a yellow. The only way the human eye can judge a color is by making contrasting comparisons to other colors or hues.

Another more difficult dimension of color is the saturation of a color. *Saturation* is often referred to as purity and will further define a given hue by its strength. Saturation is the difference between a vivid blue and a dirty or gray blue. The eye must compare the two shades of blue side by side to achieve accuracy in identification.

Furthermore, not all human eyes are alike in their ability to respond to the various wavelengths of light. Some people are born completely color blind, and others are considered partially color blind to different parts of the light spectrum. Persons involved in the evaluation of color reproduction should be tested for color deficiencies, Fig. 15-4.

It is almost impossible for the human eye to make color comparisons unless under exactly the same viewing conditions. For this reason, the industry has set a standard of 5000 Kelvin power lighting for viewing color work. The industry uses this controlled light source in viewing booths, in the pressroom, pre-press areas, and even in the customer's facility, Fig. 15-5.

Fig. 15-5. Many factors determine the way different people view and evaluate color reproduction. Color viewing booth will help keep evaluation more constant. (USA Today)

Other conditions that can affect the viewing of color reproductions are:
1. Angle of viewing the color work.
2. Angle of illumination for viewing.
3. Size and shape of color area.
4. Texture of the surface being viewed.
5. Glossy color versus flat color.
6. Health and mental attitude of the observer (rested or tired).
7. Adaptation ability of the eye of observer.

Color is unique in that it can affect our moods and general behavior. Color can fall into the realm of psychology because it is difficult to identify where color vision stops and the mental process begins.

Another factor controlling color work evaluation is color fatigue or eye fatigue. As the nerve cells in the eye become fatigued, the ability to judge color is impared. An example of this is when first looking at a bright color for a period of time, then immediately looking at a second color of a different hue. The second color will appear different as eye fatigue subtracts some of the first color from the image.

COLOR SEPARATIONS

Color separation is the process of dividing the many colors of an original image into the four primary printing pigments. This process requires four halftone film images. Each is

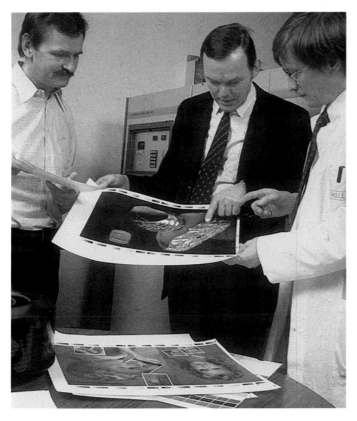

Fig. 15-4. Color reproductions will appear slightly different when inspected by different people. For this reason, it is important that all factors, especially lighting, be kept constant.

237

Fig. 15-6. This is an enlargement of a halftone separation dot structure within a four color reproduction. Note how each separation is used to print one color of ink. When two colors overlap, new color is produced.

The *green filter* is used in the reproduction of the magenta printer. Magenta ink, being a green light absorber, will represent an image of the green light absorbed by the original, when printed in positive form. For the eye to see magenta, the green light must be absorbed by the ink, and only the red and blue reflected.

To reproduce the cyan printer, the *red filter* is used. The red light image on the pan film is in negative form. When the negative image is plated, it becomes positive for printing cyan ink (red light absorber). When the eye sees the cyan ink, it only identifies green and blue light reflection because the red light from the paper is absorbed by the ink layer. See Fig. 15-8.

Fig. 15-8. This is an illustrated set of progressives for a color separation.

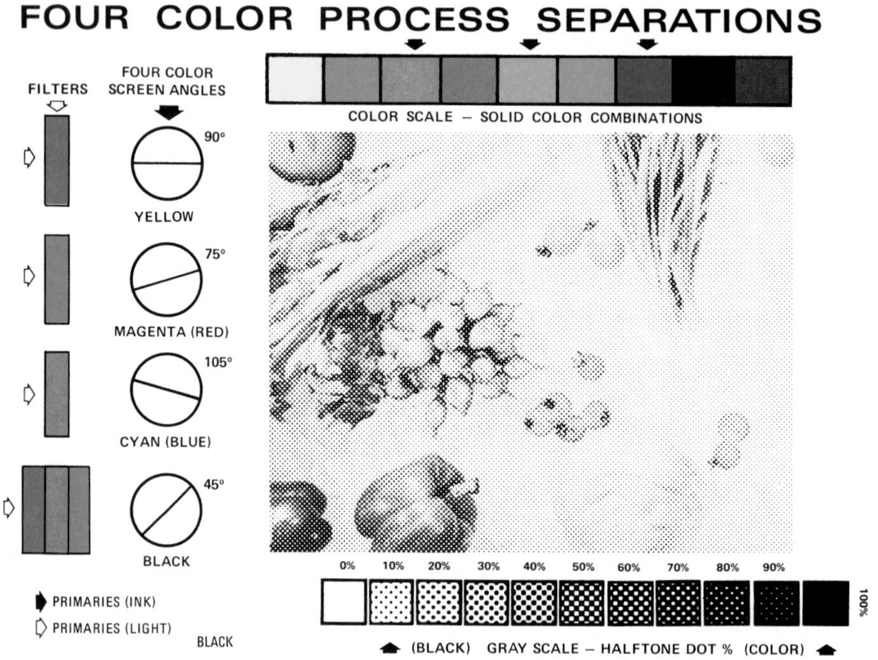

exposed at different screen angles, on pan film so that each represents a different primary printing ink, Fig. 15-6.

The exposures creating the four different halftones are each altered through the use of color separation filters. To reproduce an image that represents each of the three subtractive primary inks, the complementary additive color filter is used. The black printer, often referred to as the *skeleton* or *detail printer,* can be created in different ways, through the use of different filters. The role of the black printer will be defined later in this chapter.

The *blue filter* is used to reproduce the yellow separation printer because it represents only a blue light image on the negative. When the blue light image is printed in positive form on the paper with yellow ink (a blue light absorber), only the red and green light rays will stimulate the eye and allow the brain to identify the color yellow, Fig. 15-7.

FOUR COLOR PROCESS SEPARATIONS

Fig. 15-7. This chart shows filters used for making separations.

Narrow and wide band filters

The typical color separation filters have been identified as the additive primary colors that are complementary to the subtractive primary printing inks. The red filter is for the cyan separation. The green filter is used to produce the magenta separation. The blue filter will reproduce the yellow separation.

To be more specific, the normal color separation filters include the No. 25-red, No. 47-blue, and the No. 58-green. The specific numbered filters are considered to be pure and are called *narrow band filters*.

The narrow band filter is considered to be monochromatic. For color separation work, the narrow band filter is one that will reproduce only pure colors. For example, when photographing a clean green that flows into a dirty or off shade of green (grayish green), the narrow band only reproduces the pure green value. The use of narrow band filters is beneficial if color correction systems are limited.

Other color separation filters can be used that will reproduce broader parts of the light spectrum. These filters are considered to be *wide band filters*. Some examples of wide band color separation filters include: No. 61-green, No. 49B-blue, No. 23 and 29-red. It is recommended that the color separation system used have a good masking technique if wide band filters are used.

Screen angles for color reproduction

Color reproduction uses four halftone negatives, each representing a different screen angle. The rotation of screen angles is designed to eliminate or minimize the undesirable moire pattern. Each of the four screen angles are assigned to one of the separation colors.

YELLOW is assigned to the 90° angle for two reasons. The first reason is that the 90° screen angle is only 15° away from the 75° and 105° angles that represent a moiré. The slight moiré is not very noticeable when a light yellow pigment is used. The second reason is that the eye aligns images either on a horizontal or vertical format, and the light yellow dot structure is not as visible. The normal screen angle assignments are illustrated in Fig. 15-9.

When printing separations containing considerable amounts of flesh tones and browns, it is recommended to print both the cyan and yellow at 105°. Screen angles can be varied to favor specific colors in the original.

Black printer

In pure color reproduction theory, the three process colors of ink each subtract one color of the visible spectrum and reflect the other two. The difficulty with this theory lies in the ink impurities. The inks used in the pressroom do not entirely absorb one part of the spectrum, and only reflect a percentage of the other two parts. For this reason, when the three subtractive primary pigments are overlapped, they do not produce black, but a dark brown color.

The role of the process black printer serves a dual purpose. First, the *black printer* is used to extend the shadow details or density ranges. Printing a black ink density over the three primaries will improve and enhance the shadow details of the reproduction. The second purpose is to provide fine detail outlines and to simplify register problems of the three color overprints, Fig. 15-10.

Fig. 15-10. The role of the black printer can be seen in the shadow areas of a three-color separation, top, as compared to a four-color separation with black, bottom.

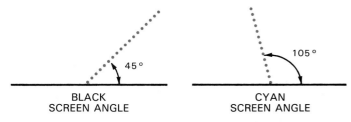

Fig. 15-9. These are normal screen angle assignments for average copy.

Under color removal

The technique of *under color removal,* abbreviated UCR is a process of color correction or compensation, typically associated with high-speed web printing. The shadow details of a four color separation will typically be represented as the three process colors overprinted with black. When printing with high speed presses, it is not desirable to overlap too many layers of ink. Drying problems as well as ink trapping problems can occur with multiple ink layers.

The theory of under color removal is to reduce the shadow dot structure in the normal three color overlap of yellow, magenta, and cyan inks. The use of a full range black printer will produce the density required in the shadow details. Under normal circumstances, the black ink will be the least expensive ink of the four process colors. Thus, under color removal will reduce ink costs and produce acceptable shadow densities by utilizing the role of the black printer to its fullest capacity. Look at Fig. 15-11.

Under color removal can be accomplished by photomechanical masking techniques or through the use of an electronic scanner.

The UCR mask, in positive form, is made from the color corrected black separation negative. Then, the UCR mask is pin registered with the color corrected yellow, magenta, and cyan separation negatives when converted to a positive image.

The electronic scanner has UCR enhancement features which allow for intensity and range alterations with adjustments of the scanner controls.

With the advent of newer scanners and digitized storage of information, the principle of under color removal has been refined. The more modern versions of UCR include *Gray Component Replacement* (GCR), and in Germany, *Achromatic Color Reduction* (ACR).

The word *achromatic* refers to the less dominant hue in a three color overprint. This color of ink is less dominant than the other two and is used to determine the grayness or purity of the desired hue in the separation. The achromatic gray pigment can be removed from the separation and replaced with the black printer.

In the United States, the accepted term in the industry is gray component replacement. Many of the leading manufacturers of current scanners and electronic pre-press equipment are developing specific software packages for GCR and storage of digitized information.

Perhaps one of the simplest ways to understand the theory of color separation is to perform the work of the color filters by hand. The use of separate rubylith cuts and tint screens is one method referred to as *fake color.* Another more popular and economical way is the use of gamma gray retouch paints to create continuous tone separations by hand. Both of these systems are not typically practiced in the industry, but are valuable as an initial experience for a student studying color separation.

To complete the hand-mechanical separation, six or seven shades of gamma gray retouch paints are used to create a gray scale from white to black. A halftone reproduction is made of the gray scale using time and temperature controlled development. Later, evaluate what number or color of the paints recorded different dot percentages.

Select a simple black and white line copy cartoon or artwork and reproduce four contact positives. The original is then colored or painted with simple colors. These colors are matched to a process ink tint percentage chart, Fig. 15-12, and the dot percentages for the appropriate colors are recorded. Using each one of the four contact positive prints to represent each of the different process color printers, paint the artwork with the appropriate gamma retouch paint.

After the four printers have been painted with the appropriate gamma retouch paints, produce four halftone reproductions. Use ortho film and the proper screen angles for the halftone negatives. Finally, the separation negatives are proofed with a pre-press color proofing system.

Direct screen color separations

The *direct screen* method of producing color separations is considered to be one of the fastest and most cost effective techniques. Just as the name implies, the halftone screening process is completed during the same color separa-

Fig. 15-11. This illustrates the difference between a full range color separation, left, and a thirty percent under color removal separation, right. (Pardini slide)

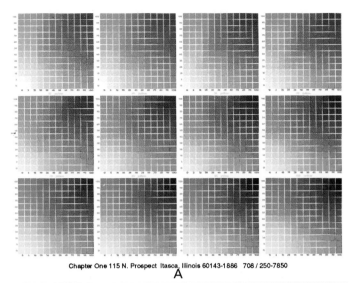

A

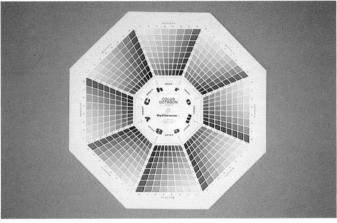

B

Fig. 15-12. A—This is a process ink tint percentage chart. B—With this see-through color octagon, it is possible to view the tint as it would appear on the selected stock. Keep it next to the electronic imaging unit and compare the CMYK color to the RGB color on the monitor.

COOLING SYSTEM

LIGHT SOURCE

COLOR HEAD

CONDENSERS

TRANSPARENCY HOLDER

PANCHROMATIC HIGH CONTRAST FILM

LENS

VACUUM EASEL

CONTACT SCREEN

Fig. 15-13. Simple drawing shows exposure during direct screen separation process.

tion exposure. The direct screen exposure can be color corrected with masking techniques or can be done with no color correction and the use of narrow band filters.

Depending on the original used and the aim points selected, pleasing color reproductions can be accomplished without color correction or masking. It should be understood that systems of color correction are normally used to ensure facsimile reproduction of the original, Fig. 15-13.

Direct screen separations can be accomplished by contact methods in a vacuum frame. This is the simplest technique and the equipment required is relatively inexpensive. The use of a contact frame will also assist in production when the cameras or enlargers are busy, as separations can be *"ganged"* (photographed) together.

Another advantage of contacting is the filter requirements are not as critical as in the process camera. Older filters once used on the process camera can be used in the contact frame. Filters tend to warp, change thickness, and fade in color with use, and should be discarded after a period of time. One major drawback to the contact method of direct screen separation is the one to one size ratio during reproduction. See Fig. 15-14.

Direct screen separations are commonly produced on a process camera or a direct screen enlarger. The advantage to using these two pieces of equipment is the lens or optical system. Incorporating a lens will allow for changes in reproduction size, unlike the contact frame. These lenses are designed to photograph flat copy, either reflection or transparent, and are fully color corrected to avoid lateral color aberration.

Fig. 15-14. Open contact frame and light source can be used for making color separations but scanners are becoming more popular. (nuArc)

Indirect methods of color separation

The use of the *indirect method* of color separation requires two separate photographic operations. In one operation, the original is color separated through the appropriate filters. In the second operation, the halftone screen is incorporated.

If a color correction system is used, the masks are made from the original. Later the masks are used to produce the first operation, which is the color separation process using continuous tone film. The color corrected continuous tone separation negatives can be modified or further corrected if necessary. The negatives are then converted during the second operation, to produce halftone positives using a contact screen.

The advantage to this system over the direct screen, is during the second reproduction operation, the size can be further reduced or enlarged. Two disadvantages, the indirect method is more complex or time consuming and it uses more film. See Fig. 15-15.

The indirect method of color separation can be accomplished in the contact frame as well as the process camera and enlarger. The use of continuous tone emulsions will require total darkness or altered safelighting conditions for the separation work. The halftone screen exposures can be completed with orth film and will require normal red safelights.

Electronic scanning method of color separation

The electronic scanner has proven to be one of the most efficient ways to perform color separation work, with respect to color correction and tone reproduction. The major difference between the scanner and the process camera or other reproduction equipment is the imaging method, Fig. 15-16.

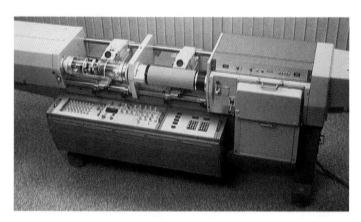

Fig. 15-16. Color scanners are replacing conventional methods of producing separations with filters. Scanner will convert original image into computer data representing microscopic, pixel dot pattern. Then, it will output same image or modified image onto film. (Linotype-Hell)

PRINCIPLE OF COLOR SEPARATION FOR THREE COLOR
AND FOUR COLOR PROCESS WORK

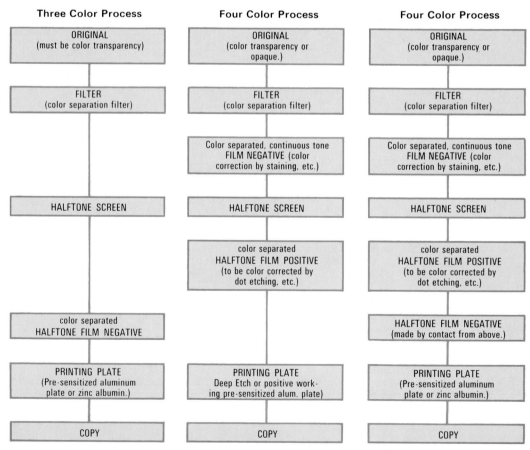

Three Color Process	Four Color Process	Four Color Process
ORIGINAL (must be color transparency)	ORIGINAL (color transparency or opaque.)	ORIGINAL (color transparency or opaque.)
FILTER (color separation filter)	FILTER (color separation filter)	FILTER (color separation filter)
	Color separated, continuous tone FILM NEGATIVE (color correction by staining, etc.)	Color separated, continuous tone FILM NEGATIVE (color correction by staining, etc.)
HALFTONE SCREEN	HALFTONE SCREEN	HALFTONE SCREEN
	color separated HALFTONE FILM POSITIVE (to be color corrected by dot etching, etc.)	color separated HALFTONE FILM POSITIVE (to be color corrected by dot etching, etc.)
color separated HALFTONE FILM NEGATIVE		HALFTONE FILM NEGATIVE (made by contact from above.)
PRINTING PLATE (Pre-sensitized aluminum plate or zinc albumin.)	PRINTING PLATE Deep Etch or positive working pre-sensitized alum. plate)	PRINTING PLATE (Pre-sensitized aluminum plate or zinc albumin.)
COPY	COPY	COPY

Fig. 15-15. Diagram shows indirect color separation method.

The process camera reproduces the entire image all at once. The scanner will reproduce the image using small increments of the image a little at a time. By scanning the image at either 500 or 1000 scans an inch, the electronic impulses from the original copy can be massaged or corrected as needed during the exposure.

Early scanners were known as the first and second generation types, and typically delivered continuous tone results at the original or same size. These scanners required a separate scan for each color separation.

Newer scanners are capable of making halftone separations, multiple scanning, different size ratios, better resolution, and more color correction or special effects.

The early scanners used a glow lamp or vacuum tube for a light source. The light sources in newer scanners include a halogen lamp, argon-ion laser (blue-green light), and helium-neon laser (red light). The newer light sources, such as the laser, allow for electronically generated halftone screens. The newer more intense light sources also allow the scanners to use a less expensive grade of ortho film. Look at Fig. 15-16.

Scanner principles

The color scanner has become the most popular way to produce color separations. The initial investment usually will be very large, but the speed and quality control factors will return the investment. The working principle of the color scanner can be simplified and diagrammed, as in Fig. 15-17.

The original copy, either reflection or transparent, is mounted on the scanning drum. The original is then scanned from reflected or transmitted light. The light record of the original highlights, midtones, and shadows will pass through the appropriate color filters and be absorbed by the proper photomultiplier tubes (PMT).

The purpose of the *photomultiplier tube* is to transform the light to an electronic signal that the computer can read. The computer is preprogrammed with color correction, undercolor removal, unsharp masking, and tone reproduction information based on the evaluation of the original. The computer modifies the electronic signal as required, and controls the light source intensity used to record an image on the film. Look at Fig. 15-18.

The scanner can be programmed to produce either negative or positive film images and right or wrong-reading images. The size of the reproduction separations can be changed by altering the speed of revolution between the input drum (original) and output drum (film).

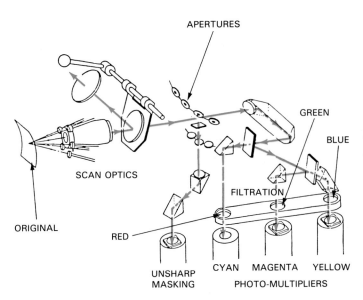

Fig. 15-18. Details of optics of color scanner shows how light from original is picked up by photomultiplier tubes.
(Linotype-Hell)

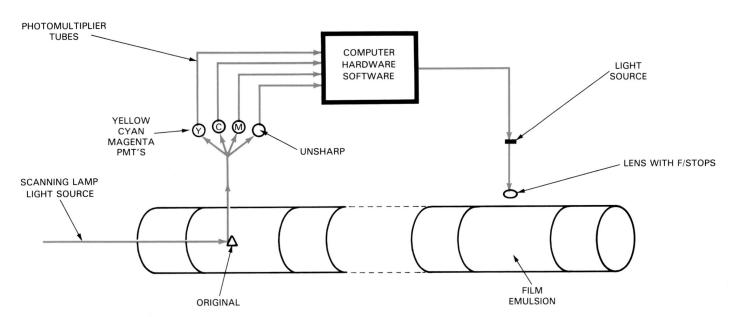

Fig. 15-17. Drawing shows basic principle of a color scanner. Light from original is picked up by sensing tubes for each color. Electrical output from tubes is sent to computer and then stored. After size change, color correction, or other modifications, computer can output image using light source on right side of scanner. Lens directs light onto film to produce desired image.

243

Scanner types

There are two basic types of scanners: the rotary scanner and the flatbed scanner.

The *rotary scanner,* just discussed, mounts the image and the film on a round drum. Then the drum spins in front of stationary reading and output devices. Presently, this is the most common type of scanner.

The *flatbed scanner* mounts the image and film on a table-like surface. It will allow you to mount rigid originals, such as an oil painting, on the scanner without bending them around a scanner drum. This prevents damage to the original, Fig. 15-19.

As the color scanner progressed, extreme enlargement or reduction capabilities became possible. Later generation scanners included the ability to produce halftone separations from either transparent or reflection copy. Major tone reproduction adjustments became possible, along with detail enhancement features.

Today's scanners are primarily digital and have the ability to scan the originals and store the electronic data on a disk or magnetic tape, Fig. 15-20. Current scanners used in the industry have custom color correction capabilities, and either improved under color removal (UCR) or gray component replacement (GCR).

Fig. 15-19. *This is a monochrome flat bed scanner. Original image lays flat as it is being scanned. This design has some advantages over rotary scanner.   (Screen - USA)*

Fig. 15-20. *After scanning, the original image can be stored digitally on magnetic disk or tape. Electrical signals from scanner computer magnetize microscopic areas on disk or tape. Image can then be stored, modified, or recalled. Here operator is removing a magnetic storage disk after scanning.*
(Lehigh Press)

Operating the electronic scanner

The purpose of this section is to provide you with an opportunity to understand the basic operating procedures of the color scanner. This section is not designed to provide you with detailed information about one particular scanner, but a generic approach to all scanners.

Color scanners are categorized by their output. There are three major scanner classifications:
1. Continuous tone.
2. Halftone by contact screen.
3. Electronic dot generated halftone.

Regardless of the scanner classification, the basic setup procedures, linearization tests, mounting techniques, and reproduction controls are similar.

The early or first generation scanners had many limitations. Some of the limitations included 1:1 reproduction ratio limitation, only transparent originals could be scanned, and panchromatic film was a requirement.

The flat bed scanner is a trend in scanners, especially in countries outside the U.S. Mentioned earlier, it will yield more accurate reproduction data because the image and the scanner head are on a single, flat plane. The original and the film do NOT have to be curved around a scanner drum. It also allows you to scan originals, like an oil painting, that cannot be bent.

Preview system

A *preview system* uses a color monitor, a computer, and the digital data from the scanner to show the color separations prior to output. Detailed in later chapter, this allows the image to be checked for color, color corrected, or even modified while in digital form. Then the improved or altered image can be placed on film and used to make the printing plate. One type preview system is shown in Fig. 15-21.

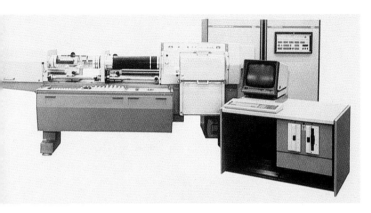

Fig. 15-21. Preview system has color monitor that will let scanner operator inspect or alter image before going onto film. Note preview system hardware, monitor, computer, etc., on right of scanner.

Fig. 15-22. A good scanner operator is very skilled and well trained. He or she must know how to use scanner to fullest potential to reproduce images properly.
(Chapter One, Screaming Color)

Scanner environment

The environment that houses the color scanner is a critical concern. The ideal temperature for electronic pre-press equipment, like the color scanner, is between 62° and 70°F (17° and 21°C).

Proper lighting or safelighting is critical for film handling, evaluation of originals, and ease of control board operation. Studies have suggested that soft or subtle music be provided to reduce the potential operator stress associated with the sophistication of the equipment.

Scanner operators

There are two basic profiles or job descriptions for color scanner operators in the industry.

The first type of scanner operator is one that has been trained to push buttons in a common sequence. This individual is capable of producing quality color, but lacks the knowledge to problem solve difficult separations.

The second type of scanner operator in the industry includes the individual who has a solid background in the basics of color reproduction and has problem solving ability. This operator can evaluate originals and compensate for the problems inherent to all printing processes, Fig. 15-22.

The scanner operator must always be mentally aware of the sequences involved in producing a quality separation. This individual should be able to mentally visualize the results of color correction or modifications in tone reproduction prior to processing the separation.

The required mathematical skills include the ability to add, subtract, multiply, and divide, along with a working knowledge of the metric system. The operator should be able to pass a color blindness test as a basic requirement of the job. Furthermore, the scanner operator must have a working knowledge of densitometry and photographic film processing.

Color scanner setup

Prior to the operation of any color scanner, basic setup procedures must be followed. These setup procedures involve calibration of densitometers and stabilizing either a lith or rapid-access film processor. Most scanners will have a night mode and a day mode.

The *night mode* is for when the scanner is not in production and provides a dim light source to keep the photomultiplier tubes warm or active.

At the beginning of a production workshift, the scanner is placed in the *day mode* which activates the main program and microprocessors.

Film linearization tests should be performed at the beginning of any workshift. *Linearization* simply refers to the calibrated output of an exposing unit (laser light source) to a given film emulsion as interpreted by densitometry after controlled processing. It is a process of consistently aligning the scanner exposure with the film processor and transmission densitometer for a specific type of film.

Successful linearization provides consistency in halftone dots or tone values for each of the separations. Figure 15-23 gives an example of a linearization test.

Fig. 15-23. Scanner operator is doing processed linearization test that includes a 21 and 13 step gray scale from each of the different settings for the laser output unit.

Mounting originals on scanner

It should be understood that about 80% or more of the originals used in the color separation process are transparencies.

Transparent originals offer a longer density range from the highlight to the shadow, and are *first generation originals*.

Color photographs, often called "C-Prints" in the industry, are considered *second generation originals* because an intermediate negative was required to produce the positive image.

Remember! For every photographic generation, a little of the integrity or sharpness and tone quality of the original is lost.

The procedure for mounting transparent copy on a scanner drum requires an initial evaluation of the original. This evaluation should be done under the proper lighting conditions and will determine the best highlight values and any imperfections in the original, Fig. 15-24.

Fig. 15-25. Here operator is mounting a 35 mm transparency in oil to help reduce the refraction of light when scanning.

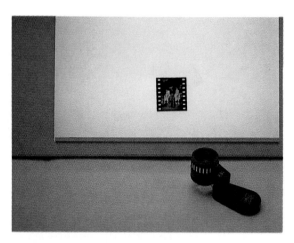

Fig. 15-24. Evaluation of original image before mounting will help determine best highlight values and find any imperfections. Viewing must be done under proper lighting conditions.

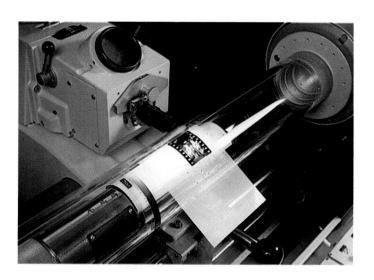

Fig. 15-26. Transparency should be mounted with sprocket holes on each side. Then, they cannot affect scanning signals because of adjacency effect.

As a rule of thumb, transparent copy should be mounted in oil when the reproduction is to be more than 600% in size. Mounting in oil will hide any scratches in the original, as well as reduce the refraction of light that occurs during the scanning procedure, Fig. 15-25.

Always follow the scanner manufacturer's recommendations when mounting in oil or cleaning the scanner drum.

Prior to mounting the transparency and required control guides (gray scales), use film cleaner to clean the drum and original. Anti-Newton ring powder should be used in a huffer (atomizer) when not mounting in oil. Mount the transparency with the EMULSION DOWN using a removable transparent tape. When mounting 35mm transparencies, it is suggested that the sprockets of the film be placed vertically on the drum to avoid any *adjacency effects* (holes upset adjacent image area). See Fig. 15-26.

Optically clear plastic should be used to mount reflection copy such as color photographs or oil paintings. Some scanners require that the reflection copy and gray scales be placed on black paper to stop the light source from passing through the original, Fig. 15-27. Care must be taken to secure the original and clear plastic to the scanning drum. Masking tape is often used to secure the composite artwork to the drum.

It is critical to check the focus adjustment on the lens of the scanning head when changing from transparent to reflection copy. Remember that the color scanner has a maximum focal adjustment of around .12 in. (3.0 mm) thickness for the original artwork.

To focus the color scanner, a magnification lens is used to examine the shadow structure, Fig. 15-28. The shadow of the transparency will show grain structure, and the reflection copy will show detail in the pigmentation.

Scanner operating steps

After the original copy has been mounted on the scanning drum and focused, the following procedures must be followed:

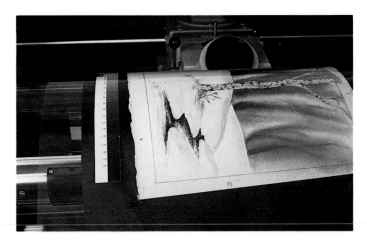

Fig. 15-27. Optically clear plastic and black paper are often used to mount reflection copy or photographs.

Fig. 15-29. Here scanner operator is measuring length and width of original using a flexible metric tape. This is needed to determine exposure window or recording format of the final separation.

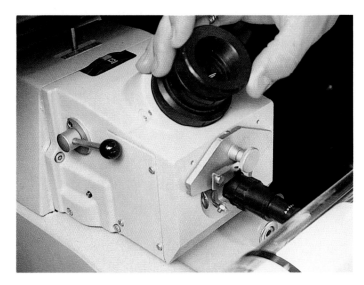

Fig. 15-28. Operator is using scanner's magnification lens to focus scanner on original. This must be done when changing originals.

Fig. 15-30. Operator is using scanner's microprocessor or computer keypad to program in reproduction parameters. Keypad controls will vary with specific type of scanner. These are typical.

1. Select the proper F/stop or aperture opening based on the percentage of enlargement or reduction.
2. Set the unsharp-masking filter accordingly.
3. Align or "wake-up" the photomultiplier tubes according to the manufacturer's instructions for the desired F/stop. Many scanners require adjustments when changing light intensity for different reproduction ratios.
4. Size the original that has been mounted on the scanning drum with a metric calibration tape. Determine the exposure window or recording format of the final separation, Fig. 15-29.
5. Key in the desired border size and density if required.
6. Key in the desired percentage of reproduction, and direction of scanning, Fig. 15-30.
7. Set the scanner for either negative or positive film exposure. Most scanners will have a universal symbol for selecting transmission or reflection copy, Fig. 15-31.
8. Energize the scanning light source and adjust the mir-

Fig. 15-31. Depending upon programmed data, scanner will generate separations in either a positive or negative orientation.

Fig. 15-32. Transparency can be viewed through scanning head.

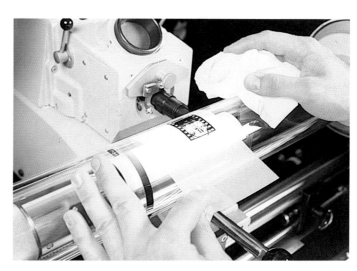

Fig. 15-33. A neutral continuous tone gray scale is used to calibrate the selected aim points for tone reproduction.

ror for viewing through the scanning head, Fig. 15-32.

9. Use the neutral continuous tone gray scale to establish the selected aim points for tone reproduction and gray balance, Fig. 15-33. Examples include:

	Highlight(A)	Midtone(M)	Shadow(B)
Cyan	6% dot	60% dot	96% dot
Magenta	3% dot	48% dot	93% dot
Yellow	4% dot	50% dot	94% dot
Black	−20% dot	20% dot	80% dot

This procedure may be in the form of pre-programmed software in some of the newer scanners.

10. Additional gradation control can be made with one-quarter tone and three-quarter tone adjustments on most scanners. This adjustment allows the operator to have a psuedo five aim point system of tone reproduction. The scanner provides more control or enhancement in the separation process than any other piece of production equipment, Fig. 15-34.

11. After establishing the reproduction standards against the neutral gray scale, the operator begins to examine the color original. This procedure includes checking for color correction and adjusting the white (unwanted) colors and black (wanted) colors. Additional correction can be made by adjusting the main color computer. Look at Fig. 15-35.

12. If required, the operator can make additional adjustments for: under color removal (UCR) or grey component removal (GCR), under color addition (UCA) or grey component addition (GCA), density limiters, catchlight dropouts, white line and black line detail enhancement, starting point, and gray balance.

13. Find the *north pulse* or *starting point* for the exposing drum. Align the beginning or top of the original with the scanning lamp as per manufacturer's instructions. Set the scanning head and exposing head to the proper stops and engage any couplings, Fig. 15-36.

Fig. 15-34. The one-quarter tone and three-quarter tone adjustments allow the scanner to enhance the tone reproduction on the separation.

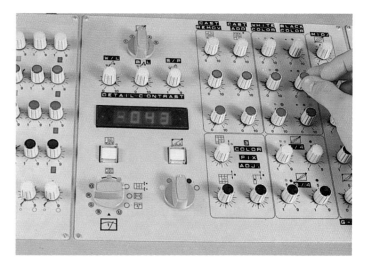

Fig. 15-35. Correction can be done with the white and black colors with main controls of color computer.

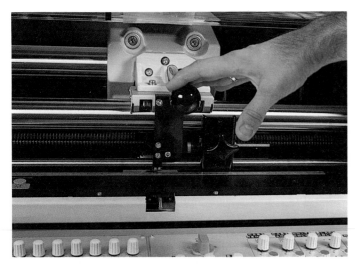

Fig. 15-36. Prior to exposing film, operator may need to align scanning head and exposing head.

Fig. 15-38. Now operator is programming keys for auxilliary register marks, gray scales, and color designations. This can vary with specific model of scanner.

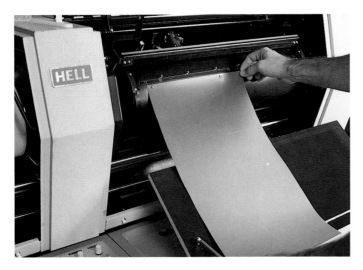

Fig. 15-37. Film is normally loaded on right side of scanner. If contact screen is used, instead of computerized screening, it must be loaded with film.

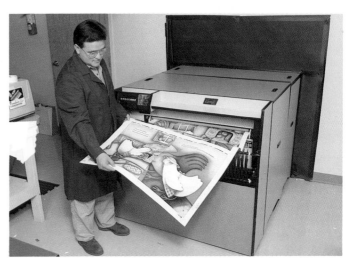

Fig. 15-39. Pre-press color proofing system may be used to evaluate quality or success of color separation prior to customer approval. (Chapter One, Screaming Color)

14. Load the film, and contact screens if necessary, as per the manufacturer's instructions. See Fig. 15-37.
15. Program any necessary register marks, gray scales, and color designations, Fig. 15-38.
16. Select the separation color(s) and depress the start button. After the scan has been completed, the scanner will automatically stop. Remove the film and process in the same environment as the linearization test.
17. A *pre-press color proofing system* may be utilized to determine the quality of the separation before printing. See Fig. 15-39.

Further applications of electronic scanner

The electronic scanner is currently being used as an integral part of the new integrated pre-press systems, Fig. 15-40. The scanner is used not only to produce color separations, but black and white halftones, and text matter or line copy in an effort to electronically digitize the information.

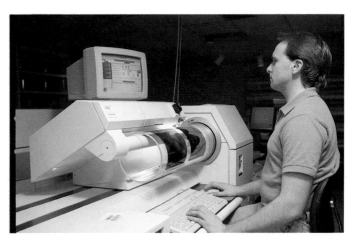

Fig. 15-40. Mentioned earlier, pre-press systems are gaining in popularity because they let operators see and alter images while still in digital form. Image data can also be transmitted to other locations electronically. (Chapter One, Screaming Color)

The digitized information can be further modified, stored, or transmitted via satellite to another output station or printing facility.

Another application of the color scanner is to generate color separated information from an original to be used in the electronic cutting of a gravure cylinder. Faster and more economical gravure cylinder preparation is accomplished with electronic impulses that bypass the film stage. Refer to Fig. 15-41.

As newer technologies are developed, a trend toward filmless imaging of printing plates or cylinders will evolve. Pre-press proofing from digitized information is currently available, but with limited results. Resolution (the ability to render fine details), pigmentation, and customer acceptance, are major concerns of the current electronic proofing system.

The term *"soft proofing"* refers to the ability to proof color editing and pagination work on the display terminal.

It should be understood that film is still considered the most efficient and economical medium of storage for graphic images. Furthermore, it is projected that film will remain the leading method of storage for small and medium size printing firms due to the cost factor of digitized equipment.

SELECTING A COLOR SEPARATION SYSTEM

The task of selecting a color separation system is difficult because there are a variety of production methods and equipment combinations. As different as one printing facility is from another, a single system of color separation would not be feasible for all printers. It should be noted that with competent personnel, quality originals, and good control in the production sequences, all the previously mentioned systems will produce comparable color separation quality.

Included below are eight major considerations for the selection of a color separation system or justification of equipment purchases.
1. What is the typical price the customer expects to pay for separations?
2. What is the level of quality the customer expects?

3. What will the completed turnaround time be for separations?
4. What is the facilities outlay of capital investment?
5. What level of personnel training is required for the equipment in the system?
6. What type of copy does the customer furnish: ganged catalog pages, original paintings, individual large format or 35 mm transparencies, or color corrected originals?
7. What is the quantity of weekly production?
8. What type of color correction is necessary?

In many cases the levels of quality between the direct separations, indirect separations, and electronic scanners are so close that the operating personnel can make the difference. However, the best color reproduction quality and speed are the results of using the newer generation color scanners.

COLOR CORRECTION

In an effort to obtain facsimile reproduction of a color original, most systems of color separation include color correction. The amount of color correction is best determined by the results in the pressroom. The inks used for process color printing contain impurities.

Primarily, *color correction* alters original colors to compensate for ink impurity in the different process colors. It can also be used to enhance weak colors on an original.

Color correction can be accomplished with photomechanical masking, both wet and dry dot etching, and the adjustment of *black* (wanted colors) and *white* (unwanted colors) *color controls* on the electronic scanner.

Dot etching is a system of local color correction used for modifying isolated locations.

Wet etching of the dots involves the use of chemicals to erode or build up the silver deposits on the film that form the different dot sizes.

Dry etching refers to contacting techniques used to spread or choke the dot structure. This technique can be used in the contact frame with diffusion sheeting and burning-in techniques for local corrections.

Fig. 15-42 shows a dot etcher at work.

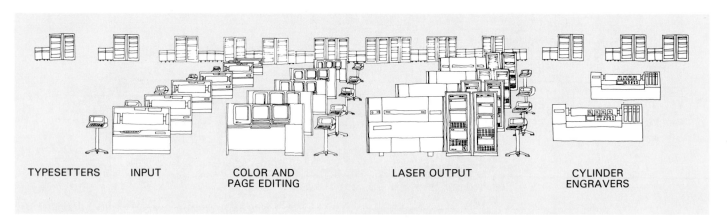

TYPESETTERS   INPUT   COLOR AND PAGE EDITING   LASER OUTPUT   CYLINDER ENGRAVERS

Fig. 15-41. This represents advanced network that will go directly to making the printing cylinder for gravure process. Film is not needed and complete system interacts electronically. (Scitex)

Fig. 15-42. Here a dot etcher is at work on separations.

2. MAGENTA PRINTER (Wanted Colors = Magenta, Red, and Blue.) (Unwanted Colors = Cyan, Green, and Yellow.)
3. CYAN PRINTER (Wanted Colors = Cyan, Blue, and Green.) (Unwanted Colors = Red, Yellow, and Magenta.)

The *photographic mask* is a film image created from the original using the proper filters to reduce the ink impurities. The use of masking film will reproduce the image in a diffused or soft focus for registration purposes.

The mask is measured in a percentage of light stopping ability. Thus, a 100% positive mask would block out all illumination from a light table if it was overlapping a negative image in register. The percentage of masking or electronic scanner adjustment is determined by an evaluation of the process inks.

The most popular methods of color correction are photographic masking and electronic scanning adjustments. The two reasons for a mask or scanner adjustment are to make the unwanted colors equal to white and to equalize the wanted colors to equal black. The principle behind these adjustments is derived from the "rule of thirds."

The *Rule Of Thirds* is based on the concept that for every color separation there should be three wanted colors that equal black (ink density), and three unwanted colors that equal white (paper density). The black or white colors are located on a color bar used as a quality control tool on the press sheet, Fig. 15-43.

1. YELLOW PRINTER (Wanted Colors = Yellow, Red, and Green.) (Unwanted Colors = Cyan, Magenta, and Blue.)

GRAY BALANCE

Color correction is also responsible for the gray balance in a color reproduction. In pure color theory, the overlapping of yellow, magenta, and cyan inks will equal black. Thus, it could be assumed that overlapping 50% tints of the three process inks would equal a perfect gray value.

In practical color reproduction, the three color overlap will NOT produce black, just as the three color tint overlap will NOT equal gray.

To achieve proper gray balance in the three color reproduction of a gray scale, the halftone dot sizes of the three separations should be properly unbalanced.

The extent of the unbalance in the separation dot sizes depends largely on the inks used and their impurities, as well

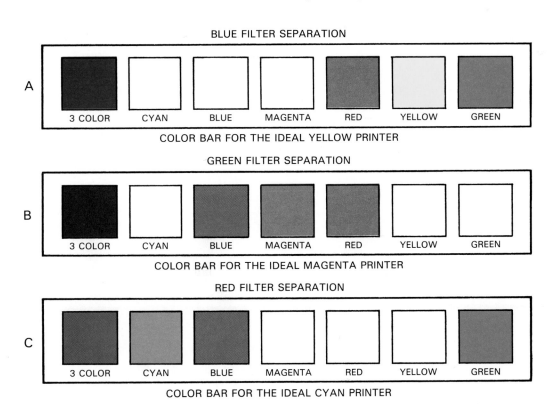

Fig. 15-43. This chart illustrates Rule Of Thirds and ideal color printers.

	Highlight	Mid-tone	Shadow
Separation	(.10)	(.70)	(1.60)
Yellow	2%	50%	80%
Magenta	2%	45%	80%
Cyan	6%	60%	90%

Fig. 15-44. This is an example of halftone dot geometry to achieve gray balance.

as the paper and press variables. Typically, the cyan separation dot sizes will print larger in the highlights, mid-tones, and shadows, than the yellow or magenta separations. A set of typical dot sizes used to achieve gray balance for a specific set of inks are illustrated in Fig. 15-44.

One method used to determine the gray balance requirements include printing a *standard tint chart* using a common paper and set of process inks. It is important to run the tint charts at the normal ink density on a printing press usually reserved for process color printing.

From the printed tint chart, select a series of grays from light to dark. Visually select the gray values using a reflection gray scale or a densitometer and the appropriate filter readings. If the grays are not completely neutral, the dot percentages for yellow, magenta, and cyan can be interpolated.

Determining gray balance on the electronic color scanner can be achieved by producing five or six, three-color

separations of a continuous tone gray scale. To perform the test, normal scanner linearization and set-up procedures are followed. Depending on the type of scanner, all five or six separations of each of the three colors can be placed on one sheet of film. The difference between each of the separations will be an equal interval change on the gray balance adjustment. It is important to record the different gray balance settings for each of the separations.

After processing the films, proof the separations with the use of an accepted pre-press proofing system and determine which of the separations represent a neutral gray value. When examining the proofs in the assigned sequence, a *cold* (blue) *cast* or *warm* (red) *cast* should be visible at either end of the aligned separations.

Process ink analysis

Any color reproduction system should be engineered from the pressroom back to the color separation facility. Thus, the first step in the engineering of a color reproduction system is the analysis of process inks. Understand that a set of process inks (yellow, magenta, cyan, and black) may differ from one ink manufacturer to another. To evaluate the set of inks used in a specific printing facility, simply run a set of color bars under normal printing conditions. Many large color separation houses will furnish films or plates with test patterns for printing, Fig. 15-45.

Using a reflection densitometer and the red, green, and blue filters, record the ink film density readings, Fig. 15-46. The densities recorded can be used to determine the work-

Fig. 15-45. This is an example of an ink analysis test pattern. (American Color Corp.)

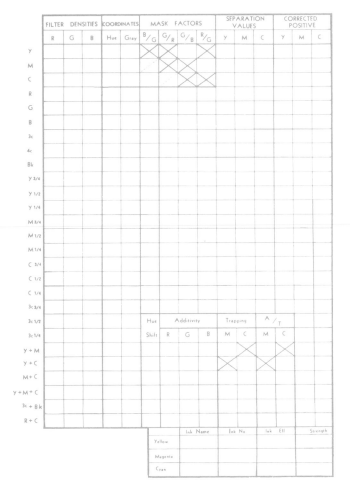

Fig. 15-46. Process ink data sheet can be used to record information concerning methods used to produce separations.

ing characteristics of a set of process inks. The four factors that best describe the working characteristics or impurities of the inks are:

1. Strength.
2. Hue.
3. Grayness.
4. Efficiency.

Ink strength is important because it will identify the range and depth of colors that can be produced from a set of inks. This factor can be determined by visually comparing the density readings, and selecting the highest reading for the yellow, magenta, and cyan inks.

Ink hue error determines the percentage of reflection of colored light from a specific color of ink. A hue or color is determined by the eye in terms of cone stimulation to colors of light. The color or hue of magenta ink should absorb and prevent green light from reflecting off the paper surface, and allow all of the blue and red light to reflect. The ink impurities in the magenta ink pigmentation that distort this normal reflection ratio can be measured as a percentage of hue error.

To determine the *hue error* for the measured set of inks, use the following equation for one color of ink and its red, green, and blue filter readings.

$$\text{Hue Error} = \frac{\text{Medium Filter Reading} - \text{Low Filter Reading}}{\text{High Filter Reading} - \text{Low Filter Reading}}$$

The grayness factor for a set of process inks identifies the purity for the process colors. A color is considered *gray* when it reflects less light of its predominant color than the white sheet of paper it is printed on. For example, cyan should reflect 100% blue and green light, but is considered gray in percentage because it reflects less blue than the white paper.

Use the following equation to determine the extent of grayness for a given color of ink—the lower the percentage or grayness factor, the higher the purity level.

$$\text{Grayness Factor} = \frac{\text{Low Filter Reading}}{\text{High Filter Reading}}$$

The *ink efficiency* is similar to the hue error, but instead of measuring the percentage of error in the reflection of light, a positive percentage is expressed. Earlier in the chapter, it was determined that each color of process ink filtered out its complementary additive color, and reflected the other two-thirds of the spectrum. The ability of the ink's color to do this is the measurement of efficiency—the higher the percentage of an ink's efficiency, the less color correction will be required.

The following equation will determine a specific ink color efficiency percentage.

$$\text{Ink Efficiency} = 1 - \frac{\text{Low Filter Reading} + \text{Medium Filter Reading}}{2 \times \text{High Filter Reading}}$$

Color diagrams for ink evaluation and color correction

When performing process ink analysis, it is beneficial to plot the information on a *color diagram* for the purpose of visual evaluation or comparisons. Data such as hue error or grayness factor can be calculated and plotted on the color hexagon, circle, or triangle diagram. These plots, representing ink data, can be visually compared to ideal colors located on the diagram. There have been many diagrams constructed for the purpose of ink evaluation and color correction requirements.

Three popular diagrams accepted in the industry are the Graphic Arts Technical Foundation color hexagon, color circle, and color triangle.

The *color hexagon* is one of the only diagrams that requires no major computations or formulas. It is used to plot the color strength and hue differences. It is one of the easier and quicker diagrams to use. It is best suited for quality control or press control of primary printers and overprints, Fig. 15-47.

The *color circle* is designed to visualize the hue error and grayness factor of actual colors in relationship to ideal colors. It is also of value in determining the color correction system requirements for different inks and substrates. See Fig. 15-48.

Finally, the *subtractive color triangle* is designed to illustrate the gamut of pure color that is possible with a set

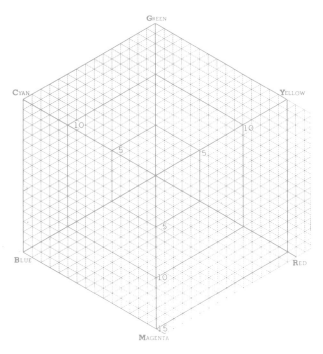

Fig. 15-47. Color hexagon is used to plot color strength and hue differences to improve quality control. (GATF)

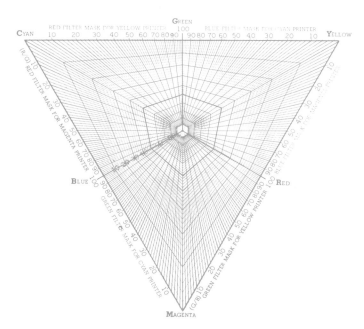

Fig. 15-49. Color triangle will illustrate the gamut of color possible with a set of process inks. Mask percentages are located on side of triangle to show requirements for color correction of inks. (GATF)

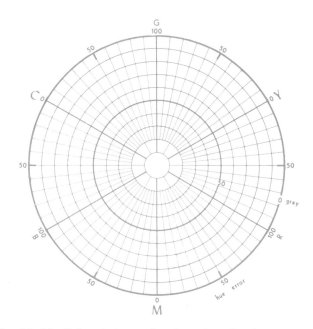

Fig. 15-48. Color circle can be plotted so that hue error and grayness can be visualized and compared to ideal colors. (GATF)

of process inks. The plots of ink data will also identify under or over-trapping and predict overprints. Mask percentages are located along the sides of the triangle to identify masking requirements for color correction of the specific inks. Refer to Fig. 15-49.

Ink impurities

The data derived from the analysis of a set of process inks will determine the exact masking or color correction requirements.

Usually, the yellow pigment will be the purest in color. The magenta ink will usually contain a color impurity of yellow. Magenta ink can either be rubine or rhodamine in color. The rhodamine is a blue-magenta which is more expensive and produces better fleshtones. The rubine magenta is more red in color.

The cyan ink contains the most impurities, and will usually have a major impurity of magenta. If the cyan appears to have a magenta impurity, then it must also contain a certain amount of the yellow that is already in the magenta. Thus, it is said that cyan ink has a major impurity of the color magenta, and a minor impurity of yellow.

For purposes of color correction, the cyan printer separation will receive the least amount of correction. Because you cannot remove the magenta impurity or yellow impurity in the cyan ink, you must print less magenta and even much less of the yellow. The yellow impurity is in both the cyan and magenta ink. Thus, it must be reduced the most and receives more masking or correction. The percentage of color correction is best determined by actual ink density readings and evaluation of the four basic ink characteristics.

COLOR PROOFING SYSTEMS

After the color separations have been produced, the use of a pre-press proofing system is suggested. The probability of error is high in color separation work because every original is different and the process is usually performed under time restrictions.

The primary purpose of a *color proofing system* is to catch errors or mistakes prior to the press run, where corrections would be expensive. Mistakes will reduce profits and could prevent potential future work from a customer.

There are two traditional methods of proofing color separations, and a third technique that is evolving with the new electronic technologies.

The first traditional method is to proof with a set of inks on the press. The second is to use a photographic or photo-mechanical proofing system. The photo-mechanical proofing systems are more popular and more economical.

Photo-mechanical proofing systems are categorized into single sheet or laminate color proofing systems and overlay color proofing systems.

The advantage of single sheet or laminate proofing is that the viewing light is reflected from a single surface and light refraction is limited.

A major advantage of overlay proofing is that individual colors, secondaries, and three color overprints, can be examined independently. With the increase of undercolor removal in four color separations, overlay proofing is becoming more important to the press crew that must compare the press sheet to the proof.

The third technique of pre-press proofing is emerging from electronic pre-press technology. The electronic or digital color proofing systems can be either *soft proofing* on the visual display terminal, or *hard copy proofing* using recorders, cameras, or ink jet printers.

Many pre-press proofing systems are available. Each of these systems have their own advantages to the industry.

Regardless of which proofing system is selected, some basic requirements should be observed. Basic requirements of a proofing system include:

1. The proofing system should match the press run or ink capabilities.
2. The proofing system should have consistency in results.
3. The proofing system should have a minimum of operator skills required.
4. The proofing system should have customer acceptance.
5. The proofing system should be practical for in-plant use (pressroom).
6. The proofing system selected should work from both negative and positive final films (separations).

Most large color separation houses will use several different systems of pre-press proofing. This is done in an effort to give the client a selection or choice.

KNOW THESE TERMS

Color separation, Complementary printer, Chromatic colors, Achromatic colors, Visible light spectrum, Nanometer, Primary additive colors, Primary subtractive colors, Hue, Saturation, Skeleton printer, Blue filter, Green filter, Red filter, Narrow band filter, Wide band filter, Black printer, UCR, GCR, Fake color, Direct screen, Ganged, Indirect separation, Photomultiplier tube, Rotary scanner, Flat bed scanner, Preview system, Night mode, Day mode, Linearization, First generation original, Second generation original, Color proofing system, Soft proofing, Rule Of Thirds, Gray balance, Standard tint chart, Cold cast, Warm cast, Ink strength, Ink hue error, Ink efficiency, Color diagram, Color hexagon, Color circle, Color triangle.

REVIEW QUESTIONS—CHAPTER 15

1. _____ contains all of the colors of the visible spectrum.
2. Explain the color separation process?
3. A color separation can be made _____ or _____.
4. Each color filter will separate the necessary colors of light to produce its:
   a. Subtractive color.
   b. Additive color.
   c. Complementary color.
   d. Opposite color.
5. The cones in the eye are receptors for _____ _____ such as red, green, and blue.
6. The cylindrical rods in the eye are receptors for _____ _____ or shades of gray.
7. List the wavelengths for six basic colors.
8. What is a nanometer?
9. List seven conditions that will affect the viewing of color reproductions.
10. Explain the function of blue, green, and red filters.
11. What is the purpose of the black printer?
12. A _____ _____ uses a color monitor, a computer, and digital data from the scanner to show color separations prior to output.
13. Define the term "linearization" as it relates to the color scanner.
14. This image would produce the highest quality reproduction when scanned.
   a. Transparency.
   b. Glossy photograph.
   c. Second generation original.
   d. Pre-screened original.
15. Why should 35 mm transparencies be mounted with the sprocket holes aligned vertically?
16. _____ _____ is a term referring to the ability to proof color editing and pagination work on a display terminal or monitor.
17. Color correction alters original colors to compensate for _____ _____ and to enhance _____ _____ on an original.
18. What is a standard ink chart?
19. This is important because it will identify the range and depth of colors that can be produced.
   a. Ink hue error.
   b. Ink efficiency.
   c. Ink strength.
   d. Ink tack.
20. In your own words, explain the use of a color hexagon, color circle, and color triangle.

Electronic scanner has changed color correction and modification technology tremendously. Scanner will convert image into electronic data. Once in electronic form, image can be modified easily. (Lehigh Press)

Chapter 16

PHOTOMECHANICAL AND ELECTRONIC MODIFICATIONS

After studying this chapter, you will be able to:
- Explain the process of producing different classifications of posterizations.
- Produce a detailed outline reproduction from a continuous tone image.
- Describe the techniques available for producing duotones.
- Create graphic appeal by using special effects screens.
- Explain the fundamentals of modifying images electronically.

This chapter will discuss the most common methods of modifying or altering images, both photomechanically and electronically. The first section of the chapter will cover photomechanical techniques for making posterizations, outlines, duotones, phantom halftones, screen patterns, and other special effects. The last section of the chapter will review more modern electronic means of making color corrections and other changes using computerized equipment.

PHOTO MODIFICATIONS

Photo modifications include any method used to change or alter continuous tone originals. Many unusual, special effects can be created photomechanically, by either a modification or conversion using standard techniques. These modifications and special effects are a designer's effort to capture an audiences' attention.

For a designer to properly use special effects, he or she must understand the photomechanical processes involved. Due to the processes, some original artwork lends itself to the desired effect better than other artwork. For this purpose, the designer and reproduction people must understand the limitations of the effects.

Often, the standard modification techniques, such as posterizations and duotones, are inexpensive attempts at imitating four-color process reproduction. Without the expense and time factor of color separations, many reproduction facilities can offer the client the impact of color through these special effects.

In some cases, the client will only furnish black and white photographs. Then the designer will find that more effect

is needed to convey a message to a perspective audience. This is where the applications of special effects photography becomes important to the industry.

CAMERA MODIFICATIONS

Photographic modification techniques can take place in the professional photographer's camera. Some applications can also be created with the use of an enlarger or in a processing tray. There is often more latitude for special effects when the photographer first captures the original image on continuous tone film, and later photographic paper. In process photography, the camera person must create the effects from a furnished original. Depending on the quality of the original, the camera person will typically make the conversion on orthochromatic film using different photomechanical techniques.

It should be emphasized that before any modifications to the normal reproduction take place, the basic line and halftone calibrations must be made for the specific facility. The camera person must have the basic reproduction variables under control. These variables include exposures, the type of film or chemistry used, as well as the source of illumination on the camera.

Most important, proper records should always be kept of the reproduction activity. Many special effects can be the result of mistakes or miscalculations. Accurate record keeping will promote consistency in results.

Remember! Any special effects created one day, should be repeatable in the future.

POSTERIZATION TECHNIQUES

Posterization is the technique of changing a black and white, continuous tone picture into a multi-color or multi-tone reproduction. In this process, the continuous tone original must be converted into selected tone values. These selected tone values should enhance the details of the original continuous tone. The abstract reproduction will attract the attention of an individual by virtue of color or contrast.

Posterization is a common special effect used by experienced designers to convey USUAL messages using the realm of the UNUSUAL.

The success of the posterization technique will greatly depend upon the proper selection of the original continuous tone photograph. An ideal black and white photograph should have good contrast, with fine line detail. Photo texture or grain can also be useful for posterization, Fig. 16-1.

Fig. 16-1. When making a posterization, original image must have good contrast and plenty of detail.

Posterization classifications

A posterization is classified by the selected number of tone values or colors of ink. A posterization may involve different colors of ink or different tone values using a hard dot tint screen. The number of tone values or colors can include the paper substrate for the posterization.

For the purposes of this textbook, the paper surface or color will be considered a tone or color value.

A *two-tone posterization* is a line reproduction of a continuous tone original that is printed on a white or colored sheet of paper, Fig. 16-2.

Fig. 16-2. This two-tone posterization is a line reproduction of a continuous tone original.

The *three-tone* or *three-color posterization* will involve two reproductions of the original, each having a different density and will overprint the paper value. See Fig. 16-3.

The *four-tone posterization* will be a reproduction of the original using three films, each with a different density. The density of these films can be controlled by either exposure or development. The three films can be represented on the paper with colors of ink or tint screen values, Fig. 16-4.

Fig. 16-3. This is an example of a three-tone posterization.

Fig. 16-4. This is a four-tone posterization.

Other *multiple-tone posterizations* can be created using similar techniques. The most popular posterizations, from the design and economy standpoint, are the three and four-tone or color reproductions.

There are three different techniques for reproducing a photomechanical posterization of a continuous tone photograph.

Posterization using percentages of basic line exposure

Probably the simplest method of producing a posterization is to use different percentages of the basic line exposure and controlled processing. This technique is the easiest and fastest of the three methods. However, it does not afford predictable results in the separation of tone values.

Select a suitable black and white photograph with good contrast, fine details, and a subject matter that is recognizable WITHOUT all the middle tone values. For the purposes of explanation, the example of a four-tone posterization will be identified as the white paper plus yellow, red, and black ink. The required line exposures will be based on a percentage of the normal basic line exposure.

For the four-tone posterization, three film negatives will be required. The exposures will be at 50%, 150%, and 300% of the normal line exposure. For example, if the normal line exposure is 20 seconds (20 units) at f/22, the exposures required to make the different tone values in the posterization will be 10 units, 30 units, and 60 units.

After making the three different film exposures, process the film following manufacturer's recommended time and temperature. Agitation can be controlled by processing all three sheets of film simultaneously in the same tray.

After washing and drying the film, examine the density differences on a light table, Fig. 16-5.

Fig. 16-5. The negatives must be evaluated by examining their densities before making a posterization.

To determine the success of the four-tone posterization, proof the film negatives with any negative acting pre-press proof system. The negative with the least density (50% exposure) will be assigned the lightest color pigment, in this case yellow. The 150% exposure negative with medium density will be red and the darkest negative will be for the black or detail printer, Fig. 16-6. Mount the pre-press color proof on the selected paper stock for final evaluation.

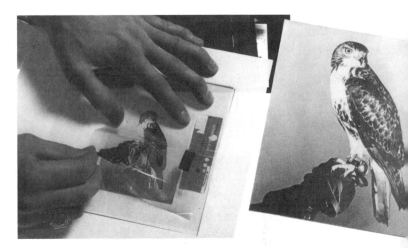

Fig. 16-6. A color key proof can be used to make the final evlauation of the posterization.

Posterization using a reflection gray scale and inspection processing

The second method of producing a posterization involves a reflection gray scale. It will allow the camera person more control in determining the starting point for tone values.

The selected original is evaluated prior to reproduction with the tone values on the gray scale. The camera person will select a high light value on the photo where the first color (yellow) of a four-tone posterization will appear.

Next, match the selected highlight value to a gray scale step, this will later become the quality control step used when processing the film, Fig. 16-7.

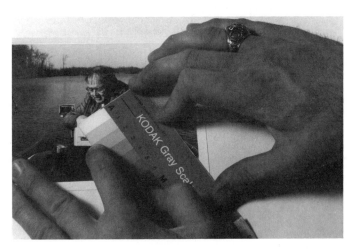

Fig. 16-7. Here a gray scale is being used to match the selected highlight densities.

Use the same cross evaluation technique to identify the mid-tone and shadow values with gray scale densities or processing steps.

When making the posterization, the basic line exposure time will be given for all three pieces of film. To process the film, use the selected gray scale steps in determining length of development for each negative. After processing is complete, evaluate the negatives on a light table. Remember that opaquing or scribing images can be done on line reproductions to enhance the results.

Again, the use of a pre-press proofing system will allow for final evaluation of the posterization on the selected paper stock, or fourth-tone value in this case. The lightest pigment color should usually be assigned to the negative with the least density or development time.

Posterization using reflection density values and exposure calculator

The third method of producing a posterization will provide the most control and consistency in results through the use of an exposure calculator, Fig. 16-8.

In this procedure, evaluate the original photo with either a reflection gray scale or a reflection densitometer to determine a density value for the different tone values. For example, if the camera person selects a mid-tone value for a tint or color to begin, that color or tint will appear on any location in the reproduction where the density value or higher values appear.

To use an exposure calculator, first calibrate the device by rotating the dials to align the basic line exposure with the normal gray scale density step used for processing, usually around .30 for density (4th step).

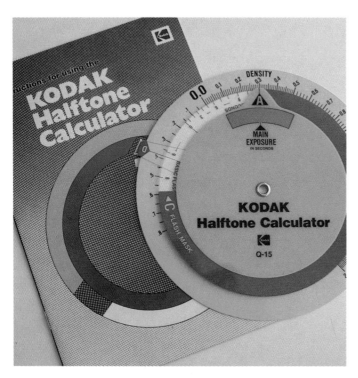

Fig. 16-8. An exposure calculator provides another way of making a posterization.

After pre-calibrating the exposure calculator with the normal development density and basic line exposure, identify exposure times by reading across from the different selected densities and their appropriate exposures.

If the calculator does not have dials as illustrated, proceed to program it with the same data, then follow manufacturer's instructions to call up specific density exposure combinations.

To produce the required negatives for a specific pre-determined density value, use the calculated exposures, and process by film manufacturer's time and temperature specifications.

In tray processing, it should be pointed out that still development techniques (discussed in Chapter 17) will bring out more details from the continuous tone copy. This method of posterization is more complicated than the two previous methods, but it is more accurate in the multiple color or tint screen posterizations.

For the final evaluation, use the same information and proofing techniques described in the two previous methods of posterization.

Posterization using screen tints and positives

Most posterizations are created for color applications, but if color is too expensivae or not a part of the design, tint screens may be substituted. Hard dot tint screens, not halftone contact screens, come in different percentages, and may create the illusion of specific gray tones.

A 10% tint screen (light gray) may be used in place of a light pigment, such as yellow ink. The 40% tint can be used as a mid-tone and a solid black for fine details. The dot percentage represents the ink value on paper.

If tint screens are used, the percentage values must be far enough apart to differentiate the tone values. Furthermore, the tint screens must be rotated or angled to prevent the visually distasteful moiré pattern. The use of an angle indicator will help to align the rows of dots. A 30 degree rotation or angle difference is suggested.

Fig. 16-9 shows a halftone screen determiner for finding out screen size. Study how it is used to quickly measure a screen.

Fig. 16-10 shows how a 30 degree triangle can be used to set the screen angle.

Some examples of incorrect screen angles and the resulting moiré patterns are pictured in Fig. 16-11.

Another effect can be created in the posterization using film positives contacted from the line negatives. The positives will, in selected cases, fill in the background areas with color or tint values. The use of positives can create very abstract and different effects. However, this should be reserved for specific design applications.

To make the positive, first select the line negative that best enhances the desired effect. Then, make a contact in the vacuum frame. Position a fresh piece of film with its emulsion up. Position the selected line negative with its emulsion up.

With the negative emulsion up, the positive will have the same film orientation as the negative. After processing the

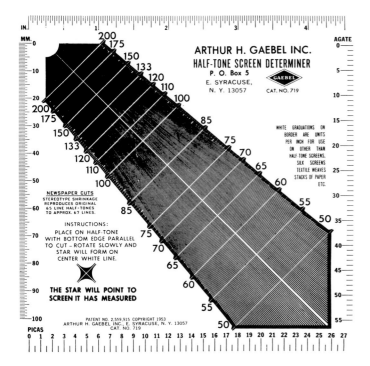

Fig. 6-9. *This halftone screen determiner can be used to quickly measure screens. Read the instructions.*

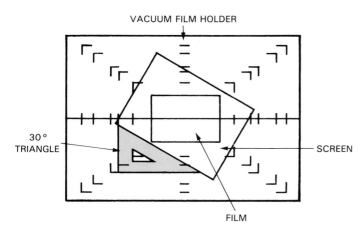

Fig. 16-10. *A 30 degree triangle can be used to set screen angle on copyboard.*

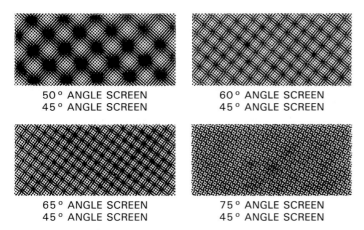

| 50° ANGLE SCREEN | 60° ANGLE SCREEN |
| 45° ANGLE SCREEN | 45° ANGLE SCREEN |

| 65° ANGLE SCREEN | 75° ANGLE SCREEN |
| 45° ANGLE SCREEN | 45° ANGLE SCREEN |

Fig. 16-11. *Note the unwanted moiré patterns produced with these screen angles.*

film positive, use a pre-press proof to evaluate the desired effect.

Tone-line technique

The *tone-line process* is used to create a detailed outline reproduction of a continuous tone original. This effect will remove the gray tone values.

The original tone-line process involves a line conversion technique using a continuous tone, ortho-reacting film. Processing of this film in a continuous tone developer will yield a high contrast negative image of the original continuous tone. Contacting this film negative with fresh ortho film produces a line positive.

The line negative and positive, with several sheets of mylar or acetate, are contacted to produce a spread or "fattie" on film or photographic paper. The contacting procedure involves a light source at an angle with the contact sandwich being spun on a turntable.

Another modification of this tone-line process is called a bas-relief image. The *bas-relief image* is similar to the tone-line. However, the sandwiched negative and positive images are positioned slightly OUT OF REGISTER by design.

Another newer method of producing a tone-line image is to select a high contrast, fine line, continuous tone original. The original can be either color or black and white. Both reflection and transparent copy will work. Using either a camera or enlarger, produce four different line negatives (reflection copy) on panchromatic high-contrast film. Each negative should be exposed to reproduce a specific density value of the original. Later, make contact positives of each of the four line negatives.

Using a light table, evaluate different combinations of a negative and positive until the desired effect is achieved. With tape or pin register, position the films base-to-base over a piece of fresh ortho film in a contact frame. Using a point light source, expose the ortho film with several thicknesses of diffusion sheeting over the tone-line films. Process the final film and the tone-line effect will be complete. An example is given in Fig. 16-12.

Fig. 16-12. *Note how a tone-line only shows an outline of the original image. It is a very striking special effect but is only applicable in certain situations.*

DUOTONE TECHNIQUES

The *duotone* is a modification or special effect requiring two halftones, each with a different screen angle and tone range of the continuous tone original. There are four different classifications of duotones.
1. A black-on-black, sometimes referred to as a *two-impression black duotone.*
2. A full tone color halftone with a *black skeleton halftone* printer.
3. A color on a *second color duotone.*
4. A *fake duotone,* usually constructed with a color tint screen value, and a normal halftone overprint.

The designer can use duotones to create a mood or simulate process color separations. Duotone colors can add warm tones to a normal black and white illustration.

Successfully making duotones

The difficulties in producing a desired effect or a successful duotone come from the camera person's abilities in evaluating tone values. The camera person is given a continuous tone original from which to make a full tone normal halftone and a second skeleton or shadow detail halftone. The density value, where the skeleton or detail halftone starts to overlap the semi-normal halftone, is the critical judgment or decision.

Another factor contributing to the success of a duotone is the choice of colors. In the realm of special effects, there are no hard rules, but past experience can offer suggestions to the novice.

For example, blues and greens will combine well with black for seascapes. But the designer must remember that a seashore in Califonia is often sunny, depicting the color blue. The seascape in New England may be cloudy, and better represented with green hues. Warm hues, such as yellows and reds, are often appropriate for sunsets or sunrises.

Two-impression black duotones

The major reason for black-on-black duotones is for exact facsimile reproduction of an original continuous tone photograph. Many professionally produced photographs have a maximum density of 1.85 and higher. The normal single impression of black ink, produces a press sheet density of about 1.40 to 1.60. The two impression black duotone will have facsimile qualities of the original photo.

The first halftone negative should be exposed to reproduce nearly the entire range of the original. The highlight, middle tones, and nearly all shadows should be represented on the first run. The second halftone negative should be extremely dense and reproduce only the mid-tones to the darkest shadows of the original. The overprint technique will improve the printed density value in the shadows.

To determine exposure times for the two halftones, simply calibrate the exposure computer as for a normal halftone. In evaluating the original, locate the whitest highlight and almost the darkest shadow. These density figures will be used in conjunction with the exposure computer in determining the first halftone exposure requirements.

For the second, black printer or the shadow detail halftone, select a mid-tone value on the original to be used for the main exposure requirement and the darkest shadow density for the flash exposure.

Note! The detail halftone should NOT reproduce the highlight values. This is to prevent white tones from becoming muddy or too dense.

Duotone production

The procedures used in the production of a duotone are similar to the normal halftone. The major difference will be in the angle of the halftone screen or original copy. To prevent a moiré pattern when printing two screen images at the same angle, rotate either the contact screen or original artwork. The contact screen can be purchased in different screen angles or in a circular screen to eliminate the need for measuring rotation.

It is best to rotate the screen rather than the copy because smaller film sizes can be used and the copyboard will not be moved. The screen angle difference between the two halftones should be 60 degrees for elliptical dot screens and 30 degrees for conventional or square dot screens.

Remember that for any multiple exposure of the same original, the copyboard percentage must NOT change. Even the slightest movement can cause registration problems.

After exposing the two halftone images, process the films by time and temperature techniques or by using an automated processor. Proof the final film negatives using any negative acting pre-press proofing system.

Using a magnification lens, determine if the dot structure creates the desired effect. The use of a reflection gray scale located next to the original copy during reproduction will assist in the final evaluation, Fig. 16-13.

One-color and black duotone

The one-color and black duotone is often referred to as a *true color duotone.* These are perhaps the most common duotones used in design work. The use of color with black details creates moods and almost simulates four-color process reproduction. The creative judgment of the designer or camera person becomes more critical with this type of duotone.

The procedures used in the production of a one-color and black duotone are the same as outlined for the two impression black printer. The first halftone will represent the entire tonal range of the original from highlight to shadow, and will be the assigned color. The second halftone will again represent a selected mid-tone to shadow range. As the role of the black printer, it will add the details.

Color-on-color duotone

Working with process color inks, the designer and camera person can create a visually stimulating effect. The choice of colors will be dependent upon the desired results. The selection of color hues should exhibit contrast to insure all the details are visually reproduced. The technique for the process of color-on-color duotones is the same as for color-on-black, Fig. 16-14.

| A | 1 | 2 | 3 | 4 | 5 | 6 | M | 8 | 9 | 10 | 11 | 12 | 13 | 14 | 15 | B | 17 |

Fig. 16-13. This is an example of two separate halftone printers with the gray scales and final printed duotone.

Fake duotone techniques

The *fake duotone* is a simulation technique of a color and black duotone or a color-on-color duotone. It is an inexpensive way to add color appearance on the printed work.

The original photograph should have good contrast because the highlight value will be the background screen tint value. In a fake duotone, the full tone halftone (black) overprints a 10 percent to 20 percent screen tint (color). The fake duotone is practical for layouts requiring many duotone images, Fig. 16-15.

SPECIAL EFFECT SCREENS

The large assortment of special effect hard dot and contact screens provide the designer an easy and inexpensive means to create a new dimension, or add appeal to the

Fig. 16-14. This is an example of a color-on-color duotone. Compare it to the others.

Fig. 16-15. This is a fake duotone. It is an inexpensive way to add color to the printed work.

graphic product. Often, the use of tint screens and texture screens act as a background to an overprint. Type matter or a dense image may be photomechanically superimposed over a soft background.

There are many special effect screens available including geometric patterns, such as: the wavy line, straight line, concentric circle, oval, and ring. Others include: wood grains and fabric designs, such as: denim, burlap, and mesh. Some halftone contact screens are available in the messotint, straight line, steel etch, and concentric circle.

The same basic exposure tests must be done to work with these contact screens. Fig. 16-16 shows several special effect screens.

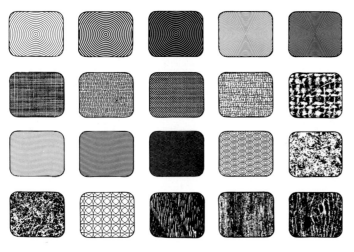

Fig. 16-16. You should be familiar with the many special effect screens available today.

Diffusion transfer modifications

Many special effects can be created by using diffusion transfer products. The use of special effect screens can produce prescreened halftone images. The use of tint screens during the different posterization exposures will produce the complete effect on one piece of photographic paper. Look at Fig. 16-17.

Fig. 16-17. Here the same photo used earlier has been altered using a diffusion transfer product.

By the nature of most diffusion transfer products, the receiver sheet will keep accepting the silver transfer images from new sheets of negative paper. Thus, multiple images or overprints are easy to produce with this method of reproduction. One popular technique using a receiver sheet, with two exposed negative sheets, is called *phantom halftones* or *ghost halftones*.

To create the phantom halftone, a continuous tone image is converted through normal halftone procedures, but the flash exposure is increased 4 to 5 times the calibrated exposure time. More light striking the diffusion transfer material will decrease the density to form a weak halftone image when transferred to the receiver sheet. Using a registration system, the type matter or overprint image is then photographed under normal conditions using a fresh piece of negative paper.

After carefully aligning the new exposed negative paper with the previously processed receiver sheet, reprocess the materials in the processor. Wait the recommended development time and separate the two sheets, Fig. 16-18. The desired effect can then be evaluated.

Fig. 16-18. This is an example of a phantom halftone using a diffusion transfer product.

Diffusion transfer modifications can include posterization, multiple exposures or transfers, and the phantom halftone. The *phantom halftone*, was defined as an overprint using one receiver sheet and two negative sheets. The background halftone was given an excessive flash exposure to soften the tones and reduce the density. The image to be overprinted was reproduced on diffusion transfer materials as normal, but a registration system must be used.

ELECTRONIC MODIFICATION

Electronics has spread to various parts of the printing industry during the last two decades. Today, it is possible to have the whole pre-press area automated. Because of the demand for quality and economy, the automated electronic, pre-press systems have been developed into fast, accurate, and reliable methods of preparing films and plates.

The pre-press system is capable of converting process copy and line art into finished separation films. Tints, masks, retouching, dot etching, image assembly, and proofing can all be done electronically. See Fig. 16-19.

This is all made possible by using digital electronics. Systems can take in all the colors simultaneously, or one separation color per scan. This depends on the type of scanner used, Fig. 16-20.

The scanned images are stored in digital form. The images that are not currently needed can be set aside or saved in a library or archive. Proofs can be made whenever needed.

With this system, it is possible to display the color images and modify them as the images are displayed on a VDT (Visual Display Terminal). It is also possible to assemble whole pages and view them without putting the images on paper or film, Fig. 16-21.

A TV-like color screen shows the images as they take form. The operator can mix colors and do progressive proofing. The operator can also display a whole image on the screen or magnify any portion of the image for close work on detail. It is also possible to look at the image with any combination of inks, paper, or press factors. This makes the image flexible.

Electronic modifications allow the operator to display and manipulate tonal gradation for the whole image or part of the image. This replaces manual retouching and dot etching. Color can be electronically air brushed, Fig. 16-22.

Fig. 16-19. Operator is using an advanced pre-press system to capture and modify an image electronically.

Fig. 16-21. Once the image is on the visual display screen, operator can alter color, contrast, or anything about image by programming in new electronic data.

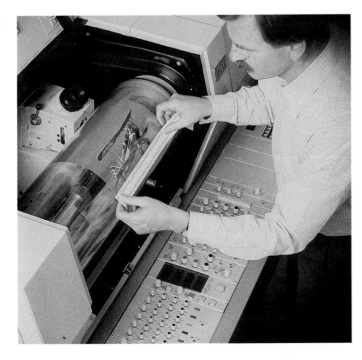

Fig. 16-20. Scanner is used to convert continuous tone original into electronic data. Then, electronic data can be used to show image on visual display screen.   (Linotype-Hell)

Fig. 16-22. Note how color can be added or changed electronically.

Page makeup is accomplished by electronic image assembly operations. Systems can mask process copy and line art, automatically generate geometric forms, insert standard elements from disk memory (such as company logos), produce shrinks, spreads, reverses, and tints. Pictures can be automatically cropped, rotated, sized, and positioned.

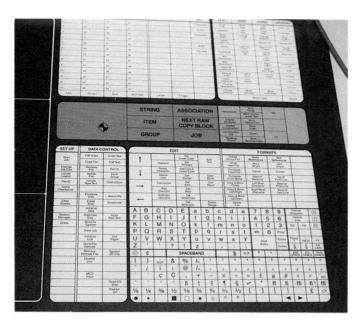

Fig. 16-23. This is a control panel for a modern pre-press system. Special training is needed to use such a pre-press system. Operating procedures also vary with the type or model system.

Fig. 16-24. Only part or all of the image can be viewed on the visual display terminal. Operator can change shade of sunglasses, change the color of the person's eyes, etc., all by pushing buttons.

Once the total page is modified to meet the customer's specifications, the finished materials are exposed as a total unit. A laser plotter is a fast exposing unit. The plotter exposes fully assembled pages individually or as imposed signatures.

Tints and picture areas can be screened automatically by the plotter in any screen ruling, dot shape, and screen angle desired.

ELECTRONIC IMAGERY

Electronic imagery is generally stated in terms of digitization; by this process, the data can be captured and managed by a computer. To understand the basics of digitization, three factors need to be considered. They are: image acquisition, image processing, and image recording.

Image acquisition

Capturing a variety of data from many sources is the basic concept of *image acquisition*, Fig. 16-24. These images must be converted into electronic form. This can be accomplished by two means: raster scanning and vector digitization.

The *raster scanning system* is a straight line principle of forming images. This *line* (light beam scan across screen) is broken up into elements called *pixels*. The total image has

many of these pixels in each scan. One of these lines of pixels is called a *raster*.

Raster image acquisition is possible for continuous tone photography, line work, and most materials given to the printer. The source material is placed on a drum or flat bed scanner in reflective or transparent form. The resolution of the final image can vary greatly. The greater the number of pixels per inch, the greater will be the *resolution* (detail) or quality of the image. A typical range would be from 1000 to over 2000 pixels or lines per inch.

When analyzing image acquisition, one can quickly realize that a great amount of information must be captured to proceed to the next step.

Vector images are generally associated with computer assisted design/computer assisted manufacturing (CAD/CAM) since point-to-point lines are generated as segments. These segments are called *vectors*. This system of electronic imagery is NOT common to the printing industry.

Image processing

Once the image acquisition is completed, the next step is to manipulate this information. This comes under the heading of image processing. Image processing, as you will learn, is becoming more "electronic."

Image processing refers to such features as: sizing of images, determining wanted areas, zooming, assembling of a variety of images, creating masks, determining color or shading corrections, creating a variety of dot shapes, electronically creating vignettes, and changing tonal values. Fig. 16-25 is a typical system capable of processing features.

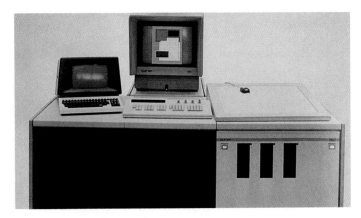

Fig. 16-25. This is another pre-press system. (Linotype-Hell)

Image recording

After the images have been processed, they need to be recorded. This means the images must be recorded as copy by a variety of output devices. The text and pictorial materials are placed on a substrate as hard copy. The recorded material can be made available as proofed material on plain paper or deposited directly onto laser sensitive plates for printing.

KNOW THESE TERMS

Photo modifications, Posterization, Two-tone posterization, Three-tone posterization, Multiple-tone posterization, Tone line technique, Duotone, Black-on-black duotone, Second color duotone, Fake duotone, True color duotone, Special effect screens, Diffusion transfer modifications, Phantom or ghost halftone, Electronic modifications, Image acquisition, Image processing, Image recording, Raster scanning, Pixel, Resolution.

REVIEW QUESTIONS—CHAPTER 16

1. Why would a designer want to use photo modifications?
2. _____ is the technique of changing a black and white, continuous tone picture into a multi-color or multi-tone reproduction.
3. What is the simplest method of producing a posterization?
4. In your own words, how do you make a posterization using a reflection gray scale?
5. Explain the tone-line process.
6. What are four types of duotones?
7. Why is it better to rotate the screen rather than the copy when making a duotone?
8. In your own words, how do you modify an image electronically?
9. Electronic modification replaces manual _____ and dot _____.
10. An image with 1000 pixels per inch would have more resolution than one with 2000 pixels per inch. True or false?

SUGGESTED ACTIVITIES

1. Select two publications and identify modification techniques.
2. Visit an ad agency and find out how they determine when to use special effects.
3. Use a pre-press system to acquire, process, and record an image.

For proper reproduction, color transparencies must be viewed in light of the proper color temperature. A color viewing booth like this one makes selection of transparencies easier. (Chapter One, Screaming Color)

Chapter 17

PROCESSING PHOTOGRAPHIC MATERIAL

After studying this chapter, you will be able to:
* Identify the equipment needed to process film.
* Explain manual and automatic developing processes.
* Summarize the chemical solutions necessary to process film.
* Identify the basic steps required to process film.
* State the precautions to follow when mixing and working with chemicals.
* Develop film using the manual tray development technique.
* Summarize the operating procedures for an automatic film processor.

Film processing is needed to make the latent images from exposure visible. The invisible images are created when the lights of the process camera are turned on. The light reflects, or is transmitted, from the copy through the camera lens to the photosensitive material. The latent image can also be produced on a scanner, as was discussed in Chapter 15. The film emulsion is chemically changed by its exposure.

Various methods are available to process this film in a chemical solution. Before describing typical processing techniques, however, you should be familiar with processing facilities.

DARKROOM

A *darkroom* is a light-tight or light-free work area for processing film. Any white light in this area could expose and ruin the latent image. A darkroom is used to develop film, make contact prints, and other tasks that cannot be done in normal light. Fig. 17-1 shows a basic layout of a typical darkroom.

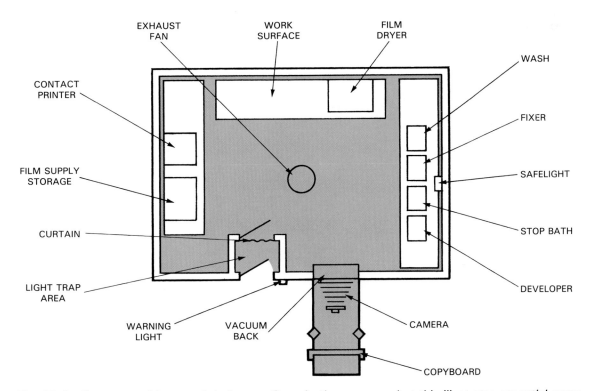

Fig. 17-1. Note general layout of darkroom. Organization can vary but this illustrates essential areas.

The term *roomlight* refers to the normal, full spectrum light found in areas other than a darkroom. *Safelight* refers to special, limited spectrum lighting that will not expose films.

Darkroom equipment

Certain pieces of equipment are commonly found in a darkroom. You should be familiar with these.

The *camera back,* for holding and exposing film, varies with the darkroom camera manufacturers. Fig. 17-2 shows

Fig. 17-2. Process camera back is normally inside darkroom. Then film can be loaded and unloaded in safelight area.

a typical unit. It has the normal vacuum frame for drawing the film down flush against the glass. A vertical camera or contact printer are also common but they require extra darkroom space.

Another important piece of darkroom equipment is the *processing sink* for containing the developing chemicals. Some factors to consider when buying a sink are:
1. Size of trays to be used.
2. Ease of cleaning.
3. Corrosive resistance.
4. Proper draining.
5. Ease of installation.
6. Maintenance requirements.

Stainless steel and fiberglass are two very popular materials used to construct a processing sink. Temperature controls are essential to maintain the proper cooling or heating of the water in the sink.

A *film processor* automatically processes or develops the photosensitive materials. These machines are found in many facilities, especially in high volume plants. The amount of chemicals used make it a costly item. Where consistency and control are essential, the film processor must be considered. This piece of equipment will be discussed later in this chapter.

Processing trays hold the chemicals for processing film. These trays come in various sizes. The two most common types of materials used in trays are stainless steel and plastic. In some cases, the cost of the stainless steel trays is prohibitive.

Film dryers are for rapid moisture removal from film. They are available in various sizes and styles. Fig. 17-3 shows one type. Some facilities will have a simple system of hanging up film to let it air dry.

Fig. 17-3. Film can be hung up in darkroom to air dry. However, film dryer will speed up operation.

Storage of chemicals and photosensitive materials can be a problem. Planning is essential for an efficient and effective darkroom. Most chemicals require a cool, dry area. Film is stored in *film storage cabinets* or, in some cases, a refrigerator.

Note! Storage of chemicals and photosensitive materials in the same area might affect film emulsions. Keep them stored separately.

A working surface in the darkroom is often very desirable since *trimmers* and/or *cutters* are often needed in the darkroom.

Safelights for proper illumination, without film exposure, in the darkroom are also essential. The type of safelight is determined by the type of photosensitive emulsions or film that will be used in the darkroom, Fig. 17-4. Usually, it is necessary to have several different filters which can be placed in or over the safelight. Then the light frequency emission will not affect the emulsion.

Fig. 17-4. Many types of safelights are available for working with film. Selection and use must be given high priority. (NuArc)

DARK ROOM

KEEP DOOR CLOSED!!

IF IT IS LEFT OPEN
ALL OF THE DARK
LEAKS OUT.

Fig. 17-5. If darkroom does not have light tight entrance, a sign or warning light is needed to prevent accidental exposure of film to room light from someone opening door.

Darkroom ventilation

Proper *ventilation* is required in the darkroom to prevent a buildup of chemical fumes. The amount of air exchange is set by federal, state, and local regulations. These regulations must be followed to be in compliance with the law.

In some cases, the system includes the removal of dust particles from the air. This too is important for quality assurance and safety in the darkroom.

Warning! Do not work with darkroom chemicals in an unventilated area. Chemical fumes, if inhaled, can be harmful.

Darkroom entrances

The darkroom is intended to be light tight, Fig. 17-5. The *darkroom entrance* must NOT let light enter the darkroom. Several types of entrances are very practical.

One of the simplest accesses to a darkroom is the open passage. The "C" or "S" pattern is often used as a darkroom entrance when ventilation is a consideration. Rapid entry and exit is another reason for its desirability. However, this entrance requires extra space consideration. See Fig. 17-6.

The double entrance door is another means of making the darkroom light tight. It requires less space. Opening both doors at one time could be a problem, however. Sometimes, darkroom cloth is used in place of one of the doors or both in some cases. See Fig. 17-7.

Revolving doors are also available from suppliers. These systems require very little space, but are more expensive. Refer to Fig. 17-8.

The size and type of entrance primarily depends on the type of facility. Choose the one which allows for an efficient operation. Planning is essential!

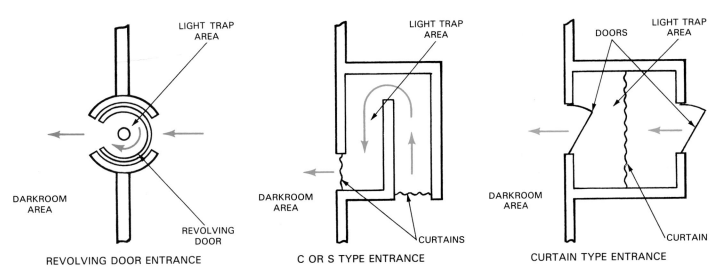

Fig. 17-6. Here are a few types of darkroom entrances.

271

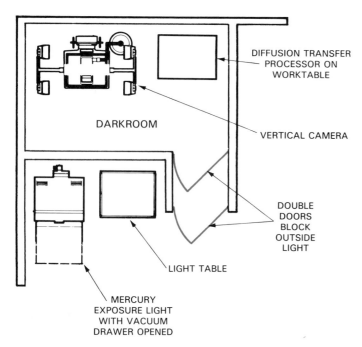

Fig. 17-7. Note use of this double-door darkroom entrance. Vertical camera and diffusion transfer processor are located in this darkroom.

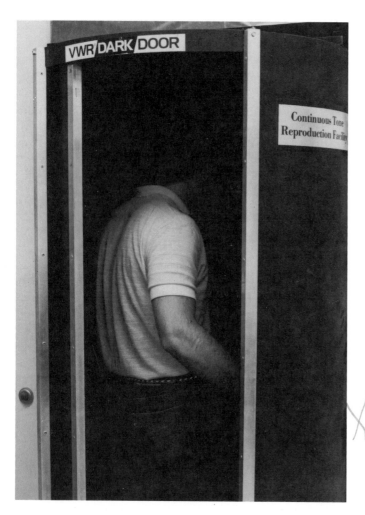

Fig. 17-8. Here worker is entering darkroom through revolving door.

CHEMICAL PROCESSING MATERIALS

Chemicals are necessary to process light sensitive materials. Many different kinds of light sensitive materials are on the market today. Each of the materials has recommended processing chemicals.

Mixing the chemicals properly is very critical. Each manufacturer has a recommended formula to follow. Exact measurement is important to assure consistency.

The containers for holding chemicals must be clean. Contamination can be a problem if someone is careless.

Note! If the same container and stirring rods are used for each chemical, make sure they are thoroughly cleaned before the mixing of each chemical.

Chemicals are necessary for mixing developer, stop bath, and fixing solutions.

Developer

Several chemicals make up the developer solution. They also vary according to their specific purpose.

The main ingredient in developer is *water* and it acts as the *vehicle*. It carries the material that develops the silver bromide crystals in the film. The water also has the function of swelling the film gelatin so that the solution can easily reach the crystals.

Another ingredient is the *developing agent*. The purpose of this ingredient is to change the latent image to a visible image. This is accomplished by changing the silver halide crystals to dark black metallic silver. The developing agent works best in an alkaline solution.

A more alkaline solution increases the developing action, therefore; it is called an *accelerator*.

The development of the photographic material becomes more rapid when the alkaline solution is increased. Developing agents are very susceptible to oxidation. The oxygen in the water destroys the developing agent. When this occurs, the developing action stops.

Because of this action, another chemical must be added to stop oxidation. This chemical is called a *preservative*. A typical preservative is sodium sulphite.

Another chemical is necessary to lessen the fogging tendency of film. *Fogging* means that the unexposed crystals have a tendency to develop in the developing solution. The chemical to help eliminate this process is called a *restrainer*. A typical restrainer is potassium bromide.

Again, proper mixing of chemicals is essential. Follow the manufacturer's instructions. Each developer has a specific and important purpose. Look at Fig. 17-9.

Stop bath

The *stop bath* is an acidic solution used to neutralize the developer solution remaining on the film. The chemical used for this purpose is acetic acid. About 2 ounces (59 mL) of 28 percent acetec acid, added to one gallon (3.78 L) of water, will make stop bath solution.

Acetic acid is one of the safest acids to use to make a stop bath. Extreme care must still be taken when mixing chemicals. Make sure all containers are labeled.

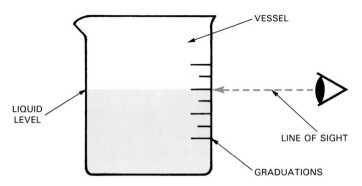

Fig. 17-9. Measurement is critical when mixing processing chemicals. When measuring liquids, hold vessel level and have eye even with graduations.

Warning! It is suggested that you wear eye protection when mixing and developing chemicals. This could prevent painful eye burns if accidentally splashed in your face. Gloves and chemical aprons are also recommended.

Fixing

A *fixer* is another solution needed to make the photographic image permanent. The prime purpose of the *fixing solution* is to remove the unexposed and/or underdeveloped crystals to clear and fix the film emulsion. The fixer also has a water vehicle. The water carries several ingredients. The chemical that dissolves out the exposed crystals is thiosulfate. Often, sodium thiosulfate is used and is commonly referred to as *hypo*.

A preservative is needed to stop the formation of sulphur. Sodium sulfite works well. The fixing solution needs to be acid. Acetic acid is often used for this purpose although boric acid can be added to help eliminate sludge.

The emulsion is soft and easily damaged; therefore, a hardener must be added. The *hardener* makes the emulsion more compact and dense.

PROCESSING FILM

Several processing techniques are used today. The three most common types are: tray, tank, and automatic. The two most common in the printing industry are tray processing and machine processing.

Tray processing, although slow, is still very evident in industry. However, machine processing is becoming more prevalent. Tray processing will be with the industry for a long time as a technique for specialized processing as well as a backup for machine processing.

Machine processing is intended for high volume output. Machine processing also gives consistent quality when properly monitored.

Processing is a critical operation because of the many variables. The object is to photographically convert the image with the results being very precise. The gray scale will be an aim point. It is one way to have quality control and assure consistency. This step will be illustrated after describing how the film is developed.

As illustrated in Fig. 17-10, most facilities that process film by hand will use the following steps:
1. Development.
2. Stop bath.
3. Fix.
4. Wash.
5. Dry.

Using developer

Once the film has been exposed, an invisible latent image is physically placed on the film. The developing process makes this image visible.

Developers may be purchased in powder or liquid form. Both types must be mixed with water, but extreme care must be taken not to splash the liquid or breathe the dust from the powder.

FILM PROCESSING

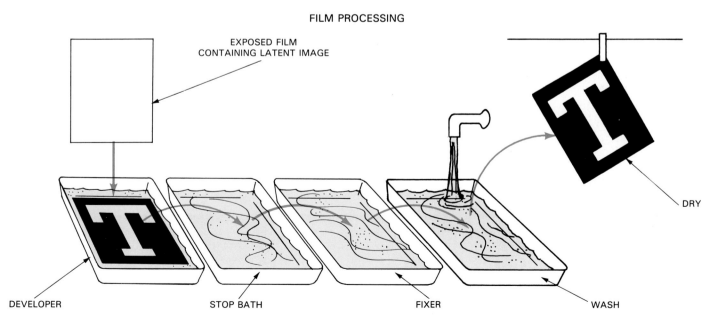

Fig. 17-10. Most film processing techniques require development, stop bath, fixing, washing, and then drying.

Warning! Wear appropriate protective devices when developing film. Also, add the chemical to the water, NOT the water to the chemical.

Once the developer chemicals are mixed, place the recommended amounts in the developer tray. Most film manufacturer's recommend that the temperature of the developer be at 20°C or 68°F.

For tray processing, the film is placed in the developer with the emulsion side up. This eliminates the possibility of the tray scratching the film, Fig. 17-11. At this point, the emulsion is soft and is very susceptible to damage.

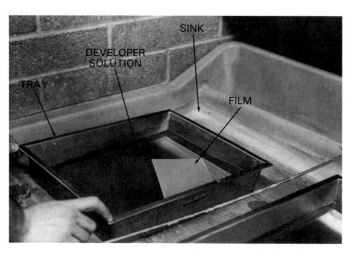

Fig. 17-11. Film is normally placed in developing solution with the emulsion side up. This helps prevent scratches on emulsion from tray.

The developing time must be established. The *timer* is one device that can be used to make sure the film is developed for the established time. The manufacturer will give the recommended development time.

Manufacturers normally recommend that the developer tray be continually rocked during the development processing stage. The motion is called *agitation*, Fig. 17-12. The

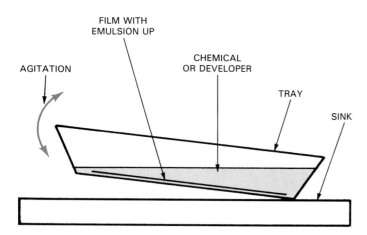

Fig. 17-12. Agitation is commonly used to prevent the image area from using up the chemicals in one area of the solution. Agitation keeps the chemicals equal in strength, even next to image area that uses more chemicals.

main reason for agitation is to keep the developer strength evenly distributed during the development of the film. If left stationary, the image areas requiring more development than others will make the chemicals become weak or spent.

The *gray scale,* which was used as an aim point, is really a sensitivity guide. It is used to show when the film has reached an acceptable density. The data sheets distributed by each manufacturer will give recommended densities. A solid step four, on a 12-step gray scale, might be a typical recommendation. Look at Fig. 17-13.

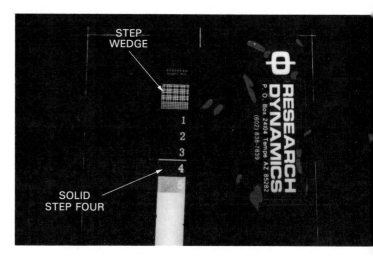

Fig. 17-13. Step wedge is a control device for checking chemicals and other variables. Wedge is run through chemicals and solid step four or recommended step should result. This is a quality control method of assuring good copy.

Note! Developer weakens with every processed piece of film. Some manufacturers will give you an idea of how many square inches of film can be processed in a given amount of developer.

Always have enough developer to completely cover the film.

The typical structure of film is illustrated in Fig. 17-14.

Time, temperature, developer strength, and agitation will affect film processing. They are critical considerations when developing film because image areas should remain white while nonimage areas must turn black (black and white film). See Fig. 17-15.

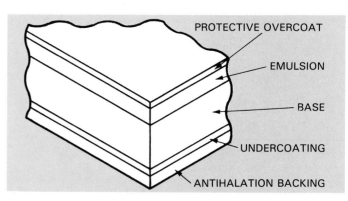

Fig. 17-14. Review basic structure of film.

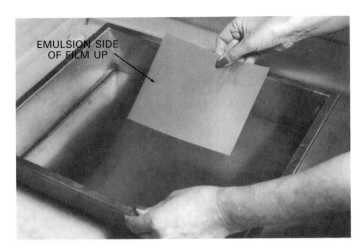

Fig. 17-15. Place film in developer so that all of the emulsion is covered. Agitation of tray is commonly used to make sure chemical works evenly.

Developer also oxidizes very rapidly. Covering the liquid with a piece of wax paper or a piece of plastic will increase the life of the developer when not in use. Do this carefully to prevent contamination.

The carriers for most types of ortho emulsions are: acetate, polyester, and polystyrene (plastic). The *acetate bases* are the least stable but are good films to be used for scribing. The *polyesters* are very stable base films while the *polystyrene* are somewhat in between.

The two most common *carrier thicknesses* are .003 and .005 inch (0.08 and 0.13 mm). Much of the halftone work uses .003 inch (0.08 mm) while .007 inch (0.18 mm) is often used for circuit board work.

Film manufacturers will also designate a development time. This development time requires that the chemicals be mixed according to their specifications. The temperature must also be at specs, typically 20 °C or 68 °F.

Proper handling of the tray is also a basic requirement. Every piece of film must be developed in the same manner. Look at Fig. 17-16.

Using stop bath

Once the film is developed to the proper density, it should be removed from the developer and placed in the stop bath tray. Bringing the film over the edge allows most of the solution to drain back into the developer tray, Fig. 17-10.

The stop bath is a weak acid solution. As stated earlier, the most common type is acetic. Twenty-eight percent is a very common percentage or strength to have in stock.

Usually, one to two ounces of 28% acetic acid, added to a gallon of water, will make a very adequate solution to be used as a stop bath.

The intent of the solution is to stop all developing action. A period of eight to ten seconds in the stop bath should remove all traces of the developer. After that time, the film is removed and placed in the fixing solution. Use the same suggested means of removing the film from the tray.

Warning! Do NOT contaminate the developer with stop bath solution.

Using fixer

The fixer for ortho type films must be capable of dissolving the unexposed silver salts and hardening the nonimage areas. The hardening of the emulsion helps eliminate the possibility of scratching the surface. The milky-looking area is the image area and it must be cleared.

The amount of time allowed for fixing the emulsion varies. Some camera operators will say that double the length of time it takes the image area to clear is satisfactory time for many fixers. In some situations, the operator will remove the film as soon as it clears.

Sometimes, the production rush will not allow proper fixing. If the film is not properly fixed, however, it cannot be stored for any length of time because the image area will lose its transparent quality.

Washing

The film must be thoroughly washed to remove the chemicals, Fig. 17-17. A constant flow of fresh water is suggested. The length of time recommended by manufac-

Fig. 17-16. Slowly slide film out of developer so that chemical drains back into tray.

Fig. 17-17. Here film is being washed in tray.

turers varies. Twenty minutes, in a tank of moderately flowing water, is typical. It is possible that discoloration will take place if the chemicals are not totally removed.

When a film dryer is used, it is important that the chemicals are fully removed because the unremoved chemicals will deposit on the machine rollers. Dirty film dryer rollers could then damage the film.

Squeegee the film to remove the water and then hang it up to dry, Figs. 17-18 and 17-19. This is a very slow way of drying film. Using a film dryer, Fig. 17-20, is a much quicker way to dry film.

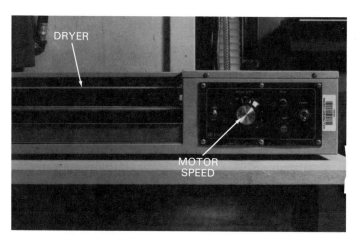

Fig. 17-20. Film dryer is needed when job is on tight deadline. Machine feed speed must be set properly for efficient operation of dryer.

TYPICAL TRAY PROCESSING PROCEDURE

The following procedure is commonly used to process litho type films.

Insert the exposed film in the developer with the emulsion side up. Not all manufacturers will recommend this method. Some recommended that you insert the film so that the emulsion touches the solution and then flip the film over. As stated earlier, scratching the film may be a problem until you gain experience.

The tray should be rocking in both directions or a circular motion. Rocking from left to right and front to back tends to distribute the developer evenly. Agitate until the proper gray scale step or the time specified has been reached (typically about 2 1/2 minutes).

Remove the film from the developer and transfer it to the stop bath.

Be careful not to contaminate the solutions. Try not to transfer developer into the stop bath. The best way is to take a corner of the film and slowly draw the film over the edge of the developer tray. This will not harm the film since the emulsion is up and will not be scratched.

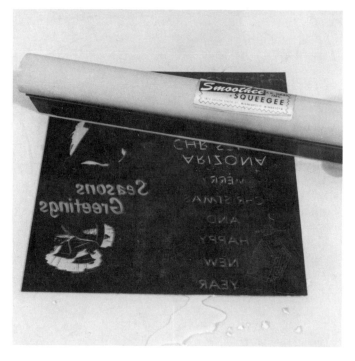

Fig. 17-18. Squeegee can be used to remove water from film before final drying.

Warning! Developer and other chemicals often tend to irritate the skin. If possible, use a pair of tongs or wear gloves that are compatible with the solutions. When the tongs or gloves touch another solution, contamination results. Wash your utensils thoroughly before placing them in any solution.

The film is placed in the stop bath with the emulsion side up. The time for the stop bath varies with the manufacturer. Five to ten seconds usually is sufficient time to stop all developing action.

Place the film in the fixer to dissolve the unexposed silver salts. The film should remain in the fixer for four to eight minutes for best results. Once cleared, it is possible to turn on the white lights if needed.

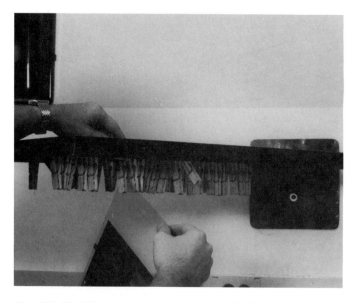

Fig. 17-19. Film can be hung up to dry if time is not critical for completion of job.

Remove the film from the fixing bath and place it in the wash sink. The water should be circulating. Generally, the minimum time is ten minutes, while the longest time is approximately thirty minutes. Twenty minutes is an average time but the water must be flowing during the washing time.

Remove and squeegee the film. Hang it up or place it in a film dryer. When dry, the film is ready to be used for the next step in the production process.

Still-tray development

As the name implies, *still-tray development* means the tray is NOT agitated during the developing process. The technique is used for heavy and fine line work and sometimes for halftone processing.

Place the film in the developing solution, emulsion up. First, agitate it and then leave it without movement. The recommended still time is suggested by the manufacturer of the developing solution or photosensitive material.

Using a fine line developer is also recommended for some types of images. The steps following the developing process are identical to the agitated-tray development method. Although this procedure is a hand-tray developing process, and slow, it is still commonly used today.

MECHANIZED PROCESSING

Mechanized processing uses a machine to automatically send the film through the chemicals for development, Fig. 17-21. The exposed film enters the processor dry and leaves the processor dry.

The typical steps for mechanized processing are:
1. Film travels through the developer.
2. Film travels through all solutions.
3. Film enters the wash cycle.
4. Film is dried.

To keep the developing solution in proper balance, a blender system is often used, Figs. 17-22 and 17-23. Many of the systems require a large quantity of chemicals. This can be very costly when the volume is not sufficient to keep the processor in constant operation.

Each processor is equipped with a system to control time for each step. Usually, the speed of film travel determines the time. The temperature and agitation is also automatically

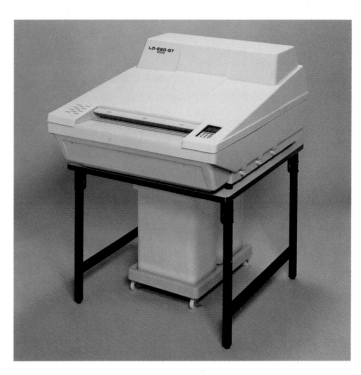

Fig. 17-22. This tabletop film processor has an automatic chemical replenisher for processing line film, contact film, RC paper, and high contrast rapid access film. This prevents developer fatigue and oxidation. (Screen - USA)

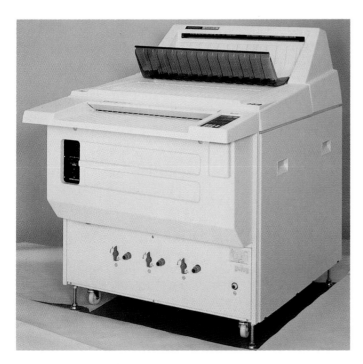

Fig. 17-21. This is a computerized rapid access film processor for processing contact, line, daylight, and scanner films. (Screen - USA)

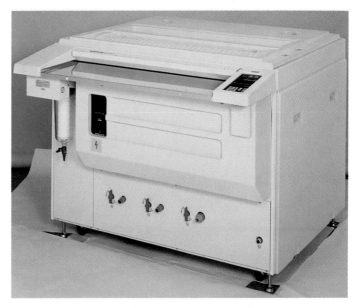

Fig. 17-23. Here is another model of a rapid access film processor for processing contact, line, daylight, and scanner films. (Screen - USA)

controlled. The time the film is in the machine varies from one machine to another, but a typical time is from six to twelve minutes.

Processor start-up

The following steps should be followed when placing all chemistry in the processing machine:

1. Clean all parts of the processor.
2. Make sure all filters are clean.
3. Mix fixer according to manufacturer's specifications.
4. Transfer fixer to processor.
5. Mix developer as specified by the manufacturer (continuous tone or lithographic).
6. Transfer developer to processor; use extreme care not to allow contamination.
7. Fill wash section of processor.
8. Set control settings.
9. Process control strip.
10. Mix and add replenisher to replenisher tanks.

Follow the specific operating instructions manual for the specific model of processor, Fig. 17-24. The temperature must be properly set. The speed must also be regulated. The flow system must also be regulated. Correct machine settings are essential for assuring quality.

Process control strips are essential to establish the machine settings and quality control, Fig. 17-25. Once the specific

control is attained, consistency will be assured. This means that every piece of photosensitive material is meeting quality standards. Any time the development of the control strip is above or below the recommended step, the automatic processor must be readjusted.

SPECIAL TYPES OF PROCESSING

Contacting is one of the special techniques requiring processing. *Contacting* results from taking an original negative or positive and contacting (exposing) it to a photosensitive material. The contact is the same size as the original. The processing of the materials can be by tray or machine.

Contact duplicate means the negative or positive is being duplicated. The processed image will be the same as the original.

Reversal processing is another method of making a positive from the original copy. It is not commonly found in the industry.

Stabilization

Many of today's photocomposition systems use a stabilization process to develop the photosensitive materials. The exposed material is passed through two solutions. The first is an *activator* that develops the materials and the second solution is a stabilizer. The *stabilizer* solution dissolves the unexposed emulsion and also acts as a fixer. The result is a permanent image on a photosensitive material, Fig. 17-26.

Most stabilization processors are in the darkroom, unless a light tight compartment is attached to the processor. The light tight area acts as a darkroom for the cassette holding the exposed photosensitive paper.

DIFFUSION TRANSFER

Diffusion transfer, also called PMT (abbreviation for *photomechanical transfer* by Kodak) is a means of creating

Fig. 17-24. Close-up of automatic processor for high volume work. It requires little space in the darkroom and can handle a large quantity of film, making it a good investment in most facilities.

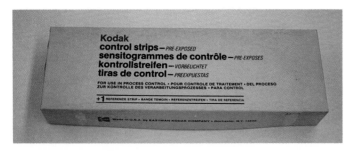

Fig. 17-25. Control strip is an indicator of processing chemicals, temperature, speed, and other variables. Read the directions provided with the specific control strips.

Fig. 17-26. Stabilization process develops and fixes the image. With improper stabilization, image could become "dirty" after a short period of time.

images directly on another carrier. It can be done with a contact printer or a process camera.

Diffusion transfer is commonly used in industry to make a duplicate of a pasted-up image. Then, if the image is lost or damaged, there is another copy of the original, Fig. 17-27.

The final diffusion transfer image can appear on an opaque surface or a transparent base, Fig. 17-28. The image can also be produced on a plate, ready for printing.

Chemical warning!

When anyone is mixing processing chemicals, extreme care must be taken. To fully understand the chemicals used to make developing solutions, follow the recommendations supplied by the solution manufacturer.

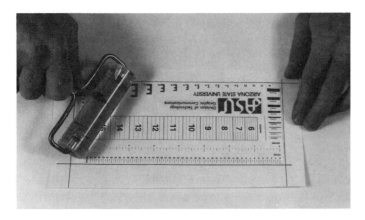

Fig. 17-27. With diffusion transfer, image is placed on another substrate as a single unit. This provides protection and a backup image in case the original is lost or damaged.

Fig. 17-28. When using diffusion transfer material, follow the suggestions given by the manufacturer. This will result in good reproduction of the original image.

KNOW THESE TERMS

Processing, Developing, Darkroom, Roomlight, Safelight, Camera back, Processing sink, Film processor, Film dryer, Processing tray, Film cabinet, Developer, Vehicle, Accelerator, Preservative, Stop bath, Fixing solution, Hardener, Machine processing, Tray processing, Agitation, Gray scale, Acetate base, Polyester base, Process control strips, Contacting, Reversal processing, Contact duplicates, Activator, Diffusion transfer.

REVIEW QUESTIONS—CHAPTER 17

1. The area normally used to process film is called the _____.
2. What are two materials commonly used to make processing sinks?
3. Explain six factors that should be considered when purchasing a processing sink.
4. Hand-processing in trays is more efficient than an automatic film processor and it produces higher quality results. True or false?
5. _____ _____ are for rapid removal of moisture from developed film.
6. Explain three types of darkroom entrances.
7. Water, also called the _____, is a main ingredient in the developer solution.
8. How does the developing agent make the latent image visible?
9. This is an acetic solution used to neutralize the developer.
    a. Fixing solution.
    b. Agitation solution.
    c. Restraining solution.
    d. Stop bath solution.
10. A preservative is needed to stop the formation of _____.
11. When mixing developer and water, you should pour the water into the developer. True or false?
12. What is the main reason for agitation?
13. In your own words, describe how to do tray processing for litho film.
14. When is still-tray development used?
15. List ten steps to follow when placing the chemistry in a processing machine.

SUGGESTED ACTIVITIES

1. Identify five light sensitive materials and identify the techniques normally used to process them.
2. While visiting a facility, check the technique used to process materials automatically.
3. Use the tray technique to develop film.

Stripping involves attaching films to a base sheet. The resulting flat is used to make the printing plate. (Foster Manufacturing)

Chapter 18

STRIPPING AND IMPOSITION

After studying this chapter, you will be able to:
- Explain the purpose of stripping.
- Identify the materials, tools, and equipment commonly used by the stripper.
- Explain the three basic imposition layouts used in industry.
- Explain the basic steps required to produce a single color flat.
- Explain the reason for accurately positioning of materials to assure quality.
- Describe the various types of flats.

Lithographic imposition is the layout and stripping of the films made from the original layout sheet. The *layout* is needed to indicate the positioning of all negatives or positives on the flat, Fig. 18-1. The *flat* consists of assembled images (films) on a support sheet. One type of support is called a *masking sheet.*

Stripping is the process of image assembly. Image assembly requires the positioning and attaching of all types of films to the support sheeting. The person doing this type of work is called a "*stripper.*" The flat is used to make the printing plate.

Making the flat is a very critical part of the pre-press activities. Therefore, planning is essential for an efficient and effective department. Following directions and working accurately is critical. Any mistake becomes very obvious because it shows up on the finished product. Reruns of the product are very costly.

The stripping department is an area of the printing facility that is changing. Automation and electronic applications are eliminating the stripping activity in large facilities. Even with these changes, manual stripping will be around for some time.

STRIPPING TOOLS AND EQUIPMENT

Since accuracy is an essential element of stripping, the equipment must be of high quality. This means it must be durable and rugged, but designed to be efficient, accurate, and convenient.

Stripping tables

The *stripping table* or *light table* is an illuminated work surface, Fig. 18-2. It allows the stripper to see the film better. The illumination should be even throughout the total working area. The glass surface should have diffused light with no evidence of *hot spots* (brighter areas). Many stripping tables have edges that are true on all four sides, for use with a T-square.

Layout and/or *line up tables* are precision pieces of equipment. They are used to accurately prepare layouts or check finished flats. One is shown in Fig. 18-3.

Many of the line up devices have micrometer adjustments and have the capability of holding scribing and ruling devices. Storage equipment must also be considered when it is necessary to store finished flats, films, tools, and other materials.

Punches are also needed to make holes in the masking sheet as well as the plate to assure exact alignment, Fig. 18-4.

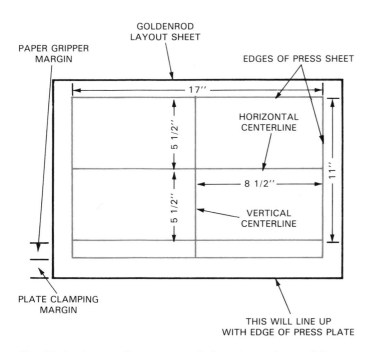

Fig. 18-1. Layout lines are needed on base sheet of flat to properly locate film and to locate sheets on press.

A

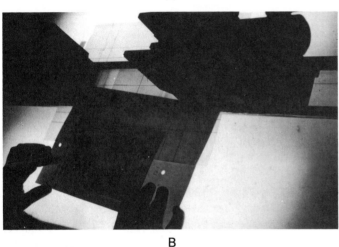

B

Fig. 18-2. A—A light table is commonly used for stripping films onto base sheet. Light shines through paper and film to make positioning of images easier. B—Stripping using light table with copy punch attachment.

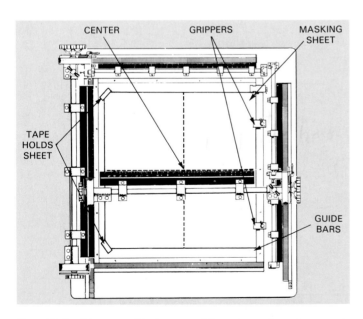

Fig. 18-3. Line up table is a precision piece of equipment. It will help align images when stripping. Line up table is useful when working on several masking sheets with same guide lines. (NuArc)

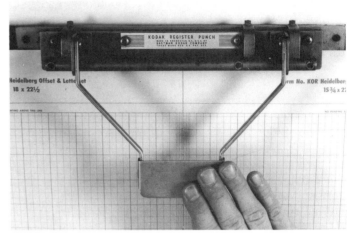

Fig. 18-4. This register punch will accurately make holes in goldenrod or base sheet. Then register pins can be inserted through holes to keep everything in register. This can also be used to punch alignment holes in the plate.

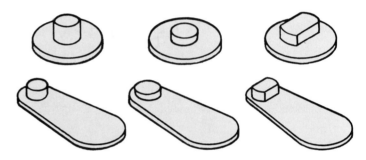

Fig. 18-5. These are a few types of register pins.

Register pins are used to hold the sheets for the stripping of photographic materials, Fig. 18-5.

Many of the tools used by strippers have been discussed in earlier chapters. Therefore, the description will be very limited for some tools.

The measuring devices, rules and scales, must be chosen according to the accuracy required by the stripper for the job. Steel and plastic are two types of material used as measuring instruments, steel being more common in stripping. Many of the scales or rules can be used as a straightedge as well as a measuring device, Fig. 18-6. The

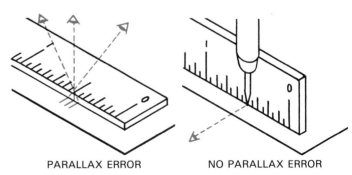

PARALLAX ERROR   NO PARALLAX ERROR

Fig. 18-6. Accuracy is critical when stripping. When drawing lines, scribing lines, or making measurements, view straight down at the scale. This will prevent parallax error.

straightedge must have a true smooth edge. The edge should not be affected by knives, scribers, pens, pencils, and needles.

T-squares and triangles are needed to align film and other materials, Fig. 18-7. They are also needed to be a true edge for drawing layout lines, control marks, outlines, or any other activity required for layout or stripping the flat.

Irregular curves are used in the stripping department to act as a guide for opaquing irregular shapes, Fig. 18-8.

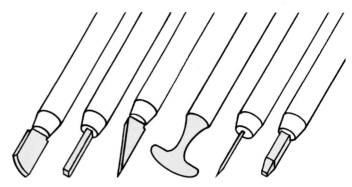

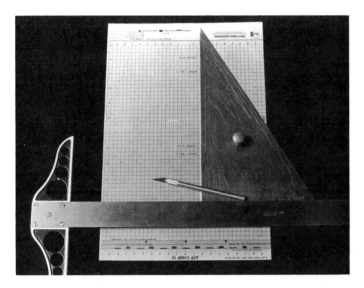

Fig. 18-7. Pre-printed masking sheets can be purchased but they must match the plate size of the press.

Fig. 18-8. Irregular curve is sometimes needed for forming irregular lines or shapes.

Dividers and other drafting tools such as compasses, ruling pens, and protractors are also useful to the stripper.

Stripping knives, Fig. 18-9, and sturdy scissors are essential as cutting tools. Fine felt tip and ball point pens and mechanical pencils are basic marking devices.

Screen angle indicators are needed to determine screen angles of halftones and tints, Fig. 18-10. Whenever a tint or halftone area overlaps, the indicator will help determine the correct angle to eliminate a moiré pattern, Fig. 18-11. Some screen angle indicators will also assist in determining the screen ruling of materials.

Fig. 18-9. These are the shapes of some of the scribing and cutting tools used by the stripper.

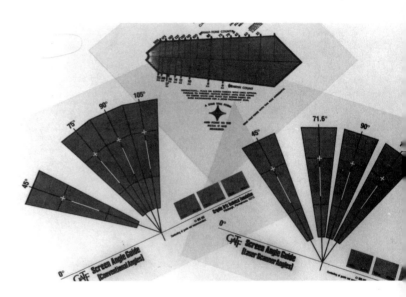

Fig. 18-10. Many types of screen angle indicators are used by the stripper. They allow correct screen angles to produce a high quality image.

MOIRÉ PATTERN

Fig. 18-11. If screen angles are incorrect, it can cause an unwanted moiré pattern that forms a muddy dot pattern on the image.

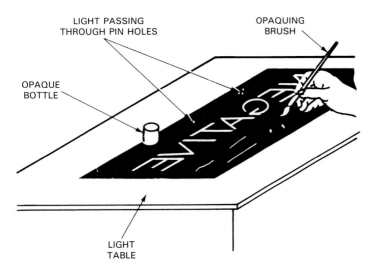

Fig. 18-12. Opaque solution is used to touch up tiny imperfections in the negatives. Any unwanted light passing through a negative will cause ink to deposit on the plate and printing substrate.

Brushes are also needed by the stripper to opaque film, Fig. 18-12. The brushes should be made of high quality hair. Low quality brushes are difficult to control when fine, quality work is required. Care of brushes is very important. Brushes for other types of operations are also used in some facilities, such as applying rubber cement for adhering materials together.

Magnifiers and collimators are used to examine the film. Refer to Fig. 18-13.

Magnifiers with a power of 10x or 12x (ten or twelve times actual size) are very typical. They are used for general examination of film, Fig. 18-14.

The *collimator* is used when the visible line of sight is in a straight line. This assists in eliminating parallax error. The collimator would be used to make sure the register marks are properly lined up when two or more overlays are used. Sighting with a regular magnifier cannot assure that the marks are lined up properly. An illusion can result because of the viewing angle.

Fig. 18-14. Here stripper is using magnifier to inspect quality of images for a job.

Materials for stripping

The first material to be discussed is the base substrate used to support the photographic materials. The most common support, commonly called *base material,* is *photo-mask paper.* This material blocks all actinic light when preparing a negative flat. The color of the material blocks all light that will expose light sensitive coatings. It is available as a goldenrod, orange, or red color.

The most common, goldenrod paper, is often purchased preprinted to meet the size requirement of a specific press, Fig. 18-15. Goldenrod unprinted stock is available in various sizes and can be cut to meet the press plate specifications. Often, a master sheet is laid out and used as a base for all flats. Larger presses seldom use preprinted base sheets.

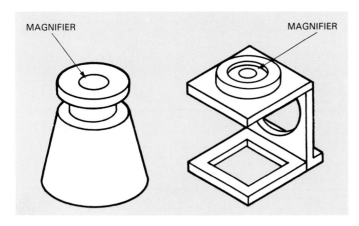

Fig. 18-13. A magnifying device will help you examine images. They help you to look straight down at surface and enlarge image for better inspection.

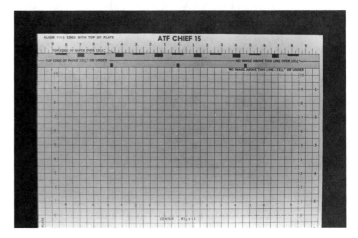

Fig. 18-15. The pre-printed press sheet size is determined by the size of the printing press.

Paper vs plastic base

Two types of base materials are commonly used by the stripper. They are paper and plastic.

The *paper base* is very satisfactory for many jobs but it lacks high STABILITY. This means the paper is affected by moisture and heat. A size change is possible.

For this reason, goldenrod *plastic sheeting* is used for jobs that need a high degree of accuracy.

The goldenrod paper and plastic is used for negative type stripping. Whenever positive film flats are needed, a clear plastic sheeting is used. *Vinyl sheeting* is affected by temperature. Because of this, the stripper might choose an acetate or polyester sheeting.

Most would consider the goldenrod and plastic materials as one-time-use materials. Selecting the masking material will be determined by the specifications on the job.

Photographic films

Film negatives and positives are used by the stripper to produce flats, Fig. 18-16. These films must be of high quality to produce sharp printing detail.

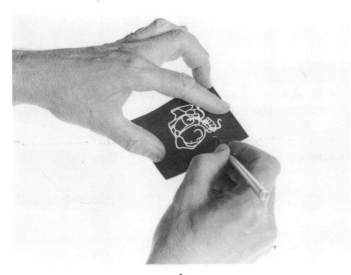

A

B

Fig. 18-16. Stripper can be required to work with both negatives and positives. A—Here stripper is scribing line on negative. B—Negatives attached to light table.

The thicknesses of the film will vary. The most common thicknesses are from .003 to .007 in. (0.08 to 0.18 mm). The thinner films are generally used when the two films are over each other. The materials must lie flat so they do not distort the image.

The base side of the film is in contact with the masking sheet. The emulsion side is in contact with the plate or proofing material.

Supplies for stripping

Some of the many supplies used by the stripper include: adhesives, ink, opaque, control marks, register pins, etc.

Tapes of various types are used to hold the base material. *Drafting tape* is recommended for that purpose, although *masking transparent* or *translucent tapes* are also used by the stripper. *Lithographer's tape* is an effective means of holding film on the masking sheet. This tape is also used to block out areas on the negative that are not going to print.

Double-coated tapes are sometimes used to adhere one film to another or to the masking sheet. Some double-coated tapes require a special dispenser.

Dispensers are available for most tapes. They are a convenient and efficient way to remove the required amount of tape.

Various colors of ink are also needed. Non-reproducing blue and black are the two most common types.

Opaquing solutions, in both red and black, are used by the stripper to block out unwanted images on negatives. The solution is used to touch up detail on positives. Which type of opaque to use depends on the type of work. The selection should be made by the stripper. The opaque is usually applied with a brush, but pens and applicators are also available.

Control marks, as well as *pins, tabs,* and *dowels,* are also used by the stripper. They assist in correct positioning for complimentary flats. This is imperative to assure register with each plate or proof. The tabs or pins are also valuable guides for *step-and-repeat work* to expose the same image more than once.

Cleaning solutions are available for cleaning the films. The solution must not leave a residue. Most commercial cleaners are very satisfactory.

MECHANICS OF LAYOUT

Fundamentals of page location and their numerical position and bindery folding sequence must be understood by the stripper. To assist in positioning pages, the stripper should make a "dummy."

Dummy

The *dummy* is a folded representation of the finished job, Fig. 18-17. Right angle and parallel folding are the two most common types of dummies.

The *right angle fold* is one in which each succeeding fold is made at right angles to the preceding one, Fig. 18-18A.

The *parallel fold* is one where all folds are parallel with the other. The first fold is made from the center out, Fig. 18-18B. The final page size with the correct fold is important.

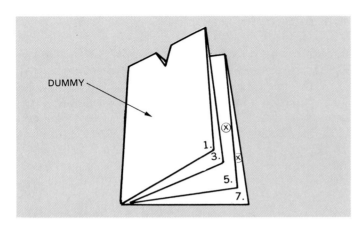

Fig. 18-17. The dummy is a folded representation of the form or signature.

For example, the booklet may have 16 pages. Three folds will be required and the binding side has been indicated. Follow this procedure:

1. Fold the dummy.
2. Cut three sides of a rectangle in the dummy.
   a. The first cut is parallel with the top.
   b. Make a vertical cut opposite the fold side.
   c. The third cut is made parallel to bottom, Fig. 18-19.
3. Fold the cut sections open. The sides to be folded are toward the fold of the booklet.
4. After the rectangular cuts have been folded, number the pages, Fig. 18-20.
5. Draw a line under each number, Fig. 18-20. The head of each page is now easily identified.
6. The dummy can then be unfolded to clearly show the page sequence.

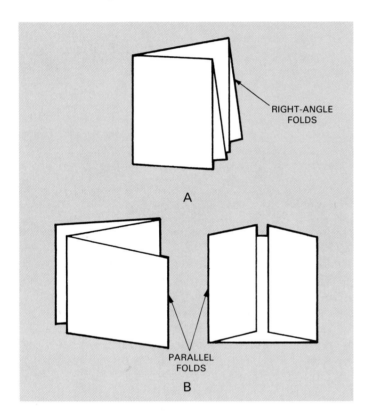

Fig. 18-18. A—Right angle fold means that each fold is at right angles to the preceeding fold. B—A parallel fold has all folds parallel with each other.

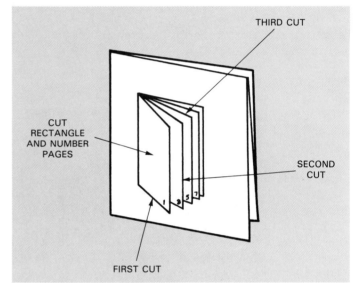

Fig. 18-19. Here windows have been cut in dummy. Cuts can be folded out and numbered. Then, the dummy can be opened up to see positioning of each page on flat.

Whenever page sizes are given, follow the rule that states the specific width measurement is given FIRST. The height measurement is given SECOND. This is called *printer's custom.*

When the printer wants to designate the binding dimension, the binding dimension is underlined, such as: 8 1/2 x 11 inch or 3 x 5 inch.

Page sequence

The layout of the pages can be confusing. Establishing the page sequence can be easily accomplished by folding a dummy. The number of pages must be known.

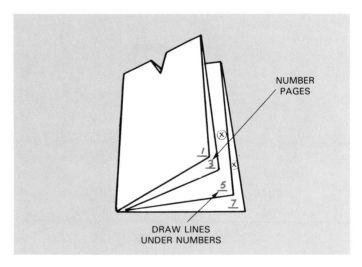

Fig. 18-20. Always draw a line under the numbers because the top of the number indicates the head of the form.

Choosing imposition format

Jobs must be positioned to fit a specific press. Printers have a variety of presses, yet each plant might have a limited number of presses. *Imposition* is the laying out of images to match the job to the available equipment. Different size formats, page configuration, and the number of pages must be given consideration.

Several terms must be considered before discussing the popular press layouts. They are one-up, step-and-repeat, and combination.

One-up means that one impression will be made on a side of the substrate.

Step-and-repeat is the term referring to the same image being repeated on the plate. Sometimes, a small form is stepped and repeated to fill the image area of the plate. Images are also stepped and repeated when a long run is required. Repeating the images reduces press time.

A combination layout is sometimes used to utilize the full area of a plate. Step-and-repeat is the same form, a *combination* is made up of various size forms on the same printed sheet.

PRESS LAYOUTS

Three types of press layouts are commonly used in the industry: Sheetwise, work-and-turn, and work-and-tumble. You should understand their differences.

Sheetwise

A *sheetwise layout* is generally used when two sides of the sheet are to be printed with a separate form. The front side of the sheet would have one image while the back side would have another image. Since the images are different, two separate printing plates are required.

The press gripper edge is the same for both plates but the guide edge will change. The first image would use the left guide while the back up image would use the right guide since the sheet has been turned over. In this case, pages one and two are printed on one side while three and four are printed on the second side. Look at Fig. 18-21.

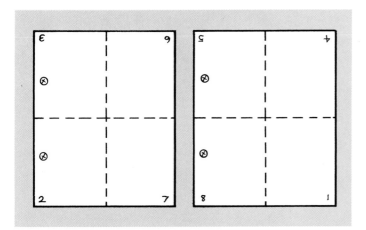

Fig. 18-21. The sheetwise layout uses same gripper edge but different press guides. (NuArc)

Work-and-turn

The *work-and-turn* is twice as large as would be needed for running the job sheetwise. All of the images that appear on one side of the sheet will be repeated on the reverse side. Pages one, two, three, and four would be printed on one side and then printed on the reverse side. The sheet has been turned end for end. The gripper edge is the same for both sides but the press guide is changed. Refer to Fig. 18-22.

Work-and-turn saves half the time as sheetwise imposition and uses only one plate. The work-and-turn imposition requires a larger press size, however.

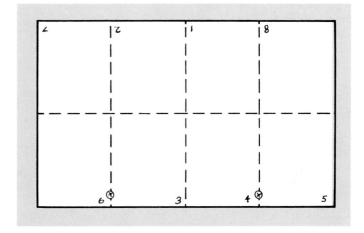

Fig. 18-22. With work-and-turn, all of the images printed on one side of the sheet will be printed on the other side.

Work-and-tumble

Work-and-tumble imposition also requires the sheet to be twice as large as sheetwise imposition. The top half and the bottom half become a set.

Work-and-tumble imposition requires different press gripper edges. The top becomes one gripper edge and then the sheet is tumbled and the bottom becomes the gripper edge. Only one side guide is used. Work-and-tumble imposition uses only one plate and requires only one press make ready. See Fig. 18-23.

The two gripper positions requires that the sheets must be trimmed and squared on all four sides.

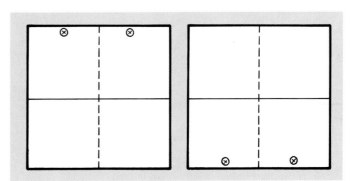

Fig. 18-23. With work-and-tumble, the top and bottom of the sheet become gripper edges.

Bleed

Several other techniques must be known by the stripper. The first of these is the term bleed.

Whenever any type of image extends to the edge of the printed page, it is called a *bleed*. Because it runs to the very edge of the page, an allowance must be made. This requires that the printing area extend slightly beyond the trim-page size. The little extra allows the person cutting the stock to make sure all of the image is off the page.

Creep

Whenever a thick saddle-stitched booklet is folded, a problem develops called *creep*. A thick saddle-stitched booklet causes the center pages to be a different dimension than the outside pages. A size difference exists. Fig. 18-24 gives an example.

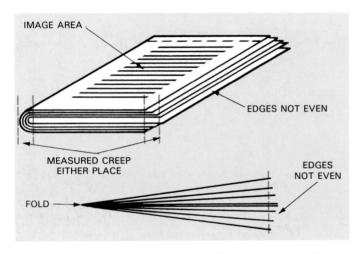

Fig. 18-24. Creep results from folding of signature. Center sheets stick out more than front and back sheets.

Creep allowance must be considered. The stripper can allow for creep by requesting a complete folded dummy. The paper for the dummy must be the same as planned to be used for the job.

Many booklets are not critical enough to consider creep. Whenever alignment is required, however, creep must be considered.

Signature

A *signature* is a sheet printed on both sides and folded in a sequence of 4, 8, 16, or 32 pages. One is shown in Fig. 18-25.

An eight page signature, for example, would have four pages printed on one side and four pages printed on the other side. The sheet would be folded and ready for trimming and binding.

Various terms are used to indicate the parts of a signature. There terms are used by both the stripping and bindery departments.

The various terms relating to a signature include:

1. The *head* is the top portion or edge of the signature, Fig. 18-25.

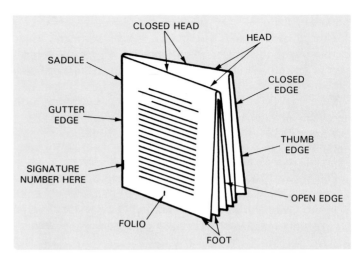

Fig. 18-25. Note basic parts of folded signature.

2. The *thumb edge* is the edge where you would touch or spread the signature to turn the pages.
3. The *bind edge* is the outside edge, opposite the thumb edge. It is the same as the *saddle edge* or *spine edge* that forms the backbone of the finished booklet.
4. *Gutter* is sometimes used to refer to the inside of the bind edge or saddle edge.
5. An *open side* or *edge* is an edge that is NOT folded and the pages can be opened without cutting or trimming.
6. A *closed side* or *edge* is an edge that is folded and must be cut or trimmed to separate the pages.
7. The *foot* is the bottom of the signature.
8. The *signature number* or *mark* is printed on the spine or saddle edge to designate the sequence of the signatures. It assures that all of the signatures are in order for binding.
9. The *folio* refers to the page number of the signature.
10. The *front folio* is the lowest page number in the signature.

STRIPPING PROCEDURES

Basic black and white stripping is the assembling of negatives in a prescribed location and attaching them to a base, masking, or goldenrod sheet. The finished product, as mentioned, is called a flat.

The reason for assembling the negatives is to hold them in place while making an appropriate printing process image carrier or proof. This section of the chapter explains how to establish correct positioning of the printing image.

Stripping preparation

Preparation is the first step or stage of stripping. The stripper must check all of the negatives for opacity and opaquing. All dimensions must be checked. Control marks must be in their correct location—both register marks and cut marks.

The *job ticket* gives the stripper the information needed to do the job. When preparing, the stripper will use the ticket as a reference. A sample ticket is given in Fig. 18-26. Note the information on the ticket.

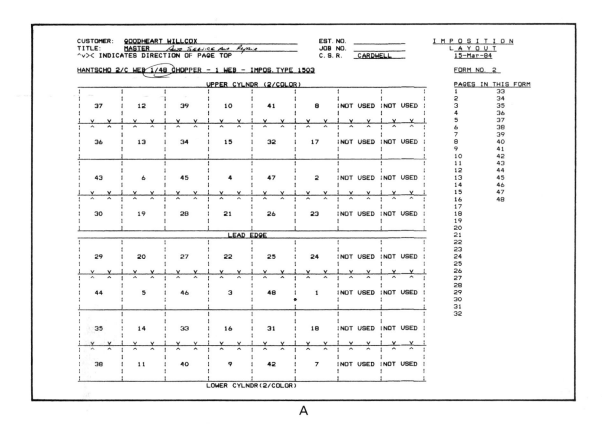

A

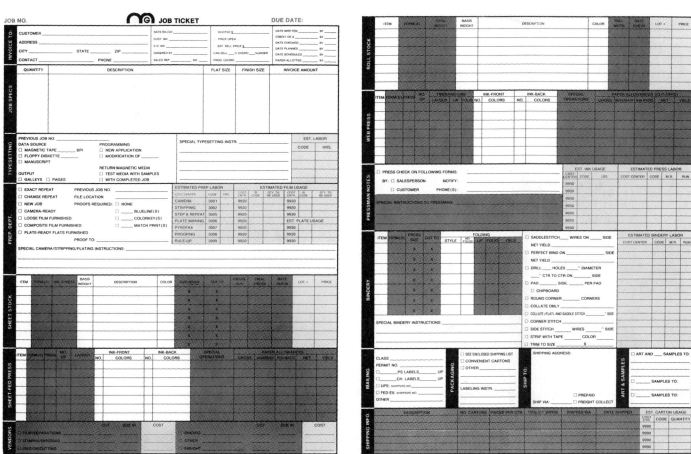

B

Fig. 18-26. A—This is a job ticket for imposition of a specific job. Stripper will use it as a guide for doing job.
B—General job ticket that includes stripping or prep department check sheet.

It is easy to make a mistake when stripping. The stripper should always double-check all work. It is very costly if mistakes are found after the job is completed.

SINGLE AND MULTIPLE PAGE STRIPPING

Two basic kinds of stripping will be considered. The first is the assembling of line and halftone images to create a single page. Commonly referred to as a *single page imposition,* Fig. 18-27A.

The second is the assembling of images to form several pages. The type of imposition requires the folding of pages and is commonly referred to as *multiple page imposition,* Fig. 18-27B.

Single page stripping

The flat must be prepared according to the specifications of each press. Most of the duplicator type presses have preprinted masking sheets. These goldenrod sheets are purchased to cover the plate size for a specific press, Fig. 18-28.

The preprinted masking sheets have all of the reference lines located on the sheet. Since most larger presses do NOT have preprinted sheets, a plain goldenrod sheet may be used.

When single page stripping, the following steps are suggested:

1. Square the sheet. The goldenrod sheet must be squared and fastened to the light table with masking tape, Fig. 18-29.
2. Locate the gripper edge. The side of the flat which will enter the press first is the gripper edge or margin.
3. Locate the plate bend. Every press requires some of the leading edge of the plate to be inserted into some type of plate holding device. The three types of holding devices

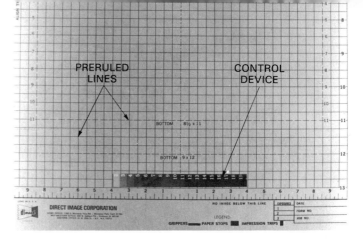

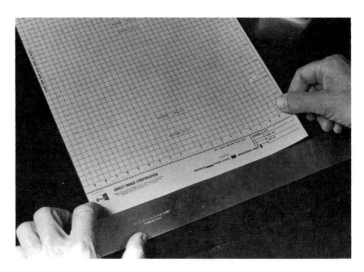

Fig. 18-28. Pre-printed masking sheets are commonly used for flat used to make a plate for an offset duplicator. Note control device for assuring accuracy.

Fig. 18-29. Stripper is accurately positioning goldenrod sheet on work surface.

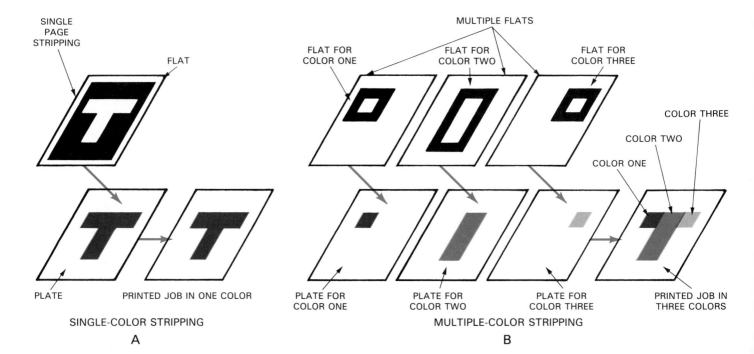

Fig. 18-27. Compare single and multiple color stripping.

are: pin bar, slotted or serrated, and clamp. This area is commonly called *plate bend allowance* and varies with each press, Fig. 18-30.

4. Consider the gripper allowance. Allowance must be made for the mechanical fingers that hold the printing sheet as it goes through the press, Fig. 18-30.

The allowance must also be located on the flat. The allowance indicates that no printing detail can be printed in this area, Fig. 18-31. The allowance will vary with the press, but an allowance of 1/4 to 3/8 inch is very common. Since images cannot be printed in that area, you must allow for any work that extends or bleeds.

5. Know the maximum sheet size. The maximum paper size that can be run on the press must be known. The press manual is the best source of information. If needed, you must draw margins on the masking sheet, Fig. 18-32.

6. Locate the control and/or reference lines. Control and/or reference lines are necessary to assure the highest accuracy in positioning of negatives. They are also used to assist in registering the flat on the plate. Sometimes, trim and registration marks are printed on the press sheet. These marks are also important to the bindery operation.

7. Cut a V-shaped notch in the lead edge of the flat. The wedge is called a *tick mark* and identifies the gripper edge.

8. Trim the negatives. Allow at least 1/2 inch film to remain around the image area. The area is needed to allow for taping the negative to the goldenrod sheet. This is not always possible, but lesser distance could create contact problems. Less space might also be needed because negatives should NOT overlap on the flat. See Fig. 18-33.

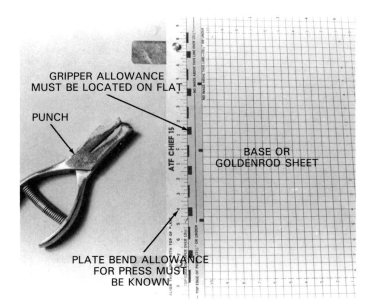

Fig. 18-30. Note allowances on goldenrod sheet for press grippers and plate bend. This can vary with type of printing press.

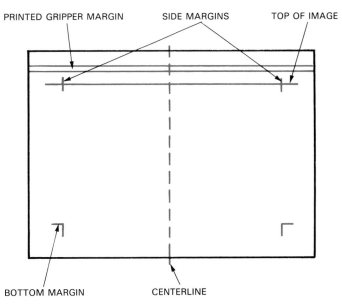

Fig. 18-32. These are the basic lines of concern to the stripper.

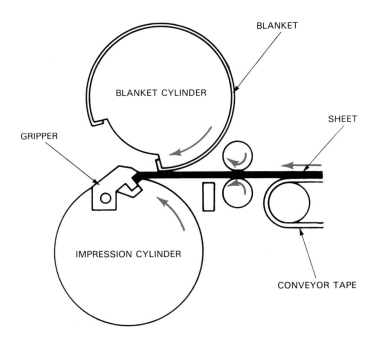

Fig. 18-31. Press grippers hold sheet as it goes through press. Stripper must allow room on flat for grippers.

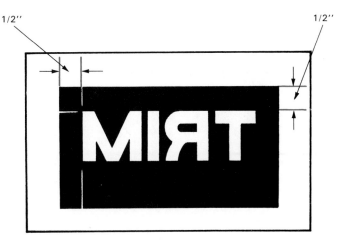

Fig. 18-33. With emulsion-up stripping, image will appear in reverse. Note how reference lines have been scribed on film.

9. Strip the first negative. Two film assembly techniques are commonly used. The first technique requires the strippers to work with the negative emulsion side up. The second has the stripper working with the emulsion of the negative down.

Emulsion up stripping

With the emulsion of the negative up, position the negative on or OVER the goldenrod flat. The base side should be toward the goldenrod. When looking at the negative, the image will appear wrong reading, Fig. 18-34. Attach the negative using lithographic tape. The ruby tape should be used very sparingly. The materials have different coefficients of expansion which could cause buckling because of size changes. Remember that paper size is affected by moisture and heat.

Emulsion down stripping

WITH THE EMULSION OF THE NEGATIVE DOWN, the negative is placed UNDER the goldenrod sheet, Fig. 18-35. The base side is placed next to the goldenrod. This requires a small area to be cut in the goldenrod sheet, as shown in Fig. 18-36. The opening allows the stripper to move the negative in the position indicated by the layout.

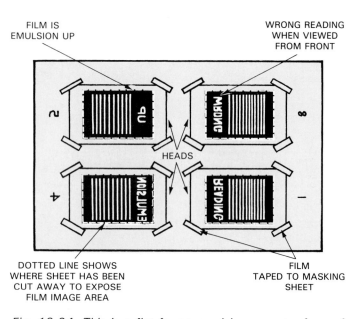

Fig. 18-34. This is a flat for an emulsion up outer form of 8-page signature.

Fig. 18-35. This is a flat for an emulsion down outer form of 8-page signature.

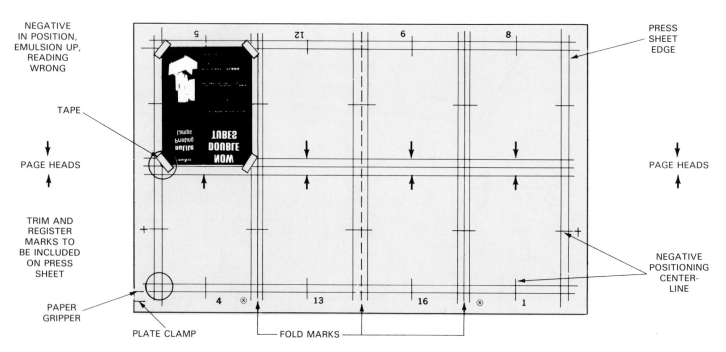

Fig. 18-36. Note how center lines, trim marks, and registration marks are sometimes needed to print on the press sheet in the margins.

When in place, tape is placed across the opening, Fig. 18-37. This holds the negatives as the flat is turned over. Then the negative can be fully secured. The lithographers tape is used in each corner and on the sides when needed, Fig. 18-38.

Emulsion up vs emulsion down

There are several advantages and disadvantages of each stripping method.

With emulsion up stripping, the film is easily removed and can be easily taped. This method is normally recommended with film positives. However, emulsion up stripping is awkward, lining up is difficult, and reference lines can be obscured by the film. Also, the emulsion is more easily damaged.

With emulsion down stripping, the reference lines are easily seen and the base side of the film is up for opaquing. This method is normally recommended with film negatives. However, emulsion down makes the film more difficult to move and tape.

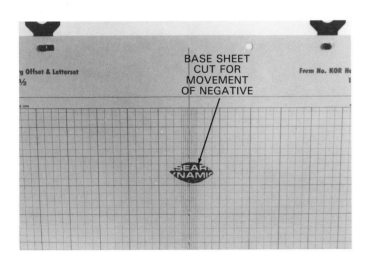

Fig. 18-37. Area cut in base sheet allows stripper to move negative.

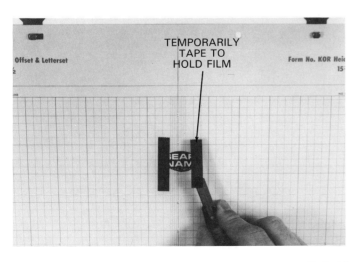

Fig. 18-38. Small amount of tape is used to temporarily hold negative while turning it over to permanently tape on other side.

Cutting masking materials

As mentioned, those areas of the negatives which are to print must not be covered with the goldenrod sheet. Called a *window,* the masking material covering printing images must be cut away, Fig. 18-39.

A sharp knife is a common tool. Since the base of the film is toward the goldenrod sheet, the negative will not be damaged. Extreme care must be taken not to cut through the negative. Practice is suggested before making the first cut on the flat.

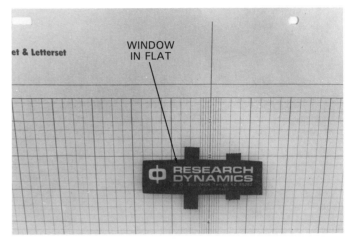

Fig. 18-39. Window or hole must be cut in goldenrod sheet where light is to pass through clear part of negative.

Adding quality control devices

It is important to control the development of the plates as well as the press sheet. The quality control device is stripped onto the base of the goldenrod sheet.

Common control devices are the sensitivity guide, star target, slur gauge, the dot gain scale, and the color control bars. All of these devices were developed by the Graphic Arts Technical Foundation, Fig. 18-40. They are placed in the non-image area of the press sheet.

An explanation of each type control device is given with the control device. Read this information carefully!

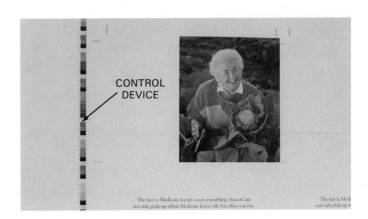

Fig. 18-40. Control devices are needed to detect ink spread, slur, and doubling of image as it leaves press.

Opaquing

Once the windows have been cut, some unwanted light-emitting areas could appear. The *opaque* covers these defects or pinholes in the negative, Fig. 18-41. The opaque blocks out all actinic light. Pinholes can occur in the negative because of a dirty copyboard or original.

Opaquing is usually the last photo conversion step. A water soluble red or black pigment is normally used as the solution. Water can be added to dilute or thin the opaque solution if needed. Alcohol- and petroleum-based opaques are also available. The opaque material is distributed with a ruling pen or a brush.

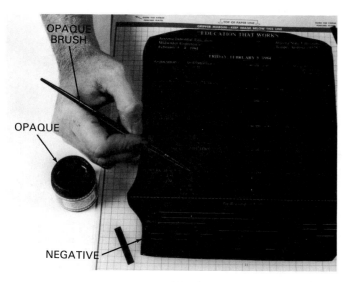

Fig. 18-41. Stripper must opaque any imperfections in negatives so unwanted light does not reach plate or proofing material.

Note! Without proper opaquing, ink spots would appear on the printed image any place unwanted light passed through the negatives.

Opaquing on the base side is usually recommended. Then it is easier to scratch off unwanted opaque and not damage the emulsion. Also, there is less chance of image distortion, Fig. 18-42.

The flat is now ready for proofing. You should double-check all specifications.

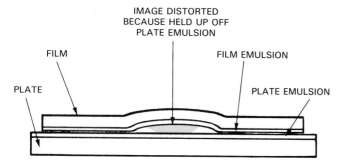

Fig. 18-42. If opaque is applied too thick, it could cause film to be held away from plate when burning plate.

Complementary flats

Complementary flats are stripped with material that will be exposed in successive "burns" (exposures), onto the same plate. One of the typical reasons for having more than one flat is that several negatives must be pieced close together. An example is a halftone with close fitting captions. Complementary flats are also suggested when the plate exposures times vary.

A typical illustration of a complementary flat is shown in Fig. 18-43. In this case, the line work is stripped in one negative while the halftones are stripped in the second flat.

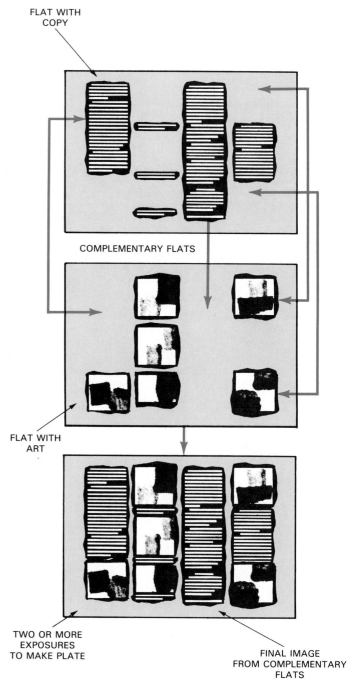

Fig. 18-43. Complementary flats are used when images are extremely close together. Each is exposed onto same plate separately. (NuArc)

The procedure described earlier is used for each flat. The only additional step would be the placement of register pins. Holes are punched in the goldenrod base sheet, Figs. 18-44 and 18-45. Once the holes are punched, the pins are taped in place, Fig. 18-46.

The pins are used to make sure each goldenrod sheet is in the same location for stripping and platemaking. This assures proper alignment during all the required steps.

Many times ruby sheeting is used as masks for halftones. The sheeting is punched and placed over the pins. The lineup material becomes the guide for cutting the windows in the ruby. The window area is removed by peeling off the ruby material, Fig. 18-47.

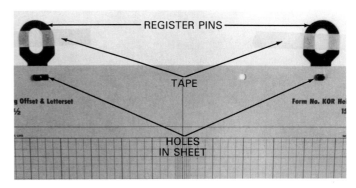

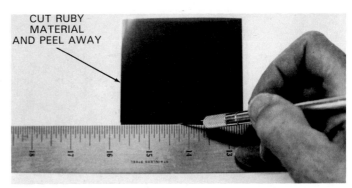

Fig. 18-46. Register pins are taped down to hold flats while working.

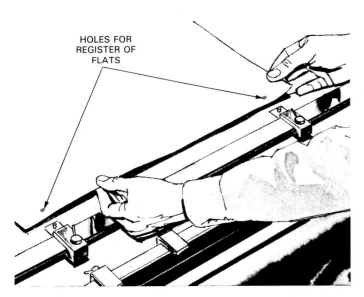

Fig. 18-44. Holes punched in goldenrod sheet assure that everything aligns.

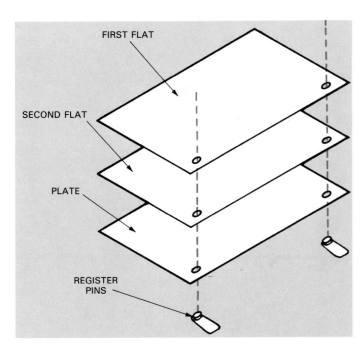

Fig. 18-45. Register pins fit through holes in plate and flats. This keeps them in alignment when exposing plate.

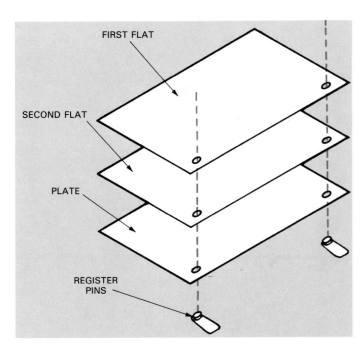

Fig. 18-47. After cutting with sharp knife, ruby material can be peeled off clear plastic base to form a window.

The same cutting procedure can be completed with a sheet of goldenrod stock. The windows are cut in the goldenrod sheet. This system can be used to attach halftone materials, tints, or other material requiring complementary flats.

Many times separate printing flats are needed. This is true when successive pages of multiple forms booklets are to be printed. These are called *multiple flats*. The complementary and multiple flats are proofed before the plates are exposed.

Stripping positives

Since film positives are the opposite of negatives, the image areas are opaque and the nonimage areas are clear. The stripping base is clear. A sheet, on which the reference lines are located, is placed down first. All of the sheets are punched to assure register. The same technique is used for positive flats as was used for negative flats.

The film positives are trimmed and positioned. Quality assurance is an important factor. Therefore, appropriate quality control devices are positioned on the flat. Normally, all of the film and control devices are attached with the emulsion up.

Step-and-repeat work

If the same image is to appear many times on the same page, the image is often *stepped and repeated*. It is exposed the number of times indicated in the job specifications. Many step-and-repeat systems are used in industry. Fig. 18-48 illustrates basic step and repeat work.

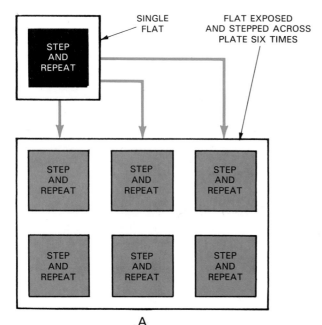

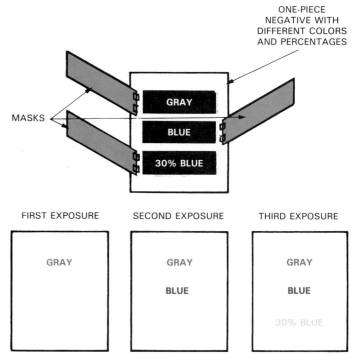

Fig. 18-49. Note how flaps can be used so one flat will expose different color images or different plates. This saves stripper from making different flats for each color.

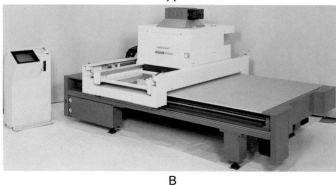

Fig. 18-48. A—Step-and-repeat is used to produce same image more than once on same plate. B—Platemaker used for automated step and repeat exposures.   (Screen - USA)

Color stripping

To reproduce process color negatives and positives, a set of flats are required. Each color requires a separate flat. This means that all of the flats must be in register.

Sometimes the job calls for simple color work. If the colors do NOT overlap, a single flat can be used. When each color plate is being exposed, the other colors are masked out, as in Fig. 18-49. Again accuracy is very important.

Registering color flats

Two techniques are commonly used to register more than one process color flat. The first is stripping up to a *drawn layout*. All of the other flats are keyed to the first flat.

The second type uses a proof as a *key*. A blue line flat is an example. The blue line is used as the key. A variety of techniques and materials can be used. When the goldenrod is used as the base for the key, the technique would be similar to stripping a single color flat.

As in single color printing, the layout must be drawn. Very often, the black printer negatives are positioned and used as the key. Once the key flat is finished, each color is positioned over the key flat one at a time.

Close register

With close register, each flat must be accurately positioned. The control marks must line up perfectly. Sighting down directly over the register marks is essential. Parallax displacement is possible. To eliminate this problem, a collimating magnifier should be used. This magnifier directs the sight straight down. Once all of the negatives have been checked and fastened down to the goldenrod, the windows are cut in the goldenrod to allow light to pass through clear areas when burning the plate.

Clear base

Whenever a clear base is used for negative flats, the goldenrod windows are cut accurately to correspond to the negative placement when burning the plate. Some strippers prefer this system because visibility is increased.

As described earlier, positive flats must be stripped up on clear base material. The layout is often drawn on a translucent paper. The clear plastic sheet is positioned over the layout. Transparent tape is used to adhere the positives to the clear plastic base sheet. Use a collimating magnifier to align the film positives.

After the flats are completed, they must be carefully checked and then proofed. The type of proof will vary according to the wishes of the customer.

ELECTRONIC STRIPPING

Electronic stripping involves using a computer, visual display screen, and mask cutting machine to generate flats automatically. Systems vary. Some can go directly from electronically scanned data to the printing plate. Others are less sophisticated and use a machine to cut conventional mask overlays for the flat.

Fig. 18-50 is an operator using state-of-the-art equipment to strip a job. The mouse is used in conjunction with the menu keypad to produce different shapes on the display screen. The resulting electronic data can then be used to run a mask cutting machine or other output device.

Fig. 18-51 shows an automatic mask cutting machine. It uses the computer input to move a cutting head. The cutting head slides over the masking sheet to cut windows for the flat.

Fig. 18-50. Operator is using computerized equipment to electronically make masks. Mouse and control keypad will allow operator to make various mask shapes and sizes quickly and easily. (Screaming Color-Chapter One)

Fig. 18-51. This is an automatic mask cutting machine. It uses computer input to move cutter across ruby sheet to cut windows accurately. (Lehigh Press)

As technology advances, you will see more and more electronics in striping departments. Someday, conventional hand-stripping techniques may be totally replaced by electronic systems.

KNOW THESE THEMS

Lithographic imposition, Stripping, Collimator, Base material, Dummy, Right angle fold. Parallel fold, Printer's custom, Step-and-repeat, Combination, Sheetwise layout, Work-and-turn, Work-and-tumble, Bleed, Creep, Signature, Head, Thumb edge, Bind edge, Gutter, Open edge, Closed edge, Foot, Signature mark, Folio, Job ticket, Gripper edge. Gripper allowance, Reference line, Opaquing, Complementary flats.

REVIEW QUESTIONS—CHAPTER 18

1. What is a flat?
2. Why is a flat needed?
3. The _____ is used to eliminate parallax error when checking alignment of images.
4. This is used by the stripper to block out unwanted images on negatives.
   a. Tabs.
   b. Double-coated tape.
   c. Opaque solution.
   d. Lithographer's tape.
5. When is step-and-repeat desirable?
6. A _____ is made up of various size forms on the same plate or printed sheet.
7. Explain the three types of press layouts commonly used in the industry.
8. When any type of image extends completely to the edge of the printed page, it is called a _____.
9. What causes creep?
10. List ten parts of a signature.
11. What is a gripper allowance?
12. What would happen if a stripper failed to opaque a small flaw or mark on a negative?
13. _____ _____ are stripped with material that will be exposed in successive "burns" onto the same plate.
14. Since film positives are opposites of negatives, the image areas are _____ and the nonimage areas are _____.

SUGGESTED ACTIVITIES

1. Visit a plant and describe the materials and techniques used to strip a process color job.
2. Describe the control devices used by a stripper at a plant having a large printing press.
3. Inspect the binding of this textbook. Note how it consists of several 32-page signatures bound together.

Operator of color proofing system is positioning a piece of photoconductive film in signature toning console, seen through piece of film from which proof is laminated. (Kodak)

Chapter 19

CONTACTING AND COLOR PROOFING

After studying this chapter, you will be able to:
- Explain the process of contacting.
- Identify the equipment needed for contacting.
- Determine the proper exposure for various light sources and contacting materials.
- Make a conventional contact.
- Describe unusual contacting methods.
- Make a duplicate.
- Make a spread and a choke.
- Make a diffusion transfer negative or positive.
- Make an overlay and transfer proof.
- Explain modern color proofing systems.

This chapter starts out by discussing contacting and how it can be used to reproduce or modify images. A *contact* is a reproduction made by exposing film or other light sensitive material touching the original.

The last section of the chapter discusses the various methods of making proofs. *Proofs* are commonly used to check the layout or flat before the press run.

CONTACTING

Contacting exposes film or photographic paper by passing light through an existing negative or positive image. This process commonly uses a vacuum frame and controlled light source to expose the light sensitive material. The positive or negative actually touches or "contacts" the film or photo paper during the exposure.

Once a negative or positive is produced using a process camera, a need may exist to develop new films from those originals. These new films are made by contacting the original to another photosensitive material.

An accurate 1:1 size reproduction is almost assured because of the nature of the contacting process. A basic contacting setup is very simple, as shown in Fig. 19-1.

Contacting applications
Some of the reasons for contacting are to:
1. Make negatives from positives.
2. Make positives from negatives.
3. Change contrast and tonal values.

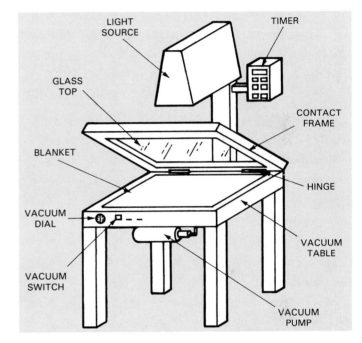

Fig. 19-1. This is a common type of vacuum contact frame with light source and light control device. It is usually located in the darkroom.

4. Make proofs and plates.
5. Produce spreads and chokes.
6. Make screen tints.
7. Make step-and-repeat images.
8. Make original screened separation negatives for direct screen color work.
9. Create masks.
10. Use duplicating film.

This list is not exhaustive, but it does indicate some of the situations when contacting is required. It will also remove some of the work load from the process camera operator.

Contacting facilities
The contacting activities should be separated from other photomechanical operations when a conflict exists. These conflicts include: competition for operator time, bottlenecks in film processing, overcrowding of the facility, and work

flow problems. Therefore, some plants will have a separate area or they will designate an area for contacting. This area is usually within the darkroom.

Location of the contacting or printing frame will vary. When positioning one, care must be taken so that objects in the surrounding area do NOT reflect light. Also, air currents should NOT pass over the frame. The frame should NOT be placed in a passage or high traffic area.

One of the worst problems within the contacting area is the control of dust. Keeping everything dust free is essential for quality assurance of the final product. Dust tends to be attracted to glass. Inspection for cleanliness should be part of the initial setup procedure.

CONTACTING EQUIPMENT

Three pieces of equipment make up a basic contacting system: contact frame, light source, and timer. The basis of contacting revolves around the light source and the contact or printing frame. See Fig. 19-2.

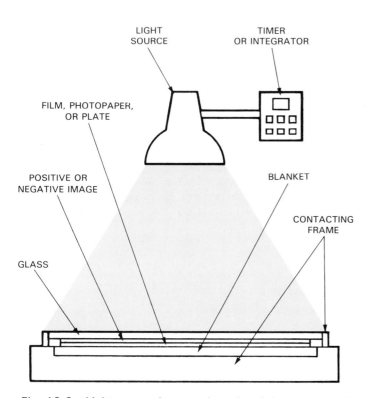

Fig. 19-2. Light source is spaced so that light covers total frame area with equal intensity. This assures proper exposure of material in frame.

Contact frames

A *contact frame* can use a vacuum or a spring load action to hold the image and light sensitive materials together. Most applications for contacting require the use of a vacuum type contact frame rather than a spring-loaded frame.

Three types of vacuum contact frames are commonly used in industry. They are: glass or covered, acetate overlay, and open type. The most common is the glass or covered frame, Fig. 19-3.

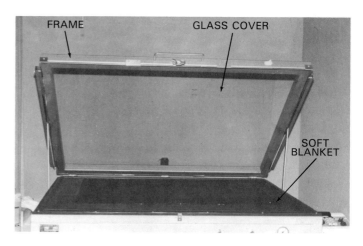

Fig. 19-3. Glass covered vacuum frame is most common type. Blanket in vacuum frame must be resilient to conform to surfaces in top of frame.

A glass top contact frame requires that the glass must be cleaned before exposures. Care must also be taken not to scratch or break the glass. Glass can also bend light, especially if the glass is dirty or covered with a residue left by a glass cleaner. A recommended graphic arts glass cleaner must be used with a soft cloth or special material to clean the glass on a contact frame.

The *drawdown time* or time vacuum is applied must be sufficient to allow trapped air to escape between the materials in the frame. The drawdown time for the acetate overlay type frame is less than glass.

The open-faced vacuum frame, as the name implies, does NOT have a cover over the vacuum surface. Cleaning the cover material is eliminated. Multiple exposures are easier using the openfaced frame. Problems can arise, however, when trying to expose several small pieces of film onto one large, single sheet. The reason being that the uppermost film must extend at least one inch beyond any lower films.

Frame size selection should be based on the plant requirements. Allowance should be made to insure the frame size is at least four or five inches larger than the largest film to be used in the facility.

The rubber blanket, utilized on the glass vacuum frame, must be pliable enough to conform to the glass when under vacuum. See Fig. 19-3. The bead around the edge of the blanket must also be uniform. An uneven bead will not hold a good vacuum.

The surface texture of the blanket can cause undesirable patterns on exposed film. Because of this, a *backing mat* or *backing sheet* might be needed. Commercially produced sheets are available. The backing sheet should exhaust air freely. The backing sheet will also help avoid problems with alignment when using register pins.

Vacuum systems

The *vacuum system* is used by the contacting frame to hold the film or photosensitive material in place. The suction of the vacuum system forces contact between surfaces to assure good reproduction. Refer to Fig. 19-4.

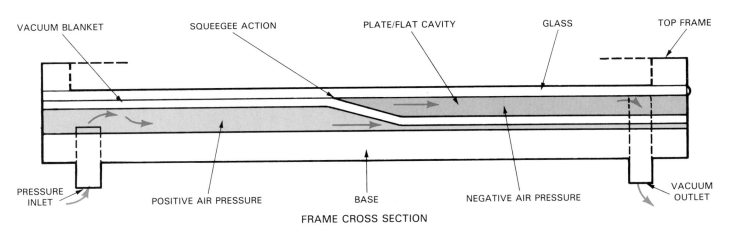

VACUUM BLANKET · SQUEEGEE ACTION · PLATE/FLAT CAVITY · GLASS · TOP FRAME

PRESSURE INLET · POSITIVE AIR PRESSURE · BASE · NEGATIVE AIR PRESSURE · VACUUM OUTLET

FRAME CROSS SECTION

Fig. 19-4. Vacuum pump draws air out of vacuum frame. The resulting suction forces blanket up towards glass. This pushes light sensitive material and film image up to create good contact with glass.   (Teaneck Graphics)

The pump must maintain a designated amount of vacuum. Most newer pumps are the oil-less type that require little maintenance, Fig. 19-5.

Some units have sealed bearings while others require periodic lubrication. The manufacturer's recommendations should be followed to insure proper performance of the vacuum unit.

Most of the systems have a *bleed valve* to release the vacuum. The vacuum scale or gauge is usually in inches of mercury or kilopascals. The vacuum range generally required for proper drawdown is between 15 and 25 in./Hg or 50 and 85 kPa.

Proper drawdown is viewed at an angle. The backing sheet must be sealed against the glass or overlay. If air pockets are trapped, release the vacuum, and restart the drawdown.

Sometimes, colored rings (Newton rings) will appear on the glass of a contact frame. When they appear between the top film and the glass, good contact is being made.

If Newton rings appear between the contact materials and the material to receive the image, they will appear on anything contacted after that stage. Under these conditions, they are undesirable.

LIGHT SOURCES

Light sources used for contacting are divided into two basic categories. These are the point source lights that are used with the high speed category of films. The films do NOT require a large amount of light for exposure. The second type of light source is the high intensity type commonly used to expose printing plates.

Point source light

The *point source light* forms a narrow cone of light, Fig. 19-6. This is very beneficial when using emulsion-to-base exposures since this type of light path insures a close application of dot-for-dot reproduction.

The films used with point source lights are of the darkroom type. This type of light source also lends itself to applications using filters.

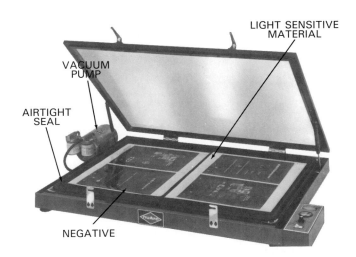

Fig. 19-5. This is a small vacuum frame useful for many jobs. Note film laid over light sensitive material.   (nuArc)

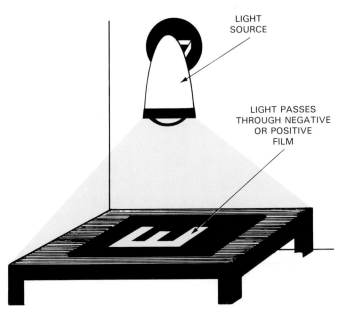

LIGHT SOURCE

LIGHT PASSES THROUGH NEGATIVE OR POSITIVE FILM

Fig. 19-6. A small cone of light is formed by point light source. This provides most accurate reproduction since light passes straight down through image area and onto light sensitive material.

A typical point source setup would have a constant voltage regulator, a three-stepped transformer, an accurate timer, and a lamp housing that is capable of holding a filter.

A multiple filter turret style lamp housing might also be used in place of the single filter holder. If color separation work is involved, the multiple filter setup would be used.

High intensity light source

The *high intensity light* source has brought contacting out of the darkroom and into the daylight or yellow light environment, Fig. 19-7. This process has many advantages

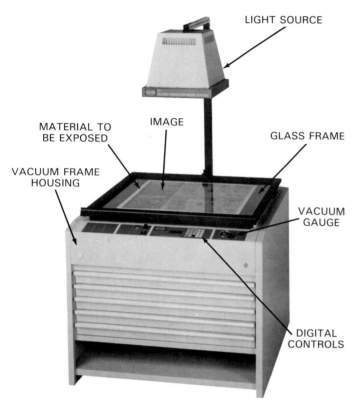

Fig. 19-7. This contact frame has a high intensity light source that is recommended for many contacting jobs. (nuArc)

because operators have a better view of what is taking place and they are not curtailed by the confinement of the darkroom.

Whatever high intensity light source is used, an integrator is a basic requirement. Line voltage fluctuations can cause a change in the amount of light that strikes the photosensitive material. An *integrator* insures that a consistent amount of light strikes the contact frame surface with each exposure.

Illumination devices vary greatly, therefore, a reliable supplier should be consulted to give recommendations based on needs.

The light source for a contact frame is generally considered to be *"white light."* This means the wavelengths have a very broad range. Wavelengths of various types of light sources have been explained and illustrated earlier in this text.

Broad light source

A *broad light source* is widely distributed light coverage and less directional than a point source light. If a diffusion sheet is placed in the filter holder of a point light source, it will have the same effect. See Fig. 19-8.

A broad light allows for some dust or unwanted objects on the glass or acetate overlay of the contact frame as the light undercuts the unwanted particles.

The broad light source is commonly used for altering line and image widths and dot sizes by contacting intermediate materials. This is explained later.

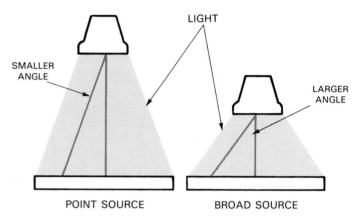

Fig. 19-8. Broad source light hits image at a larger angle. It can be used to alter reproduction image.

CONTACTING EXPOSURES

Proper *contacting exposures* are determined by light intensity and time. Variations in either changes the final product. The intensity of the light source is based on several factors. They are:
1. Light source-to-film distance.
2. Wattage of bulb.
3. Light reflectors.
4. Consistency.
Refer to Fig. 19-9.

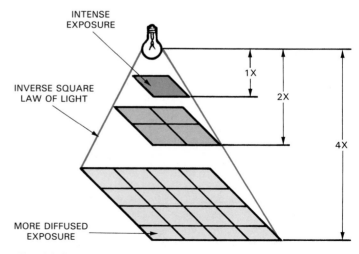

Fig. 19-9. Note how light intensity or brightness is inversely proportional to square of distance.

The duration of the exposure is often determined by a *timer*. The timer must be able to produce an exposure that is the same each time the contact frame is used. When the timer is set at 20 seconds or 20 units, it must result in the same exposure every time.

Short exposures tend to be difficult to control. Therefore, filters are recommended to give greater time for controlling the exposure.

> WARNING! Protect your eyes from the exposure lights on a contact frame. Do NOT look directly at the exposure lights. The light source may be powerful enough to cause eye damage!

Determining exposure

An *exposure test* should be conducted occasionally to check for changes in conditions. Light sources will age with time. This can change the exposure time if a light integrator is not a part of the system.

Changing to a different type of film, different manufacturer, new emulsion number, or even a new box of film may require an exposure test to determine basic exposure for the film.

The correct exposure will produce an accurate image size on the contact or duplicate with a minimum amount of defects. Fine serifs of letters and the correct size of halftone dots are indicators of a proper exposure.

Improper exposure will render low density film, pinholes, and inaccurate reproduction of the original.

Contact exposure test

The *contact exposure test* consists of a series of increasing exposures on a single sheet of film, Fig. 19-10. By moving a mask across the frame at fixed intervals, a stepped effect will be produced on the processed film.

Determine the time of exposure by viewing the step offs. The most representative image is the one to choose. The time is added and this determines the basic exposure for that specific application.

If the correct exposure appears to be between two different steps, an additional step test will be required. Use the steps in question as the low and high for the second exposure test.

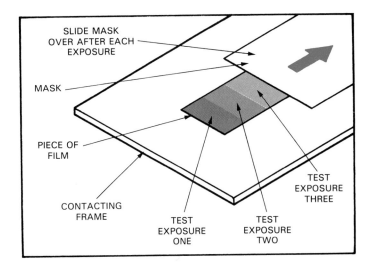

Fig. 19-10. Step-off exposure test is essential to verify exposure times for given lamp distances and film. Test should be made periodically to see if conditions have changed. Mask is slid over test strip of film and progressively exposed. Then you can calculate best exposure time for conditions.

Other methods can be used to test for the best exposure time. They include the use of a resolution guide or a projection exposure indicator as the original copy. However, the step-off method is very common in today's industry.

Once the basic exposure has been determined for the specific type of film and contacting conditions, then control guides will help maintain quality, Fig. 19-11. Most film manufacturers produce film control guides that should be utilized when exposing their specific products. There are some differences among guides, but the goal of each is the same. The exposure guides allow the contact frame operator to be in control of the process, instead of "being controlled by the process."

By becoming more familiar with the different types of guides available and the specific purposes and applications of each, it will enable the operator to become much more proficient at contacting. The establishment of standards within the facility itself and maintaining set procedures will reduce time and costs in the long run. Operators will be working together, rather than against each other.

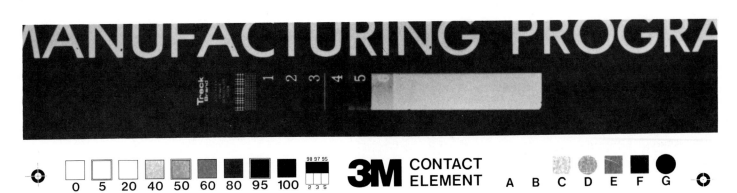

Fig. 19-11. Two control device variations. Contact control device is stripped into film flat just as other components. Place control strip as close to images as possible. Remember to position control device emulsion to correspond to other components. (3M)

Note! Too much attention is sometimes given to results from the control guides rather than the actual film being reproduced. Remember that exposure guides are an aid and are NOT the end result or final product.

CONTACTING CONSIDERATIONS

There are some basic considerations that apply to contacting in general. These considerations apply to all types of applications and should be part of any adopted procedure.

1. If using a glass or acetate overlay type frame, make sure the glass or acetate is free of dust, tape residue, opaque solution, etc.
2. Avoid scratching the frame's surface with razor blades when cleaning tape residue.
3. Use an approved backing sheet, and place the film in the frame with the desired side facing up, Fig. 19-12.
4. Always include a target control aid appropriate to the work being conducted.
5. Be careful not to place fingerprints on the photosensitive material.
6. Make sure that the exposed film is dust free.
7. Position the exposed film in such a manner as to avoid scratching the film emulsion.

8. Apply the vacuum slowly and visually inspect when possible to insure good contact or drawdown.
9. Make certain that the vacuum gauge reads properly.
10. Before exposing, wait at least thirty seconds after the vacuum gauge has reached maximum reading for less critical work. Wait up to two minutes for the more demanding jobs. This delay is very important and exposure should NOT take place until all air is exhausted between films and overlays.
11. Even lighting of the frame, over the entire surface, is imperative.
12. Set timer to the established values for the type of work and film being used.
13. Processing of exposed film should be done according to an established format for the type of film and application intended. Both tray and machine processing can be used with films used for contacting.

CONTACT IMAGE ORIENTATION

The contact operator must be aware of the three types of image orientation: emulsion-to-emulsion, base-to-emulsion, and emulsion-to-base, Fig. 19-13.

One of the most common film contacts is a reversal of image orientation and it is made with an EMLUSION-TO-EMULSION exposure, Fig. 19-14. In this case, the original negative would be wrong-reading when viewed from the emulsion side and right-reading when viewed from the base side. The finished product of an emulsion-to-emulsion exposure would result in a right-reading positive when viewed from the emulsion side.

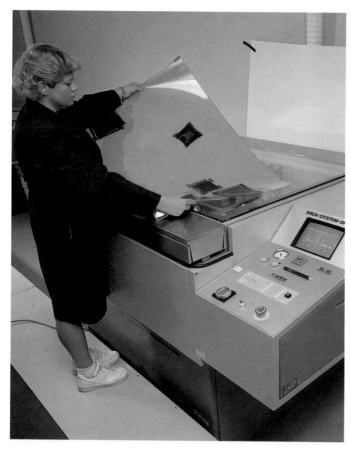

Fig. 19-12. A modern contact printer in use. Be sure to place film in frame with correct side up. Always work carefully to avoid leaving fingerprints on glass and to prevent scratching film or glass. (Chapter One, Screaming Color)

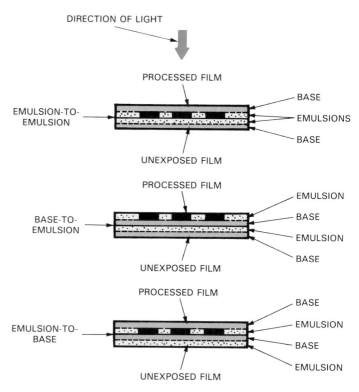

Fig. 19-13. These are the three emulsion positions for contacting. Emulsion-to-emulsion is most accurate.

Fig. 19-14. Depending upon contacting application, positive can make negative or vice versa. Negative can also make a negative or duplicate a positive.

If the final negative or positive is to be used for platemaking, the correct image orientation requires the emulsion to be TOWARD the plate. This is a very important point to remember!

An emulsion-to-emulsion contact requires that the emulsion of the unexposed film faces the light source. The emulsion of the processed film, which is placed on top, faces the exposed film. This procedure will give the HIGHEST QUALITY reproduction. A negative working film is required for this type of process.

Contact reversal

The *contact reversal* process is used to produce negatives from positives or vice versa. It is accomplished by placing an ortho-type contact film with the emulsion up in the contact frame. The film negative or positive is placed over the ortho-type film with the emulsion side up. Once exposed, the film is processed in the same manner as other ortho-type films. See Fig. 19-15.

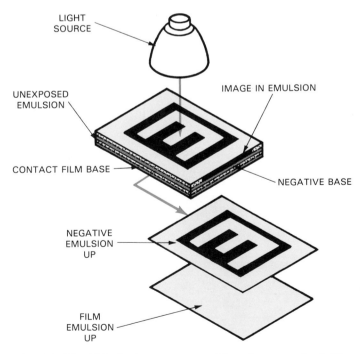

Fig. 19-15. This is how you would make a contact film reversal.

Contact duplicates

The word *duplicate* refers to making the same image as the original, such as: a negative to produce another negative. The unexposed areas of duplicating film remain black when developed. This makes the duplicate the same as the original.

To make a left-to-right reading duplicate the same as the original, it would require that the emulsion of the duplciate and original face in the same direction. When the emulsion of the duplicate film and the original are facing each other, the resulting duplicate will be a LATERAL REVERSAL.

Contacting films

Much of today's film used for contacting is called *daylight film*. This does NOT mean it can be handled in daylight. However, daylight film can be handled in a yellow light environment without exposure. This makes it ideal for use with a contact frame because of improved visibility in the work area.

If duplicates of an original, either negative or positive, are required, use a *duplicating film*. This film is of a *positive working nature* which means that light or exposure subtracts density from the film. *"Dupes"* are commonly made when a multiple number of copies are needed on one press sheet.

Processing is the same as with regular lithographic film. The same care must be taken.

CONTACT MASKING MATERIALS

Care should also be taken when choosing masking materials for applications involving contacting and duplicating film. The film has an exposure threshold that might be exceeded by multiple exposures on the same film if a high quality masking material is NOT employed.

Masking material can be checked by first determining the maximum number of exposures that will be given to the film times the time per exposure. This will give the total or maximum exposure of light.

Cover the exposed film with the mask material and expose for the maximum calculated time. If the processed film shows exposure through the mask, then the masking material is NOT appropriate for that given task. Care should be taken in selecting the right type for the specific job.

SPREADS AND CHOKES

A *spread,* sometimes called a "fatty," is made by a process in a contact frame that makes the original image slightly larger. The light source spreads out to expose more of the light sensitive material.

A *choke,* also called a "skinny," is a process of making the original image slightly smaller. The light source angles inward to expose less image area.

Both create an overlap of the images, as shown in Fig. 19-16. When the image's outline is complex, contacting is usually used to create the overlap rather than by using handwork.

Spreads are made from NEGATIVE FILM IMAGES while chokes are made from POSITIVE FILM.

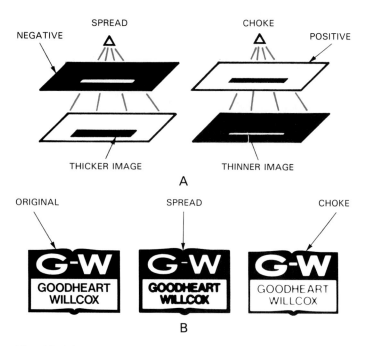

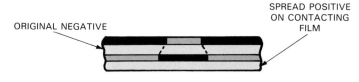

Fig. 19-16. A—Note how light can be used to enlarge and spread or reduce and choke image. B—Note effects of choked and spread copy.

Diffuser sheets are usually frosted acetate, matte drafting film, or one-eighth inch thick, white plexiglass. Sometimes, the amount of spread or choke is such that spacer sheets are placed between the film sandwich in order to provide even greater undercutting of the image. Acetate is a common spacing material.

An example of the spread and choke concept is given in Fig. 19-18.

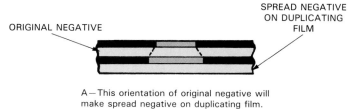

A—This orientation of original negative will make spread negative on duplicating film.

B—This orientation of original positive will make choked positive on duplicating film.

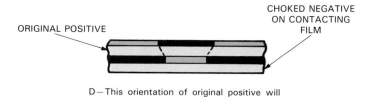

C—This orientation or original negative will make spread positive on contacting film.

D—This orientation of original positive will make choked negative on contact film.

Fig. 19-18. Study techniques for making spreads and chokes.

The amount of choke or spread should be specified for any given job, and may be influenced by the type of press used to print the image. If lettering is involved, then the width should be considered when specifying the amount of overlap. Spreads and chokes are measured with control guides.

What actually takes place when making spreads or chokes is that the light is spread as it passes through the layer of film, Fig. 19-17. Therefore, it does not produce an accurate image, but instead a somewhat larger or smaller one depending on the method or orientation of materials, Fig. 19-18.

By placing a diffuser on top of the frame, the natural tendency of light to spread is multiplied and the image is undercut. Exposure times are increased in order to achieve this undercutting.

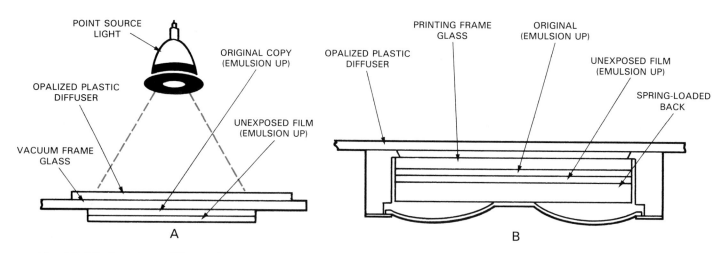

Fig. 19-17. Note how diffuser sheet is used to spread light for undercutting image. A—Orientation for vacuum frame. B—Orientation for pressure frame. (Kodak)

CONTACT FRAME SCREENING

An unscreened continuous tone negative or positive can be screened in a contact frame by using a contact screen. The technique is similar to the regular camera procedure. A white light source is used to make the main exposure while the flash exposure is also used to extend the range.

The correct exposure is determined by making a step-off. This has been illustrated earlier.

PROOFING

Three reasons are generally stated for proofing material. The first is to make a reproduction proof. The proof is made from relief images and is seldom used today. The second is for correction which has been covered in another chapter.

The third is for *representation* — to give an idea of what the final product will look like. Generally, this is considered to be *color proofing*. These proofs are used for customer inspection.

The Graphic Communication Association has defined two classifications of proofs. The first is a contact proof that must have halftone dots and meet industry color specifications. Examples would be digital halftone proofs and press proofs. The second classification would be a pre-proof, which lacks measurable halftone dots and is often the first look at color.

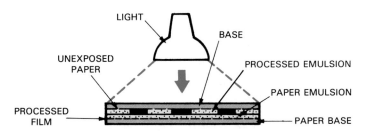

Fig. 19-19. Vacuum frame is used to make paper proofs. Proofs are then used to check for accuracy before printing job.

Overlay proofs

An *overlay proof* is made by placing a light sensitive proofing material under an image overlay. The light sensitive proof material is then exposed to a light source to produce an inexpensive proof. See Fig. 19-19.

A popular overlay system, developed by 3M, is called "Color Key." The proofing material comes in many colors as negative or positive and as transparent or opaque light-sensitive materials.

The proofs are made by the contacting method and require a light source strong in ultra-violet wavelengths. A contacting frame is needed to support the materials.

The material is taken from the light-tight container, making sure only one sheet is used. This is sometimes difficult since the material is very thin.

The sheets may be handled in regular room light for a short period of time but a yellow light environment is recommended.

Single-sheet proofs

A *transfer proof,* or *single-sheet proof,* forms an image by depositing and treating a special powder substance so that it represents the original image. The colored powder transfers and bonds to the image areas. This produces a very accurate color proof of the original image. Transfer type proofing systems are manufactured by several firms. A transfer color proofing system gives the printer added control over the color production process. This also allows the client to see an accurate rendition of the color original.

DuPont makes a system called "Cromalin," which produces full color, pre-press proofs from halftones. See Fig. 19-20.

The system consists of film, process color toners (powders), and transfer equipment. Cleanliness must be stressed at all times.

Cromalin film is a tacky, photopolymer layer between two base sheets, Fig. 19-21. Exposure of the transfer sheet is made through a positive. The cover sheet is removed and

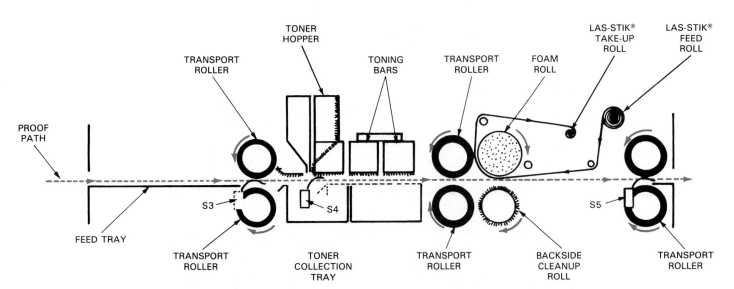

Fig. 19-20. Study diagram of automatic Cromalin or transfer proof process.

307

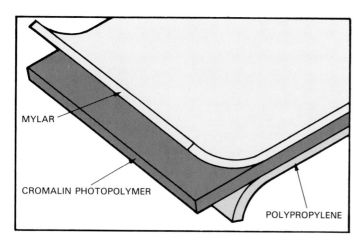

Fig. 19-21. Cromalin film has protective layers over photosensitive material.

the photopolymer layer is coated with a Cromalin process toner (colored powder). The toner adheres onto tacky non-exposed image areas.

The Cromalin transfer machine transfers the image to a receptor, such as paper, using heat and pressure. The image is hardened after each transfer by exposure to ultra-violet radiation. The process is repeated for each process color.

Another type of single-sheet color proofing system has been developed by 3M. The system uses water-based chemistry in the processor. The material is exposed, processed and laminated, and the final image appears on a single sheet. After exposure, the proofing equipment processes the film, Fig. 19-22, and the laminator, Fig. 19-23, creates the final proof.

Fig. 19-23. This unit laminates the material after it has been processed. (3M)

Digital proofing

With the advances in electronic production, proofing technology has also changed. The 3M Desktop Color Proofing System is representative of this change. It consists of proprietory software that controls the printer from a Macintosh computer and a thermal dye sublimation output unit, Fig. 19-24. Using digital input from the desktop system, four-color images are created with dyes on specially coated paper or transparency stock.

Fig. 19-22. This proofing processor can handle either negative or positive films. (3M)

Fig. 19-24. This is the workstation of a 3M Desktop Color Proofing System. Color proofing technology is changing very rapidly. (3M)

This proofing technology simulates the press results from commercial sheet-fed, publication, or newspaper printing. It produces color proofs with continuous-tone pixels and prints with yellow, cyan, magenta, and black dyes. This system is also designed to accept jobs from most standard design and page layout applications.

Another system, the 3M Digital Matchprint Color Proofing System, also uses digital data. See Fig. 19-25. It produces a high resolution halftone proof without the use of an intermediate film and allows calibration to match most proofing situations. It also has the flexibility to create proofs to customer specifications.

Dot sizes and shapes can be simulated to give the required appearance of a given press sheet. This proof appears on the actual printing stock specified by the customer.

The Matchprint system consists of three main components: the Systems Controller, VIP II Versatile Image Processor, and the Direct Digital Writer, Fig. 19-26. The Systems Controller uses menu-driven commands that make it possible to work with every element of the process. The Image Processor manages interfacing and image processing, halftone generation, and text and graphics integration. The Digital Writer, Fig. 19-27, is the graphics output recorder that creates the final image using infrared lasers and optics.

Systems have been developed by other manufacturers to work with the desktop environment, Fig. 19-28.

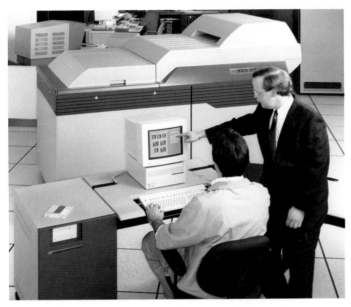

Fig. 19-25. This Digital Matchprint proofing system allows proofing on the actual stock to be used for printing.

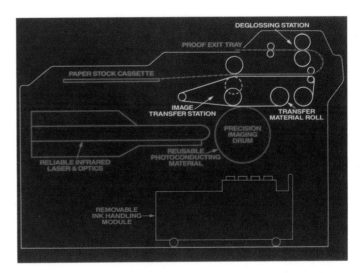

Fig. 19-27. Inside the digital writer, the full-color image is created on a photoconductor and transferred to the paper stock by an offset process. (3M)

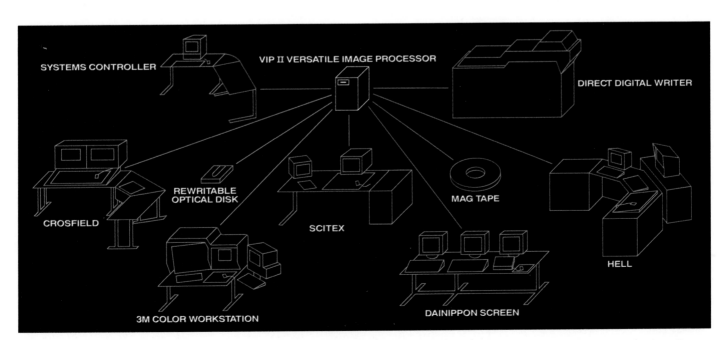

Fig. 19-26. The image processor is designed to accept jobs from most standard design and page layout applications. It manages everything from interfacing and image processing, to halftone generation and text and graphics integration. (3M)

Fig. 19-28. This is another system that is designed specifically for color desktop publishing. (nuArc)

KNOW THESE TERMS

Proof, Contacting, Vacuum frame, Backing mat, Point light source, High intensity light, White light, Broad light source, Exposure test, Emulsion-to-emulsion, Contact reversal, Contact duplicate, Daylight film, Duplicating film, Spreads, Chokes, Diffuser sheet, Contact frame screening, Contacted tints, Color proofing, Overlay proof, Transfer proof, Cromalin, Matchprint, PostScript.

REVIEW QUESTIONS—CHAPTER 19

1. What is contacting?
2. List nine reasons for contacting.
3. How does a vacuum contact frame work?
4. This refers to the amount of time needed for sufficient vacuum to be produced in a vacuum frame.
   a. Buildup time.
   b. Exposure time.
   c. Developing time.
   d. Drawdown time.
5. The required vacuum for contacting generally ranges between:
   a. 5 and 15 in./Hg (17 and 50 kPa).
   b. 50 and 75 in./Hg (169 and 252 kPa).
   c. 15 and 25 in./Hg (50 and 85 kPa).
   d. None of the above.
6. A _____ _____ light is beneficial when using emulsion-to-base exposure orientation.
7. A broad light source is a common application for altering line image _____ and _____ _____.
8. How do you use a mask to do a contact exposure test?
9. What is a contact reversal?
10. Daylight film can be handled in normal room light without exposure. True or false?
11. How can you find out if the mask material is sufficient when contacting?
12. What is a spread?
13. What is a choke?
14. How does a diffuser sheet work?
15. In your own words, explain two types of color proofing systems.

SUGGESTED ACTIVITIES

1. Visit a facility and identify all of the operations that require contacting materials.
2. Use a contact frame to make a spread and a choke.
3. Visit a facility and observe the use of a transfer type proofing system.

Chapter 20

OFFSET LITHOGRAPHIC PLATEMAKING

After studying this chapter, you will be able to:
- Develop a variety of lithographic plates.
- Identify various types of platemaking equipment.
- Identify the main parts of lithographic plates.
- Describe the carriers associated with surface plates.
- Identify problems commonly associated with the platemaking process.

This chapter is concerned with the making of the lithographic plate. Most of the personnel in printing call the image carrier a "plate." The *plate* or *carrier* is used for printing multiple copies on a press. Each process uses a different type of plate. The lithographic plate will be discussed in detail in this chapter.

The *lithographic process* is based on the principle that grease and water do NOT readily mix. The generic term is *planography* which means printing from a flat surface. In other words, the nonimage and the image areas are on the same plane. Technically, this is not true since the image area is ever so slightly above the nonprinting area.

The plate has a *nonimage area* that must be moisture receptive and refuse ink. The *image area* must accept grease (ink) and refuse water. Fig. 20-1 illustrates how ink and water act for litho printing. NOTE: *Waterless lithography,* which uses ink viscosity to keep image and nonimage areas separate, is growing in popularity.

PLANOGRAPHY—AN ART FORM

Planography could once be classified as an art form. Lithography means "stone writing." The artist had to hand draw the image directly on a lithographic stone with an ink receptive material. The stone was then moistened and inked. The paper was placed on the stone, and pressure was used to transfer the ink to it. The artist had to remember that the image reversed because it was a direct method of printing. The image was not *offset* to another surface (blanket) and then transferred to the paper, Fig. 20-2. This was a very slow, demanding process.

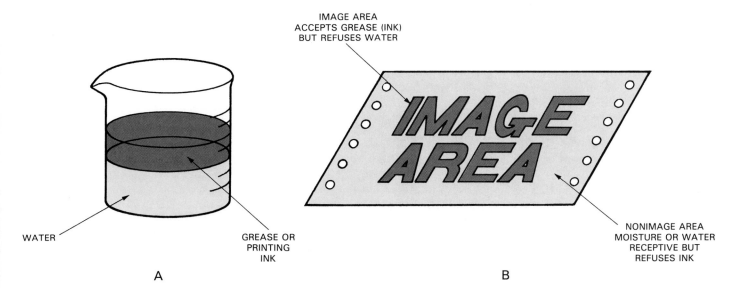

IMAGE AREA
ACCEPTS GREASE (INK)
BUT REFUSES WATER

WATER

GREASE OR
PRINTING
INK

NONIMAGE AREA
MOISTURE OR WATER
RECEPTIVE BUT
REFUSES INK

A

B

Fig. 20-1. A—Water and ink do not readily mix. If you pour ink into a jar of water, ink would normally float to surface and separate from water. B—Lithographic plates use principle of ink-water repulsion for printing. Image area accepts ink but rejects water and nonimage area accepts water but rejects ink.

311

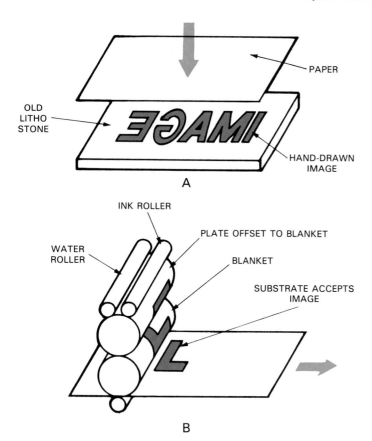

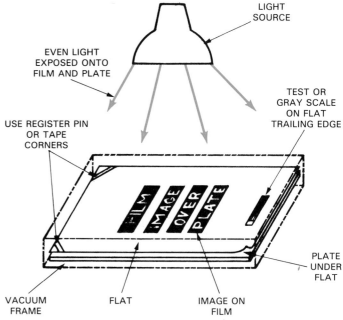

Fig. 20-3. When burning a plate, film is registered over plate. Light source then shines through image on film to expose light sensitive substance on plate surface. As you will learn, camera can also be used to expose plate.

Fig. 20-2. A—In early lithography, a thick, flat stone was used as the plate. Artist hand-formed image on litho stone in reverse. B—In litho printing today, plate transfers right reading image to an offset blanket. Blanket then transfers image to substrate.

Today, a light source is used to activate a light sensitive substance on the plate surface. The film is placed over the plate and the plate is exposed. This makes forming an image on the printing plate quick and easy, compared to hand-drawing the image on stone.

In the future, it is likely that the intermediate (film) will be eliminated and the image transferred from the original copy directly to the plate. Several such systems are being used currently.

PLATEMAKING EQUIPMENT

A basic platemaking department will have the following equipment: a light source, a vacuum frame, and a developing sink. Automatic plate processors and other equipment may also be used in a platemaking department.

Light source

Several types of light sources are used to expose plates. The light must be high in the ultraviolet and visible blue light rays. The light source must also give even illumination across the plate area, Fig. 20-3.

To assure constant and consistent light, an integrator is commonly installed. The system of controlling the exposure time of a plate is extremely important. This subject was covered in earlier chapters. Refer to the index for more information.

Vacuum frame

The *vacuum frame* holds the plate and flat (films) in close contact during the exposure. The printing frame must be sturdy. The hinged metal frame must hold the glass securely in place. The rubber blanket is connected to a vacuum pump. The air is sucked out from between the blanket and the glass. The blanket forces the plate and flat up against the glass, Fig. 20-4. This holds the image and plate in a flat or straight plane. Once they are in close contact, the exposure is made.

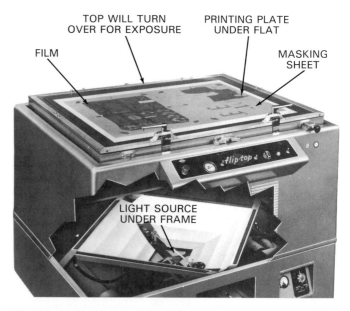

Fig. 20-4. Light source for this contact frame is inside unit. Frame flips over so bright exposure light is confined. (nuArc)

Some of the platemaking units are self-contained. The light source reflector, integrator or timer, vacuum frame, vacuum pump, and motor are all in one unit. The flip-top platemaker is an example of the self-contained unit, Fig. 20-5. This design simplifies the platemaking process.

Developing sink

The *plate developing sink* is especially designed for convenient and easy development of plates. The surface is smooth, with a sloping drainboard, Fig. 20-6. A water mixing control should be available and attached to the sink.

Fig. 20-5. This is a modern flip-top platemaker. It has electronic control of exposure for accurate burning of plate. (nuArc)

Fig. 20-6. This is a plate developing sink. It is needed when hand-treating the exposed plate surface with processing chemicals. (nuArc)

Automatic plate processors

Many of today's facilities use automatic plate processors, Fig. 20-7. The processor is very useful in a high volume type operation since automating the developing process saves cost and improves productivity. Care must be taken when purchasing a processor since some are designed for specific types of plates.

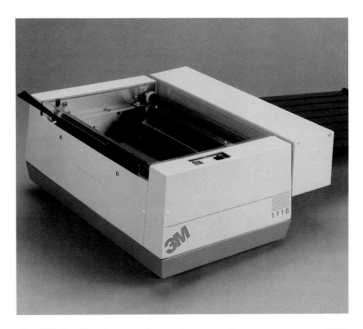

Fig. 20-7. This is a modern automatic plate processor.   (3M)

The processing chemicals may be automatically applied and replenished when needed.

Many of the carrier manufacturers have developed processing units. The carrier is transported through the unit at a determined rate of speed. It is fully processed and completely finished when it ejects from the processor.

Process monitoring is needed to make sure the chemicals are a proper strength to assure consistent development. The internal parts of a typical processor are shown in Fig. 20-8.

Fig. 20-9 shows an operator feeding a plate through an automatic processor.

LITHOGRAPHIC PLATES

Lithographic plates, as discussed for stone planography, are based on the same principle that grease and water do not mix. The image and nonimage areas are maintained chemically. This is required because the images are essentially on the same plane. The image area repels moisture and accepts ink while the nonimage area is water receptive and refuses ink.

One of the most common materials used to make present-day plates is aluminum. Plastic, paper, and metal are also found as *carrier* (plate) materials. Aluminum is used more because it prefers water over grease. It is also flexible, lightweight, and can be easily grained.

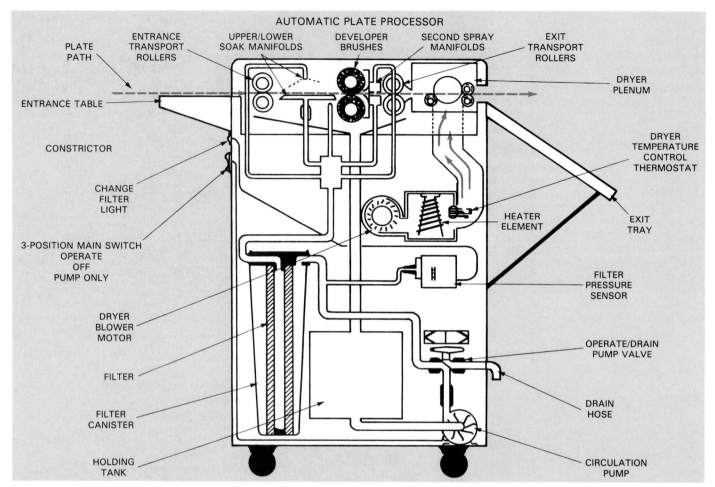

AUTOMATIC PLATE PROCESSOR

PLATE PATH

ENTRANCE TRANSPORT ROLLERS

UPPER/LOWER SOAK MANIFOLDS

DEVELOPER BRUSHES

SECOND SPRAY MANIFOLDS

EXIT TRANSPORT ROLLERS

ENTRANCE TABLE

DRYER PLENUM

CONSTRICTOR

DRYER TEMPERATURE CONTROL THERMOSTAT

CHANGE FILTER LIGHT

HEATER ELEMENT

EXIT TRAY

3-POSITION MAIN SWITCH
OPERATE
OFF
PUMP ONLY

FILTER PRESSURE SENSOR

DRYER BLOWER MOTOR

OPERATE/DRAIN PUMP VALVE

FILTER

FILTER CANISTER

DRAIN HOSE

HOLDING TANK

CIRCULATION PUMP

Fig. 20-8. Diagram shows how an automatic plate processor works. Exposed plate is fed into machine on left. Rollers feed plate into soaking manifolds, developing brushes, and second spray manifolds. This chemically treats surface of plate. Before leaving processor, hot air is forced over plate to dry it.

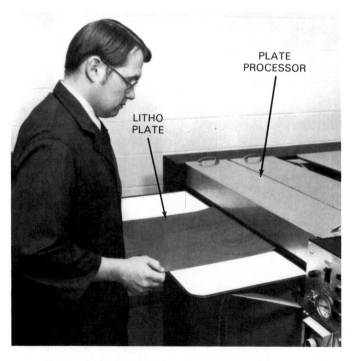

PLATE PROCESSOR

LITHO PLATE

Fig. 20-9. Automatic plate processors are commonly used in high volume printing facilities. (3M)

Lithographic plate parts

Generally speaking, offset lithographic plates have three parts: base or grain, covering, and coating. It is important for you to understand these parts.

Graining of base

Grain refers to the surface texture of the plate base. It can be very smooth or rough appearing when magnified. Several types of grains are used today. Each places a texture on the surface of the plate.

Three are *mechanical type grains:* ball, brushed, and sand blasted grains are the mechanical means of giving a textured surface to the plate. Fig. 20-10 shows several plate grain classifications.

Chemical graining is the fourth means of changing the surface of the plate. This is a chemical etching or anodizing process.

Paper and plastic plates are considered to be *grainless plates.* The surfaces of these plates are manufactured to hold moisture on their surface.

Plate covering

The plate can also be a COMBINATION of plastic, paper, or various types of metal. A *covering* is bonded to

SURFACE PLATES

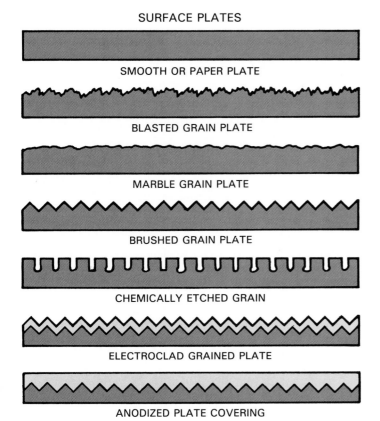

SMOOTH OR PAPER PLATE

BLASTED GRAIN PLATE

MARBLE GRAIN PLATE

BRUSHED GRAIN PLATE

CHEMICALLY ETCHED GRAIN

ELECTROCLAD GRAINED PLATE

ANODIZED PLATE COVERING

Fig. 20-10. These are some of the types of grains found on plates. Blasted grain uses air pressure to shoot abrasive onto plate surface to form texture. Brushed grain has abrasive rubbed over plate with brushes to produce texture. Chemicals can be used to etch and texture plate surface. An electrical process is used to texture electroclad and anodized plate grains.

the base of grained plates. This covering assists in holding the image area on the surface plate.

Plate coatings

Four kinds of presensitized plate coatings are commonly used in the industry. They are: negative, positive, additive, and subtractive working plates.

The *negative-working coatings* on a plate are those that cause an image to remain on the plate where light strikes the coating during the exposure. Negative film would be stripped and exposed with negative-working plate coatings.

The *positive-working coating* on a plate base is also light sensitive and the area struck by light becomes the nonimage area. Positive film is contacted to the positive-working plate for exposure.

The *additive surface plate* has the ink receptive material ADDED or APPLIED during processing.

The *subtractive plate* has the ink receptive material already applied to the image area surface. During processing, the ink receptive coating is REMOVED from the nonimage area.

Types of coatings

Different types of coatings are used by the manufacturers of plates. You should understand their differences.

One of the very common coatings is called diazo. It can

be negative as well as positive acting. Once the active light strikes a *diazo coating* on the plate, it becomes inactive. The nonimage areas remain active and can be removed during plate processing. The inactive image area remains as a part of the plate for printing the image.

Photopolymer coatings are used where the images must be long lasting and do NOT require added protection. When light strikes the coating, a strong linking of the coating's monomers results, forming a very tough image area.

The *silver halide coating* is another type of lithographic plate. The coating contains silver salts. After light strikes the surface and during the developing process, the image areas are converted to metallic silver. This type of coating is used with diffusion transfer plates.

Electrostatic plates have carbonized powders or liquids applied to the surface. The coating is placed on the lithographic plate *electrostatically* (using electricity and a static electrical charge). Although the surface of the plate is NOT light sensitive, a light sensitive material is used during the platemaking process.

When using silicone- and polymer-coated aluminum plates, the silicone rubber that is under the polymer coating hardens after exposure and processing. The unexposed silicone dissolves and is removed in the processing operation.

Other types of plates are also available but the ones discussed are the most common. Refer to manufacturer descriptions on more specialized plate coatings.

Handling plates

It is imperative that the personnel handle plates with care. Fingerprints or dirty roller marks will appear on the plate if cleanliness is not considered at all times.

All lithographic plates have some means of being attached to a printing press. The three types of holding means are: straight, pinbar, and serrated (slotted). These types are illustrated in Fig. 20-11. All three are commonly found in duplicator type presses but the larger presses tend to use the straight bar type of plate.

The *straight bar* is a press clamping device that holds the plate over the entire cylinder or plate length. The pinbar and the serrated are punched plates. The punched areas are positioned over the protruding devices on the leading edge of the cylinder and the trailing edge of the cylinder. If too much tension is put on the plate, the holes or slotted areas will tend to tear out.

It is imperative that personnel follow the manufacturer's suggestions for detailed information on how to get the most out of each lithographic plate. This subject is explained in detail later. You should also refer to the plate manufacturer's instructions for more information.

SURFACE PLATES

Two types of lithographic plates will be discussed—surface and deep etch types. This section of the chapter will present several of the most commonly used surface plates. The first is the direct image lithographic plate. Deep-etch types will be explained later.

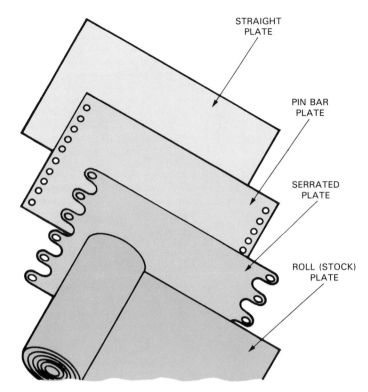

STRAIGHT
PLATE

PIN BAR
PLATE

SERRATED
PLATE

ROLL (STOCK)
PLATE

Fig. 20-11. Plates can also be classified by how they are attached to a press or their physical shape.

The *surface plate* is very prevalent in the industry. The name *surface* refers to the coating of light sensitive material.

The length of run varies according to the type of carrier and the developing process.

As pointed out earlier, two categories of surface carriers are commonly found in today's facilities—additive and subtractive. These carriers are available in many sizes. The short run plates are made of paper, plastic, or foil which is mounted on paper or plastic base materials.

Both categories of plates are classified as *presensitized,* which means the surface has been coated with a diazo or photopolymer material.

Photo direct platemaking

Most of today's *photo direct image carriers* are projected through a lens to a photosensitive plate. These are often fully automatic, computerized daylight systems, Fig. 20-12.

The camera-ready copy is placed face up in this system, Fig. 20-13. This allows the operator to see exactly where the copy is positioned. An automatic point-light registration allows the operator position the copy accurately and easily. Systems often permit automatic centering, which positions copy for consistent gripper edge when enlarging or reducing. The operator inputs the information on the control panel, Fig. 20-14. This is a totally automatic system. An older system appears in Fig. 20-15.

After the plate is exposed, it is automatically processed and ready to be positioned on the press. Fig. 20-16 shows this process.

Fig. 20-12. This is a direct photographic platemaking system. (3M)

Fig. 20-13. With direct photographic system, original image or layout sheet is placed on copyboard. Camera lens then directs reflected light onto plate to expose image on plate surface. (3M)

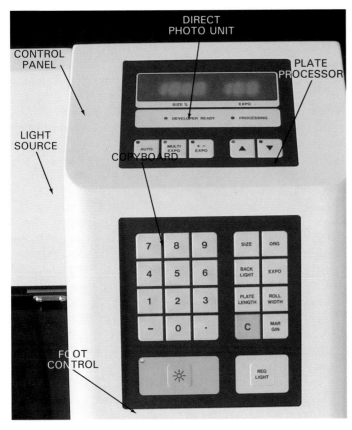

Fig. 20-14. Control panel of automatic direct platemaker. (3M)

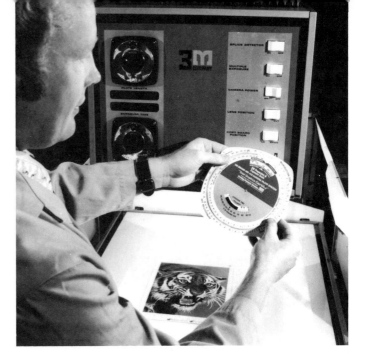

Fig. 20-15. Correct exposure is critical to platemaking. Here operator is using an exposure wheel or computer to calculate exposure time. (3M)

Once the plate is on the press, Fig. 20-17, the roll up procedure might vary with each type of system. Fast ink roll up is usually possible.

The photo direct plate process eliminates the use of a film intermediate. Also, the plate does not require special dampening systems or special inks. See Fig. 20-18.

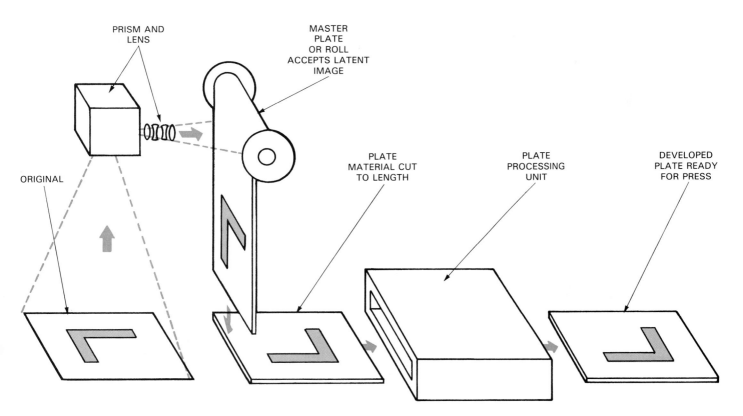

Fig. 20-16. Here is a simple diagram showing the principle of a plate exposure-processing system. First, original image is reflected through lens and prism onto plate's light sensitive coating. Roll of plate material is then fed down and cut off to size. Sheet of exposed plate is fed through automatic processing unit, dried, and then fed out of machine. Plate is then ready to be mounted on press.

Fig. 20-17. The image on the surface of the printing plate can easily be damaged by careless handling. Use care when handling a plate at all times.

Direct image plate

The *direct image plate* is made of plastic or paper. An ink receptive material is applied to the image carrier.

The most common piece of equipment used to put an image on the *master,* as this plate is sometimes called, is a strike-on machine which uses a carbon ribbon or overlay. The typewriter is commonly used for this purpose.

The image carrier is positioned in the machine and the carbon is deposited on the image carrier. It is also possible to place an image on the carrier with a grease pencil or a reproducing pen or pencil.

Sketching on the carrier is possible by using a non-reproducing pencil. This technique is NOT widely used, except in schools for low quality printing of teaching materials. It is a very satisfactory method to convey the concept of planography when a photomechanical technique is not available or possible.

Processing additive plates

The *additive plate* category has a coating which is hardened when exposed to ultra violet (UV) light rays. It is a two-step process.

The typical procedure for using additive plates is as follows:

1. Remove the plate from the package, Fig. 20-19. Be careful NOT to scratch the plate as it is removed from the package. The plate surface is light sensitive and time becomes an important handling factor. Working in a yellow light area will allow greater handling time.

    WARNING! The corners of the printing plates are very sharp. Extreme care must be taken to avoid being cut and injured. Severe lacerations have resulted from careless handling.

Fig. 20-18. Plate must be mounted correctly on press cylinder to prevent damage to plate or rollers. Make sure you know how to use the press properly.

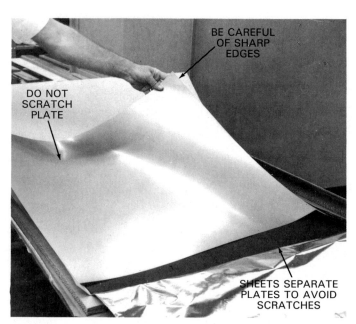

Fig. 20-19. Plate edges are very sharp and can cause painful cuts. Also, be careful not to scratch plate surface or the print job could be ruined. Sheets are used between plates to help protect them.

2. Position the plate in the light source equipment, Fig. 20-20. It is possible that the plate must be double burned. If this is true, the flats and the plate must be *pinned*. This is accomplished by lining up the flats and plate. Then punch them while they are in register. Register pins are then placed in the vacuum frame with the plate in place. The flat is then positioned properly over the carrier.

Fig. 20-20. Before exposing a plate, make sure glass is perfectly clean. If more than one exposure is going to be made on a plate, it must be pinned to assure good register.

3. Clean the glass before closing the light frame, Fig. 20-20. Turn on the vacuum. Wait 20 to 30 seconds to make sure the air has escaped and good contact has been made.

4. Even though most manufacturer's recommend an exposure time, it is a good practice to make a sample exposure with a negative step wedge, Fig. 20-21.

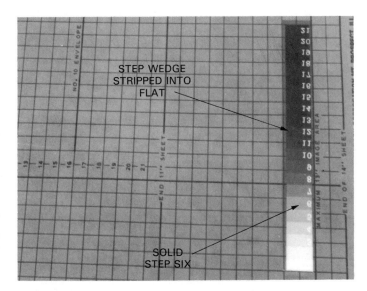

STEP WEDGE STRIPPED INTO FLAT

SOLID STEP SIX

Fig. 20-21. A negative step wedge is commonly stripped into the flat to assure and double-check for correct exposure of plate.

5. After development, a solid step six or seven will indicate a correct exposure. The correct solid step will be recommended by the manufacturer.

6. Clamp the plate for developing, Fig. 20-22. The clamps help eliminate plate movement. Absorption type paper is often placed between the carrier and the surface of the developing table.

Securing the plate is important because the sharp edges of the plate are capable of cutting the person developing the plate if slippage occurs.

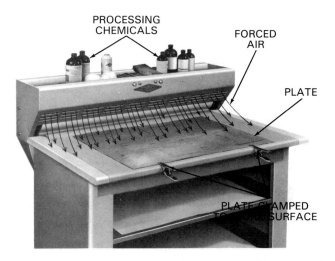

PROCESSING CHEMICALS

FORCED AIR

PLATE

PLATE CLAMPED TO TOP SURFACE

Fig. 20-22. Note how plate is clamped to plate finishing table. This will hold it while chemicals are applied to hand-develop light sensitive material. (nuArc)

7. Desensitize the lithographic plate. The *desensitizing solution* (gum-acid) is placed on the plate or on a slightly moistened graphic arts sponge and rubbed over the entire surface of the plate, Fig. 20-23. Some manufacturers will recommend other means of application. The main point to remember is that the surface must be totally densensitized.

Fig. 20-23. Here plate is being rubbed with desensitizing solution. (3M Company)

Note! The longer the plate is stored, the harder the coating is to remove.

8. Excess densitizer should be removed with the sponge. The plate must remain moist until developed.

9. Develop the lithographic plate. The amount of developer placed on the plate will vary with the plate size. For example, a small 10 x 15 inch image carrier should require no more than about a teaspoon of developer. The sponge or developing pad should be slightly moistened before coming in contact with the developer. "Rub up" the image by using circular movement, Fig. 20-24.

10. The balance between moisture and developer is very important to develop a plate properly. This will assure the maximum press run. Practice is required to become very proficient at processing the plate, Fig. 20-25.

11. Wash the plate. Wash off the excess developer. Some manufacturers will recommend that you squeeze the image carrier to remove the moisture. Care must be taken NOT to scratch the plate, Fig. 20-26.

12. Protect the surface of the plate. *Gum arabic,* at 14°Baumé, is commonly used as a solution to cover the surface of the image carrier while it is off the press. *Baumé* is a hydrometer measurement of liquid density or specific gravity. Fifty percent distilled water and fifty percent gum makes a good solution density.

Fig. 20-24. Note how light sensitive material is remaining to form image and nonimage area is removed to produce blank, nonprinting areas. Would this be an additive or subtractive plate? (3M)

Fig. 20-25. A small amount of developer is placed on a sponge and then rubbed over plate in even motion.

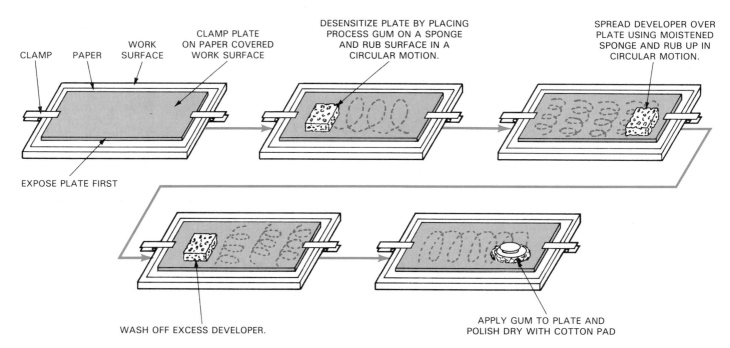

Fig. 20-26. This a summary of how you would process an additive, negative plate.

13. Buff the plate dry with a disposable wipe or cotton pad.
14. Store the plate properly, Fig. 20-27. One way to store the image carriers is to hang them up. Sometimes special cabinets are available or simply a bar is all that is needed to hang the plates.

    If the plates are to be stored flat, it is a good practice to place a sheet of paper between each image carrier to prevent scratches. When properly stored, plates can be kept for months without deterioration. However, many plants do NOT find it practical to store plates.
15. This technique for processing an additive lithographic plate is generally referred to as a two-step process. One

Fig. 20-27. Plates can be stored by hanging them up as shown. They can be stored lying flat on shelves if separated by protective sheets. (Foster Manufacturing Co.)

step is also available. The densensitizer and lacquer act as one solution.

16. Whatever plate is to be used, it is suggested that the manufacturer's recommendation for processing be followed.
17. If both sides of the plate are to be used, expose both sides before processing the plate.

    Now that the plate is processed, it is easy to understand why it is called an additive image carrier. The *developer* (lacquer) is ADDED to the image and makes the image become more ink receptive and last longer.

Processing subtractive plates

The *negative subtractive plate* requires only one processing step. These carriers are precoated. After exposure, the coating is removed from the nonimage area.

The technique is very similar to the additive process. The basic procedure is as follows:

1. Remove plate from the package. Again, do not scratch the surface of the image carrier and be careful because the plate edges are sharp. It is also suggested that handling occur in a yellow light environment. Work rapidly but carefully!
2. Expose the plate. Use the same instructions as listed for the additive procedure. Remember to test for the proper exposure time by using a negative step wedge positioned on the flat.
3. Develop the plate, Fig. 20-28. Apply the developing solution to a developing pad and rub over the entire sur-

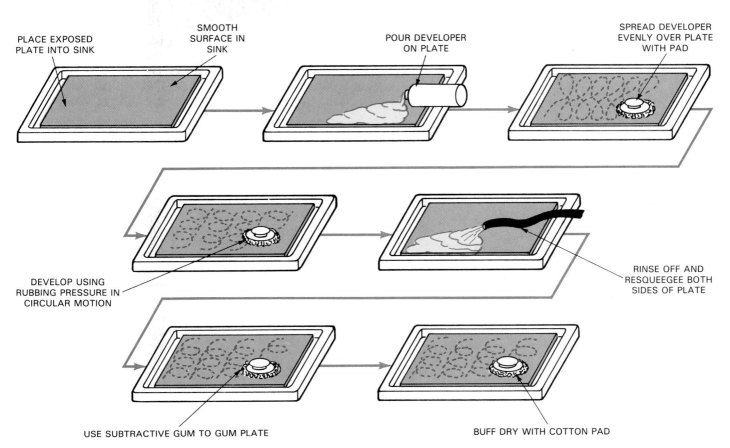

PLACE EXPOSED PLATE INTO SINK

SMOOTH SURFACE IN SINK

POUR DEVELOPER ON PLATE

SPREAD DEVELOPER EVENLY OVER PLATE WITH PAD

DEVELOP USING RUBBING PRESSURE IN CIRCULAR MOTION

RINSE OFF AND RESQUEEGEE BOTH SIDES OF PLATE

USE SUBTRACTIVE GUM TO GUM PLATE

BUFF DRY WITH COTTON PAD

Fig. 20-28. Note basic steps for processing a subtractive, negative plate.

face of the image carrier. Allow the solution to do the work. Wait for approximately 20 seconds and then rub in a circular motion. The coating must be removed from the nonprinting area.

4. Wash the plate. Wash the solution from the surface of the carrier. Again, use extreme care if a squeegee is used to remove excess moisture as it can scratch the image area easily. Wash the solution from the developing pad. Thorough washing is very important!

5. Gum the plate after it dries. Place the plate on a dry surface. Spread subtractive gum over entire carrier. Then buff dry.

6. Store the plate. The technique is the same as that described in the additive procedure.

Processing Hydrolith plates

One of the newer developed plates is called the Hydrolith plate. It is a process that only requires water to develop the plate.

The following steps are required for processing the Hydrolith plate.

1. Expose plate. Use a high intensity light source. The exposure should be made so that a solid step six appears on the gray scale. The step six gives a very durable image. The second side is also usable and its exposure should be made following the first exposure.

2. If you do NOT have an exposure for the second side, expose it to approximately one-quarter of the normal time. This will prevent coating removal on the second side when developing the plate.

3. Develop the plate. Use yellow safe lighting around the plate developing area. Remember that the area in which you develop this plate must be clean and free of contaminating materials. Saturate a developing pad with water and distribute the water evenly over the plate. Use very light pressure and a circular motion to develop the plate.

4. Rinse the plate. Rinse the Hydrolith plate thoroughly with water using a spray or hose if possible.

5. Squeegee the plate. Squeegee the Hydrolith plate on both sides. Then take a soft cotton pad and wipe the plate dry. This must be done on both sides.

6. Gum the plate. The Hydrolith plate must be gummed immediately with Hydrolith plate finisher. The total plate area must be covered. The gum is actually desensitizing the plate.

   Remember, the plate must be gummed immediately after development. If this is not done, you cannot be assured of clean, fast roll-up on the press.

7. Buff the plate dry. Using a plate wipe, buff the plate surface dry. This completes the processing of the Hydrolith plate. As you will note, it is a very simple process. Cleanliness plays a very important role in the process.

Positive-working surface plates

A positive-working surface plate makes it possible to expose a positive film image to a plate and the image area remains ink receptive. This is the opposite of the negative-acting surface plate. The film must be positive to have it work on a positive acting plate.

Diffusion-transfer plates

Diffusion-transfer is a generic term. The process is more often called by a trade name. This method of making an image carrier eliminates the *intermediates* (films) used to make conventional surface plates.

If time is a major factor, this system allows the printer to go from camera-ready copy to carrier in less than ten minutes.

Negative paper is placed in the camera, just as film. It is then exposed as line copy, Fig. 20-29. The negative can also be made by the contact method.

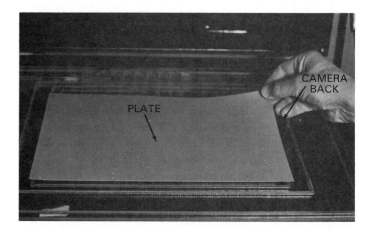

Fig. 20-29. Operator is mounting diffusion transfer plate on camera-back for exposure. Unlike contact frame, camera can be used to enlarge or reduce image on plate.

After exposure, a diffusion-transfer lithoplate is positioned with the emulsion side of the negative toward the litho plate. Both the negative and carrier are processed in a diffusion-transfer processor. See Fig. 20-30.

The exposed negative image is diffused from its surface to the carrier. After a designated period of time, the negative and carrier are pulled apart and treated with a solution that makes the image area receptive to ink.

The image carriers are of two types. The *short run* image plate (up to 2000 impressions) is made of PAPER. A METAL PLATE is also available for *longer run* lengths to approximately 25,000 impressions.

The metal plate surface image is easily scratched, so care must be taken when handling. Follow the manufacturer's recommendations when working with diffusion-transfer litho plates.

Waterless plates

The Toray Waterless Plate™ is distributed by Polychrome and is a presensitized plate designed to be used on a lithographic press without a dampening solution. The plates are manufactured in both negative and positive working formats.

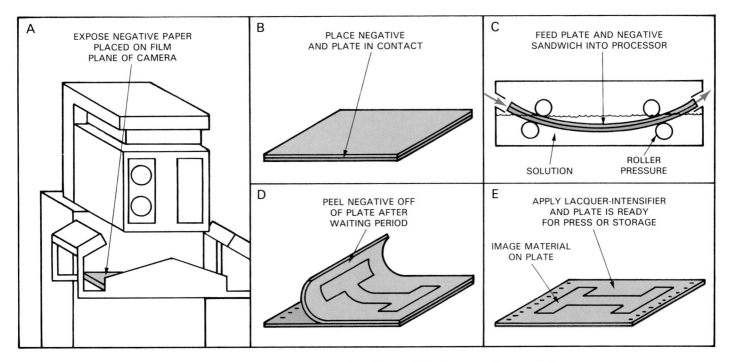

Fig. 20-30. This is a summary of making a diffusion transfer metal plate.

When exposed and processed, the nonimage area is covered with an ink-repellent silicone rubber layer, while the image area is slightly recessed and presents an ink receptive polymer surface. See Fig. 20-31.

The following are typical steps to process the plate:

1. Expose. Use a conventional exposure frame or step and repeat machine. A conventional light source is recommended.
2. Develop. The plate may be developed by hand or a special automatic processor. Special chemicals are used to develop the plate.

The plate does not require gumming, if used within a month of processing. The surface is resistant to oxidation, but it is recommended that the plate be stored in a protective paper slip sheet to help prevent scratching. If the plate is to be stored for an extended period of time, a Toray plate conserver should be used. Plates should be cleaned before storage.

The waterless plate may be run on a conventional offset lithographic press, but it is recommended that the press be equipped with a temperature control system. When the right temperature is maintained, toning can be controlled.

Electrostatic image carriers

Electrostatic printing is commonly used for lower quality work and also for short runs. However, excellent quality images, maps for example, are sometimes printed by this method.

The two common methods of making electrostatic plates are by exposing the carrier with an arrangement similar to a process camera and by a contact type image plate. Look at Fig. 20-32.

The camera process allows the reflected light to strike the carrier. When the light strikes the nonimage area of the plate, the positive charge is eliminated from the nonimage area. The image area remains positively charged. A resin powder, which is negatively charged, is attracted to the image area and fused to form an ink receptive image area.

A couple of the systems have been designed as automatic units. The copy images are automatically positioned on a

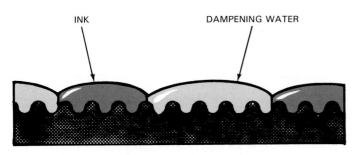

CONVENTIONAL WET OFFSET PLATE

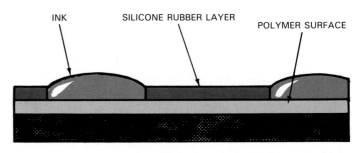

TORAY WATERLESS PLATE

Fig. 20-31. Comparison of new waterless plate and conventional wet offset plate. (Polychrome)

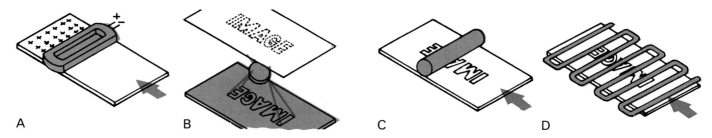

A B C D

Fig. 20-32. Basics of making an electrostatic plate. A—Surface of plate is first charged with electrostatic energy. B—Image is exposed on plate and only image area remains electrically charged. C—Plate is fed over drum that deposits developer onto plate surface. Toner only adheres to image area with static charge. D—Heating element is used to bond developer to image area.

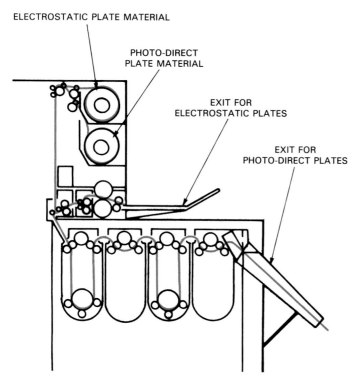

ELECTROSTATIC PLATE MATERIAL

PHOTO-DIRECT PLATE MATERIAL

EXIT FOR ELECTROSTATIC PLATES

EXIT FOR PHOTO-DIRECT PLATES

Fig. 20-33. This is a cutaway of an electrostatic plate attachment.

carrier and processed automatically. Special attachments are used to position the carrier on the press for printing. Refer to Figs. 20-33 and 20-34.

Laser lithographic plates

The *laser lithographic platemaking system* is in limited use today. However, it is possible that this process will change the newspaper and magazine operations of the graphic communications industry.

Very simply stated, the pasted-up material is scanned, Fig. 20-35. The sensing device sends electronic signals to a

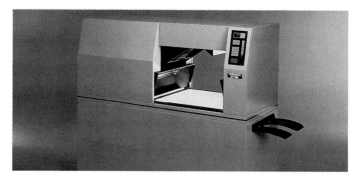

Fig. 20-34. This is an electrostatic platemaker. (AM Multigraphics)

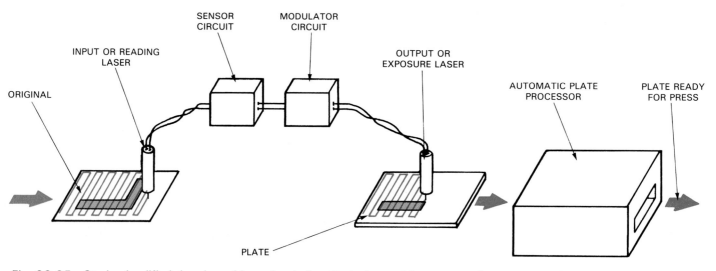

SENSOR CIRCUIT

MODULATOR CIRCUIT

INPUT OR READING LASER

OUTPUT OR EXPOSURE LASER

ORIGINAL

AUTOMATIC PLATE PROCESSOR

PLATE READY FOR PRESS

PLATE

Fig. 20-35. Study simplified drawing of laser facsimile offset platemaking system. Laser scans original image and converts image into electrical data. Sensor circuits and modulator amplify and modify this data to operate exposure laser. Exposure laser is moved over plate to burn same image or modified image on light sensitive coating. Plate is then processed and ready for printing.

modulator. The information is then digitized into computer language (binary system). The digitized material is directed to a plate by the exposure laser.

Each line is exposed to a plate by the laser. Once all of the images of a page are on the plate, the plate is automatically processed.

With this system, one location can scan all of the images sent by microwave or telephone to satellite exposure stations.

The images that appear on the plate are identical to the original pasted-up material. With this process, the need for phototypesetters could be reduced in some types of graphic communications facilities.

DEEP-ETCH PLATES

As the name implies, *deep-etch plates* have the image area slightly recessed below the surface of the base material. The most common base metal is aluminum, although steel or some other metal alloys could be used.

The image area is chemically coppered and lacquered, making the image area very ink receptive.

Deep-etch, single metal plates are positive working and produce high quality images. They are also very dependable. The carriers are intended to be used for long runs of over one-half million copies of a product.

Multimetal plates

Multimetal plates are for run lengths above the needs of the single metal deep-etch plate. These carriers use a base of aluminum or steel and they then have a second or third metal electroplated to the base. These metals are copper, brass, or chromium.

Two of the most common multimetal plates are: bimetal and trimetal. Fig. 20-36 shows these types.

The base material or nonimage areas of both types are either made of aluminum or steel. The image area of the bimetal plate is copper or brass. The trimetal carrier image is made of layers of copper and chromium.

Processing of these carriers is also very involved. Follow manufacturer directions.

MACHINE PROCESSING

Most printing firms have changed to machine processing of plates, since it is very difficult to control the variables associated with manual plate processing.

The automatic plate processor develops, rinses, gums, and dries the plate in one simple operation, Fig. 20-37. Many systems are available that use aqueous-based chemistry. This chemistry is nonflammable and can be disposed of in conventional wastewater treatment systems. It meets most local, state, and federal volatile organic compound (VOC) requirements.

VARIABLES IN PLATEMAKING

Most of the self-contained plate making units are not concerned with the plate-to-light distance. The distance is set

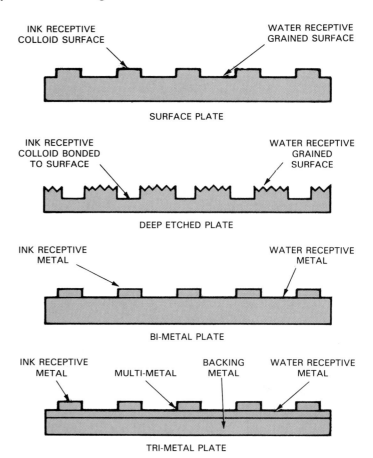

Fig. 20-36. Note different plate surface materials, especially multimetal plate surface.

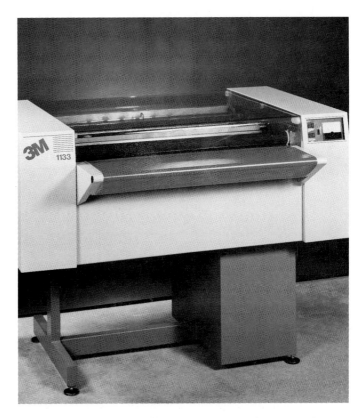

Fig. 20-37. This is a typical automatic plate processor found in printing plants.

and cannot be changed. The equipment is designed to eliminate the need for setting light distance.

Whenever the vacuum frame, light source, and reflector have free movement, the best light distance must be calibrated. If the frame is TOO CLOSE to the light source, overexposure of the image on the plate will result. When the distance is TOO GREAT, underexposure results when the same time is used.

Contact is another variable to be considered. Insufficient contact changes the size or sharpness of the image. A soft, pliable vacuum blanket assists in assuring good contact.

Improper stripping may also cause poor contact. Improper stripping refers to excessive use of tape and overlapping of the pieces of film. Opaquing solution should be a very thin film and not a built up layer of solution.

The vacuum should be consistent from one plate to another. The vacuum gauge should read in the 22 to 25 inch/Hg range. Check for collapsed hoses, plugged hoses, or a blocked air outlet if the vacuum indicator is less than the desired reading.

Litho plate problems

Greater productivity is a high priority in today's industrial environment. Plates that perform satisfactorily are essential. The best platemaking department might occasionally produce plates that create problems in the pressroom. When this happens, a troubleshooter or problem solver can save many hours of searching. Too often, the problem is not correctly identified and unnecessary work takes place.

Once the problem is identified, possible causes must be listed. Then, each possible cause must be systematically eliminated.

Some of the more common plate related problems are explained in this section.

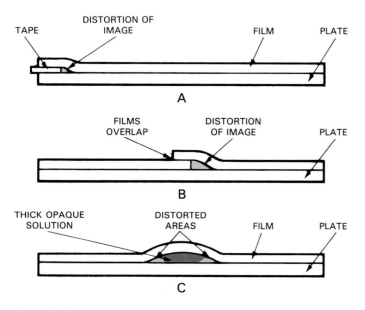

Fig. 20-38. All of these practices can cause printing problems. A—Too much tape has lifted image so plate image is distorted. B—Films overlap and image on plate is not accurate. C—Too much opaque solution can also keep film off of plate and distort image.

Soft image

To process a good lithographic plate, the film intermediate must be of high quality.

One of the most frequent problems is a *"soft image."* This occurs when the outside edges of an image have a density that is NOT as great as the inside portion of the image. This problem is apparent with many halftones. With a soft image, the dots appear to be vignetted. This often is called a *veiling, halo,* or *fringe dot.* It is imperative that the film intermediate represent the original copy.

The softness of an edge can be checked with *darkfield illumination.* This technique requires the viewing of the image intermediate with a black background, with the light source at the side. If the image on the intermediate appears to be very dense in the center and brownish around the edge, this is the first indicator that the press person will have problems with a soft image.

The platemaker must have an integrator control device to assure that each contact has the same amount of light striking the carrier. Making the film intermediate over again is very costly.

Contact problems

When exposing the plate, it is essential that the film intermediate be in contact with the plate. If good contact is NOT made, the image will have greater size than the original because of light escaping under the edges and exposing the carrier. See Fig. 20-38.

Remember that the drawing-down process does NOT take place immediately. Allow at least 20 or 30 seconds for trapped air to escape before exposing a plate. Large carriers might require as much as two minutes for maximum contact.

Scumming

A very common problem is *scumming*—the nonimage area has ink adhering to it. Several typical causes for scumming are: ink/water not in balance, high acid fountain solution, or a poorly desensitized plate.

One of the first steps would be to thoroughly clean the plate and regum. If scumming is still a problem, the poor results are probably caused by the press operation.

Gum blinding

Gum blinding is an image loss type of problem. A large amount of gum is on the image area. Because of this, the image will not accept ink. Usually, it is very evident at the beginning of a run.

Image loss can also be caused by having moisture on the carrier before it is exposed. Storing the carriers in a cool, dry place is imperative.

Contamination

Contamination with other types of chemicals is also a possible trouble source. Make sure the carrier developing area is clean.

Scratches

Improper handling of carriers often results in scratches on the plate surface. Sliding carriers over each other or another surface is NOT recommended. A sheet in between each carrier is a suggestion to help eliminate scratching problems.

Equipment problems

Choosing the correct equipment is important. A good vacuum printing frame is essential for proper drawdown and good contact. The frame should be large enough so that it will accommodate the largest carrier in the facility without interfering with the drawdown system.

A recommended light source with a light integrator, is critical where line or supply voltage to the light could fluctuate. A voltage regulator will control voltage change.

The reflectors and glass must be kept clean. Use extreme care and make sure the light source is disconnected when cleaning the unit.

A timing device is a critical unit to assure consistent exposure times for various plates. It is a valuable measuring device.

Illumination in the area should be considered because the sensitivity of each carrier will vary. Too much light can cause possible exposure. Most carriers can be handled safely in a yellow light environment.

Masking materials (goldenrod) should have the proper light stopping ability. If not, partial exposure of the nonimage area can result. In all operations, it is suggested that a pin register system be incorporated to assure proper placement of images on each carrier.

Correcting problems

It is possible that a carrier will NOT perform in the manner expected. If problems arise, you must:
1. Make sure you have identified the problem.
2. List the possible causes of the trouble.
3. One by one, eliminate the possible causes.
4. Control the process so that it does NOT occur again.
5. Try to prevent problems before they occur.
6. Keep a record of problems and corrections.

KNOW THESE TERMS

Plate, Carrier, Lithographic process, Planography, Litho stone, Plate developing sink, Automatic plate processor, Grain, Base, Covering, Coating, Mechanical graining, Chemical graining, Grainless plate, Negative-working plate, Positive-working plate, Additive plate, Subtractive plate, Diazo coating, Photopolymer coating, Silver halide coating, Electrostatic plate, Straight bar, Surface plate, Presensitized, Direct photographic plate, Starter solution, Desensitizing solution, Gum arabic, Baumé, Developer, Lacquer, Hydrolith plate, Diffusion transfer plate, Intermediate, Laser litho plate, Deep-etch plate, Multimetal plate, Soft image, Veiling, Darkfield illumination, Scumming, Gum blinding, Contamination.

REVIEW QUESTIONS — CHAPTER 20

1. How does the lithographic process work?
2. This material can be used in the manufacture of litho plates:
   a. Aluminum.
   b. Plastic.
   c. Paper.
   d. All of the above.
   e. None of the above.
3. Grainless plates hold moisture and they are made of _____ and _____.
4. A negative-working plate coating causes an image to _____ on the plate where light strikes the coating.
5. With a positive-working plate, the area struck by light during exposure becomes the _____ area.
6. Explain the difference between a subtractive plate and an additive plate.
7. This type of plate has a carbonized coating of powder or liquid applied to its surface.
   a. Photopolymer.
   b. Silver Halide.
   c. Diazo.
   d. Electrostatic.
8. What is starter solution?
9. In your own words, how do you process an additive plate?
10. A _____ plate only requires water for development.
11. What is a laser lithographic plate?
12. Explain the difference between a surface plate and a deep-etch plate.
13. A _____ _____ is a problem where the outside edges of an image are weak or do not have as great a density.
14. _____ is a problem where ink adheres to the nonimage area.
15. _____ _____ is a problem of image loss because of too much gum on the image area.

SUGGESTED ACTIVITIES

1. Prepare an additive and subtractive plate using an intermediate design to be a finished product.
2. Visit a plant and prepare a statement giving a description of the platemaking process used to produce lithographic plates.

Is 'printing quality' what you think it is? If, when discussing or describing printing quality concepts, you find yourself at odds with others (customers, peers, competitors, employees)--there is an obvious communications gap. Who is right...who is wrong? It really doesn't matter, if the confusion results in hurting your business. Perhaps the primary cause bears a direct relationship to the fact that you have yet to address and confirm in your own mind...what your enterprise really represents. What is the principal reason for the existence of your company?

A

D

B

E

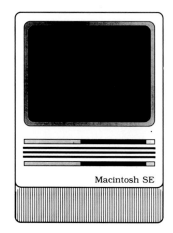

Meet "*Mac*" at

Arizona
State
University

Graphic Arts Department Tempe, Arizona

C

F

Compare various types of images. A—Line copy created by typesetter with hard copy output on photopaper. B—Pen and ink drawing created by an artist. C—Graphic images and copy generated by a PC with hard copy output using a laser printer. D—Line work combined with shading material. E—Halftone created from a photograph. F—Images in reverse.

Chapter 21

RELIEF PLATES

After studying this chapter, you will be able to:
• Identify the various types of relief plates.
• Explain basic processes needed to make relief plates.
• Follow the steps needed to make a rubber plate.
• Describe how to make a photopolymer plate.
• Explain how to make an electrotype.

The *letterpress* or *relief process* prints from a raised surface. The non-image area is recessed or relieved below the printing surface, Fig. 21-1. This is unlike the lithographic process that basically has the image and nonimage areas on the same plane.

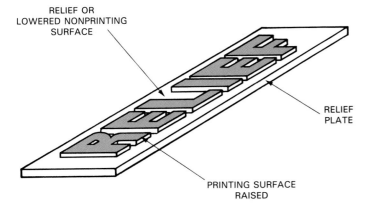

Fig. 21-1. The relief process prints from a raised surface that takes ink. Nonimage area is recessed below printing surface.

Relief printing is an older process that has been primarily replaced by lithography. However, since it is still found in some areas of printing, you should have a basic understanding of how and when letterpress is used in the industry.

Note! Letterpress and relief printing are also discussed in other chapters of this text. Refer to the index for more information as needed.

ORIGINAL AND DUPLICATE RELIEF PLATES

Plates for printing relief images can be classified as two basic types: original and duplicate plates.

The *original plate,* also called the *master* or *primary* plate, or original "lockup" (composed characters). It is generally made of zinc, copper, or magnesium. The original plate can be used directly for printing or it can be used to make a duplicate plate.

The *duplicate plate* is a copy of the original plate. It can be made of plastic, rubber, stereotype (metal casting forms mold), or electrotype (electro-chemical exchange forms mold).

A duplicate plate is needed for long press runs. If the original were used on the press, it could wear out before the end of the run and another plate would have to be made from the negative or lock-up. Several duplicate plates can be made from the original. Also, duplicates can be made from the master and then sent to different printing locations.

Relief plates come in various shapes depending upon the type of press. They can be flat, curved, or wrap-around types, as shown in Fig. 21-2. When a wrap-around plate is used, it can be termed *dry offset, letterset printing, flexography,* etc.

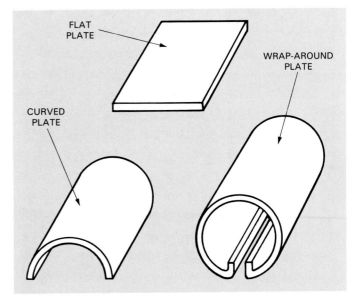

Fig. 21-2. Relief plates come in various shapes: flat, curved, and wrap-around.

Original plate production

Original plates can be made in several ways. These techniques include:

1. PHOTOMECHANICAL MASTER PLATES (light sensitive coating on plate is exposed through negative to form relief or recess nonimage area below printing surface).
2. MECHANICALLY-ENGRAVED MASTER PLATE (electronic device scans negative and mechanical arm cuts out nonimage area, leaving raised printing surface).
3. MANUALLY-PREPARED MASTER PLATE (foundry type, machine composition, or hand carving is used to produce plate).

Duplicate plate production

Duplicate plates, made from the master, can also be made using several methods of production. The most common of these are:

1. STEREOTYPES (a mat or reverse of the original is made out of soft material; then the mat is used to cast the duplicate out of metal).
2. ELECTROTYPES (complex process of casting original and then using electro-chemical process to form duplicate out of metal).
3. FLEXOGRAPHY or FLEXIBLE PLATES (plastic or rubber plates are molded from original using various techniques).

Photoengraving

Photoengraving is one of the older photomechanical processes for producing a relief printing plate, Fig. 21-3. The plate could be made up of line images or halftone images. It is also possible to have a combination of the two.

An etching process takes place to make the relief image by photoengraving. The plate is coated with a light sensitive coating. A negative is placed next to the coating and the plate is exposed.

The coating in the exposed area acts as a *resist* that protects the image area. The nonimage area is etched to a designated depth, Fig. 21-4.

The developing process requires exact controls. This is required to maintain the correct size dots and line widths at the proper etched depths. This conventional method is time consuming and requires close observation.

Fig. 21-4. This is another photoengraved metal relief plate. Once processed, it is ready to be mounted on press.

Powderless etching

Powderless etching has replaced the conventional etching technique. The metals commonly used are zinc, magnesium, and copper. The principle for each metal is the same even though the etchout will change.

During the etching process, a gelatinous precipitate adheres to the sides of the image elements. This prevents the etching from undercutting the image elements.

Photopolymer plate

A *photopolymer plate* is a precoated, plastic relief plate. A very hard, light-sensitive polymer or plastic is bonded to a base or backing material. See Fig. 21-5.

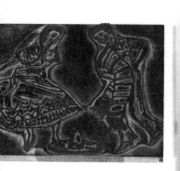

Fig. 21-3. The photoengraving can be made of various materials. Note how image area is raised above nonimage area.

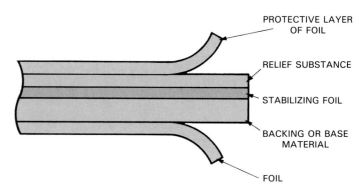

PROTECTIVE LAYER OF FOIL

RELIEF SUBSTANCE

STABILIZING FOIL

BACKING OR BASE MATERIAL

FOIL

Fig. 21-5. Note the basic structure of a photopolymer flexographic plate.

Basically, the polymer hardens when it is exposed to high intensity, ultraviolet light. When exposed with the negative, the image area is hardened while the nonimage area remains soft and can be washed off (processed) and lowered below the printing surface. Refer to Fig. 21-6.

Photopolymer plates are being used in newspaper production and on the relatively new Cameron belt press. The *Cameron press* can print a complete book or newspaper with a single pass through the press.

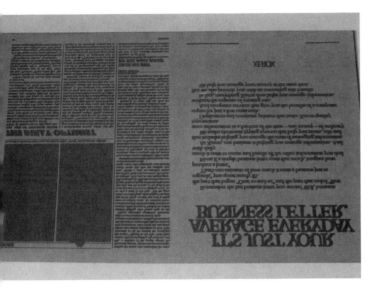

Fig. 21-6. This photopolymer plate is also a direct plate. You can tell it is direct because the image is wrong-reading.

The plastic plate will see changes in the coming years. More and more plates will be developed as flexographic printing increases. Great changes are expected in the future as the press designs are changed to print high quality four-color work. The plates are lightweight and the relief plate can be made directly from the photographic negative. The method of preparing the material is the same as used to produce an offset lithographic plate.

Photopolymer plate production

The photopolymer plate is exposed while in contact with the negative. Then the plate is processed. The plastic plate is etched and washed in a processor. The washed plate is dried and sometimes returned to the exposure unit for additional hardening by more exposure. The light source hardens the relief images to make them last longer on the press.

Fig. 21-7 illustrates the basic steps for making a photopolymer plate.

In some cases, the plate needs to be trimmed. After trimming, the plate is ready for mounting. Most of the newspaper type presses have a clamping device on the saddle to hold the plate or plates in place.

These carriers also have the capability of being used flat. The type of base material depends on the thickness of the plate. To be printed on a flat bed type press, the base and the plate must equal a thickness of .918 inches.

When the plate is to be used for direct printing, the image is WRONG-READING. If the relief image is to be used for letterset printing, the image must be RIGHT-READING.

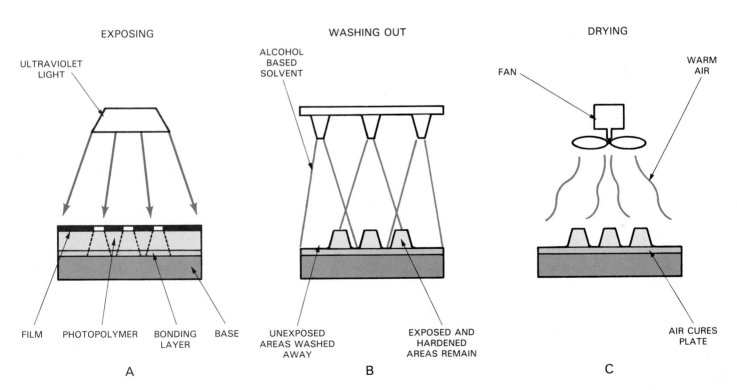

Fig. 21-7. These are the basic steps for making a photopolymer relief plate. A—Image film is placed over plate. Light exposes image areas and changes them chemically. B—During processing, solvent is used to wash off nonimage areas. Image area has been hardened by exposure and is not removed. C—Plate is then dried and usually exposed to more light to make plate ready for press or storage.

The letterset printing method uses an intermediate as in offset lithography. The image is transferred to an *intermediate,* called a *blanket,* and then it is transferred to a substrate. In this case, with the change of a cylinder, the press can be used for letterset as well as offset lithography, Fig. 21-8.

Fig. 21-8. This press is designed to be used for letterset or offset lithographic printing.

Stereotype

Sometimes, the original or primary printing plate is NOT the one used in the printing process. A *duplicate* is made from the original. These are commonly called *stereotypes, electrotypes, plastic plates,* or *rubber plates.*

The *stereotype* is made by pouring molten metal (lead, tin, and antimony) into a mold or *mat,* Fig. 21-9. The stereotype is either poured to form around a cylinder or to be used flat. The letterpress newspaper presses commonly used curved stereotypes but today this is changing to the wrap-around photopolymer plate.

The *matrix* or *mat* is made by placing the blank rubber sheet over a type form or other relief form. With extreme pressure, the images are pressed into the mat material. This forms an intaglio (reversed) image.

The mat has high moisture content and must be dried and formed as a curved or flat mat. The term commonly associated with this step is *scorching.*

After the mat has been scorched, it is placed in position for casting. The poured molten metal forms an image in the intaglio portion of the matrix. The edges are trimmed and sometimes the nonimage area must be routed to a greater depth so that it will not print.

Electrotype

An *electrotype* is a high quality relief plate that can be made flat or curved, Fig. 21-10. The method generally used to make an electrotype is molding, electroforming, backing, and finishing. This process is illustrated in Fig. 21-11.

Vinyl sheeting is placed over the original relief images and then heated. Once the vinyl sheeting has formed an intaglio image, this image is sprayed with silver. The silver forms a very thin layer on the surface of the sheeting.

The silver is a conductive material. By electroforming on a layer of metal, such as copper, the plate surface is built up slightly to a given thickness. This is an electrochemical process that forms the relief image.

Fig. 21-9. This is an example of a mat that was used to create a stereotype.

Fig. 21-10. This is an electrotype, a relief plate that can produce high quality images and very long press runs.

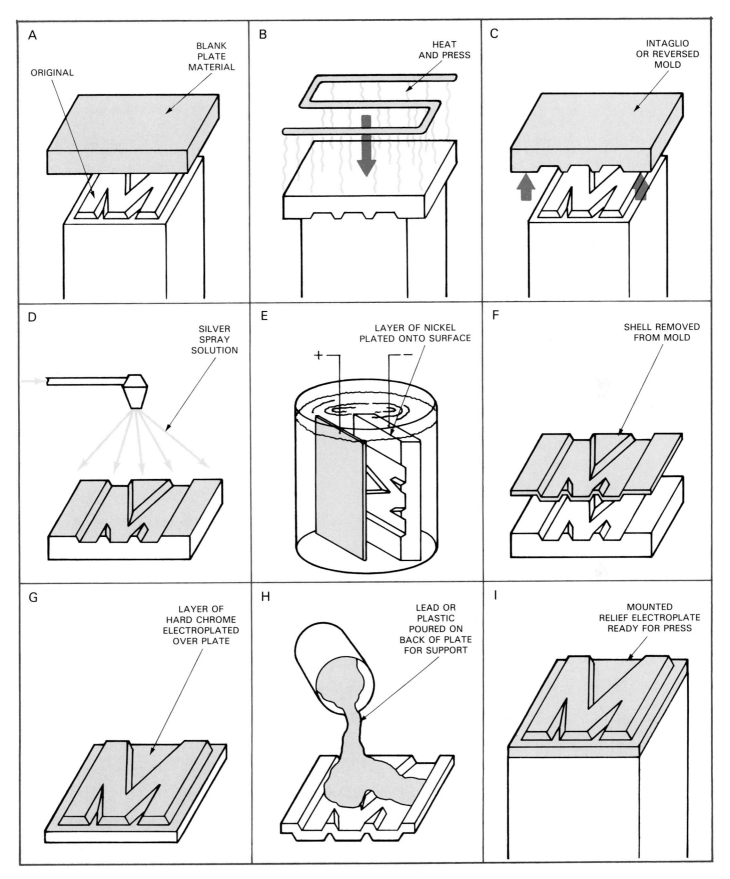

Fig. 21-11. *Study the basic steps for making an electrotype plate. A—Blank plate material is positioned over original image. B—Heat and pressure are used to form image in plate material. C—Plate with reverse image is removed from original. D—A coating of silver is sprayed over plate. E—A layer of nickel is electroplated onto plate surface. F—Thin shell of metal is removed from mold. G—Layer of hard chrome is electroplated onto plate. H—Lead or plastic is poured onto back of plate to give strength. I—Plate is machined to proper thickness and is ready for press.*

This thin image material cannot take abuse so it is backed with lead or plastic. This gives the plate its thickness. The electrotypes are finished by shaving the backs of the plates to make them have an equal thickness. The electrotypes are attached to a base and ready to use.

Because of the present de-emphasis in industry, this has been a very brief explanation. It does not include the many details to complete the finished product.

Rubber and plastic plates

The process of making rubber or plastic plates is very similar and the end product of the two materials can be used in much the same manner. They are commonly called *flexible plates* and nearly all of them are the duplicate type.

The use of plastic type plates has increased recently. An example of a plastic plate is found in Fig. 21-12. Fig. 21-13 gives an example of a rubber plate.

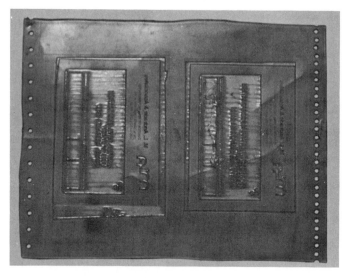

Fig. 21-12. The plastic plate, like this one, is becoming more common to the industry.

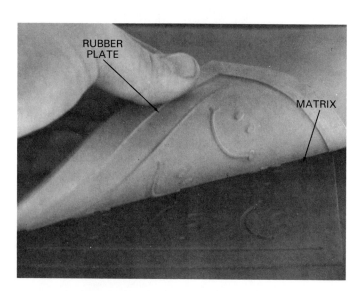

Fig. 21-13. The rubber plate has been used successfully as a rubber stamp or as a flexo plate.

The rubber and plastic plates are used to print on various substrates. Examples are: package printing, foil, wrapping paper, bags, paper, and sometimes fabric materials.

The latest means of making rubber flexographic plates is by using a laser. The laser tracks the original image. A computer can use laser input to operate a cutter. The engraving or cutting head removes the nonimage areas of the printing roller or plate.

RUBBER STAMPS

The *rubber stamp* is an easy to understand example of the use of a rubber plate. The rubber stamp press is generally small, Fig. 21-14. The presses used to make rubber plates are larger.

The presses have two flat platen surfaces. One of the platens must have a controlled heating element. The two flat surfaces must be parallel and pressure is required to bring the surfaces together. Fig. 21-15 shows the general relationship of the parts.

Fig. 21-14. The rubber stamp press has flat top and bottom surfaces. A heating element is located in the top surface of the press.

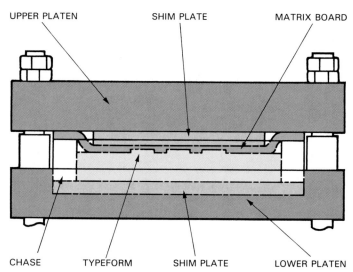

Fig. 21-15. Note the relationship of parts on a rubber stamp press for making the matrix.

Making a rubber stamp

Since "flexo" is becoming more prevalent in the industry, the making of a rubber stamp can be related to the industrial application of flexography. Typically, the following procedure would be used:

1. The rubber stamp press must be turned on and heated to approximately 300 °F to 350 °F (149 °C to 177 °C).
2. The relief form must be composed. Special type, such as service type, is recommended since it will withstand the heat and pressure. Ordinary foundry type is softer and might be smashed under the pressure.
3. The form must be locked up in a chase or holding device, Fig. 21-16.

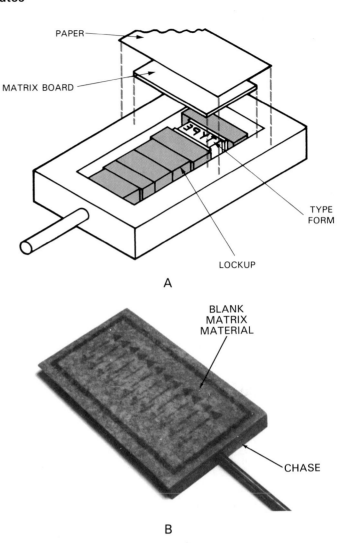

Fig. 21-17. Matrix board and paper are positioned over form. A—Lockup. B—Blank over chase.

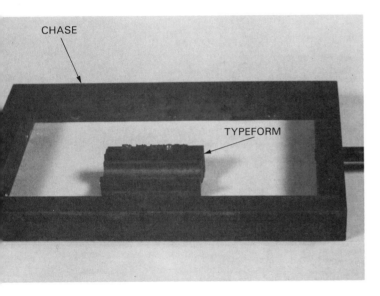

Fig. 21-16. Typeform must be set and locked up in chase.

4. Cut the matrix to size. Matrix material can vary in thickness depending on specification requirements. The matrix should be cut larger than the typeform. Follow manufacturer's recommendations.
5. Place the cut matrix on the typeform. Make sure the correct side is toward the typeform, Fig. 21-17. Some presses require a sheet of paper to be placed over the matrix. Another type will use a shim plate.
6. The shim plates must be determined and positioned in the press. Other types of presses have limit stops on the chase.
7. Position the chase, matrix, etc. in the opened platens, Fig. 21-18.
8. Allow the typeform and matrix to preheat for approximately three minutes before closing the press.
9. Close the platens. Follow manufacturer's instructions.
10. The amount of time ranges from eight to ten minutes in a closed position. Since the matrix material is a thermosetting plastic, it will harden only once. Once the relief image is forced into the softened plastic to the given depth, it will not change shape when cooled and reheated.
11. Open the press and remove the chase.

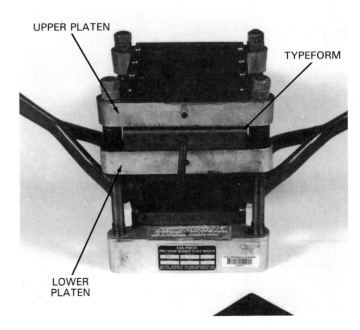

Fig. 21-18. Preheat press as recommended. Note how chase slides into press.

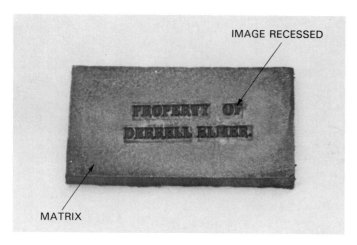

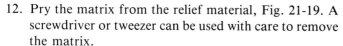

Fig. 21-19. This is a matrix as it comes out of the press. Note how molten rubber would fill recessed image.

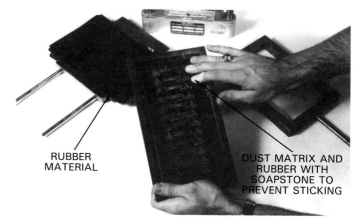

Fig. 21-21. Two image surfaces should be dusted with soapstone. This will act as parting agent so sticking is prevented.

12. Pry the matrix from the relief material, Fig. 21-19. A screwdriver or tweezer can be used with care to remove the matrix.

WARNING! When making a rubber stamp appropriate apparel must be worn to protect you from hot parts and molten rubber. Special heat resistant gloves, safety glasses, and an apron are recommended.

Vulcanizing the rubber stamp

1. Prepare the press. The procedures will vary with the manufacturer. Remove shims and place compensating block in press if needed. See Fig. 21-20.
2. Cut the *raw gum* (rubber) the size of the matrix.
3. Dust the matrix and the rubber with soapstone, Fig. 21-21. The *soapstone* acts as a parting material. Remove excess soapstone.

4. Place materials on the top and bottom to keep them from sticking. Use paper or holland cloth as recommended by the manufacturer.
5. Insert materials into the press.
6. Close the press until the surfaces touch. Wait a short time and completely close the press. The pressure forces the rubber into the image areas of the matrix.
7. The raw gum should be *vulcanized* with heat and pressure for approximately ten minutes. The time should be specified by the manufacturer.
8. Open the press when the recommended time is over and remove the rubber plate from the matrix, Fig. 21-22.
9. Separate the rubber plate from the matrix, Fig. 21-23. They can be very hot! Do not attempt to touch them without proper protective equipment or allow them to cool, Fig. 21-24.

Mounting the rubber stamp

1. The rubber stamp or plate must be trimmed.
2. Select and cut the molding or handle material to size. Look at Fig. 21-25.

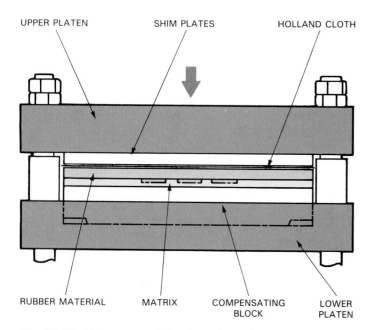

Fig. 21-20. Stamp material and matrix are inserted into press. Platens are brought together to form image into softened rubber stamp material.

Fig. 21-22. Be careful when working with hot parts of press and matrix. They can cause painful burns. Here matrix and rubber stamp are being removed from press.

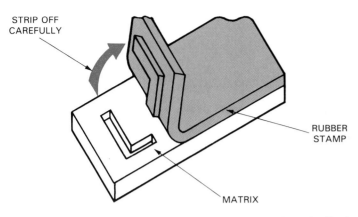

Fig. 21-23. Rubber stamp must be carefully stripped off of matrix to prevent damage.

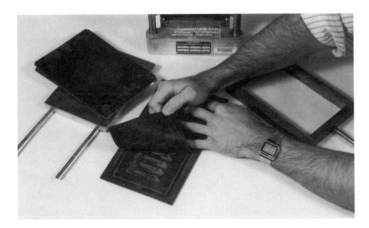

Fig. 21-24. Again, the stamp and matrix can be very hot.

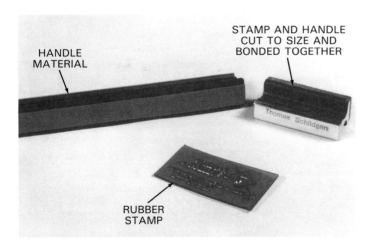

Fig. 21-25. Rubber stamp and stamp handle must be cut to size and adhered together.

3. Coat the mold surface and the rubber stamp surface with rubber cement. Allow it to partially dry.
4. Once the surfaces are almost dry, mount the stamp on the surface of the molding or handle. Make sure they are aligned before coming into contact.
5. Pressure should be applied to assure proper adhering.
6. Test or proof the rubber stamp, Fig. 21-26.

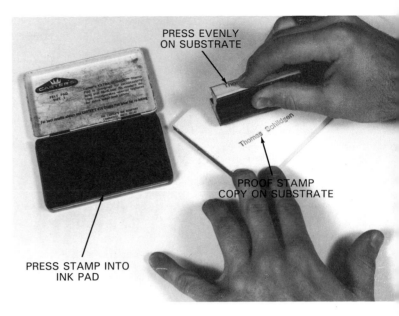

Fig. 21-26. Here proof of rubber stamp image is being made on a piece of paper. Check for letter breaks and filled letters.

KNOW THESE TERMS

Letterpress, Relief, Original plate, Duplicate plate, Dry offset, Photomechanical master plate, Mechanically-engraved master plate, Manually-prepared master plate, Stereotypes, Electrotypes, Flexography, Photoengraving, Powderless etching, Photopolymer plate, Intermediate, Matrix, Scorching, Flexible plates, Stamp press, Rubber stamp, Raw gum, Matrix, Soapstone.

REVIEW QUESTIONS—CHAPTER 21

1. The letterpress or relief process prints from a _____ surface.
2. Relief printing is an older process that has been primarily replaced by lithography. True or false?
3. Why is a duplicate plate sometimes needed?
4. Explain three ways to make original relief plates.
5. Describe three ways to make duplicate relief plates.
6. How does a photopolymer plate work?
7. When a plate is used for direct printing, the image is _____-_____.
8. In your own words, how do you make electrotype?
9. What is a Cameron Belt Press?
10. _____ is commonly used as a parting material when making a rubber stamp.

SUGGESTED ACTIVITIES

1. Prepare a rubber stamp and relate it to the flexography process.
2. Visit a printing facility with a Cameron belt press to observe its operation.
3. Visit a printing facility and note what kind of relief processes are used.

The control panel on the press assists to assure quality of color printing. *(Heidelberg Harris)*

Chapter 22

LITHOGRAPHIC PRESS SYSTEMS

After studying this chapter, you will be able to:
* Identify the five basic image transfer systems.
* Follow the substrate path of travel through a lithographic press.
* Describe the function of each cylinder in the impression system.
* Explain the function of the fountain solution.
* Compare sheet-fed and web presses.

This chapter will introduce the various types of lithographic presses. It will detail the basic sections of a press and how each functions. The chapter will also compare sheet-fed and web presses. The next chapter explains how to use or operate an offset press.

LITHOGRAPHIC PRESSES

The lithographic system is commonly referred to as an *indirect method,* Fig. 22-1. In this process, the plate is dampened, then inked. The image is then transferred to a blanket, and in turn, the inked blanket transfers the image to the substrate.

The term *offset* is used because the transfer process is referred to as being offset from one cylinder to another, Fig. 22-2. The *intermediate,* in this case, is the blanket.

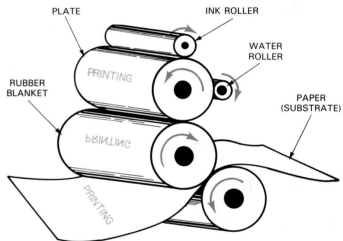

Fig. 22-2. *Note how water and ink are placed on plate. Plate transfers inked image to intermediate or blanket. Blanket then transfers image to substrate which is usually paper. (A.B. Dick)*

The offset lithographic press usually makes one impression with each revolution of the cylinders. The design of most offset lithographic presses is very similar. This chapter is concerned with the systems that make up the offset press.

Sheet-fed and web presses

Lithographic presses can be classified as sheet-fed and web types. Each has a specific purpose. See Fig. 22-3.

A *sheet-fed press* uses individual sheets of paper. They are picked up, one at a time, and fed through the press.

A *web press* uses one long, continuous roll of paper that is fed into the press. As the roll unwinds, the images are placed on the sheet as the ribbon of paper feeds through the press.

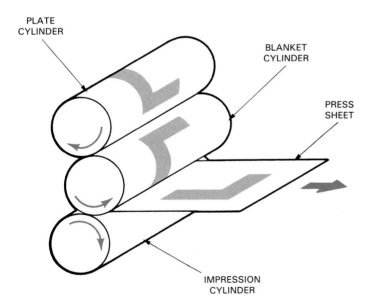

Fig. 22-1. *In offset lithographic printing, plate is dampened and then inked. Moisture bonds to nonimage area and ink to image area. Since blanket is normally used to transfer ink to substrate, this is an indirect printing method.*

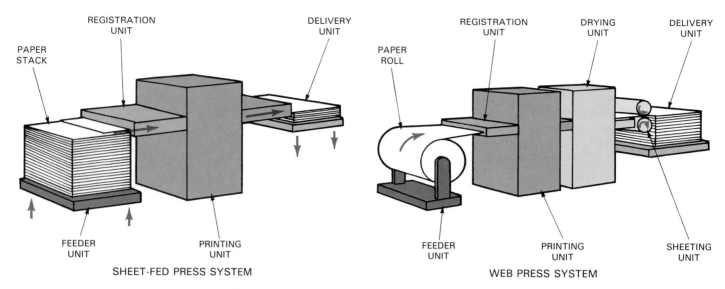

Fig. 22-3. Compare the basic sections of sheet-fed and web presses.

Press equipment for offset lithography varies in size. Sheet fed presses come in duplicator sizes which generally start at the 10 x 15 inch size, Fig. 22-4. While the large printing presses are available in many sizes up to 54 x 77 inches.

Web presses are also available in many sizes. Up to 66 inches wide or wider are presently being used in industry. See Fig. 22-5.

LITHOGRAPHIC PRESS SECTIONS

A lithographic press can be divided into sections or systems, Fig. 22-6. Each system must perform a basic function. The five basic systems of a litho press include:
1. FEEDING SYSTEM (mechanism for sending paper or other substrate into press).

Fig. 22-5. Web presses are used for longer runs, sometimes with hundreds of thousands of impressions. (Heidelberg Harris)

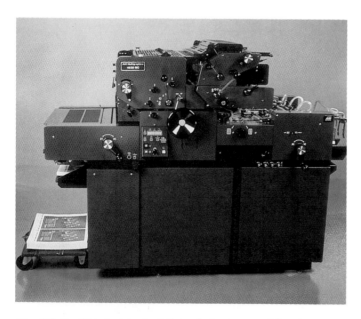

Fig. 22-4. This is a typical sheet-fed press used for short runs. (AM Multigraphics)

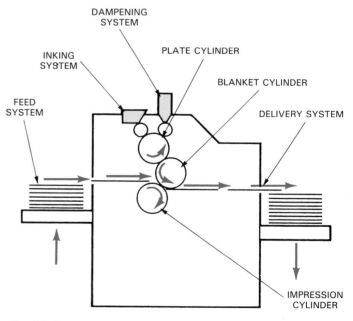

Fig. 22-6. Note basic flow of paper through this basic sheet-fed press.

340

2. DAMPENING SYSTEM (mechanism that feeds water solution onto plate).
3. INKING SYSTEM (mechanism for feeding ink onto plate).
4. IMPRESSION SYSTEM (mechanism of printing image on substrate).
5. DELIVERY SYSTEM (mechanism for feeding paper out of press).

As you will learn, these systems can vary with the press design. Also, these systems must be working properly to accurately reproduce the image on the substrate.

SHEET FEEDING SYSTEM

The first system or press component is commonly referred to as the *feeding system* or *feed unit*. Most of today's printing duplicators or presses are equipped with automatic feeders. Production speeds require the use of automatic systems.

The feeding principle requires the system to take one sheet and place it in position for printing. This can be accomplished by lifting a sheet of substrate off of a stack of paper.

The system is divided into sections: First, a stack of paper must be placed in position and the first sheet removed from the pile of paper. The separator must separate the top sheet from the rest of the pile. The sheet is then transported to the register and insertion mechanism.

Successive sheet feeding occurs when each sheet of paper is fed into the press separately. No two sheets overlap while feeding. This is shown in Fig. 22-7A.

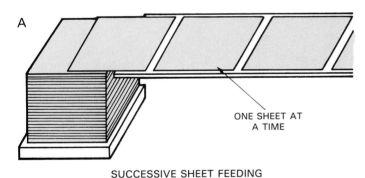

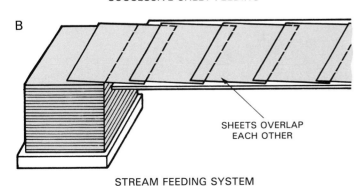

Fig. 22-7. A sheet-fed press can use successive or stream feeding. Stream feeding will usually allow greater press speeds.

Stream feeding occurs when the sheets partially overlap each other while entering the press. This method can be used with some high speed presses, Fig. 22-7B.

Continuous feeding sheets

Some presses have continuous loading. This type of press allows for loading while the press is running, Fig. 22-8. Since the press need NOT be stopped to reload paper, production is increased.

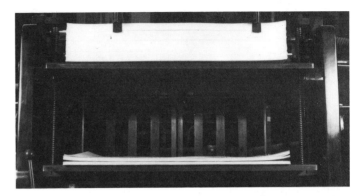

Fig. 22-8. Many sheet-fed presses allow the loading of stock during the press run.

Generally speaking, when stock is properly positioned and aligned, the sheets will not become misaligned and cause a jam. Any variation will cause the operator to stop the press.

Most manufacturers will indicate how most stock should be placed on the platform.

Pile adjustment

When the press is running, the stack of paper must remain at a given height for best operation. The type of control devices will vary with each manufacturer. The setting of these controls will vary with different stock. Gauges are available for the operator to observe. They help in determining the best operating height for each stock.

Sheet separation

The air blast is used to separate the top sheets. Air nozzles direct streams of air toward the edges of the paper to separate them. This also assures that the top sheet can be picked up and transferred to the next stage on the press. Look at Fig. 22-9.

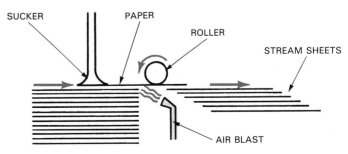

Fig. 22-9. Air blast nozzles, used to separate sheets, can be found at various locations around delivery pile.   (A.B. Dick)

Many of the devices are mechanical but as presses are becoming more sophisticated, electronic devices are becoming more common.

Nozzles for air blasts may be found at the lead edge of the sheet or from the side, Fig. 22-10. The location of the nozzles will depend on the design of the press, Fig. 22-11.

Sheet separators are also found on presses. Some are very simple feather-like brass or spring-steel fingers, Fig. 22-12.

To hold the sheet in alignment, *sheet guides* are found on the sides and back of the sheet. Very often, the *rear guide* is weighted to assist in controlling that only one sheet is fed at a time.

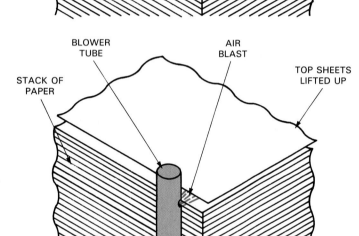

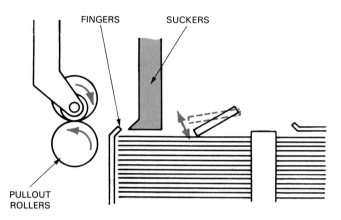

Fig. 22-12. The finger devices also help assure that only one sheet feeds onto transfer table.

Sheet transfer

Once the pile is at proper height and all adjustments have been made, the sheet must be transferred from the pile to the impression point on the press.

Suckers are the most common type of devices used by sheet-fed presses to raise up the sheet and position it for the pull out device. The smaller presses have the suckers at the lead edge of the sheet, Fig. 22-13. Another type of feed unit

Fig. 22-10. Note action of combing wheel and air blast nozzle. Both help assure that only one sheet at a time is fed into press.

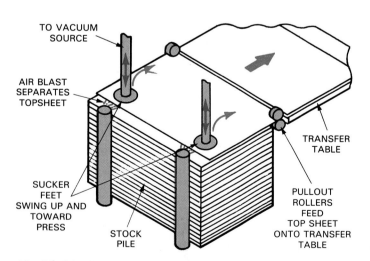

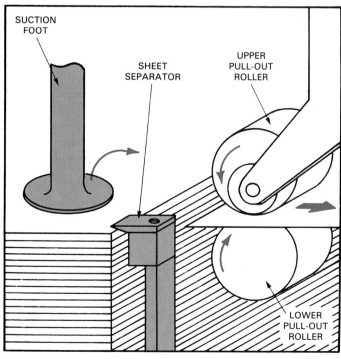

Fig. 22-11. Here you can see action of sucker feet, air nozzles, and pullout rollers. Transfer table carries sheet into printing unit of press.

Fig. 22-13. This is a closeup showing action of sucker, sheet separator, and pullout wheels.

will pick up the sheet at the back edge of the sheet. This type is called a stream feed system. The suckers pick up the sheet at the back edge and move it forward to the pull-out wheels or rollers.

The amount of vacuum present in the sucker feet must be adjusted for each type of stock. Some manufacturer's supply a variety of sucker feet adapters to comply with stock needs. See 22-14.

Pull-out rolls or *pull wheels* take the sheet from the suckers and place it on the feed ramp, Fig. 22-15. At this point, another control device plays an important role. The device is called the *double-sheet detector,* Fig. 22-16. A varie-

ty of types are used but most are the caliper type. If all settings to this point are accurate, the double-sheet detector is a back up that keeps the sheets from being printed. The detectors are adjusted to paper thickness. Refer to Figs. 22-17 and 22-18.

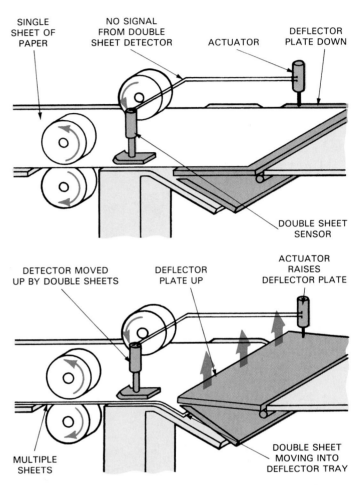

Fig. 22-14. Sucker feet can be in different locations to meet needs of press run and stock used.

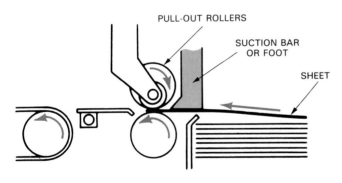

Fig. 22-15. Note how sucker feet will feed stock into pullout rollers.

Fig. 22-17. Here is a more detailed illustration of how a double-sheet detector works. When sensor detects excess thickness, it activates a solenoid. Solenoid can then open deflector plate to move twin sheets out of press.

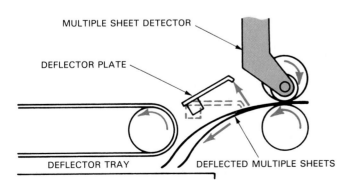

Fig. 22-16. Double-sheet detector will kick out two sheets if they try to pass into press. This press uses a deflector plate to alter direction of double sheets.

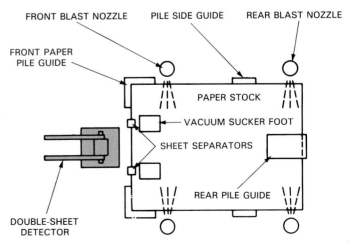

Fig. 22-18. Top view of double-sheet detector shows its location in reference to the other delivery components.

Register board or table

The *register board* or *table* carries the sheet to the image transfer position. The most common means of feeding the sheet is on cloth tapes. Refer to Figs. 22-19 and 22-20.

To help control the sheet, various devices assist in assuring that the sheet will travel in a straight line. Designs will vary but typical devices are: steel or glass balls, brushes, or wheels. Often, the brushes and wheels are in combination.

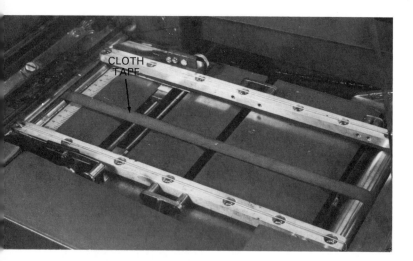

Fig. 22-19. Cloth tapes are common means of carrying sheets to the image transfer or printing system of press.

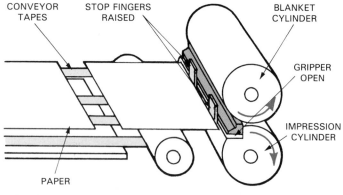

Fig. 22-20. Note how tapes carry sheet to grippers on press cylinder.

Some of the presses feed the sheet directly to register stops, Fig. 22-21. This is considered to be a very positive delivery.

Delivery of the sheet to the register point is very critical. Register systems will vary. The most common will have front stops and side guides, Fig. 22-22.

The setting of each control device is very important. Follow the manufacturers manual as improper adjustments generally means lost time and less profit for the owner.

WEB FEEDING SYSTEMS

The feeding system for a web press is obviously not the same as for a sheet-fed press. The web press operator is very concerned with the paper tension device, Fig. 22-23. Since

Fig. 22-21. Some presses have positive feed that carries sheet directly to register stop.

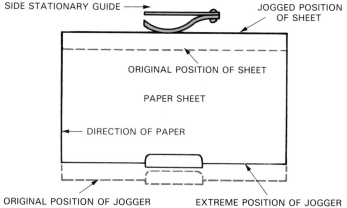

Fig. 22-22. Front stops and side guides are commonly used to register the sheet before it is carried through printing unit.

Fig. 22-23. The delivery system of a web press is obviously quite different than for the sheet-fed press. Note how the web winds around rollers on the top of this web press.
(King Press Corporation)

Fig. 22-24. *This photo shows the splicing unit for the web press. Note festoon rollers that allow slack to build up right after infeed roll. This gives operator enough time to stop used roll and splice on new roll while slack is being taken up on festoon rollers as press continues to operate.*

the web press requires a continuous stream of paper to be fed through the press, Fig. 22-24, the tension of the paper web must be closely regulated. Improper web tension could cause the roll of paper to break. Any time this happens, paper is wasted and the downtime is very costly.

Various devices are found on web presses to control tension, Fig. 22-25. One of the most common is the *braking mechanism*. Usually, the mechanism is attached to the roller shaft. It produces a slight friction or drag on the roller.

As the web is fed into the first unit, it must be flat. The web must also be in-line. The press has a tilting mechanism

Fig. 22-25. *A friction device or brake mechanism is sometimes used to maintain correct web tension.*

which acts like the guides on a sheet-fed press. This tilting device adjusts to make sure the paper is in line. Some of the presses have electronic devices that will automatically make this adjustment.

Each roll of paper tends to be a little different even if it is the same grade. Adjustments must be made to conform to the paper characteristics. Web presses feeding adjustments include: web tension, web line-up, web roll, and web guides.

Web splicer

When one roll is emptied, another roll must take its place. To eliminate threading the web through each printing unit, the paper is spliced. *Splicing* involves bonding the end of the first roll to the start of the next roll. This must be done accurately. A bad paper splice could cause a web break.

There are two basic types of web splicing mechanism: zero speed splicer and flying splicer.

The *zero speed splicer* uses a set of festoon rollers to draw out slack or extra web paper. This web slack is often called *festooning*, Fig. 22-26. This extra slack allows the two large rolls to be stopped while the press takes up the slack.

Fig. 22-26. *This is a closeup view showing festoon rollers for auto splicer.*

When stopped, the end of the new roll can be taped to the end of the old roll. The new roll is then rotated up to speed before the paper on the festoon rollers is used up. This keeps the large web press in operation. It also eliminates the need to hand-thread the new roll through the press.

The *flying splicer* does NOT stop either roll but bonds the new roll to the old one with everything in motion.

Double-sided tape is usually applied to the end of the new roll of paper.

When the old roll is about used up, the new roll is swung out so it is next to the moving web, Fig. 22-27. The new roll is spun so that it is moving at the same speed as the press web. A cutter blade moves out to shear off the old roll and the tape end is pushed against the moving web. This makes the new roll bond to and follow the first web ribbon through the press.

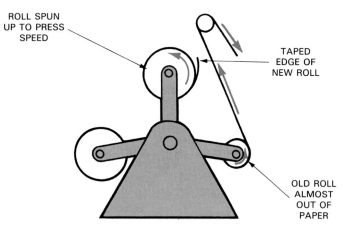

A—Roll is almost used up. New roll is on splicer and is ready to be moved into position. Double-sided tape is applied to end of new roll. New roll is then rotated up to press speed.

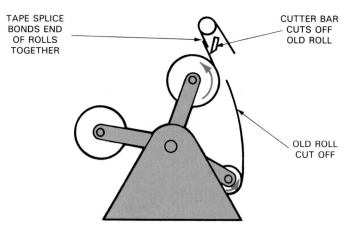

B—Flying splicer has rotated new roll against moving web. At same time, cutter slices off end of old roll and new roll end is pushed into web. Double-sided tape bonds two sheets together and new roll follows old roll sheet through press.

Fig. 22-27. Note principle of flying splicer.

Web break detector

A *web break detector* will automatically shut the press down if the web snaps or tears. With modern web presses running at tremendous speeds, a web break can be disasterous. The incoming ribbon of paper could jam into the press and wrap around rollers.

A sensor is used to detect a break in the web. Instantly, the break detector will kill power to the press. It will also activate a mechanism that cuts the incoming web off ahead of the first printing unit. Then, any incoming paper is not allowed to enter the rollers in the printing units. This all takes place in the "blink of an eye."

IMPRESSION SYSTEM

The placing of an image on the surface of the stock to be printed is the purpose of the impression system. The *impression system* takes the paper from the feed system and transfers ink to the stock being printed. The components for the system are large cylinders. All web or sheet fed lithographic presses run on cylinders. These include the plate cylinder, blanket cylinder, and impression cylinder, Fig. 22-28. This is a three-cylinder impression system.

Plate cylinder

The *plate cylinder* holds the printing plate on the printing press. It has a main cylinder body, bearers, bearings, and a gear. However, some duplicators do not have bearers. See Fig. 22-29.

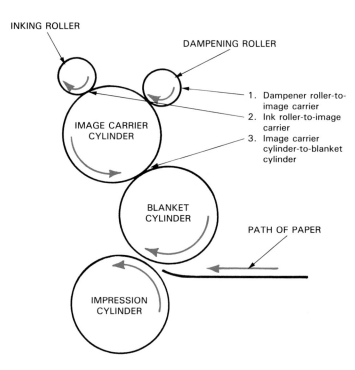

1. Dampener roller-to-image carrier
2. Ink roller-to-image carrier
3. Image carrier cylinder-to-blanket cylinder

Fig. 22-28. This is a typical arrangement of three component cylinders making up the impression system of a lithopress.

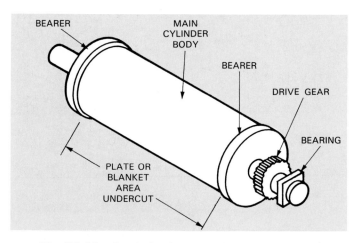

Fig. 22-29. Study basic parts of a press cylinder.

This cylinder supports the image carrier or printing plate, Fig. 22-30. This cylinder has a variety of methods of holding the plate in place.

Most printing presses have jaw type clamping devices, Figs. 22-31 and 22-32.

Duplicators might have a pin bar, serrated, slotted, or clamp type holding devices, Fig. 22-33. These devices are used to tighten or loosen the plates. Proper tension is very important. Excessive tension will place too much stress on the plate and could crack or tear it. Insufficient tension could cause poor registration and a poorly printed job.

Plate bend at the leading edge and tail of the plate must be accurate and properly done. Bending jigs are essential for proper plate bend on larger presses, Fig. 22-34.

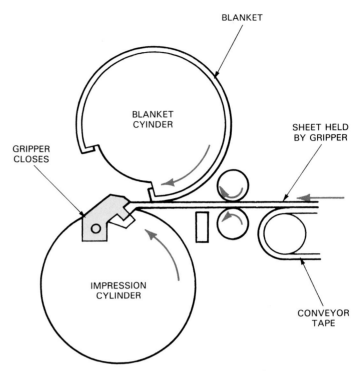

Fig. 22-32. Gripper has clamped down on paper to hold it as blanket cylinder deposits inked image. This is a jaw type clamp or gripping device.

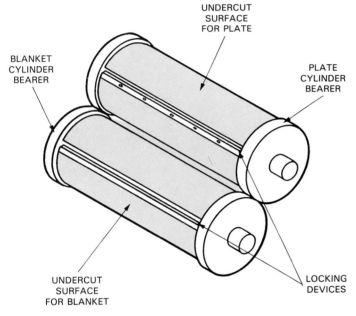

Fig. 22-30. Plate and blanket cylinders both have locking devices. Their surfaces are undercut to accept plate thickness and blanket thickness. Bearers hold cylinder center areas apart during rotation.

Fig. 22-33. Other holding classifications of plates are pin bar, serrated, and clamp types.

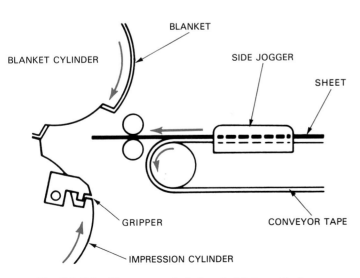

Fig. 22-31. Here paper is being fed into cylinders. (A.B. Dick)

Fig. 22-34. Plate bender can be seen in center of this photo.

The portion of the plate cylinder that supports the plate is a smaller diameter than the bearers, Fig. 22-35. This undercut allows for plate thickness and packing. The manufacturer specifies the total thickness to place around the cylinder. The thickness is determined by the diameter of the bearers. The bearers of each cylinder ride on each other. This requires the cylinder to be *packed* properly to allow for excellent transfer of the image. The amount of undercut is stamped on the cylinder or printed in the press manual.

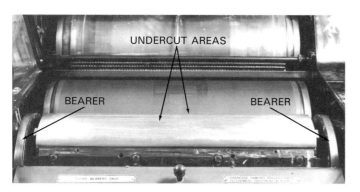

Fig. 22-35. Plate cylinder is undercut to allow for plate thickness plus packing to produce proper pressure on paper.

If cylinder undercut is unknown, measure the diameter of the cylinder and the diameter of the bearers, Fig. 22-36. Packing gauges are also available and should be used to accurately measure the undercut, Fig. 22-37. The operator now knows how much room is available for the plate and packing of the plate cylinder.

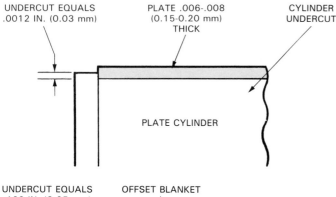

UNDERCUT EQUALS .0012 IN. (0.03 mm)

PLATE .006-.008 (0.15-0.20 mm) THICK

CYLINDER UNDERCUT

PLATE CYLINDER

UNDERCUT EQUALS .120 IN. (3.05 mm)

OFFSET BLANKET

UNDERLAY BLANKET

PAPER UNDERLAY

BLANKET CYLINDER

Fig. 22-36. Note typical dimensions of this plate cylinder and blanket cylinder.

Fig. 22-37. This dial indicator setup can be used to measure packing under plate.

Blanket cylinder

The *blanket cylinder* holds the blanket on the press. It has the same components as the plate cylinder, Fig. 22-38. The main body of the cylinder holds the blanket in place. The surface of the blanket is made of a resilient material and supported by a cloth woven base, Fig. 22-39.

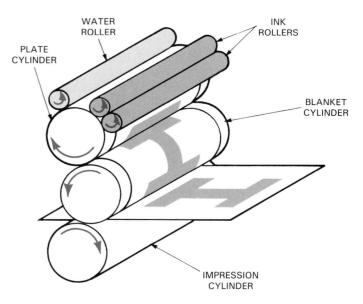

WATER ROLLER

INK ROLLERS

PLATE CYLINDER

BLANKET CYLINDER

IMPRESSION CYLINDER

Fig. 22-38. This is another illustration of basic rotary offset press with water roller and ink rollers. Note direction of rotation of rollers.

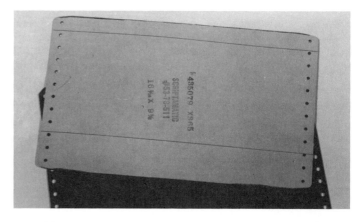

Fig. 22-39. Surface of blanket is resilient and strengthened by being attached to a woven cloth base.

The size of the blanket is determined by the size of the press. The press manufacturer will specify the size of the blanket. Since the blanket has thickness, the blanket cylinder is also undercut to accommodate this thickness plus packing.

The blanket is clamped in position, Fig. 22-40. The clamping devices will vary just as the clamping devices for plates. Blankets are elastic. The proper amount of tension is very important.

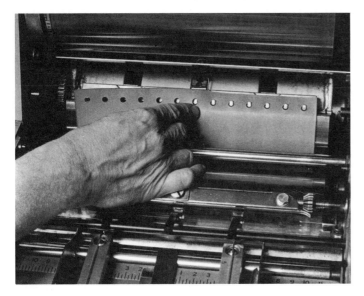

Fig. 22-40. Press operator is attaching blanket to its cylinder.

Packing is done according to press specifications. This is a good starting point. An experienced operator will be able to make the necessary adjustments.

Impression cylinder

The *impression cylinder* takes the sheet from the feed stops and brings the stock in contact with the blanket cylinder, Fig. 19-41. The image on the blanket is then transferred to the paper.

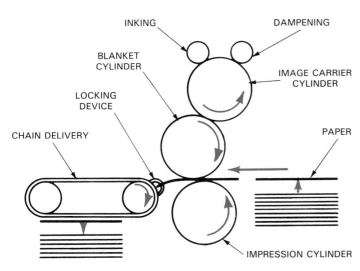

Fig. 22-41. Note how impression cylinder brings paper or other type substrate into contact with blanket. (A.B. Dick)

Another cylinder found on some presses is a *transfer cylinder*. This cylinder carries the sheet-fed paper from the printing unit to another unit.

These cylinders will vary in design. Some presses have *skeleton* or *delivery cylinders* to carry the paper from the impression cylinder to the delivery unit.

Twin-cylinder image transfer

Most printing presses have three cylinders as just explained, but another system does exist. This design uses only two cylinders because the plate and impression cylinder are combined to form one cylinder, Fig. 22-42. This cylinder is twice the circumference of the blanket cylinder. For each impression, the blanket cylinder must revolve twice while the combination cylinder makes one revolution.

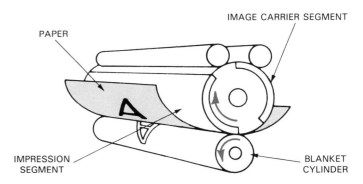

Fig. 22-42. Two cylinder system combines plate and impression cylinders into one cylinder. (A.B. Dick)

Perfecting press

A *perfecting press* prints on both sides of the substrate at once. As shown in Fig. 22-43, two blanket cylinders and two plate cylinders are used on top and bottom. The paper is moved between the two blanket cylinders to simultaneously print images on both sides of the stock.

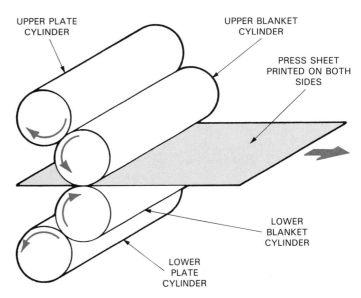

Fig. 22-43. Perfecting press prints on both sides of substrate at one time.

DAMPENING SYSTEMS

A *dampening system* is needed to apply moisture to the nonimage area of the plate. The basics of dampening systems is very similar for all printing presses. The two most common types of dampening systems are: conventional and continuous.

Conventional dampening system

The basic components that make up the *conventional dampening system* are a dampening fountain, a fountain roller, a ductor roller, an oscillating (vibrating) roller, and a form roller. These parts are shown in Fig. 22-44. Each one of these components must be kept in excellent condition.

The dampening solution is placed in the fountain. To keep the solution at the same level, many presses use a gravity feed to refill the fountain. See Fig. 22-44.

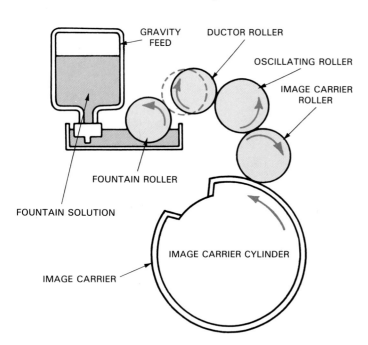

Fig. 22-44. Dampening system can use gravity to feed solution into fountain.

The *fountain roller* revolves in the fountain to pick up the solution. This roller can be chrome, stainless steel, or fabric-covered. Since the moisture is picked up by the fountain roller, it is transferred to the ductor roller.

The *ductor roller* is often covered with a molleton or paper material to retain the fountain solution. Since this component is intended to transfer the moisture to the oscillating roller, the contact is intermittent.

The *vibrating roller* or *oscillating roller* is used to help spread out the solution. As the roller moves back and forth, the solution is distributed on the rollers more evenly.

From the vibrator roller, the fountain solution is transferred to the form roller or rollers. The *form roller* or *rollers* place moisture on the printing plate. The form rollers may be covered with a molleton or sleeve cover. Some systems use a *bareback roller* which means it is NOT covered.

All of the dampening system rollers must be adjusted for proper pressure. Too much pressure could cause excessive wear on machine parts as well as printing plate surfaces. The manufacturer's manual is the source of information for proper setting.

Continuous dampening system

The two popular types of continuous dampening systems are the Dahlgren or brush systems. Alcohol is part of the fountain solution, Fig. 22-45. The amount will vary, but generally, from 15 to 25% of the solution will be made up of alcohol. Alcohol reduces surface tension in the water.

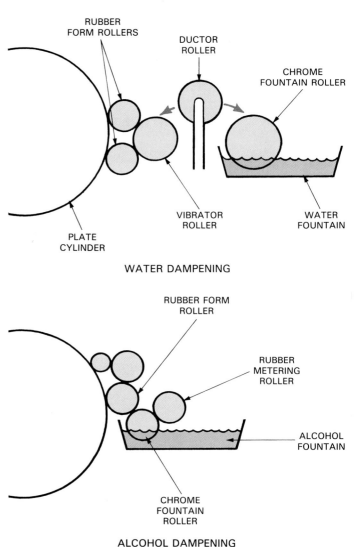

Fig. 22-45. Compare water and alcohol dampening systems.

The *Dahlgren continuous system* eliminates the ductor roller, Fig. 22-46. The transfer roller is in direct contact with the fountain roller and form roller. The Dahlgren system uses a metered fountain roller. This system responds very quickly to changes in fountain settings.

WARNING! Proper ventilation is required with an alcohol dampening system. Ventilation must meet federal, state, and local safety and health regulations.

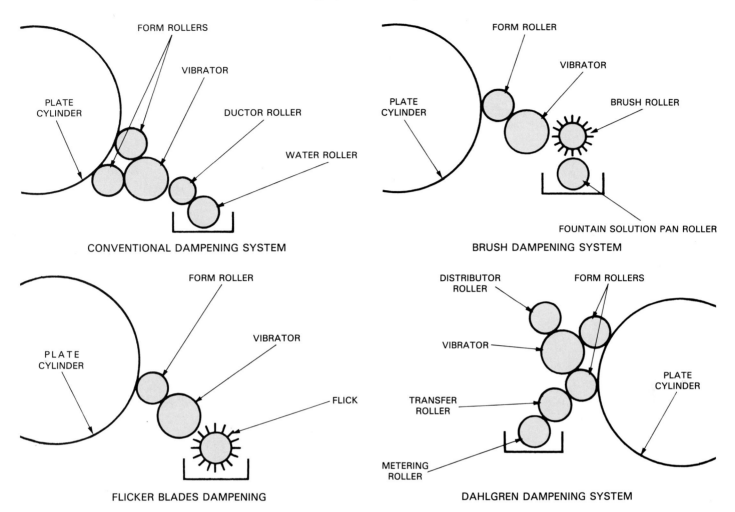

Fig. 22-46. *Note different types of dampening systems.*

The *brush system* is very similar to the Dahlgren system — the Dahlgren system transfer roller is replaced with a brush roller. The brush roller flicks the solution onto a vibrator roller that transfers the solution to a form roller. The moisture control is very accurate. Look at Fig. 22-46.

Fountain solution

All fountain solutions must have controlled pH. The *pH scale* measures the alkalinity or acidity of a solution, Fig. 22-47. The pH scale ranges from 1 to 14. Seven is the neutral point. Distilled water is neutral. Acidity is measured from one to seven while alkalinity is the other end of the scale.

Fountain solutions are on the acid side. The *fountain solution* pH should be in the range of 4.0 to 5.5 for most systems.

The pH scale is logarithmic; therefore, a small figure change can have a tremendous affect on the solution. As an example, a pH reading of 3.0 is 10 times more acid than a pH of 4.0. The control of pH will greatly assist in trouble-free press operation. Low pH can cause emulsification, tinting, scumming, and plate wear. High pH may cause plate sensitivity, emulsification, and plugging of halftones. These problems will be discussed later.

INKING SYSTEM

The *inking system* of a press places a thin film of ink on the image area of a lithographic printing plate, Fig. 22-48. Each manufacturer appears to have a different inking roller

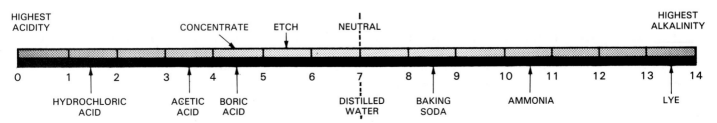

Fig. 22-47. *The pH scale measures the acidity versus alkalinity of the solution. A large number would be more alkaline and a smaller number more acid; seven would be neutral.*

configuration. This is true of sheet-fed as well as web presses.

The ink is stored in an *ink fountain*. Many of the larger presses will have an *agitator* which revolves and moves along the fountain. Its purpose is to stir the ink and keep the ink at the same flow level.

The *fountain roller* transfers the ink to the ductor roller. The *ductor roller* carries the ink to a *vibrator* or *distribution roller*. The ink is further split by *intermediate rollers* which distribute the ink to the form rollers. The number of ink, form, or image carrier rollers will vary with the press design. Some presses will have one while others could have as many as four. The diameter of the rollers will also vary.

The *form rollers* place the final ink film on the image area of the lithographic printing plate. Moisture, NOT ink, adheres to the nonimage area on the printing plate. The inking system is often referred to as the *ink train*. As stated earlier, each manufacturer will have a special design to provide uniform ink flow to the plate, Figs. 22-48 and 22-49.

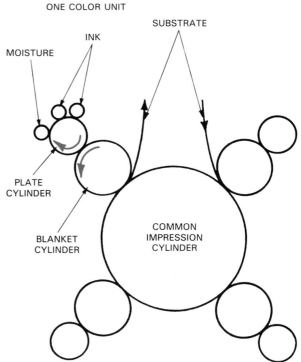

ONE COLOR UNIT

Fig. 22-49. With this press design, four separate color printing units are common to one impression cylinder. (CIC)

The maintenance of rollers is very important. Proper settings and cleaning are essential to quality reproduction. The rollers must have an affinity for ink. They must also transfer ink and withstand long wear.

Web press inking systems

Although many principles apply, the web press must have a very high volume inking and dampening system. With its tremendous speed, pumps are commonly used on large web presses to keep the fountains full during a press run.

Fig. 22-50 illustrates a simplified system for pumping ink into the fountains of a four-color web press. Note how a separate printing unit is needed for each color on this design.

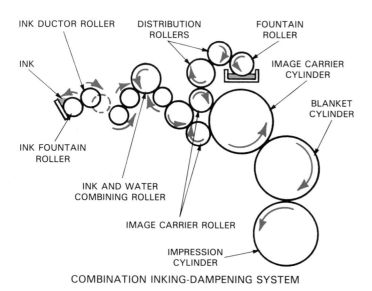

COMBINATION INKING-DAMPENING SYSTEM

Fig. 22-48. This aquamatic system is a good system common to one press manufacturer. (A.B. Dick)

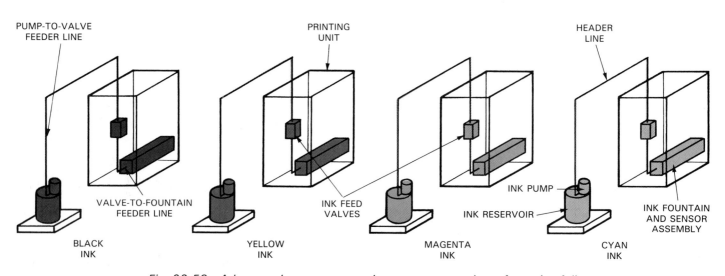

Fig. 22-50. A large web press commonly uses pumps to keep fountains full.

As the continuous web feeds through each printing unit, a selected color ink is printed on the substrate. By printing these four colors on top of each other, all colors can be duplicated.

A *drying system* is commonly used to rapidly cure the ink after the web leaves the printing units. If not dried quickly, the ink could be smeared as it leaves the press. See Fig. 22-51.

DELIVERY SYSTEM

The *delivery system* must remove the printed substrate from the impression system of the press. Obviously, the delivery system for a sheet-fed press would be quite different than for a web press.

Sheet-fed delivery system

The *sheet-fed delivery system* must remove and stack each sheet after printing. Sheet delivery systems vary.

Duplicators will often have a chute delivery system. As shown in Fig. 22-52, the small duplicator will use a skeleton

cylinder to carry the printed stock to the delivery pile. Fig. 22-53 shows an example.

The most common delivery system is the chain drive. Delivery gripper bars are powered by the skeleton cylinder, Fig. 22-54. The grippers grasp and remove the sheets from the impression cylinder and delivers them to the delivery pile.

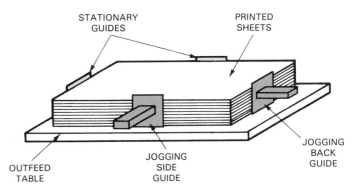

Fig. 22-53. Note guides used to help align stack of paper.

Fig. 22-51. This photo shows printing and drying units of a large web press. Drying unit helps cure ink quickly.

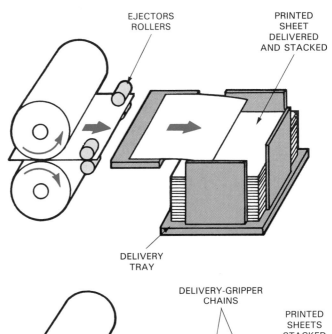

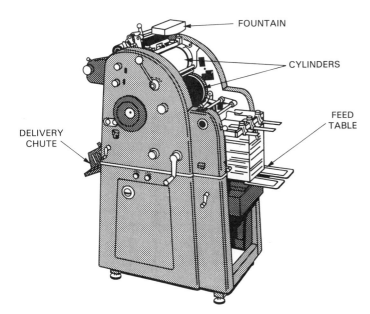

Fig. 22-52. Small duplicators commonly use a chute type delivery system.

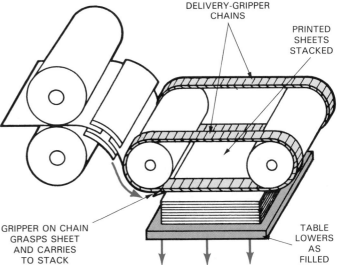

Fig. 22-54. Compare two systems commonly used to transfer printed stock to delivery tray or table.

Once the gripper bars release a sheet, the sheets are aligned in the delivery pile by jogging the sheets and by guides. See Figs. 22-55 and 22-56.

Proper alignment of the sheets is critical. It will assure that there are less problems in the bindery area of the facility.

Fig. 22-57 summarizes the main systems of the sheet-fed press. Review how each system functions.

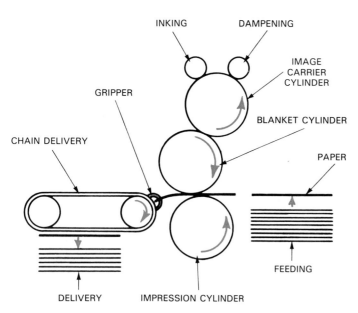

Fig. 22-55. Sheet must be removed from grippers once they are released by impression cylinder.   (A.B. Dick)

Fig. 22-56. This press uses a chain drive to deliver stock after printing.

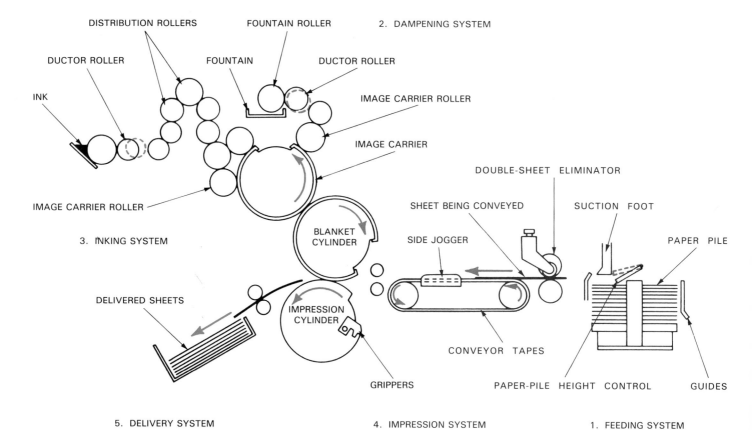

Fig. 22-57. Study complete sheet-fed press system. Trace flow of stock through each component on press.

Web delivery system

A web press can deliver rolls of paper. This usually is not the final step. The delivery system on a web-fed press usually includes a sheeter or various folding operation.

A *former board* is a curved surface that can be used to fold the web as it leaves the press, Fig. 22-58.

The *sheeter,* as the name implies, is used to cut the web or roll of paper into sheets of paper.

The *folder* on the press can make combination folds to form a signature. The finished signature is usually delivered by conveyor on delivery tapes.

Again, delivery systems on web presses vary in design. Some use a moisturizing unit to return water content to the paper. The paper would lose its moisture in the drying unit. Some moisture is needed to prevent bindery problems. Look at Fig. 22-59.

Fig. 22-60 summarizes web press operation. Trace the flow of paper from roll to finished signature.

Note! For more information on web presses, refer to the index.

KNOW THESE TERMS

Sheet-fed press, Web press, Feeding system, Dampening system, Inking system, Impression system, Delivery system, Successive sheet feeding, Stream feeding, Air nozzles, Sheet separators, Sheet guides, Suckers, Pull-out rollers, Double-sheet detector, Register board, Web braking mechanism, Web splice, Zero speed splicer, Flying splicer, Web break detector, Plate cylinder, Packing, Blanket cylinder, Impression cylinder, Perfecting press, Conventional dampening, Fountain roller, Ductor roller, Vibrating roller, Form roller,

Fig. 22-58. Former board is just one example of how a printed web can be folded. Other binding operations can also be done right after printing. (King Press Corporation)

Fig. 22-59. This is a large web with bindery type equipment. (Miller Machinery Co.)

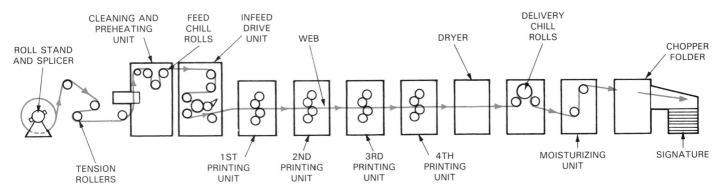

Fig. 22-60. Study this illustration showing web press operation. Follow the ribbon of paper as it flows through web.

355

Water dampening, Alcohol dampening, Dahlgren dampening, Brush dampening, Fountain solution, pH, Intermediate rollers, Ink train, Drying system, Former board, Web sheeter, Web folder, Moisture unit.

REVIEW QUESTIONS—CHAPTER 22

1. How does a sheet-fed press only deliver one sheet at a time to the impression systems?
2. What carries a sheet to the image transfer position?
3. Explain how a web zero speed splicer operates.
4. How does a web break detector work?
5. The _____ _____ takes the paper from the feed system and transfers the ink to form the printed image.
6. Why is a blanket cylinder undercut?
7. A _____ _____ prints on both sides of a sheet at once.
8. How does a dampening system work?

9. Which of the following would be a typical fountain pH?
   a. 9.
   b. 1.
   c. 4.5.
   d. 3.5.
10. Explain the five systems of a lithopress.

SUGGESTED ACTIVITIES

1. Visit a sheet-fed printing firm and observe if the presses are the three cylinder type. Trace the five basic systems.
2. Identify the type of dampening systems found in the plant.
3. Visit a web press operation and compare its systems. Describe the type of delivery system found on the press or presses.
4. Print a two-color job on a lithopress that requires the use of register marks.

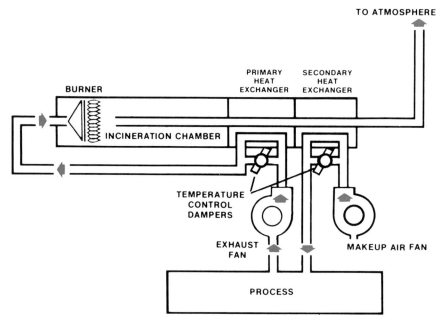

Diagram shows a thermal incinerator that can be used to burn pollutants and also produce useful energy for facility. Polluting compounds are burned in incinerator chamber and are expelled as non-harmful substances through stack to atmosphere. Heat exchangers capture heat energy to be used for drying of ink after presswork. (TEC Systems)

Chapter 23

OFFSET PRESS OPERATION
AND TROUBLESHOOTING

After studying this chapter, you will be able to:
- Explain the basic principles needed to operate a sheet-fed offset press.
- Make the adjustments needed to operate the feeding system of an offset press.
- Prepare the various cylinders before running an offset press.
- Prepare dampening solutions for duplicators and offset presses.
- Prepare and adjust inking system of an offset press.
- Summarize the procedure for using a sheet fed press.
- Summarize the operation of a web press.
- Explain common press related problems.

The major units of an offset press were identified in the previous chapter. This chapter will summarize the operation of an offset press. Each type of press common to today's industry has similar components. As a result, you can transfer basic knowledge from one type of press to another.

OFFSET DUPLICATOR AND PRESS DIFFERENCES

The offset duplicator is a small press, Fig. 23-1. Although many manufacturers have devised many controls, the duplicator has limited devices compared to the larger presses.

Fig. 23-1. Many styles of duplicators are available for smaller runs. Their operating procedures are similar.

The duplicator is considered to be a short run press. Even though it is seldom used for long runs, the duplicator can run at speeds of over 10,000 impressions an hour. The duplicator is often found in the small commercial plant and in-plant printing operations.

Many of the adjustments found on large presses are common to some duplicators. The knowledge gained from operating a duplicator can be used to help run larger presses.

The basic principle of the offset press is the same as the duplicator. The sheet-fed, offset press is considerably larger than the duplicator, Fig. 23-2. Even though many of the duplicator models are very sophisticated, the control devices on the offset press are considered to be very functional. Accuracy is essential. This qualifies the press for a wide variety of products.

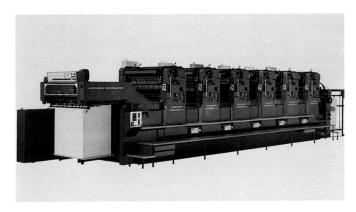

Fig. 23-2. Offset presses also come in many styles. However, if you understand the operating principles of one, you can transfer this knowledge to other presses. (Heidelberg USA)

Since size is the major difference between the duplicator and the printing press, the term "press" will be used throughout this chapter.

The principle of sheet and web presses is the same but the web's continuous flow of paper is obviously a major difference. Since smaller web offset presses are being manufactured, many more are found in the industry.

The basic operation of both sheet-fed and web presses will be discussed in this chapter.

OPERATION OF SHEET FEEDING SYSTEM

All presses require some means of stacking paper so that it can be delivered to the transfer or impression system. Proper adjustment and placement of the stock is essential to assure control as the paper enters the impression system.

The location and type of adjustment devices may vary with each press. Also, the tasks described might not always be in the same sequence. It is important for you to choose a sequence that is effective and efficient. Once a sequence has been established, following the same sequence for each press run will reduce the possibility of forgetting a task.

The following is a typical example of an operating procedure for an offset press. Some person must be designated the responsibility of placing the stock in the press. This could be the press operator or a helper. Proper handling of the paper is essential as handling the stock is a critical factor for eliminating feeder stops.

FEEDING SYSTEM SETUP (Sheet-fed press)

Placing the stock on the platform requires that the stock be perfectly straight, Fig. 23-3.

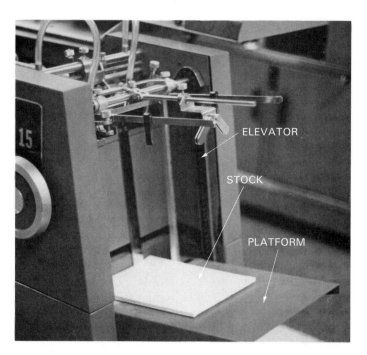

Fig. 23-4. *Platform can raise automatically or by hand. The automatic platform is more common.*

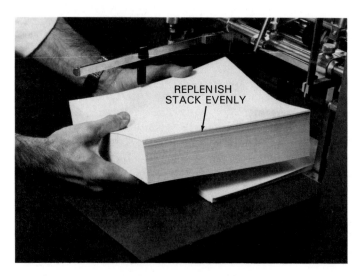

Fig. 23-3. *When placing stock on the platform, fan the paper and try to keep it stacked straight.*

The manner in which the platform lowers will vary with each press. You can lower a typical duplicator paper platform by pushing on the handwheel and turning.

Set the side guides to correspond to the size of the sheet, Fig. 23-4. Adjust the guides for about 1/16 in. (1.5 mm) clearance between the edge of the stock and guide. Jog the paper and position it on the platform.

Position the back guide so that the forward wings are on top of the stock while the back wings are holding the sheets from moving out of the feeding position, Fig. 23-5.

Position the front guides in from each side of the front edge of the stack. The air blower is usually located in the center of the top sheets. However, the air blast may be located in a variety of positions depending on the press design.

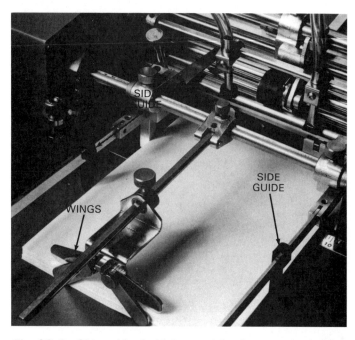

Fig. 23-5. *Side guides hold the stock in alignment for feeding into press. The forward edge of the sheet is held by arms called "wings."*

Align the suction feet with the front guides, although this will change with different types of paper. The sheet is picked up at the front edge and the next sheet is picked up when the back edge has cleared the front edge.

Another system is called stream feed. The stream fed system picks up the sheet at the back. The sheets overlap as they travel to the transfer position. The sheets move slowly which assures greater accuracy. This system is generally found on larger equipment.

The pile height of the stock must be adjusted for proper operation of the press. The weight will vary with different kinds of stock, Fig. 23-6. Gauges are available for some presses. The smaller press may have *elevator control knobs* for raising or lowering the platform.

Before turning the press on to adjust paper height, sheet separation must be assured. The air blast nozzles must be properly positioned, Fig. 23-7. This will vary with the model of press.

Fig. 23-6. The height of the stock must be maintained at all times during the press run.

Fig. 23-7. The air nozzles must be positioned so that they separate the sheets from the side. Proper height of paper will vary with each manufacturer.

Turn on the drive motor switch and adjust the elevator manually or with the automatic mechanism for raising of the paper stock. Duplicator type presses generally are regulated so that the stock is within one-fourth of an inch (6.4 mm) from the whisker. Most pile height regulators are mechanical but more amd more presses are being designed with electronic regulator devices.

If the stack of paper is uneven, wedges are used to level out the paper. Care must be taken on placement. If contact is made with a stationary part of the press, the press part might be broken.

Once the vacuum motor switch is turned on, suction is applied to the suckers, Fig. 23-8. This suction is activated by some type of control mechanism. The amount of vacuum can be controlled. If the sucker feet cannot be changed for the kind of stock being used, the amount of vacuum should be controlled. Excess vacuum could distort the sheet.

Fig. 23-8. Various devices are placed on press to assure that only one sheet feeds in at a time. Adjustments must be made for paper thickness.

When the feed lever is on, the sheet should be picked up and fed to the feed ramp.

Press adjustments are critical. The double-sheet eliminator or detector is one of these control devices. This is often set by a thumb screw and a locking device. If properly adjusted, only one sheet will go through the press. With some duplicator type presses, the second or third sheet would open a gate which directs the sheets into a storage area.

Larger presses have a trip device. This shuts off the press when more than one sheet is fed to the transfer unit.

Pull wheel(s), place the sheet on the feed board or table, Fig. 23-9. The tape and balls, brushes, or wheels align the sheet. Proper settings are required.

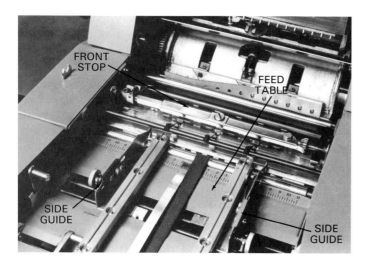

Fig. 23-9. On this press, stock travels along feed ramp or table. It hits front stops and then side guides move sheet into position. Limit stops make it possible to move image up or down on sheet.

Once the sheet is delivered to the front or limit stops, the side guides and/or jogger control go into action, Fig. 23-9. The purpose of the side guide is to place the sheet in proper position to be in exact register.

The guides are generally set to guide from the operator side or the lay side of the press. This control device varies with each manufacturer. The adjustments at this point will be identified in the press's operating manual.

Most presses have the capability of adjusting the limit stops. This makes it possible for the image to be raised or lowered on the sheet. The amount of movement will vary with the press.

Emphasis must be placed on terminology. Technical terms will vary with many of the publications and press manuals. This makes identification of specific controls very difficult.

WARNING! When applicable, all adjustments should be made when the PRESS IS STOPPED! Injury or press damage could result if recommended procedures are not followed.

IMPRESSION SYSTEM SETUP (Sheet-fed press)

At this point the sheet is ready to be taken by the impression system. All of the systems are important but transferring of the image to a substrate is the purpose of the press. The appearance of the image on the final product is either acceptable or unacceptable. Therefore, this system has critical adjustments.

The three-cylinder impression system will be introduced because it is prevalent in the industry.

Plate cylinder setup

The plate or image carrier cylinder supports the printing plate. The holding devices are available in several different designs. They are the straight bar clamp device, the serrated or slotted type, and the pin bar type. Operator's preference

varies. Generally, the top of the carrier is held by the stationary side of the cylinder clamping device, Figs. 23-10 and 23-11.

Turn the press by hand until the tail or bottom of the plate can be inserted in or on the holding device, Fig. 23-12. Tighten if the holding devices are movable, Fig. 23-13. Some holding systems are spring-loaded and only tension holds the carrier in place. See Fig. 23-14.

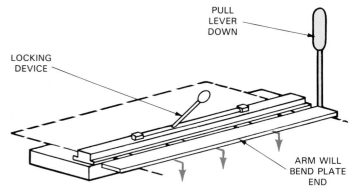

Fig. 23-10. Some plates must have ends bent before being mounted on press. Plate bending fixture will make square, even bend.

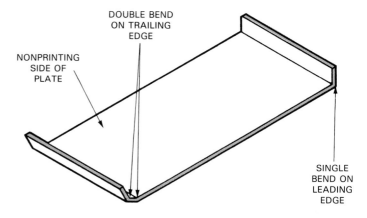

Fig. 23-11. These are the types of bends required for a typical mounting on the press cylinder.

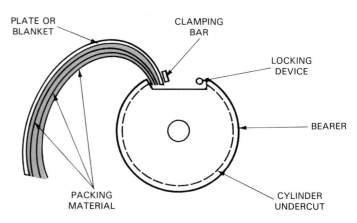

Fig. 23-12. Packing material is sometimes needed to raise blanket or plate to required height on cylinder for good impression.

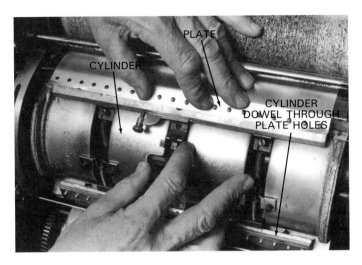

Fig. 23-13. *Top or lead edge of plate is stationary and generally is not moved. Many presses have holding devices that tighten the plate onto the cylinder.*

Fig. 23-14. *Note basic principle of how a plate may be secured or held onto its cylinder.*

The plate cylinder can be loosened on many presses. This provides another way to lower or raise the image on the sheet. The vertical positioning knob is loosened and turned while engaged, Fig. 23-15. A pointer sometimes indicates the location based on a scale. The scale shows the direction to raise or lower the image. The control knob must be securely tightened and then released.

Fig. 23-15. *Plate cylinder is normally movable and image can be raised or lowered on substrate. Press controls vary so refer to the specific operating manual.*

If the cylinder undercut is greater than the thickness of the plate, additional packing is placed under the plate. Many manufacturers identify the amount of packing for a proper transfer of the image. Fig. 23-16 gives a typical example.

Blanket cylinder setup

The blanket cylinder should be free of scratches and damaged spots. Inspection is essential.

Blankets also have a variety of attachment methods — pin bar, serrated, slotted, or straight.

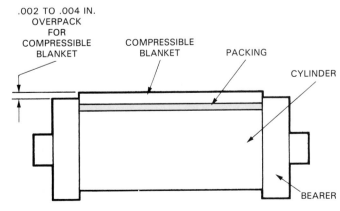

Fig. 23-16. *Note typical packing for blanket. Packing spec may be stamped on press near cylinder bearers.*

The blanket can be replaced by turning the press by hand or by using an inching mechanism. Rotate the cylinder until the lead edge of the blanket can be attached to the blanket clamp, Fig. 23-17. Again, turn the press by hand or by the inching mechanism until the tail clamp is in position so that the other end of the blanket can be attached. Tighten the blanket according to the manufacturer's specifications.

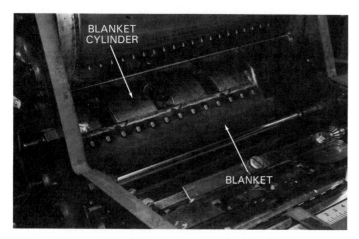

Fig. 23-17. Blanket is attached to its cylinder in much the same way as the plate.

When tight, it is suggested that the press be run on impression for fifteen or more revolutions because a new blanket has a tendency to stretch. Then, retighten the blanket if necessary.

The blanket cylinder is also undercut. Measure the blanket or read the specifications supplied by the manufacturer. Pack under the blanket to bring the thickness up to specifications. Packing sheets of varying thicknesses are available from some paper suppliers.

Seek assistance from a supplier to determine the proper blanket. Some blankets are compressible while others are conventional, Fig. 23-18.

Any additional thickness, as from crumpled paper, going through the press can damage some blankets. Materials are available to fix low spots in blankets. Sometimes placing the blanket in water and allowing it to dry will help in salvaging a damaged blanket.

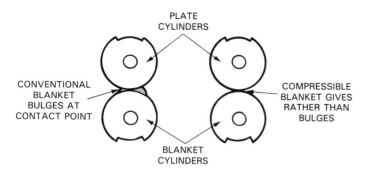

Fig. 23-18. A conventional blanket will bulge at contact point. A compressible blanket will handle more pressure without deformation.

Impression cylinder setup

The third cylinder is the impression cylinder and its main purpose is to hold the paper while the image is being transferred from the blanket cylinder.

Since the impression is regulated by the cylinder, the surface of the cylinder must be kept free of foreign material.

Since the paper is held by impression cylinder grippers, the grippers must be properly set to maintain good register. When the grippers are too tight, they will mark the sheet. All of the grippers should have the same tension.

The image carrier cylinder and the blanket cylinder are adjustable to make sure proper contact is made. To check the impression, ink the plate or image carrier. Remember the dampener rollers are NOT to be in contact with the plate. When completely inked, drop the cylinder for contact. The manufacturer's manual will detail the procedure. An even coverage is imperative for good transfer.

To readjust, you must commonly loosen the locking screw. Turn the adjusting screw clockwise to increase pressure and counterclockwise to decrease pressure. Tighten the lock screw when properly adjusted. Again, specific methods will vary with the exact press manufacturer.

Checking impression

The impression cylinder is spring-loaded on some presses, while on others the impression cylinder is adjustable. This adjustment varies the amount of pressure between the blanket and impression cylinder. Use the manual for exact procedures.

A manual impression adjustment is possible by tightening the lock screw by hand, and then loosening the locking screw, Fig. 23-19. Turn the impression adjusting screw to increase or decrease the impression. When the impression is correct, tighten the locking screw.

Fig. 23-19. The impression can usually be adjusted with some type of manual control.

TWO-CYLINDER IMPRESSION SYSTEMS

The difference between the two-cylinder and the three-cylinder systems is that the large cylinder has the plate as one-half the segment. The impression segment is the other half of the cylinder. The blanket cylinder is the small cylinder and it revolves twice for each complete turn of the large cylinder.

The plate segment of the large cylinder is dampened and then inked. In turn, the image is transferred to the blanket. The impression half of the cylinder grips the paper and the second half of the revolution transfers the image from the blanket to the substrate. The substrate is supported by the impression segment of the large cylinder.

Adjustments are critical. You should always follow the manufacturer's manual.

FOUNTAIN SOLUTION INGREDIENTS

Many companies manufacture the ingredients necessary to make the fountain solution. These are considered to be concentrated solutions. The concentrates are added to water, preferably distilled water. Different concentrates are recommended for different kinds of presses.

Duplicator type presses use a variety of fountain solutuion concentrates. You must add the solution to the water in the amount prescribed by the manufacturer.

As stated in the previous chapter, many of the printing presses use an alcohol type fountain solution. Special consideration must be given to these systems to be in compliance with local, state, and federal regulations.

An often overlooked purpose of the fountain solution is to keep the nonimage area of the printing plate clean. It must keep the image area clean and free from scum. This can only be accomplished if the plate is properly prepared.

The control of the fountain solution is essential. TOO MUCH ACID can make the background area sensitive, which allows it to be ink receptive. High acid content will cause the ink to emulsify.

When *ink emulsifies* (fountain solution and ink has mixed to a higher degree than acceptable), it will not transfer from one roller to another. Too much acid could also cause an ink drying problem on the printed stock. It will also cause the life of the plate to be reduced.

The gums or glycerine must also be measured carefully to assure proper receptivity. Gum has been the standard antioxidant of the graphic communications industry. It is highly receptive to the nonprinting areas of the plate. The amount of gum is a critical factor when mixing fountain solutions. The type of plate makes very little difference because the function of gum arabic is to prevent ink from adhering to the nonimage areas of the plate.

Solution pH

As discussed, the symbol pH indicates the acidity or alkalinity of a solution. The pH scale has a range from 0 to 14. The smaller the number, the greater is the amount of acid. The center of the scale is neutral.

More technically speaking, pH is the acidity of an aqueous solution. It is determined by the concentration of hydrogen ions in the solution.

A press fountain solution should usually be on the acid side of the scale and usually ranges from 4.0 to 5.5 pH. It is suggested that the fountain solution be close to neutral.

The pH scale is logarithmically calculated. Therefore, a slight change in the pH is really a great change in the solution. A reading of 4.0 pH is ten times as acid as a fountain solution with a reading of 5.0 pH. If the pH reading is 3.0 pH, this means it is 100 times as acid as a reading of 5.0 pH. A reading of 2.0 pH would be 1000 times more acid than a reading of 5.0 pH.

When the pH has been formulated to specs and placed in the fountain of the press, the pH should be double-checked. The solution can also change after the press is run.

Paper and ink influence the correct pH of the fountain solution; therefore, it is important to check the pH of the solution and reformulate if necessary.

Checking pH

There are several ways of checking the fountain pH. Two common methods are litmus paper and the electronic pH meter.

Litmus paper will change in color or darkness depending upon the pH of the solution. The litmus paper is dipped into the solution. This will change the appearance of the paper. Then, the paper is compared to a standardized scale. The scale darkness that matches the litmus paper darkness equals the fountain pH reading. See Fig. 23-20A.

The *electronic pH meter* is a very accurate means of taking the pH reading of a solution. First the meter must be calibrated. This might be done by taking a reading of distilled water. The meter should read seven when in distilled water. This will assure meter accuracy. Then, the test probe can be submerged in the fountain solution. A digital readout will give the pH of the solution, Fig. 23-20B.

Fountain additives blended with the fountain solution tend to change the pH. For this reason, the pH reading should be taken BEFORE additives are placed in the solution.

Note! Do NOT add additives unless a true need exists because they often cause other problems.

DAMPENERS

Many press systems use some form of a cover that fits over the dampener rollers while other systems use a bare, rubber roller. Whether the *dampener cover* is a molleton or a paper cover, its main purpose is to absorb and hold the fountain solution. Many manufacturers make excellent covers, but a cover that tends to lint, should be avoided as problems will be the result. See Fig. 23-21.

Even fountain solution distribution is imperative. Usually, the minimum amount of moisture is the most desirable.

A desirable characteristic of a cover is that it picks up dirt and scum from the surface of the plate. Many covers can be cleaned at the end of the day. Always follow the manufac-

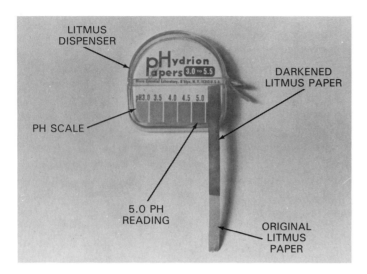

A—Litmus paper can be submerged into fountain solution. This will change darkness of paper. By comparing paper darkness to standard scale, you can determine pH of solution.

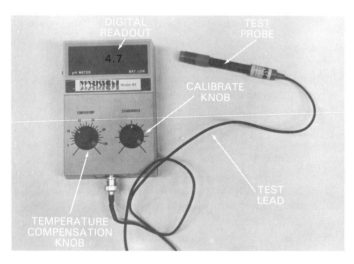

B—Electronic pH meter is more accurate way of checking fountain solution. You must normally calibrate meter before using it.

Fig. 23-20. Two methods of checking fountain pH.

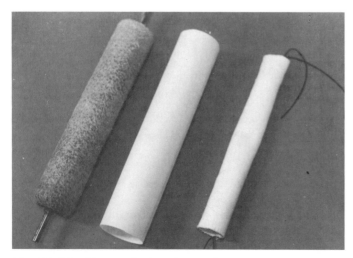

Fig. 23-21. Many of the dampening system rollers are covered.

turer's recommendations when cleaning a cover. Some covers are intended to be discarded when they are dirty.

The method of installing covers varies with the manufacturer. Follow their directions and problems will be minimal.

Dampening preparation

Place the fountain solution in the storage container. Position the container in the fountain tray.

As discussed, the fountain solution is tranferred from the tray by means of a fountain roller to the ductor roller. The turn or rotation of the fountain roller is regulated by a pawl or other type metering system. This determines the amount of moisture transferred. It is usually intermittent but continuous systems are also used in industry. The metal or covered fountain roller must be clean and water receptive.

The ductor roller transfers moisture from the fountain roller to the oscillating roller. The oscillating roller is usually metal.

The oscillating roller transfers the moisture to the plate (form) roller or rollers. The oscillating roller must be perfectly parallel to the image carrier roller.

Roller pressure adjustment

The plate roller or rollers might require adjustment. A slight impression is recommended. One way to make the adjustment is to take two, one inch strips of .003 inch (0.08 mm) stock and position them at both ends of the plate roller in the dampening position, Fig. 23-22. An even drag or resistance on each is desirable when the strips are pulled free.

The means of adjusting roller pressure varies with different presses. Typically, use a small wrench to loosen the locking nut, and an Allen wrench or screwdriver to increase or decrease roller pressure. Repeat the impression test until proper roller pressure is achieved.

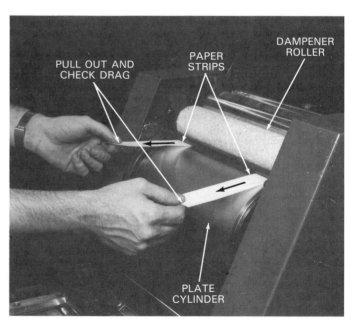

Fig. 23-22. Roller pressure is critical. By pulling two sheets of paper between rollers, you can check amount of pressure and whether pressure is even on both ends of rollers.

Some newly covered rollers will reduce in size after running. Frequent checks must be made of impression pressure.

Fig. 23-23 shows how to check distribution roller pressure. Three strips of paper are needed on each side so the center strips will pull out.

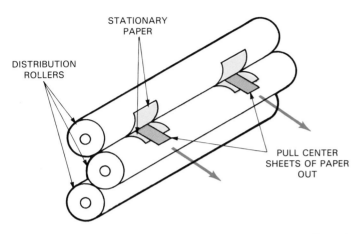

Fig. 23-23. When checking distribution rollers, you will need to place paper between strips to be pulled out of rollers. The paper will allow the strips to slide between sticky rubber rollers.

INKING SYSTEM SETUP

Choose the ink that is compatible with the fountain solution, the press, and the stock being printed. Before inking the unit, make sure that the rollers are free of dried ink, lint, dust, and glaze. The procedure might vary on some presses but the preparation of the inking system is very similar and the following procedure is quite typical.

Check the distance between the blade and the ink fountain roller. This is shown in Fig. 23-24.

Fig. 23-25. Ink is placed in the ink fountain of the press. (Heidelberg Harris)

Place ink in the ink fountain of the press, Fig. 23-25. An ink knife is commonly used to remove ink from the cans. Make sure all dried ink is removed from the top of the can. Dried ink can cause obvious printing problems. An ink cartridge gun may also be used to fill the fountain with ink.

By turning the ink fountain roller control, the ink film can be observed on the roller. The thickness of this film can be controlled by the ink fountain adjusting screw, Fig. 23-26. Volume control is also adjusted by the roller revolving con-

Fig. 23-24. Distance between ink blade and fountain roller can also be checked by pulling strip of paper between blade and roller.

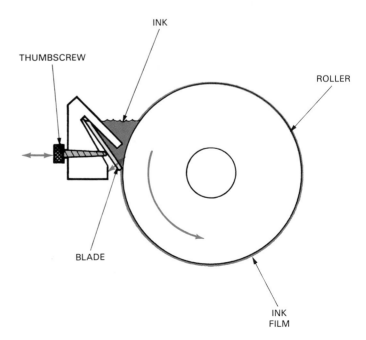

Fig. 23-26. Note how thumbscrew can move blade into or away from roller. This will control ink film thickness on roller.

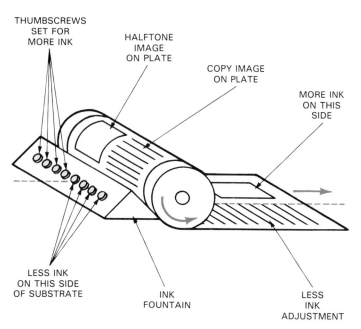

Fig. 23-27. *Thumbscrews are frequently provided for adjusting amount of ink that deposits on roller. If one side of image needs more ink, it may have to be adjusted accordingly.*

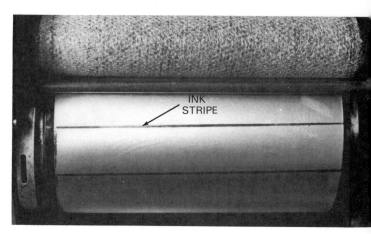

Fig. 23-28. *Inked rollers are dropped onto the plate. Inspect the resulting ink stripe. It should be the correct width and even. If uneven, there is a problem with the adjustment or the roller itself.*

trol, Fig. 23-27. For best results, a thin, even film of ink should appear on the ink fountain roller with a long sweep on the volume control.

In some cases, however, more ink should be fed from one side of the fountain. See Fig. 23-27.

Large presses have agitators that constantly stir the ink while it is in the fountain. The ink fountain roller transfers the ink to a ductor roller. The ductor roller carries the ink to the distributor rollers.

A requirement of the system is that the ink must be split into a very thin film of ink. To distribute the ink more evenly, the diameter of the rollers often vary.

Distributor rollers are made of various materials. The material must have the capability of releasing the ink evenly. Rubber, nylon, steel, and copper are used as materials for distributor rollers.

Rubber rollers are intermediates to distribute ink to the form rollers. The number of form rollers varies generally from two to four. The diameters of these rollers should also vary. This allows for overlapping of ink sufficiently to eliminate the possibility of lines across the image. These marks are referred to as *image ghost marks.*

The adjustment of all rollers is very critical but the form rollers must be set so that a specific width stripe appears on the image carrier. Adjusting the form rollers is accomplished by dropping the inked form rollers onto a clean plate, Fig. 23-28. Both stripes should be very close in appearance and approximately 1/8 to 3/16 of an inch (3.18 to 4.76 mm) in width.

To adjust the rollers, follow the directions described in the press manual. When the stripe is too wide, excessive roller bounce occurs which tends to wear the plate and causes uneven inking of the image. Fig. 23-29 shows several roller adjustment problems.

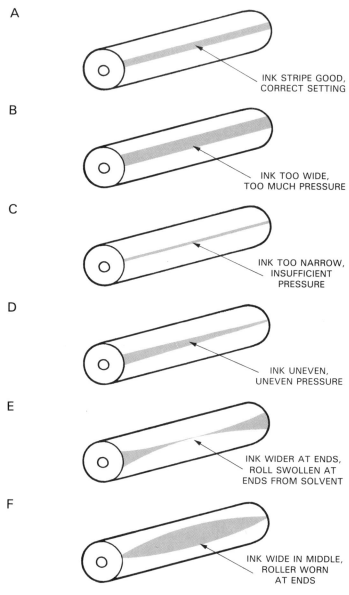

Fig. 23-29. *Note the types of problems indicated for the different ink stripes.*

Combination dampening and inking system

In this system, the ink is tranferred to the rollers and then the fountain solution is transferred to the plate rollers. The fountain solution rides on the surface of the ink.

The fountain solution is transferred to the plate first and then the ink is transferred to the image areas of the plate. This is commonly referred to as an *aquamatic system*. Proportion is critical. The system is common to one major manufacturer of duplicator type presses.

DELIVERY SYSTEM SETUP (sheet-fed press)

The delivery system of a sheet-fed press transfers the printed sheet from the impression cylinder to the grippers of a chain delivery or to the spider of the skeleton cylinder for chute delivery.

The sheets are grasped firmly from the impression cylinder. The sheets have a tendency to stick to the impression cylinder. All of the grippers must have even pressure. If slippage occurs, the sheets could be torn or nicked.

Once the sheets are released from the impression cylinder, they are delivered to the delivery pile, Fig. 23-30. The grippers open and drop the sheet.

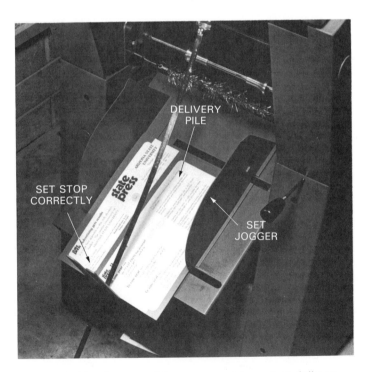

Fig. 23-30. Stops and joggers must be set at delivery.

The sheet stops must be set to correspond to the sheet size, Fig. 23-30. This is true of both chain and chute delivery.

The jogger must also be set to align each sheet as it is positioned on the delivery pile. The jogging system will vary with the manufacture.

The setting of the joggers is critical. Each sheet must be aligned and evenly stacked. Even stacking eliminates problems in the bindery area. The back joggers and side joggers must align the sheet as it settles.

Some types of paper and ink require an anti-offset powder to prevent ink smear or set-off. The powder is sprayed between the delivery of each sheet. The spray prevents the ink from being smeared or set-off on the back side of the sheet as it comes in contact with the previously printed sheet. Use powder sparingly as it can cause press run problems.

Another means of eliminating set-off is the use of a heat lamp. This helps in setting up or drying the ink.

Anti-static bars or tinsel are used to eliminate static electricity from the sheets. Static causes the paper to stick and sometimes curl. This makes it difficult to jog and align the sheets. The anti-static devices must meet local, state, and federal regulations.

When removing stock from delivery pile, extreme care must be taken not to smear the ink. This is especially true of the chute system. The reason for this is the limited number of sheets before they are removed.

SAMPLE PRESS OPERATION

Since all of the systems have been identified, one type of sheet-fed press will be used for procedure familiarization. By seeing how to run one specific type press, you will be able to transfer basic procedures to other kinds of presses. Follow manufacturer operating instructions, however.

Again, for specific technical information for each press, the specific press manual should be studied.

Note! Today's presses have safety devices that must be operational for the press to be started. Check these features carefully or injury or press damage may result.

Loading feed table

1. A handwheel usually lowers the feed table. Once it is lowered, the automatic upward feed knob must be raised.
2. The guides, Fig. 23-31, are moved to correspond to the size of the stock. Once they are positioned, lock them in place.

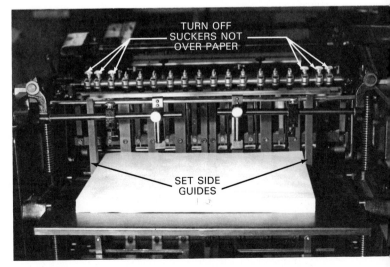

Fig. 23-31. Side guides position the sheet in place. Turn off any suckers that extend beyond the sheet size.

3. Fan the stock before placing the sheets on the automatic feed table.

4. The sucker bar can be positioned to be parallel with the sheet when the air is on, Fig. 23-32. All suckers that are not over the sheet must be turned off.

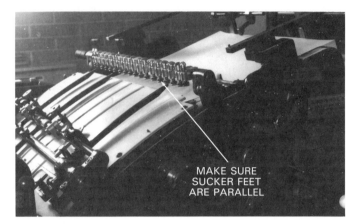

MAKE SURE
SUCKER FEET
ARE PARALLEL

Fig. 23-32. Sucker bar feet must be parallel to pick up the sheet.

5. The amount of air can be regulated by a control dial. Set it properly according to manual directions.

6. The height of the feed table must also be regulated. Thin stock requires a slower raising speed while thick stock, like card stock, would need very rapid raising of the table.

7. The sheet calipers must be adjusted to eliminate the possibility of more than one sheet feeding into the machine. Whatever system is used, secure the locknut to make sure that the space is limited and additional sheets are restricted. As illustrated earlier, many additional devices can be positioned to smooth out the sheet and allow free travel.

8. The register guide and the sheet thickness caliper must be set, Fig. 23-33. Movement of the sheet more than 1/8 of an inch (3.18 mm) is discouraged. The type of

register guide varies with presses. This example is a push type while some are a pull type.

9. The front or stop guides have very accurate adjustment capabilities. The margin can be increased or decreased but only two of the guides should be used. Which two will be determined by sheet size and thickness.

10. Many special operations are possible with most presses. Consult the manual for special applications.

Operating dampening system

1. The pH value must be checked regularly, Fig. 23-34.
2. Keep the fountain roller and fountain clean.
3. The intermediate dampening ductor roller need not be removed unless the cover must be cleaned or replaced. Make sure safety latches and any shields are in place after the roller journal is in place, Fig. 23-35.

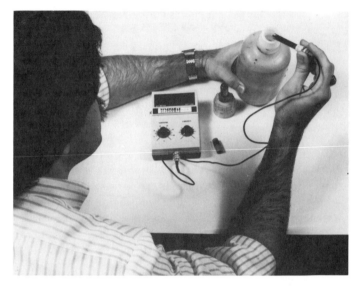

Fig. 23-34. The pH must be checked before start of run. It should also be checked periodically during press run.

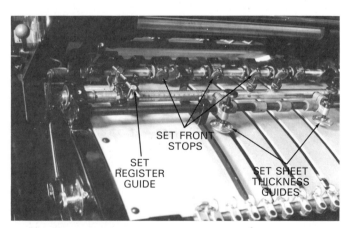

SET FRONT
STOPS

SET
REGISTER
GUIDE

SET SHEET
THICKNESS
GUIDES

Fig. 23-33. Register and sheet thickness guides must be set. Front stops must also be set properly because they position sheet for impression unit on the press.

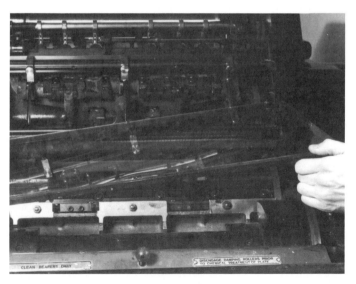

Fig. 23-35. All safety shields and latches must be in place before starting the press. Many will not run if these safety devices are removed.

4. The ductor roller must be clean and positioned in the operator's side first and then into the journal of the drive side. Make sure the sliding, needle bearing sleeve is in position so that the knob is properly engaged in the locked position. This sleeve is on all rollers and keeps them in exact running position.

5. The two form rollers are placed in the journals in the same manner as the ductor roller. A safety device is placed over the top form roller. When this is open, the press will not operate, Fig. 23-36.

Fig. 23-36. The safety device over the fountain form rollers must be closed before press will operate. You could lose finger in press rollers.

6. Roller pressure adjustments are critical and should be made according to the manufacturer's specifications. A disconnect lever allows for dampener rollers to be in contact with the plate or to allow the rollers to be disengaged.

7. A clutch system commonly regulates the amount of fountain roller turn. This determines the amount of moisture distributed through the system. Presses also have attachments which limit the amount of moisture on given areas of the fountain roller.

8. Refer to the press manual if in doubt about any operating procedure!

Operating inking system

1. The ink fountain can usually be dropped for easy cleaning. While open, check to make sure the blade is perfectly clean, Fig. 23-37.

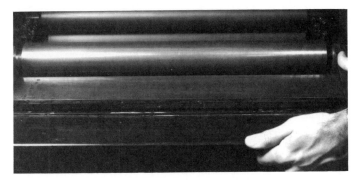

Fig. 23-37. Make sure the ink fountain well and rollers are perfectly clean before placing ink in the fountain.

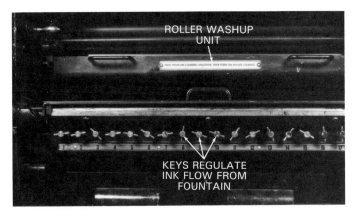

Fig. 23-38. Keys on ink fountain control flow of ink. Note roller washup unit for cleaning press after the run.

2. The ink keys must be turned to produce an even film on the ink fountain roller, Fig. 23-38. Usually, a thin film with a long turn is most desirable.

3. A clutch system turns the fountain roller when engaged. This makes for a very accurate means of ink feeding for the roller system.

4. A disengaging mechanism is part of the roller system, which eliminates the possibility of low spots on the rollers when the press sits idle at night.

5. As has been previously stressed, correct roller setting is extremely important. Ink the press as prescribed and place the proper packing on the plate cylinder. Inch the press so that all image rollers are on the plate. Drop the inked rollers by throwing the lever on the operator's side of the press. Then return to the off position.

Turn the press and look at the roller stripes, Fig. 23-39. The width should be between about 1/8 and 5/32 of an inch (3.18 to 3.40 mm). To adjust the rollers, follow the directions in the manufacturer's manual. On this press, three roller adjustments appear on the operator side of the press. One roller is adjusted from the dampening system end.

Fig. 23-39. Remember to check ink stripe by dropping inked rollers onto the plate cylinder.

6. The distributor rollers have an on and off position. When not in operation, the distributor rollers should be in the off contact position.

7. A *roller washup unit* is used to clean the ink system of most presses. Use a recommended solvent that meets local, state, and federal regulations. The solvents are usually called *blanket* and *roller washes.*

   Make sure all rollers are clean. Remove the washup unit and thoroughly clean the unit. Remember to give the blade special attention.

8. Thoroughly clean the ink fountain and ink fountain roller. It only takes a few extra minutes to do a good job. Taking time now will pay off on the next press run. It will also add to the service life of the press.

9. Make sure the solvent is in a safe storage place and that the dirty rags are placed in an approved, fireproof container.

10. Some of the smaller presses use a clean-up sheet. The material is placed on the plate cylinder. It is made to absorb the solvent and ink.

Preparing impression system

All of the press cylinders must be packed to manufacturer's specifications. If this information is NOT located on the press, the specifications are listed in the manual.

1. Before mounting the plate on the press, the thickness must be measured so that the total thickness of plate and underlay can meet the manufacturer's specifications. The correct printing height is typically .005 inches (0.13 mm) above the bearers. On larger presses, each cylinder rides on the end supports or bearers which are accurately machined, Fig. 23-40.

2. Loosen the clamp bolts and insert the plate and packing in the carrier clamps, Fig. 23-41. Make sure the carrier is in the exact position and tighten the clamp properly. Smaller presses might have another system, as illustrated earlier.

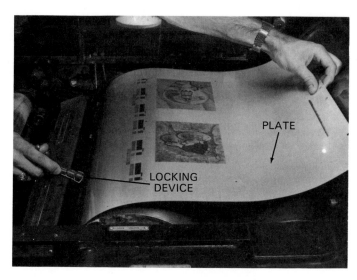

Fig. 23-41. Mount plate in cylinder using press operating manual prescribed methods.

3. Inch the press forward until the tail clamp is in position to receive the plate. The plate should be inserted until the plate touches the clamp stops.

   The packing should NOT be the same length as the carrier and should NOT be clamped into the tail clamp. Tighten the tail clamp with the bolts on the surface of the clamp.

4. Tension bolts tighten the carrier around the cylinder, Fig. 23-42. Do NOT apply too much tension or the carrier could break. Tighten the tension bolts alternately to keep an even tension.

5. The blanket and underblanket should be in good condition and meet thickness specified for good, even image transfer. The blanket is also held in position by a clamping system, Fig. 23-43.

6. The impression cylinder sometimes has a shell around it to allow for packing to press specification, Fig. 23-44.

Fig. 23-40. Bearers are on each end of cylinders. They keep the plate and blanket accurately positioned as the press operates.

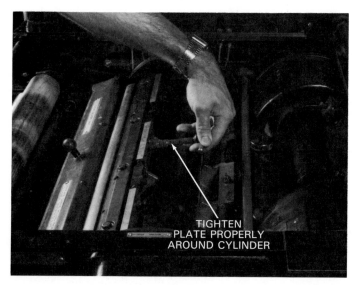

Fig. 23-42. Tighten the plate down properly to produce recommended tension. Tension bolts are typically provided.

Fig. 23-43. Mount the blanket on its cylinder properly. Again, refer to the manual for the press and any instructions from the blanket manufacturer.

Fig. 23-44. This press has a shell around the cylinder. Many presses have a solid cylinder.

7. Adjustments for off bearer printing for the cylinders is often possible on the operator side of the press. It is recommended that the cylinders be run on bearer.

Again, special and some specific applications have not been discussed but are available in the press operating manual.

8. While working on the cylinders, a safety device must be raised. While this device is raised, the press will NOT run continuously. Only inching of the press is possible.

9. It is possible to make a circumferential register adjustment. The adjustment device is usually on the drive side of the press. Loosen the bolts and move the indicator arm to make the desired change.

DANGER! Do NOT make adjustments while the press is in operation. Make sure the electricity is off to eliminate the possibility of someone starting the press.

Adjusting delivery system

1. The delivery table can be raised and lowered. The front stops can also be set for the length of the sheet. Refer to Fig. 23-45 for an example.
2. Side joggers assure even stacking of the printed sheet, Fig. 23-45. All adjustments should be fully studied in the operator's manual as misalignment or wrong placement of devices can be dangerous if they release during the press run.

WEB PRESS OPERATION

Web presses have become more prevalent since the advent of the mini-web and medium sized web presses, Fig. 23-46. Previously, the web press had been designated as doing long run work.

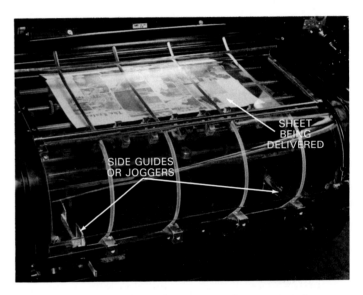

Fig. 23-45. Delivery must be set to stack paper evenly to prevent possible problem in binding.

Fig. 23-46. A small web press has become very practical in many facilities. (Didde Web Press Corporation)

371

Many of the smaller webs are doing short to medium runs and are very competitive with sheet-fed presses.

Some of the typical items that are being printed by the web offset printing method are: newspapers, business forms, monthly magazines, brochures, inserts, catalogs, annual reports, and packaging. See Fig. 23-47.

The presses have versatility since they are capable of delivering cut sheets, folded signatures, or rewound as rolled printed stock.

Discussed briefly in the previous chapter, three common types of image transfer units are in use today: unit, blanket-to-blanket, and common-impression-cylinder (CIC) press.

The unit type press has the web run between the blanket and impression cylinder. More than one unit can be used with the web traveling from one unit to another. Each unit could supply one color for the run. If the web is to be printed on the other side, the web must be turned over to print on the other side by another unit. Before it can be printed on the other side, the previously printed images must go through a drying cycle.

The blanket-to-blanket type press is a perfector and it prints on both sides at one time. The web runs between the two blanket cylinders and prints both images.

The common-impression-cylinder type of press has blanket cylinders positioned around the one large impression cylinder. More than one color can be printed as the web travels around the impression cylinder or drum. As many as five blanket cylinders can be positioned around the common-impression-cylinder to print on one side of the web.

Many of the web presses have very sophisticated control systems, Fig. 23-48.

The web offset printing operation requires that each press have an infeed unit, an image transfer unit, a drying system, and a delivery system.

Web feeding system

Since web printing requires the substrate to be in roll form, the roll must be held in the proper position. This part of the press is called the *infeed unit*. The equipment which

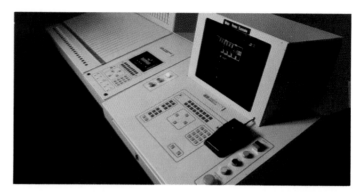

Fig. 23-48. The control panel of a large press can be very impressive. (Heidelberg Harris)

Fig. 23-47. You would need on-the-job training to learn the specifics of operating this large web press. (MAN Roland)

supports the roll of stock is called a *roll stand*. The configuration can vary from a one roll to a two roll stand. Auxiliary rolls can also be added to increase flexibility.

Once the roll of stock is in place, it is threaded through a series of rollers to the first printing unit. The roll must revolve at varying speeds, therefore a braking unit is used and is regulated by the dancer roller. The *dancer roller* moves up or down to regulate the braking action of the paper roll. This determines the speed of the stock roll and also maintains the proper web tension.

Once the roll is unrolled to a designated diameter, another roll of stock is spliced to the old roll so that the press does not need to be stopped. Not all presses have automatic splicers but the new presses generally come with the automatic splicer.

Sensing devices monitor the rolls and determine when the contact is made to transfer the new web through the press. The pasted strip on the roll attaches itself onto the web and continues on through the press. It is important to remember that paper is drawn through a web press. The press person must control web tension as it travels through the press.

The paper remaining on the old core is considered waste and should be kept to a minimum.

Web printing unit

The printing unit of web offset press is made up of elements: a dampening system, an inking system, a plate cylinder, and a blanket cylinder. The concept is the same as sheet-fed, offset printing.

Web dampening system

Dampening systems vary with the configuration of the web press. The concept is the same as with the sheet-fed press. The system must supply moisture to the plate for the non-image area.

The water roller is in contact with the fountain solution. The rotation of the water roller can be regulated. The ductor roller transfers the moisture to the vibrator roller. In turn, the vibrator distributes the moisture to the form rollers.

The water roller is a brass or chrome-plated roller but it is sometimes covered with cloth to increase its moisture carrying power. The ductor roller is molleton covered as is true of the form rollers. The vibrator is a chrome-plated roller.

This system does not have a continuous moisture feed since the ductor roller oscillates periodically. Other forms of intermittent moisture feed systems are also available for web presses.

The continuous moisture feed system eliminates the ductor roller. The most common is the brush system. The brush roller is set to the pan roller so that the brushes flick the solution to the vibrator roller.

Another form of continuous moisture system uses flicker blades to distribute moisture to the vibrator roller.

The Dahlgren Dampening System is a continuous moisture feeding system which requires replacement of about 20% of the water with isopropyl alcohol or some other substitutes. The system utilizes the first form roller as an inking as well as dampening roller.

Two rollers transfer the moisture to an ink form roller. The form roller carries the moisture directly to the plate. Other continuous-flow dampening systems are available but the concept of directly moistening the form roller is the same.

Web inking system

The concept of the web offset inking system is the same as the sheet-fed offset press. Several requirements of the inking system are that it must deliver an even film of ink to the plate and that the film must be deposited on the plate as needed. The color must also be consistent from one impression to another. The inking system must pick up some moisture as the press is in operation. This balance between ink and moisture must be carefully controlled, Fig. 23-49.

Fig. 23-49. Operating principles of a sheet-fed press often can be related to the web press. (Heidelberg Harris)

The ink used in web systems varies from the sheet-fed system. The most common type of ink used for commercial, web offset printing is called *heatset ink*. Many types of paper are compatible with heatset inks.

The *drying system* is often made up of a hot air or flame dryer which evaporates the solvent. This solvent is very volatile. Therefore, special exhaust systems are used to meet local, state, and federal regulations.

The remaining solid pigments which are a part of the semi-soft resin must be cooled. This is accomplished by having the printed web in contact with the *chill rolls*. The number of chill rollers may vary with the press. The rollers are chilled by having cold water circulating through them. It is important that the chill rollers be cold enough to harden the resin. This sets the ink, but final drying takes place after it leaves the press.

The vapor created in the drying unit must be exhausted and meet the requirements established by the Environmental Protection Association.

Some types of web offset printing requires an ink that dries by penetration. This type of ink does NOT require a drying system. This is generally true of forms and newspaper operations. The paper allows the solvent to penetrate the paper surface and this leaves the pigments and resins on the surface of the paper. This type of ink leaves a much duller finish than the ink which requires a drying system.

As in sheet-fed offset printing, the plate must be dampened before it is inked and then the plate transfers the image to a blanket. The image is transferred to the paper from the blanket.

The blanket-to-blanket press prints one color on each side of the web as it passes through the unit. It is a perfecting type press since both sides are being printed at the same time as it goes through the press. Each color would have another unit to print on both sides.

The blanket-to-blanket press is classified as a *rotary press*. Each revolution of the plate cylinder is considered to be an impression. This allows for very rapid continuous printing of an image.

The CIC press uses a central drum. As the web passes through each unit, a color is printed on the web. Note that this system only prints on one side. To print on the other side, the web must be turned over and printed on another central drum with four units for a four-color press. Between each run, the web must go through the drying unit.

Web bindery section

Once all of the images have been placed on a substrate in the press section, the bindery section takes over.

The operation most often found after the printing unit is the folding of the web. This is accomplished by using a former board. The *former board* determines where the fold will be. This was explained in the previous chapter.

Systems are also available on the press to make additional folds such as parallel and ninety degree folds.

Slitters and perforator wheels can be placed against the roll top of the former board. The slitter or perforating is in the direction of travel of the web.

The cutoff of the sheet or sheets is accomplished by having *cutoff knives* on one cylinder and having a *female die* on another cylinder. Called a *chopper,* the sheet length is determined by the diameter of the knife and die cylinders. This is a typical system to make sheets out of the continuous roll of paper.

HOUSEKEEPING AND MAINTENANCE

Whenever a knowledgeable person enters a plant to assist in seeking a solution to a problem, the housekeeping and maintenance of equipment often is a good indicator of print quality.

Keeping equipment clean is the first step in providing quality. Clean rollers, clean cylinders, clean ink fountains, a clean dampening system, a lint free area, and orderly work areas eliminate many of the troubles associated with the printing plant. Rollers must be round and have the proper resilience.

The equipment must also be oiled, greased, and properly adjusted to eliminate excessive wear. The operator must recognize any unusual noises or uncommon mechanical actions.

Remember! Follow carefully the maintenance recommendations of the manufacturer! A few minutes keeping equipment in good operating condition will save time by preventing press run problems and it will save money on down time.

PRESS TROUBLESHOOTING

Any press run problem that occurs must be reviewed or studied in a logical manner. Turning all the knobs usually increases the problem. Understanding each system is essential and proceeding in a step-by-step manner within each system is imperative. Analyzing problem symptoms carefully can help identify the source or cause of the trouble.

Press operators often encounter problem conditions due to the many pressure settings, feed adjustments, varied materials used, and the maintenance demands of the press itself. For this reason, the following guide is offered on problem conditions, their causes, and corrective possibilities.

The following problems are common to the industry. Study their causes and corrections.

Image losses—Called a break, small image area fails to print.

	CAUSE	CORRECTION
1.	Blanket becomes thin under pressure.	Repack blanket.
2.	Wrong type blanket used with heat-set or quick-set inks.	Change to proper blanket.
3.	Blanket surface glazed.	Scrub to soften blanket or replace.
4.	Swollen blanket.	Check for removal of packing or replace.
5.	Blanket smashed.	Build up smashed area or replace blanket.

Web break—Ribbon of paper tears in half during press run.

CAUSE	CORRECTION
1. Tension on one edge of web, due to tapered roll.	Turn roll end for end. Change roll.
2. Roll dented.	Sand out dent or print to area of dent, and then cut out problem area.
3. Bad splice.	Splice inside register.
4. Press out of alignment.	Check alignment to make certain everything is in line.
5. Manufacturing variations in paper.	Check with supplier.

Misregister—Two images do not align when printed over each other, Fig. 23-50.

MISREGISTER

Fig. 23-50. Misregister is when two overprinted images do not line up properly. Note how color is not inside this line image.

CAUSE	CORRECTION
1. Excess ink tack, causing ink not to release from blanket properly.	Reduce tack. Increase tension (web). Reduce press speed.
2. Curling and wrinkled paper stock.	Check paper for humidity problems—adjust pressroom or storage humidity.
3. Printing pressures stretching paper stock.	Adjust impression pressure and/or tension (web).
4. Image improperly positioned on plate.	Remake plate with careful register of image.
5. Web tension too low.	Increase tension.
6. Change in web tension during run.	Adjust infeed tension on web roll.
7. Plate mounted improperly (cocked).	Adjust plate and check bending jig for square.
8. Paper grain run short.	Jobs should be run grain-long to decrease register problems across cylinder.
9. Plate image.	Check prepress area for film, stripping, and vacuum problems.
10. Loose blanket.	Tighten blanket.

Hickies—Round, white spot surrounding an ink spot, Fig. 23-51.

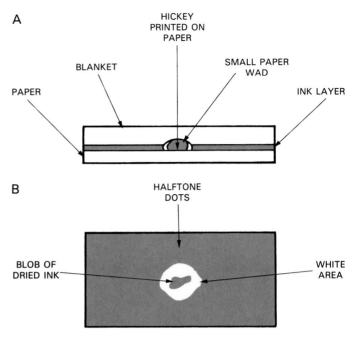

Fig. 23-51. Hickey appears as ink blob with white or unprinted area around it.

CAUSE	CORRECTION
1. Particles of dried ink.	Remove dried ink skin when skimming ink from cans. Clean press and remove all dried ink in fountain and on rollers. Prevent ink caking on roller and lids by thorough cleaning. Web—use heat-set inks with resin and solvent with better-drying oil. In large presses, use a grained rubber roller as a "hickey-picker" (less maintenance than leather). Clean often.
2. Particles of roller composition.	Remove glazed rollers and deglaze by scrubbing with pumice and ink solvent. Use rubber rollers as "hickey-pickers" (less maintenance than leather). Clean often. Replace rollers.
3. Dust specks, plaster, and other materials.	Improve cleanliness in pressroom. Use rubber roller as "hickey-picker" (less maintenance than leather). Clean often.
4. Slitter dust.	Check paper pile in sheet-fed press for loose edges.

Poor ink trapping — Ink related problem that can cause several symptoms.

CAUSE	CORRECTION
1. Too much tack in comparison to the ink on prior unit (multi-color job).	Reduce the ink that fails to trap. Reduce the color strength of the ink that fails to trap. Check with ink supplier for ink with less tack.
2. Wrong drier used on first color down.	Change drier on first color. (Check with ink supplier.)
3. Ink and fountain out of balance (halftone and dot spread).	Reduce ink feed in problem areas: then reduce fountain to a minimum.
4. Ink tack increased due to heat from rollers on drums (web).	Use heat-set oil in problem ink to decrease heat problems in unit. Increase the ink's feed and reduce its color strength. Cool vibrating drums to prevent heat-up (preheated web).
5. Inks not balanced properly for color strength. (One color is run full and another is run so that the spare doesn't trap.)	Reduce color strength of the spare ink but run more of it.
6. On single-color runs, too much time between printing of succeeding colors.	Colors should be run as soon as possible.

Slow ink drying — Ink not curing quickly enough after printing.

Dry inks by:

1. *Oxidation.* (If an ink dries by oxidation and is slow-drying, add more drier to ink.)
2. *Solvent evaporation.* (If ink dries by solvent evaporation, use a more volatile solvent or high dryer temperature in web.)
3. *Absorption into stock.* (If absorption ink dries too slowly, apply a thinner ink film.)
4. *Precipitation.* (Precipitation ink-drying can be made to occur faster by use of steam or by adding a faster glycol solvent.)

CAUSE	CORRECTION
1. pH in fountain too acid.	Check pH and adjust pH to 4.0 to 5.5 if necessary.
2. pH in paper too acid.	Check pH and replace paper stock if necessary.
3. Not enough ink drier.	Add ink drier.
4. Wrong ink for paper used.	Pick correct ink for correct paper.
5. Heat-set inks (web) having too high boiling a solvent.	Improve rub and scuff resistance. Check ink maker.

6. Low pressroom temperature.	Drying is more effective at higher temperatures. Drying time is reduced approximately 25 percent for each increase in temperature of 10°F.

Plate cracking — Plate breaks or splits during press run.

CAUSE	CORRECTION
1. Plate not tight on the cylinder.	When mounting plate on cylinder, check for snug fit.
2. Packing short or askew.	Check packing length. Check that packing does not move during run, causing bulge. Carefully align sheets in initial packing.
3. Bending jig not square.	Check alignment.
4. Wrong mil spec on plate.	Check mil spec of plate for proper size needed.
5. Sharp cylinder edge.	Smooth the edge.
6. Reel-bar areas loose during run.	Check the reel locks for wear.
7. Lead edge of plate improperly bent.	Check plate bend for fit in cylinder gap.
8. Trail edge of plate improperly bent.	Check fit.
9. Cylinder gap dirty.	Clean gap.

Misting — Ink flies off press into atmosphere as fine spray, Fig. 23-52.

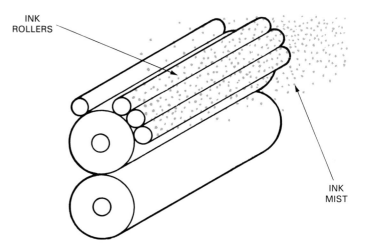

INK ROLLERS

INK MIST

Fig. 23-52. Ink mist is ink vapor being thrown off of rollers. It can be hazardous.

CAUSE	CORRECTION
1. Ink too soft.	Stiffen ink with body gum or varnish.
2. Press speed too high.	Reduce speed.
3. Excess ink.	Run less ink or use a stronger-color ink.

4. Ink rollers out of round. — Inspect and replace.

5. Ink too long in body. — Add anti-misting compounds to shorten ink.

6. Poor lateral distribution of ink on rollers. Vibrating drums allowing inks to form ridges on rollers and then to fly or mist. — Adjust sideways motion of vibrating drums.

7. Excess fountain, causing emulsification. — Lower fountain setting.

Setoff—Ink smears off of one sheet and onto back of another sheet, Fig. 23-53.

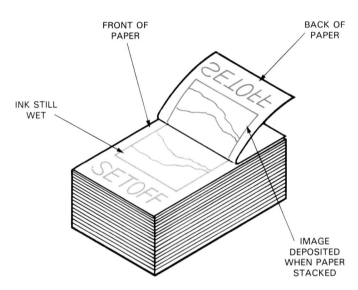

Fig. 23-53. Setoff is when wet ink transfers to back of upper sheet on stack.

CAUSE	CORRECTION
1. Too much ink carried.	Readjust ink settings.
2. Excess acid in fountain.	Low pH retards drying. Change pH to recommended level.
3. Stiff ink.	Add light varnish to ink.
4. Insufficient ink drier.	Increase drier.
5. Improper ink for stock.	Check ink supplier.
6. Static electricity—stock causes paper attraction.	Use static eliminator.
7. Delivery pile too high, causing pressure and setoff.	Reduce delivery pile height.

Ink drying on rollers—Dry ink on rollers ruins image on substrate.

CAUSE	CORRECTION
1. Too much ink drier in an oxidizing ink.	Reduce drier in oxidizing ink.

2. Heat-set ink solvents too volatile (web). — Check for less volatile heat-set ink or add a higher boiling solvent, if running.

3. High humidity. —
a. Check moisture in pressroom.
b. Reformulate ink for humidity conditions.

Poor distribution of ink on rollers—More or less ink on one area of ink rollers.

CAUSE	CORRECTION
1. Ink rollers glazed.	Deglaze, regrind, recover, or replace rollers.
2. Ink rollers out of round.	Regrind or replace rollers.
3. Ink too stiff or tacky.	Add ink-reducing compounds to this ink.
4. Uneven fountain distribution.	Readjust ink flow by ink-fountain keys.
5. Improper roller settings.	Readjust roller settings.

Plate will not roll up properly—Plate surface will not take ink or water normally.

CAUSE	CORRECTION
1. Gum dried on plate or asphaltum too thick or too thin when applied over gum.	Clean plate.

a. Wash plate with clean, warm water and sponge.
b. Wash ink off image with solvent or while plate is still damp with water. Do not let plate dry.
c. Wash solvent or cleaner off plate.
d. Rewash with water.
e. Regum and buff plate.
f. Sponge plate. Start press. Drop ink rollers.
g. Ink plate. Drop dampeners, and print.
Remake plate.

Chalking—Dry ink rubs off sheet because ink improperly bonded to substrate.

CAUSE	CORRECTION
1. Ink needing more ink drier.	Add ink drier suggested by ink manufacturer.
2. Ink absorbed by paper stock before setting properly on surface.	Add binder to stop absorption.
3. Job printed with improper ink for stock used.	Overprint with varnish.
4. Web dryer temperature too high.	Increase circulation for lower temperature.

Setoff in web heat-set inks — Image transferred from one substrate surface to another.

CAUSE	CORRECTION
1. Dryer temperature too low for web speed. (Ink solvent does not vaporize completely.)	Raise temperature in dryer. a. Adjust flame bars in dryer. b. Raise circulating air temperature in dryer. Change to faster drying ink. Reduce press speed.
2. Ink not drying tack-free.	Increase dryer temperature. Reformulate ink.
3. Ink resins not setting hard.	Lower chill temperature. Reduce press speed.
4. Heavy ink film.	Run less ink. Increase color strength.

Blind image — Image does not take ink.

CAUSE	CORRECTION
1. Excess gum in dampening solution.	Check manufacturer's recommended mix for gum in fountain solution — generally one ounce or less per gallon.
2. Too low a pH in dampening solution.	Check pH — recommended 4.0 to 5.5.
3. Excess plate-to-blanket pressure.	Check pressure with packing gauge — reduce pressure.
4. Glazed rollers.	Deglaze or replace rollers.
5. Contamination from cleanup pail.	Change pail twice daily.
6. Improper ink tack — image not accepting ink.	Rework ink — consult supplier.
7. Plate cleaners dry on plate.	Thoroughly rinse plate and do not allow cleaners to dry on plate.
8. Gum arabic substitutes.	Return to 14° Baume gum arabic.
9. Paper sizing in fountain.	Replace paper stock.
10. Contamination of plate during platemaking.	Clean developing area by water; flush where multiple chemicals are used.
11. Excess use of phosphoric acid for plate cleanup.	Dilute concentrate or use substitute cleaner.
12. Ink emulsification affecting ink rollers.	Clean up press and start again with proper ink and water balance.
13. Aired gum or image.	Wet-wash plate. Clean and regum.

Plate wear — Image area physically or chemically disappearing from plate.

CAUSE	CORRECTION
1. Excess form roller pressure.	Check form roller setting by checking ink stripe.
2. Excess plate-to-blanket pressure.	Follow press manufacturer's recommendation for packing, using a packing gauge.
3. Abrasive ink pigments whose particles are not ground properly, are too highly pigmented, or lack lubrication.	Rework ink to reduce pigment sizes. Change ink.
4. Bearer pressures too light.	Check manufacturer's recommended pressure settings.
5. Harsh solvent or blanket washes.	Test solvents selected.
6. Excess durometer reading (hard rollers).	Rollers with durometer readings above 40 are too hard. Replace.
7. Abrasive particles from pumice on blanket or rollers, causing plate to wear.	Rinse both blanket and rollers thoroughly before reuse.
8. Too little ink.	Check ink laydown. Correct ink fountain setting.
9. Length of run too long.	Choose plate designed for run length required.
10. Abrasive residue or debris from paper stock.	Clean blanket. Check paper.

Picking — Lifting of small bit of paper while printing. Fig. 23-54 shows an example.

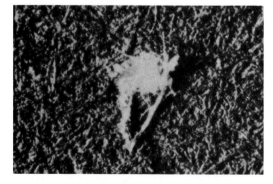

Fig. 23-54. *Picking is where small bit of paper fibers is pulled out.*

CAUSE	CORRECTION
1. Ink too tacky.	Reduce ink tack with reducer.
2. Excessive blanket-to-impression-cylinder pressure.	Decrease pressure.

3. Poor paper quality. — Use a better grade paper or use a stock with a higher pick test.
4. Rollers too hard. — Check durometer readings.
5. If preheater used, ink temperature possibly too high (web). — Cut down on preheat or install chill rolls after preheater at feed.
6. Excess moisture on plate, causing paper to weaken and pick. — Reduce plate dampening with printing pressure.
7. Tacky blanket surface. — Treat surface to reduce tackiness. Replace blanket.

Piling—A dry accumulation or cake on the printing plate.

CAUSE	CORRECTION
1. Ink too stiff or tacky.	Reduce tack by adding a reducing compound.
2. Emulsified ink.	Clean up press. Balance ink and fountain.
3. Poor paper quality. High-absorbent stock removing ink vehicle from the plate, leaving ink film unable to carry the pigment. The pigment left on the plate is piling or caking.	Change stock.
4. Ink waterlogged, improperly ground, or having too coarse a pigment.	Reformulate ink.
5. Blanket packed improperly.	Correct for either overpacking or underpacking.

Streaks—Gear streaks. Roller and blanket streaks.

CAUSE	CORRECTION
1. Improper packing of plate or blanket cylinder (loose).	Check plate and blanket packing.
2. Rollers out of round.	Check roller uniformity.
3. End play in form rollers.	Check form rollers (both ink and fountain).
4. Rollers hard or glazed.	Deglaze rollers and check durometer readings. Replace if durometer reading is above 40.
5. Bearer pressure.	Use manufacturer's suggested settings.
6. Roller pressure.	Check: a. Ink form roller pressure to plate and to vibrator roller. b. Dampening form rollers.
7. Cylinder bearings (wear).	Check pressure.

8. Form roller bearing (wear). — Check pressure.
9. Gear teeth worn or too much backlash. — Replace worn gears and/or adjust backlash.

Slurring—Filling of halftone shadows and bleed at the back of solid areas.

CAUSE	CORRECTION
1. Slippage in the impression.	Reduce back cylinder or impression cylinder pressure to a minimum.
2. Too much plate-to-blanket pressure.	Reduce pressure.
3. Excess ink on coated stocks.	Reduce ink feed or get stronger ink and run less.
4. Piling of paper. Coating on the blanket in the second or third unit of the press.	Check paper stock. Use a moisture-resistant stock.
5. Plate too loose on the cylinder.	Check for snug fit of plate.
6. High ink tack, making paper stick to blanket at the trailing edge.	Add reducing varnish to ink or change to ink with lower tack.
7. Ink too "soupy."	Add varnish to increase ink tack. Change ink.
8. Excess back cylinder pressure.	Reduce pressure.

Tinting—Emulsified ink suspended in the fountain appearing on the printed sheet.

To test for tinting: Tint can usually be washed off with water, but reappears after start-up. Wet-hone a spot in the problem area. If spot takes ink, it is a tinting condition. If not, it is usually a scum condition.

CAUSE	CORRECTION
1. Ink not water resistant.	Add heavy varnish to soft or soupy ink to increase tack. Add water-resistant varnish to ink.
2. Improper pH.	Adjust pH to 4.0 to 5.5.
3. Alkaline paper.	Adjust pH to needs of stock or change stock.
4. Ink and water out of balance.	Clean up and readjust ink and water balance.
5. Plate not properly desensitized.	Prepare new plate or rework.
6. Excess plate-to-blanket pressure.	Check pressure and reset.

Mottling—Solid portions of the dried print appear uneven, blotchy, or cloudy.

CAUSE	CORRECTION
1. Ink not absorbing uniformly on paper stock.	Formulate ink to be less penetrating. Change coated stock.

2. Running excess ink on hard paper stock.	Use greater color-strength ink, allowing less ink run.
3. Too much blanket-to-impression-cylinder pressure.	Reduce pressure, stiffen ink, or soften ink.
4. Excess fountain dampening (reducing tack and causing snowflaking).	Run less fountain.
5. Improper ink tack.	Add body gum.

Misregister on web press—Images do not line up properly when printed.

CAUSE	CORRECTION
1. Improperly stored rolls.	Store rolls on end.
2. Wavy roll.	Change roll.
3. Initial wind.	Change roll.
4. Moisture in roll.	a. Check humidity.
	b. Preheat.
	c. Adjust to balance edge tension.
	d. Increase web tension.

Scumming on plate—Scum film or ink is visible on nonimage area of plate and cannot be removed with water sponge.

To test for scum:

Wet-hone trouble spot. If area stays clean, it is generally a scum condition. If honed area takes ink, the condition is usually tinting.

CAUSE	CORRECTION
1. Ink too soft.	Add body gum or run stiffer ink.
2. Too much ink.	Adjust ink and water balance.
3. Abrasive ink pigments.	Regrind ink.
4. Sensitive plate.	a. Rework (wet-wash, ink, etch, and gum plate).
	b. Remake plate.
5. Incorrect fountain pH.	Bring pH to 4.0 to 5.5.
6. Too much ink drier.	Use less ink drier.
7. Glaze on offset blanket.	Clean or replace blanket.
8. Excessive printing pressure.	Reduce plate-to-blanket and back cylinder pressures.
9. Improve ink roller hardness.	Use rollers with proper hardness.
10. Glaze or dirt on ink rollers.	Clean or replace rollers.
11. Overpacked blanket.	Check packing and pressures.
12. Blanket too hard.	Replace blanket.
13. Ink from rollers.	Reset rollers.

Ink roller stripping—Rollers do not accept ink.

CAUSE	CORRECTION
1. pH below 3.5 acid.	Increase pH to 4.0 to 5.5.
2. Too much fountain.	Decrease fountain setting.
3. Vibrator rollers desensitized.	Clean and copperize rollers. Work thoroughly. Ink rollers and repeat wash.
4. Gum arabic content in fountain too high.	Replace fountain and reduce gum arabic ratio.
5. Rollers glazed or roller too hard.	Deglaze rollers; check durometer reading. Anything above 40 should be replaced.
6. Alcohol percentage above 30 percent, causing roller hardening.	Reduce alcohol level.
7. Acidic solutions on plates get on rollers.	Clean rollers or replace.
8. Ink additives desensitize rollers.	Clean rollers or replace.
9. Cleaners and detergents in dampeners.	Clean dampeners or replace.

Ghosting—Faint, second image appears next to original solid or halftone image.

CAUSE	CORRECTION
1. Glazed or hard ink rollers.	Clean or replace if durometer reading is above 40.
2. Excess fountain.	Recheck fountain settings.
3. Blanket embossed from previous job.	Install new blanket.
4. Form-rollers ink loss due to the printing of a narrow solid ahead of or behind a wider solid.	a. Run minimum fountain.
	b. Use opaque inks if possible.
	c. Lessen vibrator-drum oscillation.
	d. Add additional form rollers, if possible to lessen problem.

KNOW THESE TERMS

Offset duplicator, Offset press, pH, Litmus paper, Electronic pH meter, Fountain additives, Dampener cover, Roller pressure adjustment, Aquamatic system, Cylinder packing, Dancer roller, Heatset ink, Chill rolls, Image loss, Web break, Misregister, Hickey, Plate cracking, Misting, Setoff, Poor ink distribution, No rollup, Chalking, Blind image, Picking, Piling, Streaking, Slurring, Tinting, Mottling, Scumming, Ink roller stripping, Ghosting.

REVIEW QUESTIONS — CHAPTER 23

1. Typically, with a sheet-fed press, set the side guides of the feeding system for approximately _____ inch or _____ mm clearance from the stock.
2. It is commonly acceptable to make most press adjustments with the press running at a very low speed. True or false?
3. How do you check the impression on a typical press?
4. Explain two ways to check the pH of the fountain solution.
5. How do you check roller pressure?
6. When would you use anti-setoff powder?
7. These are commonly used to help harden the resin of the ink on a web press.
   a. Form rolls.
   b. Flicker rolls.
   c. Heat rolls.
   d. Chill rolls.
8. _____ is a problem that has two images improperly aligned over each other.
9. What is a "hickey?"
10. Explain three possible causes and corrections for the following press problems: plate cracking, misting, setoff, chalking, picking, piling, streaking, mottling, scumming, and ghosting.

This is a densitometer that is scanning the control devices (color bars) of a printed sheet. (X-Rite, Inc.)

This is a software system used to collect data on electronic imaging operations.   (Covalent Systems Corporation)

Chapter 24

LETTERPRESS IMPOSITION AND LOCKUP

After studying this chapter, you will be able to:
- Explain the need for arranging the letterpress elements carefully before lockup.
- Identify layouts for most common impositions.
- Summarize various lockup systems.
- Follow a typical procedure for locking up a type form.

This chapter will summarize the steps for mounting individual type characters before running a job. It will explain lockup and review multi-page imposition.

Although hand-setting of type is no longer common in industry, it will help you develop a better understanding of printing in general. For this reason, this small chapter will review the most important steps for imposition and lockup.

LETTERPRESS IMPOSITION

The term *imposition,* discussed in earler chapters, refers to the arrangement of pages or image elements for the printing process. Letterpress or relief imposition is done with metal type, wood type, or original plates, instead of film. The more modern stripping of film is similar to the imposition for letterpress operations.

Several pages of a pamphlet or book can be printed together on a large sheet of paper. This arrangement of pages is called a *signature.* The arrangement of pages in the signature is called a *lay of pages.*

An *imposition layout* must be made to show how the pages must be arranged on the sheet to produce the correct results after folding, Fig. 24-1. This plan shows how the job will be printed as well as all bindery and finishing operations. After the signature is folded, each page must be in proper position.

SIGNATURE PRINTING METHODS

The metal type and photoengravings are assembled into page forms. As stated in the stripping chapter, with the relief process, there are three methods of printing signatures of pages. They are:
1. Sheetwise.
2. Work-and-turn.
3. Work-and-tumble, sometimes called work-and-flop.

Sheetwise

To briefly review, the *sheetwise method* prints one form or forms on one side of the sheet. Another form or set of forms is printed in register on the other side of the sheet. The same press gripper and guide edge is used.

If more than one page is printed, the form that has the first and last page is called the *outside form.* The other form is called the *inside form.*

Work-and-turn

The *work-and-turn method* has forms that have all of the pages of a signature locked up together. The sheet is then turned over endways and printed on the back or other side with the same form. The gripper edge is NOT changed. The side guide is moved to the other side of the press. This retains the same guide edge of the paper. The sheet is cut in half, making two identical signatures.

Work-and-tumble

The *work-and-tumble method* also prints on a double-size sheet. After printing the first side, the sheet is turned side

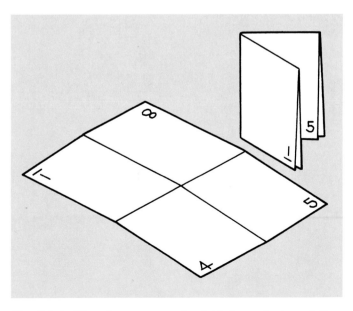

Fig. 24-1. The signature can be folded, marked, and then unfolded to indicate the location of pages for imposition.

383

to side instead of end forward. The gripper edges are changed. This method can present problems in register since the gripper edge is changed. The guide remains on the same edge, however.

The layouts shown in Fig. 24-2 illustrate the most common impositions for 4, 6, 8, 12, and 16-page forms. Study them carefully. Note the difference between each of the impositions.

Allowance for trim

After the signature has been folded and in many cases, gathered and sewed or stitched, it must be trimmed (cut) on three sides. Allowance must be made for cutting of these sides so the signature will have smooth edges. The fourth side or *gutter* does NOT need additional space and is not trimmed. A *trim allowance* of 1/8 of an inch (3.18 mm) is very common.

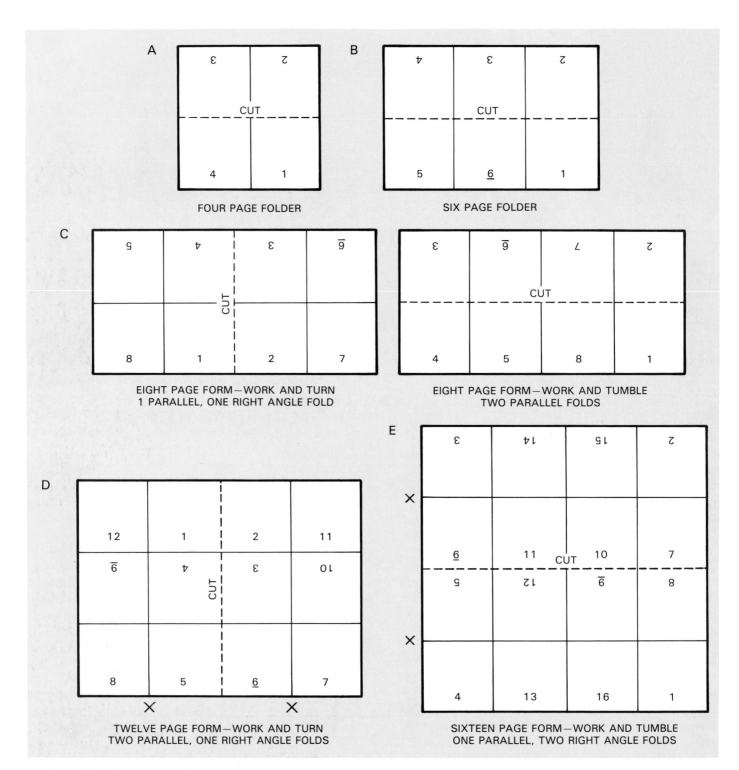

Fig. 24-2. The common impositions for 4, 6, 8, 12 and 16-page forms. A—Four page form. B—Six page form. C—Eight page form. D—Twelve page form. E—Sixteen page form.

Imposition for web presses

The first planning factor for web imposition is the width of the roll of paper. This is commonly referred to as the *width of web.*

Smaller webs are becoming common to the industry. The mini and middle size webs are very practical for certain types of printing. The distance across the web determines the amount of space that is available for the printing area.

The second consideration is the *length of cutoff.* The circumference of the press cylinder determines the size from one edge to another. The cylinder cuts or chops the web of paper into sheets. The cutoff length is constant since the circumference of the cylinder is not changed.

A *perfecting press* prints both sides of the web. The size and number of printed sheets depends on the size of the web and how the sheet is folded. The top side is called the *top deck* while the other side is printed on the *bottom deck.*

The number of units must be considered when planning imposition for web presses. The size of the booklet or printed object is determined by web size, length of cutoff, and the number of web folds.

LOCKUP OF RELIEF IMAGES

Once the relief images have been positioned, the next step is to hold the images in position as they are printed. This task is referred to as *locking up the form.* This is accomplished on a "stone." This smooth surface table is called an *imposing stone.* See Fig. 24-3.

Lockup equipment

The following equipment is commonly used to lock up a *form* (hand-set type): chase, furniture, reglets, and quoins.
1. The *chase* is a frame that supports all of the other equipment.
2. The *furniture* and *reglets* are used to fill in the blank spaces around the form.
3. The *quoins* are the locking devices.

Lockup systems

Two types of lockups are very common. They are the chaser method and the furniture-within-furniture method.

Variations do exist and are necessary with certain presses and with the imposition of the same forms.

As the term implies, *lockup* is a method of securing the type form or forms within the support device or chase. The equipment will be described as each step is explained in the lockup procedure.

Lockup procedure

Typically, the form is removed from the galley as shown in Fig. 24-4. Carefully place the form onto the cleaned stone. Position the head (top) of the form toward you if the form is shorter in length (from top to bottom) than the width. If the form has greater length than width, the head should be placed to the left, Fig. 24-5. In this case, the form is hot metal type. The same would be true of a cut or engraving.

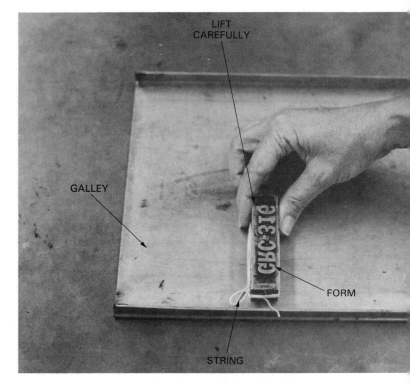

Fig. 24-4. Carefully remove the form from the galley. String is tied around form to hold it together.

Fig. 24-3. Imposing stone is a smooth table for locking the form in the chase.

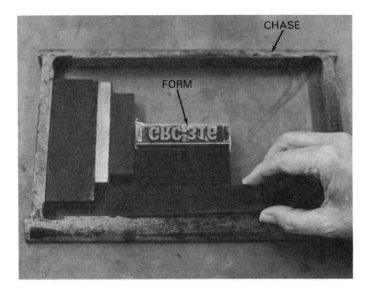

Fig. 24-5. The head of the form is placed to the left or to the bottom depending on which is longer, the width or the length of the form.

The decision must be made as to the type of lockup to be used. In most incidents, if the form has the SAME WIDTH as the LENGTH of the furniture, the furniture-within-furniture method will be used. If the form WIDTH IS NOT the SAME as the furniture length, the chaser method is suggested.

The furniture is made of metal, plastic, or wood. The length is measured in picas and the common lengths are: 10, 15, 20, 25, 30, 40, 50, and 60 picas. The width is also in picas and measures 2, 3, 4, 5, 6, 8, 10 picas. The furniture is usually stored in a rack located as part of the base supporting the stone, Fig. 24-6.

Place the chase over the form with the bottom side toward you, Fig. 24-5.

The furniture-within-furniture method will be used to illustrate a typical lockup.

In this situation, the form is shorter than it is wide (line length) and the form width is twenty picas. The first piece of furniture should be twenty picas long with the width as great as possible. Place it next to the side of the form closest to you.

Place the second piece of furniture next to the first piece. This piece of furniture is often the same length or slightly longer than the first piece. The width depends on the space. The third piece of furniture is placed on the left side of the form. The length must be greater than the length of the form. The fourth piece is the same as the third. Fill in the total area from the top of the form to the bottom of the chase with furniture that pyramids as it gets closer to the chase, Fig. 24-7.

The next step is to fill in the area to the left of the form. Position the locking devices, called quoins. The quoins are placed to the top of the form and to the right of the form. Refer to Fig. 24-8.

Several types of quoins are available. Some of the more common types are: Wickersham, Hempel, and Hi-Speed, Fig. 24-9. The Hempel works on the inclined plane principle while the other two operate on the cam principle. For this example, the Wickersham type will be used.

Place one quoin on the right side of the furniture and one next to the furniture away from you. Generally, quoins are positioned between the first and second piece of furniture next to the form.

The remaining area on both sides must be filled in with furniture in the same manner as previously stated. If the exact width of furniture is not available, reglets are used.

Fig. 24-6. Furniture is usually stored in a rack below imposing stone.

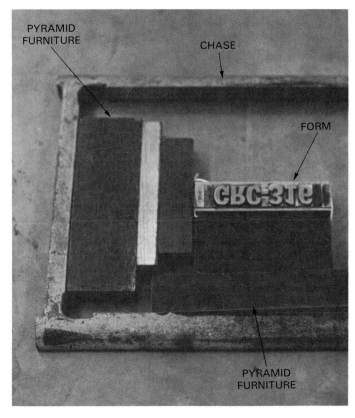

Fig. 24-7. The chase is positioned over the form. Furniture fills in space around form.

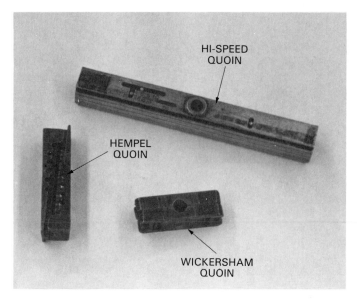

Fig. 24-9. Quoins are used as the locking devices. Note variations.

Reglets are thin wooden strips that are available in pica lengths, and pica as well as half pica (nonpareil) widths or thicknesses. Whenever possible, the reglets are placed between the quoins and the furniture. Refer to Fig. 24-10.

Once the area is filled in, the quoins must be tightened. Tightening is accomplished by taking the appropriate quoin

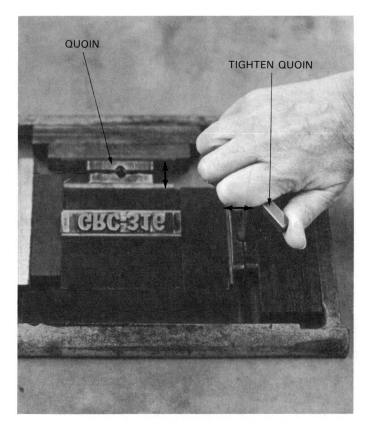

Fig. 24-8. The quoins are placed toward the top and right side of the form. When tightened, they expand to lock furniture against chase and form.

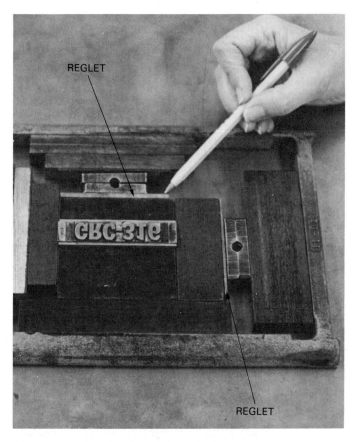

Fig. 24-10. Smaller materials, called reglets, are available to fill between the quoin and furniture.

key and tightening each quoin intermittently until the image form will not move, Fig. 24-8. It is imperative that the images are parallel to the base to give an even image for impression.

A *planer block* is used to even or level out the form characters, Fig. 24-11. The planing is done before the form is securely locked up. Tap down with the planer block to push all characters down onto the imposing stone.

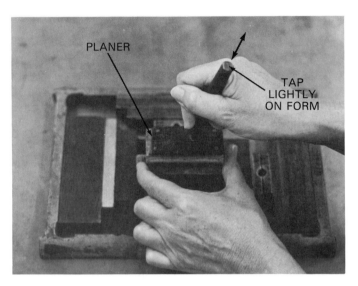

Fig. 24-11. The planer block is tapped to even the surface of the form. Stone must be perfectly clean.

After planing, tighten each quoin, one at a time, back and forth until the form is tight. To check tightness, place a quoin under the edge of the chase and tap the form lightly, Fig. 24-12. None of the materials should move.

WARNING! If the quoins are forced too tight, it is possible to break the chase. The chase will usually crack in the corners. Be careful when locking up the form.

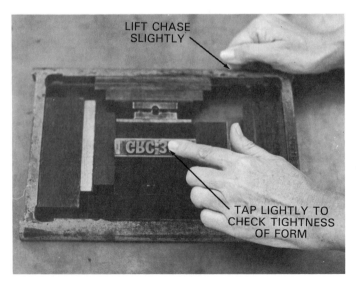

Fig. 24-12. The form is lifted slightly and tapped to make sure none of the images fall through.

The chaser method of lockup is shown in Fig. 24-13. This method is commonly used when the length of the lines and the length of the furniture do not coincide.

Another lockup variation exists when the bottom and the left side of the form are NOT the constant sides. This method is shown as a lockup for a Heidelberg platen press, Fig. 24-14. Type placement is critical. Follow the manufacturer's specifications.

Fig. 24-13. Another system of lockup uses the chaser method.

Fig. 24-14. The Heidelberg platen press requires the quoins to be placed to the top and left of the form.

CYLINDER PRESS LOCKUP

Lockup for large presses will vary, but the principle is the same as the platen press lockup. The placement of the form is critical since the grippers have set positioning. The paper line and the type line become locations for placement. The type must clear the gripper area. Larger presses usually have squared chases and are not beveled. The top and/or bottom is marked or indicated by the manufacturer. The quoins are often positioned all around the form.

It is imperative that the lockup person know the press that is being used for the job. When in doubt, refer to the press operating manual.

KNOW THESE TERMS

Imposition, Signature, Lay of pages, Sheetwise, Outside form, Inside form, Work-and-turn, Work-and-tumble, Gutter, Trim allowance, Width of web, Length of web cutoff, Perfecting press, Top deck, Bottom deck, Imposing stone, Chase, Form, Furniture, Quoins, Lockup, Chaser method, Furniture-within-furniture method, Reglets, Planer block.

REVIEW QUESTIONS—CHAPTER 24

1. Hand-setting of type is still very common in today's printing industry. True or false?
2. _____ refers to the arrangements of pages or image elements on a sheet for the printing process.
3. The compiled pages for a booklet or pamphlet is called a _____.
4. The same gripper and guide edge are used with the sheetwise method. True or false?
5. A trim allowance of _____ of an inch or _____ millimeters is common.
6. What are the two more important considerations when doing imposition of a web press?
7. The _____ is the frame that holds the form and other lockup devices.
8. The _____ and _____ are used to fill the space around the form.
9. The _____ are locking devices that expand to hold the form in the chase.
10. Why is a planer block needed?

SUGGESTED ACTIVITIES

1. Lock up a letterpress form.
2. Make a dummy. Illustrate all of the information necessary to clearly inform the prepress department, press department, and bindery department on how to produce the product.

A—On left, you can see web being fed into belt press. Finished folded signatures are coming out on right and are moving to binding area.

B—Closeup shows relief belt as it separates from paper web.

Although conventional relief presswork is on the decline, the Cameron belt press, which uses a relief principle, is increasing in use. The belt press uses two long, rubber belt-plates to print on both sides of the web at once. A complete book can be printed in one pass. (Cameron-Somerset Technologies)

Chapter 25

RELIEF PRINTING PRESSES

After studying this chapter, you will be able to:
- Identify the common types of relief presses.
- Explain the methods used to transfer the image for all types of relief presses.
- Summarize the basic procedures to operate basic types of relief presses.
- Explain flexographic printing.
- Describe how a Cameron belt press operates.

Relief printing, more commonly called *letterpress,* is a graphic reproduction method using a raised image surface. The process requires the inking of a relief image plate. Then the inked surface is pressed against the paper or other substrate. The printed image is in direct contact with the raised plate surfaces but not with the nonimage areas.

This chapter will review the operation of platen presses, cylinder presses, flexographic presses, and belt presses. The chapter will start out by covering older, simpler presses and progress to more complex, advanced presses, like the Cameron Belt Press. As a result, you should be well versed in the presses that use the relief printing process.

PRESSES FOR LETTERPRESS PRINTING

Graphic reproduction by the relief method can be accomplished by using any of three types of letterpress presses: platen, flat bed cylinder, and/or rotary. All relief presses fall into one of these categories. The principle upon which each operates is shown in Fig. 25-1.

As discussed under offset presses, they use four basic systems: inking, printing, feeding, and delivering.

Platen presses

The basic principle of a *platen press* is that it has two flat surfaces that move into each other. The type or form is locked up and placed in the *bed* of the press while the substrate is held on the surface of the *platen.* After the image is inked, the two surfaces come together and make a "kiss" impression on the substrate (usually paper). An excellent image transfer results.

A wide variety of platen presses are available. The hand-operated platen press is small and slow, Fig. 25-2. Larger

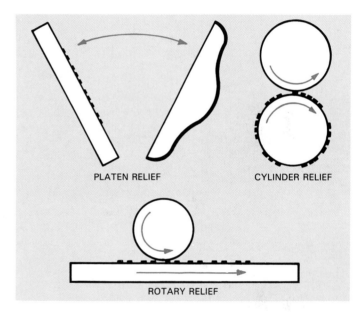

Fig. 25-1. These are the three types of relief presses. They are the platen, cylinder, and rotary. Note their basic principles.

Fig. 25-2. The hand-operated platen press was once used to print a few copies of small forms. It is seldom used in the printing industry; however, it can be used to illustrate printing principles easily.

motorized models feed automatically and are capable of printing more copies per hour.

For specific jobs, platen presses can be an efficient and economical method of printing. The power-operated automatic platen press is commonly used as one means of doing letterpress printing. Platen press sizes are usually 10 x 15 inches or 12 x 18 inches.

An older power platen press is pictured in Fig. 25-3.

Fig. 25-3. The power platen press is applicable for some printing and finishing operations. It too has been replaced by more efficient press designs.

WARNING! The hand-operated power platen press has been declared unsafe by OSHA standards. Obtain instructor permission before running this type press. When operating a hand-operated press, use care!

The hand-operated press will be used to identify the tasks needed to complete a job. The same procedure would be used to prepare a power platen press.

PARTS OF PLATEN PRESS

The parts of a power platen press are similar to the hand-operated platen press. However, the hand-operated press does NOT have a throw off lever or brake.

Fig. 25-4 shows the basic parts of a platen press. Refer to this illustration as the components are explained.

1. CHASE — The *chase* is the metal frame that supports the type form.
2. PLATEN — The *platen* is a smooth metal surface. Material is attached to the surface to hold the paper to be printed. With each revolution of the press, the platen comes in contact with the inked type form.

Fig. 25-4. Study basic parts of this platen press. This type can be used to teach basic printing methods if safety rules are followed.

3. BAILS — The *bails* are arms that hold tympan paper on the platen. The material used to support the printing paper is *tympan paper*.
4. FEEDBOARD — The paper to be printed is fanned out and placed on the feedboard.
5. DELIVERY BOARD — Once the paper is printed, it is removed from the tympan paper and placed on the *delivery board*.
6. GRIPPERS — The *grippers* of the press close at each revolution and hold the paper in place. Make sure the grippers are placed so that they do not touch the type form. If they fall in line with the type form, the type will be smashed. The type can be ruined.

Throw-off lever

The purpose of the *throw-off lever* is to take the press OFF impression or to place it ON impression. If the paper is fed in such a way that it is not in its correct position, the lever can be pushed. This will take the press off impression. An image will NOT be printed on the sheet or on the tympan paper.

Ink rollers

The number of rollers will vary with the press. The *ink rollers* distribute ink to the form. The source of ink for the roller distribution on a hand-operated press is the *ink disk*. Another type of ink distribution system uses the roller as the ink distribution source.

Rollers must be handled with care as they are easily damaged. Proper cleaning is essential. Follow the manufacturers' recommendations. Make sure the roller cleaning solvent meets federal, state, and local regulations.

Flywheel and footbrake

The *flywheel* is a large wheel, usually mounted on the shaft on the left side of the press. The flywheel provided momentum and facilitates smooth operation of the press. It is pushed by hand to move the rollers, bed, and platen of the press. When starting the hand-operated power press, it is wise to assist rotation by pushing on the flywheel in the correct direction of travel.

A *footbrake* is provided to stop the press after the power has been turned off.

Inking the press (platen)

To ink up the press, place the rollers in the lowest position. Make sure the ink disk is clean. Wipe it with a clean rag if needed. Turn the press by hand using the flywheel. Clean the rollers with a recommended solvent on a clean rag.

A small amount of ink is applied to the left side of the disk. An *ink knife* is used to take ink from a can. Remove all *livered* (dried) ink and throw it away. Scrape out some ink and place a small amount on the disk, Fig. 25-5.

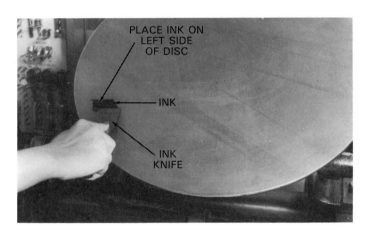

Fig. 25-5. A small amount of ink is placed on the left side of the ink disk using an ink knife.

It is best to ink up the press before the form has been placed in the bed. This allows for better ink distribution and prevents the form from being clogged by deposits of ink.

Remember! Ink should be added in small quantities with an ink knife. The frequency that ink is added depends on the amount used by the images on the specific form.

Roller service (platen)

Rollers must be kept in excellent condition. Proper cleaning must always be stressed. The height of the rollers should be checked before the form is placed in the bed of the press. A type high *roller gauge* may be used to check the height of the rollers above the surface of the bed, Fig. 25-6.

If any changes in roller height are required, use either larger or smaller roller *trucks* (spacers) on the ends of the roller shaft.

On jobs of any length, an in ink fountain must be used. As in all printing, the ink chosen should suit the stock and the nature of job being printed.

Fig. 25-6. This gauge can be used to check for proper roller height or distance on platen press.

MAKE-READY (PLATEN)

Make-ready is the process of preparing the press and regulating the pressure required to give an even impression on the substrate. This requires close attention.

Preparing the platen

Remove all of the previous make-ready from the platen of the press. Select the tympan sheet and position it on the platen. Open the bails, Fig. 25-7, and place the tympan so it can be clamped in the lower bail of the platen.

Cut a press board slightly smaller than the platen along with *hanger sheets* (hard surface stock). These sheets are called the *packing*. The amount of packing needed should be determined before inserting it under the tympan sheet on the platen. Pull on the tympan sheet and clamp the bail in place. Remove excess tympan paper. The thickness of the packing must be adjusted for each form.

Start with a packing that gives a very light impression. Add more sheets to accommodate the size of the form.

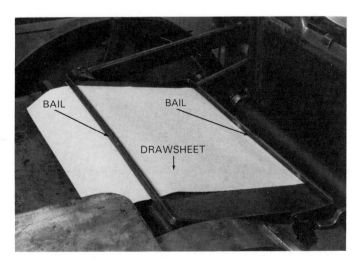

Fig. 25-7. Bails are generally used to hold tympan paper in place on platen presses.

The packed tympan paper is now referred to as the *drawsheet*. The drawsheet will withstand normal cleaning of the printed image with solvent on a rag.

Trial impression (platen)

Place the throw-off lever on impression and turn the press to make an impression on the drawsheet. A slight impression should appear on the drawsheet. The *trial impression* locates the images so that guides can be located and margins established, Fig. 25-8.

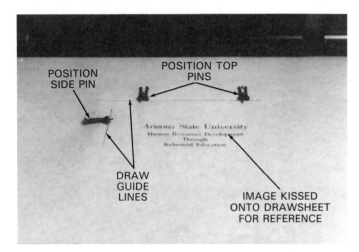

Fig. 25-8. Gauge pins are inserted into drawsheet to hold paper while being printed. Gauge pins are placed on bottom and left edges of sheet.

Positioning gauge pins (platen)

Having selected the type of substrate to be used for the job, the stock must be held in position by *guides* while it is being printed. The comprehensive tells the operator the proper location of the image. The most common type of guides are called *gauge pins,* Fig. 25-9.

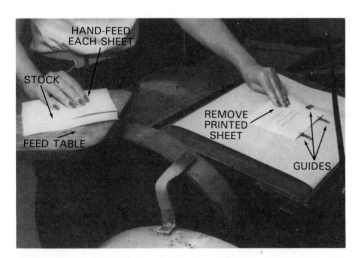

Fig. 25-9. Location of gauge pins will control location of image on paper. Blank sheet is lifted from feed table and placed against guide pins with right hand. Left hand then removes printed sheets.

The method used to find the position of each pin varies. When the image is to be centered on the paper, a very common practice is to take the distance of the form and subtract it from the size of the paper. That figure is divided in half to give an even margin on each side of the form.

The gauge pins are positioned at the bottom and left sides of the image area. Once the location has been determined, draw a line at the bottom of the paper on the drawsheet. Repeat on the left-hand side, Fig. 25-9.

Two gauge pins are positioned at the bottom approximately one-quarter of the distance in from each end of the sheet. The left gauge pin is placed approximately one-third of the distance up from the bottom of the sheet.

Insert the point of the pin approximately 1/4 inch (6.4 mm) to the bottom or left of the sheet position. Push the point through the sheet and allow enough space so that the end of the guide will return through the drawsheet to stabilize the gauge pin, Fig. 25-10.

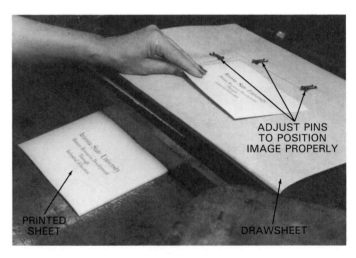

Fig. 25-10. After being printed, sheet is pulled from platen and placed on delivery board. Remember that the platen press can cause severe hand injury. Keep hands away from closing platen.

Take an impression on a sheet to check the location. If the margin needs to be increased, move the gauge pin away from the image. Once everything is correctly positioned, tap the gauge pin with a quoin key to set the points into the drawsheet, hanger sheets, and pressboard.

If the pins tend to move, a sealing wax is available. The pin can be sealed to the drawsheet with sealing wax. The type form does not move, only the paper moves. Clean the drawsheet image area with solvent.

Equalizing the impression (platen)

Having positioned a clean sheet of paper in the press and pulled an inked impression, the image should be transferred to the substrate.

If the form has a slightly uneven surface, the image will not have the same ink coverage. Some areas will print while others will not. Building up all the areas until an even ink coverage is visible is part of the process called make-ready.

Placing thin make-ready stock under the drawsheet or in back of the form is the manner in which evenness is corrected. To eliminate the very abrupt edge of the make-ready paper, tear the paper so that it has a featheredge. Build up the areas very gradually until an even impression results.

OPERATING THE PRESS (PLATEN)

Before running the press, a routine maintenance check should be made. Make sure the press has been properly lubricated.

> DANGER! Remove any apparel that could be caught in the press. This includes rings, watches, bracelets, apron ties, and neck ties. Roll up loose long sleeves. Always follow press instructions and operate the press with extreme care!

The substrate (paper stock) is placed on the feed board or table. The stock is fanned out, allowing the operator to grasp a single sheet, Fig. 25-10. The feeding process requires that the operator take a sheet from the feed board and place it on the drawsheet so that it touches the three gauge pins. Sometimes, glycerin is placed on fingertips to eliminate slipping.

> WARNING! When using a power press, never reach for a piece of paper on the drawsheet. The press could crush your fingers or hand. A sheet of paper can be replaced, but you cannot replace parts of your body.

The freshly printed sheets are removed with the left thumb and second finger and stacked on the delivery board. An efficient operator will jog the sheets as they are printed.

If the ink must be added by hand, do it sparingly and again in the left hand corner of the disk. The reason for placing ink in the lower left area allows the ink to be dispersed before coming in contact with the type form. Large amounts of ink can fill in the counter area of the type.

> Never allow a power press to run without an operator in the immediate area!

Cleaning the press (platen)

Before cleaning the press, check to see if the right number of copies have been printed. If everything checks out, remove the chase from the press with the rollers in the down position.

Clean the form with a recommended solvent and rag. Immediate cleaning is essential because the ink will dry and cleaning problems will result.

Clean the ink disk with a recommended solvent. Next, clean the rollers by rubbing the solvent rag back and forth while inching the rollers around, Fig. 25-11. This process may be repeated as many times as needed to thoroughly wash the rollers and disk.

> Place solvent rags in a recommended self-closing metal container, Fig. 25-12. This will help prevent a possible fire.

Unlocking the form (platen)

Before unlocking the form, make sure the type is thoroughly cleaned. Use a recommended solvent on a cleaning rag.

Fig. 25-11. *After job has been run, carefully clean ink disk, form, and rollers. Use an approved cleaning solution.*

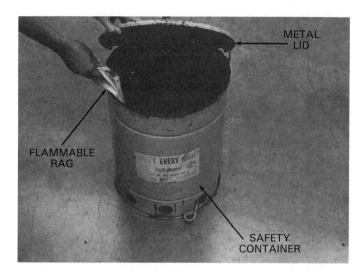

Fig. 25-12. *To prevent a serious fire hazard, place all solvent-soaked rags in an approved container with a fireproof, self-closing lid.*

If the type or form is to be stored, the form is *tied up* (string wrapped around form) and placed in a galley. If the need for a repeat printing does NOT exist, the form is *distributed* (returned to storage) or scrapped. Put the furniture, reglets, chase, and quoins in their proper places.

Remember! Cleanliness is essential in the printing industry. A few minutes time cleaning can save hours if a print job were to be ruined by poor equipment maintenance.

AUTOMATIC PLATEN PRESS

The *automatic platen press* picks up and feeds the sheets mechanically. An automatic platen press that is very typical to the industry is the Heidelberg platen press. This press is often referred to as the "windmill" and has many adaptations. Its methods of operation can be transferred to other automatic platen presses, even though the configuration may vary.

Presses are highly machined pieces of equipment. Proper care will assure longer press life with less printing problems. Understanding and using the manufacturer's manual is critical.

The following steps are basic to the operation of an automatic platen press.

Packing the press (auto platen)

The tympan sheet for each press is ordered precut. Cutting it to fit would require too much time and the folding might not meet accuracy requirements.

The number of press sheets is determined by a set figure. All of the packing, including the printing stock, is approximately .040 of an inch (1 mm) thick. Pack as described by the press manufacturer, Fig. 25-13.

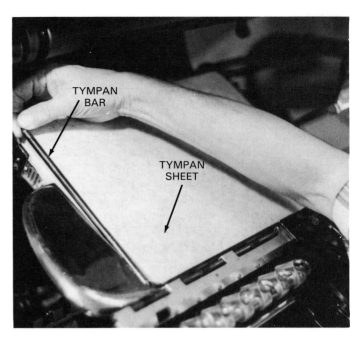

Fig. 25-14. Bars, similar to bails, are used to hold tympan sheet on this press.

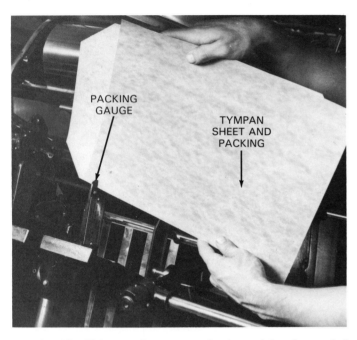

Fig. 25-13. This press has a gauge for determining the needed packing.

Clamping the drawsheet (auto platen)

Bars are used to hold the tympan and make-ready sheets at the bottom, top, and left-hand sides. Place the bottom bar in position first and next draw another bar over the drawsheet to make sure it does not have slack. The left-hand bar is positioned last in the same manner. See Fig. 25-14.

Two clamps hold the gripper side of the tympan. Insert the tympan and tighten down the thumb screw and the clamp.

Adjust the impression (auto platen)

It is possible to adjust the impression for slight changes. Typically, you can use the knurled rings on the impression on or off lever. By lifting and pulling out on the lever, the impression is on. Pushing in usually disengages the typeface from the drawsheet. By turning the lower ring clockwise, the impression is increased. Other presses have a different arrangement.

Positioning (auto platen)

For close register, guides are used. The procedure outlined will not include the use of guides. The press operating manual will graphically show the necessary tasks to be followed to use guides.

When the form is locked up, it is positioned according to the center markings. The form position determines the image location on the substrate.

Loading the press (auto platen)

The location of the stock on the feed table will also determine the image location on the sheet, Fig. 25-15. Fanning the stock before placing it in the feed table will make the operator's job easier. Sheet steadiers, and sometimes a hold-down finger, will keep the stock from inching forward while side guides keep the sheets in alignment.

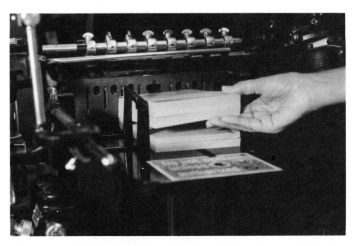

Fig. 25-15. Paper must be carefully positioned according to image location.

The sucker bar provides the pick up of the stock and transferring of the sheets to the gripper. The amount of suction can be regulated with sucker bar slides. Experimenting is necessary for thin, smooth, and heavy stock. It is also possible to move the bar laterally.

The feed blower should be adjusted by using the control device and the press manual directions. The sucker bar can also be tilted to adjust to the form of the paper. The height of the pile can be controlled for continuous smooth feeding.

Running the job (auto platen)

Turn the power switch on. This starts the motor but does NOT engage the press. The press is typically engaged by pushing the clutch lever with the front guard in the down position. The clutch lever is pushed away from the operator. The gripper will revolve with the clutch engaged. The press will automatically stop if the front guard is in the vertical position.

WARNING! Do not lean over the press when it is running. Severe injury could result.

Whenever the press is NOT in use, it is suggested that the guard be left in the vertical position because this eliminates the possibility of starting the press.

The press is equipped with a suction trip which allows the press to run without picking up sheets to be printed. When the suction trip is pushed in, the sucker bar will transfer a sheet to the gripper. When the trip is pulled out, the suction is off. Below the knob controlling the suction trip is an automatic stop control.

Delivery setting (auto platen)

Run a sheet through the press and stop it while the gripper is holding the sheet. Adjust the side guides. Also position the rear sheet guide and the jogger according to manufacturer's directions.

Running up ink (auto platen)

Ink is placed in the fountain, but it is not automatically transferred to the rollers and the form. The lever must first be pushed down so the ductor rollers transfer ink to the drum and the form rollers. All rollers must be engaged and the fountain feed lever must be set to have the press ink up for use.

Again, it is always easy to add ink, but it is difficult and time consuming to take off excess ink. Place the chase in the press and take an impression. If the impression is uneven, make-ready is required.

Press wash up (auto platen)

Many auto platen presses have a wash up device, which must be positioned so that the safety latch does not allow movement. Place recommended solvent on the rollers and apply pressure to the clean-up blade. Add solvent until the rollers are clean.

Thoroughly clean the ink fountain. The wash-up basin and blade must be thoroughly cleaned after each wash up. Do not allow the ink to dry on the blade and in the basin. Place the clean up rag in the proper safety container.

CYLINDER PRESS

The *cylinder press* has one flat surface and a cylinder. The flat portion is positioned horizontally on some presses and vertically on others. The flat portion is the bed of the press and supports the chase holding the form. The cylinder transports the substrate (paper) during the printing of an image.

Flatbed cylinder presses are available as single color unit, multiple units, or as *perfectors* (both sides printed during one pass through press). Various types of letterpress presses are in use today.

The Miehle is a vertical press. At one time, it was considered to be one of the workhorses of the industry. The basic principles are the same for horizontal and vertical letterpresses. Its use will be summarized since it is a typical cylinder flatbed press.

Operating procedure (cylinder flatbed)

The controls of the press have important functions and each should be thoroughly understood. A few are the start and stop buttons, the belt-tightening lever, the trip mechanisms, and the feeder control handle. Study the press operating manual to learn about each control.

It is imperative that the press be lubricated before any production takes place. Preventive maintenance is an essential part of the operating procedure. For specific maintenance tasks, again consult the press manual.

The power should be off. To assure that the motor cannot be started, open the cylinder guard. When the guard is open, the press power cannot be activated. The belt tightener lever should be in the release position. The speed of the press is frequently regulated by pulley size. Start out at the lowest speed. See Fig. 25-16.

Fig. 25-16. Note parts of this cylinder, relief press. Feed table is swung back to give access to other press components. Guard is an important safety device that will prevent press operation when opened.

The automatic stop control knob must be in the down position to make sure the press will trip off as needed. The side guide shifting dam determines whether the left or right guide is used to jog the stock for proper image position.

The chase is positioned in the vertical bed of the press. Alignment devices are located at the bottom of the chase. The holding device at the top of the chase must be in position, Fig. 25-17. The paper line and image line are indicated on the chase.

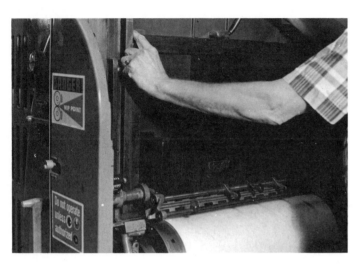

Fig. 25-17. Press operator is installing the chase in the bed of this cylinder press.

The transfer table must be attached to the cylinder journal caps. The transfer table holds the sheet from the feeder and allows movement so that the sheet is properly transferred to the impression cylinder.

Set the side guide based on the positioning of the form in the chase and size of the sheet. The feeder table front pile guides must be positioned to align with the form. The position is based on sheet size, Fig. 25-18. Place the stock on the feeder table. Set the rear and side guides to hold the

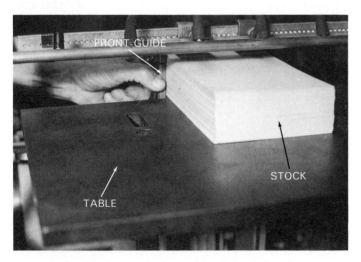

Fig. 25-18. Front guides must align with form and sheet size for proper location of image on sheets.

sheets in position. The feeder table should be raised to within a one-half inch (13 mm) of the pile guide.

The separator shoes must be positioned to within one inch (25 mm) from the edges of the sheet, Fig. 25-19. The shoe type will vary with the type of stock being run.

Pull the belt tightener lever. Using the flywheel, turn the press over by hand. Turn the flywheel in the direction indicated by the arrow. This step is to assure that everything is properly positioned.

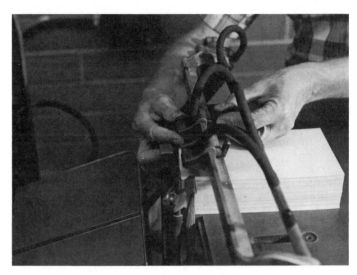

Fig. 25-19. Operator is adjusting shoes to assure that each sheet is picked up and fed properly.

Close the cylinder guard and start the press. Push the feeder control air valve in to activate it. Slowly bring the belt-tightener lever toward you. After the sheet has passed the impression cycle, stop the press by releasing the belt-tightener lever just before the sheet is released by the delivery grippers.

Position delivery side and rear joggers to fit the sheet size. Specific tasks that also need careful attention include the inking adjustment and the impression cylinder adjustment.

Inking adjustment (cylinder flatbed)

For ink adjustment, the impression cylinder should be at the uppermost stroke. The feeder table must be swung to the open position, Fig. 25-20.

Loosen the fountain lock wheel, and swing the fountain away from the press. Place rollers in proper position. Then check to make sure that each roller is mounted and locked in the roller box. Damage could occur if a roller were to release during the press run. Extreme care is essential!

The ink fountain sometimes has a "drop blade" feature which makes for easier washups.

When closing the blade, be careful not to place your fingers between the blade and the ink fountain roller or severe finger injury could result. Use extreme care!

When the blade is closed, the ink fountain screws can be tightened. Do not overtighten ink fountain screws. Overtightening will damage the blade and roller. See Fig. 25-21.

398

Fig. 25-20. To adjust ink fountain on this cylinder press, cylinder must be run up to the very top of its stroke. This allows access to fountain.

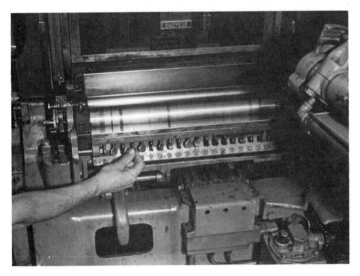

Fig. 25-21. On this press, ink fountain must be adjusted using thumbscrews to produce proper ink coverage on sheets.

Place the desired amount of ink in the fountain. Distribute ink evenly and turn the ink fountain roller to assure an even, thin film on the fountain roller.

The amount of ink fountain roller turn with each impression is variable. The cam set-wheel determines the amount of roller turn.

Return the ink fountain to the operating position and follow the procedure for starting a press to distribute ink from the ink cylinder to the rollers.

From time to time, check the roller settings for proper contact.

Cylinder adjustments (cylinder flatbed)

The press manual should be checked for the cylinder packing requirements. Generally, this is around .050 of an inch (1.3 mm), but always check specs.

Run the press so that the cylinder is on the down stroke and about one inch (25 mm) from the top. The location is usually marked on the cylinder end guard.

Open the cylinder guard as a safety precaution. Pull out the spring pin and turn it so that it stays in the out position. This disengages the cylinder.

WARNING! Never move the press while the cylinder is disengaged.

Turn the cylinder, using the large pin wrench, until the reel rod can be turned. Use the small pin wrench to release the pawl, Fig. 25-22. The packing sheets can then be removed.

The cylinder must be turned with the large pin wrench until the gripper bar is facing forward. The small pin wrench is used to remove the gripper from the cylinder, Fig. 25-23. Then you can remove the packing.

Fig. 25-22. This press uses pawl and reel rod to hold tympan sheet and packing on cylinder. Pawl must be released to free rod and packing.

Fig. 25-23. Operator is adjusting the cylinder-holding device, or gripper, so that packing is secure and smooth.

Cut new packing sheets to the size of the press. The tympan sheet (drawsheet) is often purchased precut. Follow the manufacturer's cylinder packing sheet requirements.

Position the packing, one at a time, on the cylinder pins. Replace the gripper bar with care and tighten down. Smooth the packing sheets as the cylinder is turned.

Tuck the drawsheet under the reel rod, and turn backward to crease at every corner. This assures even pressure when rewinding on the reel rod, Fig. 25-23.

Turn with small pin wrench until tight and engage the pawl ratchet.

Turn the cylinder until the spring pins align with the cylinder. When fully released, the cylinder is engaged. Close the cylinder end guard for press operation.

Some special adjustments have been omitted. It is suggested that you read the press manual to fully acquaint yourself with the total operation of the specific model of press.

WARNING! Follow the prescribed manufacturer procedures to assure safe and efficient operation of any press. If you fail to follow prescribed equipment methods, damage or injury could result.

ROTARY RELIEF PRESSES

The printing units of a rotary system consist of round cylinders. In other relief systems, it has been possible to directly print from the plate. The cylinder configuration requires that the plate or image carrier be curved. Typical image carriers are curved duplicator plates or curveable plates.

An impression cylinder and a *carrier* (plate) cylinder are required for the printing units in the rotary system. These presses are commonly used in magazine and newspaper publishing where longer press runs are required. These two types of presses use a roll of paper or web. The web is fed through the press continually, which differentiates it from a sheet fed system, Fig. 25-24. This was detailed under offset presses.

Sometimes, the speed at which the web travels through the press is expressed in *feet per minute* (fpm) or *impressions per hour* (iph). The NEWSPAPER press usually indicates the speed as impressions per hour, while the MAGAZINE press commonly refers to speed as feet per minute.

These systems are very complicated with electronically controlled panels to regulate the operation of the press. The size of a magazine press can be enormous. Others are moderately large, Fig. 25-25.

Fig. 25-25. Some relief web presses are very large.

FLEXOGRAPHY

Flexography is one classification of the relief process, but it uses a rotary process with a flexible plate, Fig. 25-26. In the older, more conventional relief process, a rigid metal or synthetic material was used as the plate. Flexo uses a comparably soft, pliable plate.

A faster drying ink is also used in flexography. The substrate used in flexography might be paper, plastic, metal, or almost any substance.

Flexography applications

Flexography is an ideal process for many printed products. It is one of the only relief processes that is still very common in today's industry.

Flexography is frequently used to print many packaging products. The flexible rubber or plastic relief plate will print very well on a variety of products: plastic bags, foils, wrapping papers, and other similar types of products. This pro-

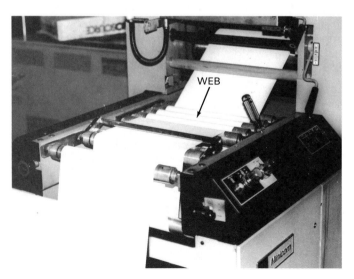

Fig. 25-24. For high speed production using relief, a web is fed through the printing unit.

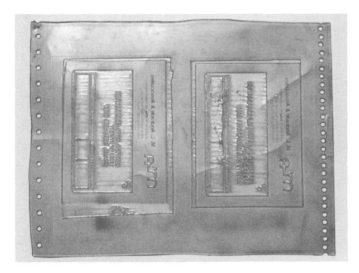

Fig. 25-26. The flexographic plate is pliable. This makes it ideal for printing on many different substrates. More and more work is being done by the flexo process.

Fig. 25-27. Flexo process can be used to print on paper, plastic, metal, and other products.

cess can also be used to print paperback books, boxes, business forms, cups, drinking straws, and other specialty items. See Fig. 25-27.

Flexographic image carriers

Flexographic image carriers or plates are usually made from rubber, plastic, or a similar synthetic substance. The rubber or synthetic plates are usually made by an etching or photographic process. After being cured, using heat and pressure, the plate is shaved to an exact thickness. The flexographic plate can be attached to the press cylinder by mechanical anchors or a special adhesive.

Cameron belt press

The *Cameron belt press system* is designed to go from web roll to a produced book in one continuous pass through the system, Fig. 25-28. It is largely used to produce mass market paperback books, coloring books, catalogs, cards, and similar items. The Cameron belt press sytem is a form of flexographic printing.

Some of the manufacturer's statements about the belt press include claims that this form of manufacturing requires only one press make-ready, eliminates costly gathering operations, and requires no inventory of unbound signatures.

Fig. 25-28. This Cameron belt press system converts a roll or web of paper into a finished book in one continuous pass or operation. (Cameron-Somerset Technologies)

Books printed by the belt press system are usually long-run, adhesive-bound, single color books. Although halftone quality has improved greatly since the introduction of this system, the photopolymer plates do not yet allow top quality with screens above 100 lines.

Paper grades that are used normally range from a 35 lb. newsprint to 120 lb. bulking book paper. Although not the most used, enamel-coated, size-coated, and coated groundwood paper are sometimes being used on the belt press.

Belt press construction

The Cameron belt press derives its name from the use of its two printing belts to which flexible, shallow-relief, photopolymer plates are attached. The flexo belt plate ranges in thickness from 0.020 to 0.030 inches (.50 to .76 mm). The plates are produced from photographic negatives and secured with a special adhesive, Fig. 25-29.

Fig. 25-29. Individual plates are bonded onto continuous belt with special adhesive. Each plate prints one page of a book or other product. The printing belt and web move through the printing unit or cylinders together. (Cameron-Somerset Technologies)

A special plate mounting machine is used to mount the pressure sensitive-backed plates to the belt. The machine applies pressure to secure the plates to the belt.

The plates are full page size and imposed on the belts in the long-grain direction to permit collating of completed books at the delivery end of the press.

The first unit or belt prints one side of the web and the second unit or belt prints the other side. As stated earlier, the complete book is printed in one pass on a web of paper. It is slit, folded, and cut into a stream of two or four-page

Fig. 25-30. Note how belt and web are moving through nip point together at very high speed.

signatures that are continuously collated and conveyed into an in-line adhesive binder. Look at Fig. 25-30.

Belt printing process

The schematic drawing in Fig. 25-31 shows the flow of paper through the Cameron belt press system.

At the beginning of the line, an automatic zero-speed splicer feeds the paper from the mill roll into the metered infeed. Next, the web passes through an edge guide; after which, it enters the printing unit.

The printing unit is made up of an impression cylinder, a plate cylinder, and a precision letterpress inking system. The belt passes around the plate cylinder and the plates are inked by three form rolls. They then transfer their image to the paper. The image transfer takes place at the printing nip. The nip is where the web, coming around the impression cylinder, meets the freshly inked plates traveling on the belt.

After the first printing, the web passes through a high velocity hot-air dryer, over chill rolls, and around a pair of turn bars to the other side of the machine. The web then is guided through a second printing unit. Here the back-up pages of the book are printed as the belt makes one complete revolution.

An electric eye controls registration and the side registration is controlled by pneumohydraulic (pneumatic-hydraulic) side register controls.

The speed of the plate is synchronized with the web by sprockets that engage holes along both edges of the belt.

Folding and cutting

After passing through a second dryer and set of chill rolls, the web is again side-guided and slit into either one or two-page wide ribbons, Fig. 25-31. The ribbons are directed around individual angle bars and former folders. The ribbons are score-perforated in the center to insure accurate and flat folding.

The folded ribbons then take a 90° turn toward the right and are married one above the other in page alignment. They are then fed to a rotary cutoff cylinder that cuts them into a stream of packets consisting of a group of four or two-page signatures.

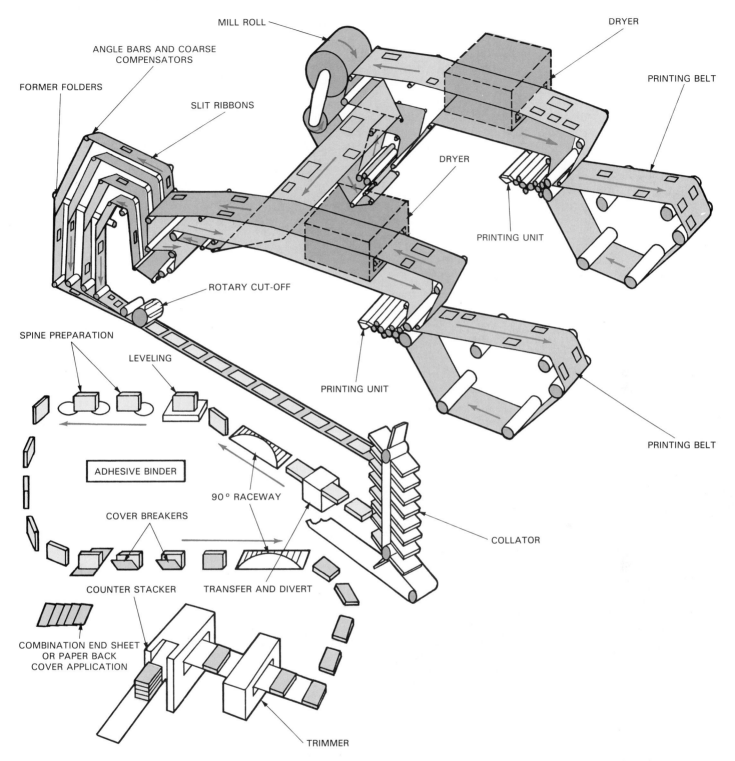

MILL ROLL

ANGLE BARS AND COARSE COMPENSATORS

FORMER FOLDERS

SLIT RIBBONS

DRYER

PRINTING BELT

DRYER

PRINTING UNIT

PRINTING UNIT

ROTARY CUT-OFF

PRINTING BELT

SPINE PREPARATION

LEVELING

ADHESIVE BINDER

90° RACEWAY

COVER BREAKERS

COLLATOR

COUNTER STACKER

TRANSFER AND DIVERT

COMBINATION END SHEET OR PAPER BACK COVER APPLICATION

TRIMMER

Fig. 25-31. This diagram shows complete Cameron book production system. Note how the web is printed, cut, collated, bound, covered, and then trimmed. (Cameron-Somerset Technologies)

After cutting, the signatures are lapped and then flow into a device that continuously collates them into complete sets. The conveyor, synchronized to the collator, delivers the sets in a lay-flat condition to an adhesive binding system.

Finishing

For adhesive binding, sets of signatures enter the binder infeed and are turned spine-down in a 90° raceway. They are jogged to bring all signatures down to the spine. They are then delivered into the bindery clamps and pass through a backbone preparation station. Only a minimal amount of paper (1/6" or less) is removed. The sets continue in the clamps around to the other side of the binder, where an adhesive is applied to the spine. For paperbacks, the cover is then drawn on. The adhesive can be a one-shot or two-shot melt or a cold emulsion, or a combination of both.

After covering, books are delivered to a three-knife trimmer that cuts them to size. After trimming, the books are delivered into a counter/stacker from which they can be either cartoned as finished paperbacks, or skidded for subsequent casing-in.

For books intended for case binding, hot-melt adhesive can be applied to the spine just before covering with a combined end sheet. It might also be possible to have end sheets added from the feeders ahead of the binder clamps. Adhesive applications are made just after spine preparation. Stretch cloth is applied as a cap to the book assembly. Refer to Fig. 25-32.

KNOW THESE TERMS

Relief, Platen press, Bed, Platen, Chase, Bails, Feedboard, Delivery board, Throw-off lever, Ink rollers, Flywheel, Footbrake, Livered, Roller gauge, Make-ready, Hanger sheets, Packing, Drawsheet, Trial impression, Guides, Gauge pins, Distribution, Perfectors, Drop plate, Tympan, fpm, iph, Flexography, Belt press.

REVIEW QUESTIONS—CHAPTER 25

1. List the three types of relief printing presses common to the industry.

2. Which of the three types of printing presses in question 1 has two flat surfaces?
3. Preparing the press so that an even impression results is called _____.
4. A cylinder and a flat surface is common to what type of press?
5. What is the safety device on a vertical press that eliminates the possibility of the press being started?
6. What two cylinders are required for the printing unit of the rotary press?
7. When a roll of paper is continually fed through the printing unit of the press, it is referred to as a _____.
8. What type of relief printing unit has the plates positioned on a belt?
9. What is flexography?
10. In your own words, explain the Cameron press system.

SUGGESTED ACTIVITIES

1. Identify the types of letterpress presses and where they would be best used.
2. Visit a letterpress facility and identify the types of presses and plates being used.
3. Observe the setup and operation of a belt press.
4. List some advantages and disadvantages of a belt press system.

Fig. 25-32. Here operators are preparing this belt press to produce finished paperback books. (Cameron-Somerset Technologies)

Chapter 26

GRAVURE PRINTING

After studying this chapter, you will be able to:
- Describe the many applications of the gravure printing process.
- Recognize the advantages and disadvantages of the gravure process.
- Identify the reproduction requirements essential to print a finished product with gravure.
- Choose the proper ink and substrate for reproduction of various substrates using gravure.
- Summarize the methods used to prepare a gravure cylinder.
- Explain the electrostatic assist process.

This chapter will review the most important aspects of gravure printing. Gravure is widely used and is very desirable for many print jobs. The chapter will summarize the advantages and disadvantages of gravure and discuss the processes involved during gravure printing. See Fig. 26-1.

DEVELOPMENT OF GRAVURE

The gravure or intaglio method of printing dates back to the year 1873, when Thomas Bell, from Scotland, patented an intaglio engraved cylinder. The cylinder Thomas Bell developed was designed for printing textiles. The *intaglio printing process* was the forerunner to gravure, and is distinguished by the hand or manual preparation techniques of the image carrier.

Intaglio, like gravure, prints from a sunken image carrier, but the image area is generated by hand or hand-mechanical operations. The intaglio process lends itself well to line illustrations or type matter because of the image carrier preparation techniques.

With the advent of the first grain screen, photo-gravure etching in 1878, by Karl Klietsch (pronounced Klic), the printing of continuous tone illustrations was made possible. Klietsch, of Austria, further refined the gravure pro-

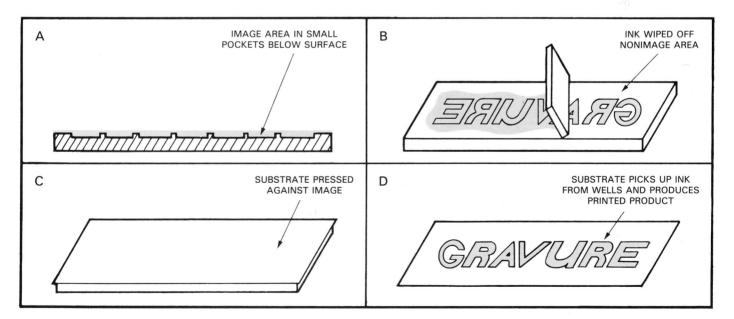

Fig. 26-1. These are the basic steps for printing with gravure. A—Side view of gravure image shows that small ink wells are formed below surface. Ink is deposited over entire image carrier surface. B—Doctor blade is slid across image carrier to remove ink from nonimage area. C—Substrate is pressed against inked image. D—Substrate absorbs or attracts ink to print image on paper.

cess using the newly invented crossline screen, and a sheet of light sensitive tissue (carbon tissue).

Klietsch sold his new process in England. In the year 1890, he developed the first rotogravure press.

Much of the gravure printing today is produced on a rotary cylinder press. Thus, the name *rotogravure* is frequently used.

THE GRAVURE PROCESS

Gravure printing is accomplished by the image area being broken down into microscopic ink wells recessed below the nonimage surface. This is shown in Fig. 26-1.

The most common image carrier configuration for gravure printing is the metal cylinder. The cylinder can have as many as 22,500 ink wells per square inch. All the image area, including continuous tone reproductions, line illustrations, or type matter, are screened to construct the ink well structure for printing, Fig. 26-2.

The gravure cylinder is then rotated at a high speed in a fountain of ink. The excess ink in the nonimage area is removed by the *doctor blade,* Fig. 26-3. The doctor blade is usually made of a thin piece of stainless steel.

The paper, usually fed by a web traveling at about 30 miles per hour (48 km/h), acts like a blotter and absorbs the remaining ink in the microscopic wells. The amount of ink absorbed into the paper surface depends on the size and depth of the ink wells, Fig. 26-4.

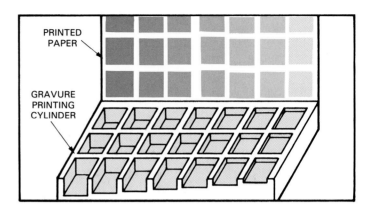

Fig. 26-4. Size and depth of ink wells determines how much ink will deposit on substrate. A deeper well will produce a darker, more dense image area for example.

Gravure as an industry

Gravure is considered to be one of the major printing processes. It is usually reserved for long press runs, due to the long life of the cylinder or image carrier. Gravure is capable of the highest quality printing, and usually at the lowest unit cost on extremely long runs.

The United States Department of Commerce has identified gravure printing as an industry in itself and now has

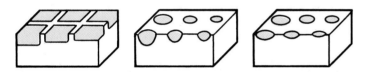

Fig. 26-2. Magnified many times, this represents microscopic ink wells in gravure plate or cylinder. Ink fills these small wells. (Gravure Association of America)

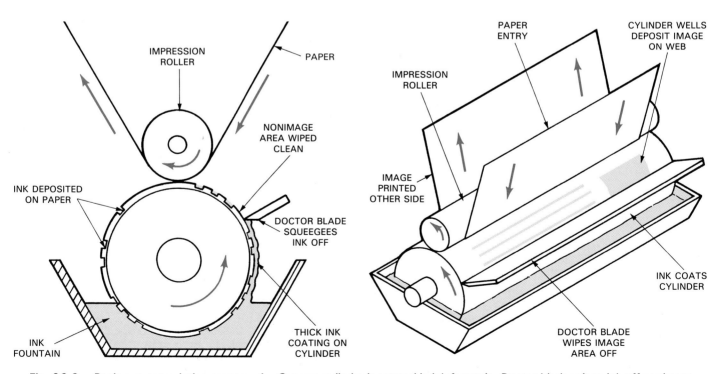

Fig. 26-3. Basic gravure printing process. A—Gravure cylinder is rotated in ink fountain. Doctor blade wipes ink off nonimage area. Impression roller pushes substrate into contact with gravure cylinder and image is deposited on substrate. B—Note how complete cylinder is covered with ink before doctor blade. After doctor blade, only the ink wells and image are inked.

its own classification code number. Gravure printing is currently a 12 to 14 billion dollar industry, employing tens of thousands of people. It is responsible for 15 to 18 percent of all printing in the United States.

The gravure industry is divided into three major markets: publication and advertising, packaging, and specialties. Look at Fig. 26-3.

Some printed products typical of the publication and advertising market would be:
1. Newspaper supplements.
2. Magazines.
3. Catalogs.
4. Advertising promotional material.
5. Coupons or stamps.

Other printed products using the gravure process would be classified in the packaging market. Examples of packaging products would be:
1. Folding cartons.
2. Wrapping paper for gifts.
3. Flexible packaging such as nylon, cellophane, and foils.
4. Labels.

The final classification of gravure printed products are specialty items. Gravure printing can be accomplished on a wide variety of substrates, including inexpensive stocks.

Some examples of gravure specialty printing would include:
1. Wall covering.
2. Floor coverings.
3. Auto windshield and glass tints.
4. Plastic containers.
5. Decorative laminates (furniture and counter tops).
6. Sanitary tissues.

Advantages and disadvantages of gravure

Typical of any printing process are production advantages and disadvantages. Gravure has many advantages, with one of the most important being its SIMPLICITY.

Gravure or rotogravure is a direct printing process that has NO ink and water balance, such as with offset lithography. By eliminating the different production variables typical of the other printing processes, gravure presses can run at higher production speeds.

Letterpress is a direct printing process that requires pressure for the transfer of the image. The gravure image transfer utilizes the natural tendency of the paper to absorb ink out of the tiny ink wells in the plate.

Another advantage to the gravure process is the consistent high quality reproduction during extremely long production runs. The microscopic cell structure of the image results in an almost continuous tone appearance on the press sheet. Due to the long life of the gravure cylinder, high quality reproduction is sustained. The inks used in gravure printing dry extremely fast and also allow for faster press speeds.

The disadvantages of gravure are inherent to the gravure printing cylinder. The cost and time involved in the preparation of the cylinder makes gravure prepress operations more costly than the other printing processes. If the gravure cylinder has been engraved and then becomes damaged during shipping or production, the entire cylinder or set of cylinders may have to be re-engraved.

Because the entire gravure image is to be screened for the cellular ink well structure, the fine details of type matter and line work are of critical concern. When using type styles containing serifs, use of a type size smaller than eight point is not recommended.

GRAVURE PREPRESS CONSIDERATIONS

There are several factors you must consider during prepress for a gravure job. The most important considerations will be summarized.

Gravure paste-up requirements

Unless you are using a flat bed scanner, copy preparation and paste-up should be prepared on flexible board stock. The advantage of using flexible stock with gravure artwork is in the mounting of the mechanical to the copy drum of a rotary, color scanner. Layouts requiring color separation should not be thicker than 3 mm or about 1/8 of an inch. Multi-layered paste-ups can also cause focusing problems with the scanner.

Both line work and continuous tone images are reproduced with a screen pattern in gravure. As mentioned, the selection of typefaces becomes important with type eight points or smaller. The screen pattern will disrupt the uniformity of fine line structure. Thus, the use of medium to bold faces is suggested with smaller type sizes. Furthermore, small sans serif type styles will reproduce better than small type styles containing a hairline serif structure.

Reproduction films used in gravure are like those used in offset lithography, and they will NOT reproduce light blue guide lines. Type matter should be proofed for consistency of density and image structure. Some of the newer typesetting systems will output directly to film. If the type galley is in the form of film, the films should match the same quality or density level required of the engraver.

Gravure continuous tone and color requirements

Continuous tone photographs or copy should be selected for gravure reproduction based on average contrast and good tonal separation. Photographs should NOT be enlarged more than 500% or reduced to less than 20% to avoid a loss in quality.

Color photographs, to be printed in a single color or monotone should be avoided when possible because of the color compensation required during the photomechanical reproduction process. Traditional reproduction techniques avoid the use of prescreened prints or halftone images in substitute of continuous tone originals.

Copy to be reproduced for four-color gravure can be either reflection copy or color transparencies. The advantage of using transparency copy is its sharpness or focus as an original image. Common sizes for transparencies are 35 mm, 2 1/4 x 2 1/4 in., 4 x 5 in., and 8 x 10 in. It is often better to select darker transparencies than light ones for reproduction. A color scanner should be used when the enlargement has to exceed 500%. To reduce the grain effect achieved during enlargement, the original photographer should use a slower speed film.

Dye transfers are often the most desirable form of reflection copy. Color photographs should be color corrected prior to reproduction. Due to some of the reflection problems caused by original oil paintings, it is often suggested that a color transparency be produced for reproduction purposes.

Color evaluation and viewing for both originals and reproductions should be completed under uniform lighting conditions. The gravure industry uses the American National Standards Institute's standard of 5000 degrees Kelvin lighting for viewing, Fig. 26-5.

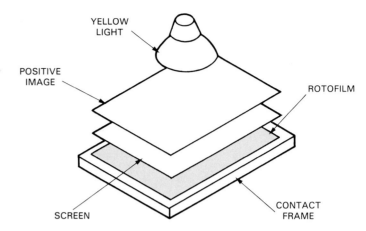

Fig. 26-6. Rotofilm provides one method of making a gravure image carrier or cylinder. It must be exposed to original image. Rotofilm is being exposed in a vacuum frame.

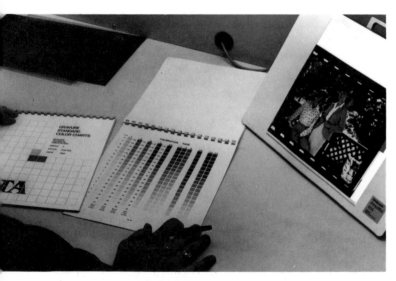

Fig. 26-5. Here operator is using a standard color chart provided by the GAA and a controlled light source. This will help assure acceptable print quality.

The electromechanical processes use a scanner to read image densities. Then, through the use of a computer, it controls a cutting unit (diamond stylus) laser light source, or electron beam to prepare the cylinder image. See Fig. 26-7.

Typical of any printing process, four-color separations require that the printers be assigned different screen angles. The common screen angles for gravure work are illustrated in Fig. 26-8.

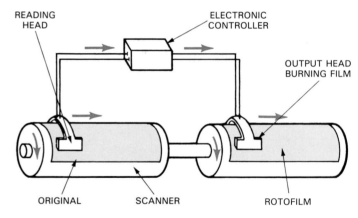

Fig. 26-7. Scanner is being used to read original image. The scanner can then burn the rotofilm using an output laser on the other scanner drum.

Traditional film preparation for gravure

The original continuous tone images are usually reproduced on continuous tone panchromatic film in negative form. The normal density range in the negative will have a density value of .30 in the shadows and a 1.70 in the highlights.

The type matter and line art are produced in negative form on separate line films. After the film negatives are retouched, the films are stripped in combination with the continuous tone films, in respect to proper imposition. The film negatives are then contacted to form one final film positive used to expose the cylinder or tissue.

Exposures and reproductions are usually completed in the contact frame, unless enlargements or reductions are required. See Fig. 26-6.

Today, the use of the color scanner is becoming popular for both color and black and white work. The electronic scanner information can be stored or sent via satellite to other locations. New technological innovations are bypassing the film stages and are preparing gravure cylinders faster and more economically.

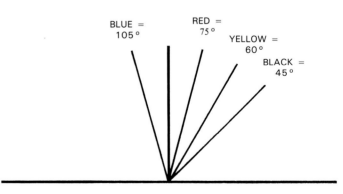

Fig. 26-8. These are the common screen angles used in the gravure printing process.

Gravure image carrier configurations

The cylinder is the most common image carrier configuration for gravure printing. In addition to the cylinder, the gravure industry sometimes uses flat and wrap-around image carriers. See Fig. 26-9.

The flat image carrier or printing plate is used on sheet-fed gravure presses. The flat plate prints from a sunken surface and is used for limited runs requiring high quality results. This can be used for printing certificates of stocks or bonds and limited editions of fine art originals.

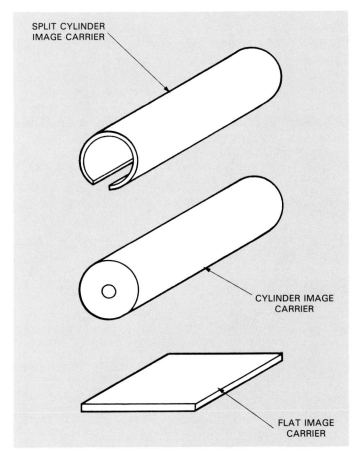

Fig. 26-9. These are the three basic gravure image carrier configurations. The cylinder is the most common because it will produce a continuous image. Split cylinder would have a blank area where plate is open.

The wrap-around plate is thicker than an offset plate. However, like the offset plate, it is flexible and is designed to bend around a cylinder. The plate is used for limited runs and cannot produce an edgeless or continuous design because of the clamp area.

The cylinder is the most popular image carrier because it can print a continuous pattern. This is beneficial in printing products such as laminates for furniture and floor coverings. The cylinder core is reusable after the press run.

There are two basic categories of cylinder construction, mandrel, and integral shaft, as illustrated in Fig. 26-10.

Because the cylinder is the most popular image carrier in gravure, this chapter will examine only the cylinder design.

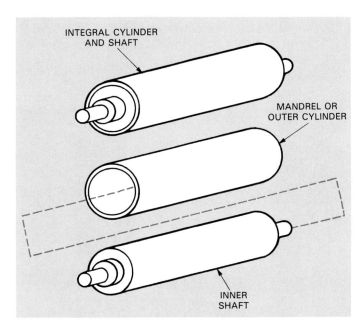

Fig. 26-10. Gravure cylinder can be integral with shaft, or more commonly, a mandrel or outer cylinder mounted on an inner shaft.

GRAVURE CYLINDER ENGRAVING

Gravure cylinder imaging is currently experiencing a rapid transition period. Traditionally, cylinders were produced using continuous tone films, carbon tissue, and chemical etching.

Today, we have the technology to image or prepare gravure cylinders without using photographic films. The original artwork is electronically scanned and is combined with typematter through digital, electronic color page make-up systems. The digitized data is then sent to the electronic cylinder engraving system, which can be a mechanical or stylus engraver, or more recently a laser or electron beam engraving system.

Currently, the industry is in an intermediate stage of cylinder imaging. This stage usually requires the use of film to store graphic image data.

Halftone gravure is the process that allows the use of halftone separations, made for offset printing or directly for gravure. The halftone separations are used instead of the more expensive continuous tone films. Halftone gravure lends itself to either chemical etching or electromechanical engraving.

Electromechanical engraving is the current technology, with some chemical etching still being done by smaller service houses and the packaging and specialty sectors of the industry. In the immediate future, cylinders will be imaged by the use of laser or electron beam systems.

Gravure base cylinder

Gravure base cylinder refers to the cylinder before it is imaged. It must be ground, and then polished smooth.

The gravure cylinder size is the main difference between the packaging and publications cylinders. There are many different size diameters and cylinder lengths in the packaging segment of the gravure industry, as compared to the standard sizes in publication work.

The base cylinder is made of steel or aluminum. It is ground and polished to a tolerance of .001 inch (0.025 mm). See Fig. 26-11.

Fig. 26-11. Photo shows a gravure cylinder being turned on a cutting lathe. This trues cylinder surface and brings it to rough size. (Gravure Association of America)

The base cylinder is then copper plated to an increased thickness of .006 inch up to .030 inch (0.15 to 0.76 mm). The copper plating is applied in a electrical-chemical process known as *electroplating*. Fig. 26-12 shows this process.

The copper plating is usually oversize by around .006 inch (0.15 mm) in thickness. With grinding and polishing techniques, the cylinder is ground down to its final diameter. A 1,000 grit abrasion is used to polish the copper-coated cylinder perfectly smooth. The copper plating on the cylinder is usually tested for hardness, tensile strength, grain structure, and percent of elongation.

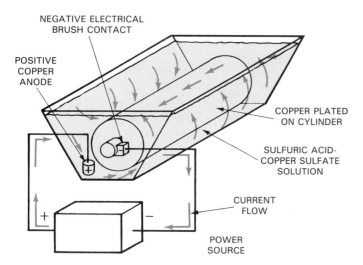

Fig. 26-12. This illustrates the fundamental way that gravure cylinders are copper plated. Cylinder is submerged in acid-copper sulfate solution. Then current is fed through solution and cylinder. This causes copper to electroplate onto cylinder surface.

Cylinder etching with rotofilm or carbon tissue

The image transfer process to the cylinder can be accomplished by using either diffusion etch, direct transfer, or electromechanical methods. Many gravure plants have their own techniques. The carbon tissue or rotofilm system is probably one of the more popular processes in the industry. The *carbon tissue* or *rotofilm* is a diffusion etch method of preparing a gravure printing cylinder. The image is exposed on the tissue or rotofilm. After development, the tissue or rotofilm is mounted on the gravure cylinder.

The carbon tissue is not sensitized until treated with potassium bichromate (3 1/2 to 4% solution). Once treated, the tissue should be handled in yellow light and stored at about 45°F. Currently, some experimentation is being done with carbon tissue that is purchased as a presensitized film.

Rotofilm is a popular presensitized film that is composed of four different layers. The first layer is a light sensitive, thin emulsion or resist. It is mounted on a clear support, base layer, with a waterproof stripping membrane or layer between. The fourth layer is a dark anti-halation backing similar to most photographic films, Fig. 26-13.

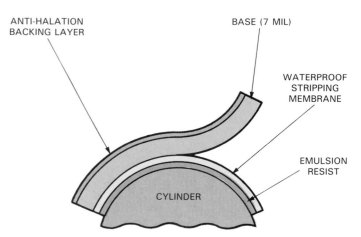

Fig. 26-13. Diagram of rotofilm shows its different layers. (Ronar)

The rotofilm method has been used by many large gravure printers and is associated with the Hurletron Altair Process of gravure.

The rotofilm is first given a fine line screen exposure (150 to 300 crossline screen) using a yellow filter in a vacuum frame. Another yellow light exposure is made with the film positives placed on top of the screen and rotofilm in the vacuum frame.

The *second exposure* determines the size of ink cells that will be etched between the lines.

The third and final exposure is made without the screen, using only the film positive and ultraviolet light. The *final exposure* determines the depth of ink cells to be etched.

Processing the rotofilm will develop the exposed image and harden the emulsion layer to different degrees, as determined by the amount of light exposure through the positive. The processed rotofilm is then mounted on a clean cylinder with a moisture bond, Fig. 26-14A.

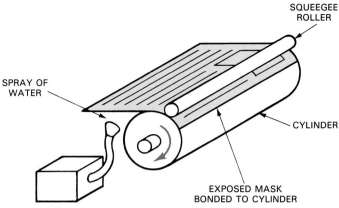

A—Rotofilm is applied to clean base cylinder with a water bond. Squeegee roller smooths and presses rotofilm onto cylinder for good adhesion.

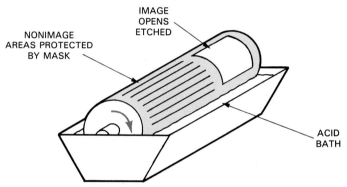

B—Once rotofilm is treated to remove image areas, cylinder is submerged in acid. Acid eats ink wells wherever rotofilm is removed. Rotofilm covers and protects cylinder surface on nonimage areas.

Fig. 26-14. Imaging gravure cylinder with rotofilm and acid bath.

After all the processed pieces of rotofilm are positioned on the large cylinder, a pressure roller is used to secure the film or resist to the copper surface. The base layer of the rotofilm is then peeled off while the emulsion and waterproof membrane remain secure.

Later, the waterproof membrane is removed from the cylinder with an *alcohol solution*. Using a stream of hot water, the unhardened or soft emulsion is removed leaving only a hard *frisket* or *mask* to control the etching of the acid. The other non-coated nonimage areas are covered with a protective *asphaltum* before etching.

The direct transfer method of cylinder etching involves the use of a light sensitive mask coating on the cylinder. A special machine rotates the film positive against the cylinder during exposure. The mask is then processed in a bath or tank and is ready to be acid etched, Fig. 26-14B.

The acid used for etching the cylinder is typically a solution of iron chloride. The acid eats small ink wells on the unprotected image areas of the cylinder.

After the acid bath, the cylinder is rinsed and inspected. The entire etched cylinder is inspected for imperfections with a 12x or greater magnification lens.

Electromechanical cylinder preparation

The use of a scanner tied to an engraving machine is another method of preparing the gravure cylinder for printing, Fig. 26-15. The two machines are wired together. The scanner reads the original copy and converts it into electronic data or impulses.

The *engraving machine* is controlled by a computer and by these electronic impulses. It uses a *diamond stylus* to form

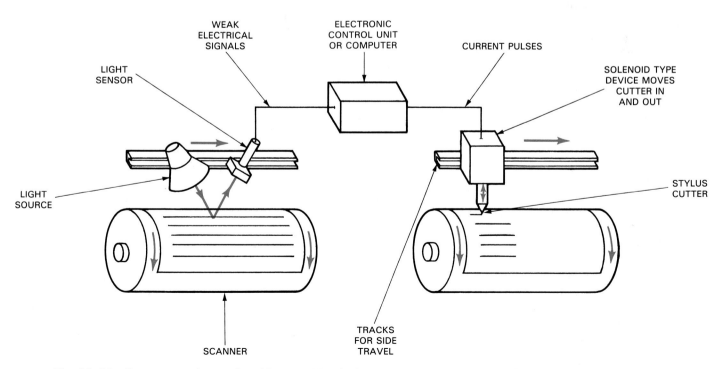

Fig. 26-15. Scanner can be used to drive a mechanical engraver to cut image on gravure cylinder. Scanning head reads original image and converts image into computer data. Computer can use this data to drive engraver. Impulses from electronic control unit make stylus move in and out very quickly as gravure cylinder rotates. Microscopic cuts produce ink wells that form image in cylinder surface.

or cut the tiny ink wells on the metal cylinder surface. The diamond stylus vibrates or engraves at around 4,000 oscillations per second. See Fig. 26-16.

The ink cell structure is controlled in depth and size by the strength and duration of the impulses from the scanning drum pickup. The precision in the oscillating or cutting frequency is controlled by a quartz crystal, like those used in expensive wrist watches.

Most of these machines have multiple engraving heads that work simultaneously. This technology currently takes about 40 minutes to engrave a four ribbon page on a cylinder.

Fig. 26-16. Mechanical engraver is cutting image in copper plated gravure cylinder. Diamond stylus moves in quickly to cut ink wells to correct size and depth.

Laser engraved cylinders

In the late 1970s, research work was started to engrave cylinders by laser. Special epoxy coatings were developed to work with a laser and still withstand the long run requirements of gravure cylinders.

Today, the industry is working with carbon dioxide laser beams to engrave cylinders at a rate of about 32,000 cells per second. Typical screen ruling is about 250 lines per inch. The engraving time for the same four page ribbon (11 inches long) is about 4.4 minutes. The epoxy coating is still being used because the highly polished copper coating would reflect about 95% of the laser output, and leave only 5% for engraving.

Electron beam engraved cylinders

The most recent engraving technology uses a high energy electron beam. It is referred to as *Electron Generated Beam* (EGB). The electron beam engraves by melting the copper and forcing out small crater-like cells by plasma pressure. A diamond stylus removes any imperfections surrounding the cells.

The electron beam engraving process has been demonstrated for several years now. The future for this pro-

cess appears to be very good. Quality engravings have been produced at a very high rate of speed ranging from 75,000 to 150,000 cells per second. The new process also decreases setup time for gravure cylinder engraving.

As you see in Fig. 26-17, the EGB machine is very large. The bed of the machine is made of heavy cast iron for stability. The cylinder is centered in the machine bed. A pillow block, on each end, supports and drives the cylinder.

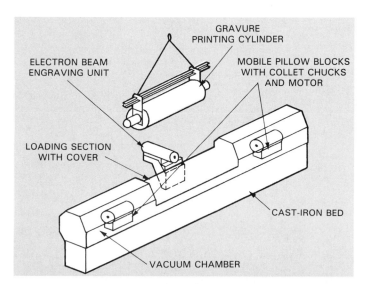

Fig. 26-17 Electron beam engraving machine is very large. Base is made of heavy cast iron so that vibration does not affect engraving of image. Gravure cylinder mounts in center of machine. Pillow blocks hold and rotate cylinder. (Hell)

Fig. 26-18 shows the cylinder in place. The chamber area, which holds the cylinder, must be covered. The vacuum cover forms the processing chamber for the copper cylinder. A vacuum is needed for the electron beam to function properly.

The cylinder spins and the electron beam gun is stationary. The gun can be initially moved to accommodate different sized cylinders. Once the setup is completed, the remaining operations are automatically controlled by microprocessors.

Fig. 26-18. Cylinder is rotated inside EGB machine. Powerful electron beam gun "burns" tiny ink wells cells at a tremendously fast rate. Cylinder must be enclosed in vacuum tight chamber for electron beam to work properly. (Hell)

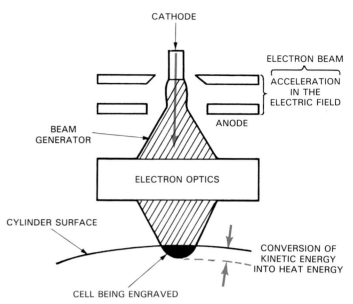

Fig. 26-19. Note how electron optics is used to direct powerful electron beam onto surface of gravure cylinder. (Hell)

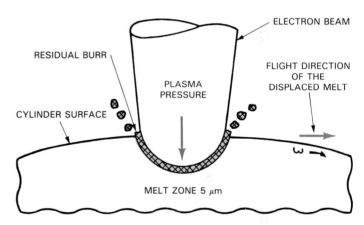

Fig. 26-20. As electron beam strikes copper surface, it melts and blows out tiny ink wells. Molten copper is thrown outward by plasma action and centrifugal force produced by spinning cylinder. (Hell)

Typical operations include: closing the cover of the vacuum chamber, clamping the cylinder, producing required vacuum in the processing chamber, positioning and rotating cylinder, activating electron beam, begin engraving.

Cylinder size generally determines the engraving time. Approximately 15 minutes is required to engrave a cylinder with an engraving length of 95 in. (2 400 mm) and a circumference of 31 in. (780 mm).

Following the engraving, the electron beam is deactivated. The cylinder is stopped. The chamber must be filled with air before the cylinder is declamped.

The electron beam gun is the main component of the EGB engraving machine. The beam generator and the beam optics are shown in Fig. 26-19. The tremendous power of the electron beam is focused by the beam optics on the surface of the copper cylinder. The high energy electrons penetrate the copper. The energy is delivered to the copper and produces a superheated copper melt, as illustrated in Fig. 26-20.

The electron beam plasma pressure drives the melted copper out of the sides of the ink wells. The rotating speed of the cylinder causes the droplets to fly away because of centrifugal force.

After the beam has been deactivated, the cells recrystallize or harden to a fairly smooth surface. Slight edges remain around the cells but they are cut away using a diamond shaver.

This system appears to be feasible for large printing houses. A schematic representation of EGB cylinder engraving is shown in Fig. 26-21.

Cylinder evaluation and finishing techniques

Mentioned briefly, once the gravure cylinder is etched or engraved, it must be closely inspected. Under magnification, it is checked for flaws in the ink cell structure. Cylinder correction can be accomplished by spot plating, burnishing with charcoal, lacquer, and by many other methods.

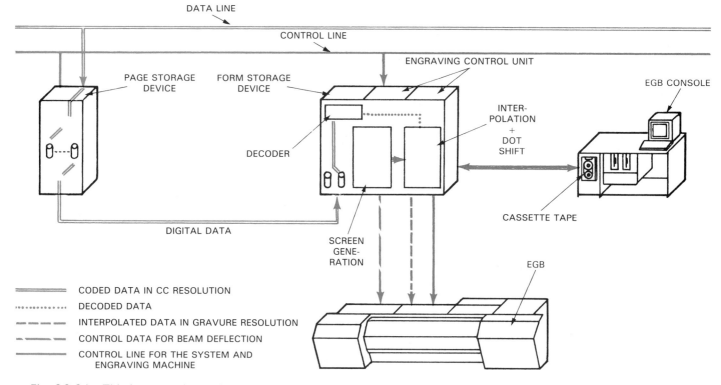

DATA LINE

CONTROL LINE

PAGE STORAGE DEVICE

FORM STORAGE DEVICE

ENGRAVING CONTROL UNIT

EGB CONSOLE

DECODER

INTER-POLATION + DOT SHIFT

CASSETTE TAPE

DIGITAL DATA

SCREEN GENE-RATION

EGB

CODED DATA IN CC RESOLUTION

DECODED DATA

INTERPOLATED DATA IN GRAVURE RESOLUTION

CONTROL DATA FOR BEAM DEFLECTION

CONTROL LINE FOR THE SYSTEM AND ENGRAVING MACHINE

Fig. 26-21. This is a complete schematic of an electron beam engraving system. Note how it uses electronic means of image input and storage.

If correction is NOT necessary or is completed, many finished cylinders are chrome plated to increase the life of the image carrier. The chromium metal coating is harder than copper. It can better withstand the friction of the doctor blade.

Cylinders can be chrome coated in horizontal or vertical immersion tanks, Fig. 26-22. The chrome plating on a gravure cylinder is usually around .0003 inch (0.008 mm) thick.

Proofing of the gravure cylinder is typically done on the proof press or the job press. Cylinder proofing on a press is probably one of the more important stages of evaluation. The press proof is evaluated for color registration, quality of color reproduction, and type or line work imperfections. The final press proof must meet customer approval.

The gravure industry uses three different types of proof presses to evaluate the cylinder: The single-impression drum press, the roll press, and the sheet-fed press, Fig. 26-23.

Fig. 26-22. After imaging, gravure cylinders can be chrome plated. The hard chrome plating will wear much better than the soft copper.

Fig. 26-23. This is a gravure proof press. It can be used to run off an image to check cylinder for problems.

Halftone gravure technology

A current trend associated with electromechanical engraving is halftone gravure. *Halftone gravure,* occasionally called *offset gravure,* uses halftone separations rather than continuous tone separations on the mechanical or stylus engraving machine. The gravure industry is developing the technology to use a generic or universal halftone film, for both offset work and gravure work.

The gravure industry is reporting a 50% savings in time and materials cost through the use of halftone gravure. Halftone gravure requires a minimum of a 4 to 5% highlight dot and up to a 98% dot in the shadows of the separation. These requirements are slightly different from offset separations, but represent the tone reproduction necessary for cylinder engraving.

Another advantage of using the halftone positive is in the proofing systems available. The offset lithography industry uses halftone images in its many proofing systems. The offset prepress proofing systems, such as chromalin, match print, color key, and others, have excellent abilities to identify facsimile color reproductions. These prepress proofing systems are far more economical to use than the current gravure proofing methods.

GRAVURE PRINTING PRESS

The gravure printing press, next to the flexo press, is considered to be one of the simplest of the reproduction processes. The gravure press does not require a dampening system like the offset press. Thus, cheaper grades of paper can be run, at higher press speeds, without the threat of web tear.

The gravure press will usually run around a 32 pound newsprint stock and a 35 to 40 pound coated stock for publication work. The paper selection for gravure work should be evaluated by strength and ink absorption. The packaging and specialty products are typically using substrates such as films, cellophanes, cloth, plastic, and corrugated board.

The inks used in gravure are typically fast drying. This allows for high press speeds while printing on a variety of substrates. The inks are either petroleum based or water based. The use of electrostatic assist and new ink formulations allow for printing on substrates that have hard surfaces and poor ink absorption.

Gravure press configuration

The *gravure printing press* is typically a web-fed or rotogravure press. These are some specialty sheet-fed gravure presses for limited production runs, such as fine art reproductions or bond certificates.

The word *"roto"* means to turn or to rotate. The rotary press is associated with the web press. The typical rotogravure press is capable of web speeds 2,000 to 2,500 feet per minute or about 30 mph. Refer to Fig. 26-24.

Printing units

The gravure press is made up of a number of *printing units,* each unit containing one printing cylinder. The com-

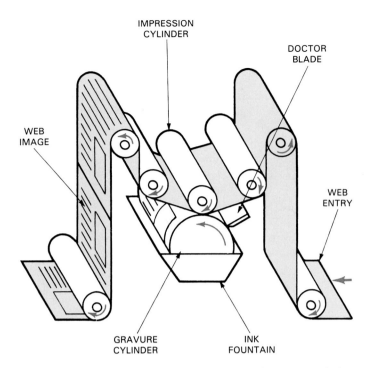

Fig. 26-24. Note how web is moved through gravure printing unit.

bination of printing units can range anywhere from four to 16 or more. The number of units depends on the number of pages being printed, and the amount of color work being produced, Fig. 26-25.

Gravure cylinder action

The printing unit of a gravure press contains the *gravure cylinder* immersed in a trough or fountain of ink. As the cylinder turns, it fills its tiny ink wells with ink. Modern gravure printing presses can have cylinders that are over 150 inches (3 810 mm) in length.

Fig. 26-25. This is a large gravure press with many printing units.

Gravure doctor blade

The *gravure doctor blade* serves the function of removing or wiping the excess ink off the raised, nonimage area of the cylinder. The doctor blade was traditionally called the *ductor blade*.

Doctor blade thickness is typically .006 inch (0.15 mm) and has a typical set angle of 20°. The blade can be stainless steel or plastic, but is usually a blue spring steel. It is as long as the printing cylinder.

The doctor blade must be sharp and free from burrs or imperfections. Unbalanced printing cylinders or poor etching of the cylinder can cause the doctor blade to function improperly.

Impression roller

An *impression roller* is used to press the paper or substrate against the printing cylinder. The point of contact between the printing cylinder, paper (substrate), and impression roller is called the *nip*. This is shown in Fig. 26-26.

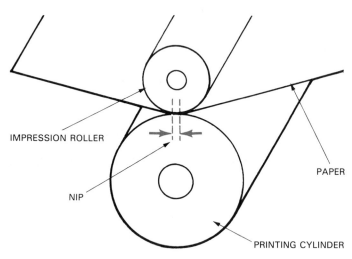

Fig. 26-26. Diagram shows impression roller, paper, nip point, and printing cylinder. Very little impression roller pressure is needed with gravure.

The impression roller serves an important function in determining the printing quality when reproducing images on a wide variety of substrates. The impression roller usually supplies between 100 to 200 lbs per linear inch of pressure at the printing nip point. Impression rollers are made of rubber, neoprene, and other synthetic products.

Impression rollers should be tested for the degree of hardness as determined by the printing substrate. Also, the amount of resilience and solvent resistance is important to the continued quality of printing.

Gravure process inks

The process color inks used in gravure printing differ in both hue and composition from the average offset lithography and letterpress inks.

The gravure inks used in color reproduction are referred to as yellow, red, blue, and black. They are a different hue than the offset yellow, magenta, cyan, and black. The magenta and cyan are considered to be lighter and cleaner colors than the heavier red and blue used in gravure. Gravure uses predetermined standards of inks. The red and blue colors have continued to meet the customer demands better than magenta and cyan.

Ink standards

Over a period of years, the Gravure Association of America (GAA) has established several major ink standards serving the major product markets. This effort has compromised the many different kinds and hues of inks that once existed. The three proofing ink standards used in the publication work are determined by the type of printing stock.

1. Group 1 (yellow, red, blue, and black for printing on newsprint stock).
2. Group III (yellow, magenta, cyan, and black for printing on coated stock).
3. Group V (yellow, red, blue, and black for printing on coated stock).

Recently, the gravure industry added a new Group VI ink. Group VI inks are cleaner and purer than the other gravure ink groups. Group VI standards require a minimum of a 133-line screen and any screen angle can be used as long as moiré patterns are avoided. The advantage of Group VI inks is in relation to the use of halftone gravure technology and the generic or universal film input for magazine advertising.

Gravure inks, like any other process ink, contain impurities. The study of the pressroom results will determine the color correction requirements used in color separation.

The GAA color charts represent one of the greatest accomplishments in the standardization of results and customer expectations. The use of the industry ink standards is voluntary, but represents a solid communication tool between advertising agencies (designers), color separation houses, and the printer.

The inks used on a gravure printing press are thinner than those used in other printing processes. The *ink viscosity* (weight) is much lower then most inks. Gravure inks will usually be diluted with 50% or more solvent when on the press.

Solvent-based gravure inks are considered highly volatile.

It should be noted that there is a major difference between fire safety in the offset pressroom and the gravure pressroom. The design of a gravure printing plant should isolate the pressroom from unnecessary production traffic and ventilation problems. The fumes from solvent-based gravure inks are filtered through beds of charcoal. The charcoal has the ability to absorb the odors or vapors.

Due to shortages and rising costs of petroleum, the demand for a water-based ink has been a top research priority. The government EPA standards have limited the amount of hydrocarbons released into the air, which makes the use of solvent inks expensive. Additional control and pollution monitoring of solvent inks has resulted in the use of water-base inks in the gravure industry.

Some common properties of gravure ink are opacity, drying speed, gloss, and fineness of pigment grind. Gravure inks are shipped to the printing plant in small five gallon steel containers, 30 to 55 gallon drums, or large 300 to 500 gallon tanks.

Inks should never run too low in the press fountain or air entrapment and foaming may occur. See Fig. 26-27.

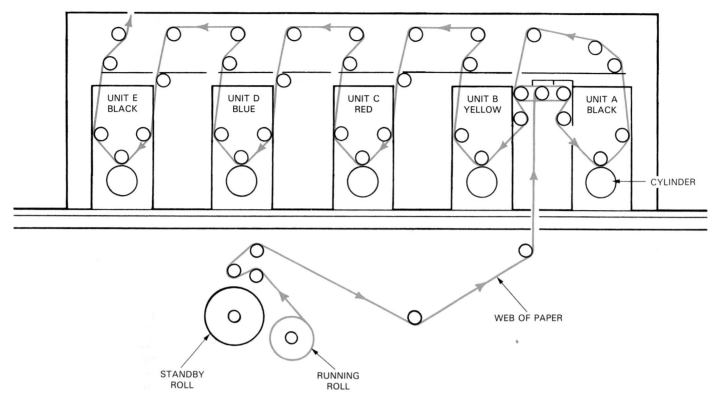

Fig. 26-27. Diagram shows how web feeds through multiple unit gravure, web press.

SWOP

The abbreviation *SWOP* stands for Specifications for Web Offset Publications. These specifications in general apply to the control of supplied material (film) for color separations, progressive proofs, and specifications for print. These specifications are designed to establish a desired level of quality. This means that each step of the manufacturing process is treated statistically and specific methods are followed. Measurements indicate the quality of the product. This is accomplished by periodic verification during the reproduction cycle.

The characteristics of publications papers are very unique. This makes web offset printing different from sheet-fed offset printing. The whole intent is to help the publications printer do a better job, more consistently, and more efficiently.

The Gravure Association of America (GAA) approved the specifications for halftone gravure. They recommend the Group VI inks just discussed and SWOP proofing inks. This means that both the proofing and production processes have control of quality for publication work.

The GAA Group VI Inks for applicable publications include the following specifications:

1. COLORS: Gravure Group VI standard colors are to match the SWOP colors (Group VI/SWOP). The stan—dard is on deposit at the Graphic Arts Technical Foundation.
2. PRESS PROOFS: The color guide for Group VI shall be an offset press proof made to Group VI/SWOP specifications.
3. SCREEN RULINGS: A 133-line screen ruling is the minimum standard. Any coarser screen is handled by mutual agreement.

4. SCREEN ANGLES: Moiré patterns are to be avoided. Colors other than yellow should avoid angles between 75° and 105°.
5. FILM SPECIFICATIONS: Group VI standards are positive right-reading, emulsion-down, .004 in. thickness film. Group VI/SWOP standard control devices are to be used.
6. GUARANTEED PRINTING TONE: The first guaranteed printing tone is a 5% film dot.
7. PROOFING STOCK: A 60 lb. consolidated fortune gloss or champion text web or equivalent is to be used.
8. OFF-PRESS PROOFS: Group VI procedures are required for an off-press proof.
9. INSPECTION PROCEDURES: Input information must comply with standard GAA Group VI material inspection procedures.

Additional statements are often found under each SWOP specification, therefore, these standards are not all inclusive.

ELECTROSTATIC ASSIST

Many gravure printing presses use an *electrostatic assist* during the actual printing to improve ink transfer to the substrate. The system of electrostataic assist was developed in the mid 1960s by the efforts of several manufacturers and the Gravure Research Institute. The electrostatic assist is called by names such as *Electrosist* and *Heliostat*. The Hurletron Altair Corporation has been licensed in the United States to sell electrostatic assists for press units.

The purpose of the electrostatic assist is to improve the ink transfer to the substrate, especially when the surface is hard or has poor link receptivity. The highlights or light tone values will often have a speckled appearance if some of the

417

ink cells do not transfer their ink. Also, the color reproduction may shift in hue if the amount of ink transfer is not consistent.

The principle behind the electrostatic system is relatively simple. The impression roller has a conductive covering, which could be carbon black in its rubber coatings. An electrical charge is connected from a power source to the impression roller. This creates an electrostatic charge behind the web. This electrical charge will pass through the paper at the printing nip point to the ink cells of the copper printing cylinder. The electrostatic charge, acting like a magnet, draws the ink out of the cells and onto the substrate being printed. See Fig. 26-28.

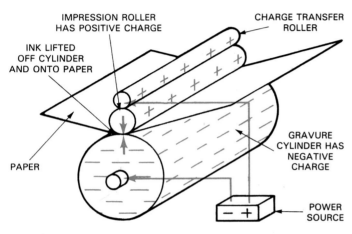

Fig. 26-28. Electrostatic assist can be used to help deposit ink on substrate. Power source feeds current into charge transfer roller. Charge roller transfers electrical charge to impression roller and paper. Since gravure cylinder has an opposite charge, a magnetic-like force helps pull ink out of wells and onto substrate. If petroleum-based inks are used, precautions must be taken because of the danger of fire.

Danger! Precautions should be taken to prevent fires on the gravure press when electrical charges are exposed to volatile solvent-based inks.

KNOW THESE TERMS

Intaglio, Gravure, Rotogravure, Doctor blade, Gravure inks, GAA, Gravure plate configurations, Cylinder engraving, Base cylinder, Copper plating, Rotofilm, Frisket, Acid etched, Engraving machine, Diamond stylus, Laser engraving, Electron beam engraving, Cylinder evaluation, Halftone gravure, Gravure press, Impression roller, Electrostatic assist.

REVIEW QUESTIONS—CHAPTER 26

1. Intaglio printing was the forerunner to gravure. True or false?
2. When a gravure press uses a cylinder, it is called:
   a. Rotointaglio.
   b. Rotogravure.
   c. Cylinder gravure.
   d. Platen gravure.
3. How does gravure deposit ink on the substrate?
4. What are the three markets that commonly use gravure?
5. The most important advantage of gravure is _____.
6. Gravure process inks are almost identical to inks used in offset lithography. True or false?
7. Explain four classifications of gravure ink.
8. How can a gravure cylinder be produced without conventional photographic films?
9. The gravure base cylinder is made of _____ or _____ and is ground and polished to a tolerance of _____ inch or _____ mm.
10. In your own words, how do you use acid to etch an image in a gravure cylinder?
11. How does a mechanical engraver operate?
12. This gravure cylinder engraving technique can cut up to 150,000 cells per second.
    a. Laser engraving.
    b. Stylus engraving.
    c. Quartz crystal engraving.
    d. Electron beam engraving.
13. How do you evaluate a gravure cylinder after engraving?
14. What is halftone gravure?
15. Explain how electrostatic assist functions.

SUGGESTED ACTIVITIES

1. Select ten major magazines and determine if any of them are printed by the gravure process.
2. Identify the changes that are taking place in preparing gravure cylinders.
3. Visit a facility and observe the methods of making the gravure cylinder.
4. Observe a gravure press run.

Chapter 27

SCREEN PRINTING AND OTHER PROCESSES

After studying this chapter, you will be able to:
* Explain the principles of screen printing.
* Select the proper fabric or other substrate to be used
* for screen printing.
* Select and prepare screen frames as support devices.
* Prepare and attach the fabric to a frame.
* Cut and prepare stencils to be adhered to the screen.
* Prepare photographic stencils.
  Summarize the use of screen presses.
* Explain the process of sublimation heat transfer.
* Summarize ink jet printing.

Screen printing is done by forcing ink through an image stencil. As a means of reproducing images, it has been known by a variety of names including: *serigraphy, mitography, silk screen, stencil printing,* and *screen process.*

Today, only two terms are in common usage. To the fine arts creative individual, *serigraphy* is the name most commonly heard. To the industrial person, *screen printing* is the preferred name for this process. Some individuals continue to refer to the process as silk screen; however, silk is little used in modern applications.

Screen printing can be a very simple process requiring only a few inexpensive tools and materials, or it can be extremely complex, requiring an array of sophisticated tools, materials, and production techniques. The deciding factor is the complexity of the product to be printed, and the required level of quality in the finished piece. This is a tremendous virtue of screen printing because the type of applications are very diverse. Everything from a simple single color poster to a multi-layer printed circuit board for electronic circuits can be done by screen printing.

SCREEN PRINTING APPLICATIONS

Almost any substrate, in almost any shape or size, can be printed by the screen method. However, substrates are usually limited to flat, relatively thin substrates such as paper, metal, or plastic.

Some screen printing applications include: posters, plastic bottles, drinking glasses, mirrors, metal surfaces, wood, textiles, printed circuits, point of purchase displays, and vinyl binders. End products are everything from a football jersey to a traffic sign. The versatility of screen printing is limited only by imagination and ingenuity. Frequently, only screen printing can provide the means of meeting the necessary printed product requirements.

SCREEN PRINTING PROCESS

In screen printing, a fabric is stretched across a frame. Portions of the porous fabric are blocked out. This leaves only the desired image areas open. An ink is poured onto the fabric and forced through the porous image areas using a rubber blade, called a *squeegee.* As the ink is forced through the fabric, it is deposited on a substrate below the fabric, Fig. 27-1.

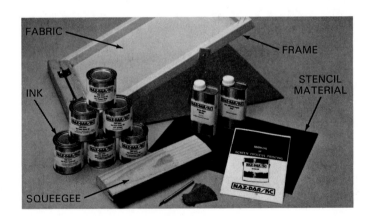

Fig. 27-1. This is the basic equipment needed to do screen printing by hand. (NAZ-DAR/KC)

Multiple prints are accomplished by repeating the squeegee action on a new substrate.

Five elements are necessary for basic screen printing:
1. Frame.
2. Stencil.
3. Ink.
4. Squeegee.
5. Substrate.

To achieve the correct printed result, each of these five elements must be matched in the proper combination.

419

Screen printing advantages and disadvantages

The principal advantages of screen printing are:
1. Versatility in types of substrates that can be printed.
2. Relatively easy production of printed products.
3. Low capital expense in relation to other printing processes.
4. Decorative capability to print with glitter, flock, and other unique finishes.
5. Strength and durability of the ink film due to the tremendous thickness of the ink deposit (up to 100 times as thick as other printing processes).

Disadvantages of screen printing are:
1. Slow production rate or speed.
2. Poor ink mileage.
3. Excessive drying times required by many inks.
4. Relative inability to print detail and fine line images when compared to other printing processes.

HISTORY OF SCREEN PRINTING

Screen printing is considered by many historians to be the oldest of the printing processes, although some individuals believe block printing to be older. The actual beginning of screen printing is vague and difficult to prove. The Chinese, Egyptians, and Japanese are generally credited with the first use of a stencil process. The Japanese were the first to combine a screen with a stencil.

In Japan, stencils were cut by the artist from two sheets of paper. Silk or hair was sandwiched between the paper sheets forming a screen. The process of stencil printing spread to Europe in the 15th century and eventually to the American colonies.

In America, many people contributed to the process by experimentation. In 1914, a multi-color screen printing process was perfected by John Pilsworth, a San Francisco commercial artist.

In 1929, Louis F. D'Autremont, a screen printer in Ohio, developed the first material for knife-cut stencils. His stencil, called Profilm, was hard to cut and adhere.

Several years later Joe Ulano, a New York screen printer, developed his own knife-cut stencil called Nufilm. D'Autremont and Ulano became involved in a court battle over patent rights, which was eventually settled in favor of D'Autremont. However, Ulano's Nufilm was a better, more easily used stencil and it became the standard of the industry.

With a working stencil now available, paint manufacturers saw the potential of a new market for their products, and screen printing became an established industrial process.

The applications for screen printing were limited by the available stencils (all hand-cut) and inks. With the advent of World War II, screen printing began to have wider application, especially as a method of identification for military vehicles and related equipment.

Modern screen printing began in the 1940s and 1950s as new materials and production techniques were developed. Today, screen printing is still the slowest printing process, yet rapid technological advances continue to improve the process and lead to expanded markets.

FABRICS

Proper screen fabric selection is critical to the screen printer if fundamental product requirements are to be fulfilled. In general, screen fabric determines:
1. True size, shape, and reproduction of the original image.
2. Edge definition.
3. Resolution of fine lines and detailed images.
4. Accurate register.
5. Durability of the screen.
6. Ink film thickness.

Originally, only silk and cotton organdy were available to the screen printer. These two natural fabrics are seldom used in industry today. Silk fabric gave rise to the old fashioned term silk screen. Instead, most modern screen printers prefer synthetic and metal fabrics. Three general kinds of screen fabrics are used today: natural, synthetic, and metal mesh.

Fabric specifications

Screen fabrics are classified according to filament, mesh count, strength, and weave pattern. *Filaments* may be either multifilaments or monofilaments, Fig. 27-2.

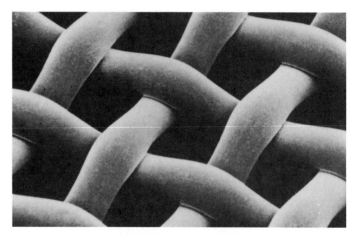

MONOFILAMENT FABRIC

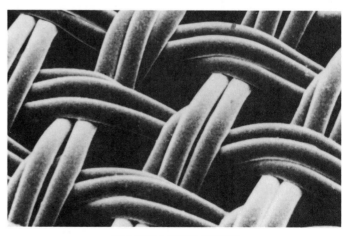

MULTIFILAMENT FABRIC

Fig. 27-2. This magnification compares 120 mesh monofilament fabric with 12XX multifilament fabric. (Autotype USA)

Multifilament means there are several strands of material per filament. This is similar to sewing thread with multiple strands.

Monofilament means each filament is one piece of material or a single thread. Fishing line is monofilament for example.

Natural fabrics are always multifilament. Individual filaments are spun into a thread. Threads are then woven into cloth fabric. Synthetic fabrics may be either multifilament or monofilament.

Mesh count

Fabric *mesh count* is specified according to the number of threads (or strands) per linear inch. The higher the fabric mesh count, the better able the fabric can reproduce fine line details. It also assists in minimizing sawtoothing effects. *Sawtoothing* relates to edge definition characteristics.

In general, as mesh count increases, fabric strength and durability DECREASES. Multifilament fabrics are specified by a one or two digit number, usually from 5 to 25.

The mesh count per linear inch is approximated by multiplying this number by 10. Thus, if the mesh count number is 12, the approximate actual mesh count will be 120 threads per linear inch (10 × 12 = 120). This number is only an approximation because there is little standardization between manufacturers. As an example, a 12-mesh number fabric could have anywhere from 115 to 129 threads per linear inch.

Monofilament fabrics are specified by actual thread count. A 160-mesh fabric will have exactly 160 threads per linear inch. This is also true for all metal mesh.

Fabric strength

Fabric strength is in direct relation to the thread diameter. Multifilament fabrics use X, XX, or XXX to specify strength. A single X is the smallest diameter, a triple X is the largest diameter. In practice, however, these are only relative specifications. As fabric mesh count increases, thread diameter must decrease or no porous areas (open cells) will remain, Fig. 27-3.

For example, a 12XX fabric will be stronger than a 12X fabric, and also stronger than a 20XXX. Only compare strength as a relative measure between fabrics of equal mesh count.

Monofilament fabrics use a different system to specify strength. Either the actual thread diameter will be given, expressed in thousandths of an inch, or a letter rating will be given. The letter specifications are: S = small, T = medium, and HD = heavy duty.

In general, most screen printers select XX-multifilament and T-monofilament fabrics.

Weave patterns

Weave pattern determines how the vertical and horizontal threads are woven into fabric. There are four different weave patterns available for screen fabrics. They are illustrated in Fig. 27-4.

The *plain* or *taffeta weave* is a general purpose weave used in most situations requiring good strength and sharp detail.

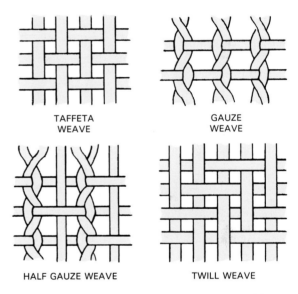

Fig. 27-4. Study these weaves that can be used for screen printing. (Screen Printing Association International)

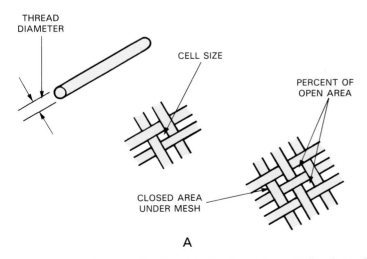

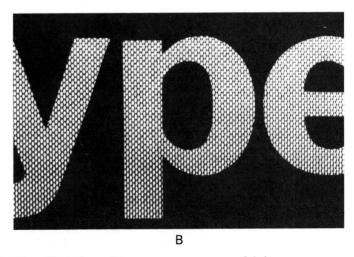

Fig. 27-3. A—Note basic fabric specifications. B—Magnified view of image area on screen fabric.

Gauze weaves are sometimes selected when an extremely long run is necessary. With this weave, the squeegee must move parallel to the double threads. This fabric weave cannot print fine detail due to the double threads. Half gauze weaves are usually NOT recommended.

Twill weaves result in an uneven ink film thickness and poor edge definition resulting in a more pronounced sawtooth effect.

Threads that run HORIZONTALLY in the fabric are called *weft threads*. Threads that run VERTICALLY are called *warp threads*.

Two other specifications, not always available, are percent open area and cell size.

Percent open area is the percentage of area per square inch through which ink can pass. The greater the percent open area, the thicker the ink film, and the weaker the fabric. This is because the greater open area requires that smaller diameter threads be used to weave the fabric.

Sometimes, *cell size* is given in thousandths of an inch. It is the distance across individual open areas between adjacent threads. As cell size increases, the percent of open area increases and fabric strength decreases.

Multifilament fabrics are sometimes used with indirect photographic and knife cut stencils. These fabrics usually print a slightly uneven ink film due to the irregular size and shape of cells. This results from the irregular cross sections of each thread. In practice, multifilament fabrics have slightly less dimensional stability due to the stretching or elongation associated with their "rope" construction.

Monofilament fabrics are generally suitable, with some caution, for use with any stencil. These fabrics usually provide better ink film thickness uniformity and dimensional stability, Fig. 27-5. Monofilament fabrics, however, usually cost more than multifilament fabrics, and are NOT as durable.

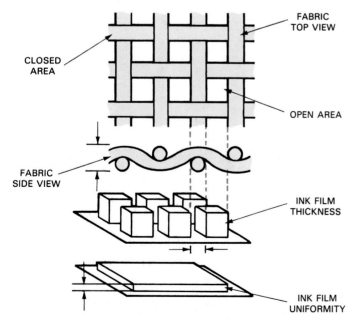

Fig. 27-5. Ink film thickness and uniformity are related to fabric weave pattern. (Screen Printing Association International)

Silk

Silk is a natural multifilament fabric once used by most screen printers. Today, it is generally only used by the serigrapher. Silk cannot be used with certain chemicals associated with some photographic stencils. Traditionally, the best silk fabric is manufactured in Switzerland. It has relatively good durability and dimensional stability.

Organdy

Organdy is a natural multifilament fabric made of inexpensive cotton. It is often used when the fabric is not to be cleaned and reused. Organdy has limited applications in textile printing. It has poor dimensional stability, but relatively good durability for short to medium runs.

Polyester

Polyester or *Dacron*® is a synthetic fabric available as multifilament or monofilament. The fabric has wide applications in almost all areas of screen printing. It can be used with any stencil. It is very durable in multifilament and monofilament, but slightly better in multifilament. Monofilament has slightly better ink film uniformity and the best dimensional stability of any natural or synthetic fabric. Polyester is a very popular fabric (particularly monofilament) in the screen printing industry.

Nylon

Nylon is a synthetic fabric available only as monofilament. Nylon has relatively good dimensional stability if used in a climate (temperature and relative humidity) controlled environment. It is the most durable of the natural or synthetic fabrics, and adapts well when printing on rough textured or uneven substrates. It also is used when printing on concave or convex surfaces due to the flexibility of the fabric.

Metalized polyester

Metalized polyester is a hybrid, monofilament fabric with a metallic (usually nickel) electroplated surface coating. The metallic coating is usually about 3 microns thick. The metallic coating increases dimensional stability for printing critical tolerances, such as electronic circuit board printing. Each thread is "welded" in position. Metalized polyester is NOT as susceptable to kinks or deformities as metal mesh fabrics. Therefore, it is more durable than metal mesh fabrics.

Metal mesh

Metal mesh is always monofilament—usually stainless steel, but may also be bronze, copper, or brass. It is used for printing heated inks (some plastic printing applications) or when the ultimate in dimensional stability is required. Metal mesh is very durable, but fragile. Any kinks or deformities usually require replacement of the metal mesh.

SCREEN FRAMES

The screen frame is often the most overlooked element in screen printing. The function of the *screen frame* is to:

1. Provide rigidity and dimensional stability.
2. Resist mechanical stress and warpage.
3. Resist chemical action and corrosion.
4. Provide a means of attaching fabric at the proper tension.
5. Provide means for register.

A variety of different materials are used to manufacture screen frames including wood, aluminum, steel, and plastic.

Wood frames

Wood frames are the most popular for general screen printing applications, Fig. 27-6. While a hardwood such as maple is ideal, costs dictate clear pine as the most frequently used wood.

Wood frames may be constructed by many different techniques using screws, corrugated fasteners, dowels, splines, and even nails, Fig. 27-7. Whichever type is used, it is wise to remember that frames are continuously subjected to mechanical and chemical stress.

Included in the area of chemical stress is the constant attack of water on the frame and fasteners. For this reason, metal fasteners should be avoided when possible or rust and corrosion will cause the frame joints to loosen and weaken. Wood frames should be glued using a non-water soluble glue if possible.

Wood frames may be constructed or purchased, either complete or in ready to assemble parts, Fig. 27-8. As frame size increases, frame sidewall dimensions should also increase to withstand the increased mechanical strain of the fabric after tensioning. Additionally, the larger the frame, the less will be the tendency for warpage.

As a rule of thumb, frame sizes up to 15 x 15 inch should be constructed of 1 1/8 x 1 1/8 inch frame lumber. From this frame size up to 24 x 24 inch, use 1 5/8 x 1 5/8 inch frame lumber. Beyond this size, 2 x 2 inch or larger frame lumber should be used.

Whenever wood is used to construct a frame, a waterproof frame sealer should be applied before the frame contacts moisture.

Aluminum frames

Aluminum frames provide greater rigidity and dimensional stability compared to wood frames, Fig. 27-9. While

Fig. 27-6. This is a basic screen printing frame for holding the fabric.

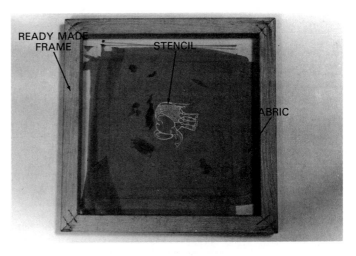

Fig. 27-8. Screen frames can be purchased or made using frame lumber.

Fig. 27-7. Screen frames can use various methods of construction which can affect their service life.

Fig. 27-9. Aluminum frame is not affected by moisture but can be damaged by some chemicals.

not susceptible to chemical attack from water, aluminum frames have poor resistance to acids and soda solutions.

Most aluminum frames are manufactured with a built in *mechanical clamp* for attaching and stretching the screen fabric, Fig. 27-10. These frames are available from many manufacturers. While expensive, they provide high quality. With proper care, they have a long life.

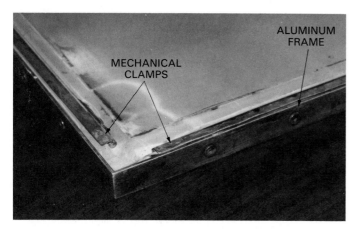

Fig. 27-10. Most aluminum frames use mechanical clamps to hold the fabric.

Aluminum frames are available in a variety of styles and sidewall dimensions. Aluminum frames are rigid enough for frame sizes up to 36 x 36 inch. Beyond this size, aluminum may be satisfactory, but steel frames are preferred. Some frames are constructed using a combination of metal (usually aluminum) and wood. The fabric may be glued to the wooden part of the frame.

Frame profiles

To compensate for the inward pull of tensioned fabric, some screens are manufactured using special sidewall profiles, Fig. 27-11. If the frame is bent inward from the force of fabric tension, the fabric will lose tension. Because of the varied fabric tension, the image may not print in register or it may become distorted.

Some screen printers intentionally deflect frame sidewalls inward. When the tensioned fabric is attached, the frame is allowed to relax. This results in an automatic outward pull of the frame sidewalls to balance the inward pull of the tensioned fabric, Fig. 27-12.

It is important to keep frames clean, and free of any ink buildup.

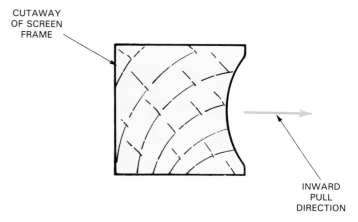

Fig. 27-12. Cutaway shows basic profile of typical wooden screen frame. Shape helps frame resist inward pull of fabric.

Print size

Maximum *image* or *print area size* is determined by inside dimensions of the screen frame. Generally, the frame should have twice the inside area as does the image, Fig. 27-13. An ideal frame size should be four times the print or image area size. This is necessary for proper fabric flex without causing excessive squeegee pressure or undesirable excessive *off contact distance* (distance from screen to substrate). See Fig. 27-14.

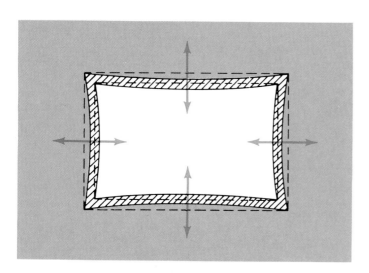

Fig. 27-11. An inward deflection of the frame results in an outward pull on the fabric. This produces fabric tension. (Screen Printing Association International)

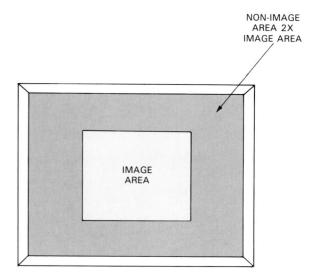

Fig. 27-13. Screen frame should have an inside area twice as large as image area to be printed.

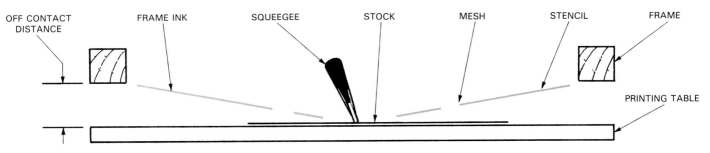

Fig. 27-14. Proper off-contact distance results in minimum fabric flex when printing. This produces necessary fabric snap back to lift fabric away from substrate after printing. (Autotype USA)

SCREEN FABRIC TENSIONING

Correct fabric tension is partially responsible for:
1. Registration.
2. Ink film uniformity.
3. Print detail.
4. Print resolution.
5. Durability of screen stencil and fabric.

In practice, fabric stretching and attaching the fabric to the frame is usually carried out in one operation. This is an extrenely important aspect of screen printing.

There are four different techniques for attaching the fabric to the frame:
1. Staples.
2. Cord and groove.
3. Mechanical clamp.
4. Adhesive.

Staples

Staples provide the least desirable method to tension and attach the fabric to the frame. It should be avoided when other techniques are available. Staples puncture the fabric and tend to tear the fabric. This weakens the fabric weave and can result in early fabric failure. It is difficult to achieve uniform and correct fabric tension with staples. Use of staple tape may provide help, but it will not solve the basic problems associated with the process, Fig. 27-15.

Fig. 27-15. Staples can be used for low quality screen printing. Staple the center of each side first. Gradually pull and tension fabric while installing staples. When finished, staples should be about one-eighth inch apart.

Cord and groove

The *cord and groove* technique is popular in small screen applications where printing requirements are not critical. Using this technique, a cord is forced down into a sized groove in the frame, Fig. 27-16.

Cotton cord is the best but plastic is also used. As the cord moves down, the fabric is stretched across the frame. Grooved frame lumber and cord are available from a variety of manufacturers, or they can be made by the printer.

It is important that groove depth and cord diameter be correct. It is recommended that the groove depth be one and one-half times the cord diameter, Fig. 27-17.

Fig. 27-16. Here fabric is being stretched using the cord and groove method. As cord and fabric are forced down into groove in frame, tension is placed on fabric.

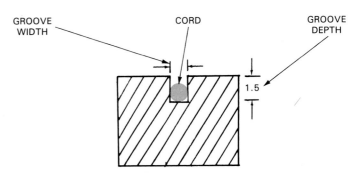

Fig. 27-17. Groove depth in relation to cord diameter is important for proper fabric tension.

425

Cords of varying sizes are available and care should be taken to correctly match cord diameter and groove width so that a tight fit is obtained without causing damage to the frame or fabric.

Mechanical clamp

Mechanical clamping of the fabric to frame is available with many aluminum frames. The fabric is clamped in position on all four sides, then screws are turned to force the movable clamps outward, resulting in fabric tension.

An advantage of the mechanical clamp is that the fabric may be tensioned to exact specifications. Care must be exercised in providing periodic lubrication of the screw threads to prevent corrosion and wear.

Adhesive

In order to attach fabric to a frame with an *adhesive,* a stretching machine is necessary. *Stretching machines* may be either mechanical or pneumatic, Fig. 27-18. The advantage of a stretching machine is that fabric may be tensioned to exact specs without cell distortion.

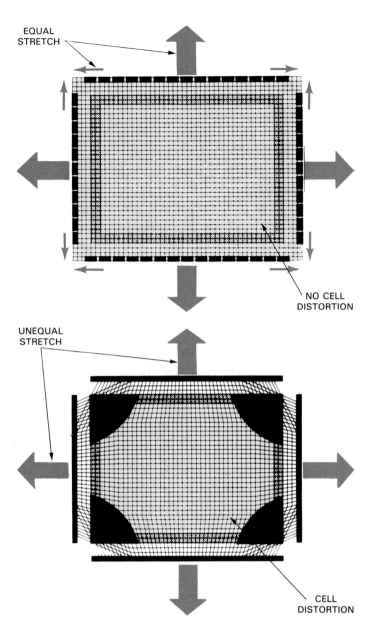

Fig. 27-19. Note difference from improperly stretched fabric and correctly stretched fabric. With equal tension, cells or openings in fabric are not distorted. (Tetko Inc.)

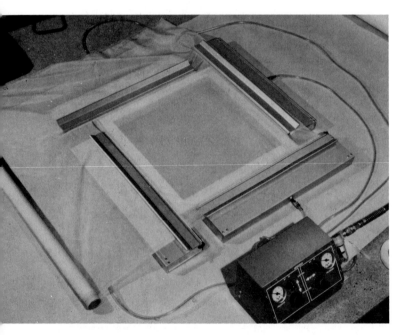

Fig. 27-18. This is an automatic or pneumatic fabric stretching machine. Controlled air pressure is used to pull out on fabric in all directions. An equal fabric stretch results which improves printing quality. (Autotype USA)

Cell distortion results when fabric openings are stretched different amounts vertically and horizontally. Cell distortion is always present when using other techniques than a stretching machine. Cell distortion is the result of tensioning the fabric one way without allowing the fabric to also stretch along the other frame sides, Fig. 27-19.

In general, stretching machines are only found where volume allows for the high initial cost of the machine. They are also needed when printing requirements are critical in relation to resolution of fine detail and ink film uniformi-

ty. An example of this would be in the production of printed circuit boards or four-color process printing.

FABRIC TENSION

Screen tension or tightness may be accurately measured by finding the percent of fabric stretch or by using a tensiometer (tension meter).

Percent stretch is a simple technique requiring very accurate measurement before and during tensioning. Then, the percent size increase is found.

As an example, a fabric at rest before tensioning is measured and marked at 10 inches, the inside measurement of the frame being 10 x 10 inches. As the fabric is tensioned, measurements are taken until the 10 inch original distance has been stretched to 10 1/2 inches, Fig. 27-20.

Fig. 27-20. The percent of stretch can be measured with a yardstick. Mark and measure fabric in at least six different locations. Measure before and after tensioning to calculate percent of stretch.

This procedure of marking and measuring should be made in at least six different locations. It should be done adjacent and parallel to each of the four frame sides, and in the middle of the frame, in both vertical and horizontal directions.

The percent stretch procedure is possible when stretching fabric by either the cord and groove, mechanical clamp, or stretching machine techniques.

When tensioning fabric using a *tensiometer* or tension meter, measurements are taken from all areas of the tensioned fabric. Tension meters usually measure tension in Newtons per centimeter. The reading is displayed as a number value, and can be compared to other areas of the fabric, and to the manufacturer's specifications, Fig. 27-21.

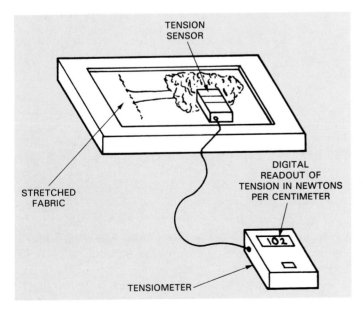

Fig. 27-21. Tensiometer can be used to quickly measure tension or stretch of fabric. Modern types will give digital readout of fabric tension.

It is important to allow a *relax time* between tensioning and measuring to allow the fabric to reach equilibrium at the new tension level. Tension meters are generally used in conjunction with mechanical or pneumatic stretching machines.

FABRIC TREATMENT

For the image stencil and fabric to adhere to each other, the fabric must be properly cleaned. In some instances, stretched fabric must be chemically and/or mechanically treated. Cleaning of fabric removes surface grease, airborne contaminents, and residue.

Chemical treatment alters the adhesion characteristics of the fabric. This allows for better bonding between the stencil and fabric.

Mechanical treatment changes the physical properties of the fabric to enhance the bond between stencil and fabric.

Usually, chemical and mechanical treatments are done only once with new fabric. Repeated use of these treatments will degrade the fabric causing early fabric failure.

Cleaning the fabric is usually referred to as *degreasing,* and should be completed just before each new stencil is adhered to the fabric. The following treatments are suggested:

1. SILK—No mechanical or chemical treatment. Degrease with 2% solution of trisodium-phosphate (TSP) or other caustic soda.
2. NYLON—No mechanical treatment. Chemically treat, only once, with 5% solution of metacresol (cresylic acid). Use skin and eye protection with this solution. Remove from screen with cold water. Degrease with 5% solution of trisodium-phosphate (TSP) or other caustic soda.
3. POLYESTER—If monofilament, mechanically treat with silicon carbide to roughen threads. Do NOT use household cleaners. These substances damage threads and can clog mesh. Do this only once with new monofilament fabric.

   Multifilament polyester does NOT require mechanical treatment or chemical treatment. Degrease with 5% solution of acetic acid; then rinse with cold water.
4. STAINLESS STEEL—No mechanical treatment. Chemical treatment by flame treating is an optional procedure always following manufacturer directions. Degrease with 5% solution of trisodium-phosphate (TSP) or other caustic soda.

   Danger! Follow all precautions when handling and using chemicals.

STENCILS

Proper fabric selection will enable the printer to reproduce images with the necessary production quality in edge definition, image resolution, ink film thickness, and ink uniformity. The stencil, however, determines if the quality level available in the selected fabric will be reached.

No matter how small the fabric mesh, the wrong stencil or an improperly processed stencil will not give the desired

427

results. Each stencil has advantages and disadvantages which must be analyzed in relation to printing and production requirements, Fig. 27-22.

KNIFE-CUT STENCILS

There are three types of knife-cut stencils: paper, water soluble, and lacquer soluble. Each has its applications.

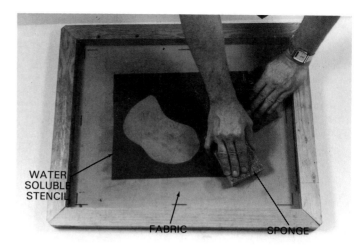

Fig. 27-23. Water-soluble stencil is being adhered to fabric. Use sponge to moisten and then dry stencil to adhere it to fabric.

Fig. 27-22. Gelatin layer is being removed after hand-cutting of this screen printing stencil. (Autotype USA)

Paper stencils

Paper stencils are cut from thin durable papers, such as vellum. They are inexpensive and can provide excellent results. The amount of detail depends on the stencil cutter's talent. Generally, paper stencils are used for relatively simple designs, especially if the production run is limited.

After the stencil has been cut, the paper is placed beneath the screen frame. Ink is then spread across the fabric. The tack (stickiness) of the ink causes the stencil to adhere to the underside of the fabric.

Water-soluble stencils

Water-soluble stencils are composed of a water soluble gelatin material coated onto a plastic support sheet. To create an image area, cut the stencil and remove the water soluble gelatin. Do not cut into or remove the plastic support.

After stripping away all image area gelatin material, position the stencil beneath the frame with the gelatin side in good contact with the underside of the fabric. Use a wet sponge to moisten and dry the stencil in small sections, Fig. 27-23.

Generally, it is suggested that adhering take place diagonally, from corner to corner. After a suitable drying time, the base support is peeled off leaving the adhered stencil, Fig. 27-24.

After printing and ink removal, the stencil may be removed with a warm water spray. If a spray unit is not available, allow the stencil to soak in warm water until the

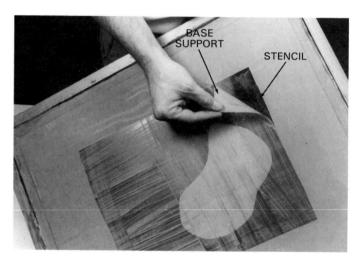

Fig. 27-24. Peel away the base support sheet. Always follow the stencil manufacturer's directions when processing.

stencil can be flushed from the fabric. Water-soluble stencils provide excellent results, but cannot be used with water-base inks.

Lacquer-soluble stencils

Lacquer-soluble stencils are essentially the same as water soluble stencils, except they are only soluble in lacquer thinner or other lacquer-based solvents. Lacquer-soluble stencils are composed of a lacquer-soluble material coated onto a plastic or paper support sheet.

To create an image area, cut the lacquer coating into the image. Then remove the printing areas. Care must be taken not to cut into or remove areas of the support sheet. Refer to Fig. 27-25.

After stripping away all image area material, position the stencil beneath the frame. The lacquer side must be in good contact with the underside of the fabric. Using a cloth wetted with the proper lacquer adhering liquid and also a dry cloth, wet the stencil and then dry it in small sections. Again, it

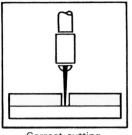
Correct cutting.

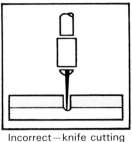
Incorrect—knife cutting into base.

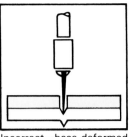
Incorrect—base deformed.

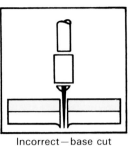
Incorrect—base cut through.

Incorrect—tapered cut.

Fig. 27-25. Note correct and incorrect ways of cutting a stencil. Do not cut into base support.   (Autotype USA)

is suggested that adhering take place diagonally from corner to corner, Fig. 27-26. After a suitable drying time, peel off the base support leaving the adhered stencil, Fig. 27-27.

The stencil may be removed using lacquer thinner. This stencil provides excellent results, but cannot be used with lacquer base inks. It is ideal for water base inks.

Fig. 27-26. Lacquer-soluble stencil is being adhered to fabric.

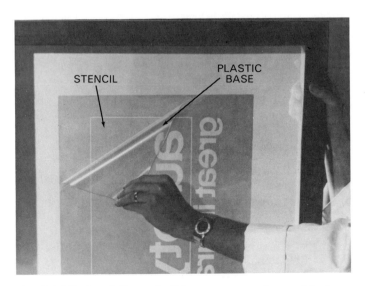

STENCIL

PLASTIC BASE

Fig. 27-27. Carefully peel off base support sheet while leaving stencil adhered to fabric. (Autotype USA)

Burned edges

Both water soluble and lacquer soluble stencils can produce imperfect results if burned edges are present. *Burned edges* are the results of poor cutting or adhering techniques.

Ten reasons for burned edges are:
1. Cutting with a dull knife.
2. Poor fabric and stencil contact during adhering.
3. Using new fabric which has not been degreased.
4. Using old fabric that is not clean.
5. Using the wrong adhering liquid.
6. Using rough, abrasive rags to apply adhering liquid.
7. Using the wrong adhering technique.
8. Failure to rapidly dry the screen after adhering.
9. Failure to keep stencil clean while cutting.
10. Kinks and creases in stencil.

PHOTOGRAPHIC STENCILS

Photographic stencils provide the detail, durability, and process flexibility required for the majority of screen printing applications. Photographic stencils are classified as either indirect, direct, or direct-indirect. Photographic stencils are made sensitive to light, then exposed using a positive film image.

Positives for photographic stencils

Positives used to prepare photographic stencils must block light in the image areas, and pass light through the nonimage areas. Diffusion transfer positives are adequate if enough density exists to prevent exposure in the image areas.

Other types of positives include contact film positives made from film negatives, high speed duplicating film positives exposed on a process camera, and cut rubylith masking film.

For most applications, it is necessary that the film positive be right-reading on the emulsion side. The exceptions to this are when printing a textile transfer, or when printing a transparent substrate (glass). When printing on a transparent substrate, it may be desirable to see a right-reading image when viewing the image through the substrate from the unprinted side.

Indirect stencils

Indirect stencils are exposed off of the fabric; they are not in direct contact with the fabric. These are the oldest of the photographic stencils, and date back to the 1930s. With the use of knife-cut stencils, certain restrictions apply. An example is the inability to cut detailed images and halftones. Indirect stencils allow more detailed images to be produced.

Today, indirect water soluble stencils are used for relatively short production runs. Indirect stencils are excellent when extremely fine detail is to be printed.

There are two types of indirect stencils, the unsensitized and presensitized. *Unsensitized indirect stencils* are seldom used in modern industrial applications.

Three layers exist in an indirect stencil: light sensitive gelatin, the plastic support (usually polyester), and an intermediate adhesive layer to keep the gelatin and base together until after adhering to the fabric. See Fig. 27-28.

Indirect stencils are washed out with water. This allows the use of any ink other than a water base ink.

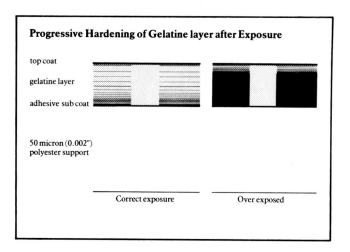

Fig. 27-28. Note three layers of gelatin in this indirect stencil. (Autotype USA)

Indirect stencils adhere particularly well to multifilament fabrics. Degreasing and mechanical treatment of monofilament polyester is essential if good adhesion is to be obtained. Indirect stencils have excellent *mesh bridging capability* which is the ability to bridge diagonally across a cell.

Indirect stencils are exposed in a contact frame (usually a lithographic platemaker). The stencil is exposed through the base, with the positive positioned emulsion down, in contact with the stencil base, Fig. 27-29.

After exposure, the stencil is placed in a hardening solution. The *hardening solution* is either a proprietary solution or a 5% hydrogen peroxide solution. Leave the stencil in the solution for the manufacturer's suggested time, usually a minimum of one and one-half minutes, Fig. 27-30.

After hardening, the stencil is then washed out using a warm water spray, as in Fig. 27-31.

After washout, the softened stencil is placed base-side down on a flat buildup. The screen fabric is wetted and the substrate side of the screen is brought into good contact. Look at Fig. 27-32.

Fig. 27-30. The exposed indirect stencil is hardened in a solution with the gelatin side face-up. This helps prevent scratching gelatin on bottom of tray. (Autotype USA)

Fig. 27-31. Water nozzle is being used to wash out the image area. Hardened nonimage area remains and is not washed away.

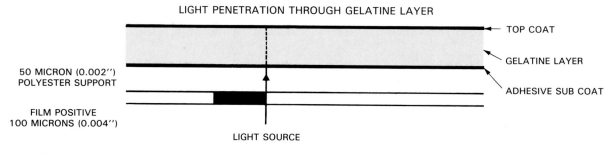

Fig. 27-29. Note process when exposing indirect stencil with a film positive. (Autotype USA)

Fig. 27-32. To adhere stencil to fabric, position stencil with gelatin side up. (Autotype USA)

Unprinted newsprint is applied repeatedly to blot off and remove excessive water, Fig. 27-33. After blotting five or six times with a folded cloth the stencil is allowed to dry. Fans or blowers are ideal to speed drying of the stencil.

A *blockout material* may be applied to the substrate side of the screen before or after the stencil has dried. However, use caution to prevent blockout from filling the image area. See Fig. 27-34.

Fig. 27-33. Use paper and roller to blot away water and adhere this type stencil to fabric.

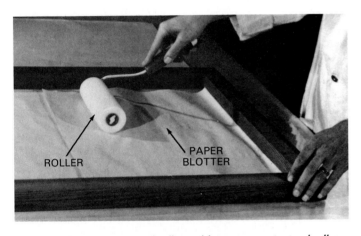

Fig. 27-34. Apply blockout solution to base side of stencil and fabric. Pinholes can be filled after peeling away base sheet.

The following steps are recommended:
1. Degrease screen fabric.
2. Expose stencil through support base with a right-reading film positive.
3. Harden stencil according to manufacturer's directions.
4. Wash out stencil using a stream of warm water spray.
5. Wet screen fabric.
6. With stencil, emulsion side up on a raised buildup, position screen in contact with the stencil.
7. Adhere by blotting out excessive water.
8. Allow to dry.
9. Apply blockout material.
10. Retouch pinholes using blockout and small brush.

Direct stencils

Direct stencils are called "direct" because they are exposed AFTER a solution has been applied to the screen frame. Direct stencils (or emulsions) are generally preferred where durability is important and thousands of prints are to be reproduced.

Direct emulsions impregnate the fabric and can withstand abrasions and chemical action over a prolonged time period.

Direct emulsions, when properly coated, will have almost the mesh bridging capability of an indirect stencil. The slight loss of mesh bridging results in a sawtooth edge, and somewhat poorer edge definition.

Direct stencils are comprised of a polyvinyl alcohol suspension and a sensitizer. Two common types of sensitizers are: bichromated and diazo, Fig. 27-35. The bichromated sensitizers are usually either ammonium or potassium bichromate.

Fig. 27-35. Bichromate sensitizer is on left and diazo sensitizer is on right.

If bichromated sensitizers are used, the direct emulsion must be sensitized, coated, dried, exposed, and washed out within a very short period of time, usually 24 hours. This is because coated screens using bichromated emulsions lose their sensitivity to light over time. Bichromated emulsions, if properly processed, provide the shortest exposure time.

Danger! Bichromates are toxic. Ventilate the area and wear appropriate gloves when handling this material.

Diazo emulsions are becoming more and more popular. One of the reasons for the recent popularity of diazo emulsions is that diazos are considered non-toxic and biodegradable. They are also safer to handle than bichromates.

Diazo sensitized direct emulsions may be stored up to six weeks in a closed container, and even longer if refrigerated. Coated screens may be stored usually up to three or four weeks before exposure.

Unfortunately, diazo emulsions are about half as sensitive to light as bichromated emulsions. Diazo emulsions require about twice the exposure time of bichromated emulsions. This is illustrated by the graph in Fig. 27-36.

Fig. 27-37. This special scoop coater is being used to apply direct emulsion to screen fabric.

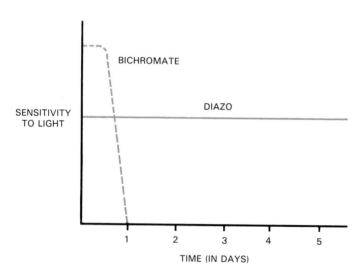

Fig. 27-36. Note exposure comparison of bichromate and diazo sensitizers.

A variety of different diazo direct emulsions are available. Some emulsions are specially formulated to be used with water base inks. Others are formulated for use with solvent soluble inks.

To coat a screen with direct emulsion usually requires a special "scoop coater," Fig. 27-37. Sensitized emulsion is poured into the scoop then applied to both sides of the screen fabric, Fig. 27-38.

To obtain a high quality print, it is necessary to apply multiple coats. An intermediate drying time should take place as the emulsion shrinks as it dries, Fig. 27-39.

If enough shrinkage occurs, then thread profiles will appear on the substrate side of the emulsion and the ink will seep out of the image area when printing. This will cause poor edge definition and a loss of resolution when printing fine, detailed images. It is important that the coating be

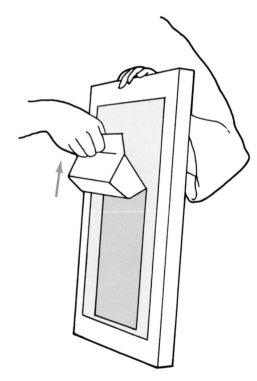

Fig. 27-38. Scoop coater is carefully pulled across screen to apply even coating of solution onto screen. (Autotype USA)

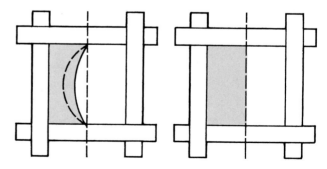

Fig. 27-39. As emulsion dries, it shrinks. This requires multiple coats for best results. (Autotype USA)

thicker than the fabric and that the substrate side of the emulsion be as smooth as possible.

To expose a direct emulsion, a special deep bottom, vacuum frame is necessary. The screen is positioned with the positive on the substrate side. The film emulsion should be in contact with the screen emulsion, Fig. 27-40.

Exposure to light causes a chemical reaction. Areas struck by light become hardened and insoluble to water. The image area, unexposed, remains soluble and can be washed out using a warm water spray, Fig. 27-41.

After drying, a blockout material can be applied to those areas not coated with emulsion. Any pinholes should also be retouched, Fig. 27-42. *Pinholes* can be caused by dust or other airborne contaminates.

To remove direct emulsions from the fabric, *reclaiming solutions* must be used. Originally, undiluted household bleach was used for this purpose. Today, better reclaimers are available and bleach should be avoided when possible.

To use the reclaiming solution, apply it to a screen free of ink and wait several minutes, Fig. 27-43. The direct

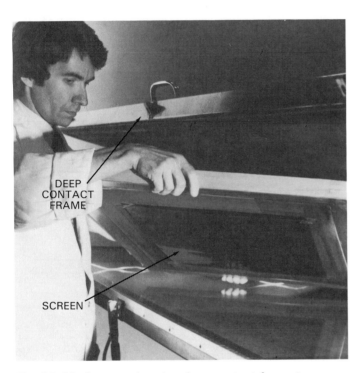

Fig. 27-40. Operator is using deep contact frame to expose emulsion.

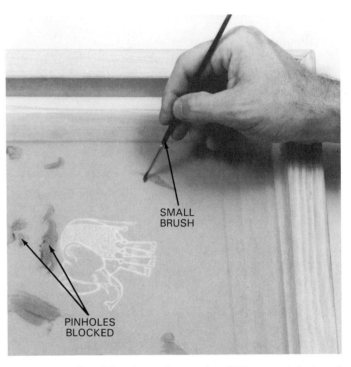

Fig. 27-42. Small brush can be used to fill in any pinholes. If pinholes in nonimage area are not filled, ink can pass through pinholes and deposit on substrate.

Fig. 27-41. After exposure, direct emulsion is washed to remove emulsion from image area of screen. (Autotype USA)

Fig. 27-43. Screen reclaimer is being sprayed on direct emulsion screen. This will dissolve emulsion and allow use of screen over again.

emulsion should gradually change color, and can be removed using a warm or hot water spray. Special high pressure screen washers are available, and they aid in the removal of the emulsion from the fabric mesh.

The following steps are used to coat direct emulsion stencil:

1. Pour sensitized emulsion into scoop coater.
2. Holding screen at an inclined angle, apply coating to substrate side of screen. Apply several coats, one in each of four different directions.
3. Turn screen around and apply one or two coats on squeegee side of screen.
4. Check that excess emulsion has been removed or forced through fabric back onto substrate side. The substrate side should appear smooth and glossy.
5. Allow screen to dry with the substrate side down (in printing position).

Direct-indirect stencils

Direct-indirect stencils, sometimes called *direct-film stencils,* are a combination of the two stencil techniques and materials. There are two types of direct-indirect stencils, the emulsion adhering type and the water adhering type (referred to as a *capillary system stencil*).

With the *emulsion adhering* type of direct-indirect stencil, a dry film or unsensitized gelatin on a polyester base support is positioned in contact with the underside (substrate side) of the fabric. A bichromate or diazo sensitized direct emulsion is spread across the screen with a squeegee. One or two passes might be needed, Fig. 27-44.

The direct emulsion is forced into the fabric mesh. As it softens the dry gelatin film, the indirect portion of the stencil is adhered and sensitized.

After drying, the polyester base support is stripped away and the stencil is exposed, Fig. 27-45. The stencil is exposed in the same manner as with the direct emulsion.

Fig. 27-45. Peel off base after drying of direct-indirect stencil emulsion.

In the *water adhering* or capillary system, the dry gelatin is already light sensitive. Water is spread across the screen to soften the stencil. This allows the gelatin to adhere to the screen fabric, Fig. 27-46. After drying, the polyester support is stripped away.

The stencil is exposed in the same manner as with the direct emulsion. Essentially, both types of direct-indirect

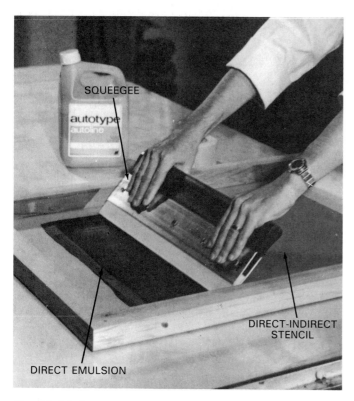

Fig. 27-44. Squeegee blade can be used to apply direct emulsion to direct-indirect stencil.

Fig. 27-46. Here a capillary system stencil is being applied using water and a squeegee.

stencils are processed in the same manner. One stencil requires direct emulsion and the other water.

Direct-indirect stencils are a compromise between an indirect and a direct stencil. Direct-indirect stencils last longer than an indirect stencil. However, they cannot match the detail that an indirect stencil can print. Also, direct-indirect stencils do not last as long as a direct emulsion stencil but can resolve and print a finer image with more detailed imagery. This is illustrated in Fig. 27-47.

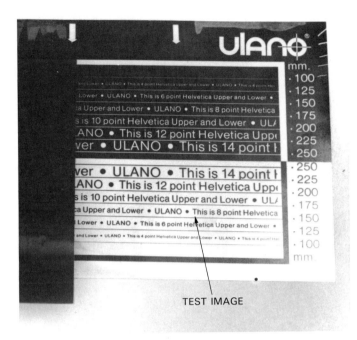

Fig. 27-48. This is an example of a test image used for the proper exposure calibration of photographic stencils.

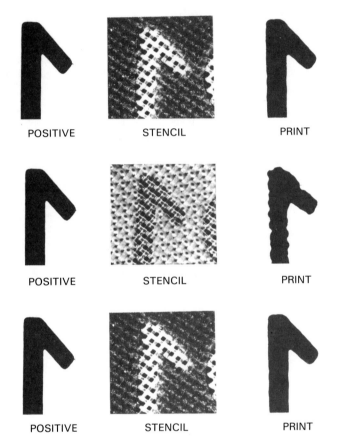

POSITIVE   STENCIL   PRINT

POSITIVE   STENCIL   PRINT

POSITIVE   STENCIL   PRINT

Fig. 27-47. Comparison of the original positives, stencils, and prints. Top. An indirect stencil. Center. Direct stencil. Bottom. Direct-indirect stencil.

PHOTOGRAPHIC STENCIL EXPOSURE CALIBRATION

All photographic stencils require a specific amount of exposure. The exposure is needed so the stencil will adhere well, be durable, and print with the best possible quality of image resolution and edge definition.

Calibration images are available and should be used to identify correct exposure, Fig. 27-48. With a change in fabric, mesh count, stencil, or exposure device, a new exposure time should be determined.

Whenever a colored fabric is used to reduce light scatter within a direct or direct-indirect stencil, the exposure time must be increased by about one-third to one-half.

Fig. 27-49 lists some of the problems associated with improper stencil exposure.

INDIRECT STENCIL	
Underexposed	**Overexposed**
1. Stencil becomes too thin after washout. 2. Excessive pinholes. 3. Early failure of stencil. 4. Images spread.	1. Stencil fails to adhere to fabric. 2. Images choke. 3. Stencil is difficult to remove.

DIRECT EMULSION STENCIL	
Underexposed	**Overexposed**
1. Stencil is soft in nonimage areas. 2. Stencil becomes too thin after washout. 3. Images spread. 4. Early failure of stencil. 5. Excessive sawtooth at edges of images (poor mesh bridging).	1. Stencil is difficult to washout. 2. Loss of detail (such as serifs). 3. Images choke. 4. Stencil is difficult to remove.

DIRECT-INDIRECT STENCIL	
Underexposed	**Overexposed**
1. Stencil is soft in nonimage areas, or washes away completely. 2. Squeegee side of stencil bcomes too thin. 3. Images spread. 4. Early failure of stencil. 5. Excessive sawtoothing at edges of image (poor mesh bridging).	1. Stencil is difficult to washout, or washes out completely due to high pressure required. 2. Loss of details (such as serifs). 3. Images choke. 4. Stencil is difficult to remove.

Fig. 27-49. Chart gives common exposure problems for three types of stencils.

FABRIC AND STENCIL SELECTION

The fabric and the stencil must be matched for good results. Indirect stencils are usually best suited to a multifilament polyester fabric. However, they can also be successfully used with virtually any fabric. Direct emulsions and direct-indirect stencils work well with any fabric, but are generally used with a colored (dyed) monofilament polyester when printing critical detail.

Ruby, orange, or yellow fabric will reduce the chance of exposure in the image areas due to light refraction in the fabric threads, Fig. 27-50. As light strikes each thread, it

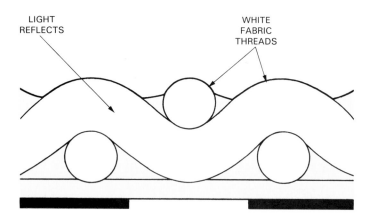

Fig. 27-50. With photographic stencil, light refraction can be a problem, especially if fabric is white.

is refracted. Light rays scatter to adjacent areas of the stencil. This could result in a loss of small detailed images. With colored or dyed fabric, each thread acts as a safelight filter, refracting a wavelength of light to which the stencil is sensitive. Colored monofilament polyester should always be used when printing halftones or process color reproductions.

SCREEN INKS

Selection of the proper printing ink should be the first step in the production of screen printed images. Ink selection will determine what fabric, stencil, and squeegee will be appropriate.

Usually, the selection of screen ink is based upon the type of substrate to be printed, and the product requirements. Should the ink be resistant to ultraviolet rays from the sun? Is moisture resistance important? These questions and others need to be answered before the proper ink can be selected. A partial list of additional concerns might be fade resistance, resistance to chipping or scratching, chemical resistance to acids and alkalines, and finally, the ability to withstand a change in shape associated with vacuum forming.

SCREEN SOLVENTS

Solvents for screen printing are classified as thinners, retarders, and washup.

Thinners

Thinners are solvents added to ink to change the viscosity of the ink. Viscosity is a measure of flow rate or thickness. Depending on the fabric mesh count, thinning is required to achieve the proper ink flow out. Thinners do NOT usually affect the drying time of the ink.

As a general rule, if an ink can be thinned, the viscosity should be approximately similar to pancake syrup, or 40 weight motor oil at room temperature. High ink viscosity can cause poor snap back and may cause a mesh pattern to appear in the printed ink film.

Retarders

Retarders are solvents added to ink to change the viscosity (thin) and to slow (retard) the drying time. This is necessary with some fast dry inks that may clog mesh openings. This is especially important in warm weather climates where solvent evaporation and drying is accelerated.

Washup solvent

Washup solvents are used to remove ink from the screen. These solvents are generally inexpensive. They have only one function, to totally dissolve a particular ink.

Danger! Whenever petroleum solvents are used, it is important to provide adequate ventilation and air exchange. Prolonged exposure to some solvent fumes can be harmful!

SQUEEGEES

Squeegees for hand use consist of a smooth wooden or aluminum handle with a rubber blade. Squeegee blades are usually between 3/16 and 3/8 inch thick, and about 2 inches high.

Squeegee blades may be purchased by durometer or hardness ratings, Fig. 27-51.

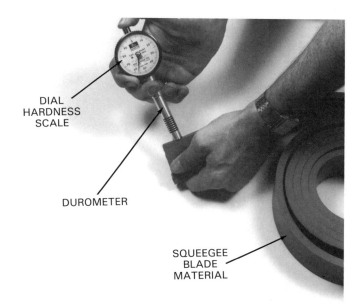

Fig. 27-51. Durometer can check hardness of squeegee blade material.

A durometer reading of 60 is considered soft, 70 is medium, and 80 is hard. For general use, a medium durometer of 70 is usually suggested for a squeegee blade. Look at Fig. 27-52.

Blades may also be purchased according to the type of material. Neoprene blades (black) are the least durable and require frequent sharpening. Plastic blades (tan) are most frequently used, and provide good durability and easy sharpening. The most durable blade is polyurethane. These blades are amber or orange, and somewhat translucent. They provide maximum durability, but are sometimes difficult to sharpen. Fig. 27-53 shows a squeegee blade sharpener.

Quality printing requires that blades be shaped with specific edges for different substrates. Shown in Fig. 27-54, there are six different squeegee blade shapes:

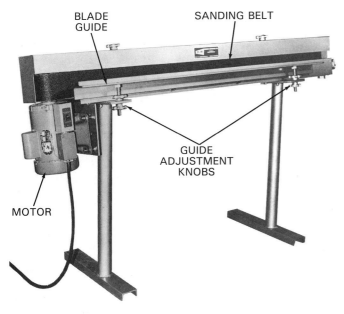

Fig. 27-52. Squeegee blade hardness determines proper blade flex when printing.

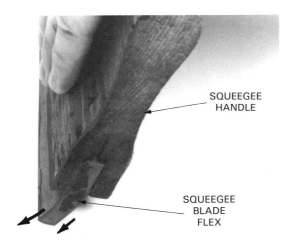

Fig. 27-53. This is a squeegee blade sharpening machine. It uses long sanding belt to grind new edge on used blades. This helps maintain image quality. (Advance)

SQUEEGEE BLADE SHAPES

Fig. 27-54. These are some of the squeegee blade profiles recommended for printing on different substrates.

1. SQUARE-EDGED—for flat surfaces and most general purpose printing.
2. SQUARE-EDGED WITH ROUND CORNERS—gives extra heavy ink deposits on flat substrates. Used when a light color will be printed on a dark substrate.
3. ROUNDED-EDGE—used primarily in textile printing where an extra heavy ink film is required.
4. SINGLE-SIDED BEVEL EDGE—used for glass.
5. DOUBLE-SIDED BEVEL WITH FLAT POINT—primarily to print clay "slip" on ceramics.
6. DOUBLE-SIDED BEVEL EDGE—for printing on cylindrical objects such as bottles and containers.

Machine squeegees are similar to hand squeegees. Usually, the machine squeegee handle is rectangular and has a thicker profile, Fig. 27-55.

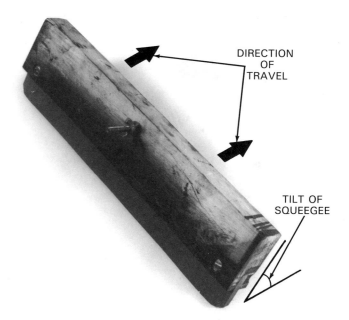

Fig. 27-55. This is a machine squeegee that mounts inside screen printing press. It is automatically pulled across image to print image.

Problems associated with dull squeegee blades include:
1. Bubbles in ink film.
2. Poor edge definition in print.
3. Excessive ink film thickness.
4. Loss of detail.
5. "Spread" images.
6. Poor ink mileage.

Always maintain the edges on squeegees. This is critical to quality screen printing.

DRYING SYSTEMS

Drying a printed ink film has always been a problem for screen printing. Large drying racks and wicket dryers were used to allow each substrate to air dry for the required time. Today, modern drying systems are available which allow much faster production speeds and more efficient use of floor space. There are three methods of heat transfer for oven drying an ink film: conduction, convection, and radiation.

Conduction is the heat generated within an object when that object is in contact with a heat source. As an example, a cooking pan in contact with a hot flame.

Convection heating starts with heating air. The warmed air transfers the heat to the object. An oven uses warmed air to bake food.

In *radiation* heating, heat is generated directly within the object by exposure to radiation. A microwave oven radiates an energy which heats objects, but does not heat the surrounding air. This technique, radiation heating, is becoming ever more popular as new inks are formulated which can be *cured* (dried) by infrared or ultraviolet radiation.

Drying the ink film requires the forced evaporation of a solvent. *Curing* relies on a chemical change called polymerization. *Polymerization* is the cross linking of molecules into a rigid or semi-rigid state.

Most drying systems use some form of conveyor, Fig. 27-56. The speed of the conveyor belt determines the period of time the ink is subjected to heat transfer. Faster drying inks use a faster conveyor belt speed and vice versa.

HALFTONE AND PROCESS COLOR SCREEN PRINTING

Whenever a screened (halftone) image is to be printed, control of screen printing variables and selection of ink, stencil, fabric, squeegee, and printing technique become even more important. In general, fabric tension, frame stability, and proper stencil processing are critical if results are to be acceptable.

Using conventional process color angles, the fabric mesh should be at least five to six times higher than the screen ruling of the halftone dots, Fig. 27-57. This ratio should eliminate any moiré pattern between halftone screen and fabric mesh. The angle between the halftone ruling and the fabric thread should be 22.5 degrees. This relationship will produce the least noticeable interference pattern between lines of halftone dots and fabric mesh.

Generally, conditions necessary for process color printing are:

SCREEN RULING IN INCHES	MESH COUNT IN INCHES
35	210
45	270
55	330
70	420
85	500

Fig. 27-57. The relationship of screen ruling to fabric mesh count should be a ratio of about 1:5.

1. All screens have the same fabric from same manufacturer. Use only monofilament polyesters with plain or taffeta weave.
2. All screens must have same fabric tension.
3. Fabric should be stretched uniformly in all directions to minimize cell distortion.
4. Squeegee should be sharp and of correct durometer.
5. Again, mesh count should be five to six times higher than halftone screen ruling.
6. Halftone dots should be positioned at 22.5 degrees from fabric threads.
7. Ink should be retarded for a very slow drying time.
8. Off-contact distance should be no greater than necessary for adequate snap back.
9. Halftone dots should range from approximately 15 percent in highlight areas to 80 percent in shadow areas.
10. Positives should be made by contacting from negatives.
11. Use precise processing of stencil.

Fig. 27-56. This is a conveyor type drying system for flat substrates. It helps speed drying of ink to speed printing process. (Advance)

SCREEN PRINTING PRESSES

Specialized equipment is necessary to print most screen printed substrates. Usually, the screen printing press is designed with respect to degree of automation and the shape of the substrate.

Semiautomatic presses require the operator to hand-feed the substrate into the printing position. The printed substrate may or may not be removed automatically. Once adjusted properly, the machine carries out all printing functions. Automatic presses infeed and outfeed automatically.

There are five types of screen printing presses:

1. FLAT BED PRESS—It is usually semi-automatic and is used for printing flat substrates made of paper, plastic, or metal, Fig. 27-58.
2. FLAT BED-CYLINDER PRESS—Designed similar to a letterpress flat bed cylinder press but it is used for long production runs when printing flat substrates of paper or plastic, Fig. 27-59.
3. CYLINDER PRESS—Used to print cylindrical or oval objects such as bottles and drinking glasses, Fig. 27-60.
4. TEXTILE PRESS—Designed to print one or more colors on T-shirts or other similar textiles, Fig. 27-61.
5. PRECISION FLAT BED PRESS—Special flat bed press used to produce printed circuit boards, Fig. 27-62.

OTHER PRINTING PROCESSES

The major processes have been discussed in this and previous chapters. However, changing technology causes constant adaptations to old techniques as well as the development of completely new concepts and processes. This changing technology makes graphic communications a very challenging and exciting field. This section of the chapter will briefly discuss newer, less common printing methods.

Fig. 27-58. This is a flat bed, semi-automatic screen printing press. Note parts of press. (M & M Research)

Fig. 27-60. This cylindrical screen printing press is used to print bottles. It also has drying systems to speed production. (American)

Fig. 27-59. This is a flat bed, cylinder automatic screen printing press. (Advance)

Fig. 27-61. This is a multi-color, semi-automatic textile screen printing press. (Advance)

439

Fig. 27-62. This is a precision flat bed screen printing press used to print circuit boards for electronic applications. (American)

Sublimation heat transfer

Sublimation heat transfers use high temperatures to adhere an image onto the substrate. The process of transferring an image from a paper surface to a cloth substrate using heat is not new. It is an important transfer system sometimes used in the graphic communications industry as well as the textile industry.

Sublimation transfer is the process of placing encapsulated dyes on a paper support by the more traditional processes of intaglio, screen process, or planography.

To do sublimation heat transfer, the transfer sheet is positioned on a synthetic fabric, as in Fig. 27-63. Dry heat, from an iron for example, is applied to the transfer sheet. The heat required for transfer is about 375°F or 180°C. The dwell time is around 30 seconds to thoroughly vaporize the dyes and produce a solubilized (melted) image on a synthetic fiber, Fig. 27-64.

Fig. 27-63. Here a household iron is being used to transfer an image to a T-shirt.

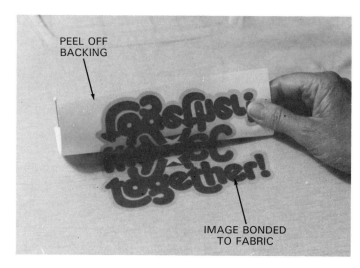

Fig. 27-64. After heating and adhering image, peel off transfer sheet.

The best results are obtained on 100% polyester fabric, but some nylons and a 50/50 cotton-polyester will also give satisfactory results. Presently, cotton is NOT a suitable fabric for the heat transfer process.

The depth and brilliance of color from a transfer sheet is dependent on the nature of the fiber as well as the type of weave. It is suggested that all intended fabrics be tested before transferring the final image.

Most of the recommended fabrics will be resistant to fading, washing, dry cleaning, etc. after the dye is transferred.

Heat transfer inks are classified as low to medium energy inks as the low range of temperature is 180°F or 80°C and the high range is 450°F to 230°C. The dwell time can range from 15 to 30 seconds. The lowest energy will produce a more brilliant color when using 100% polyester fabrics.

In most educational facilities, the planographic process will be used to place an image on a smooth offset or matte finish paper. Coated stock is not recommended. The conventional method with special inks is suggested.

The variable of ink coverage on the paper will create extreme differences. Quality control is essential. When the ink is placed on the paper, it will appear to be very dull and lack color. The heat transfer brings out the true color and must be used to identify the true color.

Whenever scumming or tinting occurs, these images will also transfer when heat is applied. The condition of the transfer sheet, the variety of fabrics, the control of temperature, and the amount of dwell are critical factors which must be controlled to produce a consistently acceptable product.

To complete a product the following materials are needed: a heat source (a household iron will do the job, or transfer press); means of holding transfer sheet in place (pins); and synthetic material.

The suggested procedure is:
1. Preheat heat source.
2. Place receiver synthetic material on bed of transfer press or flat ironable surface.

3. Place printed transfer sheet with the color side toward the receiver material and position securely.
4. Apply heating element for determined dwell time. If an iron is used, do NOT move the transfer sheet because a double image could possibly appear, Fig. 27-65.
5. Remove heating element and allow dye to cool for one minute.
6. Pull off transfer sheet in a vertical motion, Fig. 27-64.

To produce halftones, special consideration must be given to dot size as standard percentage used for other processes are not acceptable.

Fig. 27-65. This is an example of a heat transferred image.

It has been stated that approximately 20% of the textiles printed will be by the thermal method in the future. Some countries have made great strides in the area of heat transfer systems. Research is very evident in the United States and other countries. Some plastics and vinyl tiles are patterned by this method, while carpet tiles and needlepoint canvases are other production products.

Impactless printing

As the title implies, *impactless printing* is a form of image transfer which does NOT require that an image carrier transfer the image by impact or contact with a substrate.

The various processes which come under the impactless printing heading are:
1. Thermal.
2. Magnetic.
3. Electrostatic.
4. Electrophotographic.
5. Ion projection.
6. Ink jet.

THERMAL PRINTING

Thermal printing, like heat transfer, uses heat to form an image in or on the substrate. The substrate surface is treated with a colorless dyestuff. The designated image area is determined by a printing head. When heat is applied, the designated, heated areas on the substrate become visible.

The designated areas are characters or images which are determined by the printing head.

Because of the heat, the images must cool down before handling. This limits the production speed. Thermal printing creates a very acceptable image. The cost of the treated substrate is considerably more than a normal or plain substrate, however.

Magnetic printing

In *magnetic printing* a magnetic charge places an image on a tape. A powdered ink, which is magnetic, is then transferred to the substrate. The transferred magnetic ink is fused to the substrate as the image.

Keeping a clean nonimage area (background) is a potential problem with the magnetic process. Careful attention to cleanliness is imperative.

Electrostatic printing

Electrostatic printing also uses a specially coated substrate. The images are transferred by using an electrically charged stylus. This process uses a liquid or powdered toner. The toner is heated to bond it to the paper. Some copying machines use this process.

Fig. 27-66 illustrates the electrostatic process. Fig. 27-67 shows a magnified example of electrostatic printing.

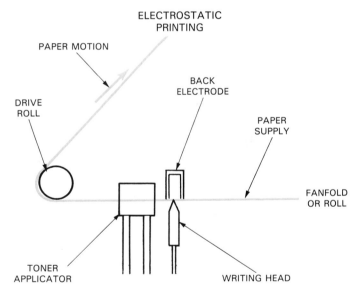

Fig. 27-66. Study basic process of electrostatic printing. Electrostatic energy makes toner stick to substrate where energized by writing head. Toner can then be bonded to substrate to produce permanent image.   (Mead Paper)

Fig. 27-67. Closeup shows an actual image printed by the electrostatic process.   (Mead Paper)

Electrophotographic printing

Electrophotographic printing is most often referred to as the *xerographic process*. It is also called the photoelectrostatic process. Its operation is shown in Fig. 27-68.

This electrophotographic unit has much greater speed than previous processes. It is also possible to have limited image style changes when using the cathode ray tube in place of the drum.

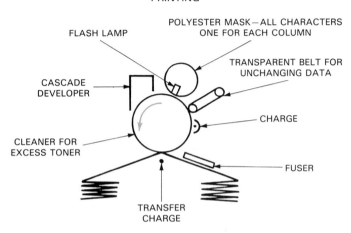

PHOTOELECTROSTATIC PRINTING

Fig. 27-68. Study diagram of photoelectrostatic principle of printing. (Mead Paper)

Ion projection printing

The *ion projection* method of impactless printing has only been demonstrated as an experimental process. Basically, the model has vaporized ink and a panel with small holes. As the substrate moves, the ion beam passes through the designated hole in the panel to direct the ink mist onto the substrate. The matrix controls the image positioning. To assist in understanding the ion projection principle, look at Fig. 27-69.

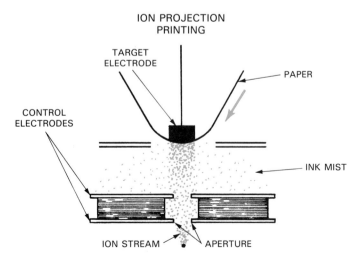

ION PROJECTION PRINTING

Fig. 27-69. Note how ion projection can be used to deposit image on substrate. (Mead)

Ink jet printing

The *ink jet printing* process is an important technological advance in placing images on a substrate using impactless principles. The images are formed by microscopic drops of ink that are electrically charged or left neutral. The droplets form images on the substrate.

Some of the systems use a single jet while others use multiple jets. Ink jet printing has a wide variety of applications. Several of the systems will be briefly explained.

One of the companies that has developed a widely used ink jet process uses the name Videojet. The schematic of this system is shown in Fig. 27-70.

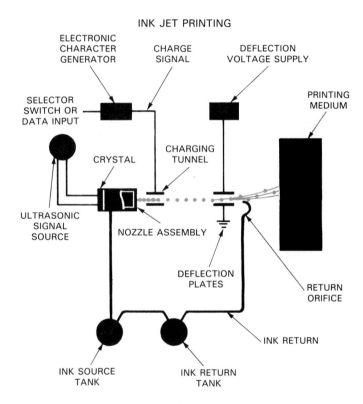

INK JET PRINTING

Fig. 27-70. Diagram shows principle of ink jet printing. (A.B. Dick Co.)

Most of the conventional printing methods are intended to be used for printing the same images over and over again. The ink jet principle is also applicable to the variable information concept. This means it is capable of printing personalized computer letters or individual address labels. The devices are capable of being mounted on web presses or assembly packaging lines.

Coding is a very practical application. An example would be placing a date code on eggs or the identification symbol on medical products. As the product moves past the printing head, the ink droplets are selected or rejected by the force of an electrical charge, Fig. 27-71. The ink droplets that are rejected are recycled by deflection plates and used again.

Inks must be specially formulated for the ink jet process. As the nozzle is very small, the ink must have low viscosity and have properties which will not clog the opening.

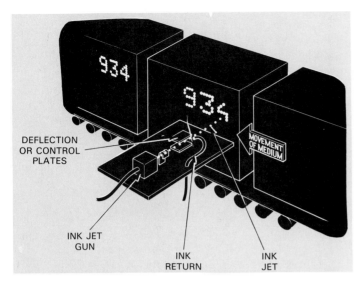

Fig. 27-71. Ink jet head is printing images on packed products. Ink jet is ideal for this type application. (A.B. Dick)

Not only the ink, but the surface materials, will determine the degree of acceptability of the final image.

Another trade name for ink jets is DIJIT (Direct Imaging by Jet Ink Transfer). The single jet is shown in Fig. 27-72. Fig. 27-73 illustrates the use of the print

The drying qualities of the ink are also a major factor of consideration. Basically, the penetration of the ink is the drying means, but evaporation is also possible. Rapid drying is essential.

The inks are on the alkaline side of the pH scale. The droplets have a tendency to splatter as they strike the surface. If this is excessive, the edges of images become fuzzy. A highly fibrous surface will also cause the images to be fuzzy. Not only the ink, but the surface materials, will determine the degree of acceptability of the final image.

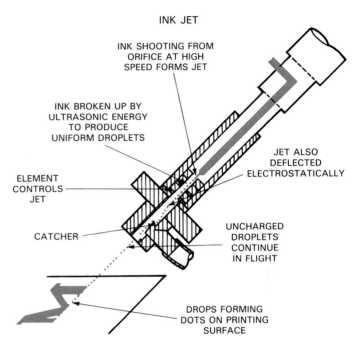

Fig. 27-72. This is another type of ink jet printing. Note its similarities and differences from the ink jet printing just illustrated. (Mead Paper)

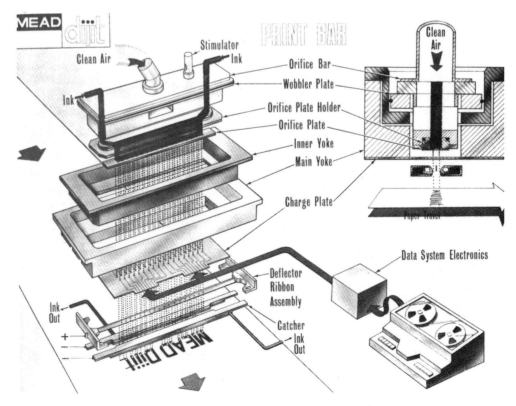

Fig. 27-73. This ink jet process uses a printing bar instead of a single ink jet stream. (Mead Paper)

bar. The ink droplets that are not charged strike the surface and create the image while the charged ink droplets are deflected and return for reuse. The number of jets per inch is one hundred and they operate at a very high rate of speed.

A drum printer can also have as many as four or five jets. The resolution of this system is much higher since up to 280 dots per inch are possible with the jet array.

The main features of DIJIT are:

1. It is programmable and uses computer information to produce individualized communications.
2. It is incredibly fast and generates over 48,000 characters per second or 45,000 lines of text per minute.
3. It employes digital fonts and gives flexibility to type design selection.

Is ink jet printing capable of becoming a major process as presently associated with planography, gravure, relief, and screen processes? What is the fastest process? A comparison is found in Fig. 27-74 of impactless printing systems and a few selected conventional printing systems. Potential applications for ink jet printing seem almost limitless.

KNOW THESE TERMS

Screen printing, Serigraphy, Mitography, Silk screen, Stencil printing, Squeegee, Frame, Stencil, Fabric, Filament, Multifilament, Monofilament, Mesh count, Sawtooth, Fabric strength, Plain weave, Taffeta weave, Gauze weave, Twill weave, Weft, Warp, Open area, Cell size, Silk, Organdy, Polyester, Nylon, Metallized polyester, Metal mesh, Mechanical clamp, Print area, Off contact distance, Fabric tension, Staples, Cord and groove, Adhesive, Cell distortion, Tensionmeter, Relax time, Fabric treatment, Degreasing, Mechanical treatment, Chemical treatment, Knife-cut stencils, Water soluble stencils, Lacquer soluble stencils, Burned edges, Photographic stencils, Indirect stencil, Mesh bridging, Direct stencil, Pinholes, Reclaiming solution, Direct-indirect stencils, Photographic stencils, Screen inks, Screen solvents, Thinners, Viscosity, Retarders, Washup solvents, Durometer, Conduction, Convection, Radiation, Screen printing presses, Sublimation heat transfer, Impactless printing, Thermal printing. Magnetic printing. Electrostatic printing, Electrophotographic printing, Ion projection printing, Ink jet printing.

REVIEW QUESTIONS—CHAPTER 27

1. What are some other names for screen printing?
2. Screen printing is no longer used in today's graphic communication industry. True or false?
3. In your own words, how do you do screen printing?
4. List the five elements needed for screen printing.
5. This type mesh is used for printing heated inks or when the ultimate of dimensional stability is needed.
   a. Organdy.
   b. Nylon.
   c. Polyester.
   d. Metal mesh.
6. How do most aluminum frames hold the fabric?
7. This is the least desirable way of holding fabric on a wooden frame.
   a. Staples.
   b. Adhesive.
   c. Mechanical clamp.
   d. Cord and groove.
8. What are two ways of finding fabric tension?
9. Chemical treatment alters the _____ characteristics of the fabric and mechanical treatment changes the _____ _____ of the fabric.
10. Explain the use of five types of stencils.
11. _____ are caused by dust and other airborne contaminants on the stencil.
12. Screen printing inks are the same as lithographic inks. True or false?
13. _____ are solvents added to screen ink to change only the ink's viscosity.
14. _____ are solvents added to screen ink to alter viscosity and to slow drying time.
15. In your own words, explain the following printing processes: Sublimation heat transfer, Thermal printing, Magnetic printing, Electrostatic printing, Ion projection printing, Ink jet printing.

SUGGESTED ACTIVITIES

1. Visit a screen printing facility and identify the type of screens and ink used. Why was this ink used to print on the specified stock?
2. Print a two-color bumper sticker or T-shirt using the screen process. The bumper sticker or T-shirt should publicize your school or a student organization.

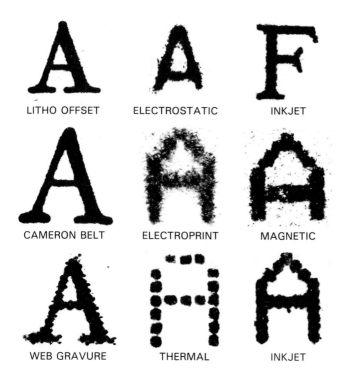

Fig. 27-74. These are images printed using conventional and unconventional printing methods. Note differences in quality.

LITHO OFFSET   ELECTROSTATIC   INKJET

CAMERON BELT   ELECTROPRINT   MAGNETIC

WEB GRAVURE   THERMAL   INKJET

This is a common use for inkjet printing. Inkjet printhead is being used to label boxes as they come off of production line. Speed and rapid change of output makes injet ideal for this application. (Diagraph Corporation)

The characteristics of the substrate can make or break a print job. The substrate, usually paper, must be selected carefully. This large web press will consume a tremendous amount of stock. Improper substrate selection could be a costly mistake!   (Rand McNally)

Chapter 28

SUBSTRATES

After studying this chapter, you will be able to:
- Trace some of the historical highlights of papermaking.
- Explain how paper is manufactured.
- Identify the basic characteristics of paper.
- Explain the basic size and weight of paper.
- Identify the common sizes and types of envelopes used for most printing materials.
- Describe basic paper types or classifications.
- Summarize the characteristics of plastic substrates.

Substrates include any material used for printing. Although paper is the most common substrate, plastic, metal, wood, and other substances can also be printed on and classified as substrates.

Matching the substrate to the application or job is very critical. For example, the highest quality layout, plate, ink, and printing technique will be wasted if low quality paper is used to print the job. You do NOT want to use expensive stock to print a newspaper or rough sandpaper to print decorative toilet paper. The substrate must be matched to the requirements of the job.

This chapter will add to the information you acquired in previous chapters. It will explain the different classifications of substrates and how their characteristics can affect printing. Knowing something about paper is essential for salespeople, designers, strippers, press operators, as well as finishing and binding personnel. Misuse is very costly because of the amount of paper consumed on today's presses.

PAPERMAKING HISTORY

For many years, paper was made by hand. Most of today's paper is manufactured using modern machine technology, although some paper is still made by hand.

The use of hand-made papers is usually limited to special applications. The science of *formulary* (percent of each substance used to make paper) is very important to the makers of these special papers.

Some of the historical highlights of papermaking are:
1. 105 A.D.—Ts'ai Lun invents paper. He is a Chinese official in the Court of HoTi, Emperor of Cathay. He used the bark of the mulberry tree and mixed it with linen and hemp to make a crude form of paper.
2. 500 A.D.—Mayans invent a paper using fig tree bark.
3. 751 A.D.—Muslims capture Chinese paper mill at Samarkand. The process spreads to European countries.
4. 1400 A.D.—Papermaking by hand flourishes.
5. 1690 A.D.—First paper mill is built in America, near Philadelphia by William Rittenhouse and William Bradford.
6. 1799 A.D.—The first machine to produce paper using an endless wire screen is invented. The machine was patented by Nicholas Louis Robert and the Fourdrinier brothers in England. It was given the name Fourdrinier machine.

The *Fourdrinier machine* is still used today to make most of the paper in the United States. The mechanical principles of the original paper machine have remained practically unchanged. Other inventions have occurred, but many are simply refinements.

MAKING PAPER

Since *cellulose* (wood) fibers are used to make paper, various kinds of trees are used to make different qualities of paper. Typical kinds are: pine, fir, spruce, aspen, beech, birch, maple, and oak. The fibers from the various sources vary in length and their selection determines the strength and other characteristics of the paper.

The process of making paper, Fig. 28-1, involves fastening the fibers together in sheet form. This process is similar for all kinds of paper.

Chipping

Logs are cut to uniform length, debarked, and sent to the chipper or grinder, Fig. 28-2. The *chipper* reduces the logs into chips that are approximately 3/8 to 3/4 inch in size. Very often the chips are stored until needed, Fig. 28-3.

Making pulp

The cooking process of the chips takes place in the digester. After the chips have been screened for size, they are placed in the *digester* which is a huge cooking kettle.

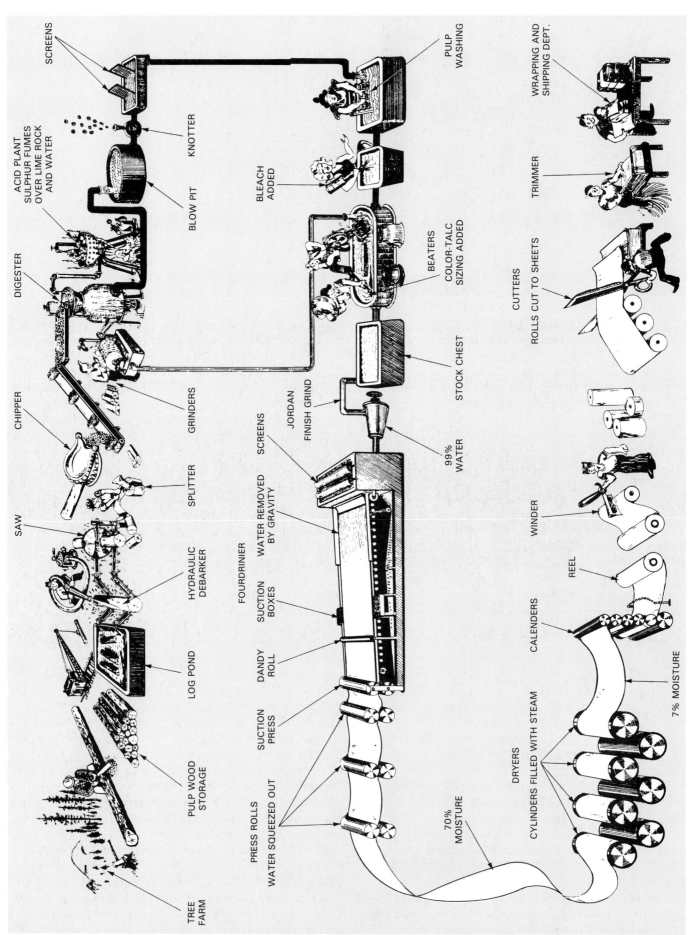

SCREENS

ACID PLANT
SULPHUR FUMES
OVER LIME ROCK
AND WATER

PULP
WASHING

KNOTTER

BLOW PIT

BLEACH ADDED

DIGESTER

BEATERS

COLOR-TALC
SIZING ADDED

GRINDERS

JORDAN
FINISH GRIND

STOCK CHEST

CHIPPER

SCREENS

99%
WATER

SPLITTER

WATER REMOVED
BY GRAVITY

SAW

FOURDRINIER

HYDRAULIC
DEBARKER

SUCTION
BOXES

LOG POND

DANDY
ROLL

PULP WOOD
STORAGE

SUCTION
PRESS

PRESS ROLLS
WATER SQUEEZED OUT

70%
MOISTURE

TREE
FARM

DRYERS

CYLINDERS FILLED WITH STEAM

CALENDERS

REEL

WINDER

7% MOISTURE

CUTTERS
ROLLS CUT TO SHEETS

TRIMMER

WRAPPING AND
SHIPPING DEPT.

Fig. 28-1. Study major steps of papermaking process.

Fig. 28-2. This huge machine rotates logs inside toothed chamber to remove bark. (International Paper Co.)

Fig. 28-3. Chipper is reducing large log into tiny bits of wood. (International Paper Co.)

Sizing and fillers

Sizing is added to the pulp to make the paper more resistant to moisture. *Rosin* is a common material used as a sizing. *Alum* is also added as a binding agent for individual fibers.

Fillers are needed to improve opacity and brightness as well as to improve the smoothness of the paper. Two common fillers are clay and titanium dioxide. *Filler additives* are also needed to improve ink receptivity and other properties.

Dyes and pigments

Dyes and *pigments* are added to the furnish to give a variety of colored substrates. Bleaching is done to make the pulp white, Fig. 28-4. All of these ingredients are mixed in vats, called *pulpers*. The pulp goes through a final beating and refining stage and is then pumped to a stock chest.

Fig. 28-4. Here wood pulp has been bleached to whiten it. (International Paper Co.)

Powerful chemicals are placed in the digester and the digester is sealed. Steam pressure is then turned on. After a period of about five to eight hours, the cellulose fibers, which look like soda straws, are free from the binding material, called *lignin*. This is known as a *chemical process* of making pulp.

The contents are next blown into a pit that thoroughly washes the "cooking liquor" (chemicals) from the pulp fibers.

The *groundwood process* uses grinding wheels to reduce the logs to fiber; it is a *mechanical means* of making pulp. This kind of pulp has high opacity but relatively low strength.

Pulp is basic to a sheet of paper, but the sheet's properties must vary based on its intended use. In papermaking terms, the pulp ingredients are known as the *"furnish."*

Removing water

At this point, the Jordan mixes the solution so that 95-99 percent of the solution is water. The solution is then pumped into the headbox of the papermaking machine.

Not all papermaking machines have the batch arrangement where individual solutions are mixed and then pumped to the headbox. Many are continuous to create a higher speed method of making paper.

The furnish is then evenly dispersed on the Fourdrinier wire, Fig. 28-5. This is known as the "wet end" of the machine. The wire is an endless screen. As the screen travels, it vibrates to line up the fibers in the direction of travel.

Water is removed as it travels the length of the wire screen, Fig. 28-6. Gravity and suction removed about 35% of the

Fig. 28-5. This shows the Fourdrinier wire section of the paper-making process. (Nekoosa Papers Inc.)

Fig. 28-6. Wet paper fibers ride on endless wire screen so water can drain off. Paper fiber is moving toward dryers. (International Paper Co.)

water. The furnish still has enough strength to leave the screen. Then it enters the second section of the machine known as the *press section* which removes more water.

Next, the paper enters the dryers. The *dryer section* is made up of large temperature controlled rollers. This is a very critical operation that removes more moisture.

Calendering

At some stage of the drying process, sizing is often applied. Then, the paper must be calendered. *Calendering* is the process of flattening and smoothing the paper by passing the paper between a series of polished rollers. Fig. 28-7 shows how calendering is done.

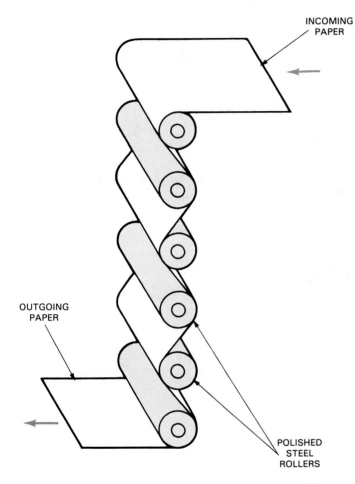

Fig. 28-7. Calender rolls are used to smooth and polish paper surface.

Watermarking

Some papers have a *watermark* which denotes quality paper and usually the manufacturer, Fig. 28-8. The watermark can be seen but not felt. The symbols or images are created by rearranging the fibers with a *dandy roll,* Fig. 28-9.

Rolling up paper

The paper is wound as a roll and is not trimmed, Fig. 28-10. The next step is to rewind the paper. Some rolls are slit and cut into lengths to make flat packages of paper, Fig. 28-11. Others remain as rolls.

PAPER TYPES

There are many types of paper. Some of these are bond, text, newsprint, mimeograph, index, cover, ledger, and offset papers. It is important that you have a general understanding of the characteristics and applications for each paper type.

Coated and uncoated paper

Coated paper is a broad classification of paper that has a mineral substance applied to it. Clay, stain white, and

Fig. 28-8. Here you can see watermark that identifies paper.

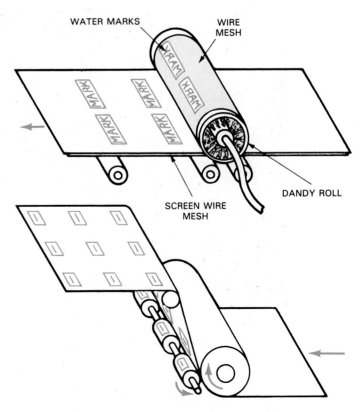

Fig. 28-9. Dandy roll is used to place watermark on paper. Watermark image is simply rearrangement of paper fibers. (J.J. Plank Corp.)

Fig. 28-10. After leaving the dryers, the paper is wound on huge rollers. (Nekoosa Papers Inc.)

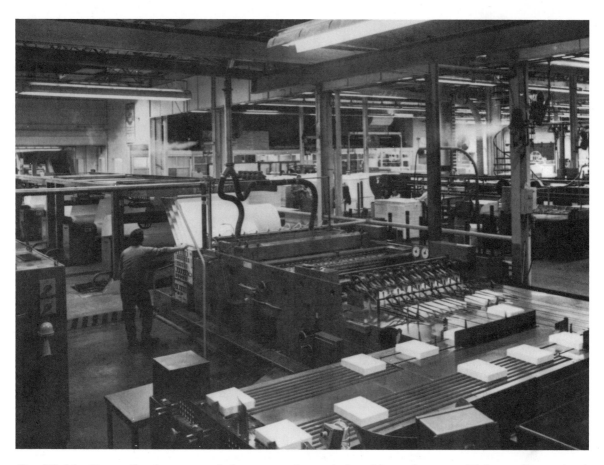

Fig. 28-11. Here rolls of paper are being cut to size and placed in packages. (Nekoosa Papers Inc.)

other substances can be used to produce coated paper. Coated paper typically has a smoother, stronger surface than uncoated paper. It is more expensive than uncoated paper and will produce better image reproduction quality.

Uncoated paper, as implied, does NOT have a mineral layer applied over its surface. It is generally a less expensive paper and its image will generally not be as good as coated stock.

Bond paper

Bond paper refers to a broad classification of quality paper with a wide variety of uses. It will have good strength, good ink receptivity, and should be easy to erase.

One type of bond paper is made from cotton fiber or rag fiber. Another bond paper is made from chemical wood pulps. Rag bond is the most expensive. They have an even, hard finish on both sides. Rag bonds often have a watermark, as is found on typewriter bonds.

Bond is used for flyers, typing paper, business forms, letterheads, stationary, and many other products.

Offset paper

Offset paper is designed specifically to be used on offset printing presses. It will have good opacity, rapid ink absorption, and permanence. Offset papers can be coated or uncoated. They are used for a wide variety of products: books, form letters, magazines, manuals, advertisements, etc.

Offset paper is sometimes called *book paper* because both have similar properties and construction methods. Book and offset papers are made from several different materials: chemical wood pulp, mechanical wood pulp, reclaimed newspapers, and even straw. Frequently, two or more of these raw materials are combined to make offset paper.

Impregnated offset paper receives a mineral film to smooth and strengthen the surface for better image reproduction. This is sometimes called *pigmentized offset paper.*

Text paper is an expensive grade of offset or book paper. It can be functional and beautiful, depending upon its surface smoothness. Smoother text papers are for accurate reproduction of halftones. Rougher or "turkish towel" surfaces are for special applications when halftone reproduction quality is not important.

Duplicator paper

Duplicator paper, as implied, is paper designed to be used in a copying machine. It can be used with mimeograph machines, spirit duplicating machines, and other types of office duplicating equipment. Duplicator paper is comparatively inexpensive and provides a cheap way of making copies of an original. See Fig. 28-12.

Duplicator paper should never be used in presses. Its surface strength and other characteristics are not suited for being run through a printing press.

Cover paper

Cover paper is commonly used for covers of books, booklets, catalogs, brochures, manuals, and similar publications. It is a thick or heavy paper, typically 85 pound.

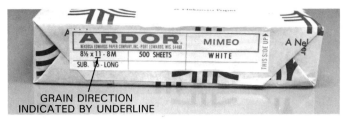

GRAIN DIRECTION
INDICATED BY UNDERLINE

Fig. 28-12. Note identification information given on this package of paper. Underlined dimension shows direction of paper grain.

Sometimes, two layers of cover paper are bonded together to produce double thickness. When pasted together, it can be sold by caliper or thickness.

Ledger paper

Ledger paper, also called *record paper,* has a smooth, matte finish that resists erasing. It will accept pen writing easily, is strong, and very durable. Ledger paper is frequently used for accounting notepads, bookkeeping forms, business ledger sheets, financial statement forms, etc.

Index paper

Index paper is a thick, stiff paper, frequently with two or more plies pasted together. It has a hard, smooth surface for easy writing or typing. Index stock can be coated or uncoated. Since its most common use is index cards, index paper must be sturdy enough to withstand frequent handling. It is also used for post cards and other similar applications. Bristol is similar to index paper.

Newsprint paper

Newsprint paper is one of the lowest quality or grades of paper used as a printing substrate. It is made by the groundwood or mechanical method of paper making. Newsprint has very short fibers which makes the paper fold easily in either direction. When new, it has a grayish color but it will turn yellow and become brittle with age. Since newsprint absorbs ink readily, a drying system is often not needed on the press.

Recycled paper

Recycled paper is made from old or used paper products. There are different grades of recycled paper. High grades can be made into quality printing paper. Low grades can be made into newsprint, cartons, and other products.

The recycled paper arena is constantly changing. Guidelines relating to the manufacturing of recycled paper are continually being reviewed by the Environmental Protection Agency (EPA). The trend is to increase the recycled content in printing and writing papers.

The term waste paper changed to recovered paper, but the American Forest and Paper Association (AFPA) is using the term "postconsumer/processed recovered fiber," which certainly expands on the traditional definition. Increasing total recycled paper content seems to be the major objective.

Many states have established guidelines that specify the required amount of recycled paper content for printing and writing papers. This has had a profound impact on the paper and recycling industries.

More and more paper is being recovered and mixed with other fibers and used as recycled paper. Mills have indicated various percentages of postconsumer recycled fibers in the finished product.

PAPER APPLICATIONS

Some papers are very adaptable to several applications, while others are very limited. The next section will briefly discuss the types of paper that are acceptable for different printing processes and applications.

Paper for gravure

Generally, gravure produced newsprint will contain mineral fillers and a calendered surface. Many mail order catalogs are a good example of this type of stock.

When higher quality is desired, the paper also uses mineral filler but with a greater percentage of the chemical pulp with short fibers.

The surfaces of the paper can be relatively softer since the gravure ink is not tacky. This eliminates the problem of picking fibers from the surface of the paper.

Coated surfaces are now very evident in gravure. The compressibility of the paper is important as the gravure cells must make contact with the paper surface.

Since packaging is also involved with the gravure process, the surface must be excellent and the stock must have dimensional stability. The thickness must also be controlled. The moisture content is another major factor to be considered with gravure.

Satisfactory printing of the stock and its reaction to the process is critical to quality and high production speeds required of gravure.

Paper for offset lithography

In offset lithography, one of the primary paper considerations must be the limitation of fuzz, lint, or dust. A wide variety of paper can be printed by the planographic process, but they must have sufficient fiber bonding strength to prevent the pulling of fibers from the stock. Because of the surface contact and the tackiness of the ink, special coatings are normally placed on the paper.

Moisture is another consideration since it comes in contact with the surface. The paper surface cannot be weakened by moisture so that fibers pick off with each successive impression.

Surface irregularity is not critical since the blanket is resilient and should return to its original shape after many impressions, even if the paper has an irregular surface. Of course, limitations do exist.

When in doubt, seek advice from a reputable firm. Paper has been developed to cover a wide range of uses.

Paper for letterpress

The relief process uses a large amount of newsprint but a great many paper grades exist for the relief process.

Rough stocks are NOT recommended because of the positive contact, high pressure required to make complete ink coverage. Very hard, smooth paper surfaces are excellent for high quality line and halftone work.

New types of inks and drying processes have forced the paper manufacturer to produce new types of paper to withstand additional punishment.

Coatings have greatly improved the surface but it has also forced a higher degree of surface levelness.

Paper for screen printing

Many kinds of paper can be used for screen printing. The end use is the most important factor to be considered. Will it be used outside as a bumper sticker or inside as a poster?

PAPER CHARACTERISTICS

Paper made by the machine method is generally considered to have grain. *Grain* is determined by the direction of the pulp fibers. It has great importance when feeding the paper through the press and during some of the finishing procedures.

Grain direction

Grain can be determined by looking at the end of a package and studying the dimensions. If one of the dimensions has a LINE under it, this dimension indicates that the grain runs parallel with this direction, Fig. 28-12.

Another way to find paper grain direction is to tear a sheet in one direction and then the other. Generally, the straightest tear is WITH the grain, Fig. 28-13.

Another means of telling the grain direction is to cut two strips from the paper, each one going different directions on the sheet. Lay them over a rod or straight surface. The one that is curved the most is ACROSS the grain.

Grain may also be found by dampening one side of the sheet. This will make the paper curl WITH the grain. Usually, a sheet of paper will fold easier and form a more even edge with the grain.

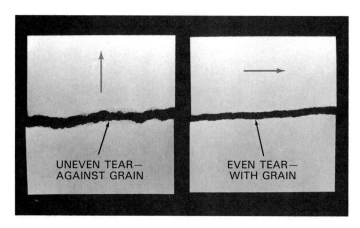

UNEVEN TEAR— AGAINST GRAIN

EVEN TEAR— WITH GRAIN

Fig. 28-13. An easy way to tell paper grain direction is to tear two sheets different ways. Straightest tear would be with-the-grain.

When binding folded paper, the grain should be WITH the binding edge so the fibers will not have a tendency to break.

In most cases, the sheets are fed through a press with the grain parallel to the cylinder of the offset press. This is commonly referred to as *grain long* when ordering stock.

Paper flatness

Paper flatness refers to how well the paper will remain straight or unwarped. The flatness of the paper is a basic requirement if the stock is to feed through a sheet-fed press without problems.

If the paper has wavy edges, the edges have a greater amount of moisture than the inside of the sheet, Fig. 28-14. Sometimes, the opposite occurs and the result is tight edges and the sheet will curl up or down.

Relative humidity and paper moisture are very important to the operation of the press. Keeping the packages of paper closed until needed will help prevent trouble.

Paper must also be square and free of dust, lint, and dirt. Paper handling must be closely supervised.

Paper size and weight

All paper has a *basic size* and dimension for length and width. The basic size is not the same for all kinds of papers. Some examples are given in Fig. 28-15.

The categories—book, writing, cover, index, Bristol, and newsprint are commonly called the kinds or *grades of paper*. Each has special characteristics and common uses. How you intend to use them will determine what kind you will buy. The printer should know about paper but a reliable paper salesperson can be a great help.

The *basis weight* is based on the weight of one ream of stock of its basic size. A *ream* is generally considered to be 500 sheets. In a few cases, 480 sheets is considered a ream.

Usually paper is referred to in its ream weight, such as 20 lb. bond or 70 lb. book. Twenty-pound bond means that 500 sheets of 17 x 22 in. writing paper will weigh 20 lb.

If an "M" appears after the weight, it means that the weight refers to 1000 sheets. An example is: 25 x 38 – 140M. This means that 1000 sheets of 25 x 38 in. book paper will weigh 140 lb., Fig. 28-16.

When the *substance weight* is given, it is the actual weight of the ream. The *equivalent weight* is the weight of one ream (500 sheets) of another size, larger or smaller than the basic size.

Papers have many basic sizes and many basic weights. This indicates that the thickness of the stock can vary for each ream based on its substance weight.

If a need arises to find the equivalent weight of paper, use the following formula.

$$\frac{\text{Length x width of sheets x basis weight}}{\text{Length x width of basis size}} = \text{equivalent weight}$$

An example is:
What is the weight of a 32 pound ledger paper size 28 x 34 inch?

$$\frac{952 \times 32}{374} = 81.4 \text{ equivalent weight}$$

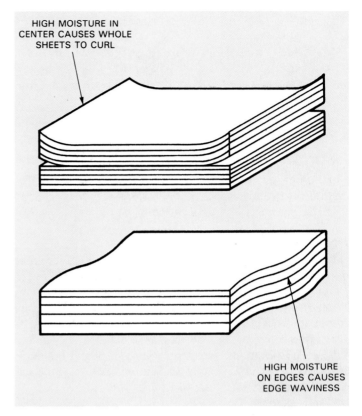

Fig. 28-14. *High moisture content can make paper warp or become wavy.*

KIND OF PAPER	SQUARE INCHES	BASIC SIZE
Bond, Ledger, Writing	374	17 x 22
Cover	520	20 x 26
Newsprint	864	24 x 36
Book, Offset, Text	950	25 x 38
Index, Bristols	778	25½ x 30½

Fig. 28-15. *These are some common types of paper and their possible sizes.*

If a need exists to find the weight of a number of sheets, use the following formula:

$$\frac{\text{Weight of 1000 sheets x number of sheets}}{1000} = \text{total weight}$$

An example is:
What is the weight of 1475 sheets of 17 x 22 in.-56M basis, 28-pound stock?

$$\frac{45M \times 1475}{1000} = 82.6 \text{ pounds or the 1475 sheets weigh } 82.6 \text{ pounds.}$$

If the need exists to figure basis weight, use the following formula when the sheet size and ream weight are known.

$$\frac{\text{length x width of basic sheet x ream weight}}{\text{Length x width of sheet}} = \text{basic weight}$$

An example is: What is the basis weight of a ream of book

TYPICAL WEIGHTS (1000 SHEETS) AND SIZES AVAILABLE									
BOOK	25 x 38	60	70	80	90	100	120	140	160, ETC.
WRITING	17 x 22	26	32	40	48	56	64, ETC.		
INDEX BRISTOL	25½ x 30½	117	144	182	222	286			
COVER	20 x 26	100	120	130	160	180, ETC.			

Fig. 28-16. Here are some typical weights of paper for common sizes.

paper with a sheet size of 23 x 29 inch, weighing 56 pounds-per-ream?

$$\frac{25 \times 38 \times 56}{23 \times 29} = \frac{53200}{667} = \text{80-pound basis weight}$$

Looking at four of the commonly used types of paper, we find that bond has a basic size of 17 x 22 inches and it might weigh 16 or 20 pounds. These are known as 16 or 20-pound papers, but 16-pound bond is thinner than 20-pound stock.

The basic size of 25 x 38 inch is associated with book paper. The substance weight of book is two and one-half times that of the weight of bond and it has two and one-half times the surface area of bond.

Cover, as the name implies, is used to cover booklets and its basic size is 20 x 26 inches. It is a very durable stock and has many textures.

Index stock has a basic size of 25 1/2 x 30 1/2 inches. It is a heavier stock often labeled and identified by *plies*. One-ply equals 90-pound substance while 110-pound stock is two-ply and 140-pound is listed as three-ply.

Paper in rolls

The length or weight of paper in rolls can be figured by applying the factor shown in Fig. 28-17 and using the appropriate formula.

The length of paper in a roll of known width and net weight (not including wrapper and core) is computed using this formula:

$$\text{Length} = \frac{41.67 \times \text{roll weight} \times \text{Factor}}{\text{Roll width} \times \text{Basis weight}}$$

Example: How many feet of paper are in a 1000 lb. roll of 75 lb. offset 35″ wide?

$$\frac{41.67 \times 1000 \times 950}{35 \times 75} = 15,080 \text{ feet}$$

The approximate weight of rolls put up on 3″ I.D. cores can be computed as shown:

Weight = roll diameter $\times$ 2 $\times$ width $\times$ roll factor*

*Roll Factors:	Bond	.021
	Smooth Finish Offset	.022
	Vellum Finish Offset	.018
	C2S Web Offset	.032

Example 1: What is the approximate weight of a 34 1/2″ wide, 40″ diameter roll of coated web paper?

$$40 \times 40 \times 34 1/2 \times .032 = 1766 \text{ lb.}$$

Example 2: What is the approximate weight of a 17 1/2″ wide, 40″ diameter roll of vellum offset?

$$40 \times 40 \times 17 1/2 \times .018 = 504 \text{ lb.}$$

Sometimes, it is necessary to figure out how many pieces of paper can be cut out of a large sheet. A typical stock cutting sheet is shown in Fig. 28-18.

To figure the number of pieces-per-sheet, place the dimensioning piece under the dimension of the sheet and divide vertically and diagonally.

An example is as follows: Stock size is 25 x 38 inch while the finished size is 6 x 9 inch. The results would be that 16 can be cut out by the vertical method and 12 out of the diagonal method.

It is more economical to cut the short dimension of the piece out of the short dimension of the sheet. However, this is only true if it is satisfactory to have the grain run the long way on the piece.

If it would be necessary for the grain to run parallel to the six inch side of the piece, it would yield only twelve pieces.

Sometimes, it is possible that the trim can be used. To find out, utilize the same type of formula.

When purchasing stock, the paper suppliers have catalogs which give the basis weight, basic size, and cost. Quality of stock varies greatly, and the cost range corresponds to the quality.

With the more frequent use of webs, a greater variety of web stocks will become a need. Presently, there are comparatively few classifications of paper available for the web presses.

Metric paper sizes

Another measuring system is becoming a part of our industry. It is called the SI metric system. One area that we will be concerned with is paper size. The letters A and B will be used to designate a series. The sizes in each series are numbered from 0 to 8.

The basic "A" series, with the designation of 0, has an area of 1 square meter. This sheet is not square but has a proportion of 5:7.

Fig. 28-19 represents the "AO" series.

Once we have the one square meter, each smaller size is determined by halving the larger size, as seen in Fig. 28-20. The standard metric sizes of paper used today are found in Fig. 28-21.

The "B" series is divided the same as the "A" series. But the sizes are between the "A" series and are to be used for unusual situations.

PAPER COMPUTATION FACTORS		
CLASSIFICATION	BASIC SIZE	FACTOR
Business Papers	17 × 22	374
Book Papers	25 × 38	950
Cover Papers	20 × 26	520
Printing Bristols	22 1/2 × 28 1/2	641
Index Bristols	25 1/2 × 30 1/2	778
Tag, News, Conv.	24 × 36	864

Fig. 28-17. These factors are used to relate to the basic size when working paper math formula. They are the square inches of one sheet in its basic size. For example: the basic size of business paper (bonds) is 17 × 22, so 17 × 22 = 374. (Inter-City Paper Co.)

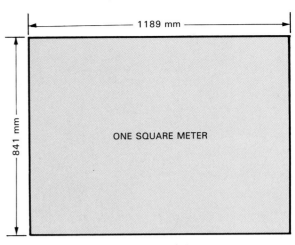

Fig. 28-19. This is a metric "AO" series size for paper. It is basis for metric paper sizes.

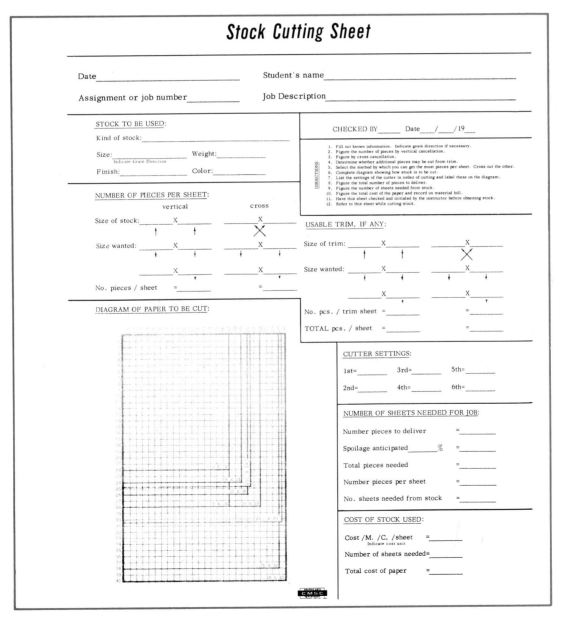

Fig. 28-18. This is a stock cutting sheet form. Note how it could be used to cut stock. (Central Missouri State University)

457

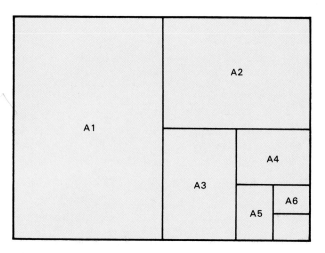

Fig. 28-20. Metric sizes are simply halves of larger sizes. Note alpha-numeric or letter-number designations.

DESIGNATION	mm	INDEX
A0	841 x 1189	33.11 x 46.81
A1	594 x 841	23.39 x 33.11
A2	420 x 594	16.54 x 23.39
A3	297 x 420	11.69 x 16.54
A4	210 x 297	8.27 x 11.69
A5	148 x 210	5.83 x 8.27
A6	105 x 148	4.13 x 5.83
A7	74 x 105	2.91 x 4.13
A8	52 x 74	2.05 x 2.91
B0	1000 x 1414	39.37 x 55.67
B1	707 x 1000	27.83 x 39.37
B2	500 x 707	19.68 x 27.83
B3	353 x 500	13.90 x 19.68
B4	250 x 353	9.84 x 13.90
B5	176 x 250	6.93 x 9.84
B6	125 x 176	4.92 x 6.93
B7	88 x 125	3.46 x 4.92
B8	62 x 88	2.44 x 3.46

Fig. 28-21. Note designations, size, and index for metric sizes sheets. Index is metric size in inches.

One advantage of the metric is that the proportion of any size in the series is always the same. Each smaller size is always half the larger size. The number represents the number of times a sheet can be folded to obtain that size.

PAPER COLOR

Paper is available in many colors, but paper color must be compatible with the color of ink. White paper is essential for full or four-color printing. It will reflect all colors of the spectrum while color paper does not. The color of the paper creates a process color value that is undesirable and the final results may not be what the customer expected. Therefore, a knowledge of paper color and the expected color of the final product is essential.

Paper smoothness

Smoothness or *texture* greatly affects *printability* or how well images will show fine detail. The degree of smoothness of a sheet varies with paper type. A smooth sheet requires

a very thin film of ink. This tends to provide for very sharp images. The opposite is true for rougher papers.

Paper strength

Paper strength is primarily determined by how well the INNER FIBERS are bonded together. For example, if a roll of paper cannot feed through a web press without breaking easily, it has low strength. This would be called the *tensile strength* of the paper.

Print or *pick strength* generally refers to how well the SURFACE of the paper is bonded together. A low print strength could allow bits of fiber to be lifted off of the paper surface by high tack inks. This could cause hickeys or specks to appear on the printed image. Coated paper normally has higher print strength than uncoated stock.

Paper brightness

Paper brightness is determined by how well the paper surface reflects light. Paper brightness affects the contrast of the printed image. A bright paper will make the colors, especially black, stand out more.

With today's transparent inks, brightness will also produce better color rendition. More light will reflect up through the ink layers to produce stronger colors.

Opacity

The *opacity* of paper determines whether you can see through the paper. It will also vary. An undesirable result of poor opacity would be *show-through*. The image from one side can be seen on the other side. This is very distracting to the reader. Look over the stock very carefully to make sure show-through will NOT occur. A high paper weight will help reduce opacity. Very thin papers will tend to produce low opacity.

EMBOSSING

Embossing is a process of pressing a shaped image into the paper or other substrate. The embossed image is raised or lowered below the normal paper surface. A simplified illustration of how an image can be embossed in paper is given in Fig. 28-22.

Basically, embossing requires a die and a counter. The *die* is the rigid metal form with the image shaped on it. The *counter* is similar, but it is an opposite of the die. The paper is crushed between the die and counter when being embossed. This stretches the paper to form the image shape.

Before embossing, the paper should be *conditioned* with moisture. The moisture will allow the paper to stretch without tearing its fibers. Sometimes, a heated die is used to aid the embossing process.

An embossed product is pictured in Fig. 28-23.

ENVELOPES

Envelopes come in many styles and sizes for many different applications. If an envelope is used for inter-office usage, there are no set standards. However, envelopes that

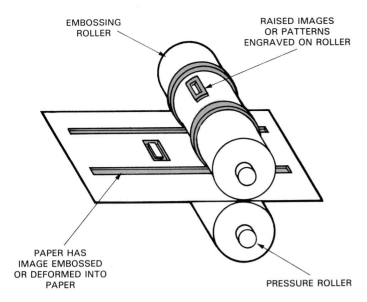

Fig. 28-22. Embossing forces a shape into the fibers of the paper or other substrate. One roller has the die and the other the counter.

Fig. 28-23. This is an embossed envelope. Note expensive or exotic appearance produced by embossing. (Ponté Engraving Co.)

are to be used for postal purposes have a minimum size of 3 1/2 x 5 inches. Also, any size over 6 1/8 x 11 1/2 inches or having a thickness more than one quarter inch is subject to additional postage fees.

Envelope styles

Common envelope styles are: commercial, baronial, booklet, and clasp. Examples of each are in Fig. 28-24.

The *commercial envelope* has many applications but the most common one is to send correspondence.

The *window envelope,* as the name implies, has an opening that allows the address to appear through the clear opening. This is a time saving and convenient feature.

The *baronial envelope* is designed to be used mostly for invitations, announcements, and greeting cards.

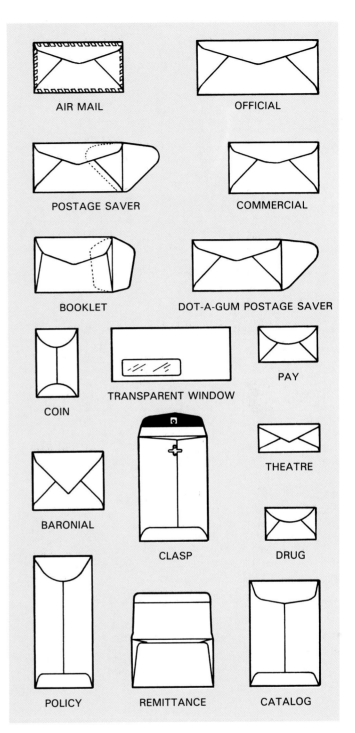

Fig. 28-24. These are typical envelope types. Study them. (Carpenter-Offutt Paper Co.)

The *booklet envelope* is commonly used to hold house publications and direct mail pieces. The opening is on the side.

The *clasp envelope* is used to mail bulky materials. The manner of fastening will vary, but it is very strong and can take abuse.

The *open end envelope* is also very sturdy and will take rough handling. Booklets and reports are typical pieces placed in this type envelope. Typical envelope sizes are given in Fig. 28-25.

OFFICE AND COMMERCIAL SIZE	
5	3 1/6 x 5 1/2
6 1/4	3 1/2 x 6
6 3/4	3 5/8 x 6 1/2
7	3 3/4 x 6 3/4
7 3/4	3 7/8 x 7 1/2
8 5/8	3 5/8 x 8 5/8
9	3 7/8 x 8 7/8
10	4 1/8 x 9 1/2
11	4 1/2 x 10 3/8
12	4 3/4 x 11
14	5 x 11 1/2
BARONIAL SIZE	
4	3 5/8 x 4 11/16
5	4 1/8 x 5 1/8
5 1/2	4 3/8 x 5 5/8
5 3/4	4 5/8 x 5 15/16
BOOKLET SIZE	
2 1/2	4 1/2 x 5 7/8
3	4 3/4 x 6 1/2
5	5 1/2 x 8 1/8
6	5 3/4 x 8 7/8
6 1/2	6 x 9
7	6 1/4 x 9 5/8
7 1/2	7 1/2 x 10 1/2
9	8 3/4 x 11 1/2
9 1/2	9 x 12
10	9 1/2 x 12 5/8
CLASP SIZE	
0	2 1/2 x 4 1/4
5	3 1/8 x 5 1/2
10	3 3/8 x 6
15	4 x 6 3/8
11	4 1/2 x 10 3/8
25	4 5/8 x 6 3/4
35	5 x 7 1/2
14	5 x 11 1/2
50	5 1/2 x 8 1/4
55	6 x 9
63	6 1/2 x 9 1/2
68	7 x 10
75	7 1/2 x 10 1/2
80	8 x II
83	8 1/2 x 11 1/2
87	9 3/4 x 11 1/4
90	9 x 12
93	9 1/2 x 12 1/2
94	9 1/4 x 14 1/2
95	10 x 12
97	10 x 13
98	10 x 15
105	11 1/2 x 14 1/2
110	12 x 15 1/2

Fig. 28-25. Note common envelope sizes.

Special envelope catalogs are available. Use them as a resource for obtaining more detailed information.

OTHER SUBSTRATES

Paper is not the only substrate used in the graphic communications industry. Metal and plastic are also used in some applications.

Printing on foil is very common in the packaging industry. It is done by several processes. Sometimes, the thin foil is laminated to the paper.

Plastic has many variations. Sometimes the plastic is a film. Other times it is a sturdy material that has good flexibility. Another type could be very stiff or rigid. The selected substrate usually determines the printing process to be used or the printing process could help determine the substrate.

Whenever a substrate is selected as a package for food, substrate, ink, etc., must meet the requirements that have been established by the Food and Drug Administration (FDA). Some inks and substrates could pose a possible health hazard if used improperly.

PLASTIC SUBSTRATES

Plastic substrates include many classifications of plastics used in printing. Plastic substrates are chemically blended from various petrochemical (petroleum or crude oil-based chemicals) and other compounds. Most plastic substrates come in both roll and sheet form. You should be familiar with their printing characteristics.

Polyester substrate

Polyester is one of the strongest plastic films used as a printing substrate. It has high clarity, toughness, durability, and dimensional stability. It must be treated for offset printing. Polyester substrates are used for decals, labels, product identification, and interior signs.

Lexan® polycarbonate film

Lexan® polycarbonate film is a substrate with a very high gloss, good dimensional stability, and good heat resistance. It has excellent light transmittance and low haze Lexan® polycarbonate film can be printed using offset without pretreatment. It is easily die cut and embossed. It is used for decals, name plates, membrane switch panels, overlays, and product identification. Lexan® is a registered trademark of the General Electric Company.

Rigid vinyl

A *rigid vinyl* substrate has good stability and is available in calendered gloss or a matte finish. It comes in white transluscent, white opaque, and standard opaque colors. Rigid vinyl is commonly used for identification cards or credit cards but is also used for shelf signs or labels, danglers, wall signs, and pocket calendars. Rigid vinyl is easily die cut and *thermoformed* (formed with heat and pressure) into shapes.

Copolyester

Copolyester is an extruded and dull finished plastic substrate. It has a high degree of dimensional stability, clarity, and formability. It is available in matte finish or transparent colors. It is a comparatively inexpensive plastic substrate. It is used for book report covers, overhead projector overlays, flip charts, etc.

High impact polystyrene

High impact polystyrene is a highly versatile and economical plastic substrate. It is offset printable and is available in natural or translucent and opaque colors. It is used for point of purchase display signs, toys, etc.

Cellulose acetate

Cellulose acetate is the original plastic film used as a printing substrate. It provides outstanding clarity but poor dimensional stability and poor tear resistance. Its softer surface permits receptivity of a wide variety of inks. Cellulose acetate is used in folders, bookjackets, audio visual transparencies, etc.

Clear oriented polyester

Clear oriented polyester is the cheapest plastic substrate. It tears and scratches easily but provides good printing clarity. It is used for short term display signs, labels, visual aids, and similar products.

Kimdura®

Kimdura® is a white opaque or translucent polypropylene film substrate. It serves as a "synthetic paper" that has been treated for offset printing. It is tough, durable, and can be folded repeatedly. Kimdura has good dimensional stability and provides a waterproof printing surface. It is used for posters, brochures, catalogs, children's books, outdoor maps, globes, menus, and instructional manuals. Kimdura® is a registered trademark of the Kimberly-Clark Corporation.

Reemay®

Reemay® is a spunbonded polyester that is acrylic coated on both sides. It has excellent UV resistance, a bright white color, and the feel of a fabric. It can be sewn and grommeted. Reemay® is used for indoor banners and other similar applications. Reemay® is a registered trademark of the E.I. DuPont Co.

Tyvek®

Tyvek® is a strong spunbond polyolefin plastic substrate. It has a smooth surface, good dimensional stability, good UV resistance, and excellent opacity. It is treated with an anti-static agent during production to aid sheet handling when printing. It is commonly used for tags, labels, maps, book coverings, etc. Tyvek® is a registered trademark of the E.I. DuPont Co.

KNOW THESE TERMS

Substrate, Formulary, Fourdrinier machine, Chipper, Digester, Lignin, Chemical process, Cooking liquor, Mechanical process, Groundwood process, Furnish, Sizing, Fillers, Dyes, Pigments, Pulpers, Calendering, Watermark, Dandyroll, Coated paper, Uncoated paper, Bond, Offset paper, Book paper, Impregnated offset paper, Text paper, Duplicator paper, Cover paper, Ledger paper, Index paper, Bristol, Newsprint, Recycled paper, Grain direction, Paper flatness, Paper size, Paper weight, Basis weight, Ream, Paper smoothness, Paper strength, Paper brightness, Opacity, Show-through, Embossing, Die, Counter, Commercial envelope, Window envelope, Baronial envelope, Booklet envelope, Polyester, Lexan®, Rigid vinyl, Copolyester, High impact polystyrene, Cellulose acetate, Clear oriented polyester, Kimdura®, Reemay®, Tyvek®.

REVIEW QUESTIONS — CHAPTER 28

1. List three common materials used as substrates for printing. *paper plastic wood*
2. What is the name of the most commonly used paper-making machine? *Fourdriner machine*
3. What is the most common source for cellulose fibers used in papermaking? *pine,fur,spruce trees*
4. The variety of paper used for offset-lithography is very limited. True or false? *False*
5. What types of stock are NOT recommended for the relief process? *Rough stock*
6. What characteristic is associated with machine-made papers? *grain*
7. How many sheets are usually in a ream of paper? *500*
8. How many sheets of 8 x 10 inch can be cut out of 17 x 22 inch sheet? *4*
9. What color paper is essential for true process color reproduction? *white*
10. List six common types of envelopes.
11. Pick or print _____ would be an important factor affecting hickeys or specks on the printed image.
12. The _____ of paper affects whether you can see through the paper and an undesirable problem called _____.
13. This is a process that presses a shape into the substrate.
    a. Watermarking.
    b. Calendering.
    c. Furnishing.
    d. Embossing.
14. Explain the characteristics of four types of plastic substrates.

SUGGESTED ACTIVITIES

1. Explore the possibility of making paper by hand.
2. Visit graphic communications facilities and notice how many different kinds of substrates are being used at the different presses.
3. Make a collection of the many substrates that have images transferred onto them. List the possible printing processes used for each.
4. Use a rubber stamp to print on different substrates. Note how paper smoothness, color, etc. affect the printed image.

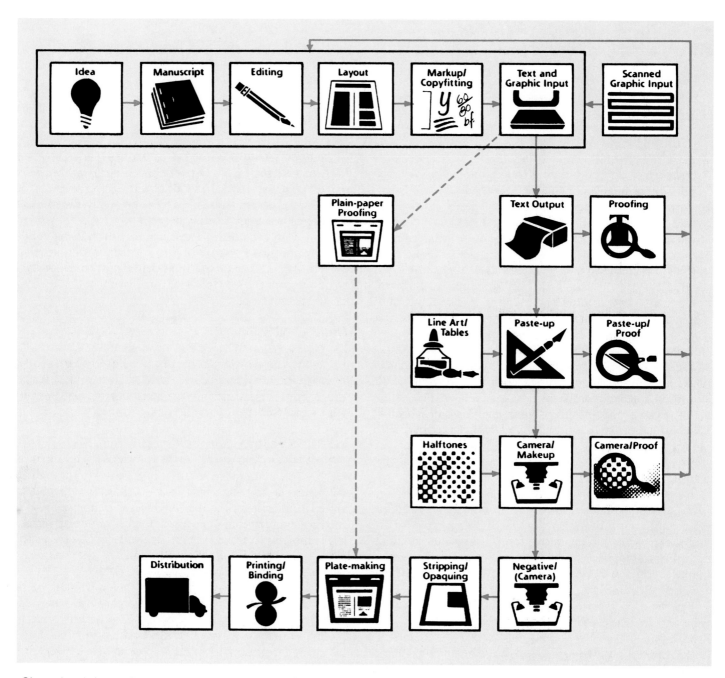

Chart shows steps that can be saved when using direct-to-press electronic technology as compared to conventional production cycle. Dotted lines show how direct-to-press cycle bypasses numerous tasks.   (Agfa)

Chapter 29

INK

After studying this chapter, you will be able to:
- Identify the characteristics of inks used for different printing processes.
- Summarize the various properties of ink.
- Mix and match ink.
- Explain how ink characteristics affect the printed product.
- Define commonly used terms relating to ink.

To make images visible on a substrate, a coating must be applied to the substrate. *Ink* is the most common coating used to place a printed image on a substrate.

Inks have many properties that can affect printing quality. Inks must flow properly, have the correct stickiness or tack, be permanent, dry properly, and have a workable consistency for the press rollers.

This chapter will discuss the characteristics of printing inks and summarize how they can affect the print job. This is an important chapter that will add to the knowledge you gained in previous chapters on substrates, presses, and other processes. Study carefully!

INK INGREDIENTS

Ink formulation refers to the amount and type of ingredients used in the printing ink. Ink formulation requires many substances. The main three ingredients of ink are: vehicle, pigment, and drier.

The *vehicle* is a binding agent that holds the ink together. The vehicle also acts as a carrier that holds the pigment. The vehicles are often solvent/resin or oil/resin combinations, but because of Environmental Protection Agency (EPA) regulations, many paste inks are soy-based to replace petrochemical oils. Compounds and additives help make inks rub-resistant or water resistant (litho inks) and reduce body tack. Oxidant agents, wetting agents, and anti-foaming agents may be added, as well.

The *pigment* is the color of the ink. A wide range of pigments is available. Pigments are opaque or transparent. They are used in a "dry" state to be ground into a vehicle or "flushed" (pre-dispersed in a vehicle). Dyes are also used as coloring agents, but used most often in flexographic ink.

The *drier* is needed to make the ink dry quickly. This is to prevent *setoff* where a printed page smears off onto the back of another sheet. The drier allows one sheet to be placed on top of another right after printing. Various devices or systems are used to assist in the drying effort. Infrared (IR) sensitivity is used to accelerate oxidation. Ultraviolet (UV) sensitivity assists in curing, which is also true of electron beam technology. Spray powders are sometimes dispersed over the surface of the printed sheet to eliminate direct contact.

INK PROPERTIES

The common properties of ink are color strength, body, length or elasticity, tack or stickiness, stability or thixotropy, and drying. It is important for you to comprehend each of these characteristics.

Color strength

Color strength is the ink's ability to cover the substrate. Strength may be needed so that you cannot see through an ink. This will make the image vivid, sharp, and give good coverage. Pigments or dyes are chosen to be compatible with the ink's base. Generally, weak colorants are not desirable chemically or economically; the colorant must be selected based on end use. Metallic, fluorescent, and pearl pigments are used for special effects.

A *transparent ink* would have less color strength. This type ink is desirable in some situations where you want something under the ink to show. It is commonly used in four-color printing so that all colors of the spectrum are produced by overprinting the four process colors. Look at Fig. 29-1.

Ink body

Ink body refers to the ink's consistency, thickness, or fluidity. Some inks are very stiff or thick while others are thinner or more fluid. This can have considerable affect on press operation.

Inks used in the relief printing or planographic process are very stiff but flow more freely after being *worked* (mixed) by the press rollers. Gravure inks are thinner so that

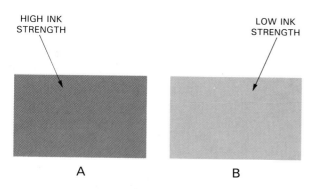

Fig. 29-1. Ink strength refers to how well ink will cover substrate. A — This image represents ink with high strength or opacity. B — This image represents ink with lower strength or opacity.

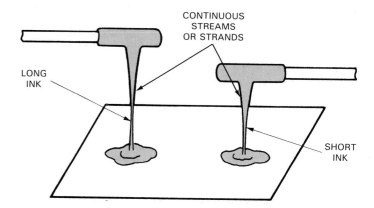

Fig. 29-2. A long ink will form longer filaments than short ink. Ink is placed on rod and then tapped on surface before lifting.

they can easily flow out of the microscopic ink wells in the gravure cylinder.

High ink body tends to thicken the deposit of ink on the substrate with lithography. A thinner ink would do the opposite. Faster (high-speed) presses use a softer body (more flow) ink, while slower presses use heavier body (less flow) ink. Ink must be formulated to the specific type of printing being done.

Ink stability (thixotropy)

Ink stability, also termed *thixotropy,* refers to how an ink tends to flow more freely after being worked. With relief, the press rollers work the ink by squeezing and depositing the ink on the press rollers before printing. The ink becomes more fluid as the rollers work the ink.

For this reason, many large presses have vibrators to work the ink in the fountain. This keeps a high stability ink more fluid while in the fountain. Lack of motion will allow the ink to become very stiff and not transfer properly.

The stirring or agitation of ink tends to break down the ink's internal cohesiveness. By agitating the ink in the fountain, it makes the ink flow more easily and distribute more evenly on the press rollers.

Good thixotropy helps keep the ink stable when not being worked. An extreme example, poor thixotropy or stability could cause the ink to drain or drip off the press rollers when the press stops.

Ink length

Ink length is the ink's ability to form a filament or strand of a different length. The filament can be long or short.

If the ink forms a *long filament,* it will have a tendency to fly out on a high speed press. *Long inks* flow more rapidly than short inks. One example, ink to be used to print on newsprint is considered to be long.

Short inks will have poor flow qualities and appear more like butter. A comparison is shown in Fig. 29-2.

Ink tack

Ink also has tack which is another very important property. In non-scientific terms, *tack* is the stickiness of ink. When ink leaves the fountain, it must split or have limited

tack. If ink did not split (too much tack) it could not be transferred from one roller to another, to the plate and blanket, or from the roller to a surface of the substrate.

The tack of an ink can be measured by an *inkometer.* It will check if the tack is too great for the surface strength of the paper. Too much tack can cause press problems. The surface of the paper could be ruptured to cause picking, splitting, or tearing. Look at Fig. 29-3.

Tack is a term generally used in planographic/relief printing, which employs paste inks. The second color down in "wet trap" may need a lower tack. On a four color press the ink sequence may need a lower tack as well.

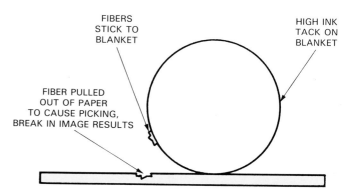

Fig. 29-3. Picking can result from ink tack not being matched to stock. High tack can pull off fibers of paper.

Ink drying

Important to any printed product is the ink's ability to dry. Some very common means of ink drying are: absorption, evaporation, oxidation, polymerization, and precipitation. These means of drying are illustrated in Fig. 29-4.

1. *Absorption drying ink,* also called *penetrating ink,* dries when the solvent is drawn into the paper. The ink does NOT dry hard but remains on the surface as a powder-like substance.

   Newspapers are a good example of inks that dry by absorption or penetration. When you rub your finger over the print, it will smear off as a black powder onto your hand.

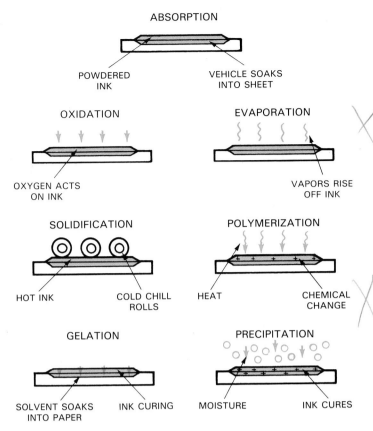

ABSORPTION

POWDERED INK | VEHICLE SOAKS INTO SHEET

OXIDATION | EVAPORATION

OXYGEN ACTS ON INK | VAPORS RISE OFF INK

SOLIDIFICATION | POLYMERIZATION

HOT INK | COLD CHILL ROLLS | HEAT | CHEMICAL CHANGE

GELATION | PRECIPITATION

SOLVENT SOAKS INTO PAPER | INK CURING | MOISTURE | INK CURES

Fig. 29-4. Note the many ways that ink can dry.

2. *Evaporation drying inks* dry as the solvent is evaporated into the surrounding air. This leaves a solid film or resin on the paper. The various printing methods require the use of different solvents for evaporation drying inks. This type ink is used where fast drying is important: flexography, gravure, web offset, etc. Fig. 29-4.

Solvent evaporative inks consist of resins, solvents, and additives. Specific types of solvent evaporative inks include poster inks, lacquers, textile dyes, and water-base inks.

3. *Oxidation drying inks* dry by absorbing oxygen out of the surrounding air. The oils in the ink absorb the oxygen in the air to make the ink solidify. Letterpress and offset printing commonly use oxidation type drying inks.

4. *Polymerization drying inks* dry by a chemical reaction which causes molecules in the ink to combine. Oxygen thickens the ink into a "gel" which allows the ink to be handled without smearing until full drying occurs. Polymerization ink can be used to print on metal.

Chemical reaction inks consist of resins, solvents, additives, and a drying oil catalyst. These inks dry and cure by evaporation of the solvent, and by oxidation. Specific types of ink include enamels and a variety of less common ink types, such as: vinyl, epoxy, and polyester.

5. *Precipitation drying inks,* also termed *moisture-set inks,* dry by reacting with water. Steam or water is sprayed on the ink after printing. This makes the ink set quickly. Glycol in the ink combines with the water and is absorbed into the paper.

Adhesion in ink is relative to the printing process. Relief and planographic inks provide best adhesion on porous substrates, while gravure and flexographic printing allows use of solvents and resins that readily adhere to nonporous substrates (such as foils, vinyl, and polyester).

UV curable ink

UV curable inks consist of resins, monomers, additives, and photoinitiators. These inks do NOT dry, but they cure. The distinction here is that with *curing,* no solvent is evaporated away. As ultraviolet light strikes the ink film, this creates a chemical reaction which converts all of the ink from a liquid to a solid. This chemical conversion is called polymerization.

Specific types of UV ink are available for paper, plastic sheets, plastic bottles, and other types of substrates.

Setoff

Matching ink to the substrate is very critical, and when properly considered, can save time and trouble. After the job has been printed, it is too late to find out that the ink does not dry quickly enough.

Sometimes, improper selection of ink or a drier can cause a setoff problem. Mentioned earlier, setoff is the transfer of ink from the printed side of one sheet to the back side of another sheet. This occurs when the paper is stacked at the delivery end of the press. Setoff is a very common problem and needs constant monitoring, Fig. 29-5.

Other ink related terms

Other ink related terms you should know include:
1. *Permanent* or *fast ink* maintains its color with exposure to sunlight. It will not easily fade and is suitable for posters, signs, and other similar applications.

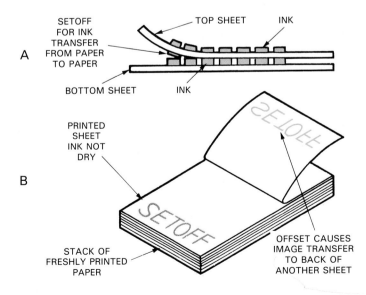

SETOFF FOR INK TRANSFER FROM PAPER TO PAPER

A

TOP SHEET | INK

BOTTOM SHEET | INK

PRINTED SHEET INK NOT DRY

B

STACK OF FRESHLY PRINTED PAPER

OFFSET CAUSES IMAGE TRANSFER TO BACK OF ANOTHER SHEET

Fig. 29-5. Setoff occurs when printed sheets are stacked on output of press. It is usually caused by improper drying of ink, but can also be caused by excessively thick ink film, paper stacked too high, improper substrate or ink combination. A—How setoff happens. B—Results of setoff problem.

2. *Resistant ink* is a very stable ink that can withstand exposure to forces that would fade other inks. It can tolerate sunlight, chemicals, heat, moisture, and gases without fading.

3. *Fugitive ink* will fade and lose its color after prolonged exposure to sunlight. It is useful for temporary signs and posters that are dated and will not be used for long time spans.

4. *Ink viscosity,* also called *body,* refers to how easily an ink will flow. High viscosity ink is thick and will resist flow. Low viscosity ink is more fluid and will flow more easily. Look at Fig. 29-6.

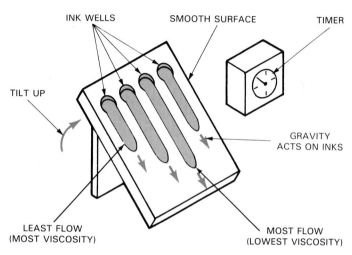

Fig. 29-6. Ink viscosity is the thickness or fluidity of the ink. Here is how to basically determine ink viscosity. Ink is placed in small wells on surface. Then surface is tilted upward so that ink flows out of wells. The ink with the most flow has the lowest viscosity and vice-versa. Flow could be timed to get accurate reading of viscosity.

5. *Lakes* are the main body colors of ink and are not very strong.

6. *Toners* are stronger ink colors that are very concentrated. Toners are almost pure pigment that is ground and mixed into an oil, usually linseed oil.

7. *Job black* refers to normal black ink used for a normal press run of average quality.

8. *Halftone black* is a higher quality black ink designed for reproducing fine detail in halftone screen images.

9. *Watercolors* are inks with a very flat or dull finish. They have a water base and do NOT contain varnish or oil base.

10. *Metallic inks* contain metal powders (aluminum, bronze, etc.) blended with an appropriate vehicle.

11. *Cleaning white* is used to wash a press when changing from a dark to a light color.

12. *Liquid tack reducer* will cut the ink's tack and body. It can be used to correct problems like picking and linting.

13. *Paste tack reducer* will cut tack but will not affect ink body.

14. *Gloss/matte finishes* are the visual effect of ink formulation. Gloss is achieved by the smoothness of the ink deposited on the substrate as well as the volume of dried ink retained on the substrate. The surface of the substrate also contributes to gloss. Matte ink is achieved by the addition of flattening agents added to the formula that creates the microscopically irregular surfaces for the eye to see it as matte.

15. *Slow-dry additive* can be used to lengthen ink drying time or skinning time in the fountain.

16. *Spray powder* can be placed on ink after printing to prevent setoff. A special press attachment sprays the powder onto the printed images.

17. An *ink mill* is a machine with steel rollers for crushing the ink ingredients into a fine substance.

18. *Non-toxic compounds,* to meet FDA standards, must be used when dried ink has direct contact with food or edible materials.

19. *Vegetable-base inks* are replacing petrochemical oils. Petrochemical solvents/oils emit VOCs (volatile organic compounds) which are considered a harmful chemical pollutant of our environment. Whenever printing ink is no longer useful in the plant and must be disposed of, it is considered "hazardous waste." Disposal must meet local, state, and federal regulations.

INK FORMULATION

Inks must be compatible with the printing process, therefore, special formulas are used to produce specific inks to match the process. To formulate the specific inks, highly skilled people are involved. This includes scientists, engineers, and technicians. The manufacturing of ink is a highly competitive business.

Different types of ink are needed for each process. The characteristics are determined by the plates, press units, and the type of substrate.

The types of ink used in producing images with the four basic printing processes will be briefly discussed.

Relief inks

Several types of ink are used in placing an image on a substrate by raised surfaces or by relief. Letterpress inks for covering the face of electrotypes, foundry type, and similar printing surfaces is generally quite tacky and viscous (thick). These inks usually dry by oxidation. However, the ink used to print on substrates, such as newsprint, dry by evaporation if heat is applied to the inked surface. Drying oils are used as vehicles to support the pigment. The pigment is often purchased in paste form.

Flexographic inks are fast drying fluid inks and are used to print on a variety of materials. The substrates range from paper to cloth and plastic to metal.

Alcohol and water are the two vehicles readily available for flexo inks. The *alcohol-based inks* dry by evaporation. The *water-based inks* dry by evaporation and/or absorption.

The inks are formulated for various types of presses and the type stock to be used for printing books, magazines, labels, packaging, or other types of commercial applications.

Typical kinds of ink are: rotary, quickset, moisture-set, water-washable, news, and job.

Job ink is found in many commercial letterpress facilities since it can be used on a wide variety of presses and papers. The quality of the ink varies with the type of images. Line work ink does NOT need to be as high in quality as a halftone ink.

Relying on a reputable ink representative is highly desirable in today's facilities. Compatability is a key word for good results. Science plays a very important role in today's quality operation.

Planographic (offset lithography) inks

The image area of offset lithography is neither raised nor recessed. It is a flat surface with an image area that accepts ink. The nonimage areas are moisture receptive. The knowledge of chemistry is important in the planographic process.

A basic requirement of the inks used in the offset lithography process is that they have high color strength. This is because the film of ink placed on the substrate has less thickness than the relief process.

The formulation of planographic ink requires that the vehicle be water resistant, although it is possible that the ink will accept about 20 to 25 percent moisture before it will emulsify. If emulsified, the surface no longer distributes the ink throughout the inking system of the press, Fig. 29-7. This means that balance between ink and moisture is essential to produce an acceptable product.

Another requirement is that the pigment does not bleed in water. None of the color should mix with the water.

Basically, planographic inks dry by oxidation. It is usually essential that the ink set very rapidly.

The inks used in planography vary greatly in formulation since many different types of substrates are used in sheet and web-fed presses. Because of the great variety, the vehicle must have different qualities. One being that they are oxidative. This requires drying oils as the vehicle while gloss type inks have very hard resins. Quick-set inks have hard soluble resins, hydrocarbon oils, and solvents. Some inks are of the penetrating type with soluble resins, drying and semi-drying oils, and varnishes.

UV-curing inks are evident in today's facilities and dry by using ultraviolet (UV) radiation. This system requires special attention from the standpoint of local, state, and federal regulations.

Web offset inks are also found as thermal curing besides being oxidative and penetrative. The ultraviolet curing technique is also used to cure this ink. Thermal curing inks have low amounts of solvents and require heat and a catalyst.

As stated earlier, the amount of moisture absorbed in the ink is critical. Too much moisture eliminates the needed tack of the ink to transfer from one roller to another. The ink must split at the nip point of the press rollers, Fig. 29-8.

Inks also are formulated and manufactured to work with Toray waterless printing plates. These DriLith™ offset inks are available in both sheetfed and heatset web formulations.

Litho ink problems

Two problems are often associated with planographic printing. The first is the fact that ink mixes with the moisture and forms an ink-in-water emulsion. The term used to express this problem is *tinting*. The nonimage area has a slight tint of ink on the printed sheet.

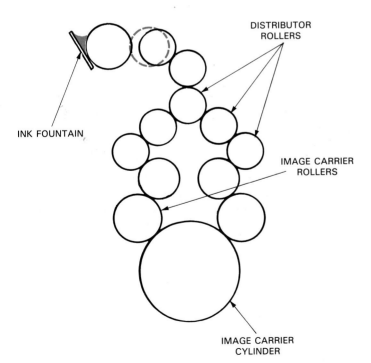

Fig. 29-7. With planographic or litho printing, ink formulation is critical. If the ink emulsifies, it will no longer distribute on press properly.

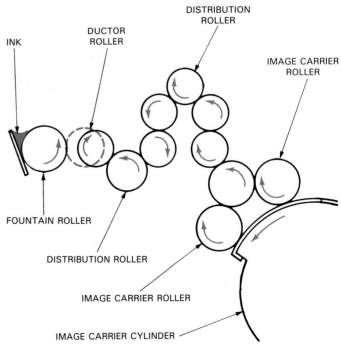

Fig. 29-8. The ink must split and transfer from one press roller to the next at nip points. This also makes ink formulation critical.

467

Scumming is the second problem that results when the nonimage area of the plate accepts ink and prints as background on the nonimage area. Abrasiveness of material and excessive acid are common faults that can make the plate lose its desensitization.

Intaglio (gravure) inks

The cells of gravure plate or cylinder are recessed. Ink must be taken or pulled from the cells and deposited on a substrate. Inking the cells is known as *flooding*. The *doctor blade* removes all of the ink from the surface of the nonimage area of the cylinder or plate.

The inks used for gravure process are very fluid and dry very rapidly after flowing out of the cells. The printing substrate must be capable of taking the ink out of the cells. Gravure ink dries mainly by evaporation.

> WARNING! Many of the inks are highly volatile and require special fire prevention precautions. Special ventilation and pollution problems require close compliance with local, state, and federal regulations.
>
> Drainage of the solvent must meet regulations; therefore, many facilities have implemented a solvent recover system.

Screen printing inks

Originally, screen printing used paint to produce the image. Screen printing inks are now available.

The film thickness of the screen process ink is greater than ink used in other processes. The ink must have properties that allow it to flow evenly through the screen when forced downward by the squeegee.

The conventional screen process inks contain pigments, binders, and solvents. The *colorant* (pigment) is held together by the binder which also assists in adhering the ink to the substrate. The solvents dissolve the resins and form a pliable material.

Screen ink formulas vary greatly since the substrates are numerous in number. Examples of screen process substrates and products are shown in Fig. 29-9. Typical substrates are paper, cloth, plastics, metal, and glass.

Fig. 29-9. These products were printed by the screen method. Since substrates are quite different, ink selection must be carefully made to match the application.

Screen ink problems

Screen clogging can be a problem; therefore, the solvent cannot evaporate too rapidly. Screen inks are formulated in a number of different varieties, each suitable for one or more different substrates. It is important to communicate clearly with suppliers and vendors of inks. They will help you select the correct ink, the one to satisfactorily meet specific product requirements.

MIXING, MATCHING, AND PROOFING

Mixing systems are available for all types of printing inks. These systems allow the person to blend basic inks together. They are weighed to a prescribed amount based on information indicated on a catalogued color selector.

The equipment basic to manual color mixing and matching includes a hard smooth surface, mixing knives or spatulas, scales, a color chart, and a record card.

Color matching can be done as it has been for years; by evaluating the color as well as the substrate to be used. The selection of pigment/dyes requires a very talented eye and the knowledge of a colormatcher. Small additions of other colors can bring the color to the exactness that satisfies even the most critical of color specifiers. Another technique is to read the color values of a sample to be matched by using a sophisticated instrument called a spectrophotometer. It is interfaced with a computer that correlates these values to those of the pigment/dyes available. This data gives you the formulation based on the sample.

Proofing of relief or planographic ink is accomplished by a variety of instruments found in an ink manufacturing company. Some are sophisticated, custom-built presses that simulate various equipment and are able to determine the volume of ink used, others are small hand-operated presses, still others are manual applicators called brayers.

Custom-built presses are also available for flexographic proofing. Proofs can also be made with a small hand brayer that has both a rubber plate type roller and a metering steel roll that simulates the "squeegee" application of ink on a full size flexographic press.

Gravure can be proofed very successfully on custom built proofing presses and on press-simulating instruments.

Typical procedure for mixing and matching ink

Many color books are available from ink manufacturers, Fig. 29-10. The books normally contain samples of ink on coated and uncoated stock. The example will indicate the printing or color results of each ink.

Weigh out the designated amounts of ink on the scale. Use the ink manufacturers' figures. Remember to include the weight of the stock placed on the scales. Place the inks on a glass plate or smooth area and thoroughly mix them with an ink spatula. Mix until the color is uniform. Tap out some of the ink onto the stock to be used and compare it with the desired sample.

Select and weigh out the ink based on the directions indicated by the color system. Continue until the color is an exact match.

Fig. 29-10. Color matching charts or manuals are available. They are used to make sure ink matches desired sample.

Use only a very small amount to mix a trial batch. After the ink is thoroughly mixed, pull a proof. Compare the proof with the sample.

When matching a tint, it is essential that the color be added to a white base in very small quantities until the desired tint is reached. Cleanliness is essential at all times.

Ink mileage

How much ink is needed for a specific sheet fed lithographic job? Finding the amount needed *(mileage)* is not an exact science, but here are a few points of reference. Full strength lithographic inks will cover between 350,000 square inches to 450,000 square inches per pound on a coated stock. On an uncoated sheet, use 280,000 to 360,000 square inches. It is possible to lose 20% or more mileage to the absorption of the paper. Remember to include ink for the makeready, as well as the amount left in the ink fountain and on the rollers when you finish. Running out of ink can be a disaster. Consult the ink representative.

Finding the amount of ink required for a specific job is not easy. Tables give the approximate number of square inches a given amount of ink will cover. Factors governing the amount of ink needed include the specific gravity and color strength of the ink, the stock surface, the work to be printed, the ink needed to prepare press, the type of press, and the ink film thickness.

Ink can be purchased in tubes, cartridges, cans, pails, drums, and tanks. Selection depends on the kinds, amounts needed, and uses of the ink. Care must be taken to close containers of ink that dry when not covered. The chemical change is NOT reversible. The dried ink is often referred to as *livered ink*. The dry flakes should NOT be placed in the ink fountain because this would cause print run trouble.

Ink should also be stored in a cool, dry place for longer life. Remember to close containers to prevent ink contamination and livering. Waste is costly!

Ordering ink

When ordering ink, you and the ink salesperson must consider the following questions:

1. What colors are going to be used to produce the job?
2. What printing process will be used: gravure, offset, etc.?
3. What are the product requirements: long lasting, exposed to weather, etc.?
4. What substrate will be used: smooth paper, rough paper, paper weight, plastic, metal?
5. Is ink cost a consideration?

Asking these kinds of questions will help you and the sales representative select the appropriate ink for the job.

INK-RELATED CHALLENGES

Inks can cause a wide variety of printing problems. However, ink is a common excuse or alibi when there is a press problem. Sometimes, ink is at fault; sometimes not.

Setting and drying

Set is that point when the ink is dry enough to touch lightly without smudging and the sheet can be handled. *Dry* is that point where the ink is free of all volatiles and has polymerized to its total solid state.

Ink will dry relative to the substrate. Ink on substrates that have no absorption must dry by oxidation. This may take from 6 to 24 hours.

Chalking

Chalking is an ink problem that allows the dried ink to rub off the substrate. For example, newspapers will have a chalking type ink by their nature. This does not pose a problem, since the newspaper is only used once and is then discarded. Chalking could be a serious problem with a more permanent product, like this textbook.

Chalking can be prevented by using a varnish that does not penetrate into the paper. The varnish will stay on the substrate surface to hold the pigment. If a chalking problem happens on a large job, you might be able to print a clear protective coating over the image.

Strike-through

Strike-through is an ink penetration problem; the ink soaks into the paper too much and shows on the opposite side of the sheet. Usually, strike-through is caused by an excessively long ink drying time. The excess drying time allows the ink to soak into the paper. A highly absorbent paper can also cause strike-through.

Strike-through should NOT be confused with show-through. Strike-through is caused by excess ink absorption and show-through is caused by thin or non-opaque stock. With show-through, the ink does not absorb too much into the paper as with strike-through.

Setoff

Mentioned briefly, *setoff* is caused by wet ink printing off onto the back of another sheet stacked on top of the previously printed sheet. Setoff can be caused by an excessively thick ink deposit on the paper, improper ink, by stacking the paper too high, drying system problem, etc.

Ink sticking

Ink sticking can occur if two layers of ink film, on two different sheets, bond together. This problem is similar to setoff—both are caused by improper drying of the ink.

Plate wear

Plate wear can be caused by inks that are not fully ground to a fine substance. The unground particles in the ink can act as an abrasive to wear away the surface of the plate. The pigment can be too coarse or there could be too much pigment in the ink. Always check the ink grind when plate wear is excessive. Note! Excessive roller pressure or an abrasive paper can also cause plate wear.

Off color

Off color results when the color of the printed job does not match the intended color. Off color problems have many causes. The press could be dirty and altering the colors of the ink. The substrate color (not true white) can affect the printed color. Also, the ink itself can cause an off color problem. Ink thickness, opacity, translucence, or other ink qualities can affect the color of the printed product. Improper ink mixing also can result in an off color problem.

An *ink drawdown test* can be used to check for proper ink mixing. A standard ink and the newly mixed ink are placed on the stock. Then, a thin blade is used to spread the inks down over the surface of the stock, Fig. 29-11. After drying, the standard ink is compared to the newly mixed ink for proper color match, tone, and strength.

Specking

Specking causes tiny dots or unprinted areas to appear next to halftone dots or next to line art. The ink can be con-

taminated with paper fibers, or other foreign material, or not ground properly. The ink film could be too thick.

KNOW THESE TERMS

Ink formulation, Vehicle, Pigment, Drier, Color strength, Transparent ink, Ink body, Ink stability, Thixotropy, Ink length, Short ink, Long ink, Ink tack, Inkometer, Absorption drying ink, Evaporation drying ink, Oxidation drying ink, Polymerization drying ink, Precipitation drying ink, Adhesion, UV-curable ink, Fast ink, Resistant ink, Fugitive ink, Ink viscosity, Lakes, Toners, Job black, Halftone black, Watercolors, Metallic inks, Cleaning white, Tack reducer, Gloss paste, Slow-dry additive, Spray powder, Ink mill, Relief inks, Litho inks, Gravure inks, Scumming, Colorant, Screen inks, Chalking, Strike-through, Setoff, Ink sticking, Off color, Ink drawdown test, Specking, Mixing, Matching, Non-toxic.

REVIEW QUESTIONS—CHAPTER 29

1. Explain the three main ingredients of ink.
2. _Color Strength_ is the ink's ability to cover the substrate.
3. _Ink body_ refers to the ink's thickness or fluidity.
4. Define the term "ink thixotropy." *Ink fluid*
5. This ink quality would tend to make the ink fly out on a high speed press.
   a. Short ink.
   b. Long ink.
   c. High tack.
   d. Low tack.
6. Low ink tack could cause the following problem(s):
   a. Paper tearing.
   b. Picking.
   c. Splitting.
   d. All of the above.
   e. None of the above.
7. Describe five ways that ink can dry.
8. Exlain 15 ink related terms.
9. _____ _____ can be found in many commercial letterpress facilities since it can be used on a wide variety of presses and papers.
10. What five factors should you consider when ordering ink?
11. What are VOCs?
12. Which type of press uses a softer body ink?

SUGGESTED ACTIVITIES

1. Visit an ink manufacturing company and observe the formulation of ink.
2. Place a very small amount of two kinds of ink on a sheet of glass. Tap the ink and check the length of each kind by measuring the breaking point.
3. Mix ink to match a standard color. Use the drawdown test to check the ink's color and strength.

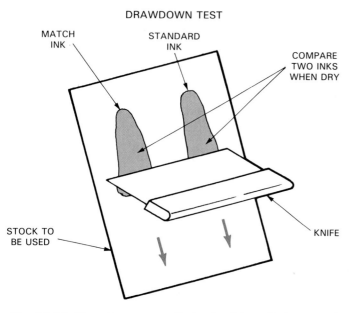

DRAWDOWN TEST

MATCH INK

STANDARD INK

COMPARE TWO INKS WHEN DRY

STOCK TO BE USED

KNIFE

Fig. 29-11. Drawdown test will check mixing of ink to match a specific color. Standard ink and match or mixed ink are placed on the stock to be printed. Then, sharp blade is used to spread inks onto stock to be used for job. After drying, you can compare ink qualities.

Chapter 30

FINISHING AND BINDING

After studying this chapter, you will be able to:
- Identify the many finishing methods for completing a multi-page printed product.
- Choose the most efficient finishing process for the specific job.
- Explain the types of equipment found in the finishing and binding section of a facility.
- Describe the various binding techniques.
- Edition bind a small book.
- Summarize the processes needed for different binding techniques.

"Finishing" is a general term that applies to the many operations done after or while printing. This would include cutting, folding, slitting, creasing, scoring, perforating, drill-ing, ruling, stamping, die cutting, varnishing, embossing, flocking, laminating, numbering, and binding. Exact finishing methods will vary depending upon the type of product and its specifications.

Binding refers to the method of holding the sheets of a product together. This is also a general term that can mean slightly different tasks depending upon the type of product being produced and the type of processes. See Fig. 30-1.

Remember! Finishing, and the many assembly methods involved, is as important as the printing itself. If even one finishing process is poorly done, the well printed job has little or no value. For instance, if 10,000 books have been printed properly in four color and they are then cut to size incorrectly, do you think the customer will pay for the books? Your company may not be paid for the job and

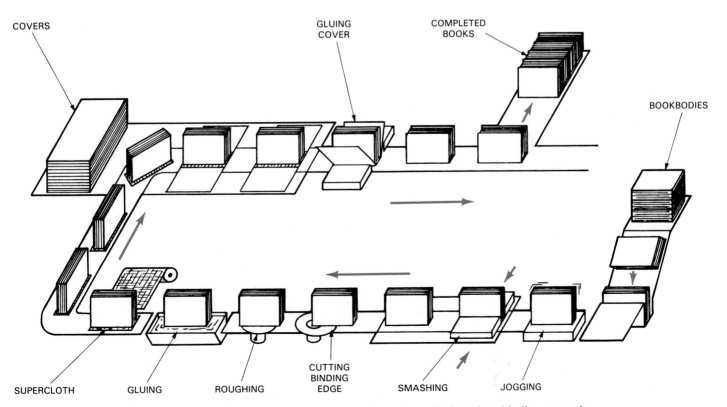

Fig. 30-1. Study flow of book as it moves through typical perfect binding operation.

could not be proud of the final product. This makes it extremely important that all finishing processes are done correctly.

CUTTING

Cutting is done to make a large sheet of paper into several smaller sheets. Cutting should NOT be confused with trimming. *Trimming* refers to cutting off uneven edges of paper, as when trimming the three sides of a book. It makes the sheets smaller, square, and even with each other.

Guillotine cutter

The most common type of equipment used to cut paper stock is the guillotine cutter. The knife of a *guillotine cutter* is forced through the paper at a slight angle to have an oblique shearing action, Fig. 30-2.

The blade must be very sharp. Any roughness of the blade will appear as a jagged edge on the sheet. Any irregularities are obviously very undesirable.

Keeping the blade in excellent condition is essential for quality trimming or cutting of stock. Most plants will send cutter blades out to be sharpened.

Extreme care must be taken to remove and install a cutter blade. Once the blade is removed from the cutter, it

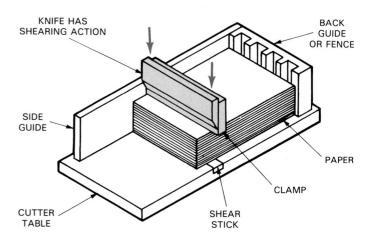

Fig. 30-2. Guillotine cutter forces blade through stock to produce shearing action. Note parts of cutter.

should be placed in a *sheath* (cover) to eliminate the possibility of someone being injured by the sharp edge, Fig. 30-3.

Danger! Respect a cutter blade's sharpness. It can cause severe lacerations and injury. Handle a cutter blade carefully!

Specific equipment instructions should be followed to correctly position a sharpened blade in the cutter. Before

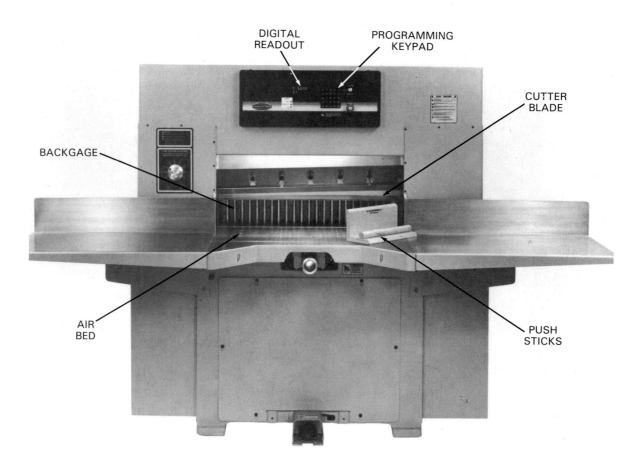

Fig. 30-3. This is a powerful computer-controlled cutter. Cuts can be preprogrammed into computer memory. It has 37 inch power backgauge cutter, with a six inch clamp capacity. It also has automatic lubrication feature for reduced maintenance and longer life. (Challenge Machinery Co.)

472

making the adjustments, a cutting stick, with no previous cutting, should be placed in the table's groove or channel. Refer to Fig. 30-4.

Cutting sticks are wood or plastic strips inserted into the cutter table. The sticks should be rotated or turned to give a new surface under the cutting edge when the cutting action no longer gives a sharp, clean cut.

Fig. 30-4. Operator is using large cutter to size large sheets of stock.   (Lawson)

Paper cutters

Today's paper cutters come in a wide variety of sizes from table top models to huge floor models, Fig. 30-5. The simplest type is usually hand-operated while other models have power clamps to hold the paper while it is being cut. Modern floor models have automatic clamps and are computer programmed to make planned cuts.

Fig. 30-5. Here is another cutter. It uses display screen to show cutting parameters or settings.

The size of the cutter is designated by the length of cut. A 30 inch paper cutter will take a sheet that has a measurement of 30 inches or less, Fig. 30-6.

A dial gauge or digital readout indicates the distance of the back gauge to the cutting edge of the blade. A properly adjusted cutter will give very accurate cuts.

Most of today's plants have power automatic paper cutters. It is also possible to have paper cutters with multichanneled electronic programming and supplied with a digital step and repeat device.

Automatic paper cutters may be equipped with:

1. *Nonrepeat device* (cutter will only come down once until reset).
2. *Two-handed operation* (two buttons on each side of operator must be pressed simultaneously to make cutter blade come down).
3. *Electric eye stop* (electric eye can detect hand, arm, or other object in the way and will stop cutter automatically).

Fig. 30-6. Care must be taken when using a cutter. If it will slice through a thick stack of paper, imagine what it would do to your hand.

All of these are safety features that help prevent loss of fingers or hands. See Fig. 30-4.

The amount of paper each cutter will pass through depends on paper type, weight, and size. Six hundred sheets of narrow paper will cut much easier than 600 sheets that cover the total width of the cutter table.

Many features are available such as: split back gauge, magnetic tape memory, air jet beds, etc.

The *air jet bed* allows for easy movement of large, heavy sheets. Air is pumped up through the table to form a cushion between the bed and the paper. The air lifts the paper so it floats over the bed for easy positioning, Fig. 30-7.

Many of today's facilities will have a *vacuum system* to remove all of the unwanted paper. The waste stock is baled as it is sucked to a receiving area. Paper dust must be held to a minimum to comply with local, state, and federal regulations.

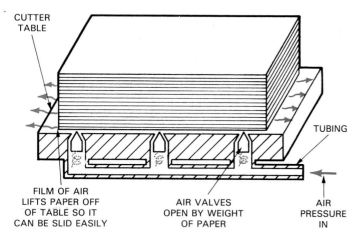

Fig. 30-7. Most large cutters have an air film on the table. Air flows up through holes in table to lift paper up for easy movement.

The cutting of paper is a very exacting task. A miscut can make a job a pile of waste—a very costly mistake. Accuracy is essential when paper is cut down to the size for a given press run. Proper allowances must also be considered when bleeds and trims are specified.

Three-knife paper cutters are used in specialized operations. Book publishing is a typical usage. Each cutter cuts one edge, such as the top, bottom, and one edge. Operation of a three-knife trimmer is shown in Figs. 30-8 through 30-10.

Fig. 30-8. Three-knife paper cutter is commonly used to trim sheets to size and to square them.

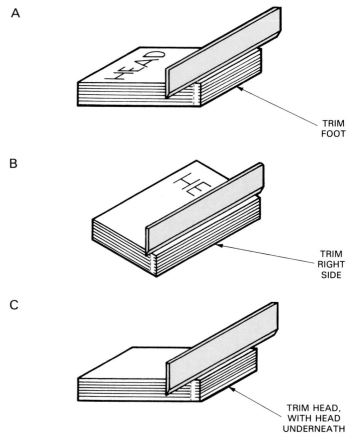

Fig. 30-9. Basic action when trimming product. A—Trimming foot. B—Trimming right side. C—Trimming head.

Fig. 30-10. A book is about to be fed into this three-knife trimmer.

A *card cutter* is another type of cutting device used to cut a limited number of sheets, Fig. 30-11. The card cutter has multiple uses since it can cut paper, film, and other materials.

A *film cutter* is another device commonly found in the graphic communications facility, Fig. 30-12. The film cutter will accurately cut negatives, positives, and other materials.

> NOTICE! Whatever the cutting device, safe operation of the equipment is essential. If a cutter will slice through a pile of paper like butter, what would it do to a hand? Always follow manufacturer directions when using cutters.

Folding

Once images have been printed on the substrate, they are often folded. Many jobs are printed as one page on one side and backed up with a second printing, commonly called sheetwise imposition. The single sheet might be folded to fit into an envelope, but often the sheet has many pages on each side. See Figs. 30-13 and 30-14.

The most common folding machine is the *buckle type* which uses roller action to buckle fold the paper. The stock is placed in the friction or suction type feeder. The adjustment on the suction type is similar to the printing unit feeder while the friction type requires a very exact setting. An example of the friction type feeder is shown in Fig. 30-15.

Fig. 30-11. The card cutter is common in most facilities and has many uses.

Fig. 30-12. This cutter is designed for film.

Fig. 30-13. A small folder can be used for numerous products. (Baumfolder)

Fig. 30-14. This is a larger, high speed folder. It is available in 18, 20, and 23 inch widths. (Baumfolder)

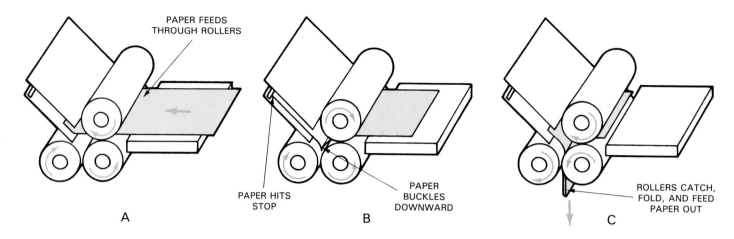

PAPER FEEDS THROUGH ROLLERS

PAPER HITS STOP

PAPER BUCKLES DOWNWARD

ROLLERS CATCH, FOLD, AND FEED PAPER OUT

A   B   C

Fig. 30-15. Study the operating principle of a buckle folder. A—Paper is fed into machine by rollers. B—Paper hits stop and buckles downward. C—Rollers catch paper and feed it down through rollers to make a fold.

As the sheet leaves the feeder, it travels on belts or rollers to two rollers that carry the sheet to the fold plate, Fig. 30-16. As the sheet is forced against the *fold plate,* the sheet buckles and another combination of rollers folds the sheet and carries it to a delivery station or to another set of folding rollers. These rollers will place another fold if necessary. The fold will be either parallel or at right angles to the first fold. The two examples appear in Fig. 30-17.

Some folders use a *knife arm* to force the paper between the folding rollers. This process is illustrated in Fig. 30-18.

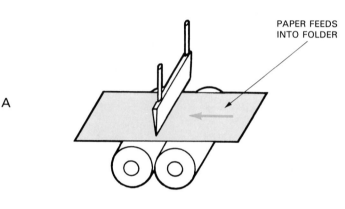

A

PAPER FEEDS INTO FOLDER

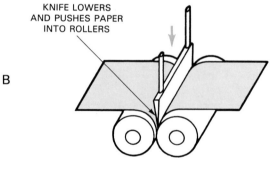

B

KNIFE LOWERS AND PUSHES PAPER INTO ROLLERS

FOLD PLATE

Fig. 30-16. This is a fold plate of a folder.

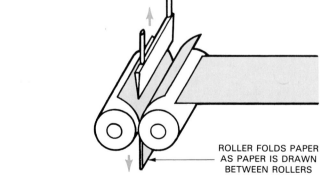

C

ROLLER FOLDS PAPER AS PAPER IS DRAWN BETWEEN ROLLERS

Fig. 30-18. Study operation of knife type folder. A—Paper is fed into folder by rollers. B—Knife comes down and pushes paper into rollers. C—Rollers fold and pull paper through machine.

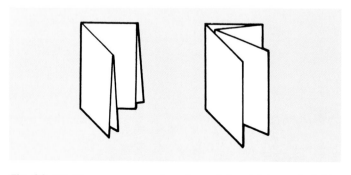

Fig. 30-17. These are examples of parallel and right angle folds.

The *floor type folder* is commonly found in graphic communications facilities.

Table models are used in many business establishments where parallel folds are commonly needed. The table model is used to fold small sheets.

Web presses use rotary folders to convert the web into folded signatures for binding operations. Two folds will make an eight page signature.

The folding requirements should be considered in the planning stage. A few folds are shown in Fig. 30-19.

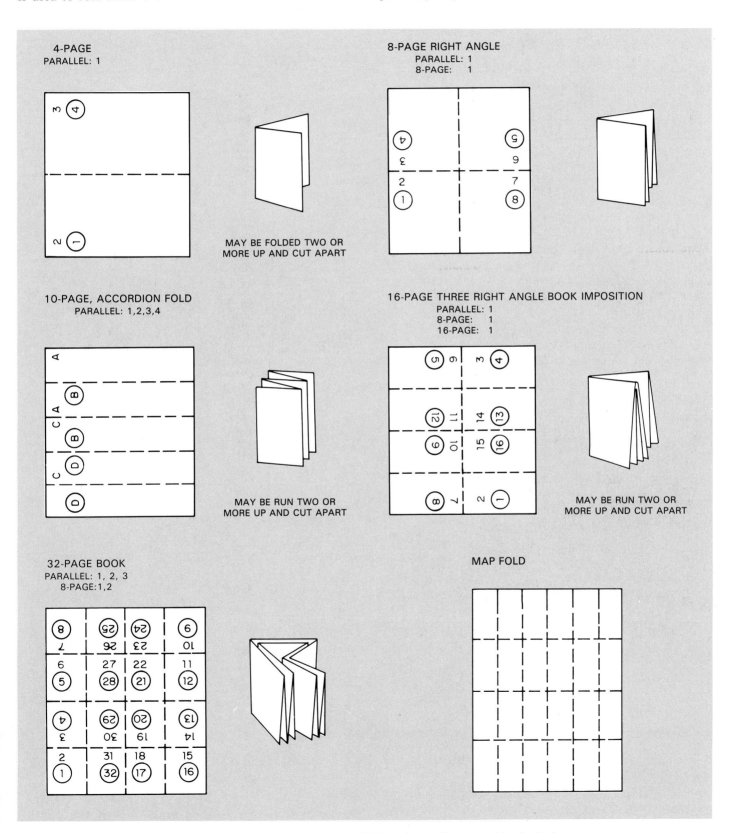

Fig. 30-19. These are a few of the folds or impositions used in the industry.

Folding terms

1. *Self-cover stitched body.* The cover is the same stock as the sheets inside the book. Sheets are folded on the long side and stitched along the spine of the book.
2. *Gate-fold book.* The front and back cover have panels that are folded in toward the spine of the book.
3. *Folder.* A picket or a flap which can be on one or both sides of the inside of the cover stock.
4. *Three-panel fold.* A sheet is folded twice to make three panels. Often used for direct mail, this format may be slipped into a standard No. 10 envelope or as a self mailer printed on 8 1/2 x 11 in. stock. Sometimes, one fold is perforated to be used as a reply card.
5. *Accordion fold.* The sheet size will vary depending on the number of folds and panel size. The sheet is parallel folded several times. The accordion fold is designated for ease of opening.
6. *Fold-out book.* A fold out in a book can fall anywhere in the book. Some books and magazines use the fold-out format.

This is not a complete list but it conveys the idea that innovative types of folds require advance planning. Hand folding is a very costly operation.

Folding area safety

Safety is important in the folding area. A few rules to remember include:

1. Long hair should be tied back because the revolving rollers could grasp the hair and pull it into the machine.
2. The edges of paper are very sharp and require careful handling. Paper cuts are painful.
3. When making adjustments, the machine should be turned off.
4. Maintenance should be performed with the machine's electrical power locked out.
5. Machine adjustments should be done following manufacturer prescribed procedures.

Slitting

Slitting is similar to the cutting concept in that a set of wheels actually cut the stock as it passes through the folder, Fig. 30-20. Many folding machines can be equipped with a slitting attachment. An example of the slitting attachment is shown in Fig. 30-21. During the folding operation, for example, a leaflet or booklet can be trimmed to finished size by slitting.

Creasing and scoring

Creasing is the process of compressing the substrate so that it will fold more easily, Fig. 30-22. This is accomplished with a creasing rule or a rotary creaser attached to the folder, Fig. 30-23.

Sometimes, creasing is a separate operation using letterpress equipment or specially designed finishing equipment. Rule thickness will vary with the stock. The correct way to crease stock is shown in Fig. 30-24.

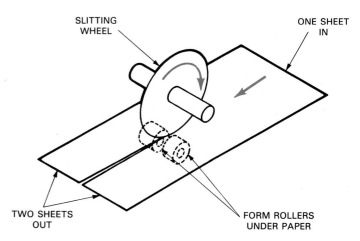

Fig. 30-20. Slitting is commonly done by sharp wheel that cuts paper sheet as it passes against wheel.

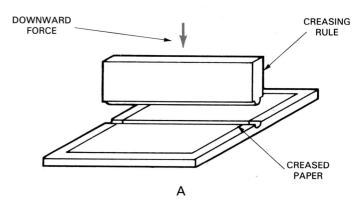

Fig. 30-21. Note one type of slitting attachment for a folder.

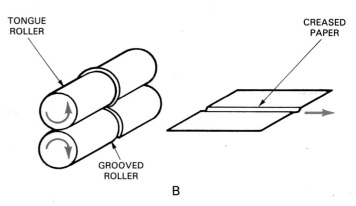

Fig. 30-22. Scoring or creasing can be done by rule or roller action. A—Principle of creasing rule. B—Principle of creasing roller.

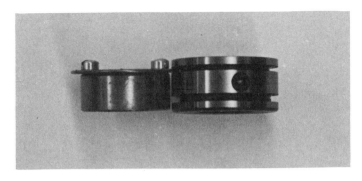

Fig. 30-23. A rotary creasing attachment is available for many folders.

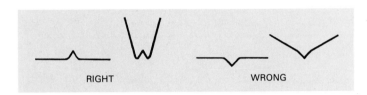

RIGHT   WRONG

Fig. 30-24. Note correct and incorrect ways of creasing stock.

The term *scoring* is used interchangeably with creasing in some operations but scoring is a slight cut in heavy stock before it is folded. The operation is commonly found in the packaging industry where the score is made at the fold point. The correct depth of the cut is important.

Perforating

Perforating places a series of small cuts or slits in the paper. Whenever it is necessary to remove a portion of the printed material, the stock is perforated or "perfed." This makes it possible to readily tear off and remove the return mailer or similar informational material. The removal of a check from the checkbook is a typical example of a perforated sheet. See Fig. 30-25. The number of teeth per inch to make the slits will depend on the type of substrate used.

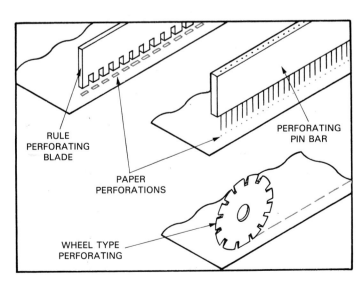

RULE PERFORATING BLADE

PERFORATING PIN BAR

PAPER PERFORATIONS

WHEEL TYPE PERFORATING

Fig. 30-25. These are some of the ways that stock can be perforated.

Fig. 30-26 gives numerous examples of perforation types. Study them carefully.

Sometimes, the task can be completed while running the job on the press. This is a common practice with relief and planographic mechanical processes. See Fig. 30-27.

The stock can also be perforated on the folder as an auxiliary process. In this case, it is very similar to the slitting process.

Stock #1706	Pinhole	2ST per inch	#1
#1707	Slot	9T per inch	#2
#1708	Slot	9T per inch	#3
#1709	Slot	9T per inch	#4
#1710	Slot	8T per inch	#5
#1711	Slot	7T per inch	#6
#1712	Slot	3 1/2T per inch	#7
#1713	Knifecut	6 1/2T per inch	#8
#1714	Knifecut	3 3/4T per inch	#9
#1715	Knifecut	2 1/2T per inch	#10
#1716	Slot	4T per inch	#11
#1717	Slot	3T per inch	#12
#1718	Knifecut	12T per inch	#13

Fig. 30-26. Here are some examples of different perforations. (Rollem)

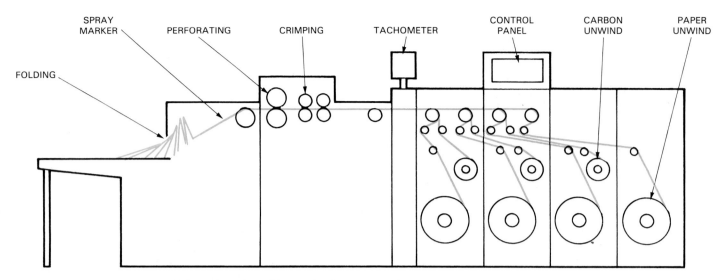

Fig. 30-27. Note that this production system has in-line perforating and folding.

A round hole punching device is also capable of perforating stock after it has been printed. Common products using this kind of perforating are the postage stamp and computer printout paper.

Drilling and punching

Drilling is the process of cutting holes in stock. The drill bit is hollow and the edges are very sharp. After placing stock on the drill table board, the revolving drill is forced through the *lift* (pile) of paper, Fig. 30-28. The waste stock is forced through the hollow center of the drill and ejected out of the drill top.

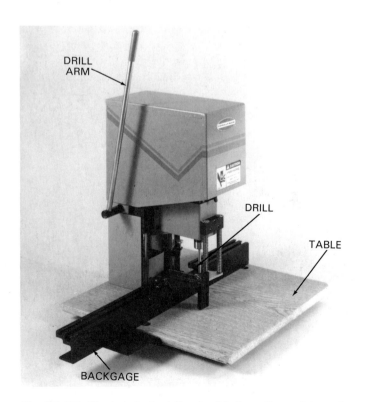

Fig. 30-28. Single spindle drill spins bit through stock to make holes. (Challenge Machinery Co.)

A dull drill will tend to overheat when forced through stock. Feeding the drill through the stock faster than the recommended rate will also cause overheating. Overheating can take the temper out and dull the drill.

A guide at the back of the board regulates the distance the holes are drilled from the edge of the sheet, Fig. 30-29. Most drills have stops to assure the proper positioning for each lift to be drilled.

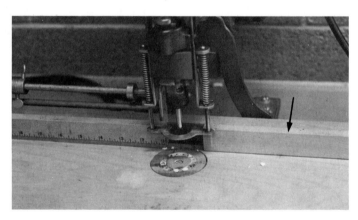

Fig. 30-29. Closeup shows gauge for determining where holes will be drilled in stock.

Drills are available in *multiple spindles* which makes it possible to drill up to ten or more holes at one time. The multiple spindle drills can be operated by hand, foot, or by hydraulic power, Fig. 30-30.

Danger! The drill spindle should be guarded. The high speed revolving action of the drill tends to draw hair toward it. This action is caused by static electricity. Hands and fingers must also be kept away from the revolving drill.

Punching forces metal rods down through the paper without rotation. This removes stock for holes. For instance, the holes required for spiral binding are usually punched. See Fig. 30-31.

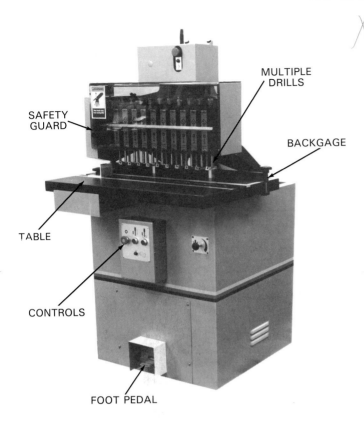

Fig. 30-30. A multiple spindle drill is needed for high speed production. This unit will drill up to ten holes at once and up to a depth of 9 1/2 inches from margin. (Baumfolder)

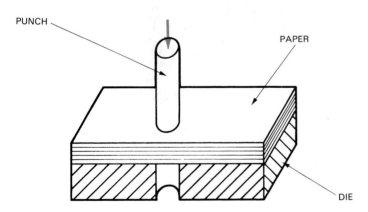

Fig. 30-31. A punch forces metal rod straight down through stock. It does not spin, as does a drill. Die is located below punch to shear off stock and form a hole.

The punched holes are usually one size, but drills are available in various diameters. Many drills have auxiliary devices as attachments. These devices make it possible to slit, round corner, or notch a lift of paper.

Ruling

Ruling is done to form or print lines on the stock. Ruling is accomplished with pens or disks that are held against the paper as it moves through the machine.

The disks are inked with felt rollers while the inking pens have a stored supply of ink. The color and type of line varies with the need.

Stamping

Goldstamping is the term commonly used for stamping foil onto a substrate. Gold or simulated gold is commonly used as a stamping material. However, silver and some other colors are also available as hot stamping materials.

Stamping is an image transfer process closely associated with the relief process. Letterpress images are placed between two jaws which tighten, Fig. 30-32, and hold the type characters. The clamping device is heated, Fig. 30-33. Before

Fig. 30-32. This is an example of a hand-operated stamping press. It is for low production quantities.

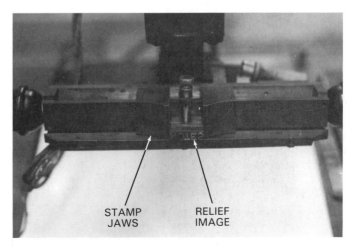

Fig. 30-33. Jaws of hot stamp press hold the relief images.

the image comes in contact with the substrate, a coated foil is placed between the type characters and the substrate, Fig. 30-34. The heated type characters are then depressed. The heat and pressure transfers the image to the substrate. The proper image transfer depends on the amount of heat, the pressure applied, and the dwell time the type characters are in contact with the foil and substrate.

Fig. 30-34. Foil is placed between type and substrate in press.

Usually, the relief images are brass or a service type. Service type is more durable and will withstand the heat and pressure longer.

In a production situation, the stamping unit is automated but it can also be a hand-operated process. Some production facilities have platen presses which have been modified for the hot stamping process.

Die cutting

Whenever an irregular shape must be cut in stock, die cutting is the process most often used to do the task, Fig. 30-35. Pressure is used to force a sharp metal die or steel rule through the stock.

For example, special dies, which look like kitchen cookie cutters, are used to slice through many sheets to form envelopes. Dies are also used to cut the irregular shapes after

screen process printing of labels, decals, and stickers. Die cutting is NOT limited to paper, but can be done with many materials.

Steel dies and rules are used on many standard relief presses. The rules are shaped and inserted in the saw kerf formed by a jig saw, or in advanced technology, by a laser on the dieboard, Fig. 30-36. Sponges release the stock from the die.

To eliminate the problem of portions of a dieboard falling out, the saw does not cut through the board in all of

Fig. 30-36. Dieboard must be prepared for steel rule properly.

the sawed areas. The unsawed areas are called *bridges,* allowing the board to stay solidly together. The steel die rule is notched in the bridged area which allows for a continuous cutting edge. Various types of presses are used for die cutting. Examples are shown in Figs. 30-37 and 30-38.

Varnishing

After an image has been transferred to a substrate, it is sometimes coated or *varnished.* The coating becomes a clear protective surface. Usually, the coating makes the surface resistant to moisture and scuffing.

Glossy restaurant menus, annual report covers, and similar products are typical examples of varnishing. The

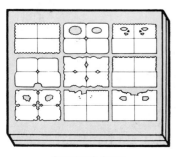

GREETING CARD
DIES FOR
AUTOMATIC FOLDING

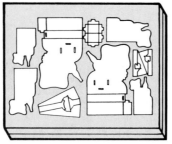

TAG AND
LABEL DIES
PRESSURE
SENSITIVE DIES

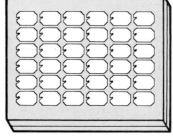

DISPLAY DIES
THAT
REALLY REGISTER

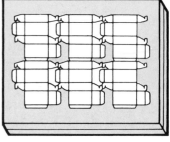

FOLDING BOX
DIES FOR
MACHINE FILLED BOXES

Fig. 30-35. Irregular shapes can be die cut. These are examples. (Accurate Steel Rule Die Mfg., Inc.)

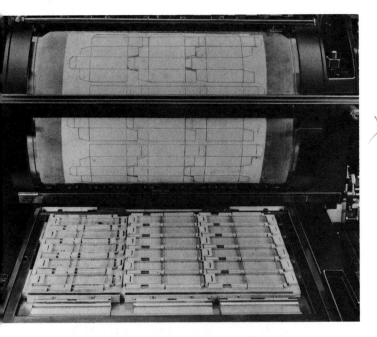

Fig. 30-37. This is a die cutting press.
(Accurate Steel Rule Die Mfg., Inc.)

coating materials vary but some of the latest coatings are epoxies that give excellent wear qualities.

Total area coverage can be accomplished by various processes but a planographic press can be used when the dampeners are removed. Letterpress and screen processes can also be used for specific varnishing jobs.

Embossing

Embossing is a term commonly used to designate a raised surface forced into the substrate, as shown in Fig. 30-39. The image is impressive and a very unusual finishing process results. Embossing requires the use of two dies. Shown in Fig. 30-40, the one die is in relief while the other is recessed. The stock (paper) is placed between the two dies. When the two are brought together, the clamping force creates a raised image on the stock.

Some stock requires heat and/or moisture to give a better, more permanent shape to the image. Many engraving plants have the capabilities of doing excellent embossed printed jobs. It is possible to foil stamp at the same time the image is being embossed. Tinted colors are available for very pleasing results.

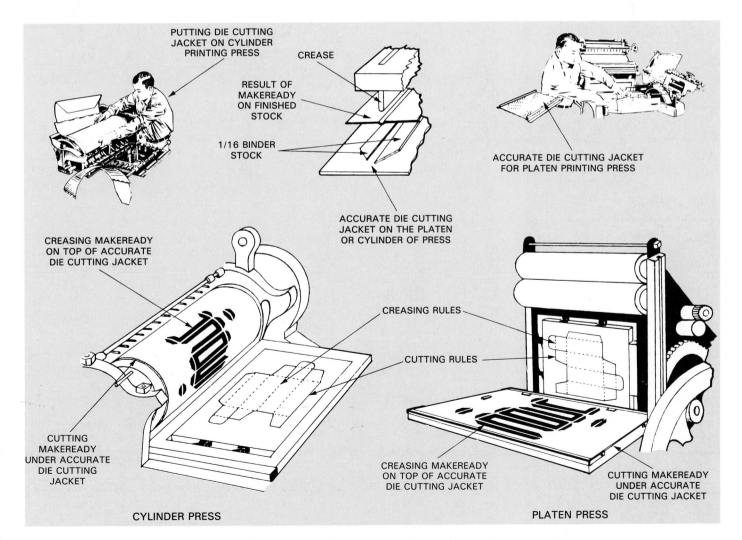

Fig. 30-38. Study principles of die cutting. Dies are very sharp and should be respected to prevent injury.
(Accurate Steel Rule Die Mfg., Inc.)

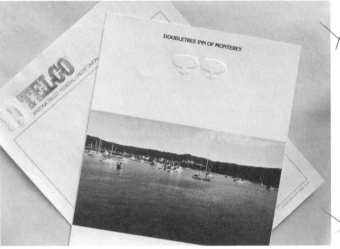

Fig. 30-39. Embossed surfaces create a very interesting pattern or design that has depth.

Fig. 30-40. Here is an example of a relief and recessed area of a die for embossing.

The dies are very expensive but it is possible to make the counter image if the recessed die has been machined. Cements are available to make the counter die on the tympan sheet of a platen press.

Note! When the stock creates the image and ink is NOT used, it is called *blind embossing.*

High quality embossing requires close tolerances and very exacting work on the part of the operator.

Flocking

Whenever the surface of a printed package, T-shirt, or greeting card is fuzzy, the inked surface has been covered with cloth fibers. This is called *flocking.*

The fibers are attached into the ink while the ink is still wet. For example, some wall coverings use this technique to give an unusual texture.

This is a highly specialized finishing process. It is NOT commonly found in the graphic communications industry.

Laminating

Laminating is the bonding of two or more materials together to become one common unit. If you have attended a conference or convention where graphic communications suppliers have booths, the suppliers of laminators might ask you for your business card. The card will be laminated in plastic. In this case, the card often becomes the identification tag for luggage.

Many of today's restaurant menus also use this process as a protective surface to prevent rapid wear and destruction of the paper.

Numbering

The process of consecutively placing a number or skip placing of figures (numbers) in forward or backward order is called *numbering.*

The figures are transferred from the inked relief images onto the stock, usually paper. The plunger is automatically depressed by the press to ratchet the numbering head. This permits forward or backward numbering, each impression changes to a different figure or digit. See Fig. 30-41.

Fig. 30-41. Various types of numbering machines are available. They are used when sequenced numbers are needed on product. Personal and payroll checks are numbered in sequence, for example.

Often, the numbering machine is set to start on the maximum amount. When printed, the last figure will be number one. This prevents an overrun and places the tickets, forms, or other numbered materials in the right order. Numbered tickets or gate passes would be a good example of sequential numbering. See Fig. 30-42.

BINDING

Once the image transfer has taken place, the product is ready for shipment or it may require *binding* to fasten the folded images or single sheets together. Fig. 30-43 shows several binding classifications.

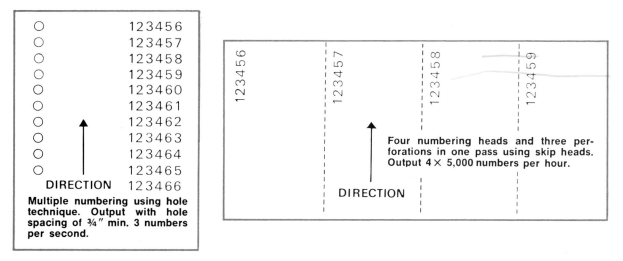

Fig. 30-42. These are examples of different numbering methods. (Rollem)

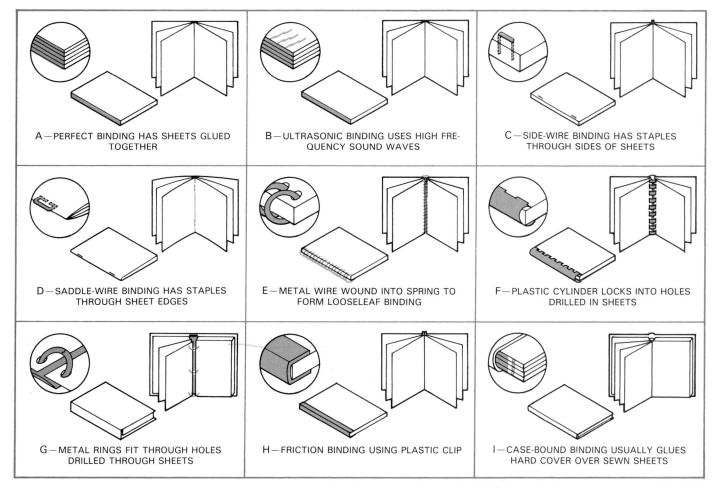

Fig. 30-43. Study typical binding methods. You should be able to identify each type.

Folding Buckle + Knife

Some general or basic types of binding include the following:

1. Adhesive binding (also called padding, is a broad classification that uses glue or adhesive to hold the sheets together).
2. Mechanical binding (devices such as spiral wire, metal posts, metal rings, plastic cylinders, etc. hold sheets together, often called or includes *looseleaf binding*).
3. Side stitching (metal wire is forced through sides of sheets and formed into staples to hold sheets together.
4. Saddle stitching (metal wire is forced through folded edge and formed into staples to hold sheets together).
5. Side sewing (threads are forced through sides of sheets to bind them together).
6. Saddle sewing (threads are forced through folded edges of sheets to hold them together).
7. Soft binding (also called *perfect binding* or *patent binding,* a flexible cloth or paper cover is glued to body of sheets; glue is also used to hold sheets together).
8. Hard bound binding (a flexible cover is wrapped around rigid piece of cardboard and then glued to body of book; body of book is held together by sewing).
9. Self-cover binding (same material as body of book is glued over sheets to hold sheets together).

Many of the printed press sheets are very large and must be folded, gathered and collated, stitched, and trimmed. The fastening process can be divided into pamphlet binding, edition binding, perfect binding, and mechanical binding.

PAMPHLET BINDING

Most of today's magazines, folders, catalogs, and booklets fall into the *pamphlet binding* category. One of the simplest techniques is saddle wire stitching. Sheets are folded, gathered, and stitched through the CENTER or saddle of the folded sheets, Fig. 30-44. Many booklets, magazines, are fastened by this method.

Fig. 30-44. These magazines are being gathered and stitched automatically for high production run. (Muller-Martini Corp.)

The maximum number of pages is regulated by the limit of the stitcher and/or the pamphlet thickness which allows the booklet or magazine to lie flat.

The folded sheets are placed one over the other and then placed on the saddle of the stitcher.

When larger publications are bound, the machine is capable of gathering the signatures, and cover. They are then stitched and trimmed, Fig. 30-45.

Fig. 30-45. Stitching machine uses roll of wire to produce staples that hold sheets together.

Gathering and collating

Gathering is a general term associated with the assembling of signatures. Discussed earlier, a *signature* is a large sheet that has been folded into smaller groups of pages, Fig. 30-46. The term *collating* usually means the assembling of single sheets. However, the term *collate* can also mean the checking of signature placement after gathering.

The basic process of gathering is illustrated in Fig. 30-47. It involves using a gathering machine to stack the signatures on top of each other in the correct order. Note that one type uses a rotating gripper bar and the other uses a gripper arm. Both place the signatures on a moving conveyor. Other variations are also available.

Fig. 30-48 shows a gathering machine placing a booklet in proper sequence. A rotary collator is in Fig. 30-49.

Fig. 30-46. A signature is a larger sheet that has been folded to produce a series of pages.

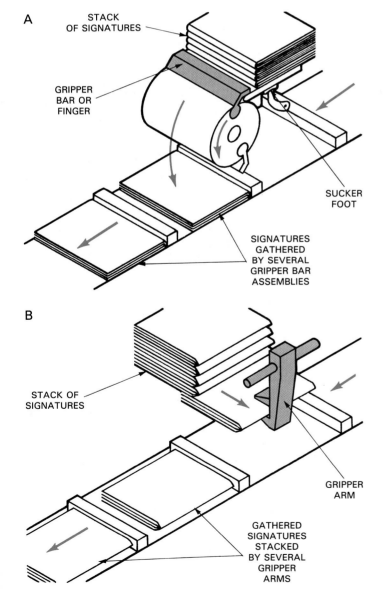

A

STACK OF SIGNATURES

GRIPPER BAR OR FINGER

SUCKER FOOT

SIGNATURES GATHERED BY SEVERAL GRIPPER BAR ASSEMBLIES

B

STACK OF SIGNATURES

GRIPPER ARM

GATHERED SIGNATURES STACKED BY SEVERAL GRIPPER ARMS

Fig. 30-47. Note two methods commonly used to gather signatures. A—Rotary gathering. B—Gripper arm gathering.

Fig. 30-48. A sheet gathering machine places all pages of product in order. Photo shows one station and a part of another. There will be as many stations as there are sheets. (Muller-Martini Corp.)

Fig. 30-49. This is modern rotating collating machine. It is computerized and has digital readouts. (Challenge Machinery Co.)

A suction feed collator with on-line stitching, folding, and trimming is pictured in Fig. 30-50. A form collator is in Fig. 30-51. Note how it feeds from four stacks of paper.

Collating marks can be used on signatures to check the accuracy of signature sequence. Illustrated in Fig. 30-52, the collating marks should be aligned one after the other, forming a diagonal line. If the marks do not align, one or more signatures is out of sequence.

Stitching

Mentioned briefly, *stitching* is a binding method that holds the sheets together with staples. *Sewing,* explained shortly, is another binding method that uses thread instead of wire staples. Both methods of binding are common. Stitching is used on publication with fewer pages and sewing is limited to thicker books with more pages.

Saddle stitched booklets or magazines are common because they tend to lie more flat than side stitched products

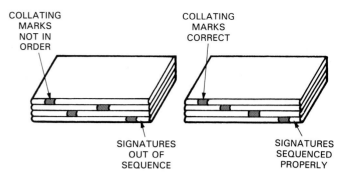

Fig. 30-52. Collating marks can be placed on folded edges of signatures so visual check of sequence can be made. Marks must line up in sequence.

when opened. When the thickness increases, the amount of creep becomes more evident. The thickness of the folded area determines creep.

Most of the high production stitching machines have a multiple stitching head. This increases binding speed or volume.

The side wire stitching technique is another method of fastening several signatures or many sheets, Fig. 30-53. The cover could be of the same type of stock or a specially printed substrate. One of the drawbacks of this type of binding is that the booklet or magazine does not want to lie flat when opened.

Fig. 30-50. This is a suction feed collator with on-line stitch, fold, and trim units. (Challenge Machinery Co.)

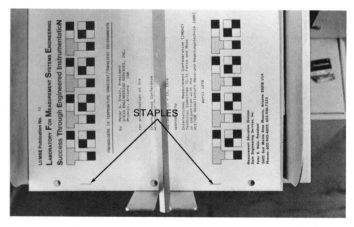

Fig. 30-53. This is a side stitched product. It will not lay as flat when opened as will a saddle stitched product.

Side stitch machines might be multiple head or single head, as shown in Fig. 30-53. Consideration must be given to the distance required from the edge of the booklet to the staple. The inside margin might need more space so that it can be seen when the pages are opened.

Danger! Never place a finger or hand under a stitcher head. A staple could be driven through your finger or hand if the machine is activated.

Edition binding

The *edition bound* or *case bound* book must take more abuse and is considered to be more permanent, Fig. 30-54.

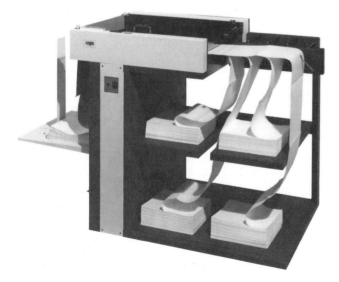

Fig. 30-51. This unit is collating computer forms from four stacks. Holes in sheets keep sheet together or in sequence. (A.B. Dick)

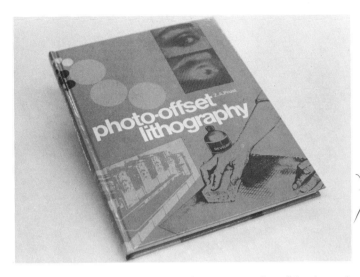

Fig. 30-54. High quality textbooks are normally edition bound. The book you are reading is edition bound. Study how its pages are sewn together.

The signatures (folded, printed pages) are sewn together to make up the total number of pages in the book. These sewn signatures make up the *body* of the book. Refer to Figs. 30-55 and 30-56.

The *case,* or cover for the book, is made separately. Pieces of binder's board are cut to size. Then, bookbinder's cloth is glued to the board to make a strong protective surface for the book body. The process of positioning and attaching the signatures to the case is known as *casing in* the book. Refer to Fig. 30-57.

Binding a book

High production bookbinding facilities have automatic machines to make a finished product. However, so you will understand binding and book construction better, a typical procedure to bind a book by hand will be summarized.

1. Select ten sheets of 11 x 17 inch stock (newspaper or bond) and fold them into signatures. The fold should be sharp.

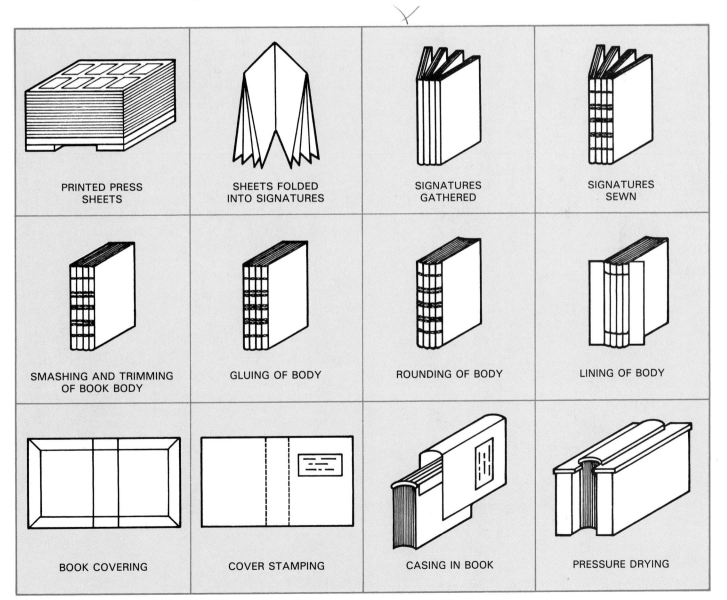

Fig. 30-55. These are the major steps for edition or case binding a book. Study them.

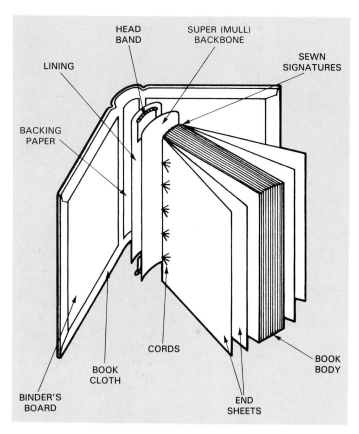

Fig. 30-56. Study the basic parts of a hard cover book.

Fig. 30-57. With edition binding, the signatures are placed in order and then sewn together with thread.

2. Clamp the ten signatures with wood stock on each side. Starting at one end, mark the signatures at the following measurements: 1/2", 1", 1/2", 1 1/2", 1/2", 1", and 1 1/2 inch. This is shown in Fig. 30-58.

3. Make a saw kerf across all signatures at the marked positions. Depth of each kerf is determined by the number of folds. Merely cut through the folds, Fig. 30-59.

4. Position the sewing tapes on the sewing frame. The inside one-half inch marks designate the tape locations.

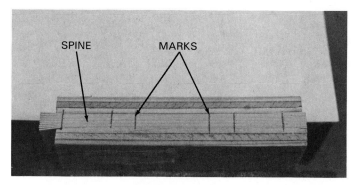

Fig. 30-58. To hand bind a book, mark the edges of the signatures first.

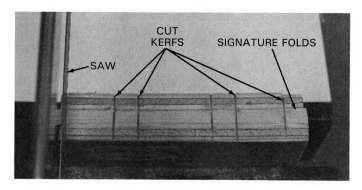

Fig. 30-59. Use a saw to make a small cut on the spine at each of your marks.

5. The first signature is positioned on the platform of the sewing frame with the head or fold to the left. Using a linen or other type of thread, thread a large sewing needle. Insert the needle from the outside through the first saw kerf. Leave at least a three inch tail of thread. Determine the amount of thread needed by measuring one length and multiply it by the number of signatures. Continue sewing in and out until finished with the first signature, Fig. 30-60.

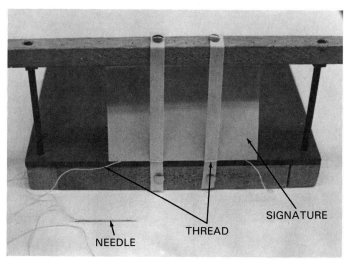

Fig. 30-60. Sew the first signature.

6. Place the second signature over the first in the same direction. Insert the needle through the kerf opposite the final kerf of the first signature. Continue sewing each kerf. When finished, tie the first and second signatures with the loose end of the first signature, Fig. 30-61. The third signature and those thereafter require another step. Rather than tying one signature to another, a kettle stitch is used to fasten at the end of the signature.

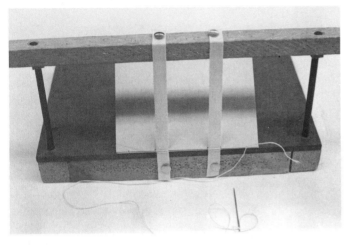

Fig. 30-61. Sew and attach the first signature to the second.

Fig. 30-63. Next, attach the end sheets to the sides of the book body.

The *kettle stitch* is a looping of the needle end of the thread under the prior signature. The last signature must be tied.

Fig. 30-62 shows how a machine can sew a book together.

7. The *spine* of the book is glued with bookbinder's glue. When dry, apply a ribbon of glue to one side of the folded edge of the end sheets, Fig. 30-63. The *end sheets* are usually made of slightly heavier stock and placed on both sides of the combined signatures (first and last pages).

8. Trim the top, bottom, and outside edge of the book with a hand or power guillotine cutter.

9. Round and shape the spine or back edge of the book. Look at Fig. 30-64.

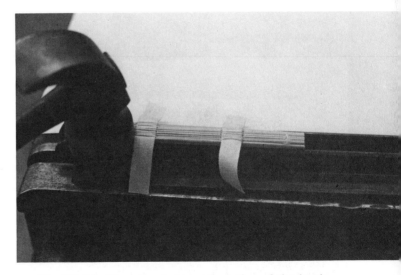

Fig. 30-64. Round and shape the spine of the book.

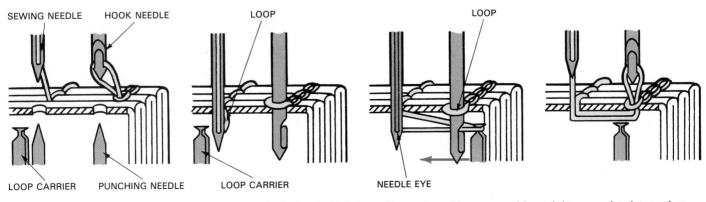

Fig. 30-62. A kettle stitch is used to hand bind a book. This is an illustration of how a machine might sew a book together.

Padding — Released
Tipping —

10. Glue the headbands to the top and bottom of the book, Figs. 30-65 and 30-66. The *headbands* are the finishing touch to hide the glue and folded portion of each signature. They should be cut to correspond to the distance of the rounded and shaped back.

11. Cut super cloth approximately one-half inch shorter than the book. It should extend one to two inches on each side of the back. Using bookbinder's glue, center the super cloth in all directions and glue it to the back of the book, Fig. 30-67.

12. Cut a thin piece of paper the size of the book and position it over the glue portion of the super cloth. Allow the glue to dry before casing the book.

Making the case

1. Cut two bookbinder's boards. The suggested size is determined by measuring from the shaped or flared edge to the opening edge of the book and adding 1/8 inch. Also measure the distance from the top to the bottom of the book and add 1/4 inch.

2. Position the boards on each side of the book body. Moisten two pieces of gummed tape large enough to go over the book spine or back. Position them around the boards as shown in Fig. 30-68. The tape holds the boards in place. Accuracy is important!

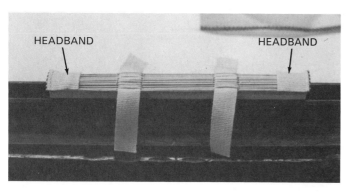

Fig. 30-65. Apply the headbands to the body of the book.

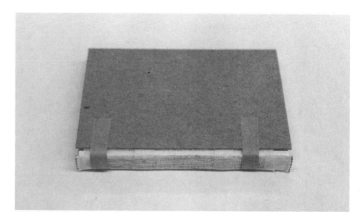

Fig. 30-68. Use tape to hold the boards in position.

3. Stretch the boards so that the tape is tight. Measure horizontally and vertically. Cut the bookbinder's cloth or paper two inches larger than the binder's board.

4. Using the wrong side of the cloth or paper, position the boards to that the distance around the outside is equal, Fig. 30-69. Mark around the edges of each binder's board and remove the gummed tapes.

5. Cover the side of each board next to the cloth or paper with a thin coat of bookbinder's glue. Press them firmly in place.

6. Cut a paper strip with the grain going the long way. It should be the exact length of the case boards and the exact width of the rounded back. Center and glue the strip between each board, Fig. 30-70.

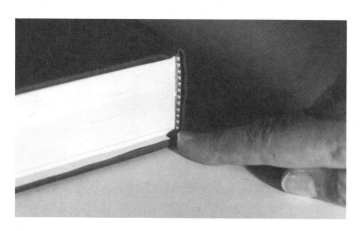

Fig. 30-66. Headband is fabric glued to book edges of pages inside the cover.

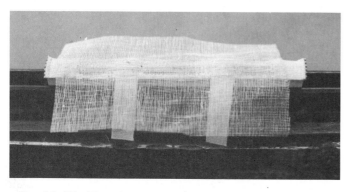

Fig. 30-67. Glue the supercloth to the back of the book.

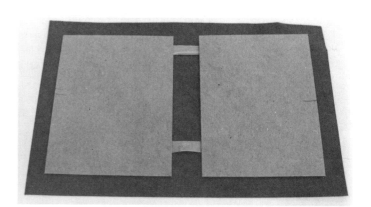

Fig. 30-69. Position the binder's board on the cloth or paper.

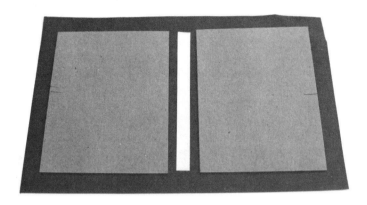

Fig. 30-70. Position a paper strip between the case boards.

7. Shape the corner by using the cut corner or library corner technique. The library method is shown in Fig. 30-71 and involves gluing and folding the corners. Glue the sides, one by one, starting with the long sides. Fold over and stretch into position. Sometimes, the case is put into a book press until the glue is dry, Fig. 30-72.

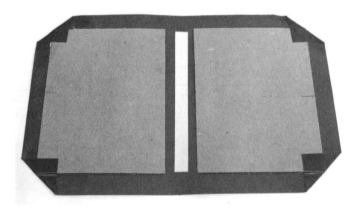

Fig. 30-71. Shape or fold over the corners of the case.

Fig. 30-72. Sometimes, you must place the case under pressure until the glue dries.

Casing-in

1. Cut wax paper larger than the end sheets and place it between both end sheets.
2. Cut the sewing tapes to equal the distance of the edge of the super cloth. Apply bookbinder's glue to the outside surface of both end sheets. Make sure the tapes are glued to the end sheets and coated with a thin film of glue. Carefully position them and press the case covers against the glued end sheets, Fig. 30-73. Adjust the end sheet and repeat this operation on the other side.

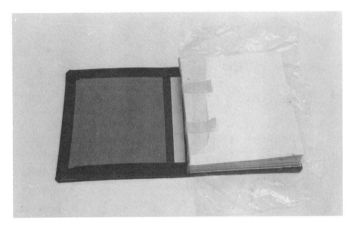

Fig. 30-73. Carefully position the case on the end sheets. Glue them together.

3. Close the book and crease it for the hinges. Carefully position the press boards on both sides of the book. The metal parts of the press boards must fit into the hinges of the book.
4. Place the book body and press boards in the book press or similar device, Fig. 30-74. Close the press and allow the glue to dry for eight hours.

   Although this summary describes a slow hand operation, some facilities still do hand binding of short runs, special editions, or when repairing old, valuable library books. This will also help you understand book construction.

Fig. 30-74. Place the book in the book press with the press boards in position.

PERFECT BINDING

Perfect binding has been a very successful form of binding printed materials. A typical example of perfect binding is a paperback book. Another product using this binding process is a telephone directory.

The perfect binding process eliminates the need for sewing and constructing a hard cover. Perfect binding is not as long lasting or rugged as edition binding. After prolonged use, the pages can fall out when the book is opened. The main advantage of perfect binding is low cost.

The signatures or single sheets are gathered, and/or collated. While being held together, the machine grinds or saws the binding edge of the book body to roughen the surface. A flexible glue is then applied to the edge. The cover is placed in contact with the glue and clamped in place until set. The book is then trimmed, usually with a three knife trimmer.

A typical perfect binding machine is shown in Fig. 30-75.

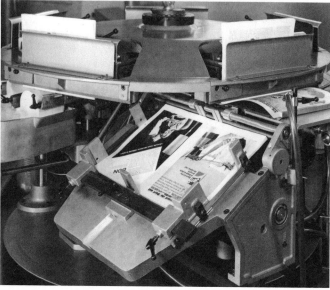

Fig. 30-75. This typical perfect binding machine is very fast and efficient. (Muller-Martini Corp.)

MECHANICAL BINDING

Discussed earlier, *mechanical binding* uses a mechanical device (metal spring, plastic fastener, etc.) to hold the sheets together in looseleaf form.

The *plastic fastener* is commonly used in a wide variety of publications. Rectangular holes are punched along the edge of the printed material. After the sheets are punched, they are positioned over the spread or expanded plastic teeth of the fastener. When released, the plastic teeth insert into the punched holes and bind the publication.

The finished product with a plastic fastener should look like the illustration in Fig. 30-76. The plastic fastening unit can be purchased in longer lengths and cut, but the 19 hole punch is common for an eleven inch side of the stock.

The *spiral binding* is very similar to the plastic method but the punched holes are smaller and wire is spiral fed through the booklet automatically. The finished book should appear as in Fig. 30-77. The ends of the wire are crimped to eliminate the probability of unraveling. The diameter of each type of binding wire varies with the need.

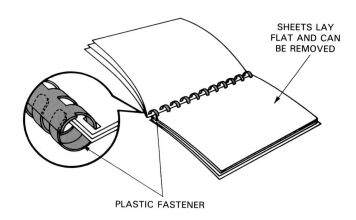

Fig. 30-76. Finished plastic bound book uses pronged plastic device that inserts through holes in stock. This allows booklet to lay flat. It can also be taken apart to add or remove pages easily. (A.B. Dick Co.)

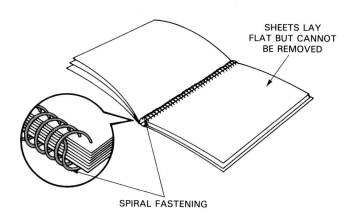

Fig. 30-77. Spiral fastening uses metal wire wound into a spring to form looseleaf binding. Sheets will lay flat but cannot be removed and installed from binding. (A.B. Dick)

A big advantage of the mechanical binding is its ability to open flat and remain that way. The plastic type allows for the removal and adding of a sheet very quickly. The spiral allows for the tearing out of a page but not insertion of sheets.

PACKAGING

In graphic communications, *packaging* basically involves enclosing or strapping the printed pieces together for shipping. For example, books can be enclosed in boxes that are taped shut. Several boxes can be stacked on a pallet and then strapped in place before shipping. This can vary with the type of printed product.

A *banding machine,* also called a loop press, will strap and bond a plastic or metal band around a bundle of booklets, books, boxes, or other products. This holds the products together for shipping.

Fig. 30-78 shows one type of banding machine or loop press for small products. It is computer controlled and will

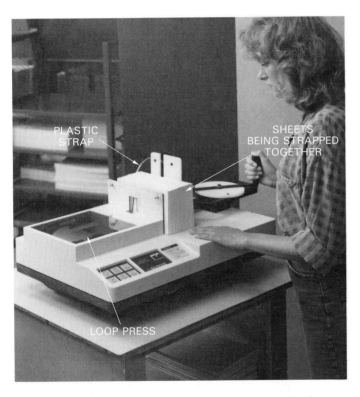

Fig. 30-78. Operator is using loop press to wrap plastic strap around sheets before shipping. (Signode)

automatically compress the sheets together and then wrap and join a plastic strap around the sheets. The computer will "remember" the size of the product for automatic banding.

Other banding machines are much larger and will strap full stacks of books or other printed materials before shipping. They can be hand operated or automatic.

A *taping machine* will automatically apply adhesive tape to seal the tops of boxes. One is pictured in Fig. 30-79. As

the boxes are fed through the machine, a series of rollers and brushes apply the adhesive tape to the top of each box. A cutter also slices off the tape to the correct length. Two belts force the boxes through the taping machine. This helps automate the shipping department of a facility.

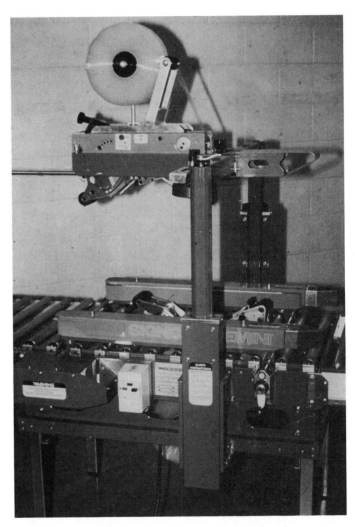

Fig. 30-79. Taping machine will speed up packaging area by automatically sealing boxes with tape. (Signode)

BINDERY PRODUCTION CONTROL SYSTEM

A *bindery production control system* uses a computer to monitor the bindery equipment as a means of increasing efficiency. For example, one system uses a personal computer to communicate with one or more electronic input device(s) in the bindery. This allows production performance data to be fed back to the computer, Fig. 30-80.

When the data is in the computer, bindery production efficiency and progress of a specific job can be analyzed. Data such as total job time, job cost, downtime, etc. for a specific piece of bindery equipment or for an equipment operator can be collected. It is possible to also eliminate the conventional bindery job ticket with a bindery production control system.

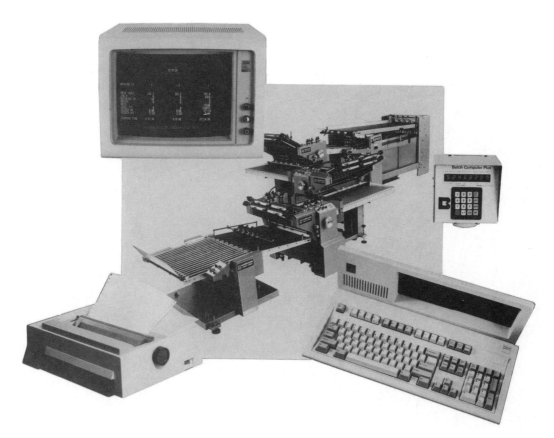

Fig. 30-80. Computers can be used to improve efficiency of binding area. Computer can check progress of product, check efficiency of each binding operation, etc.   (Baumfolder)

KNOW THESE TERMS

Finishing, Binding, Cutting, Trimming, Guillotine cutter, Sheath, Cutting stick, Nonrepeat device, Two-handed operation, Electric eye stop, Vacuum system, Three-knife cutter, Card cutter, Film cutter, Air jet bed, Buckle folder, Knife folder, Fold plate, Floor folder, Table folder, Self-cover stitched body, Gate-fold book. Three-panel fold, Accordion fold, Fold-out book, Slitting, Creasing, Scoring, Perforating, Drilling, Punching, Multiple spindle, Ruling, Stamping, Die cutting, Bridges, Varnishing, Embossing, Blind embossing, Flocking, Laminating, Numbering, Adhesive binding, Mechanical binding, Side stitching, Saddle stitching, Side sewing, Saddle sewing, Soft bound, Hard bound, Self-cover binding, Pamphlet binding, Gathering, Collating, Collating marks, Edition binding, Case, Casing-in, Kettle stitch, Spine, End sheets, Headbands, Bookbinder's boards, Perfect binding, Plastic fastener, Spiral binding, Packaging, Banding, Taping, Bindery production control system.

REVIEW QUESTIONS — CHAPTER 30

1. Define the term "finishing."
2. This term refers to when three sides of a book are made even and square.
   - a. Cutting.
   - b. Flocking.
   - c. Sheathing.
   - d. Trimming.
3. What is a cutting stick?
4. Explain three means of protecting a cutting machine operator.
5. The _____ _____ _____ lifts heavy stacks of paper off of the cutter table for easy movement.
6. How does a buckle folder work?
7. _____ is similar to cutting but it can be done by a set of wheels as the sheet passes through the folder.
8. Explain the difference between creasing and scoring.
9. Describe the difference between punching and drilling.
10. What is one product that is commonly laminated?
11. Summarize nine classifications of binding.
12. _____ is a general term associated with the assembling of signatures.
13. _____ usually means the assembling of single sheets while to _____ means checking signature placement or sequence after gathering.
14. Why are collating marks sometimes used?
15. How can a computer be used to improve the efficiency of the bindery department?

SUGGESTED ACTIVITIES

1. Complete an edition binding project.
2. Visit a commercial bindery and list all of the bindery operations and finishing operations performed by the plant.
3. Visit a library and study types of binding.

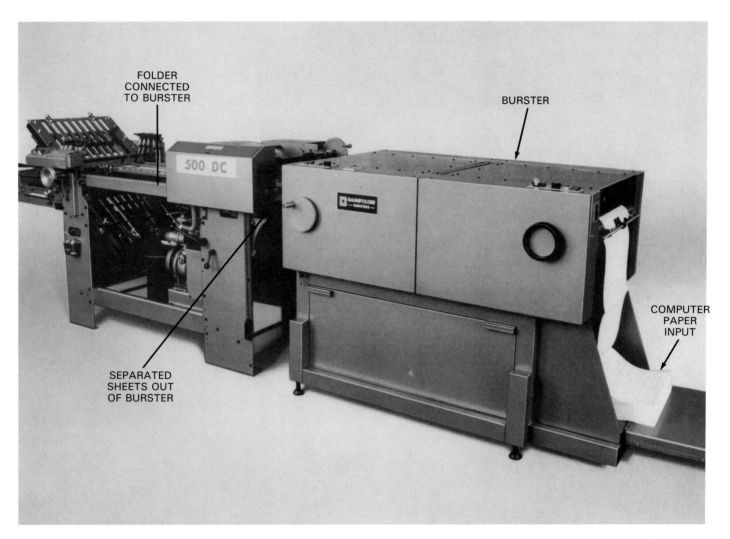

FOLDER
CONNECTED
TO BURSTER

BURSTER

500 DC

SEPARATED
SHEETS OUT
OF BURSTER

COMPUTER
PAPER
INPUT

This burster will tear perforated sheets of computer paper apart and separate them. Burster can then be tied to folder.   (Baumfolder)

Trade customs are implied laws or rules that regulate the printing industry. Those working in graphic communications should understand these customs so they can protect themselves and satisfy their customers.

Chapter 31

TRADE CUSTOMS

After studying this chapter, you will be able to:
- Explain the statements that uphold the trade customs in the graphic communications industry.
- Describe the most common trade customs in graphic communications.
- Summarize copyright laws.

This chapter will overview the most important rules that govern the printing industry. It would be time consuming and inefficient to write a contract that covered all aspects of each new print job. Trade customs are therefore used and understood by those working in the industry. It is important for you to grasp the meaning of trade customs if you are going to be employed in this field.

The chapter also summarizes copyright laws. A printer should understand these laws to protect the business from possible lawsuits.

WHAT ARE TRADE CUSTOMS?

Trade customs are understood rules or implied laws used in the printing industry. After something has been in use for a long time, it has the same effect as a law.

A trade custom does not spring up overnight. Just because an act is done over and over does not make it a custom. The act must be recognized by all parties as a contract and that their rights and responsibilities are established by the custom.

Trade customs have been backed up by the courts as binding agreements. At times, specific contracts are issued when other additional terms are desired.

The National Association of Printers and Lithographers (NAPL) have written statements that uphold trade customs. These include:
1. Printer should publish trade customs on the back of estimates and other order acknowledgments.
2. State on the order acknowledgment that all work is subject to trade customs.
3. Make sure that custom-made terms and conditions are no less strict than trade customs.
4. Make sure that salespersons are knowledgeable of trade customs and how they protect the printer.

The trade customs of the Printing and Lithographic Industries have been accepted by the National Association of Printers and Lithographers (NAPL) and the Printing Industries of America (PIA). These associations reaffirm the trade customs at their business meetings and, from time to time, create a committee to study proposed changes to the customs.

An example of trade customs on the back of a quote are given in Fig. 31-1. Read through each carefully.

Trade customs are usually printed on the back of estimates or quotes for printing jobs. Many companies use the traditional trade customs written by the NAPL and PIA. However, some firms modify the trade customs slightly and also add *riders* or additional stipulations to the conventional trade customs.

Fig. 31-2 gives some examples of riders that supplement trade customs. Riders are important to the printer and to the customer since they can affect the responsibilities and outcome of the job as well as the costs of the job if difficulties arise.

COPYRIGHT LAWS

As the term implies, a *copyright* protects people from having their work copied or plagarized. Literary materials (printed words, books, etc.), music, art, film, video, and drama are common examples of works protected by copyright. In the U.S., a copyright is in effect for the life of the author or producer, plus 50 more years after his or her death. In graphic communications or printing, you should be primarily concerned with copyrights on printed matter.

For example, a textbook, like this one, will have the copyright information on the title page or on the page right after or before the title page. The copyright should say "copyright" or use the symbol "©" followed by the name of the copyright owner and the year the work was first published.

Fig. 31-3 gives the copyright information from the front of a textbook. Compare it with the copyright data in the front matter of this book.

When someone brings in materials (sign, poster, ad, etc.) and asks the printer or copy service to reproduce it, they may

Printing Trade Customs

Trade Customs have been in general use in the Printing Industry throughout the United States of America for more than 50 years.

1. QUOTATION: A quotation not accepted within thirty (30) days is subject to review. Materials are quoted based on current costs and are subject to change.

2. ORDERS: Orders are not deemed accepted until customer credit has been approved. Orders regularly entered, verbal or written, cannot be cancelled except upon terms that will compensate printer against loss.

3. PREPARATORY WORK: Sketches, art work, composition, plates, negatives, positives, dies and other items when supplied by the printer shall remain his exclusive property unless otherwise agreed in writing. Experimental work performed at customer's request will be charged for at current rates and may not be used without consent of the printer.

4. CONDITION OF COPY: Estimates for typesetting are based on the receipt of original copy or manuscript clearly typed, double-spaced on 8½" x 11" uncoated stock, one side only. Condition of copy which deviates from this standard is subject to re-estimating and pricing review by printer at time of submission of copy, unless otherwise specified in estimate.

5. ALTERATIONS: Alterations represent work performed in addition to the original specifications. Such additional work shall be charged at current rates and be supported with documentation upon request.

6. PROOFS: Proofs shall be submitted with original copy. Corrections are to be made on "master set", returned marked "O.K." or "O.K. with corrections" and signed by customer. If revised proofs are desired, request must be made when proofs are returned in writing. Printer regrets any errors that may occur through production undetected, but cannot be held responsible for errors if the work is printed per customer's O.K. or if changes are communicated verbally. Printer shall not be responsible for errors if the customer has not ordered or has refused to accept proofs or has failed to return proofs with indication of changes or has instructed printer to proceed without submission of proofs.

7. PRESS PROOFS: Unless specifically provided in printer's quotation, there will be an additional charge for press proofs. An inspection sheet of any form can be submitted for customer approval, at no charge, provided customer is available at the press during the time of makeready. Any changes, corrections or lost press time due to customer's change or delay will be charged for at current rates.

8. COLOR PROOFING: Because of differences in equipment, paper, inks and other conditions between color proofing and production pressroom operations, a reasonable variation in color between color proofs and the completed job shall constitute acceptable delivery.

9. OVER RUNS AND UNDER RUNS: Over runs or under runs not to exceed 10% on quantities ordered up to 10,000 copies and/or the percentage agreed upon over or under quantities ordered above 10,000 copies shall constitute acceptable delivery. Printer will bill for actual quantity delivered within this tolerance. If customer requires guaranteed "no less than" delivery, percentage tolerance of overage must be doubled.

10. CUSTOMER'S PROPERTY: The printer will maintain fire, extended coverage, vandalism, malicious mischief and sprinkler leakage insurance on all property belonging to the customer, while such property is in the printer's possession; printer's liability for such property shall not exceed the amount recoverable from such insurance.

11. DELIVERY: Unless otherwise specified, the price quoted is for a single shipment, without storage, F.O.B. local customer's place of business or F.O.B. printer's platform for out-of-town customers. Proposals are based on continuous and uninterrupted delivery of complete order, unless specifications distinctly state otherwise. Charges related to delivery from customer to printer, or from customer's supplier to printer are not included in any quotations unless specified. Special priority pickup or delivery service will be provided at current rates upon customer's request. Materials delivered from customer or his suppliers are verified with delivery ticket as to cartons, packages or items shown only. The accuracy of quantities indicated on such tickets cannot be verified and printer cannot accept liability for shortage based on supplier's tickets. Title for finished work shall pass to the customer upon delivery to carrier at shipping point or upon mailing of invoices for finished work, whichever occurs first.

12. PRODUCTION SCHEDULES: Production schedules will be established and adhered to by customer and printer, provided that neither shall incur any liability or penalty for delays due to state of war, riot, civil disorder, fire, strikes, accidents, action of Government or civil authority and acts of God or other causes beyond the control of customer or printer.

13. CUSTOMER FURNISHED MATERIALS: Paper stock, camera copy, film, color separations, proofs, and other customer furnished materials shall be manufactured, packed and delivered to printer's specifications. Additional cost due to delays or impaired production caused by specification deficiencies shall be charged to the customer.

14. TERMS: Payment shall be net cash thirty (30) days from date of invoice unless otherwise provided in writing. Claims for defects, damages or shortages must be made by the customer in writing within a period of thirty (30) days after delivery. Failure to make such claim within the stated period shall constitute irrevocable acceptance and an admission that they fully comply with terms, conditions and specifications. Printer's liability shall be limited to stated selling price of any defective goods, and shall in no event include special or consequential damages, including profits (or profits lost). As security for payment of any sum due or to become due under terms of any Agreement, printer shall have the right, if necessary, to retain possession of and shall have a lien on all customer property in printer's possession including artwork, film plates, work in process and finished work. The extension of credit or the acceptance of notes, trade acceptances or guarantee of payment shall not affect such security interest and lien.

15. INDEMNIFICATION: The customer shall indemnify and hold harmless the printer from any and all loss, cost, expense and damages on account of any and all manner of claims, demands, actions and proceedings that may be instituted against the printer on grounds alleging that the said printing violates any copyright or any proprietary right of any person, or that it contains any matter that is libelous or scandalous, or invades any person's right to privacy or other personal rights, except to the extent that the printer has contributed to the matter. The customer agrees to, at the customer's own expense, promptly defend and continue the defense of any such claim, demand, action or proceeding that may be brought against the printer, provided that the printer shall promptly notify the customer with respect thereto, and provided further that the printer shall give to the customer such reasonable time as the exigencies of the situation may permit in which to undertake and continue the defense thereof.

Fig. 31-1. These are the accepted Trade Customs used in the printing industry. Read through them carefully. They are sometimes printed on the back of quotes and bills.   (Viking Press—A Minnesota Co.)

RIDER

C & S Company will accept orders for printing, binding and other book manufacturing services only upon the following understandings and agreements of Customer:

Risk of loss and insurance coverage on material supplied by Customer and on work produced and billed by C & S or delivered, including film and unfinished as well as finished books, are Customer's responsibilities. Customer releases and forever discharges C & S and its employees from any and all claims or causes of action whatsoever founded upon loss of or damage to such material or work, if such loss or damage is caused by fire or other insurable peril, whether or not attributable to the fault or negligence of C & S, its employees or agents, and whether or not Customer has obtained insurance coverage therefore. Insurable perils are those perils such as sprinkler leakage, explosion, riot/civil commotion and building collapse, in addition to fire and such other risks that are insurable under the standard form of ALL RISKS insurance currently in use.

C & S prices are based on the present cost of materials involved and C & S current labor rates. If there are any changes in the cost of materials or in C & S scale of wages prior to the completion of any portion of this work, said increases or decreases will be reflected in C & S charges for that portion of the work.

All applicable personal property, sales, use of other taxes now in effect or hereafter imposed on this sale and on the use or ownership of the finished goods covered by this proposal, shall be filled as an extra and will be borne by the Customer.

It is understood that five percent (5%) overrun or underrun of a single binding shall constitute complete delivery and that C & S charges are based upon quantities delivered.

No agreements or instructions shall be binding upon C & S unless accepted in writing by C & S. Printing orders shall specify the quantity of each title to be printed at one run; binding orders, the quantity of each title to be bound at one time. C & S retains the right to reject Customer's order based on any proposal, without liability, upon mailing Purchaser written notice of such rejection within thirty (30) days after C & S receives it. Once accepted, orders cannot be cancelled by Customer except on terms that will compensate C & S for all expenses incurred for materials purchased, services performed and unrecovered production time attributable thereto.

C & S warrants the articles manufactured by it will conform to specifications and be free from defects in workmanship and materials attributable to the labor performed and materials furnished by C & S which render the articles unmerchantable. THERE ARE NO WARRANTIES THAT EXTEND BEYOND THOSE STATED. In the event of breach of warranty, Customer's exclusive remedy and C & S liability and responsibility will be limited, at C & S option, (a) to repairing or replacing such defective articles at no cost to the Customer, or (b) if such repairing or replacing is not practicable, then to reimbursing Customer for the cost of any paper or other materials furnished for such articles by Customer and for the cost of labor and materials furnished by C & S and paid for by Customer, including shipping, upon receiving actual notice of the nature of the defect and the quantity involved. In no event shall C & S be liable for consequential damages resulting from breach of warranty or any other default.

It is understood that all Customer-owned material, paper, sheets or books remaining in C & S custody, will be subject to a five percent (5%) inventory shrinkage allowance for each year said material is in C & S possession.

Customer agrees to indemnify and hold C & S harmless from all loss, damage and expense (including attorney's fees) incurred by Rand in defending against any claim alleging that C & S has libeled or violated the privacy of any individual or has infringed any copyright, or contributed to such wrongs, by reason of C & S performance in accordance with Customer's order or instructions.

C & S shall not be liable for any default or delay which is due to any act or neglect of Customer or Customer's agents or employees, or which is due to a shortage of materials or energy, labor difficulties, flood, fire, governmental action or control, a delay of common carriers, act of God or any cause beyond Rand's control. Should C & S performance be delayed by any one or more of such occurrences it may be completed as soon as practicable after such disabilities have ceased, but C & S shall give seasonable notice to Customer of the delay.

C & S acceptance of Customer's order shall result in a contract made in Illinois and shall be construed according to Illinois Law.

Customer hereby agrees that this Rider is incorporated as part of Customer's Purchase Order # _____ dated _____ any any other order that may be placed with respect to the subject matter thereof, and supercedes any terms and conditions in conflict herewith.

_____   Dated: _____
Customer

By_____

Title: _____

Fig. 31-2. These are stipulations given by one printer. They protect both the printer and the customer.   *(NAPL)*

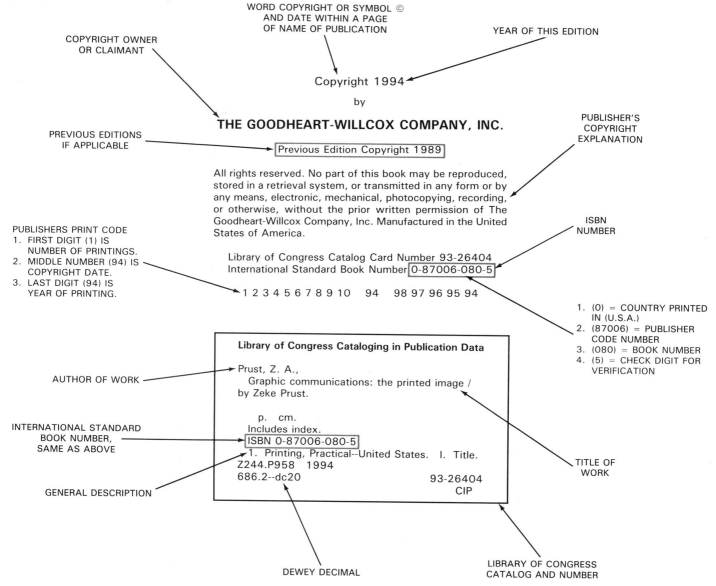

COPYRIGHT OWNER OR CLAIMANT

WORD COPYRIGHT OR SYMBOL © AND DATE WITHIN A PAGE OF NAME OF PUBLICATION

YEAR OF THIS EDITION

Copyright 1994

by

THE GOODHEART-WILLCOX COMPANY, INC.

PREVIOUS EDITIONS IF APPLICABLE

Previous Edition Copyright 1989

PUBLISHER'S COPYRIGHT EXPLANATION

All rights reserved. No part of this book may be reproduced, stored in a retrieval system, or transmitted in any form or by any means, electronic, mechanical, photocopying, recording, or otherwise, without the prior written permission of The Goodheart-Willcox Company, Inc. Manufactured in the United States of America.

PUBLISHERS PRINT CODE
1. FIRST DIGIT (1) IS NUMBER OF PRINTINGS.
2. MIDDLE NUMBER (94) IS COPYRIGHT DATE.
3. LAST DIGIT (94) IS YEAR OF PRINTING.

Library of Congress Catalog Card Number 93-26404
International Standard Book Number 0-87006-080-5

ISBN NUMBER

1 2 3 4 5 6 7 8 9 10   94   98 97 96 95 94

1. (0) = COUNTRY PRINTED IN (U.S.A.)
2. (87006) = PUBLISHER CODE NUMBER
3. (080) = BOOK NUMBER
4. (5) = CHECK DIGIT FOR VERIFICATION

Library of Congress Cataloging in Publication Data

AUTHOR OF WORK

Prust, Z. A.,
   Graphic communications: the printed image / by Zeke Prust.

   p.   cm.
   Includes index.
   ISBN 0-87006-080-5
   1. Printing, Practical--United States.   I. Title.
Z244.P958   1994
686.2--dc20   93-26404
                                        CIP

INTERNATIONAL STANDARD BOOK NUMBER, SAME AS ABOVE

GENERAL DESCRIPTION

TITLE OF WORK

DEWEY DECIMAL

LIBRARY OF CONGRESS CATALOG AND NUMBER

Fig. 31-3. This is an example of the copyright information given in the front of a textbook.

be asking the printer or copy service to break a copyright law. Illegal requests for duplication are commonly made of printers. However, this is in violation of copyright statutes.

The Copyright Act of 1909 was revised on October 19, 1976 and went into effect on January 1, 1978. Under the new law—"A copyright is automatically secured when work is created and a work is created when it is fixed as a copy. Copies are material objects from which a work can be read either directly or with the aid of a machine."

This means that the copyright owner determines who is able to use the material. Permission for use must be initiated by the requestor, usually in writing.

Exceptions for duplicating copyrighted materials do exist and they are listed in the Fair Use Clause of the Copyright Act and House Report #94-1476.

A typical example of this often take place in the school classroom when a teacher photocopies copyrighted material for classroom use by students. This act falls under this exception clause. Students can also copy protected material

if it is used to assist in a lesson, or for private study or research. For a complete use statement, the copyright laws should be read.

The factors commonly used by the courts to determine if infringement of copyright has taken place are:
1. How material has been used.
2. Type of work copied.
3. Amount of material copied.
4. Content of material.
5. Value of material.

LEGAL CONSIDERATIONS

It is the printer's responsibility to receive proper clarification that the copyright law is not being broken. It is illegal to copy some material unless proper channels for permission are secured.

The material supplied by the customer must comply with copyright regulations. The printer cannot be expected to make that decision; therefore, the customer should be asked to make any inquiries. For a small fee, a search can be requested from:

Reference and Bibliography Section
Copyright Offices
Library of Congress
Washington, DC 20559

It may be necessary to seek legal counsel to determine if an infringement exists. It might be wise to have a release form for customers to sign that releases the printer from liability for copyright infringement.

If the printer is found to have infringed on a copyright, the penalties are determined generally by two methods: the first is Actual Damages and Profits and the second is Statutory Damage.

The *Actual Damages and Profits* method is done by calculating the actual damages and profits that have been made, based on the infringement.

The *Statutory Damage Method* identifies the liability of the infringer. The courts can set the fee of not less than $250 or more than $10,000. If the courts determine that the act was willful, the court may assign a fee of not more than $50,000. This can vary with unusual situations, however.

To fully understand the implications of the act, it is advisable that the printer read the act and seek information from various associations. This makes good sense and is essential if owners are to operate a printing facility in a professional manner.

KNOW THESE TERMS

Trade custom, NAPL, PIA, Rider, Quotation, Order, Preparatory work, Alterations, Proofs, Press proofs, Color proofing, Over runs, Under runs, Customer's property, Pro-duction schedule, Customer furnished material, Terms, Indemnification, Copyright.

REVIEW QUESTIONS—CHAPTER 31

1. Define the term "trade customs."
2. Trade customs change from day to day. True or false?
3. Write the statements given by NAPL that uphold trade customs.
4. What do the abbreviations NAPL and PIA mean?
5. In your own words, explain what each trade custom means to you. (Refer to Fig. 31-1.)
6. _____ are additional stipulations governing the responsibilities of a job.
7. If you are working for a printer and someone brings in a poster with a copyright, can you legally reproduce the poster without fear of legal action?
8. Define the term "copyright."
9. What materials can be copyrighted?
10. Where do you write to get a copyright search?
11. Art, type, and plates supplied by the printer, are the property of the _____.
12. What is the period of time that quotations are typically accepted?

SUGGESTED ACTIVITIES

1. Visit a large printing plant and inquire if they use the published information on trade customs supplied by NAPL and PIA.
2. Review trade custom cases that have appeared in courts of law.
3. Observe and note how copyright is stated on books, television shows, videos, and other materials.

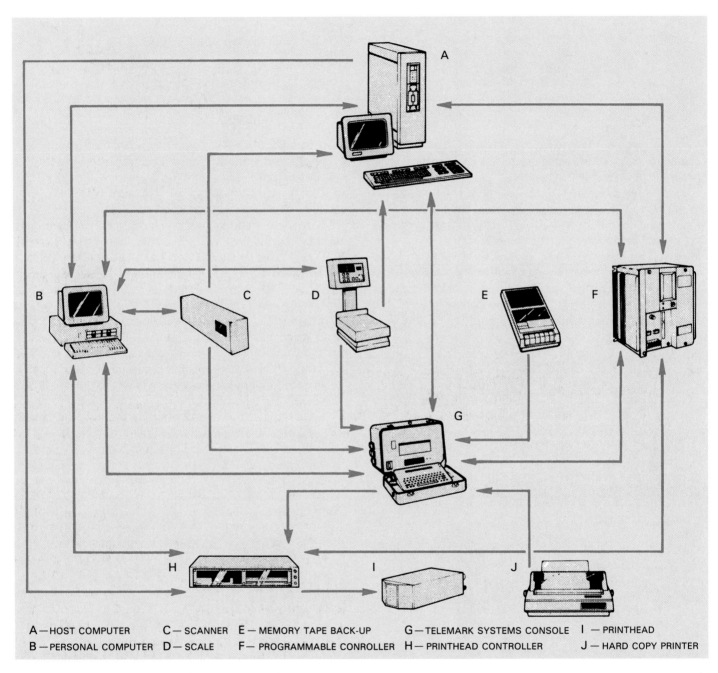

A — HOST COMPUTER   C — SCANNER   E — MEMORY TAPE BACK-UP   G — TELEMARK SYSTEMS CONSOLE   I — PRINTHEAD

B — PERSONAL COMPUTER   D — SCALE   F — PROGRAMMABLE CONROLLER   H — PRINTHEAD CONTROLLER   J — HARD COPY PRINTER

Diagram shows computerized network for running inkjet printhead for labeling products in shipping department. System will interface with electronic sales, programmable controllers, scanners, and other packaging equipment.   (Diagraph Corporation)

Chapter 32

DESIGNING FOR EFFICIENCY, ENTREPRENEURSHIP

After studying this chapter, you will be able to:
- Write the objectives for planning a graphic communications facility that meets specific business goals.
- Determine the space needed for the facility.
- Make decisions about company expansion based on the data available.
- Outline the questions that must be answered when determining whether to expand an existing facility or build a new facility.
- Utilize job tickets and other business forms.
- Summarize the abilities of an entrepreneur.

If you ever move into upper level management in a graphic communications facility, you may have to take part in planning the growth of the company. You may be required to make decisions about new equipment, flow or handling of materials, building an addition to the building, or starting a new company. You might also want to start your own business some day.

This chapter will outline the types of things you must consider when expanding or developing a graphic communications facility. The chapter outlines the types of questions or information you must have to make logical business decisions.

After reading this chapter, your instructor may want to have a class discussion on this topic or may want you to simulate the business decision making process as an assignment.

FACILITY EFFICIENCY AND GROWTH

The efficiency and success of a graphic communications operation is dependent upon many factors. Every employee, every process, every supplier, every piece of equipment, all play a vital role in the growth or downfall of a company!

The location of the various departments, the placement of equipment, employee attitudes, the location of the facility geographically, these factors and many others affect business success. For this reason, careful planning is tremendously important. If a planner or manager makes mistakes, it can cost the firm time, money, and personnel.

The growth of a graphics firm is primarily dependent upon the finished product's cost and quality. In turn, the employees, raw materials, and equipment control the cost and quality of a printed product.

An old wise saying goes, "A chain is only as strong as its weakest link." Relating to the planning of the growth or development of a graphics company, every phase of production must be well thought out and reviewed periodically. If one phase of production is "weak," the final product will also be "weak."

The growth and success of a company is dependent upon many numerous interacting factors. From a progressive management viewpoint, some of these include:

1. Using efficient cost-effective equipment to produce better products at a lower cost.
2. Using a "team effort" mental attitude where all employees work and communicate as a cohesive unit to outperform competing companies.
3. Using worker feedback to analyze and improve production steps; if someone does the same task over and over, they should have ideas that might help improve that workstation.
4. Partially base pay increases on company profits. This will help employee "peer pressure" improve job performance. If someone is not producing their fair share of work, it can affect everyones pay increases. As a result, worker interaction will affect and improve work output.
5. Make it obvious that advancements and salary increases are dependent upon job performance; use objective criteria like dependability, work quality, work speed, efficiency, cooperation, initiative, innovation, etc.
6. When possible, provide for advancement within the company, to reward good workers and discourage insufficient job performance.
7. Analyze and select outside sources of supplies and services carefully, weigh cost versus quality factors.
8. Incorporate modern quality control and production control methods to evaluate all activities within the company.
9. Constantly train employees to keep them up-to-date with advances in technology. Then, the employees can use this knowledge to help strengthen the company.

505

10. Make employment with the company a life-long goal through profit sharing plans, pleasant working conditions, etc.

GROWTH PLANNING CHECKLISTS

A *growth planning checklist* will help assure that all criteria is considered when determining the considerations for facility growth or the development of a new facility. The checklist is designed for use in developing the technical and financial data necessary to determine whether plant expansion or new plant construction is more cost effective. It represents both an outline of the questions that need to be answered and a guide for assigning responsibilities for various aspects of the work.

The checklist applies to commercial printing plants, book publishing, newspaper and magazine printing, and with some adaptations, it also applies to in-plant operations.

Determining facility objectives
1. What dollar volume of annual sales must the plant (expanded or new) be able to accommodate at peak efficiency?
2. What levels of production does the target sales volume (projected sales goal) equal?
   a. By product line.
   b. Reflecting annual change from present to design (goal) year projected sales.
   c. Reflecting seasonal variations in production.
3. When will this sales volume be achieved, according to present projections?
4. Is the time span projected between existing sales levels and design year sales:
   a. Too brief to allow sufficient use of facility (expanded or new) before additional space is required—less than five years?
   b. Too long to justify capital investment in expanded or new facilities—more than 5 years?
5. Based on topic 3, should a different design level of sales be adopted as the facilities planning target?

Translating sales goals into space requirements
1. What is the present space usage and percentage utilization of space in the various departments?
   a. Art department.
   b. Composition.
   c. Photo conversion.
   d. Intermediate prep.
   e. Platemaking.
   f. Stripping.
   g. Printing.
   h. Binding and Finishing.
   i. Mail room.
   j. Advertising.
   k. Circulation.
   l. News room.
   m. Raw material storage (paper, film, plates, ink, other).
   n. Finished product storage.
   o. Service areas.
   p. Offices.
2. Do any specific congestion areas exist in the present layout? Determine area size and percent overload.
3. Are there any functions NOT now included in the plant that should be added to increase efficiency or incorporate new production methods?
   a. Photo composition.
   b. Editing.
   c. Electronic publishing.
   d. Scanning.
   e. Binding.
   f. Other.
4. Will any new equipment be added to improve operating efficiency or to incorporate new production methods?
   a. Art department.
   b. Composition.
   c. Photo conversion.
   d. Intermediate.
   e. Platemaking.
   f. Stripping.
   g. Printing.
   h. Binding and Finishing.
   i. Material handling.
   j. Other.
5. Are there any regulations for which applicable codes (building codes, OSHA codes, etc.) will affect space allocation and layout in a new or expanded facility?
   a. Size of areas permitted within fire walls.
   b. Separate storage of flammable materials.
   c. Noise control areas.
   d. Ventilation requirement.
   e. Other (underwriters insurance codes, state codes, OSHA, EPA, other).
6. Are there any operational requirements that will affect space allocation and layout in a new or expanded facility?
   a. Temperature or humidity control areas.
   b. Isolated areas (intermediate preparation, platemaking, other).
7. Based on topics 2 through 6, how much space will be required to meet the target level sales; what will be the departmental net space change and revised percent utilization?
8. What affect will additional employees have on the existing facility?
   a. Additional space required.
   b. Additional service facilities to meet codes and employee comfort standards (toilets, cafeteria, lounges, locker rooms, exercise area, etc.).
   c. Additional parking.

Determining if facility can be expanded for increased production
1. Based on the revised departmental arrangement and plant layout, does sufficient space exist to accommodate all departments?
   a. Within existing building.
   b. Requiring expansion of building.

2. Where a particular department cannot be accommodated with ideal space, what compromise is necessary?
3. What percentage of the projected target sales volume can be accommodated in the expanded facility?
4. Does the proposed expansion permit a later expansion if needed?
   a. How much subsequent expansion on the site is possible after the contemplated move?
   b. What effect will subsequent expansion have on the layout planned for this expansion?
5. Does sufficient site capacity exist to accommodate the expanded facility and does it also provide for required parking?
6. If expansion is still feasible through topics 1 to 5, what building modifications will be required?
   a. Structural.
   b. Lighting.
   c. Electrical.
   d. Plumbing and mechanical.
   e. Interior finishes.
   f. Ventilation.
   g. Others.
7. What site modifications will be necessary?
   a. Clearing and grading.
   b. Drainage.
   c. Paving.
   d. Landscaping.

Evaluating investment required to expand

1. What are the intial costs?
   a. Site development.
   b. New equipment.
   c. Building addition design and construction.
   d. Building services (mechanical, electrical, etc.).
   e. Internal rearrangement (moving costs).

Considering "differential" operating costs in expanded facility

1. How will annual costs in expanded facility change over existing facility?
   a. Labor.
   b. Raw materials.
   c. Utilities.
   d. Maintenance costs.
   e. Debt service.
   f. Other.

Determining time required to complete expansion

1. How will you schedule the activities involved?
   a. Planning.
   b. Design drawings and bid documents.
   c. Equipment procurement.
   d. Construction.
   e. Move.

Considering investment feasibility

1. Do the survey results indicate expansion to be desirable? Analyze cost of owning expanded facility versus the income required to carry the investment.

ANOTHER ALTERNATIVE—A NEW FACILITY

1. What modifications to projected space allocation can be made in an ideal new layout with no previous structural constraints?
2. What modifications to plant layout would be made in an ideal facility?
3. What modifications to building configuration would be made in an ideal facility?
4. Based on topics 1 through 3, what would the ideal layout and configuration be?

Choosing a potential location

1. What factors should be considered in choosing a location?
   a. Location of potential customers.
   b. Availability of skilled and unskilled labor supply.
   c. Union conditions (wage rates and union demands relative to area-wide conditions).
   d. Convenience to employee transportation.
   e. Convenience to transportation for shipping and receiving.
   f. Other.
2. What factors should be considered in selecting a site?
   a. Potential land cost.
   b. Development cost.
   c. Potential for future expansion.
   d. Availability of required transportation.
   e. Proximity of labor as needed.
   f. Accessibility to highways.
   g. Tax structure.
   h. Utilities.
   i. Others.

Planning building to house operation

1. Based on the ideal layout and building configuration, determine the following criteria.
   a. Building materials.
   b. Design performance standards.
      Floor loads to accommodate presses and other heavy equipment.
      Temperature and humidity control (if needed) for press areas and paper storage.
      Lighting levels for composing, artwork, and other critical work areas.
      Dust control.
      Noise control.
      Other.
   c. Architectural treatment, as a basis of estimating preliminary costs.

Estimating investment in new facility

1. What are the initial costs?
   a. Site acquisition.
   b. Site development.
   c. New equipment.
   d. Building design and construction, including building services, mechanical, electrical, etc.

e. Moving costs.

f. Minus income from sale of existing building, if one is to be sold.

Considering "differential" operating costs in new facility

1. What are the new annual costs going to be?
   a. Labor.
   b. Raw materials.
   c. Utilities.
   d. Lease or mortgagae payments.
   e. Maintenance costs.
   f. Taxes.
   g. Others.

Determining time required to complete facility

1. How will you schedule the activities involved?
   a. Planning.
   b. Design drawings and other bid documents.
   c. Construction.
   d. Move.
   e. Others.

Considering investment feasibility

1. Analysis of cost of owning expanded facility versus income required to carry investment.

Making a decision

1. Did you decide to expand or build a new facility? Take into account the extenuating circumstances prompting consideration of plant expansion and construction of a new facility, such as:
   a. Plant condemnation (precludes expansion).
   b. Inability to meet current sales (because of space limitations which necessitates rapid movement into more space).
   c. Determine the relative long and short term costs and advantages of the two alternatives, based on the above developed data.

Planning a facility is no easy task. The layout must be accurate because it shows the arrangement of equipment to produce a product in the most economical way. Many of today's facilities require a high degree of flexibility. The permanent securing of most equipment is not a common practice when a functional plant layout is needed.

Nearly every factor in site selection is a compromise. This is also true within the facility because the "ideal situation" might be forced to change with the conditions encountered in each operation. The operation is looking for the optimum arrangement of the total facility.

JOB TICKETS, FORMS

Productivity is the amount of quality work completed in a given time span. It is a key word in the printing plant. *Efficiency* (maximum output with minimum effort) and *utilization* (maximum use of people and equipment) are two factors which add up to productivity. In order for this to

happen throughout the plant, understood steps or procedures are essential.

Most plants that produce printed products use some type of *form* to collect all of the information necessary to communicate to all departments, Fig. 32-1. Forms are generally designed to meet the needs of a specific company or area in a company.

The form found in Fig. 32-2 is an example where all of the personnel had input. The shaded area is filled out by personnel in the planning and purchasing departments while the clear areas are filled out by sales people.

In this example, a separate job ticket or jacket is used for sheet-fed presswork and web-press operations. If joint use is required, a symbol is placed after the job number. This is required to clearly identify the dual application.

Headings break up the form to aid in the communication process. This clearly identifies what is to be done in each special area.

Type and art forms

The type/art portion of a job form or ticket tells the people involved what must be done. A check mark is placed in the proper square. Additional or special information can be written in the space provided.

Prep department forms

The personnel in the prep department can also be informed of what needs to be done by a form. Sometimes, the job has been printed before. If so, the job may be repeated without any changes. However, if changes are to be made, the proper square on the form must be checked. The various stages are also checked to identify camera-ready copy, one piece of film, or a number of negatives or positives. "*Seps*" refers to the nickname given to the film necessary to print a full color job.

Proof forms

The types of proofs requested can also be listed on the job form. Who will be responsible for or has checked the proofs may initial the form.

Paper forms

Proper paper information is extremely important. In this case, sales personnel fill out one section of the job ticket. The planning and purchasing people are responsible for listing the basis weight of the stock, as well as the supplier of the paper. Also listed is: when paper is ordered, when it will arrive, paper lot number, quantity needed, size of stock, direction of grain, cut direction, specific size, number of pieces from each sheet, and total number of finished cut pieces.

The paper section changes slightly with the web operation since the paper is in roll form. The width of the roll and the cut allowance are two different pieces of information needed to make sure enough paper is ordered.

The sheet-fed press section is filled out by at least two different departments. Careful cross-checking is very important.

ORDER ENTRY PROCEDURES

1. After an order is placed by the customer, the salesperson will fill in a pink sheet and submit it, along with artboards, estimate form, and previous ticket, to the sales person's Production Coordinator and Estimator, explaining all details pertaining to the job.
2. The Estimator will review the pink sheet to ensure that all of the required information is on the sheet and is stated clearly. If any information is missing or unclear, the sheet will be returned to the sales person immediately.

    The Estimator will then review the pink sheet and customer supplied art with the estimate to be sure that the job is still the same as was estimated. Any changes, along with prices for the changes, will be given to the salesperson as soon as possible. The tagging form will then be completed and should include all estimated time and material. The job will then be given to the Production Coordinator.
3. The Production Coordinator will review all artboards and specifications. He or she will confirm size of copy relative to finish size requirement, check for proper sizing of photos, identify any missing copy, determine it's status, and prepare the job for entry into production. The pink sheet, estimate, previous ticket, and artboards will then be submitted to the Production Planner.
4. After reviewing the artboards, pink sheet, estimate, and tagging form, the Planner will complete the production planning areas of the pink sheet, issue purchase orders for any outside purchases and create prep layouts. The pink sheet must be checked for consistent and clear language in the description of the job and in planning instructions. The job will then be given to the Production Clerk.
5. The Production Clerk will immediately assign a job number, complete the appropriate scheduling strips, and submit both the strips and pink sheet to the Production Manager.
6. The Production Manager will verify the delivery date (or set a revised one with the agreement of the Sales Rep, or Sales Manager), establish the production schedules appropriately and then forward the pink sheet to purchasing for ordering paper, notifying the Purchasing Agent of the scheduled press date. If paper will not be available by the scheduled press date, purchasing will immediately notify the Production Manager so alternative stock or press dates can be determined. After paper has been ordered, purchasing will forward the pink sheet to the Production Clerk for typing of the Job Ticket.
7. After typing the Job Ticket and making photo-copies for distribution, the ticket will then be given to the appropriate Production Coordinator, who will forward it along with the artboards into production, explaining all necessary information to the appropriate Production Supervisor.

Fig. 32-1. This is an example of an order entry procedure sheet that summarizes the flow of a job through upper level personnel. Read through it.

Graphic Communications

JOB TICKET

Job No. _____   DELIVERY DATE: _____

INVOICE TO:

Customer _____
Address _____
City _____ State _____ Zip _____
Contact _____ Phone _____

Date billed _____
Customer No. _____
P.O. No. _____
Ordered by _____
Sales rep. _____ No. _____

☐ Quoted $_____
☐ Price open
☐ Est. sell price $ _____
Can sell ____%overs/
_____%unders
Prod. coord. _____

Date written _____ by _____
Date checked _____ by _____
Date planned _____ by _____
Date scheduled _____ by _____
Credit approved ____ by _____
Mat's. purchased ____ by _____

JOB SPECS.

Item	Quantity	Description	Flat size	Finish Size	Invoice amount

TYPE/ART

☐ Set changes only ☐ Set entire job
☐ Paste-up ☐ Create mechanicals
_____
_____

PREP

☐ Exact repeat ☐ Change repeat   Previous job No. _____   Drawer No. _____
☐ Camera ready ☐ Composite film furnished ☐ Loose film furnished ☐ Seps furnished
_____
_____

PROOFS: ☐ None ☐ ____ Blueline(s) ☐ ____ Colorkeys ☐ Chromalin/Proof To: _____ ☐ Press check: ☐ Sales rep. ☐ Customer ☐ Prod. Coord. Notify _____ Phone _____

PAPER

Item	Form(s)	Basis Wgt.	Description	Suplr.	Order date	Due in	Lot No.	No. sheets	Size/grain	Cut to	Pieces out	Final pieces
									×	×		
									×	×		
									×	×		
									×	×		
									×	×		
									×	×		
									×	×		
									×	×		

SHEET-FED PRESS

Item	Form(s)	No. up	Layout	Press	Front ink(s) No.	Front ink(s) Colors	Back ink(s) No.	Back ink(s) Colors	Gross sheets	Makeready allowance	Run-waste allowance	Net count required	Net yield

BINDERY

Folding instructions

Item	Form(s)	Fold type	Net yield

☐ Saddlestitch _____ Wires on _____ Side: Net yield _____
☐ Perfect bind on _____ side: Net yield _____
☐ Drill _____ Holes _____'' Diam. _____'' Ctr to ctr _____ side
☐ Trim to size
☐ Other

☐ Pad _____ side, per _____
☐ Round corner
☐ Eyelet
☐ Side stitch _____ wires

VENDORS

☐ Film/seps _____
☐ Dies _____
☐ Die cut/emboss _____
☐ Type _____
☐ Bindery _____
☐ Other _____

MAILING

Class: _____
Permit No. _____
☐ PS labels _____ Up: qty _____
☐ Cheshire _____ Up: qty _____
☐ Ups: shippers No. _____
☐ Fed ex: shippers No. _____

PACKAGING

☐ Band _____
☐ Wrap _____
☐ Shrink _____
☐ Box _____
☐ Labels furnished
☐ Labeling instr. _____
☐ Special skids _____

SHIP TO

Note: All jobs ship freight collect unless pre-approved: (prepaid approval by _____)

Ship via: _____

ART & SAMPLES

☐ Do not return art
☐ Art and _____ samples
To: _____
_____
_____ samples to:
_____ samples to:

Fig. 32-2. This job ticket, form, or jacket provides space for all major departments. People must fill out and check off specific steps as product moves through system.

510

The planners will indicate how many images will be placed on the same signature as well as the type of layout to be used. The press to be used is given by the planner. Sales might list the colors to be used on each side of the sheet. The total number of sheets must also be listed.

Make-ready allowances are also recorded as well as the sheet allowance for waste during the press run. After figuring the allowances, the net count is recorded.

An important part of this section of the form is the *net yield*. This is the final production total or figure after the job is completed. It is an excellent follow-up tool for control.

Whenever special instructions are needed, a space is provided on the form for that information.

Bindery forms

The bindery area of many plants is becoming more automated. However, much of the work still requires a great amount of hand work, especially in the smaller facilities.

If a printed piece is to be stapled, the personnel need to be told how many and how the staples are to be positioned (saddle stitched or side bound). An example of a binding ticket or form is in Fig. 32-3. This form is used in a printing firm that prints hardbound books. Some of the terms are only used by book printing companies.

Another form, Fig. 32-4, used by one firm is in addition to the job ticket or jacket. It is a check-in form for magazine printing. The back side of the check-in sheet indicates the layout of the magazine.

Other forms

Other form information categories, such as: vendors, mailing, packaging, shipping, and storage, are also necessary to complete the production cycle.

One type of form is planned to be backed up with categories allowing the user to record problems that occurred during the printing of the job. After analysis, corrective action can be taken by management to prevent the problem from happening again.

REMEMBER! These are only examples of forms. They are NOT intended to meet the needs of all printing facilities. Forms must be designed for each facility and area. When planning forms, it is a good idea to involve all plant personnel. Well designed forms lead to greater efficiency and increased productivity.

ENTREPRENEURSHIP

An *entrepreneur* is someone who successfully starts their own business. This might be a small print shop, typesetting service, silk screen facility, color separation house, or similar endeavor.

Thousands of new businesses are started every year. Small businesses provide over 50% of all jobs in the U.S. Service areas, such as printing, are predicted to be in demand for many years into the future.

A good entrepreneur will be a self-starter. He or she should be in good health and have high self-esteem. This person must be able to differentiate a calculated risk with a foolish chance. An entrepreneur must be responsible, dependable, hardworking, and must know how to motivate and utilize worker talents. He or she will set specific goals, and work until these goals are achieved.

Advantages and disadvantages of entrepreneurship

Before deciding to start your own business, there are several important things to consider.

Some advantages of owning a small business include:
1. You can have more control over income if the business is successful and grows.
2. You can have more control over job responsibilities.
3. You can use many talents in all aspects of running a business.
4. You will have people working for you and can develop meaningful professional relationships.
5. You can gain recognition as a leader.

Some disadvantages of owning a small business might include:
1. You may work longer hours trying to get and keep the business profitable.
2. Worry of work can come home with you since all responsibilities of success or failure are on your shoulders.
3. Can lose money, even life savings, if the business fails.
4. May have to pay back business loans for many years.
5. Income may not be consistent nor predictable.
6. Large quantity of paper work to fill out for taxes, inventory, bookkeeping, etc.
7. May have to discipline workers for unsatisfactory performance.

Starting the business

You can either buy an existing business or start a new business. When buying an existing business, you have the advantage of being able to check financial records to determine if the business has been profitable in the past. Also, you will already have customers that know about and patronize the business. Equipment costs, facility planning, and other problems are already solved.

If you decide to start a new business, much more work is involved. You must find a suitable location, rent or build a facility, order equipment, supplies, etc. Until customers start patronizing the facility, it can be difficult to meet financial obligations. Financial backing can also be more difficult to obtain with a new business because of the risk.

To get help obtaining information for buying or starting a business, you can contact:
1. Small Business Administration.
2. Chamber of Commerce.
3. Friends that own a business.
4. Trade associations in graphic communications.
5. Bankers.
6. Accountants.
7. Attorneys.
8. Librarian at a public library.
9. Realtors who might know of a business for sale, building for lease, etc.
10. Insurance agent.

BINDING TICKET

DATE _____ CSR _____ EST NO. _____ JOB NO. _____

CUSTOMER

PRINT _____ BIND _____

FOLD _____ GATHER _____

TITLE

SEW _____ HOLD _____

BMI   BK — YES   NO

TR SIZE _____ HD TRIM _____

BK CODE _____ SBN _____ UNTR SIZE _____ BACK TRIM _____

NO OF PAGES _____ BULK _____ HD MARGIN _____ BK MARGIN _____

FLAT CUT text covers covermounts endsheets jackets	**FOLD** quad baum	**MACHINE TIP, STRIP** tip es flat tip and guard es guard es with drill make es on norwood print on norwood
HANDWORK insert jacket flat tip outsert tear off	**GATHER** no of sections_____ side stitch_____ wires patent bind cap cover glue off for randlock	**SEW** smyth_____ sec mc cain moffett
SADDLE STITCH no of sections _____ no of wires _____	**TRIM, EDGEWORK, INDEX** smash, glue trim continuous in line sprinkle thumb index	**FORWARD, CASE IN, BUILD IN** round back super sgl dbl lining sgl dbl headbands ribbons tight back loose back irons-1/16 1/8 3/16 1/4
MAKE CASES endfeed sheetfed board in back	**STAMP** blind _____ oper ink _____ oper imit. gold _____ oper pigment foil _____ oper clean	
BOX 1	**BOX 2**	**FINAL OPERATIONS** inspect 1 2 3 ub inspect 1 2 3 b insert jacket shrinkwrap price sticker carton send _____ samples to csr pile on skids pallets
		BOX 3

turn over for gathering breakdown and materials
1, 2, 3, 4, 5, 6, 7, 8, 9, 10, 11, 12, 13, 14, 15, 16, 17, 18, 19, 20, 21, 22, 23, 24

Fig. 32-3. A binding ticket, for example, is more specialized and only deals with procedures in binding area. Similar job tickets can be used in other areas.

Sig	Pgs	Form	Folios

BOX 4

BOX 5

BOX 6

BOX 7

BOX 8

MATERIALS

Board _____ pt binders-chestnut-chip-pasted oak _____ pieces _____ × _____	Foil
Cover material	Jackets
Endsheets	Caping material _____ yds Muslin, Tyvek, Rope Paper _____ yds Drill _____ yds
Shrink wrap	Ribbon _____ yds

Fig. 32-3. (Continued)

Graphic Communications

CHECK-IN SHEET

Customer: _____ Job#: _____ Date: _____

Logged By: _____

Form: _____ Pages: _____ Color: _____ Issue: _____

PAGE NO.	LINE SHOT	SCREEN TINT	HALF TONES	STRIP INS	DUO TONES	LOOSE 4/C	FULL PAGE FURN.	REV.		PICK-UP	DUP NEGS	ART BOARDS	SUPPLIED PROOF	MFG PROOF	COLORS	IDENTIFICATION
																TOTALS

Fig. 32-4. This check-in sheet is used to make sure all materials are accounted for when first moving into production. Back of sheet shows imposition.

1	2	113	114
4	3	116	115
5	6	117	118
8	7	120	119
9	10	121	122
12	11	124	123
13	14	125	126
16	15	128	127

17	18	129	130
20	19	132	131
21	22	133	134
24	23	136	135
25	26	137	138
28	27	140	139
29	30	141	142
32	31	144	143

33	34	145	146
36	35	148	147
37	38	149	150
40	39	152	151
41	42	153	154
44	43	156	155
45	46	157	158
48	47	160	159

49	50	161	162
52	51	164	163
53	54	165	166
56	55	168	167
57	58	169	170
60	59	172	171
61	62	173	174
64	63	176	175

65	66	177	178
68	67	180	179
69	70	181	182
72	71	184	183
73	74	185	186
76	75	188	187
77	78	189	190
80	79	192	191

81	82	193	194
84	83	196	195
85	86	197	198
88	87	200	199
89	90	201	202
92	91	204	203
93	94	205	206
96	95	208	207

97	98	209	210
100	99	212	211
101	102	213	214
104	103	216	215
105	106	217	218
108	107	220	219
109	110	221	222
112	111	224	223

Fig. 32-4. (Continued)

11. Business, accounting, or bookkeeping teachers.
12. Computer "buffs" that can help with computerized record keeping.

Always remember to avoid the "big dream" of fame and fortune when deciding to start a business. Try to look at the "pros and cons" equally. It is easy to get excited about starting a business and overlook how much work and money is involved. You may not realize the consequences of failure. Keep in mind that there may be less "headaches" and more money working for someone else.

KNOW THESE TERMS

Weakest link, Team effort, Growth planning checklist, Facility expansion, Productivity, Utilization, Efficiency, Forms, Job tickets, Seps, Net yields, Entrepreneurship, Small business.

REVIEW QUESTIONS—CHAPTER 32

1. Why should you know something about company growth and planning?
2. Every _____, every _____, every _____, every piece of _____, they all play a vital role in the growth or downfall of a company.
3. List ten factors that can contribute to the success of a business.
4. What is a planning checklist for expansion?
5. Give five questions that should be asked when determining whether to expand and how to expand a facility.
6. Give four things that could make the operating costs of a new facility different than an existing facility.
7. _____ is the amount of quality work completed in a given time span.
8. How can forms or job tickets improve efficiency?
9. Standardized job tickets will work for most printing facilities. True or false?
10. An _____ is someone who successfully starts their own business.
11. Explain the advantages and disadvantages of owning a business.

SUGGESTED ACTIVITY

1. Visit a facility and draw a revised plan to provide a more modern functional operation.
2. Write the specifications for a facility that you would like to manage.
3. Simulate the tasks needed to plan a new business.
4. Talk to someone that owns a business. Find out what they think is important to success.

Chapter 33

THE CHANGING TECHNOLOGY

After studying this chapter, you will be able to:
* Summarize the impact the computer has made and will make on the graphic communications industry.
* Review the types of electronic equipment moving into the graphic communications.
* Explain the growth areas in graphic communications.
* Summarize what processes will be phased out and what processes will be more prominent in the future.
* List the trends to watch in the future of graphic communications.

This chapter will summarize the technological innovations discussed throughout this text. It will also discuss what the future might hold for those involved in graphic communications.

RAPID CHANGE IN TECHNOLOGY

This is an extremely challenging time for anyone involved in graphic communications. Primarily because of advancements in electronics, rapid growth in equipment sophistication has made it very difficult to keep up-to-date with equipment capabilities and operating procedures. Open any graphics related magazine and you will see advertisements for more advanced equipment. This is true in all areas of graphic communications.

Graphic arts used to be the common name for the study of the processes used in the printing industry. Now graphic communications is more accurate because of the many methods of transferring and processing the images before printing them on a substrate. Some experts want to call graphic communications "graphic science." This could also be an accurate description since so many sciences are involved: mechanics, physics, electronics, and chemistry, as well as many others.

One fact is crystal clear—"if you snooze, you lose!" If you fail to keep up with new technology, you could fall behind and not be aware of more efficient types of equipment and processes. This could let your company lose any competitive edge. The result could be antiquated techniques and inferior products or higher costs. Either could cause you to lose customers and profits.

Evaluate change and predictions carefully

Several years ago, experts stated that film would no longer be used in the printing and publishing field in the late 80s. Obviously, this prediction was not accurate. Well into the 90s, we are still using film, and more of it than ever.

This proves that you should be cautious before jumping into a new piece of equipment, process, or technique!

In some areas, change can happen almost instantly to make a process more efficient.

In other areas, change can occur more slowly, depending upon the circumstances.

It is very important to be very critical of new equipment or processes before making an investment. Make sure you analyze all of the advantages and disadvantages of new methods before purchasing. Also compare the equipment features, difficulty of operation, quality improvements, utilization time, production savings, and other factors first. This will help assure a wise investment.

Computer applications

The computer has made a very pronounced impact upon the graphic communications industry. It has applications in all areas: prepress, press, and finishing. The computer has become an important "tool" that can increase production quality and volume.

Refer to Fig. 33-1.

As you studied this text, you were introduced to computer applications in almost all areas. In composition, electronic typesetting equipment has replaced cumbersome strike-on and hand-set type. It has made typesetting a much more efficient operation. It has also improved image quality.

In the future, we will see even more use of the computer in composition. Many firms are using the personal computer for writing and editing functions. Computers are capable of automatically checking spelling, providing a thesaurus, and even allowing you to layout your work on the screen. Refer to Fig. 33-2.

Interface units are available for connecting personal computers to larger typesetting equipment or for translating PC floppy disks into the computer language used by the typesetting equipment. This can allow a writer's or editor's work to be sent in on floppy disk, edited on a PC, transferred

A

B

Fig. 33-1. Computers and electronics are moving into all areas of production. A—Instructor is illustrating the use of computerized typesetting equipment to student. B—This web press has electronic sensors and computer controls to increase efficiency. (King Press Corporation)

Fig. 33-2. Desktop and more powerful electronic publishing systems will become more common to all graphic communications facilities in the future. (Chapter One, Screaming Color)

into the typesetting equipment language, and then converted into a hard copy on camera-ready galley sheets.

Desktop publishing systems will also become more common. With some print jobs, they are ideal for typing copy, drawing simple illustrations, and organizing the material (text and art) on the screen. More and more small printing facilities will be using desktop systems for many kinds of jobs: advertisements, flyers, inserts, etc. Larger electronic publishing systems will also grow in number.

The computer is also being used to help with record keeping in graphic communications. It can be used for control of inventory, invoices, and other data. Computers can also be used to evaluate product flow as a means of improving the efficiency of the different steps of production.

Computers, as discussed in detail in the text, are also being used in the color separation process, Fig. 33-3. Not only can the computer help produce the separations but it allows the

Fig. 33-3. Operator is programming in prescanning specifications for making four-color separations. Computer keyboard is serving as input device for making high quality separations. (Chapter One, Screaming Color)

operator to modify any aspect of the image electronically. Look at Fig. 33-4.

Electronics and the computer have also provided a means of going "straight-to-plate." The images (copy and art) are converted to and handled electronically on a publishing system. All images are sized and placed into their location on the layout using the display screen and electronic controls. Then, once the layout is proofed, the computer can be used to burn the printing plate, Fig. 33-5. This eliminates the conventional processing of film, stripping operations,

A   B

Fig. 33-4. Electronics and computers have allowed the development of systems that can capture images electronically and store them on computer disks. Then, the computer can be used to modify the images electronically to alter colors or even add or remove images. A—Workstation for electronic image modification system. B—Example of how photograph of boy has been modified electronically to simulate multiple exposure.

Fig. 33-5. Customer is proofing the position, layout, and color of job from a remote color CRT workstation. Images are shown to customer as they are composed on front-end of electronic prepress system to save time and money. (Kodak)

etc. Data can also be stored on magnetic disks, saving space over having to store large sheets of film.

The computer and electronics are also moving into the camera, stripping, press, and binding areas, Figs. 33-6 through 33-9. Electronic sensors and control panels can improve equipment operation and increase total efficiency in all operations.

A *computer language* is a set of instructions used to write programs. The *program* is then used for a specific application: word processing, graphics, etc.

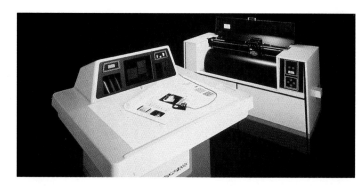

Fig. 33-8. This is an electronic stripping station. Using electronic controls, a form of a "mouse," and a monitor, system will automatically do stripping tasks.

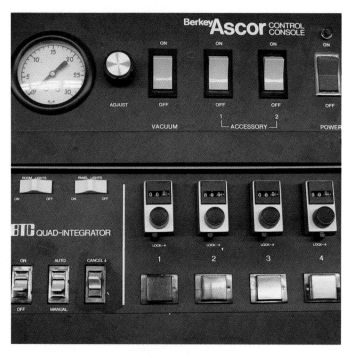

Fig. 33-6. Electronic controls are being incorporated on almost all equipment used in graphic communications.

Fig. 33-9. This large cutter has electronic controls for programming cuts to be made on substrate. (Lawson)

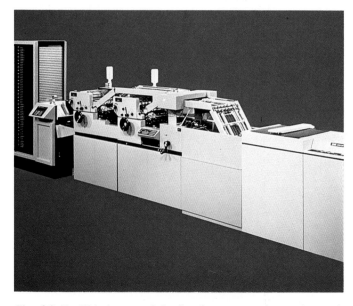

Fig. 33-7. This is a total duplicating system from platemaking through the finishing process of sorting. (AM Multigraphics)

The computer languages you might want to learn, depending upon your field of study, are:
1. BASIC (this is a general program primarily used for educational purposes).
2. FORTRAN (this is a computer language commonly used for scientific and math applications).
3. PASCAL (a general computer language with many uses).
4. COBOL (this is a computer language primarily designed for business applications).
5. C (this is a very powerful computer language with specific applications, commonly applied in data base [files, record keeping, inventory, etc.] and graphics.)

In graphic communications, the primary uses of computers are in or will be in:
1. Cost estimating.
2. Bookkeeping and associated functions.
3. Composition.
4. Editing functions.
5. Stripping applications.
6. Proofing functions.
7. Pressroom applications.
8. Binding operations.
9. Finishing applications.
10. Production, scheduling, and quality control.

This is not every use for a computer in graphic communications, but it shows that the computer is here to stay. Applications seem limitless. Try to learn as much as you can about computers and you will be much better prepared to thrive and succeed on the job today and tomorrow. The computer is and will continue to be the "graphic industries' friend."

Laser applications

The use of lasers in the graphic communications facility has taken a serious role in the last few years. Specialized facilities and the large plants appear to be today's primary users. Laser printers and other laser applications are also moving into smaller facilities.

Laser scanners have greatly changed color separation techniques, Fig. 33-10. Dot shapes can be designated by the customer and programmed by the scanner operator. The time of making separations has also been decreased dramatically. With linkage to the computer, storage and calculations of image data are important elements for repeatability and change.

Scanners come in a variety of configurations and are valuable instruments for a variety of masking techniques. The laser can also be used to create images on printing plates. The information is stored in a computer or directly transmitted to the laser platemaking system. The images are "burned" on the plate by the laser. Once the images have been placed on the plate, the plates are then processed automatically in modern facilities. Then they can be run on the press.

Laser milling is a process used to etch and make gravure cylinders. This is just the beginning of laser applications in graphic communications.

Voice input systems

A *voice input system* electronically converts human speech into computer data which can then be used to print words. At this time, its use is limited primarily to research and development but programmers are making steady progress.

Someday the voice input system could replace the keyboard on a computer or on typesetting equipment. Instead of typing, you would simply talk into a microphone and your words would show up on the display screen.

A voice input system is technically difficult to design since everyone's voice patterns are different, just as fingerprints are different. A method must be developed for programming the computer for each person's speech pattern.

Also, the voice recognition computer would also have difficulty spelling words correctly depending upon usage. For example, it might not know how to select the correct spelling of "sun" versus "son" when used in a sentence. Someday, programmers may overcome these problems.

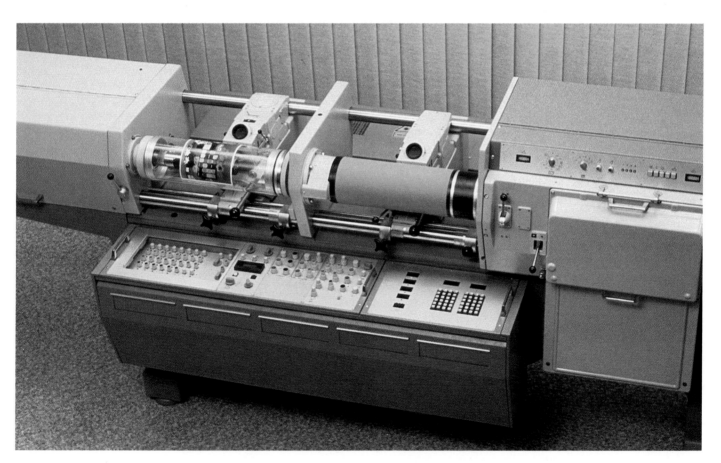

Fig. 33-10. Instead of process camera, electronic scanner is becoming the "workhorse" for making separations. This is a rotary scanner but flatbed scanners are becoming much more common. A flatbed scanner will hold art pieces without bending them and can also allow for easier mounting of images. (Hell)

Optical disk technology

Optical disk technology applications have not yet been clearly defined in the printing industry.

The compact disk is presently very expensive to produce but its use is evident in information distribution, such as in music, movies, training, libraries, manuals, and catalogs. It is an efficient means of storing a vast amount of information in a very small area. Archival material, drawings, and government documentation are typical applications of the optical disk technology today.

A five and one-quarter inch optical disk contains approximately three miles of track. The track widths on the disk are measured in *microns* (millionths of an inch or thousandths of a millimeter).

Optical waveguide technology

This technology is often referred to as *fiber optics*. A very thin strand allows verbal, visual, and written messages to be sent great distances with a high degree of reliability. It is revolutionizing the data transmission field.

This technology also is changing the printing and publishing industry. The rapidity and accuracy of data transmission is phenomenal. Another factor of great importance to the industry is optical measurement. In the future, fiber optic measurement may be very relevant as part of a quality assurance system.

Electronic document publishing

The changing technology of document publishing is greatly affecting today's business environment. The XEROX DocuTech Production Publisher, Fig. 33-11, is an example of a multifunctional machine that combines digital imaging and laser printing to publish documents from a PC environment.

The system has four main components: a scanner, a printer, a user interface, and a controller.

The scanner scans images at 600 x 400 dpi with 256 gray levels, and converts this data to a 600 x 600 binary image with no gray levels. The gray level data enables the system to perform powerful image processing on each image before it is stored and printed. This includes cropping, halftone screening, darkness adjustment, and edge enhancement.

Once scanned, the material can be printed immediately or stored on a disk to be printed later. The printer is a laser scanner. The finished product has 600 dpi resolution and the printer performs at 135 pages per minute with automatic duplexing of output as large as 11″ x 17″. It also has automatic collating, stitching, and binding.

The interface features include a mouse, a touch screen, and a keyboard that interact with the systems graphic user interface (GUI) software.

The controller has multiple processors, a resource manager, intelligent interface, and data compression.

TRENDS OF THE FUTURE

It is possible to logically predict what technical advances or changes might be seen in the future. You might want to watch for these changes in graphic communications:

1. More use of the personal computer in typesetting. The computer can be programmed to check spelling, provide a dictionary, merge text and art, etc. It is much less expensive to purchase and can evolve faster than more complex, expensive typesetting machines.
2. More use of interface units to connect personal computers to larger typesetting equipment. All writers and editors work on PCs then data is interfaced into typesetting computer for programming of parameters (typestyles, type sizes, line length, etc.).
3. Complex electronic equipment will become more standardized. Controls, internal operating principles, and construction methods should become more similar. This will reduce complexity of selecting and using equipment.
4. Prices of equipment will drop. Equipment will also become more efficient and easier to use, Fig. 33-12.

Fig. 33-11. Document publishing "on demand" is possible with a system that combines digital imaging and laser printing.

Fig. 33-12. The price of sophisticated equipment will drop in the future, making it more affordable to smaller facilities. (Chapter One, Screaming Color)

5. Reduced use of film as electronic pagination systems become more competent and user-friendly.
6. Electronic sensing and electronic controls will become more common on all types of equipment: presses, binding equipment, automatic strippers, cameras, processors, etc.
7. Laser printers will be less expensive and produce higher quality images. They will be used more for proofing and final printing with some applications, Fig. 33-13.
8. Increased use of optical character readers to input hard copy onto computer disks as means of automatically setting type, Fig. 33-14.
9. More use of digitized scanners and image processors.

Fig. 33-13. Lasers are being used in several areas in graphic communications. This laser printer is one example. Image quality of 1000 dpi is available and advancements are on the way. Laser printers will steadily replace most electrostatic processes. (Data Recording Systems, Inc.)

Fig. 33-14. Optical character readers are now inexpensive and will convert typed copy into computer data. This saves from having to manually keystroke the copy. Once in the computer, copy can then be edited or rewritten more easily. (Compu-Scan)

Their prices will drop considerably. Flatbed scanners will become more common.
10. Larger facilities will purchase and use sophisticated electronic publishing systems. Their prices will also drop and they will become easier to operate.
11. More use of four-color in all areas of printing.
12. Decreased use of electrostatic systems.
13. More sophisticated quality control and production control methods will be utilized in all areas of graphic communications.
14. Customer demands for top quality at a lower price will become even more stringent.
15. Longer press runs at higher speeds.
16. Increased use of web and belt presses.
17. Improved formulation of chemicals for safer working conditions and improved quality.
18. Process camera will become even more automatic. Use of combination camera-processor will also become more common.
19. Metric system will steadily move into U.S. market because of trade with other countries.
20. Increased use of on-screen proofing by customers.
21. Steady growth of printing industry.
22. Fierce competition between all companies in the graphic communications industry.
23. Training requirements for entry level graphics employees will become more involved.

KNOW THESE TERMS

Graphic arts, Graphic communications, Graphic science, Computer applications, Straight-to-plate, Laser applications, Voice input system, Optical disk technology, Fiber optics.

REVIEW QUESTIONS—CHAPTER 33

1. Because of standardization, electronic advancement is not difficult to comprehend in graphic communications. True or false?
2. Experts were wrong when they predicted the phasing out of film in our present facilities. True or false?
3. What must you do before buying new, sophisticated equipment?
4. Explain some present and future applications of computers in graphic communications.
5. How do you go "straight-to-plate?"
6. Describe some laser applications in graphic communications.
7. The rotary scanner may someday be replaced by the _____ scanner.
8. How would a voice input system operate?
9. An optical disk contains about _____ _____ of track with a track width measured in _____.
10. List twenty trends to watch in the graphic communications industry.

INDEX-GLOSSARY REFERENCE

This Index-Glossary Reference serves two functions. It is a conventional index for finding topics in the body of the textbook. It also provides a method of quickly finding definitions of technical terms.

A **bold typeface** is used to give the page numbers for definitions. If you need a technical word explained in one or two sentences, simply turn to the page number printed in darker type. The defined term is printed in *italics*.

The Index-Glossary is educationally superior to a conventional index because it allows you to obtain more information about the term being questioned. You can read the definition in context and then continue to read more on the subject as needed. You can also refer to the illustrations which will help you more fully comprehend the new technical term.

A

Abort key, **129**
Absorption drying ink, **464**
Accurate character count, 99
Acetate base film, **202**
Achromatic Color Reduction, **240**
Achromatic colors, **236**
Activator, **278**
Additive color, **179**
Additive plates, processing, 318-321
Additive surface plate, **315**
Adjacency effects, **246**
Adjustable triangle, **155**
Aesthetics, **235**
Agency, studio, 29
Air jet bed, **473**
Alphanumeric, **130**
American point system, **56**, 57
Analog signals, **127**
Antihalation coating, **203**
Append key, **130**
Aquamatic system, **367**
Arrow keys, **129**
Art and images, 185
Art knives, 158
Art knives, safety, 158
Artwork, **8**, 9
Ascender, **69**
Author's alterations, **172**, 173
Automatic exposure, 210, 211
Automatic platen press, **395**-397
  clamping the drawsheet, 396
  delivery setting, 397
  loading, 396, 397
  packing the press, 396
  positioning, 396
  press wash up, 397
  running the job, 397
  running up ink, 397
  safety, 397
Automatic strike-on system, **123**
Autoscreen film, **232**
Average character count, **98**, 99

B

Backing mat (sheet), **300**
Back leading, **85**
Balance, design, **91**, 92
Bails, **392**
Banding machine, **495**
Bank, relief composition, **112**
Bareback roller, **350**
Base density fog, **225**, 226
Base line, **69**
Base material, **284**
Base-plus fog, **225**
Basic flash test, 227
Basis weight, **455**
Baskerville, **71**
Bas-relief image, **261**
Beard, foundry type, **110**
Bed, 391
Binary code, **127**
Binary system, **127**
Bindery
  finishing personnel, **35**, 36
  finishing service, 29, 30
  form, 511-513
  production control system, **495**, 496
Binding, **22**, 23, **471**, 485-496
  bindery production control system, 495, 496
  book, 489-492
  case bound, 488, 489
  casing-in, 493
  collating, 486-488
  edition bound, 488, 489
  gathering, 486, 487
  making the case, 492, 493
  mechanical, 494, 495
  pamphlet, 486
  perfect binding, 494
  stitching, 488
Bit, **127**
Bitmap, 185
Bit-mapped images, **180**
Black letter, **70**
Black printer, 239

Blanket, **332**
  cylinder, **348**, 349
  cylinder setup, sheet-fed, 361, 362
  roller washes, **370**
  thickness gauge, **65**
Bleed, **288**
Bleed, illustrations, **149**
Bleed valve, **301**
Blind embossing, **484**
Blind image, **378**
Block, **127**
Blockout material, 431
Blue filter, **238**
Blue pencil, 14, 148
Blue sensitive films, **202**
Bodoni, **71**
Body, **489**
 height, **69**
 size, 80
Bond paper, **453**
Bookbinding, **489-492**
Book paper, **453**
Book publishing and printing, **25**
Book system, **170**
Border material, **163**, 164
Bottom deck, **385**
Bridges, **482**
Brightness, **83**
Broad light source, **302**
Brushes, layout, 154
Brush system, **351**
Buckle type folding machine, **475**
Buffer, **127**
Bump or no-screen exposure, **227**
Burned edges, **429**
Burnisher, **158**, 159
Byte, **127**

C

Calendering, **451**
Calibration images, 435
California Job Case, **111**
Call page key, **130**
Camera back, **270**
Camera copy classifications, **216-218**
 continuous tone, 217, 218
 linework, 217
 mechanical shading, 217
 pre-screened images, 218
Camera modifications, 257
Cameron belt press, **401-404**
Cameron press, **331**
Camera-processor, **212**, 213
Camera-ready copy, **12**
Carbon-arc, **192**
Carbon tissue, **410**
Card cutter, **475**
Careers, 27-39
 preparation, 38, 39
 proofreading, 169

Carrier, **400**
Case, **489**, 490
Case bound, **488**, 489
Casing-in, 493
Caslon, **71**
Cassette, **125**
Cathode ray tube (CRT), **127**
Cell size, **422**
Cellulose acetate, **461**
Centerlines, **166**
Chain dot, **220**
 average, 98, 99
 filling a space, 100, 101
 manuscript, 99, 100
 type size, 101
Chalking, **377**, **469**
Character count system, **97-101**
 accurate, 99
Character (image) generation, **119**
Characters, 69
Characters per pica, 99, 100
Characteristic curve, **201**, 202
Chase, **385**, **392**
Chemical graining, **315**
Chemical hazards, 45-47
 image carriers, 47
 ink mists, 47
 gases, fumes, dust, 47
 organic solvents, 46, 47
Chemicals, film processing, 272, 273
 developer, 272
 fixer, 273
 safety, 273
 stop bath, 272, 273
Chill rolls, **374**
Choke, contacting, **305**
Chopper, **374**
Chromatic colors, **236**
Cleaning white, **466**
Clean proof, **114**
Clear memory key, **129**
Clear oriented polyester, **461**
Clip art, **121**
Close file key, **130**
Coated paper, **453**
CMYK, **179**, 184
Coating, **24**
Cold composition, **11**, **119**-139
 hand composition, 119, 120
 output system, 133, 134
 photocomposition, 124, 125
 phototypesetting, 126-133
 preprinted art/type, 120-123
 processor (developer), 136-138
 strike-on, 123, 124
Collate, **486**
Collating, **23**, **486**-488
Color
 capability, 179
 circle, **253**

correction, **250**, 251
design, **91**
diagrams for ink evaluation and color
  correction, 253, 254
evaluating, 237
hexagon, **253**
light principles, 236, 237
monitor, 179, 180
proofing, **307**
proofing systems, **254**, 255
temperature, **194**
theory, **235**
vision, **236**
wheel, **236**
Color-on-color duotone, 262, 263
Color reproduction,
  color correction, 250, 251
  gray balance, 251, 252
Color sensitivity, 202
Color separations, **235**, **236**-250
  direct screen, 240, 241
  electronic scanning, 242, 243
  indirect method, 242
  mounting originals on scanner, 246, 247
  narrow and wide band filters, 239
  preview system, 244, 245
  scanner environment, 245
    operating steps, 246-249
    operation, 244
    operators, 245
    principles, 243
    setup, 245
    types, 244
  screen angles, 239
  under color removal, 240, 241
Color separation system, selecting, 250
Combination dampening and inking system, **367**
Commercial printing, **24**
Communication, **7**
Communication, importance of, 7
Comparison proofing, **173**
Compass, **157**
Complimentary color, **235**
Complimentary flats, **294**, 295
Compose key, **130**
Compose mode, **127**
Composing service, 29
Composing stick, **113**
Composition, **108**
Composition depth, 80
Compositor, **108**
Comprehensive layout, **144**, **145**
Comprehensive sketch, **14**
Compressed air, safety, 45
Computer
  applications, 517-521
  binary code, **127**
  control unit, **126**
  language, **520**
Computerized exposure, 211, 212
Computerized typesetting, **126**-133

Computers and electronics, 27, 28
Condensed typefaces, **77**
Conduction, **438**
Contact duplicate, **278**, 305
Contact exposure test, **303**
Contact film, **203**
Contact frames, **300**
Contact method, **124**
Contact reversal, **305**
Contact screen, 218, **219**
Contacting, **278**, **299**-307
  applications, 299
  considerations, 304
  equipment, 300, 301
  exposures, **302**, 303
    safety, 303
  facilities, 299, 300
  films, 305
  frame screening, 307
  image orientation, 304, 305
  light sources, 301, 302
  masking materials, 305
  spreads, 305
  spreads and chokes, 305, 306
  tints, 307
Contamination, offset platemaking, **326**
Contemporary typefaces, 72
Content editing, **11**
Continuous dampening system, **350**, 351
Continuous tone, **217**, 218
  copy, **10**, **215**
  material, 166
  originals, 221-224
Contrast, design, **92**, 93
Control keys, **129**
Controller, **38**
Control signal, **127**
Control strips, 231
Control unit (computer), **131**, 132
Convection, **438**
Conventional dampening system, **350**
Conventional dot, **220**
Conversion chart, metric, **55**, 56
Copolyester substrate, **460**
Copy, **8**, 9
Copyboard
  controls, **199**, 200
  loading, 206
  process camera, **198**
  safety, 198
Copy camera, 194
Copy editing, **11**
Copyfitting, **11**, **95**, **96**-106
  character count, 97-101
  desktop publishing, 103, 106
  electronic, 101-105
  measurement review, 95
  points/picas, 95, 96
  square-inch, 97
  word count system, 96, 97
Copyholder, proofreading, **170**

Copyright laws, **499**, 502, 503
Copywriter, **36**
Cord and groove, **425**, 426
Counter, **69**
Counter, foundry type, **110**
Cover paper, **453**
Creasing, **478**, 479
Creep, **288**
Crop marks, **145**, 146
Cropping, **145**, 146
CRT (cathode ray tube), **127**
Curing, **438**
Cursive, **75**, 76
Cursor, **127**, 131
Customer service representatives, **37**
Cut program, **102**
Cutters, layout, 159, 160
Cutting, **472**-475
  guillotine cutter, 472, 473
  paper cutters, 473-475
  safety, 475
Cutting boards, 160
Cutting sticks, **473**
Cylinder etching, rotofilm or carbon tissue
  method, 410, 411
Cylinder evaluation and finishing, 413, 414
Cylinder packing, **65**
Cylinder packing gauge, **65**
Cylinder press, **397**-400
  cylinder adjustments, 399, 400
  inking adjustment, 398, 399
  lockup, 388
  operating procedure, 397, 398
  safety, 398-400

D

Dahlgren continuous system, **350**
Dampener, 363-365
Dampener cover, **363**
Dampening preparation, 364
Dampening system, **350**, 351
  continuous, 350, 351
  conventional, 350
  fountain solution, 351
  safety, 350
Dandy roll, **451**
Darkfield illumination, **326**
Darkroom, **16**, 269-272
  camera, 196
  entrances, 271, 272
  equipment, 270, 271
  safety, 271
  ventilation, 271
Data centers, exposure computers, 228, 229
Daylight camera, **195**
Daylight films, **203**, 305
Day mode, scanner, 245
DCS, **184**
Dead copy, **170**
Decibels, **65**
Decorative typeface, **76**

Deep-etch plates, **325**
Define key, **129**
Definition, **85**
Delete keys, **129**, 130
Delivery board, **392**
Delivery system, **353**-355
  setup, sheet-fed, 367
  sheet-fed, 353, 354
  web, 355
Densitometer, **18**, **63**, 64, 222
Densitometer, using, 224
Densitometry, **224**-226
Density, **201**, **222**
Density capacity, **201**
Density-log exposure curve, **225**
Density reaction, 225
Department supervisor, **38**
Depth of copy display, 101, **102**
Descender, **69**
Design, **8**, **87**-94
Design, graphic designer, 87, 88
Design elements, **88**-91
  color, 91
  lines, 88, 89
  mass, 89, 90
  shape, 89
  texture, 90
Design principles, **91**-94
  balance, 91, 92
  contrast, 92, 93
  proportion, 94
  rhythm, 93, 94
  unity, 92, 93
Designers, **36**
Desktop publishing, 177
Desktop publishing, copyfitting, 103, 106
Developer, **126**, **136**-138, **272**
Developer, using, 273-274
Developing system, **127**
Developing unit, **12**
Developmental fog, **225**
Diazo, **205**
Diazo coating, **315**
Didot point, **57**
Die cutting, **23**, **482**, 483
Diffuser sheets, **306**
Diffusion transfer, **204**, 205, 278, 279
  exposing negative materials, 205
  modifications, 264
  plates, **322**, 323
  process, **232**
  reflex paper, 205
  silverless light sensitive materials, 205
Digital proofing, 310
Digital signals, **127**
Digitizing tablet, **177**, 178
Direct-film stencils, **434**
Direct image plate, **318**
Direct-indirect stencils, **434**, 435
Direct input, **127**
Direct input system, **130**

Direct screen color separations, **240**, 241
Direct stencils, **431-434**
Dirty proof, **114**
Disk data, 133
Disk drive, **126, 132**
Display key, **130**
Display type, 80, 85, 86
Display type, layout, 142
Distributed form, **395**
Distribution of type, **115**
Dithering, **179**
Dividers, **157**
Double-coated tape, **161**
Dot etching, **250**
Dot gain, **224**
Dot geometry, **223, 224**
Dot matrix, **76**
Dot matrix printers, 181
Double-sheet detector, **343**
Drafting board, 149, 150
Drafting tape, **161**
Drawdown time, **300**
Drilling, **480**
Drilling, safety, 480
Drop-down menus, **186**
Dropout, layout, **161**
Dry etching, **250**
Drying system, 353, **374**
Drying system, screen printing, 438
Dry transfer sheets, **121-123**
d-system, **57**
Dual disk drive, **132**
Dual-dot halftone screens, **220**
Ductor roller, **350**
Dummy, **144, 145**
Dummy, stripping, **285, 286**
Duotones, 262, 263
  color-on-color, 262, 263
  fake duotone, 263
  making, 262
  one-color and black, 262
  production, 262, 263
  two-impression black, 262
Duplicating film, **203, 305**
Duplicator paper, **453**
Durometer, **65**

E

Editing, **10, 11**
Editing keypad, **129**
Edit mode, **127**
Edition bound, **488,** 489
Editor, **36**
EDP supervisor, **38**
Efficiency, **508**
Electric eye stop, **473**
Electromechanical cylinder preparation, 411, 412
Electron Generated Beam (EGB), **412**
Electronic
  imagery, **266, 267**

layout page, 167
memory devices, exposure computer, 228
modification, 264-266
pagination, **15**
pH meter, **363**
scanning, color separation, **242,** 243
stripping, **296, 297**
Electronic copyfitting, 101-105
  cut program, 102
  depth of copy display, 101, 102
  indent program, 102
  line length display, 102
  line spacing display, 102
  parameter line, 101
  type size display, 101, 102
Electronic imaging or electronic prepress, **177**
Electronic imaging process, 182, 183
  graphic images, 183
  text preparation, 182, 183
  word processing, 183
Electronic layout page, **186,** 187
Electronic line art, 187, 188
Electronic production, 177-189
Electronic publishing
  layout page, 167
Electron beam engraved cylinders, 412-414
Electrostatic
  assist, **417,** 418
  image carriers, **322-324**
  method, **22**
  plates, **315**
  printing, **441**
Electrostatically, **315**
Electrotype, **330, 332-334**
Elliptical dot, **220**
Embossing, **23, 458, 483,** 484
Em quad, **80,** 81
Emulsion, **201**
  contrast, **225**
  sensitivity, **224**
Emulsion-to-emulsion exposure, **304**
End sheets, **491**
Engineers, 36, 37
Engraving machine, **411**
Enlarging, **206**
En quad, **80,** 81
Entrepreneur, **511**
Entrepreneurship, 511, 516
Envelopes, 458-460
  size, **58**
  styles, 459, 560
Environmental compliance, 51
EPS, **183,** 184
Equalizing platen impression, 394, 395
Equivalent weight, **455**
Estimator, **37,** 38
Evaporation drying inks, **465**
Execute key, **130**
Expanded typefaces, **77**
Exposing film, 210

Exposing negative materials, 205
Exposure
  automatic, 210, 211
  control units, **210**
  computer, **210**
  computerized, 211, 212
  test, **303**
  time, line copy, 209, 210
  time, setting, 209
Eye span, **84**

F

Fabrics, screen printing, 420-425
Fabric strength, **421**
Fabric tension, screen printing, 426, 427
Fabric tensioning, screen printing, 425, 426
Fabric treatment, screen printing, 427
Face, foundry type, **110**
Fake color, **240**
Fake duotone, **263**
Fast ink, **465**
Feedboard, **392**
Feeding system setup, sheet-fed press, 358-360
Feet, foundry type, **110**
Festooning, **345**
Fiber optics, **127**, 522
File, **127**
  disk, **133**
  keypad, **130**
  management, **127**
File formats, 183, 184
  DCS, 184
  EPS, 183, 184
  paint file, 183
  PICT, 183
  RIFF, 183
  TIFF, 183
Files, 132
File transmittal, 185, 186
Filling a space by characters, 100, 101
Film
  back, **199**
  bases, **202**
  cassette, **126**
  cutter, **475**
  dryers, **270**
  negative, **15**
  positive, **15**
  processing, **269**-279
  processor, **270**
  storage cabinet, 270
  types, 202
Filters, process camera, **203**, 204
Finishing, **23**, 24, 471-485
  creasing, 478, 479
  cutting, 472-475
  die cutting, 482, 483
  drilling, 480, 481
  embossing, 483, 484
  flocking, 484

folding, 475-478
  laminating, 484
  numbering, 484, 485
  perforating, 479, 480
  punching, 480, 481
  ruling, 481
  scoring, 479
  slitting, 478
  stamping, 481, 482
  varnishing, 482, 483
Fire prevention, 45
First generation images, 109
First generation originals, **246**
Fixer, **273**
  halftone processing, **231**
  use, 275
Flash exposure, determining, 227
Flash exposure, halftones, **227**, 228
Flat, **18**, **141**
Flat, layout, **281**
Flatbed scanner, **244**
Flat reproduction, **232**
Flexographic image carriers, **401**
Flexography, **19**, **21**, **107**-109, **330**, **400**-404
  applications, 400, 401
  Cameron belt press, 401-404
  image carriers, 401
Flocking, **484**
Floor horizontal camera, **196**
Floppy disk, **12**, **127**, **132**, 180
Fluorescing agents, **224**
Flying splicer, **345**
Flywheel, **393**
Focal length, **208**
Focusing camera, **208**, 209
Folding, 475-478
  safety, 478
  terms, 478
Fold lines, 166
Fold plate, 476
Font, **78**,79
Font disk, **133**
Fonts, **184**, 185
  formats, 184
  printer, 184
  screen, 184
  using, 185
Footbrake, **393**
Form, **385**
Formal balance, **92**
Former board, **374**
Form roller, **350**
Forms printing, **25**
Formulary, **447**
Foundry type, **107**, **109**-112
  dimensions, **110**, 111
  furniture, 112
  leads and slugs, 111
  parts, 110
  reglets, 112

spacing material, 111
storage, 111
Fountain additives, **363**
Fountain roller, **350**
Fountain solution, **351**
Fountain solution, ingredients, 363, 364
Fourdrinier Machine, 447
Four-tone posterization, **258**
Frame, 184
Frame, process camera, **196**
Front end, **127**
f-stops, **207,** 208
Fugitive ink, **465**
Function keys, **129**
Furniture, **385**
Furniture, foundry type, **112**

G

Gallery camera, 195
Galley, **12**
 relief composition, **113**
 proofs, **108, 173**
Gamma, **202, 225**
Gamma rays, 194
Ganged, **241**
"Gang shot," **148**
Garamond, **71**
Gases, fumes, dust, safety, 47
Gathering, **23, 486,** 487
Gauge pins, positioning (platen), **394**
Gauze weave, **422**
German black letter, **70**
Ghosting, **380**
Glass screen, 218
Gloss paste, **466**
Goldstamping, **481**
Grades of paper, **455**
Grain, **314**
Graining of base, 314, 315
Grainless plates, **315**
Graphic, **7**
Graphic communication, **7**
 facility planning, 505-511
 purpose of, 8
 technology changes, 517-523
Graphic designer, **87,** 88
Graphical user interface (GUI), **179**
Graphic images, 7, 183
Graphics editors, 180, 181
Gravure
 base cylinder, **409,** 410
 cylinder, **415**
 doctor blade, **416**
 inks, 467
 paper, 454
Gravure press, **415**-418
 configuration, 415
 cylinder action, 415
 doctor blade, 416
 impression roller, 416
 ink standards, 416, 417

printing units, 415
process inks, 416
safety, 418
Gravure printing, **21,** 22, 405, **406**-418
 cylinder engraving, 409-415
 development, 405, 406
 electrostatic assist, 417, 418
 prepress, 407-409
 process, 406, 407
 SWOP, 417
Gray balance, **251,** 252
Gray Component Replacement, **240**
Gray scale, **63,** 210, **222**
Gray scale monitor, 179
Green filter, **238**
Grippers, **392**
Ground glass, **200**
Growth planning checklist, **506**
Guideline system, **170**
Guides, layout, **164**-166
Guillotine cutter, **472,** 473
Gum blinding, **326**

H

Hairline, **69**
Halftone, **10, 215**
 black, **466**
 grade film, 218
 gravure, **415**
 process color screen printing, 438
 production, 229, 230
 screen, **216**
Halftone exposure computers, **227**-229
 data centers, 228, 229
 electronic memory devices, 228
 hand-operated dials, 228
Halftone reproduction, **215**-233
 autoscreen film, 232
 camera copy classifications, 216-218
 continuous tone originals, 221-224
 densitometry, 224-226
 diffusion transfer, 232
 exposure computers, 227-229
 exposures and screen ranges, 226
 flash exposure, 227, 228
 main exposure, 226, 227
 negatives, 231, 232
 processing the film, 230, 231
 rapid access film, 232
 scanner, 232, 233
 screen process, 218-221
Halftone screen process, **218**-221
 color, 219
 contact, 219
 dot shapes, 220
 handling, 221
 negative and positive, 219, 220
 percent dot size, 219
 selecting, 220, 221
 shapes, 220

special screens, 221
Hand composition, 112-114, **119**, 120
  lettering, 119, 120
  templates, 120
Handles, 181
Hand lettering, 12, 13, **119**, 120
Hand-operated dials, exposure computer, **228**
Hanger sheets, **393**
Hard copy, **12**, 13
Hard copy proofing, 255
Hard copy proofs, 185
Hard disk, **127**
Hard disk drive, **132**, 133
Hard drives, 180
Hardening solution, **430**
Hardness tester, **65**, 66
Hardware, **127**
Headbands, **492**
Heavy elements, **73**
Hickies, **375**
High impact polystyrene, **460**
High intensity light source, **302**
High-key and low-key, **222**, 223
Highlight, **221**
Highlight values, **216**
High technology, **27**
Horizontal camera, **196**, 197
Horsing, **170**
Hot composition, **11**
Hot type, **72**, 73, **107**
Hot wax adhesives, **160**
Hue error, **253**
Hurter and Driffield curve, **225**
Hydrolith plates, processing, 322
Hyphenation routine, **127**

I

IBM PC compatibles, 179
Illumination, **191**-194
  color temperature, 194
  controlling light source, 193
  light source, 191-193
  light spectrum, 193, 194
Illustration board, **150**
Illustrations, **142**
  cropping, **145**, 146
  line art, 147
  mark-up, 148
  mounting, **147**, 148
  photographs and tone material, 147
  scaling, 145, **146´**
  workmarks, 148, 149
Image
  acquisition, **266**
  area, **311**
  carriers, safety, 47
  generation, **11**
  generator, **126**, 133-135
  reversal, **201**
  losses, **374**
  processing, **266**, 267

recording, **267**
Imagesetter, **182**
Impactless (pressureless) printing, **22**, **441**
Imposing stone, **385**
Imposition, **383**
  format, **287**
  layout, **383**
Impregnated offset paper, **453**
Impression cylinder, **349**
  adjustment, 362
  setup, sheet-fed, 362
Impression roller, 416
Impressions per hour, **64**
Impression system,
  blanket cylinder, 348, 349
  impression cylinder, 349
  perfecting press, 349
  plate cylinder, 346-348
  twin-cylinder image transfer, 349
Indent program, **102**
Index paper, **453**
India ink, 154
Indirect color separation, **242**
Indirect method, **339**
Indirect stencils, **429**-431
Infeed unit, 372
Informal balance, **92**
Infinity, **208**
Ink, **463**-470
  body, **463**
  color strength (opacity), **463**
  darkness, **83**
  disk, **392**
  drying, 464, 465
  drying on rollers, 377
  drawdown test, **469**
  efficiency, **253**
  fineness gauge, **64**
  film thickness gauge, **64**
  formulation, **463**, 466-468
  hue error, **253**
  impurities, 254
  ingredients, 463
  knife, **393**
  length, **464**
  measurements, **64**
  mill, **466**
  mists, safety, 47
  mixing, 468, 469
  problems, 469, 470
  rollers, **392**
  roller stripping, **380**
  safety, 467
  setoff, 465
  stability (thixotropy), **464**
  standards, gravure, 416, 417
  sticking, **469**
  strength, **253**
  tack, **464**
  UV curable, 465
  viscosity, **465**

Inking
  template, **156**
  the press, platen, 393
  triangle, **155**
Inking system, **351**-353
  setup, 365-367
  web, 352, 353
Ink jet printing, **22, 442**-444
Inkometer, **464**
In-plant printing, **25**
Input devices, 177, 178
  digitizing tablet, 177, 178
  keyboard, 177
  mouse, 177
  pointing device, 178
  scanners, 178
Input system, **127**
Input system (keyboards), 128
Insert key, **129**, 130
Inside form, **383**
Inspection method, halftone processing, **231**
Intaglio process, 21, **405**
Integrators, **193, 302**
Intermediates, **201**
Ion projection printing, **442**
ISO sizes, **58**, 59
Italic, **76**, 77

J

Janson, **71**
Jenson type, **70, 71**
Job black, **466**
Job satisfaction, 27
Job tickets, forms, 508-511
Justifying type, **82**

K

Kelvin, **194**
Kerning, **83**
Kettle stitch, **491**
Keyboard, **126**, 177
Kimdura, **461**
Knife-cut stencils, screen printing, 428, 429
Knife arm, **476**

L

Lacquer-soluble stencils, **428**, 429
Lakes, **465**
Laminating, **484**
Lamination, **24**
Laser, **28, 29, 127**
  applications, 521
  engraved cylinders, 412
  lithographic plates, **324**, 325
  printers, 22, 181, 182
Latent image, **12**
Lay of pages, **383**
Layout, **14, 15, 141**-168
  assembling the mechanical, 166, 167
  base sheet, 150, 151
  cutting tools, safety, 160

electronic pagination, 15
  guides, **164**-166
  illustration processing, 145-149
  mechanical, 14
  methods, 144, 145
  paste-up materials, 160-164
  preplanning, 143, 144
  sheet, **141**
  stripping, **281**
  surfaces, 149, 150
  tables, **281**
  tools and equipment, 151-160
Layout elements, **141**-143
  display type, 142
  illustrations, 142
  text type, 141
  white space, 142, 143
Leading, **84**, 85
Leading display, **102**
Leads and slugs, foundry type, **111**
Ledger paper, **453**
Legibility factors, **83**-85
  definition, 85
  letter forms, 85, 86
  line spacing (leading), 84, 85
  line width, 84
  type size, 84
  visibility, 83
Length of cutoff, **385**
Lensboard, 198, **199**
Letter forms, 83, 84
Lettering guides, 12, 13
Letterpress, **19**, 21, **107, 329**
  imposition, 383-385
  imposition, signature printing, 383-385
  paper, 454
  relief printing, **391**
Letterspacing, **82**
Lexan polycarbonate film, **460**
Ligatures, **79**
Light
  elements, **73**
  hazards, 47
  integrator, **211**
  spectrum, **193**, 194
  table, 149, 150, **281**
Lighting system, process camera, 196-198
Light sensitive materials, **200**-203
  antihalation coating, 203
  characteristic curve, 201, 202
  color sensitivity, 202
  contact film, 203
  daylight film, 203
  duplicating film, 203
  emulsion, 201
  film bases, 202
  film types, 202
  prescreened film, 202
  rapid access film, 202
Light source, **191**-193
  control, 193

safety, 192
setting, 206
Lignin, **449**
Limit key, **129**
Linearization, **245**
Line art, **9,** 147, **191**
Line casting machines, 116
Line copy, **9, 170**
Line film, 218
Line gauge, **56**
Line length, 80, **84**
Line length display, **102**
Line photography, 191-194
Line photography, illumination, 191-194
Lines, design, **88,** 89
Line spacing, **84,** 85
Line spacing display, **102**
Line width, **84**
Linework, 217
Liquid tack reducer, **466**
  dampening system, 350, 351
  delivery system, 353-355
  impression system, 346-349
  inking system, 351-353
  sections, 340, 341
  sheet-fed, 339
  sheet feeding system, 341-346
  web, 339
  web feeding system, 344-346
Lithographic
  imposition, **281**
  plates, **313-316**
Lithographic press, 339-355
Lithographic process, **311**
Litho ink problems, 467
Litho plate problems, 325, 326
Litmus paper, **363**
Livered ink, **393**
Locking up the form, **385**
Lockout devices, safety, **44,** 45
Lockup, **385-388**
  cylinder press, 388
  equipment, 385
  procedure, 385-388
  relief images, 385
  systems, 385
Long inks, **464**
Logarithmically calculated, **64**
Lowercase, **69**

M

Machine guarding, safety, **42-44**
Machine processing, 273
Macintosh, 178, 179
Magnesium oxide, 224
Magnetic disks, **16**
Magnetic disk storage, **132**
Magnetic printing, **441**
Magneto-optic (M/O) storage, 180
Magnifiers, **284**
Magnifiers, layout, **159**

Main exposure
  determining, 226
  halftones, **226,** 227
  test, **226**
Make-ready,
  equalizing platen impression, 394, 395
  platen, **393**-395
  positioning gauge pins (platen), 394
  preparing the platen, 393, 394
  trial impression (platen), 394
Makeup person, **34**
Management, 32
Manually-prepared master plate, **330**
Manufacturers, 30
Manuscript, 9
Manuscript, determining space needed, 99, 100
Mark-up, illustrations, **148**
Masking film, **161**-163
Masking sheet, **281**
Mass, design, **89,** 90
Master page, 184
Materials handling, safety, 45
Matrix, 116
Measurement, 53-67
  blanket thickness gauge, 65
  cylinder packing gauge, 65
  envelope size, 58
  hardness tester, 65, 66
  ink, 64
  ISO sizes, 58, 59
  metric equipment, 66
  metric system, 53-56
  noise, 65
  paper size, 57, 58
  paper weight, 59-61
  press speed, 64, 65
  pH meter, 64
  photo conversion, 61-64
  principles, 53
  printer's, 56, 57
Mechanical, **14, 141**
  binding, **494,** 495
  pencils, 152
  shading, **217**
Mechanical hazards, 42-45
  compressed air, 45
  lockout devices, 44, 45
  machine guarding, 42-44
  materials handling, 45
  personal protection, 44
Mechanically-engraved master plate, **330**
Mechanicals,
  attaching elements, 166
  collecting elements, 166
  layout factors, 167
  overlays, 166, 167
  paste-ups, 166
  production for printing, 167
Mechanical type grains, **314,** 315
Mechanics of layout, 285-287
Mechanized processing, **277**

Mechanized processing, start-up, 27
Mercury-vapor lamps, **192**
Merge key, **130**
Mesh bridging capability, **430**
Mesh count, **421**
Metalized polyester, **422**
Metallic inks, **466**
Metal mesh, **422**
Metal relief type, **109**
Metal type, **108**, 109
Metric equipment measurement, 66
Metric paper sizes, 456-458
Metric system, 53, **54**-56
  conversion, 55, 56
  prefixes, 54, 55
  rules of notation, 54, 55
  SI, 54
Metric type size, **57**
Micro imaging, 29
Middletones, **221**
Midtone values, **216**
Millimicron, **194**
Mini-floppy disk, **132**
Minus leading, **85**
Misregister, **375**
Misregister on web press, **380**
Misting, **376**
Mitography, **419**
Modern Roman, **74**, 75
Modern typefaces, **71**, 72
Moisture-set inks, **465**
Monitor, **130**
Monitors, 179, 180
  color, 179, 180
  gray scale, 179
  monochrome, 179
Monochrome display, 179
Monofilament, **421**
Morris, **71**
Mottling, **379**
Mounting illustrations, **147**, 148
Mouse, **127**, 177
Multifilament, **421**
Multimetal plates, **325**
Multiple flats, **295**
Multiple page imposition, **290**
Multiple-tone posterization, **259**

N

Nanometer, **236**
Narrow band filters, **239**
Neck, foundry type, **110**
Negative, **201**
Negative and positive screens, 219, 220
Negatives, halftone reproduction, 231, 232
Negative-working coatings, **315**
Next page key, **130**
Net yield, **511**
Neutral density filters, **227**
New file key, **130**
News Case, **111**

Newsprint paper, **453**
Newspaper printing, **25**
Nick, foundry type, **110**
Night mode, scanner, **245**
Nip, **416**
Nip points, **43**
Noise measurement, **65**
Noise, safety, 47, 48
Nonimage area, **311**
Non-imaging, **227**
Non-pareils, **56**
Nonrepeat device, **473**
Novelty typeface, **76**
Numbering, **484**, 485
Nylon, **422**

O

Object-oriented images, **181**
Occasional typeface, **76**
Off color, **469**, 470
Off contact distance, **424**
Office proofs, **114**
Off-line, **127**
Offset, **311**
Offset duplicator, **357**
Offset gravure, **415**
Offset lithography paper, 454
Offset paper, **453**
Offset platemaking, 311-327
  contact problems, 326
  deep-etch plates, 325
  equipment, 312, 313
  lithographic plates, 313-316
  surface plates, 316-318
  variables, 325-327
Offset press (see lithographic press), **339**-355
Offset press operation, **357**-374
  dampeners, 363-365
  fountain solution ingredients, 363, 364
  inking system setup, 365-367
  maintenance, 374
  safety, 360, 367, 371
  sheet-fed, 358-371
  troubleshooting, 374-380
  two-cylinder impression system, 363
  web press, 371-374
Old English, **70**
Oldstyle Roman, **73**, 74
One-color and black duotone, 262
One-up, **287**
On-line, **126**
Opacity, **458**
Opaque, **294**
Opaqued, **147**
Opaque paper, **83**, 84
Opaquer, **34**
Optical character reader, **126**
Optical disk technology, 522
Optical exposure unit, **9**
Organdy, **422**
Order entry procedures, 509

Organic solvents, safety, 46, 47
Orthochromatic films, **202**
Oscillating roller, **350**
Output devices, 181, 182
  dot matrix printer, 181
  imagesetter, 182
  laser printer, 181, 182
Output system, **127**
Output system, phototypesetting, **133**, 134
Outside form, **383**
Overhead horizontal camera, **196**
Overlay proof, **307**-309
Overlays, **166**, 167
Owner of facility, 37
Oxidation drying inks, **465**

P

Packaging, **495**
Page, **127**
Page composers, 180, 181
Page composition, 184
  master page 184
  page grid, 184
  template, 184
Page grid, **184**
Page sequence, stripping, 286
Paint file, 183
Pamphlet binding, **486**
Panchromatic film, **202**
Paper
  absorption, halftone reproduction, 224
  applications, 454
  base, stripping, **285**
  brightness, **458**
  caliper, **61**
  characteristics, 454-458
  color, 458
  cutters, 473-475
  flatness, **455**
  forms, 508, 511
  grades, **59**
  grain, **454**, 455
  punch mechanism, **124**
  size, **57**, 58
  size and weight, 455-457
  smoothness, 458
  stencils, **428**
  strength, **458**
Paper tape, **124**
Papermaking,
  calendering, 451
  chipping, 447
  dyes and pigments, 449
  history, 447
  pulp, 447, 449
  removing water, 449-451
  rolling up paper, 451, 452
  sizing and fillers, 449
  watermarking, 451
Paper types, 453, 454
  bond, 453

  coated, 453
  cover, 453
  duplicator, 453
  index, 453
  ledger, 453
  newsprint, 453
  offset, 453
  recycled, 454
  uncoated, 453
Paper weight, **8**, **59**-61
Paper weight, ream conversion factors, 61
Parallel fold, **285**
Parameter line, **101**
Paste tack reducer, **466**
Paste-up, **14**, **141**
Pasteup artist, **33**
Pencils, layout, 151, 152
Penetrating inks, **464**
Pens, layout, 152-154
Percent dot size, **219**
Percent open area, **422**
Percent stretch, **426**
Perfect binding, **494**
Perfecting press, **349**, **385**
Perfectors, **397**
Perforating, **479**, 480
Permanent ink, **465**
Permanent memory, **127**
Periodical printing, **24**
Personal protection, safety, 44
Personnel classification, 30-32
Phantom halftone, **264**
pH meter, **64**
Photo CD, **180**
Photocomposing, **11**, 12
Photocomposition, **124**, 125
  combination equipment, 125
  photo display units, 124
  phototypositor, 125
  projection method, 125
  strip printer, 124, 125
Photoconversion, **15**-18
  darkroom, 16
  process cameras, 15, 16
  scanners, 16-18
Photoconversion measurement, **61**-64
  densitometer, 63, 64
  gray scale, 63
  screen angle, 61, 62
  screen rulings, 61, 62
  tint percentages, 62, 63
Photo-density range, **222**, **229**
Photo direct plates, **316-318**
Photo display units, 124
Photoengraving, **330**
Photograph as black, **203**, **204**
Photograph as white, **204**
Photographer, **36**
Photographic films, stripping, 285
Photographic stencils, **429-436**
  exposure calibration, 435, 436

fabric and stencil selection, 436
positives, 429
Photo-mask paper, **284**
Photomechanical
electronic modifications, 257-267
master plates, **330**
methods, **191**
Photo modifications, **257**
duotones, 262, 263
posterization, 257-261
special effect screens, 263, 264
Photomultiplier tube, **243**
Photopolymer coating, **315**
Photopolymer plate, **330**, 331
Photopolymer plate production, 331, 332
Phototext composition, **126**-133
Phototype machine, **133**-135
Phototypesetting, **126**-133
computer terminology, 126, 127
control unit (computer), 131, 132
direct input, 130
disk data, 133
disk drive, 132
editing keypad, 129
equipment components, 126
file keypad, 130
floppy disks, 132
function keys, 129
hard disk drive, 132, 133
input systems (keyboards), 128
magnetic disk storage, 132
output system, **133**-135
paper, **134**, 136
proofing programs, 133
proof printer, 133
video display screen, 130, 131
Phototypositor, **125**
pH solution, **363**
Pica, **56**, 80
Pica point, **57**
Pi characters, **79**
Picking, **378**
Pick strength, **458**
PICT, **183**
Piling, **379**
Pied type, **113**
Pigment, **463**
Pigmentized offset paper, **453**
Pin mark, foundry type, **110**
Pixelized, 183
Pixels, **180, 266**
Plain/taffeta weave, **421**
Planer block, **388**
Planographic (offset lithography) inks, 466, 467
Planography, **311**, 312
Plant manager, **37**
Plant superintendent, **37**
Plastic fastener, **494**
Plastic plates, 334
Plastic sheeting, **285**
Plastic substrates, **460**, 461

Plastic type, **108**, 109
Plate, **311**
bend allowance, **291**
coatings, 315
coating types, 315
covering, 315
cracking, **376**
cylinder, 346-348
cylinder setup, sheet-fed, 360, 361
handling, 315, 316
wear, **378, 469**
will not roll up properly, **377**
Platemaker, **34**
Platemaking, **18**
Platen, 391, **392**
Platen press, **391**, 392
automatic, 395-397
cleaning, 395
flywheel, 393
footbrake, 393
inking the press, 393
ink rollers, 392
make-ready, 393-395
operating, 395
parts, 392, 393
roller service, 393
safety, 392, 395
throw-off lever, 392
unlocking the form, 395
Platform, IBM PC and compatibles, 179
Platform, Macintosh, **178**, 179
Plotters, **9**
PMT, 278, 279
Point, **56, 69**, 80
Pointing device, 178
Points/picas, type forms, 95, 96
Point source light, **301**
Point system, **95**
Polyester base film, **202**
Polyester/Dacron, **422**
Polyester substrate, **460**
Polymerization, **438**
Polymerization drying inks, **465**
Polystyrene base film, **202**
Poor distribution of ink on rollers, **377**
Poor ink trapping, **376**
Positioning film, 209
Positive, **201**
Positive screen, **219**, 220
Positive-working coating, **315**
Positive working nature, **305**
Positive-working surface plates, 322
Posterization, **257**-261
basic line exposure percentages, 259
classification, 258, 259
reflection density values and exposure
computer, 260
reflection gray scale and inspection
processing, 259, 260
screen tints and positives, 260, 261
tone-line technique, 261

PostScript, 181
Post treatment, **201**
Powderless etching, **330**
Precipitation drying inks, **465**
Prefixes, metric, **54**, 55
Prep department forms, 508
Prepress, gravure printing, 407-409
Preprinted art/type, **120**-123
  clip art, 121
  dry transfer sheets, 121-123
Prescreened images, **218**
Prescreened films, **202**
Presensitized plates, **316**
Press
  blanket, **65**
  layouts, 287, 288
  runs, **19**
  speed measurement, **64**, 65
Presses, screen printing, 439, 440
Pressroom personnel, **34**, 35
Presswork, **19**-22
  gravure printing, 21, 22
  impactless (pressureless) printing, 22
  letterpress, 19, 21
  screen printing, 21, 22
  sheet-fed press, 19
  web presses, 19, 20
Previous page key, **130**
Preview system, **244**, 245
Primary additive colors, **236**
Primary subtractive colors, **236**
Print, **15**
Printer fonts, 184
Printer's measurement, **56**, 57
  American point system, 56, 57
  d-system, 57
  metric type size, 57
  pica, 56
  point, 56
  type height, 57
  type rule, 56
Printing, **7**
Printing units, **415**
Process camera, **15**, 16, **194**-213
  camera-processor, 212, 213
  copyboard, 198
  copyboard controls, 199, 200
  diffusion transfer, 204, 205
  filters, 203, 204
  film back, 199
  frame, 196
  ground glass, 200
  horizontal, 196, 197
  lensboard, 198, 199
  lighting system, 196-198
  light sensitive materials, 200-203
  operating procedures, 205-212
  operator, **33**
  parts, 195, 196
  vertical, 195, 196
Process control strips, **278**

Processing
  additive plates, 318-321
  chemicals, safety, 279
  halftones, 230, 231
  Hydrolith plates, 322
  sink, **270**
  subtractive plates, 321, 322
  trays, 231, **270**
Processing film, 269-279
  darkroom, 269-272
  chemicals, 272, 273
  developer use, 273-274
  diffusion transfer, **278**, 279
  fixer use, 275
  mechanized, 277, 278
  special techniques, 278
  stop bath use, 275
  tray procedure, 276, 277
  washing, 275, 276
Process ink analysis, 252, 253
Process ink, gravure, 416
Processor, **12**, **136**-138
Production manager, **37**
Production scheduler, **37**
Productivity, **508**
Program features, 186-188
  drop-down menus, 186
  electronic layout page, 186, 187
  electronic line art, 187, 188
  toolbox, 186
Programming disk, **133**
Projection method, **125**
Proof, **114**, **169**
Proof forms, 508
Proofing, 307-310
  overlay proof, **307**-309
  program, **133**, 176
  transfer proof, 309, 310
Proofing and correcting, relief composition, 114
Proof printer, **126**, 133
Proofreader's marks, **171**, 172
Proofreading, **169**-176
  author's alterations, 172, 173
  careers, 169
  checking corrections, 174
  copy correction, 170
    book system, 170
    guideline system, 170
  copyholder, 170
  marking corrections, 173, 174
  proofing programs, 176
  proofreader's marks, 171, 172
  responsibilities, 169
  skills, 169, 170
  typesetting corrections, 174, 175
  using proofs, 173
Proportionally spaced, **123**
Proportion, design, **94**
Pulling a proof, relief composition, **115**
Pulp, making, 447, 449
Pulpers, **449**

Pulsed-xenon lamps, **192**
Punches, stripping, **281**
Punching, **480**, 481
Purchasing factors, 188, 189

Q

Quality control supervisor, 38
Quartz-iodine lamps, **192**
Queue key, **130**
Quick printing/copy services, 29
Quoins, **385**
Quote, **8**
"Qwerty" keyboard, **128**

R

Radiation heating, **438**
Radio waves, 194
Rapid access film, **202**, **232**
Raster, **266**
Raster Image Processor (RIP), 181
Rasterizing, **181**
Raster scanning system, **266**
Readability, **83**
Reader, **124**
Ream, **455**
Reclaiming solutions, **433**
Recycled paper, **454**
Red filter, **238**
Reduction, **206**
Reemay, **461**
Reflection copy, **217**
Reflection densitometer, **63**, 222, 224
Reflection density range, 224
Reflex paper, **205**
Register marks, **164**
Register pins, **282**
Reglets, **112**, **385**, **387**
Regulators, **193**
Relief composition, 107-117
  foundry type, 109-112
  line casting machines, 116
  proofing and correcting, 114
  proofs for correction, 114
  pulling a proof, 115
  relief type, 107-109
  repro proofs, 114
  slug casting machines, 116, 117
  tying the form, 113, 114
  type distribution, 115, 116
  typesetting processes, 112-117
Relief inks, 466
Relief plates, 329-337
  duplicate, **329**
  duplicate plate production, 330
  electrotype, 332-334
  original, **329**
  original plate production, 330
  photoengraving, 330
Relief printing, **107**, **391-404**
  automatic platen press, 395-397
  cylinder press, 397-400

  flexography, 400-404
  letterpress, 391
  platen press, 391, 392
  rotary press, 400
Relief process, **329**
Relief type, **72**, 73, **107-109**
  composition, 108
  first generation images, 109
  materials, 108, 109
  metal, 109
  second generation images, 109
Removable cartridges, 180
Replace page key, **130**
Reproduction proofs, **108**, **173**
Repro proofs, **114**
Resin-coated paper, **136**
Resistant ink, **465**
Resolution, **179**, 181, **266**
Retarders, **436**
Reversal processing, **278**
Reverse leading, **85**
Reverse type, **76**
Revised proof, **114**
RGB, **179**, 185
Rhythm, design, **93**, 94
RIFF, 183
Right angle fold, **285**
Rigid vinyl substrate, **460**
Robotics, 23, **28**
Roller gauge, **393**
Roller pressure adjustment, 364, 365
Roller service, platen, 393
Roller washup unit, **370**
Roll-fed press, 19
Roman type styles, **73-75**
Roomlight, **270**
Rotary press, **374**
Rotary relief press, **400**
Rotary scanner, **244**
"Roto," **415**
Rotofilm, **410**
Rough layouts, **144**, 145
Rough sketch, **14**, **143**, 144
Rubber cement, 161
Rubber plates, 334
Rubber stamps, 334-337
  making, 335, 336
  mounting, 336, 337
  safety, 336
  vulcanizing, 336, 337
Rubber type, **108**
Rule of Thirds, **251**
Rulers, layout, 155, 156
Rules of metric notation, 54, 55
Ruling, **481**
Ruling pen, **152**
Rulings, **220**

S

Safelight, **270**
Safety,

art knives, 158
automatic platen press, 397
contacting exposures, 303
copyboard, 198
cutting, 475
cylinder press, 398-400
dampening system, 350
darkroom, 271
developer, 274
drilling, 480
film processing chemicals, 273
folding, 478
gravure press, 418
ink, 467
layout cutting tools, 160
light source, 192
offset press operation, 360, 367, 371
platen press, 392, 395
processing chemicals, 279
rubber stamps, 336
screen printing, 427, 432, 436
slugs, 117
stitching, 488
stop bath, 275
tray processing film, 276
Safety and health, 41-51
  chemical hazards, 45-47
  fire prevention, 45
  general safety rules, 48-51
  light hazards, 47
  mechanical hazards, 42-45
  noise, 47, 48
  program, 41
Safety rules, 48-51
Sales manager, **38**
Sales representative, **38**
Sample press operation, sheet-fed, 367-371
Sans serif, **75**
Scaling, 145, **146, 206**
Scanner, **16**-18
  environment, 245
  halftone screens, 232, 233
  mounting transparent originals, 246, 247
  operating, 244
  operating steps, 246-249
  operator, **33,** 245
  principles, **243**
  setup, 245
  types, 244
Scanners, 178
Scissors, layout, 158
Scorching, **332**
Scoring, **23, 479**
Screen
  color, 219
  dot shapes, 220
  fonts, 184
  inks, 436
  process, **419**
  process service, 29
  range, finding, 226, 227
  rulings, **61,** 62
  scale, **61**
  shapes, 220
  solvents, **436**
  special effect, 263, 264
  tension, **426**
  tint, **62,** 63
Screen angle
  indicator, **61**
  color reproduction, 239
  measurement, **61,** 62
Screened photo, **16**
Screen frames, **423**-425
  aluminum, 423, 424
  print size, 424, 425
  profiles, 424
  wood, 423
Screen printing, 21, 22, **419**-439
  applications, 419
  drying systems, 438
  fabrics, 420-425
  fabric tension, 426, 427
  fabric tensioning, 425, 426
  fabric treatment, 427
  halftone and process color, 438
  history, 420
  inks, 436, 467, 468
    applications, 468
    problems, 468
  knife-cut stencils, 428, 429
  paper, 454
  photographic stencils, 429-436
  presses, 439, 440
  process, 419, 420
  safety, 427, 432
  screen frames, 423-425
  solvents, 436
  squeegees, 436, 437
  stencils, 427, 428
Script, **75,** 76
Scroll
  down, **129**
  key, **129**
Scrolling, **127**
Scumming, **326**
Scumming on plate, **380**
Secondary file key, **130**
Second generation images, 109
Second generation originals, **246**
Selecting halftone screens, 220, 221
Semiautomatic strike-on system, **123**
Sensitometry, **201, 224**
Separations, **10**
Serif, **70, 73**
Serif, foundry type, **110**
Serigraphy, **419**
Service operations, 29, 30
Setoff, **377, 469**
Setoff in web heat-set inks, **378**
Set size, **81,** 82
Set solid, **84**

Set-width, **70**
Shading film, **163**
Shadow, **221**
Shadow values, **216**
Shape, design, **89**
Sheet-fed delivery system, **353**, 354
Sheet feeding system, **341**-346
  continuous, 341
  pile adjustment, 341
  register board, 344
  sheet separation, 341, 342
  sheet transfer, 342, 343
Sheet-fed press, **19**, **339**, **358-371**
  delivery system setup, 367
  feeding system setup, 358-360
  impression system setup, 360-362
  sample press operation, 367-371
Sheet guides, **342**
Sheet separators, **342**
Sheets-per-hour, **65**
Sheetwise, **383**
Sheetwise layout, **287**
Short inks, **464**
Shoulder, **202**, **225**
Shoulder, foundry type, **110**
Signature, **288**, **383**, **486**
Signature printing, 383-385
Silk, **422**
Silk screen, **419**
Silver halide coating, **315**
Silverless light sensitive materials, **205**
SI metric system, **54**
Single disk drive, **132**
Single page imposition, **290**
Single-sheet proof, **309**
Size and lens diaphragm setting, 206, 207
Skeleton (detail) printer, **238**
Sketches, **143**
Slitting, **478**
Slow-dry additive, **466**
Slow ink drying, **376**
Slug, **116**
Slug casting machines, 116, 117
Slugs, safety, 117
Slurring, **379**
Small caps, **79**
Soft copy, **12**
Soft image, **326**
Soft proofing, **250**, 255
Software, **127**, 180, 181
  graphics editors, 180, 181
  page composers, 181
  word processors, 180
Spacing material, foundry type, 111
Special characters, **79**
Special effect screens, 263, 264
Special screens, **221**
Specialty printing service, 29
Specifications, **8**
Specking, **470**
Spelling program, **176**

Spine, **491**
Spiral binding, **494**
Spray adhesives, **161**
Spray powder, **466**
Spread, contacting, **305**
Square dot, **220**
Square-inch copyfitting, **97**
Square serif, **75**
Squeegee, **419**
Squeegee, screen printing, 436, 437
Stabilization paper, **134**, 136
Stabilization process, **136**, **278**
Stabilizer, **278**
Stamping, **23**, 24, 481, 482
Standard tint chart, **252**
Star scale, **61**
Stem, **69**
Stencil printing, **419**
Stencils, screen printing, 427, 428
Step-and-repeat, **287**
Step-and-repeat, stripping, **296**
Step-off method, **209**
Stereotype, **330**, **332**
Still development, halftone processing, **231**
Still-tray development, **277**
Stitching, **23**, **488**
Stitching, safety, 488
Stock, **144**
Stop bath, **273**
  halftone processing, **231**
  safety, 275
  use, 275
Storage devices, 180
  floppy disks, 180
  hard drives, 180
  Magneto-optic (M/O) storage, 180
  photo CD, 180
  removable cartridges, 180
Storage system, **127**
Straight bar, **315**
Straight line, **202**
Straight line portion, **225**
Straight matter, **83**
Streaks, **379**
Stream feeding, **341**
Stress, **70**
Strike-on composition, **123**, 124
Strike-on type composers, **12**
Strike-through, **469**
Strip-ins, **166**
Stripper, **34**, **281**
Stripping, **18**, 19
  clear base, 296
  close register, 296
  color, 296
  complementary flats, 294, 295
  cutting masking materials, 293
  electronic, 296, 297
  emulsion down, **292**, 293
  emulsion up, **292**
  emulsion up vs. emulsion down, 293

imposition, **281**-297
imposition, press layouts, 287, 288
multiple page, 290, 294-296
opaquing, 294
procedures, 288-290
positives, 295
preparation, 288-290
quality control devices, 293
registering color flats, 296
single page, 290-292
step-and-repeat, 296
tables, **281**-284
Stripping tools and equipment, 281-285
base materials, 284
photographic films, 285
stripping tables, 281-284
supplies, 285
Strip printer, **124**, 125
Stroke, **69**
Stylesheet, 184
Subiaco face, **70**
Sublimation heat transfer, **440**, 441
Substance weight, **455**
Substrate, 7, 19, **447**
paper, 447-460
plastic, 460, 461
Subtractive
color, **179**
color triangle, **253**, **254**
filters, **235**
plates, processing, **321**, 322
working plate, **315**
Successive sheet feeding, **341**
Suckers, **342**
Surface plates, **316**-318
Swivel knife, **158**
SWOP, **417**
System command key, **130**

T

Table model cutters, 159, 160
Table top waxer, **160**
Tape, layout, 161
Taping machine, **495**
Technical ink pen, **152**, 153
Technical skills careers, 32-36
Technological growth, 27-29
Templates, **120**, **184**
Templates, layout, 156
Temporary memory, **127**
Text, 9
filters, **183**
layout, 141
(black) letter typeface, **75**
(body) type, 80
paper, **453**
preparation, 182, 183
Texture, design, **90**
TIFF, 183
Thermal printing, **441**
Thinners, **436**

Thixotropy, **464**
Three-knife paper cutter, **474**
Three-tone posterization, **258**
Throw-off lever, **392**
Thumbnail sketch, **14**, **144**
Tick mark, **291**
Tied up form, **395**
Tinting, **379**
Tint percentages, 62, 63
Tint screen, **219**
Toe, **202**
Toe portion, **225**
Toolbox, **186**
Tone-line technique, **261**
Tone material, **147**
Tone range limitations, 224
Toners, **466**
Top deck, **385**
Tracking, **85**
Trade customs, **499**-501
Transfer letters, **12**
Transfer proof, **309**, 310
Transfer system, **127**
Transitional Roman, **74**
Transmission densitometer, **63**, 224
Transparent copy, **218**
Transparent plastic tape, **161**
Tray processing, 273
film, 276, 277
film, safety, 276
Trends of the future, 522, 523
Trial impression, platen, **394**
Triangles, layout, **155**
Trim allowance, **384**
Trim marks, **164**
Trimming, **23**, 472
Tristimulus, **224**
Troubleshooting, offset press, 374-380
Trucks, **393**
True color duotone, 262
T-square, **154**, 155
Tungsten-filament lights, **192**
Tweezers, layout, 157
Twenty-pound bond, **59**
Twill weave, **422**
Two-handed operation cutter, **473**
Two-impression black duotones, 262
Two-person proofing, **173**
Two-cylinder impression systems, 363
Two-tone posterization, **258**
Tying the form, **113**, 114
Tympan paper, **392**
Type and art forms, 508
Type forms, 95, 96
Type height, **57**
Type size, 84
display, 101, **102**
to fit space and manuscript, 101
Type style development, 70-72
black letter, 70
contemporary typefaces, 72

German black letter, 70
Jenson, 70, 71
modern typefaces, 71, 72
Typefaces, **69-86**
 classifications, 73-77
 contemporary, 72
 display type, **85**, 86
 elements, **72**, 73
 family, **77**
 font, 78, 79
 legibility factors, 83-85
 modern, 71
 pi characters, 79
 relief type, 72, 73
 series, **78**
 special characters, 79
 terminology, 69
 typesetting measurements, 79-83
 type style development, 70-72
 typography, 69
 width, 77
 weight, 77
Typesetter, **33**, 34, **108**
Typesetting corrections, 174, 175
Typesetting measurements, 79-83
 em, 80
 justifying, 82
 kerning, 83
 letterspacing, 82
 set size, 81
 widow, 82, 83
 word spacing, 82
Typographer, **69**
Typography, **69**
Typos, **76**, **170**
Typositor, 13
Tyvek, **461**

U

Uncoated paper, **453**
Under color removal, **240**, 241
Unity, design, **92**, 93
Units, **81**
Unsensitized indirect stencils, **430**
Uppercase, **69**
Using fonts, 185
Utilization, **508**
UV curable ink, **465**

V

Vacuum back, **199**
Vacuum systems, **300**, 301
Varnishing, **24**, **482**, 483
Vehicle, **463**
Vertical camera, **195**, 196
Vibrating roller, **350**
Video display screen, **130**, 131

Video display terminal (VDT), **126**, **130**
Vignetted dot structure, **219**
Vinyl sheeting, **285**
Viscosity, **436**
Visibility, **83**
Visible light spectrum, **236**
Voice input system, **521**
Volatile organic compounds, 51, 465

W

Waist line, **69**
Warp threads, **422**
Wash, halftone processing, **231**
Washup solvents, **436**
Watercolors, **466**
Waterless plates, 322
Waterless printing, 21, 311
Watermark, **451**
Water-soluble stencils, **428**
Weave patterns, **421**, 422
Web
 break, **375**
 break detector, **346**
 delivery system, **355**
 feeding system, 344-346
 splicer, **345**, 346
Web press, **19**, 20, **339**, 371-374
 bindery section, 374
 dampening system, 373
 feeding system, 372
 inking system, **352**, 353, 373, 374
 printing unit, 373
Weft threads, **422**
Wet etching, **250**
White light, **236**, **302**
White paper tape, **161**
White space, **142**, 143
Wide band filters, **239**
Widow, **82**, 83
Width of web, **385**
Window, **293**
Window, layout, **161**
Wood type, **108**, 109
Word count copyfitting, **96**, 97
Word processing, 183
Word processors, **180**
Word spacing, **82**
Work-and-tumble, 287, **383**, 384
Work-and-turn, **287**, **383**
Workmarks, 148, 149
WYSIWYG, **179**

X

Xerographic process, **442**

Z

Zero speed splicer, **345**

ACKNOWLEDGEMENTS

A special thanks is extended to the many students, colleagues, and industry personnel who have given assistance, in some way, during the completion and revision of this text. Some of the individuals are: John Adler, Alfred (Bud) R. Anderson, Bob Baranowsky, Pat Beausoleil, Dick Benjamin, Bruce Binder, C. Ray Bradley, Blair Brouhle, Wesley Carter, Robert D. Cavin, Larry Charles, Lee Clifford, Paul Coony, Joleen Crimmins, Warren Daum, Bill Dunn, John Earle, Jon Engfer, Don Epley, Cheryl Ferrin, Michael Friel, Jim Gale, Greg Gallagher, Karen Gallik, Chris Gannon, Don Gasser, D. W. Gillmore, Joseph J. Goclowski, Mark Goddard, Lynn Glasenap, A. James Hall, Roger Halligan, Willis Hawrylkiw, Joe Hayes, R. Cameron Hitchcock, Ed Holmberg, Robert Hughes, John Jacobs, George Jenson, Vlnod Kapoor, Edward Kelly, Ty Kohnke, Julian (Red) Koren, William Lamparter, Kathryn Lauerman, Donald Marsden, James McClintick, Bill Milkowfsky, John Morton, Karen O'Brien, Stephanie Palmer, Kim Pardini, Art Petrosemolo, J. J. Plank, Frank Roys, Jack Simich, Tony Simuel, Terry Stengel, Kent Stumpe, John Sweeney, Daryl VanderHarr, Paul Volpe, Robert Walker, Bud Walrod, Paul Wasserman, Art Webb, Gordon Woodard, James A. Wilkens, Frank Woods, and Tim Young.

Appreciation is extended to Sue Fogler for typing the manuscript, to Martha Beakley Heier and Sergio Capon for artwork. Appreciation is also extended to Dr. Walter Brown and Professor Scott Williams, School of Technology, Arizona State University, for their assistance. Special thanks to Dr. Thomas Schildgen, Professor in the Department of Manufacturing and Industrial Technology, for writing the chapters relating to color theory and reproduction and gravure printing and to Dr. Ron Dahl, Professor in the Department of Manufacturing and Industrial Technology, for writing the chapter on electronic production. Thanks is also extended to Dr. Rich Hannemann, Professor at University of California, Chico, for writing the screen process chapter.

To my wife, Mary Ann, a sincere thanks for her patience and encouragement. Thanks to our sons, Donald L. Prust, printer, and Randall S. Prust, MD.

The following companies have assisted greatly by providing information and pictorial material used in the textbook:

A. B. Dick Co.; AM Multigraphics; Accurate Steel Rule Mfg.; ACTI Products, Inc.; Advance Process Supply; Agfa; American Color; American Screen Printing Equipment Co.; Arizona Printing Equipment Co., Inc.; ATF Davidson Co.; Autotype U.S.A.; Baumfolder Corp.; Brown Camera Co.; ByChrome Co.; Cameron-Somerset Technologies; Camex, Inc.; Caprock Development Inc.; Carpenter-Offutt Paper Co.; Central Missouri State University; Center for Vocational Education, Columbus, Ohio; Consolidated Papers, Inc.; Challenge Machinery Co.; Chapter One, Screaming Color; Clampitt Paper Co.; Color Masters, Inc.; Communications and Graphic Arts Leadership Council; Compuscan Inc.; Cordata; Covalent Systems; Datwyler: Diagraph; Didde Web Press Corporation; Dienes; Donihe Graphics Co.; Eastman Kodak Co,; Edwards Brothers; E. I. DuPont DeNemours and Co.; Foster Manufacturing Company; Gans Ink and Supply Co.; Garret-Buchanan; Global Equipment Co.; Graphic Arts Technical Foundation; Gravure Association of America; Gretag; Hanscho, Inc.; Heidelberg Harris; Heidelberg Pacific, Inc.; Heidelberg West; Heritage Graphics; High Technology Solutions; Hunterlab; Ilford; Information International Inc.; International Paper Co.; Ironwood Lithographers, Inc.; Kenro; Keystone; Kimberly-Clark Paper Co.; King Press Corporation; Krause; KURTA; Lehigh Press; Linotype-Hell; 3M Company; MAN Roland Inc.; Miller; Mix & Match Corp.; Morgana Systems Unlimited: Muller-Martini Corp.; Murray Printing Co.; National Association of Printers and Lithographers; National Association of Printing Ink Manufacturers; Nekoosa Paper Co.; nuArc Company, Inc.; Oliver; J. J. Plank Corp.; Polychrome Corporation; Printing Industries Association of America, Inc.; Printing Industries Association, Inc., of Arizona; Ponte Engraving Co.; Rapiline; George Rice & Sons; Rob Macintosh Communications, Inc.; Rollem; RPS; Salco, Inc.; S. D. Warren Co.; Scitex America Corp.; Screen Printing Association International; Screen USA; Shanebrook Graphics; Software Publishing Corp.; Synergo: TEC Systems; Tekra; Tobias Associates, Inc.; Type Studio; Ulano: United Graphic Products and Equipment Inc.; Unisource Corporation; Varitronics; Visual Graphics Corporation; Western Gear Corp.; Woods Lithographics; Xerox Corporation; X-Rite, Incorporated; Xyneticx-Clectroglas.